STUDIES IN PUBLIC COMMUNICATION

A. WILLIAM BLUEM, GENERAL EDITOR

INTERNATIONAL COMMUNICATION

Media, Channels, Functions

STUDIES IN PUBLIC COMMUNICATION

MASS MEDIA AND COMMUNICATION
Edited by Charles S. Steinberg

THE LANGUAGES OF COMMUNICATION
By George N. Gordon

TO KILL A MESSENGER
Television News and the Real World
By William Small

INTERNATIONAL COMMUNICATION
Edited by Heinz-Dietrich Fischer and
John Calhoun Merrill

THE COMMUNICATIVE ARTS
An Introduction to Mass Media
By Charles S. Steinberg

INTERNATIONAL COMMUNICATION

Media, Channels, Functions

Edited, with preface, special introductory
notes and suggested readings

by HEINZ-DIETRICH FISCHER, Ph.D.

and JOHN CALHOUN MERRILL, Ph.D.

COMMUNICATION ARTS BOOKS

HASTINGS HOUSE, PUBLISHERS · NEW YORK

First Edition

Published simultaneously in Canada by
Saunders of Toronto, Ltd., Don Mills, Ontario

SBN: 8038-3370-9

Library of Congress Catalog Card Number: 70-112443

DESIGNED BY AL LICHTENBERG

PRINTED IN THE UNITED STATES OF AMERICA

To
Erika J. Fischer
and
Dorothy J. Merrill

CONTENTS

Contents   ix

PREFACE

INTERNATIONAL COMMUNICATION, receiving great and increasing emphasis in the last couple of decades, is certainly nothing new—being as old as the history of men and nations. In most of the Biblical writings we find an emphasis on communication among nations, and the teachings of Christ and the practical actions of St. Paul add force to the early concern with spreading information across national borders. Missionaries, it might be noted, became some of the very first serious "professionals" in spreading messages among people of different countries, languages, and races.

In the European Middle Ages the songs of the Troubadours not only entertained the nobility but carried information of all kinds across the continent. Postmasters became another group which gathered, exchanged and distributed news. Songs and slogans of military troops and adventurers of all kinds influenced the opinions and attitudes in conquered countries. And it should be observed that the first real newspapers of the early 17th century were largely international papers because their contents came from nearly all over the then-known world. One of these pioneer newspapers of 1609 exemplified in its long title a certain internationalism. The full name of this famous German "Aviso" was (in translation): *Relation of what has happened in Germany and Italy, Spain, the Netherlands, England, France, Hungary, Austria, Sweden, Poland, and in all the provinces, in East and West Indies, etc.*

During the days of the Romans and during the Middle Ages the Latin language had the function of a *lingua franca* all over Europe, and so communication—especially between well-educated people—from country to country was rather easy. But the more Latin was pushed back and step by step replaced by various Romanic, Germanic or Slavic languages, the more complicated became the written communication among various European countries. Added to this problem was a growing censorship of publications by absolute monarchs.

The importance of international communication to a person's general education and to society generally was recognized early. Caspar von Stieler mentions in his *Zeitungs Lust und Nutz* (Hamburg 1695), the world's oldest book about the meaning and function of the press, how important it is to be well-informed about international affairs. And many of the early newspapers covered foreign affairs much better than domestic events because a strong censorship prevented them from giving emphasis to domestic news. It is only since the Glorious Revolution in England and the French Revolution a hundred years later that significant changes have occurred in press freedom and expansion.

It has largely been during the last couple or three decades that the whole realm of international communication has been opened wide for exploration. Of course, the realm was "discovered" and stressed to some degree very much earlier. August Ludwig Schlözer of Germany's Göttingen University, for example, was one of the first academics to treat the press in his history lectures. In 1777 he observed the contents and functions of news from different parts of the world and gave some critical comments on his discoveries.

During the 19th century it became quite common for historians in their lectures and writings to touch on the development of important periodicals. In the United States, for example, in 1879 David R. McAnally had a course at the University of Missouri entitled "History of Journalism," dealing with practical daily newspaper life and emphasizing not only the *New York Herald* but also London's *Spectator* and *The Times*. This was perhaps the first course in comparative journalism offered in any university.

It has been in the present century, however, that emphasis has been given to international communication, both in writings and university courses. Journalistic activities of other nations have increasingly come under the scholar's scrutiny. One of the first published works in this respect was the German *Handbuch der Auslandspresse 1918* (Handbook of the Foreign Press 1918). It was prepared by the Foreign Department of the government's War Press Office and described the main newspapers of thirteen foreign countries. Emil Dovifat of Berlin University, one of the pioneers of research about the international press, started in 1931 a *Handbuch der Weltpresse* (Handbook of the World Press), which had several later updated editions.

Dean Walter Williams of the University of Missouri, founder of the world's oldest school of journalism there (1908), organized so-called Press Congresses of the World in San Francisco (1915), Honolulu (1921) and Geneva (1926). Williams, Karl d'Ester (Germany) and Hideo Ono (Japan) belonged to the small group of journalism educators who very early recognized the need for breaking out of the provincial and nationalistic straight-jacket in which education for journalism was then confined.

In addition to Walter Williams of the University of Missouri, another professor of the same institution was one of the earliest writers to deal with foreign journalism. He was Eugene Webster Sharp who made such early studies in this area as "International News Communications: The Submarine Cable and Wireless as News Carriers" (1927), and "The Censorship and Press Laws of Sixty Countries" (1933).

Perhaps the first book to present a survey of the international press was Robert Desmond's *The Press and World Affairs* (1937) which he wrote as a Ph.D. dissertation at the London School of Economics. About this same time motion pictures and radio broadcasting had become very important in national and international communication. John E. Harley's book *World-wide Influence of the Cinema* (Los Angeles, 1941) was one of the early studies on the multi-cultural function of movies. Paul F. Lazarsfeld was one of the first authors to stress the propagandistic functions of radio broadcasting across national borders; his "Radio and International Cooperation as a Problem of Psychological Research" (*Journal of Consulting Psychology*, Jan.-Feb., 1946) was one of first studies in this area. He and some of his colleagues continued their work in this area and discovered many interesting things about the role of broadcasting in international propaganda.

The development of television since the 1950's revolutionized the cross-national relations and opened new and dramatic channels for global information. In close connection with television development is the use of communication satellites for various purposes. UNESCO's book *Communications in the Space Age—The Use of Satellites by the Mass Media* (Paris, 1968) shows some of the ways the traditional media can use this marvelous technical aid.

It can probably be said safely that it was in the late 1940's and early 1950's that the study of international communications really became important. Articles and books began to be seen more often in the 1940's, but it was not until the 1950's that the literature of international communications exploded around the world. This literature was still rather general, uneven and fragmented, to be sure, but it began to be taken seriously. A new area of concern in journalism had arrived—accompanied, of course, by a parallel interest in international communication in such fields as sociology and political science. In the 1940's and 1950's—and especially in the latter years of the 1960's—an ever-increasing number of bright young scholars have become interested in the international ramifications of communication and have brought their individual talents to bear on the subject. Psychologists, social psychologists and sociologists have studied the communication process across national boundaries (and within nations themselves) from the perspective of the individual person and of the entire social system. Political scientists have become concerned about the impact of communication on internal national politics and development, as well as on international relations. Behavioral scientists generally, taking a broad eclectic approach, have plumbed, with greatly improved research sophistication, the complex relationships between communication and human and social behavior.

One of the purposes of this book is to indicate, in a survey manner to be sure, the broad and varied aspects of the area of international communication. So far as we know, this is the first book which presents a collection of readings specifically related to international communication. In it we have tried to present articles and portions of books and theses which relate to a dozen important aspects of this area. There are many more areas and sub-areas, of course, which are not dealt with in this volume. We have begun with the broader, more general, aspects of international communication and have worked toward the end of the book to more specific concerns and areas of the field. We have tried to present readings in this book which stress the overall *international* concern and not specific national concerns; this has not been easy, and an occasional article may appear which the reader might feel presents a "national" emphasis. When this happens, however, we have felt that the article reflects an idea or concept which the reader, with a minimum of imagination, can *internationalize*.

We have tried to design a book which will be useful in a number of courses and will be of some interest to the general—especially the general *academic*—reader. A few of the articles have never been published before; however, most of them are reprints—occasionally with considerable editing or rewriting to make them more appropriate for this book. In a few cases parts of several chapters of an original book or dissertation have been spliced or interwoven so as to make a more relevant part of this anthology; and in several cases we have supplied a new title for the spliced portions.

In conclusion, we wish to thank the many persons who have assisted us, with encouragement and actual help, in bringing out this book. And there have been many such persons, both in and out of the United States and West Germany. Especially are we grateful to the individual authors and publishers who have given us permission to use portions of their material and have aided us in numerous ways. We have tried to provide—for the many teachers, scholars, practitioners and others engaged in the study of, and endeavors in, international communication—a compact and concise book which will serve as a catalyst to discussion and further research. If this book has, even in a small way, served to this end, we are more than satisfied.

Heinz-Dietrich Fischer,
Universities of Bochum and Cologne (Germany)
John Calhoun Merrill, *University of Missouri* (U.S.A.)

INTRODUCTION

Despite sometimes overwhelming evidence to the contrary, men of good intentions refuse to relinquish their hope that a system of free and open communication on a global scale will one day bring peace, justice and prosperity to all. Such a faith is not easily held, for its realization is threatened not by any failure in technological or institutional progress, but by the very nature of man. Those who believe that the mere *capacity* to communicate is sufficient to deter men from killing one another must come to grips with the haunting question of whether man really wants to communicate with his fellow beings. And beyond this lies an even more threatening possibility—that such notions as "world-community" are now being re-stated in such gross and simplistic terms as to render our traditional concepts of liberty and freedom meaningless.

Those who seriously regard the expansion of capabilities for international communications as a positive step forward might pause to consider whether the opening of new channels, the widespread battle to increase literacy, and the massive increase in application of the new electro-mechanical media guarantee that men and nations will be more favorably disposed to seek either understanding or peace. We are agonizingly aware that many nations which have the capability of making their intentions known to those with whom they have differences still persist in the use of armed force to settle matters. Note that the communicative option we call "war" has been employed among and within nations on this planet over fifty times since the arrival of the ultimate weapon in 1945 made "all future war unthinkable." Small wonder that there is growing impatience with the tenuous faith of those who feel that calm and logical appraisal of communicative systems will ultimately point the way toward reason, international sanity, and peace on earth.

Even if he can resist the forces of pessimism, the man of good will may still find it difficult to associate his aims and aspirations with those of certain of his fellow beings who have also discovered serious deficiencies in man's ability to live with, let alone communicate with, his fellow man. Rampant among us are the Global Villagers, the Computer-Technocrats and the Woodstock Nationals, all of whom have long since abandoned any hope that knowledge—at least in any of its linear, analytical and embarrassingly factual forms—will solve whatever issue they regard as paramount for this season. The more passionate among them will quickly reduce such phrases as "international understanding" to the level of other folk-song-and-cinema clichés like "war is hell," "love is all," and "heaven is near"—all of which are sure-fire hits among the sentimental young, who somehow feel that they have made a startlingly new discovery about the human condition. Their concern is natural, and might even be regarded as a hopeful sign in the battle for sanity were it not for the fact that they are ultimately used only for profit by purveyors of sentimentality in its cheapest and most stultifying forms. All who share real concern for the destiny of mankind must now consider whether such self-professed allies may not be our worst enemies.

Somewhere between the global village of savage innocence and the computer-driven world of total technological "achievement" lies a shell-pocked middle ground where some kind of stand for man's ability to defend himself must be made. The accomplishments here are seldom colorful, shocking or exciting, but it is only on such ground that communicators, students of communication, and all who believe in the intelligent use of public media may elect to stand. Something more than vague feelings of universal brotherhood—and something more than technological super-organization—is essential if we are to prevail.

In this work, two dedicated scholars of communication engage in the difficult and continuing task of mapping that ground. The work of Drs. Heinz-Dietrich Fischer and John Calhoun Merrill is a welcome addition to *Studies in Public Communication*.

A. William Bluem, Ph.D.
Professor
S. I. Newhouse Communications Center
Syracuse University

I

COMMUNICATION
SYSTEMS
AND CONCEPTS

Heinz-Dietrich Fischer
FORMS AND FUNCTIONS OF
    SUPRANATIONAL COMMUNICATION

John C. Merrill
THE PRESS AND SOCIAL RESPONSIBILITY

W. Phillips Davison
THE ROLE OF COMMUNICATION IN DEMOCRACIES

Mark W. Hopkins
THREE SOVIET CONCEPTS OF THE PRESS

James W. Markham
COMMUNIST REGIMES, MASS MEDIA AND SOCIETY

1

COMMUNICATION SYSTEMS

AND CONCEPTS

JOURNALISTIC concepts, in their broadest sense, vary widely throughout the world. One would expect the role or function of the media of mass communication to differ significantly between, say, a Communist nation and a Capitalist nation. And, indeed, this is the case. But, it should be noted that even within so-called ideological contexts—between Yugoslavia and the Soviet Union, for example, or between West Germany and the United States—there are significant differences.

In addition, within any *one* press system there is growing debate about basic communication purpose or concept; many press systems appear to be changing rather rapidly, thus bringing about interesting dialogue concerning a redefinition of basic journalistic concepts. The mid-20th century emphasis on the press' responsibility to society, not only in controlled press systems but also in libertarian press systems, is a case in point. Many observers are struck by the fact that a universal trend is growing to consider social stability and national progress more important than free discourse in a pluralistic press system.

The function of mass communication, not only within particular press systems but also among national press systems, is receiving increasing attention. In a way, this is a primary concern in any book related to *international* communication, and Heinz-Dietrich Fischer's opening article of this chapter discusses both the roles and functions of supranational communication. John Merrill follows this discussion with a more opinionated analysis of the whole concept of "social responsibility," placing it not only on libertarian foundations where it is usually found but relating it also to the closed or controlled systems, both Left and Right.

Following these two articles, W. Phillips Davison of Columbia University discusses the role of mass communication in libertarian democracies and points out interesting implications for *international* communication. Mark Hopkins, a long-time student of the Soviet Union, shows that press concepts in a socialist society not only vary among individuals at any one time, but change—albeit slowly—through the years. Perhaps the best lesson learned from Hopkins is that no press system is really as simplistic or monolithic as might be generally assumed.

James W. Markham, after studying both the Chinese and Soviet Communist press systems, provides in the final article of this chapter a fascinating overview of the similarities and differences of the two systems. Markham agrees with Hopkins that the Soviet press has been quite adaptable to change. As to China, he points out that, although changes in the press there have not been profound, there are evidences that public opinion increasingly will have an impact on social change and, along with it, on mass communication itself.

Certainly the reader will recognize that other press systems exist in addition to those in Communist and libertarian-democratic nations. These systems, usually called "authoritarian," combine the characteristics of both the Communist and "free" concepts, even though the organization or structure may differ somewhat. It is interesting to speculate on the broad global trends of ideologically based press theory: toward more free and open systems, or toward more controlled and "responsible" systems?

*   *   *   *

RELATED READING

Buzek, Antony. *How the Communist Press Works*. New York: Frederick A. Praeger, 1964.

Commission on Freedom of the Press. *A Free and Responsible Press*. Chicago: University of Chicago Press, 1947.

Davison, W. Phillips. *International Political Communication*. New York: Frederick A. Praeger, 1965.

General Council of the Press. *The Press and the People*. London: General Council of the Press, 1954.

Schulte, Henry F. *The Spanish Press 1470-1966: Print, Power, and Politics*. Urbana: University of Illinois Press, 1968.

Siebert, Fred S., Theodore Peterson and Wilbur Schramm. *Four Theories of the Press*. Urbana: University of Illinois Press, 1963.

Stephenson, William. *The Play Theory of Mass Communication*. Chicago: University of Chicago Press, 1967.

Markham, James W. *Voices of the Red Giants: Communication in Russia and China*. Ames: The Iowa State University Press, 1967.

Wright, Charles R. *Mass Communication: A Sociological Perspective*. New York: Random House, 1959.

Yu, Frederick T. C. *Mass Persuasion in Communist China*. New York: Frederick A. Praeger, 1964.

Heinz-Dietrich Fischer:

Forms and Functions of Supranational Communication

GEORGE N. GORDON has said that "various forms of communication be-tween living organisms had doubtless reached heights of sophistication long before even primitive speech (or noise) was invented." [1] The dialogue between different people and countries is as old as the history of man and nations. At least three basic elements of expression and communication have been available as "raw material" in all epochs of history: [2] the word, [3] the picture (drawing),[4] and the sound (noise).[5] And the earliest mode of communication with a larger group of people was probably speech.

Houston Peterson says that "we can be sure that tens of thousands of years ago there were individuals who cast spells over their fellows with the magic of words. At first it was not words so much as the rhythm, the sounds, the incantation that was a part of ritual. Chiefs, priests, medicine men . . . must have risen to power through skill in speech as well as skill in arms. They must have addressed themselves, in hope or in terror, to the mysterious forces of nature and to the spirits of dead relatives. Then, as now, stirring words helped to hurry men to hunt or to battle, and after-ward the defeat or the victory would be relived with those who had remained behind. Perhaps the first formal orations were delivered at the graves of heroes." [6] Political and religious aims may well have been merged in those early speeches.

As a consequence of these basic possibilities of expression we find that since earliest times there have been forms of propaganda of different

[1] George N. Gordon, *The Languages of Communication: A Logical and Psychological Examination*, New York: Hastings House, 1969, p. 237.
[2] Cf. Hanns Buchli, *6000 Jahre Werbung: Geschichte der Wirtschaftswerbung und der Propaganda*, Vol. 1: Altertum and Mittelalter, Berlin: Walter de Gruyter & Co., 1962, p. 49 ff.
[3] Cf. Lutz Mackensen, *Auf den Spuren des Wortes*, Hamburg: Verlag Nannen, 1964.
[4] Cf. Lancelot Hogben, *From Cave Painting to Comic Strip*, New York: Chanticleer Press, 1949.
[5] Cf. John Robinson Pierce, *Symbols, Signals and Noise: The Nature and Process of Communication*, New York: Harper & Row, 1961.
[6] Houston Peterson (ed.), *A Treasury of the World's Great Speeches*, New York: Simon and Schuster, 1967, p. 1.

► This is an original article done for this book by Heinz-Dietrich Fischer, Universities of Bochum and Cologne (Germany). Short portions of the article were presented at a guest lecture by the author before a class in international communications at the School of Journalism, University of Iowa, Iowa City, March 19, 1969.

kinds,[7] both political and religious. Besides good examples of political propaganda of the early cultures,[8] we have several parts in the Holy Bible which show how and why peoples communicated with each other and what the content of their communication was. Especially the Old Testament is largely composed of speeches and sermons—good examples of communication between different cultures. And in the New Testament we have of the earliest instructions in this respect. Among Jesus of Nazareth's last words on earth were those exhorting his disciples to "go . . . and teach all nations" (St. Matthew, 28) or to "go . . . into all the world, and preach the gospel to everey creature" (St. Mark, 16).

In the Ancient World the Hebrews, Greeks and Romans developed new forms of political propaganda by using—for example—heroic titles, coins,[9] specific symbols, or gigantic constructions of architecture. Flags, beacon fires and other instruments were the early transmission belts for information within or outside of the empires.[10] In many ways Greeks and Romans tried to keep contact with their neighbouring countries by using various forms of written or unwritten communication. It is said that the famous 'Acta Diurna,' founded by Julius Caesar and one of the forerunners of modern information media, was distributed nearly all over the Roman Empire.[11] In addition to political propaganda, later on religion became one of the most important parts of cross-cultural communication.

Missionaries especially became real communicators between people of different countries, languages, and races. They tried to replace the old concept of the *Imperium Romanum* by popularizing the basic ideas of Augustines' book *De civitate dei* (written 413-426 A.D.) all over Europe. The different missionary activities [12] of the Church were centralized in 1622 by constituting the famous "Congregatio de Propaganda fide," which became the first propagandistic headquarters for the then known world.[13] The "propaganda fide" was one of the reactions of the Catholic church to the Reformation and a result of the Thirty Years War (1618-1648), when the Protestants developed a press policy and several journalistic activities, especially from Sweden. In this war—which was indeed a world

[7] Cf. Alfred Sturminger, 3000 *Jahre politische Propaganda*, Vienna—Munich: Verlag Herold, 1960.
[8] Cf. Yigael Yadin, "Communication in ancient Israel," *Gazette* (Leiden), Vol. 7/No. 1 (1961), pp. 158-162. See also Fumio Yamamoto, "Reporting in ancient Japan," *Gazette* (Leiden), Vol. 2/No. 1 (1956), pp. 29-52.
[9] Cf. Carol Humphrey Sutherland, *Coinage in Roman Imperial Policy* 31 B.C.-A.D. 68, London: Methuen, 1951.
[10] Cf. Wolfgang Riepl, *Das Nachrichtenwesen des Altertums mit besonderer Berücksichtigung auf die Römer*, Leipzig—Berlin: Verlag von B. G. Teubner, 1913.
[11] Cf. J(oseph) Vic(tor) Le Clerc, *Des journaux chez les Romains*, Paris: Firmin Didot Frères, 1838.
[12] Cf. Adolf von Harnack, *Die Mission und die Ausbreitung des Christentums in den ersten drei Jahrhunderten* (2 Vols.), Leipzig: Hinrichsche Buchhandlung, 1915.
[13] Cf. *Collectanea S. Congregationis de Propaganda Fide seu Decreta Instructiones Rescripta pro Apostolicis Missionibus*, Vol. 1, Ann. 1622-1866, Nos. 1-1299. Rome: Ex Typographia Polyglotta, S.C. de Propaganda Fide, MCMVII.

war of that time—different forms of political and religious propaganda were practised and had effects in many countries.[14]

Since the Middle Ages, Latin as the *lingua franca* of Europe was pushed back step by step and replaced by various national languages. These languages became the main vehicle of communication for the European colonial powers in many parts of the world—especially for the English, Spanish, Portuguese, and French. This development, together with the growth of the press, was one of the most remarkable communication revolutions of all the times. These transplantations of communication systems around the globe had the result that an evolutionary process took place, merging the traditional form of communication of the newly conquered countries with those of the conquerers.[15] The English "Glorious Revolution" (1688/89) and especially the French Revolution (1789) were not only the starting points for political and social reforms of all kinds, but also the impulses for the growth of general freedom of communication.[16] The idea of free expression of ideas among the people of the home country and across the national borders never died since that time, although Napoleon Bonaparte tried to get control of public opinion for making his own imperialistic propaganda throughout great parts of Europe.[17] A French scholar made the observation that this "revolutionary period which we consider to begin about 1770 and to end about 1850, witnessed the development of newspapers into 'mass communication media' in the entire Western world," [18] because newspapers from then on became available for bigger groups than ever before. In connection with this remarks one has to mention the growing importance of hymns, songs and arts as forms of journalistic expression following the Revolution in France [19] and during the Belgian Revolution of 1830,[20] spreading from country to country.

[14] Cf. Elmer Adolf Beller, *Propaganda in Germany During the Thirty Years' War*, Princeton/N.J.: Princeton University Press, 1940. See also: Göran Rystad, *Kriegsnachrichten und Propaganda während des dreißigjährigen Krieges*, Lund/Sweden: C. W. K. Gleerup, 1960.
[15] See among others: Livingston Rowe Schnyler, *The Liberty of the Press in the American Colonies Before the Revolutionary War*, New York: T. Whittacker, 1905.
[16] Cf. Wilhelm Bauer, *Die öffentliche Meinung in der Weltgeschichte*, Wildpark-Potsdam: Akademische Verlagsgesellschaft Athenaion, 1930, p. 211 ff.
[17] Cf. Robert B. Holtman, *Napoleonic Propaganda*, Baton Rouge: Louisiana State University Press, 1950. See also: Robert B. Holtman, "Thought Control in Napoleon's Satellite Countries," *Gazette* (Leiden), Vol. 4/No. 3 (1958), pp. 209-218.
[18] Jacques Godechot, "The Origin of Mass Communication Media," *Gazette* (Leiden), Vol. 8/No. 2 (1962), p. 81.
[19] Cf. C(onstant) Pierre, *Les Hymnes et Chansons de la Révolution*, Paris: Impr. nationale, Champion, 1904. See also: Cornwell B. Rogers, "Songs—colorful propaganda of the French Revolution," *Public Opinion Quarterly* (Princeton/N.J.) Vol. 11/No. 3 (Fall 1947), pp. 436-444. Cf. also: David L. Dowd, "Art as national propaganda in the French Revolution," *Public Opinion Quarterly* (Princeton, N.J.) Vol. 25/No. 3 (Fall 1951), pp. 532-546.
[20] Cf. Theo Luykx, *Politieke Geschiedenis van Belgie van 1789 tot heden*, Brussels—Amsterdam: Elsevier, 1964, pp. 44 ff.

During the 19th Century one concept dominated in nearly all of the important nations and often became a mighty force and a kind of myth: *public opinion*.[21] And also mass movements can be found all over Europe as a communication factor with steadily growing importance: demonstrations, public festivities, world exhibitions, congresses, etc. With the growth of modern political forces, more and more slogans, rumors and whispering campaigns have received importance in international communication.[22] The middle of the 19th Century ushered in the so-called newsagency-epoch,[23] and it was also the time when numerous foreign correspondents spread all over the world.[24] A permanent activity in international communication since 1864 came from the different supranational communication institutions of the Socialists (Socialist International).[25]

A real bundle of international communication activities with highly propagandistic appeal was developed during and since World War I, and certain propaganda techniques were used by all nations which took part in the war.[26] During the late phase of the war a new medium was used for propagandistic purposes: the Motion Picture, which was first used as a propaganda instrument by the German War Press Department.[27] After the foundation of the League of Nations, Geneva became one of the most important communication centers of the world,[28] but the global information policy of the League was not too successful.[29] Much more activity in international communication showed, for example, the Communist International (Comintern), which was founded by Lenin in March, 1919.[30] Since the early 1920's various movements of Fascism became more and more popular in several parts of Europe with a certain international propagandistic function.[31]

[21] Cf. Frederick C. Irion, *Public Opinion and Propaganda*, New York: Crowell, 1950.
[22] Cf. Emil Dovifat, *Handbuch der Publizistik* (3 Vols.), Berlin: Walter de Gruyter & Co., 1968 f.
[23] Cf. Kent Cooper, *Barriers Down: The Story of the News Agency Epoch*, New York: Farrar & Rinehart, 1942.
[24] Cf. John Hohenberg, *Foreign Correspondence: The Great Reporters and their Times*, New York: Columbia University Press, 1964.
[25] Cf. Julius Braunthal, *Geschichte der Internationale* (2 Vols.), Hannover: Verlag J. H. W. Dietz Nachf., 1961-1963.
[26] Cf. Harold D(wight) Lasswell, *Propaganda Technique in the World War*, New York: Alfred A. Knopf, 1927. See also: James R. Mock and Cedric Larson, *Words that won the war. The story of the Committee on Public Information 1917-1919*, Princeton/N.J.: Princeton University Press, 1939.
[27] Cf. Georges Sadoul, *Histoire du cinéma mondiale des origines à nos jours*, (5th ed.), Paris: Flammarion, 1959.
[28] Albin E. Johnson, "Geneva now world's propaganda center," *Editor & Publisher* (New York), Vol. 60/April 21, 1928, p. 94.
[29] Cf. Dell G. Hitchner, "The Failure of the League: Lesson in Public Relations," *Public Opinion Quarterly* (Princeton, N. J.), Vol. 8/Spring 1944, pp. 61-71.
[30] Cf. Franz Borkenau, *The Communist International*, London: Faber & Faber, 1938.
[31] Cf. Ernst Nolte, *Die faschistischen Bewegungen. Die Krise des liberalen Systems und die Entwicklung der Faschismen*, Munich: Deutscher Taschenbuch Verlag, 1966. See also: Theodor W. Adorno, "Freudian Theory and the Pattern of Fascist Propaganda,"

At the same time radio broadcasting made its first steps to become an influential instrument for national and international communication. Especially the short-wave radio, already in its very early stage of development, was discovered for its supranational communication value. During the 1930's radio broadcasting became the most intensive vehicle for message transmissions in nearly all parts of the world.[32] The instrument was used extensively by the leading political powers, and Hitler was fascinated by the various possibilities of this medium. Journalistic and propagandistic instruments and techniques were used by nearly every nation during World War II as psychological weapons. To some extent the war was also a propaganda war, mainly led by radio broadcasting.[33] A very important instrument of international communication during and after the war became the newsreels with a rather high level of output.[34]

After 1945 a couple of organizations were established for promoting international understanding by developing the process of international communication—for example, UNESCO and the I.P.I. The communist-ruled countries established in 1947 in Bucharest (Rumania) the COMINFORM (Communist Information Bureau), which was the headquarters of the propaganda activities of the World's Communism until its liquidation in April, 1956.[35]

Along with all these mainly political institutions there were also established some international religious organizations for propagandizing the ideas of the various churches in the modern world. For example, the World Council of Churches in Geneva established a special Department of Communication. In April, 1954, the "Trans World Radio" system of several protestant churches was begun.[36] A much longer tradition in worldwide religious radio broadcasting was "Radio Vaticana" (founded 1931), which transmits in about 30 languages of the world.[37] Great emphasis to

---

in: Géza Róheim (ed.), *Psychoanalysis and the Social Sciences*, Vol. 3, New York: International Universities Press, 1951, pp. 279-300.

[32] Hans-Joachim Weinbrenner, "Grenzenloser Rundfunk," in: Kurt Wagenführ (ed.), *Jahrbuch Welt-Rundfunk*, Vol. 1:1937/38, Berlin—Heidelberg: Vowinckel, 1938. See also: John D. Tomlinson, *International control of radio-communications*, Ann Arbor/Michigan—Geneva: Edwards, 1945.

[33] Thomas O. Beachcroft, *Calling all Nations*, London: British Broadcasting Corporation, 1942. See also: John Hargrave, *Words Win Wars, Propaganda the Mightiest Weapon of All*, London, 1940; Charles J. Rolo, *Radio Goes to War*, London: Faber, 1943; Daniel Lerner, *Sykewar, Psychological Warfare against Germany*, New York: Library of Policy Sciences, 1949.

[34] See Peter Baechlin and Maurice Muller-Strauss, *La Presse Filmée dans le Monde*, Paris: UNESCO, 1951.

[35] Cf. F. Bowen Evans, *Worldwide Communist Propaganda Activities*, New York: Macmillan, 1955. See also: Denis Healey, "The Cominform and World Communism," *International Affairs* (London/England), Vol. 24/July 1948, pp. 339-349.

[36] Karl Heinz Hochwald, "Trans World Radio und Evangeliums-Rundfunk," *Communicatio Socialis* (Emsdetten), Vol. 2/No. 1 (1969), pp. 56 ff.

[37] Cf. UNESCO, *World Communications: Press—Radio—Television—Film*, New York—Paris: UNESCO Publications Center, 1964, pp. 295 ff.

the problem of global communication possibilities was given by the Second Vatican Council which concluded a special Decree on the Instruments of Social Communication ("Inter mirifica") on December 12, 1963. According to No. 18 of "Inter mirifica" [38] it was planned that a so-called "World Day of Social Communication Media" annually should be arranged by Catholics around the world. The first of these World Communication Days was declared by Pope Paul VI for May 7, 1967,[39] and a second was arranged for May 26, 1968.[40] A special declaration on "The Church and the Media of Mass Communication" was also presented to the Fourth General Assembly of the Ecumenical Council of Churches, held in Uppsala, Sweden in July, 1968. This declaration "was approved and recommended by the Assembly in its essential features. Compared with the Vatican Council's Decree on the Instruments of Social Communication ("Inter mirifica") it shows some correspondence in principle, emphasizing, however, different conditions of communication activities in various countries." [41]

As was mentioned earlier, "international broadcasting grew as the totalitarian countries began to propagandize their neighbors—frequently with the ultimate objective of conquering them—and the democratic countries began international services in response to the dictators' broadcasts. During World War II, the propaganda services of the German Reich and the British Broadcasting Corporation competed for acceptance in Europe and throughout the world. . . Just as World War I stimulated the development of radio, so the electronic advances of World War II contributed to the emergence of television which soon became the dominant electronic medium." [42] Besides radio broadcasting, which had been a real medium "without barriers" [43] for a long time, in the 1950's and especially in the 1960's television became *the* communication instrument for national and international purposes *par excellence*. Across-the-border telecasting operations became quite common, and across-the-Atlantic transmissions were possible after launching the first satellite (Telstar-1) in July, 1962. Since that time the term of "Communication in Space Age" became a synonym

[38] Cf. John W. Mole OMI, "The Communications Decree of the Second Vatican Council charter of the communications apostolate," *Social Justice Review* (St. Louis/ Missouri), Vol. 59/1966, pp. 274-350.
[39] Pope Paul VI, "Nuntius Radiotelevisificus Universis catholicis Christifidelibus, ob diem recto instrumentorum communicationis socialis usui provehendo per totum orbem terrarum dicatam," *Communicatio Socialis* (Emsdetten), Vol. 1/No. 1 (1968), pp. 53-57 (French and German version).
[40] Text in: *Communicatio Socialis* (Emsdetten), Vol. 1/No. 4 (1968), pp. 343-346 (French and German version).
[41] Heinz Melzer, "Publizistik im Spiegel von Konzilsdekret und Uppsala-Erklärung," *Communicatio Socialis* (Emsdetten), Vol. 1/No. 4 (1968), p. 295 (summary).
[42] Burton Paulu, *Radio and Television Broadcasting on the European Continent*, Minneapolis: University of Minnesota Press, 1967, p. 4.
[43] Cf. George A. Codding Jr., *Broadcasting Without Barriers*, Paris: UNESCO, 1959.

for this most modern form of communication facilities.[44] Doubtless the "Age of Television" [45] or the Space Age later in communication history will be considered a *communication revolution* because it will have many expected and unexpected influences on how people and nations communicate with each other.

So far this brief discussion has dealt with the evolution of different forms of communication. As could be demonstrated, sometimes various forms together result in a new kind of expression, but not all of these forms can be called media or even mass media. To give a systematic overview on the various areas of communication research—both in national or international context—it is necessary to present this listing [46] which includes all the possible means and forms:

● *Original Communication:*
  1. Signals (Symbols, Flags, Signs)
  2. Word and Sound (Speech, Device, Slogan, Rumor)
  3. Arrangement (Assembly, Ceremony, Demonstration)

● *Intermediatorial Communication*
  4. Press (Pamphlet, Leaflet, Newspaper, Magazine)
  5. Picture (Drawing, Cartoon, Poster, Photo)
  6. Broadcasting (Radio, Television)
  7. Film (Documentary Film, Newsreel, Movie)
  8. Stage and Literature (Political Theater, Cabaret, Political Literature, Political Song).

This overview makes clear that, for example, forms of original communication in certain cases can be merged with those of intermediatorial: *i.e.*, if slogans, symbols, signs, etc., are brought to a larger audience by press or film, or if speeches or demonstrations are transmitted by broadcasting.

Some of these media, forms and subgroups are more, and some are less, predestined for international dialogues between people and nations, but at first we must, in this context, distinguish some basic questions. Our literature and oral discourse today often is using two terms for research activities in world-wide or regional communications: some people use "intercultural communication"; others prefer "international communication"; a third group of researchers is using both of them without making

---

[44] See: UNESCO, *Communication in Space Age. The Use of Satellites by the Mass Media*, Paris: UNESCO, 1968. Cf. also: Wilson P. Dizard, *Television: A World View*, Syracuse/N.Y.: Syracuse University Press, 1966. See also: François Pigé, *La Télévision dans le Monde—Organisation Administrative et Financière*, Paris: Societé Nationale des Enterprises de Presse, 1962.

[45] Cf. Leo Bogart, *The Age of Television* (2nd ed.), New York: F. Unger, 1958.

[46] Cf. *Studium der Publizistik*: Münster/Germany: Institut für Publizistik an der Westfälischen Wilhelms-Universität, 1961, p. 5.

any distinctions. But in reality there exist two different meanings [47] which Gerhard Maletzke has defined as follows:

> *Intercultural Communication* is the process of the exchange of thoughts and meanings between people of differing cultures.
> *International Communication* is the communications process between different countries or nations across frontiers.

If one accepts these definitions, he might say: International and intercultural communication *may* be the very same, but not necessarily. Often there exists inter*national* communication between people of the same culture (often using even the same language), but separated from each other by national borders. On the other hand it is also possible to find inter*cultural* communication within one country if people of different cultures (and often with different languages—minority groups) communicate with each other. Sometimes the terms "supranational" or "comparative" communication are used as well, and there seems to be no real consensus in the use of terminology.

Hamid Mowlana seems to be a little too pessimistic when he said at a convention of communication researchers: "Although we are more able to cover International Communication systematically, I don't believe there is promise in trying to conquer it as a whole." [48] But Mowlana is quite right with his remark that for the individual researcher "there will have to be some form of specialization within the field." And in another context, Mowlana says: "The primary emphasis is on an introduction to the activities focused on the phenomena of international communication. After an examination of the range and definition of phenomena, an attempt is made to lay a foundation for an identification and critical evaluation of major approaches, theories, concepts, and propositions with particular attention being paid to problems of analytical integration within the field of study and to problems of interdisciplinary contributions and coherence." [49]

James W. Markham belongs to the group of researchers which looks to the past as a first step toward understanding the international communication situation of our time: "As for communications law and history, these subjects can adapt certain obvious international comparative approaches. Mass communication systems everywhere and in past times are usually more closely related to political and legal systems of nation-states than to other aspects of the society. The student's explorations on the

[47] Gerhard Maletzke, "Intercultural and International Communication," in chapter 12 of this book.
[48] Hamid Mowlana, *International Communication: A Probe into Methods and Approaches,* paper presented to the National Conference on the Teaching of International Communication, Racine/Wisconsin, March 27-30, 1969, p. 3.
[49] *Ibid.,* p. 8.

history of American journalism is more effectively conducted in the context of the development of world communications." [50]

Touching on the time factor in communication history, this brings up the question: Which of the journalistic concepts of our time is most-accepted in great parts of the world? The slogans of the libertarian theory of the function of the mass media have been the "self-righting process" and the "free market place of ideas," but "several types of limitation on the freedom [of communication] have been universally accepted as being consistent with libertarian principles." [51] It seems that Lenin's formula of 1901 is the best-known conception and is accepted not only by the communist countries but also by some communist-oriented groups in other nations. According to Lenin, the mass media have to be not only "a collective propagandist and collective agitator, but also a collective organizer." [52] There are, of course, several other conceptions of communication, but these two seem to be the ones which received acceptance in great parts of the world, whatever people in different countries may understand by those terms.

In any case, the main problem is what kind of content is preferred by the various media in national and international communication. Henk Prakke describes three functions of all communication as (1) information, (2) comment and (3) entertainment.[53] Information or innovation has to be the basic function from where all communication starts.[54] The comment function contains the opinionated analysis of information.[55] Entertainment in a general sense is described by William Stephenson as "Communication-pleasure." [56] Ralph Lowenstein tried to make a grouping of the "Elements of Emphasis" which he calls (a) News-information, (b) Interpretation-comment, and (c) Entertainment: [57]

> *Books:* 1. Interpretation, 2. Entertainment, 3. News.
> *Magazines:* 1. Interpretation, 2. Entertainment, 3. News.
> *Newspapers:* 1. News, 2. Interpretation, 3. Entertainment.

[50] James W. Markham, *International Communication Orientations for Professional Education*, paper presented at the Convention of the AEJ, International Communication Division, Lawrence/Kansas, August, 1968, p. 8.
[51] Fred S(eaton) Siebert, "The Libertarian Theory of the Press," in: Siebert, Theodore Peterson, and Wilbur Schramm, *Four Theories of the Press*, Urbana: University of Illinois Press, 1963, p. 70 and p. 54.
[52] Vladimir Ilych Lenin, *Collected Works*, Vol. 4. New York: International Publishers, 1927, p. 114.
[53] Cf. Henk Prakke et al., *Kommunikation der Gesellschaft. Einführung in die funktionale Publizistik*, Münster/Germany: Verlag Regensberg, 1968, pp. 65 ff.
[54] Cf. Wilbur Schramm, "Information Theory and Mass Communication," *Journalism Quarterly* (Iowa City/Iowa), Vol. 32 (1955), pp. 131-146.
[55] Cf. Charles E. Osgood, George J. Suci and Percy H. Tannenbaum, *The Measurement of Meaning*, Urbana/Illinois: University of Illinois Press, 1957.
[56] Cf. William Stephenson, *The Play Theory of Mass Communication*, Chicago and London: The University of Chicago Press, 1967.
[57] Ralph L. Lowenstein, *The Elements of Mass Communication*, paper presented to

Radio: 1. Entertainment, 2. News, 3. Interpretation.
Movies: 1. Entertainment, 2. Interpretation, 3. News.
Television: 1. Entertainment, 2. News, 3. Interpretation.

One would have to prove if this ranking could be similar or very different in the cases of international communication. But it can be said, for example, that "information is circulated internationally in three forms: as raw material, as semifinished goods, and as finished product," [58] and most of the research deals with the flow of news among countries. It is rather difficult to speak in general terms about cross-national effects of opinion expression of all kinds, but we know something about biasing and stereotyping in an international context, sometimes referred to by the expression "how nations see each other" [59] or "public opinion" in various countries. [60] Some forms of entertainment, especially sports events, have been brought to an international audience mainly by television. [61]

Very much still has to be done in this nearly unlimited area of research. Besides the books and articles dealing with the flow of news, such research has been undertaken in the fields of national and international attitudes and reactions to certain events. We do not know enough yet to make final decisions about the real corresponding functions in the international process. Making this clear, let us conclude with an observation from the controversial Marshall McLuhan about the cross-cultural influences between the United States and England: "Yet ten years of TV have Europeanized even the United States, as witness its changed feelings for space and personal relations. There is new sensitivity to the dance, plastic art, and architecture, as well as the demand for the small car, the paperback, sculptural hairdos and molded dress effects. . . . Notwithstanding, it would be misleading to say that TV will retribalize England and America. . . ." [62]

---

his "Mass Media and Society" Course, School of Journalism, University of Missouri, Columbia, Spring 1969.

[58] Llewelyn White and Robert D. Leigh, "Merchants of Words and Images," in Charles S. Steinberg (ed.), *Mass Media and Communication*, New York: Hastings House, 1966, p. 351.

[59] Cf. W. Buchanan and H. Cantril, *How Nations See Each Other*, Urbana: University of Illinois Press, 1953.

[60] Cf. Bruce L. Smith and Chitra M. Smith, *International Communication and Political Opinion*, Princeton: Princeton University Press, 1956, pp. 5-21.

[61] Cf. H.-D. Fischer, "Eurovision and Intervision Toward Mondovision" in Chapter 6 of this book.

[62] *Understanding Media: The Extensions of Man*, New York: The New American Library, Inc., 1964, p. 274.

John C. Merrill:

The Press and Social Responsibility

INCREASINGLY one hears reference to the responsibility of the press and less and less about its freedom to react independently in a democratic society. Not only has the concept permeated the authoritarian countries, where it is an expected development, but in the last 20 to 30 years it has made notable incursions into the press philosophy of the United States. On the surface this new emphasis seems notable and commendable. Many writers and speakers enthusiastically expound its virtues. But there are certain aspects of this growing concept which should be questioned and even challenged.

Four Theories of the Press, published in 1956,[1] attempted to put in intelligible language this concept of the press which has been materializing since World War II. It mentioned "social responsibility" as a press "theory" alongside Communism, authoritarianism and libertarianism. And from this book it has made its way, unchallenged in the main, into a number of assorted books, magazine articles and academic dissertations.

The Hutchins Commission's Concept

Although isolated journalists, statesmen and academicians had long been thinking in terms of "responsibility" as well as freedom for the mass media, there had really been no significant effort to place the concept as a theory—parallel in importance to "libertarianism"—until 1947 when the Commission on Freedom of the Press, headed by Robert Hutchins, discussed it in *A Free and Responsible Press.* Previously, it had been thought that responsibility was somehow automatically built into a libertarian press, that a "free press" in the Western democratic sense was responsible *per se* to its social system.

But the Hutchins Commission thought differently. After seeing a very clear danger in growing restriction of communications' outlets and general irresponsibility in many areas of the press, it offered this ominous warning: "If they (the agencies of mass communication) are irresponsible, not even

[1] Fred S. Siebert, Theodore Peterson and Wilbur Schramm, *Four Theories of the Press* (Urbana: Univ. of Ill. Press, 1956), pp. 73-103.

▶ From: Freedom of Information Center Publication 001 (University of Missouri), March, 1965, by J. C. Merrill.

the First Amendment will protect their freedom from governmental control. The amendment will be amended." [2]

For a while, it seemed that the majority of United States publishers were quite excited over the commission's "report" and the implications which they read in (or into) it; but by 1950 the issue had settled down, the journalists thinking that the best policy was to ignore it or feeling that the whole concept was simply too "fuzzy" to bother with further. Certain suggestions of the report, such as the possible need for the government to get into the communications business, had disturbed them much more than had the theoretical consideration of just what was meant by "social responsibility" of the press.

Theoretical Considerations

What does "social responsibility" mean as first used by the Hutchins group in 1947 and nine years later in *Four Theories of the Press*?

Proponents of "social responsibility" recognize that it is closely related to the libertarian press system, but they see it as going beyond the free press theory, in that it places many moral and ethical restrictions on the press.[3] It is a restrictive theory although its advocates do not stress this point. Instead of emphasizing "freedom," it stresses "responsibility" to the society of which it is a part.

If this responsibility is not forthcoming, voluntarily, then in time it will be absolutely necessary that it be imposed on the communications media by the government. According to the Hutchins group, press freedom is limited by a social responsibility to report facts accurately and in a meaningful context. Since such thinking inevitably leads to the advocacy of a regulatory system to watch the actions of the press and to keep it functioning properly (i.e., to keep it "socially responsible"), the Hutchins Commission suggested that some type of government regulation might be needed to assure that the press accept its responsibility.

The social responsibility "theory" implies a recognition by the media that they must perform a public service to warrant their existence. The main parts of the commission's report which seemed to have antagonized many American editors and publishers were those that intimated possible government involvement in the press system.

Who Defines "Responsibility?"

This so-called "theory" of social responsibility has a good ring to it and, like "love" and "motherhood," has an undeniable attraction for many. There is a trend throughout the world in this direction, which im-

---

[2] *A Free and Responsible Press* (Chicago: Univ. of Chicago Press, 1947), p. 80.
[3] If the "theory" is nothing more than an admonition to individual journalists to improve in their ethics, it can hardly be called a "theory"; at least there is nothing new in it.

plies a suspicion of, and dissatisfaction with, the libertarianism of Milton, Locke and even Jefferson. Implicit in this trend toward "social responsibility" is the argument that some group (obviously a governmental one, ultimately) can and must define or decide *what* is socially responsible. Also, the implication is clear that publishers and journalists acting freely cannot determine what is socially responsible nearly as well as can some "outside" or "impartial" group. If this power elite decides the press is not responsible, not even the First Amendment will keep the publishers from losing this freedom to government. This would appear to many as a suggestion of increased power accumulation at the national level, a further restriction of a pluralistic society.

No one would deny that the press, in one respect, would be more "responsible" if some type of governmental supervision came about; indeed, reporters could be kept from nosing about in "critical" areas during "critical" times. The amount of sensational material could be controlled in the press, or eliminated altogether. Government activities could always be supported and public policy could be pushed on all occasions. The press could be more "educational" in the sense that less hard news (crime, wrecks, disasters, etc.) would appear, while more news of art exhibits, concerts, speeches by government personages and national progress in general could be emphasized. In short, the press would stress the positive and eliminate, or minimize, the negative. Then, with one voice the press of the nation would be responsible to its society; and the definition of "responsible" would be functional—defined and carried out by government.

Government Control Inevitable

Many persons will object to this line of analysis and will say that "social responsibility" of the press of a nation does not necessarily imply government control. The writer contends that ultimately it does, since if left to be defined by various publishers or journalistic groups the term is quite relative and nebulous; and it is quite obvious that in the traditional context of American libertarianism no "solution" that would be widely agreed upon or enforced could ever be reached by non-government groups or individuals.

The only way a "theory" of social responsibility could have any significance in any country is for the government power elite to be the definer and enforcer of this type of press. Since in any country the organization of society—its social and political structure—determines to a large extent what responsibilities the press (and the citizen) owe society, every country's press quite naturally considers (or might logically consider) itself as being socially responsible.

Assuming that a nation's socio-political philosophy determines its press system, and undoubtedly it does, then it follows that every nation's press system is socially responsible. For example, the Marxist or Communist press system considers itself socially responsible,[4] and certainly it is responsible to its own social system. A capitalistic press, operating in a pluralistic context, would be diametrically opposite to what the Soviets consider a socially responsible press. It would be to the Soviets the most irresponsible press system imaginable, since "social responsibility" is roughly synonymous in Marxist theory to "party/government support." The Communist press *is* government, *is* reflective of the society, *is* an instrument for social conformity and support. As such it is "socially responsible."

All Systems "Socially Responsible"

The same thing might be said of the so-called "authoritarian" press system, exemplified in Spain. A critical press, a press which by its pluralistic nature would tend to undermine national policy and disrupt national harmony, would be anathema in an authoritarian nation like Spain. It would be considered quite "irresponsible" in that context. As it is with the Marxist press, the Spanish (authoritarian) press is conceived as an instrument of government—although in this case it might be privately owned.

The authoritarian press theory revolves around the idea that a person engaged in journalism does so as a special privilege of the National Leader. It follows that this journalist is under obligation to the leader and his government. The authority of that state, the national equilibrium, the status quo, must be supported and preserved under this theory. This is the social responsibility of the press—in an authoritarian context.

All this brings us back to the point about all press systems conceiving of themselves as socially responsible. Actually any other possibility would be unimaginable—at least over any substantial period of time. For the press of a nation is caught up in the governmental philosophy to such an extent that by an operational definition it must be socially responsible. It reflects the governmental philosophy and fits into the theoretical structure of its society. If it does not, then the politico-social structure of the country is in flux; either the government must change to fit the press (unrealistic) or the press must change to fit the government (realistic).

Those who say that the United States press is "irresponsible" are seeing in it some real or imaginary danger to the national society. Those who might view the press of the Soviet Union or Spain as irresponsible would do so if in their views the press was exhibiting mannerisms which endangered the equilibrium and ongoing of their respective national societies. Responsibility and irresponsibility are not only relative to the particular national society under consideration, but even within an individual society the terms have a multitude of meanings depending on the degree of pluralism present.

---

[4] It is also interesting that the Communist press considers itself not only socially responsible, but a free press.

"Responsibility" Implies "Control"

It is significant that in an authoritarian country nobody believes the press to be socially irresponsible. At least, if such brave critics exist, their complaints are made to one another and are not made public. Only in a libertarian nation, or in a quasi-libertarian nation such as France, are there persons who criticize the function of the press and condemn it for its "irresponsibility." This might lead one to think that in order to be "responsible" a press system *must* be authoritarian or Communist; and this is a valid assumption if one is to pursue this idea of social responsibility very far.

Following from what has been said, the following hypothesis can be made: The amount of social responsibility present in a press system is closely correlated to the amount of "control" some outside group exercises over that press system.

When Does Government Intervene?

The social responsibility proponents say that government should intervene "only when the need is great and the stakes are high." [5] They assure us that the government should not be heavy-handed. The question arises, however, as to just when is the need great enough and the stakes high enough for government to intervene. And just how much intervention by government is enough to be "heavy handed?"

According to *Four Theories of the Press* a "duty to one's conscience is the primary basis of the right of free expression under social responsibility theory." [6] This is all very well, but what relation does this have to the question of government intervention "if the need is great?" It would seem that "duty to one's conscience" is extremely relative and that a newspaper espousing the causes of Barry Goldwater, for example, would do so in as good conscience as would the newspaper espousing the tenets of Vice President Hubert Humphrey. Which is irresponsible to society? To what or which society? To which segment of what society? During the last presidential election many segments of our press were described as "irresponsible" by persons on various sides of various issues. Who would determine which segment or segments were "right" or "responsible?" The government presumably would do so.

The American press has been proceeding on unregulated initiative up until now. But the Hutchins group and its followers think it questionable, if not unwise, for this to continue, for the "citizen has a moral right to information and an urgent need for it" [7] and the implication is that the United States press is not giving it to the citizen. A moral right to *what*

[5] *Four Theories of the Press*, p. 95.
[6] *Ibid.*, p. 97.
[7] *Ibid.*, p. 101.

information? This is a significant question. Or, probably a better one: To *whose* information? Evidently the commission did not think that a pluralistic information system is good enough. Under such a system, which we now have—at least to a large degree—the citizen does get information and a wealth of it. Admittedly, there are gaps in it. But anyone vaguely familiar with information theory and semantics knows that there will always be gaps, and if different reporters observe and communicate it, there will always be variant versions.

Press Pluralism: Sound Theory

It is certainly not contended here that all information coming to the public from all mass communication outlets is reliable, honest, complete, fair and "socially responsible." Nobody really knows just how much of it is—or if any of it is. Since, in a nation such as the United States there is no ready definition for "social responsibility," there is really no standard to which our media seek to conform—even though, without a doubt, they would all conceive of themselves as "socially responsible."

Their very pluralism, their very diversity is the base of their nebulous idea that in our society they are responsible. Responsibility to our society implies a continuance of this very pluralistic communication—with all of its virtues and evils—and a constant guard against any encroachments by government on any level to "define" what is "responsible" to society and further to align the press to its definition.

This "press pluralism" concept seems much sounder, and certainly more meaningful, than "social responsibility." All press systems can claim to be responsible to their societies, but the idea of a pluralistic media system injecting a variety of opinions and ideas into the social fabric is one which only the libertarian system can reasonably claim.

Libertarianism, or press pluralism, then, if it is to be considered as a separate theory must embrace the right of, or at least the possibility for, some press units to deviate from others. If that be irresponsibility, we had better make the most it.

W. Phillips Davison:

The Role of Communication in Democracies

DOMESTIC practices affecting communications in any state held to determine both the nature of the messages from and about that state that go abroad and the impact that ideas from other countries have on its internal politics. The role of communication in democracies is a particularly complicated one, and imposes a number of limitations on the ways that democratic spokesmen can seek to influence foreign nations. It also causes difficulties for people in other countries when they try to evaluate the significance of news from democracies; and it produces a curious blend of susceptibility and invulnerability to messages from abroad on the part of citizens of democratic states.

Many of the characteristics that we associate with democracy depend on free access of all groups in a population to the channels of communication, both as senders and as receivers. These characteristics include nonviolent competition for political power among various groups within the nation (and the existence of machinery for the orderly transfer of power from one group to another), the ability of those outside the government to influence its actions, and the reliance of the government more on suasion and less on force to accomplish its domestic policies. Because of their political significance, the communication media in democracies are under constant pressure, on the one side from groups seeking preferential access, and on the other from those who feel themselves disadvantaged or who want to maintain freedom of access for all.

Democracies are also characterized by a respect for the individual, who is allowed wide latitude to seek full personal development according to his own inclinations, to pursue his own happiness, and to participate actively in a variety of groups. Satisfaction of personal desires likewise depends in large measure on access to information of many types and on freedom to communicate. Nevertheless, complete freedom for any individual can never be assured, since it may restrict the freedom of others or may conflict with strongly held group values. How much latitude each individual can be allowed is a problem with which democratic theorists have struggled since classical times; they agree only that individual freedom should be as great as possible.

Communications and the Functioning of Competing Groups

Since competing groups in a democracy have such diverse political interests, a far greater variety of media is necessary to satisfy their internal and external requirements than is the case in states where only one political point of view is permitted. Officials familiar with communications in India, for instance, have noted that, in proportion to population, much more varied information sources are required than is the case in a totalitarian country such as Communist China. Democratic states that have succumbed to totalitarianism, as Italy did in 1922 and Germany in 1933, witnessed a marked decline in the number of newspapers, magazines, and other information media that previously spoke for nongovernmental points of view. When the German press was "coordinated" after 1933, the same serial publication, by then under Nazi influence, recorded a similar decrease in the number of German newspapers, but this time explained that it was undesirable to have so many political points of view expressed, because this interfered with the formation of a single national will.

Recent trends toward the consolidation of the mass media in industrialized democracies have led to fears that in these countries, too, the media will no longer be able to give adequate expression to all principal points of view.

Perhaps equally important is the fact that many large media are hospitable to a broad range of opinions in their news coverage, even if they have become hesitant in expressing their own opinion.

Opportunities for competing groups to make use of communication channels are never perfect; some groups are better served than others. Nevertheless, most democracies have facilities for the dissemination of a wide range of information and attitudes, usually excluding material that is repugnant to moral values held by the overwhelming majority. This variety of expression enables individuals to nourish their own points of view by finding support for them in the stream of communications; it makes it possible for those with similar attitudes to learn about each other and to get in touch with each other; and it thus facilitates the growth of public opinion, the formation of new political groupings, and the modification of the programs of existing groups.

A democracy is, however, more than a network of contending groups. It is itself a larger group, and as such requires a communication network that will help ensure internal cohesion, reinforce democratic values, and assist in the formation of a national public opinion on vital issues. Plato's observation that democracy was possible only in small states may have been related to the fact that in his day effective communication via the mass media was not possible, and that a sufficient exchange of ideas through person-to-person channels could not be achieved throughout a large realm.[1]

Popular Influences on Government

Channels of communication from the citizenry to the government make it possible for those outside the governmental structure to influence official actions and policies. In democracies one channel is established constitutionally, in that all citizens are, in theory at least, assured of access to their representatives in the legislature. This channel is supplemented, and indeed usually overshadowed, by other mechanisms through which the citizen can influence officials: the public media, pressure groups, lobbies, communications to administrative agencies, and public opinion. Public-opinion polls offer a relatively new device through which popular views on a large range of issues can be made known to policy-makers.

It is characteristic of political communications in democracies that a large proportion of them are of a critical nature. Indeed, criticism is an important component in the working definition of news used by the mass media. When some institution or government agency is functioning as it should, this ordinarily remains unreported; a malfunction, however, usually merits headlines. The 999 honest government officials receive little attention; the one who proves to be corrupt may be at the center of the news for days.

Public opinion, especially, is likely to crystallize around an actual or potential grievance and to oppose something: corruption, segregation, integration, or inflation. Government officials may act or may be restrained from acting on an issue when they anticipate that their behavior is likely to mobilize a hostile public opinion.[2] This is not to say that public opinion does not also form around positive issues—better schools, a chicken in every pot, and so on. Many such examples could be cited, but they tend to be less noticeable than those that represent opposition.

The prevalence of critical communication in a democracy is often deplored. Nevertheless, criticism of things as they are, or as they might be, is vital to the functioning of a democratic order. Without them, organizations and opinions advocating change could not take shape, and an orderly transition of power from one government to another would be impossible. Even successful maintenance of an existing administration would be difficult unless malfunctions in need of correction were highlighted. While a certain ratio between expressions of approval and disapproval is necessary for stability, a preponderance of critical communications appears to be necessary to the functioning of a democracy, even

[1] Winston L. Brembeck and William S. Howell, *Persuasion: A Means of Social Control* (New York: Prentice-Hall, 1952), p. 9.
[2] David B. Truman, *The Governmental Process* (New York: Alfred A. Knopf, 1951), pp. 448-49, 511-12.

when the opinions of a majority favor things substantially as they are. Whether attention given to real or imagined malfunctioning is justified on the basis of newsworthiness or for some other reason, information media are playing a necessary role when they give an opportunity for critical voices to be heard. The status quo, if it is to be stable, must continuously be tested against possible alternatives.

Not all citizens in any democracy take an intelligent or continuous interest in the affairs of government; the circle of those interested in public affairs, and informed about them, may be relatively small. Political scientists sometimes differentiate among the general public, the "attentive public," and policy and opinion elites. The elites take the most active interest in governmental affairs, and the attentive public, which constitutes the audience for discussion among the elites, is sometimes mobilized to act with regard to one or another political issue. The general public, which may include far more than half the population, rarely communicates to policy-makers.

The dangers inherent in this situation have been noted. Without adequate citizen participation in the affairs of government, it is difficult for a democracy to find a solid basis for policy.[3] The nation may be dominated by demagogues or by selfish minorities, or its stability may be threatened as important elements become aware of their interests and power, and demand special privileges. When any group combines political interest and activity with selfishness and ignorance, the results can be disastrous, unless its influence is countered by other groups.

Governmental Dependence on Suasion

It is axiomatic that, in a democracy, laws cannot be enforced unless they enjoy the support, or at least the acquiescence, of a large majority. Indeed, the degree of compliance with some laws has been documented statistically, and it can be shown that enforcement agencies usually have to concern themselves with only a limited segment of the population.[4] If more than a small minority resists compliance, a law is likely to become a dead letter. Although most decisions are made by a few men, these usually decide on a given course of action only if they feel fairly certain that the public will support them. For they will hold power only as long as a sufficient number of citizens approve of the way it is being exercised.[5]

Communications from a government, like other communications, are subject to serious limitations when it comes to changing strongly held individual attitudes, but they are particularly important as a means of

[3] Lester Markel, "What We Don't Know *Will* Hurt Us," *The New York Times Magazine*, April 9, 1961.
[4] Floyd H. Allport, "The J-Curve Hypothesis of Conforming Behavior," *Journal of Social Psychology*, May 1934, pp. 141-83.
[5] Michael Balfour, *States and Mind* (London: Cresset Press, 1953), p. 119.

encouraging pro-government groups and rallying public opinion behind specific measures. Indeed, an official in a democracy who is unable to reach the public through the mass media and must rely on personal or official channels is deprived of a large measure of his influence.

Government information programs in a democracy often give rise to fears that democratic processes will be weakened. Yet there are also grave dangers in not maintaining facilities that enable a government to present its case and appeal for support. As with so many problems of democracy, the solution appears to lie in a proper balance—in this case between government publicity and private criticism.

Controversy Over Access to the Media

Because communications play such an important role in the functioning of groups that compete for power in a democracy, one feature of democratic life is pressure on the part of some groups for preferential access to the media of public communication, and counterpressure from others that seek greater access for themselves or for all members of the society.

The most obvious group seeking preferential access to the media is government. Indeed, many of the earliest newspapers served as official organs. The first newspaper to appear in France, Renaudot's *Gazette*, was founded with the assistance of the court, and Louis XIV himself frequently wrote for it. In most countries of Europe during the eighteenth and much of the nineteenth centuries, media expressing views contrary to those of the government were either suppressed or were subject to serious disabilities. As soon as formal government controls are removed from communication media, most governments attempt to secure preferential access to them by other means. Most states maintained similar bodies for influencing the mass media, although they were not always so well organized, and controversy has continued up to the present time about the extent to which government ought to try to influence the press and the means it should use.

Private interests, no less than governments, seek preferential access to the media of communication. In many democracies, labor and business, as well as political, religious, and social groups, support extensive public-relations programs, one of the principal purposes of which is to influence the content of the mass media. In addition, certain organs, although not officially spokesmen for economic interest groups, are believed to enjoy hidden subsidies or otherwise to be dominated by a particular point of view. Thus, the pre-Hitler *Frankfurter Zeitung*, one of the great newspapers of Europe, was considered to represent the views of a liberal industrial group that supported it.

As a matter of practice, no democracy has found a way of ensuring that communication facilities are open to all groups equally. Nevertheless, various formulas for equalizing access have been developed, and these are reflected in the laws and customs of each democracy. Many countries provide for the control of broadcasting by mixed commissions, representing both public and private bodies. Persons or groups who feel that they have been unfairly treated in the press are entitled under the laws of some states to demand space for a reply. A number of countries discourage press-radio combinations or limit the right of publishers to be involved in other businesses also.

The degree to which wide access to the public media can or should be assured by law and the extent to which preferential access of any group should be discouraged are both highly controversial questions. Certainly no one solution is the only correct one. Democracy can function (assuming its other requirements are fulfilled) as long as competing groups and interests are assured adequate use of communication media to satisfy their internal and external requirements, even though all do not have complete equality of access. A degree of preferential access for some groups is far less dangerous than the complete exclusion of others. If a government can suppress media serving other groups contending for political power, and pre-empt a major share of the communication spectrum for itself, then the threat of tyranny is imminent. Alternatively, if opposition groups enjoy a vastly preferred position, and no government is able to mobilize a favorable public opinion, then anarchy or instability is assured. American concern about the threat posed by government domination of communication channels may be explained in part by the fact that the ability of governmental leaders to reach their supporters, put their case before the country, and rally public opinion has never been seriously in doubt. Other democracies, in which political communications are primarily along tribal lines or are fragmented among splinter parties or social groups, may require a far higher degree of preferential access to the communication system on the part of government if stability is to be assured.

In states that have not yet become nations, or where the practice of democracy has only recently been attempted, the temptation for the government to impose restrictions on the media is particularly strong. The Director of the Institute of the Science of the Press at Amsterdam University has reported a large number of inquiries from emerging countries asking whether there are ways that irresponsible attacks and other misuses of press freedom can be curtailed without destroying the basically democratic character of the state. To all these inquiries he has replied that there have been many attempts to combine such restrictions with democracy but that none on record in European history has succeeded, and has concluded that "there is really no middle ground between press freedom and unchecked tyranny."

The cure for an irresponsible, divisive press appears to lie less in imposing restrictions than in encouraging a responsible, national press as a counterweight and ensuring that the government has adequate facilities for reaching the public.

Implications for International Communication

A democratic form of government implies freedom of two-way international communication as well as domestic freedom of information. Many of the groups that contend and interact in a democracy require ideas and information from abroad if they are to form and function, and individuals no less frequently seek information from other countries to satisfy personal needs. Any person who wishes to take an intelligent interest in the foreign policy of his own nation must have access to foreign news and opinions. If the democratic process is to function, the right of individuals to incoming information must be assured.

When it comes to the right of private individuals and organizations to transmit communications to foreign audiences, the requirements of democracy are less clear. Perhaps a democratic state could exist without allowing private communication to other countries as long as domestic freedom of communication and freedom for incoming information were assured. Foreign commerce, missionary activity, and travel would be ruled out except under government auspices, but domestic groups and individuals could still obtain all the information they required, and the internal democratic process might be able to function. This is, however, pure speculation, since in practice all democracies allow private citizens a wide range of opportunity to communicate with citizens of other countries. Furthermore, if all democracies restricted the *outflow* of information, this would mean that for each the range of *incoming* information would be greatly narrowed, a situation that might be expected to lead to the gradual undermining of democracy everywhere.

The hospitality of democracies to ideas from abroad means that democratic governments can be influenced indirectly by international communications that are given attention by important domestic groups. Dictatorships, by way of contrast, seek to exclude some categories of foreign ideas and are far less responsive to pressures from their own population. Consequently, a government in a totalitarian country, while it may be affected directly by diplomatic communications and propaganda from abroad, is less likely to be responsive to domestic pressures generated by ideas from outside the country. Although democracies do, in fact, attempt to influence mass opinion in dictatorships through propaganda, the paucity of upward communication channels in the latter makes it more difficult to affect their policies in this way.

Most democracies permit, and even encourage, a wide range of activities on the part of foreign publicists. In the United States, foreign advertisers, representatives of religious groups, and cultural salesmen of all kinds are usually welcomed. Foreign political spokesmen also are likely to be well received when they state their aims openly, and when they do not attempt to exert a direct influence on elections, legislation, or other political processes that are regarded as the prerogatives of citizens only.

Communications from abroad, if they are to have an effect, must find users among the population of the receiving country. Furthermore, if these ideas are to be politically influential, the users ordinarily must be organized in some way—in political parties, industrial enterprises, or groups sharing a public opinion. In economically developed democracies, the range of interests represented by organized groups is very wide; therefore, a great variety of domestic organizations are in the market for ideas they can use to achieve their purposes. In view of the intense competition for the attention of people in industrialized democracies, however, any communication from abroad that does not fill an important need is likely to be submerged in the sea of competing domestic and international communications.

Another set of implications for international communication arises from the fact that democracies impose few restrictions on messages that leave the country. Anything that is publicly said or done in a democracy may become known abroad. Foreign newsmen are accepted as a matter of course, and are permitted a wide latitude in their activities. Critical communications, which are necessary for the functioning of the democratic order, are especially likely to find their way into international channels and to be given wide currency by hostile media.

Furthermore, because democratic states allow freedom for outbound communications, the information about these states that reaches foreign audiences is likely to contain contradictions and inconsistencies. Just as the numerous domestic groups competing for power and influence require different kinds of incoming information for their own functioning, they also will have different things to say to other peoples, and their actions that become known abroad will reflect the divergences in their values and goals. Communications from or about a democracy are likely to highlight the contradictions implicit in a pluralistic society.

Mark W. Hopkins:

Three Soviet Concepts of the Press

OF THE three Soviet leaders—Lenin, Stalin and Khrushchev—whose thoughts and decisions have had a strong impact on the Soviet press system, Lenin ranks first by far. There are perhaps three reasons for his predominant influence. First, Lenin was certainly far more a brilliant theoretician than either Stalin or Khrushchev, and his interpretations as to the role of the press in achieving and maintaining political power proved of lasting use. Second, Lenin by his own journalistic career, as well as by his writings, cast the model for a centralized press system and so exercised the power of precedent. And, third, deliberate glorification of Lenin after his death in 1924 made his views on the press, and most other subjects, a sacred writ.

It was Stalin's lot to make use of Lenin's theories in practical matters of establishing a socialist state. His contribution to press theory was small, as it was to Marxism-Leninism in general. To Stalin goes the dubious credit of exaggerating the most restrictive interpretation of the role of the press in Soviet society, and of developing a carefully devised network of newspapers, under strict government censorship and party control, to propagate state policies. If Lenin supplied the ideas, Stalin applied them. It was he who really built the system, incorporating oppression, dullness, repetition and censorship, that has been associated with a state controlled press in the Soviet Union.

Khrushchev, too, had nothing really original to propose to Soviet press theory, but in contrast to Stalin's fear of dissension which resulted in a mouthpiece press, Khrushchev's more flexible nature led him to loosen controls so that to some extent the Soviet newspapers became a forum of ideas. While never denying that the press was an arm of the party, Khrushchev acknowledged implicitly that it was a social force in itself and in serving, within bounds, as a tribune for discussion could contribute to social development. In one sense, Khrushchev turned the clock back to the 1920's when a debate raged over the function and form of the Soviet press system. Stalin won that debate simply because he won the concurrent political battle and achieved a position from which he could institute the

▶ From: *Journalism Quarterly* (Iowa City, Iowa), Vol. 42/No. 4 (Autumn 1965), pp. 523-531. Reprinted by permission of the publisher and of the author.

repressive elements of Lenin's press theory. Khrushchev in a way reopened the discussion in the 1950's, but by then the press had become rooted in its ways and so the issue was not what form the Soviet press should take, but in which direction it should develop.

It is perhaps inaccurate to refer to Lenin's theory of the press as if it were an academic treatise. His collected writings on the press, which fill one Soviet collection of more than 700 pages (including, however, some very inconsequential observations and communications) are more in the realm of operating principles. He worked them out during his career as a revolutionary, often to justify or plead for certain political actions. Thus, what is Lenin's press theory today was actually a conglomeration of essays or a few paragraphs of editorials written in the heat of battle. For this reason, it is difficult if not deceptive to isolate Lenin's concepts of the press from his general political philosophy, for the former was really a facet of the latter.

In his journalistic career, too, Lenin's work as editor or writer was never far removed from practical politics. He seldom spoke about the ideal press of the future, but rather of what sort of newspaper should be published at the moment, how it should be directed and what immediate function it should serve.

As a Marxist, Lenin held the customary opinion that a society's economic system chiefly determined its legal and political institutions. Moreover, each stage of social development was dominated by a particular class, which used these institutions to perpetrate its power. In the Marxist interpretation, capitalists comprised that dominant class in the late 19th and early 20th century Russia. In Lenin's mind, and to a great extent in fact, they therefore controlled the press, subject to czarist regime surveillance. To speak of a "free press" in the Western sense was at the least to deceive oneself and at the most to contradict Marxist theory. Lenin maintained that a press always served the dominant class, which certainly was not a view original to him, but of singular importance to the development of the Soviet press.

From it sprung two ideas. One was that it was entirely justifiable after the 1917 Bolshevik seizure of power to deny those elements loyal to the old order access to the press, since they no longer were dominant in society. Rather, the press was to serve the victorious proletariat. The second idea to come out of Lenin's Marxist outlook was that freedom of the press was guaranteed not only, and not primarily, by government protection of the right to say what one would, but by public ownership of the economic structure of the press—its capital, newsprint, printing equipment, buildings and distribution network. Then, all citizens would be assured access to the press.

Early in his career, Lenin had little to say about these matters. Only in 1917, just before the Bolshevik revolution, when it seemed possible, at least, that he and his party could gain power, did he wholeheartedly express the Marxist view of a free press. It is worth quoting liberally because in one form or another the idea appears throughout the history of the Soviet press. In an article on September 28, 1917, Lenin wrote:

> Capitalists call "freedom of the press" that state of affairs when censorship is removed and all parties are free to publish any newspapers. In this very thing there is no freedom of the press, but freedom to deceive the oppressed and exploited masses by the rich, the bourgeoisie. . . . Publication of a newspaper is a large, income producing capitalist enterprise in which the rich invest millions and millions of rubles. "Freedom of the press" of a bourgeois society consists in freedom of the rich systematically, unceasingly and daily in the millions of copies to deceive, corrupt and fool the exploited and oppressed masses of the people, the poor. It is asked, is it possible to fight this howling evil and how? The means is state monopoly of private advertising in newspapers. . . . They will say: But this is destruction of freedom of the press. Not true. This would enlarge and restore freedom of the press. For freedom of the press signifies: all opinions of *all* citizens may be stated. And now? Now *only* the rich have this monopoly, and the large parties. Besides with publication of large *soviet* [*i.e.*, workers' soviets] newspapers, with all the advertising, there would be full guarantees of expression of opinion to a very much broader number of citizens, say, to every group collecting a certain number of subscriptions. Freedom of the press would in this case become a great deal more democratic, would become incomparably fuller. . . . State authority in the name of the Soviets will take *all* printing plants and *all* paper and distribute them justly, first to the government in the interests of the majority of the people, the majority of the poor, especially the majority of the peasants; . . . second, to the large parties, polling, say, in both capitals a hundred thousand or two hundred thousand votes; and third, to the smaller parties and to any group of citizens, attaining a certain number of members or collecting a certain number of subscriptions." [1]

After the Bolshevik revolution, when Lenin was directing the new Russian state, advertising was in fact made a state monopoly; almost immediately, printing plants were confiscated and various severe restrictions on the press were at once instituted. The rationale for these actions was that the press was being used by elements hostile to the Soviet regime, that is the bourgeoisie, and that the press was then in the hands of a new class, the proletariat, which should have the commanding voice in

---

[1] *Lenin o Pechati* (Moscow, 1959), pp. 578-80; italics in quotation are Lenin's.

what was published. There were sheer political reasons for establishing dictatorial control over the press after Bolsheviks seized power, but Lenin's Marxism was operating with them. There was an element of truth in Lenin's polemics concerning capitalistic control of the press and a logic in the argument that a just apportionment of economic means of newspaper publishing would permit greater numbers to use freedom of the press.

In the quotation of Lenin's above, there are certain parts which others of Lenin's writings consistently contradict. When he says that freedom of the press means the right of all citizens to state all opinions, for instance, it is correct to suspect political motivation. For not long before Lenin wrote those lines, *Pravda*, the official Bolshevik newspaper, had been closed by the provisional Russian government. Thus, Lenin had a rather obvious ulterior motive in demanding that all parties have access to the press.

In the main, Lenin tended more toward conformity of opinion than diversity, and at that conformity to *his* opinion. From almost the beginning of his revolutionary career in St. Petersburg, Lenin strove to organize a political party—at first the dissenting Social-Democrats, then later his Bolshevik wing of that group—subject to rigorous central control. He was flexible enough to alter his thinking when obstacles appeared, but after they were beaten down Lenin invariably returned to demands for centralization.

There are many episodes in Lenin's revolutionary career revealing of this point. One involved his efforts to establish an all-Russian or national newspaper, which ultimately became known as *Iskra* (The Spark); in the history of the Russian revolutionary press, this is a famous publication, described now in Soviet press histories as "the first newspaper of a new type, serving as a model for printed organs of the party established after that." [2] Lenin conceived of this national or all-Russian newspaper while he was in exile in Siberia. In the latter half of 1899, as his term of exile was ending, and the first half of 1900, Lenin wrote several articles on the role of the press. They were the first of his written statements on the function and purpose of newspapers, in this case within the immediate Russian revolutionary movement.

It was Lenin's persistent argument that a newspaper could be the center of a revolutionary organization, and could inspire the masses to oppose Russian autocracy. The newspaper in Lenin's view was simultaneously a corporate institution and a means of communication. These functions happened to meet what were, to Lenin, the major problems confronting the Russian revolutionary movement. He felt that the Social-Democrats, of which he counted himself one, were disorganized, scattered and ineffective in their isolation. At the same time, there was no single

[2] *Sovetskaia Pechat'*, No. 12, 1960, p. 4.

body of theory that could be presented consistently to the working masses and make them conscious—a favorite word of Lenin's—of their political as well as economic interests in overthrowing the autocracy. Lenin contended that a newspaper published frequently and distributed throughout Russia by a central organization could provide leadership simultaneously to the disintegrating Social-Democratic party and to the city workers. This dual role of the press is the burden of Lenin's early articles and, it should be noted, the concept meshed precisely with Lenin's overall political views.

From Lenin's early articles, those from 1899 through about 1902, emerges a clear alliance of the press and a political party. Indeed, the party's leadership and the editorial staff of its newspaper were usually comprised of the same men. This was not an uncommon repetition in the Russian revolutionary movement and society at large, for the most astute political leaders were also often the most able and willing to propagate their programs in the press, whether a newspaper or political journal. What separated Lenin's views from most others on the matter of press and politics was his insistence that the newspaper could be more than simply a channel of communication, but a political force in itself. This idea ran through Lenin's early essays on the press. The first, written in 1899 as Lenin completed his three-year exile in a Siberian village as a result of a first unsuccessful journalistic venture, were prompted by an invitation to contribute to a defunct revolutionists' newspaper called *Rabochaia Gazeta (Labor Gazette)*. This publication had been run out of business by czarist police after only two issues, but in 1899 there was a proposal to revive it. *Rabochaia Gazeta* had said in its first editorial in 1897:

> . . . We are beginning publication of a labor newspaper for all Russian workers, wherever they might live. We think that our newspaper is needed now not only because it will discuss all questions regarding the labor movement here and abroad, but because it will unite Russian workers. . . . Only after uniting in one powerful union, in one powerful powerful workers' party, will the Russian workers be victorious over the capitalists and government.[3]

Lenin elaborated at great length in his own essays on the theme expressed in this editorial excerpt. He maintained first of all that the Social-Democratic movement suffered from provincialism, narrowness of thought for lack of a central newspaper through which a body of Marxist theory adaptable to Russian conditions could be propagated. "Therefore," Lenin wrote, envisioning what the revived *Rabochaia Gazeta* should do, "we will readily devote space in our newspaper for articles on theoretical

---

[3] *Rabochaia Gazeta*, No. 1, 1897, reprinted in *Bol'shevistskaia Pechat'; Sbornik Materialov* (Moscow, 1959), Vol. I, pp. 97-99. This quotation is on p. 99.

questions, with the invitation to all comrades to discuss controversial points openly." [4] And, at another point, he contended that the chief means to develop a political program and tactics was ". . . a party organ, published regularly and connected with all groups. Without such an organ, local work will remain provincial. The formation of a party—if this party is not represented regularly in a noted newspaper—remains to a significant degree only a word." [5]

A little later, after he had returned to western Russia from Siberia, Lenin prepared a draft statement of purpose for *Iskra*, the establishment of which occupied most of his time all through 1900. While he was in exile, a number of local Social-Democratic committees or groups had emerged, some with their own newspapers (in St. Petersburg, Kiev and Ekaterinoslav, for instance). They were not likely to merge into a central organization that promised their extinction or suppression of their views. Lenin tactfully proposed that local newspapers would be useful for discussion of different points of view among party workers, while the central newspaper would be responsible for broad theory and practice. "We not only do not repudiate discussion between comrades on the pages of our organs, but on the contrary, we are prepared to allot it a great deal of space." [6] However, this thought, contained in the draft statement of purpose for *Iskra*, was somewhat altered in the final form, partly under the pressure of the old guard of Russian Marxists with whom Lenin was allied for a time, and came out ". . . we do not intend to make our organ an ordinary storehouse of diverse views. We will conduct it, on the contrary, in the spirit of a strict, definite school of thought. This school can be expressed in a word: Marxism. . . ." [7]

The concept that Lenin quite clearly was developing in these essays was a newspaper serving as a processing point for theory under the direction of a central political agency. *Iskra*, which was printed in Europe and smuggled by ingenious means into Russia and distributed there from many points, operated on this concept, as did all subsequent newspapers over which Lenin had any authority.

In 1905, when government censorship of publications was lifted to a considerable extent, central control of newspapers became paramount to Lenin. He apparently reasoned that as long as the revolutionary press was illegal it was comparatively easy to subject it to rigorous control, the chief reason being that not many underground newspapers were published and of these most were short lived. But with government restrictions lifted, new opportunities opened for every little political faction in Russia to publish a few broadsides. Lenin therefore called for strict subordination

[4] V. I. Lenin, *Sochinenie*, 4th ed., Vol. IV, *Nasha Programa*, p. 12.
[5] *Ibid.*, in *Nasha Blizhaishaia Zadacha*, p. 198-99.
[6] *Ibid.*, p. 304.
[7] *Ibid.*, p. 329.

of journalistic activity to the party. "All party literature, local as well as central, must without question be subordinate to the party congress and the corresponding central or local party organization," Lenin demanded. "The existence of party literature not connected . . . with the party is impermissible. . . ." [8]

In the same year, 1905, Lenin chastised local members of the Social-Democratic party for making insufficient use of the then central party newspaper, *Rabochii (Worker)*, for which Lenin occasionally wrote, in their own publications. He wanted these newspapers to reprint the slogans, articles and news items from the central organ and create an attitude among workers that *Rabochii* was "their own ideological center."[9]

It can be concluded from these statements, drawn from an increasing body of comments on the press, that by 1905 Lenin had really established the concept of a centralized press whose function was to propagate a doctrine. The tendency in his writings on the press to this time and after was toward conformity—not to be mistaken for mediocrity—of view. Lenin simply did not lean toward the idea that a multiplicity of opinion could have any value, but rather would have a disruptive, disorganizing effect on a revolutionary party and the new Soviet state.

There remains one facet of the press which was particularly dear to Lenin's thought. This was the matter of the newspaper as an organizational force. The now famous sentence, "A newspaper is not only a collective propagandist and a collective agitator, but also a collective organizer," Lenin wrote in 1902 not as a general guide for the press (as it is used today in the Soviet Union), but in immediate response to those in Russia who argued against Lenin that a newspaper could not be what he most adamantly maintained it could, an organizer of men and ideas. In an article titled *"C Chego Nachat"* ("Where to Begin"), published in the fourth issue of *Iskra* in May 1901, and then in a long essay called *"Chto Delat?"* ("What to Do?") a year later, Lenin began to see the newspaper and its staff as the hard core of a disciplined party. The men and women who worked for the central organ were to be not only responsible for collecting information and distributing the newspaper, but also were to be agents of the party. They were to be dedicated and resourceful, atune to local political circumstances but advised of overall party policy.

When this coincidence of professions—revolutionary and journalist—is combined with Lenin's insistence on a disciplined party organization and public ownership of means for publishing newspapers, the result is logically a press operating as an active participant in society, as an organizer of forces. To this day in the Soviet Union, the journalist is thought

[8] *Lenin o Pechati*, p. 330.
[9] *Lenin o Pechati*, p. 334, printed in *Rabochii*, No. 2, September 1905.

of as a political activist. It would be bourgeois of him to think that he could stand aside and observe social development. In "Leninist tradition" the journalist is expected to get into the fight, using the press to effect certain ends.

By the fall of 1917 when the Bolsheviks took power in Russia, Lenin had produced or processed a considerable body of principles for the press. To summarize the main ones:

1) The press served the dominant class in any society.

2) The economic bases of newspaper publishing should be controlled by the state, which in turn was directed by the party representing the proletariat:

3) Newspapers were adjuncts of, if not identical to political organizations, and journalists were political activists.

4) Freedom of the press was advanced to the extent that the *means* of publishing newspapers were available to all segments of society.

5) Diverse opinion should be permitted, but within the bounds of Marxist thought.

These principles certainly do not serve a politically independent press proposing an array of ideas and information, but neither do they inevitably dictate a press operating under stifling censorship. Based on these principles, a press could represent various facets of public opinion, provide information and stimulate thought.

The primary flaw in Lenin's principles, the one that allowed for perversion of the free press as he interpreted it, was the insistence on central control by a political organization. This meant that the whole press system depended on the good will and wisdom of the men who directed this organization. The press would function to the benefit of individual expression and to the healthy exchange of information and ideas only to the extent that these men considered the function necessary.

In the 1920's after the new Soviet state had pulled out of three years of revolution, civil war and foreign intervention, there were men of good will who hoped that the press could be a dynamic force in society, albeit to help build a certain type of society. There was not in these years the frightened silence and parrot-like press that later characterized the Soviet mass media. One can follow in the Soviet press of the 1920's rough and tumble debates.

Toward the end of the 1920's, as Stalin's political power increased, an oppressive weight began bearing down on the press. The reasons are several, but a main one it would seem was Stalin's own views on the press. As noted earlier, Stalin made no original contribution to Soviet press theory, but in the way he organized and refined the mass media system he established certain guides for the press which had all the importance of theory. That is, given the principles developed by Lenin, Stalin interpreted them in certain ways to fit his own notions of what role the press should play in Soviet society and these, in effect, became Soviet press theory.

The striking fact about Stalin's writings on the press is their shallowness. Stalin seemed to hit on an idea and hold to it relentlessly, repeating and repeating. He was not an intellectual; he revealed very little ability for original thought and very little flexibility. In the various collections of statements of Lenin and Stalin on the press, published after Stalin became supreme leader and before he was denounced in 1956, one finds the same scanty comments that he made in the 1920's. His first important commentary was in 1923, in an article titled *"Pechat kak kollektivnyi organizator"* ("The Press as a Collective Organizer"). It was a slashing rebuttal to another article on the press written by a well known Soviet journalist by the name of Ingulov. Stalin wrote:

> The organization role of the press is the most significant at this moment. It is not only that the press agitates and accuses, but that above all it has a large network of agents and correspondents through the country, in all industrial and agricultural areas. The newspaper as a collective organizer in the hands of the party and Soviet state, the newspaper as the means to bind contacts with the working masses of our country and rally them around the party and the Soviet state —in this now lies the immediate task of the press.[10]

At another time, in his report to the 12th Congress of the Communist party in April 1923, Stalin declared: "The press is the only instrument with the help of which the party daily, hourly speaks to the working class; there is no other such flexible apparatus." [11]

Four years later, in the fall and winter of 1927, as Stalin was in the process of eliminating his political opposition, he had to deal with control of the press. Trotsky had published tracts with proposals at variance to Stalin's desires. Stalin savagely attacked anyone's right to do so:

> . . . Comrade Trotsky considers that the opposition is correct, therefore it has the right to set up its own illegal printing plants. . . . If we follow in the steps of Trotsky, then it has to be allowed that each of these groups has the right to set up its own illegal printing plants. . . . It means the existence of several centers in the party, having their own "programs," their own "platforms." What is there left then of the iron discipline in our party, which Lenin considered the foundation of the dictatorship of the proletariat? [12]

[10] Reshetnikov, T. M., *Partiia o Pechati* (Sverdlovsk, 1934), pp. 16-17.
[11] Reshetnikov, p. 22.
[12] *Stalin o Pechati* (Sverdlovsk, 1932), p. 18.

Shortly after he made this statement, Stalin met with a foreign delegation in Moscow and among the questions put to him was one about freedom of the press in the Soviet state. He retorted:

> What kind of freedom of the press are you talking about? Freedom of the press for what class—for the bourgeoisie or for the proletariat? If we are talking about freedom of the press for the bourgeoisie, then we do not have it and will not have it so long as the dictatorship of the proletariat exists. If we are talking about freedom for the proletariat, then I must say that you will not find in the world another state where there would exist such an all inclusive, broad freedom of the press for the proletariat as exists in the U.S.S.R. . . . Without the best printing plants, the best publishing houses . . . there is no freedom of the press. . . . We never took upon ourselves the responsibility to give freedom of the press to all classes, to satisfy all classes.[13]

In Stalin's slim writings, there is a clear emphasis on a functional, ideologically pure press, as contrasted to a creative, diverse mass media. It is difficult to see, in Stalin's comments, how the Soviet press could become anything but a sterile obedient servant of the party. Stalin simply did not think in terms of a vibrant, broad ranging press. If one considers his general political views and his personal political career, it can be understood even better that Stalin could no more tolerate a free press, even in the Lenin ideal, than he could political opposition.

The results of Stalin's views on the press are better known than the views themselves. Gradually the press, like all elements of Soviet society, was subordinated to Stalin's goals. Censorship, which was provided for as early as 1922, and party controls were made more rigorous in the 1930s and thereafter, although they did not operate as perfectly as one would suppose, given the political centralization in the Soviet Union. But they were effective and produced a press given over to extreme glorification of Stalin's person and to parroting whatever he said or approved of.

Stalin died in 1953 and within four years Nikita S. Khrushchev gained supremacy in the Soviet political hierarchy. Exactly as Stalin interpreted Lenin's principles of the press within the context of his own political views and personal psychology, so Khrushchev's personal vision of Soviet society had an impact on the press. Under Khrushchev, the Soviet mass media lost much of its dull uniformity. Part of this must be attributed to the fresh crop of journalists that emerged after World War II from university and party schools of journalism, but ultimately greater diversity in the press must be traced to the willingness of the political leadership to allow it.

[13] Reshetnikov, pp. 10-11.

In general, Khrushchev expressed a clear Marxist view of the press. A statement he made in 1963, during an interview with 50 foreign journalists, is reminiscent of Lenin's thoughts in 1917:

> The fundamental attitude consists of this, that in capitalist countries society is divided into antagonistic classes and there a class struggle occurs. This class struggle goes on in every country where there are the exploited and the exploiters. . . . The exploiters try to instill simple attitudes, illusions in the consciousness of the people simultaneously through the press, radio and television, which are in their hands and obediently serve them.[14]

Like Lenin, Khrushchev looked on the press and the journalists' corps as instruments of the party. In 1959 he said:

> Journalists are not only the loyal helpers of the party, but literally the apprentices of our party—the active fighters for its great cause. Why apprentices? Because you are actually always at the hand of the party. As soon as some decision must be explained and implemented, we turn to you, and you, as the most trusted transmission belt, take the decision and carry it to the very midst of the people.[15]

If these words are also reminiscent of Stalin's, they should be tempered with Khrushchev's implicit respect for the press. Stalin used it; Khrushchev can be said to have elevated the mass media from its groveling servility to the role of trusted servant. "You journalists occupy an honorable place in this great cause, which under the direction of the party our people, the buildings of communism, are accomplishing." [16]

Khrushchev put emphasis, too, on broad public participation in the press and during his years in power there was, in fact, a noticeably greater involvement of many people in newspapers throughout the press structure. "The Soviet press is really a peoples' press. It is put out by the hands of the people and serves the people with the great ideals of communism," [17] Khrushchev said. The idea of the popular press should not be carried too far, even though it was more dominant under Khrushchev than Stalin. Not only did Khrushchev remain convinced that the press was subordinate to the party, it in fact continued to be so. Yet, it is also true that Khrushchev adopted the more positive aspects of Lenin's principles of the press and made some attempt to put them into action. One cannot say that Khrushchev wished for political opposition in newspapers. But he did ask for a more attractive, better written and more stimulating press within the framework established by the party.

Under Krushchev, however, as with Lenin and Stalin, a fundamental

[14] *Pravda*, Oct. 27, 1963.
[15] *Pravda*, Nov. 18, 1959.
[16] *Sovetskaia Pechat'*, No. 4, 1964, p. 6.
[17] *Ibid.*, p. 7.

flaw in Soviet press theory remained. That is, the press, while freed from those abuses arising from private ownership of the mass media, became subject to an authoritarian political party. Hence, rather than wealthy individuals or corporations controlling the press, a political machinery with the force of state power took it over in the Soviet Union. The transformation really did not result in greater freedom of the press, but less, whether judged by the Soviet or American interpretation of the concept.

James W. Markham:

Communist Regimes, Mass Media and Society

IN REGARD to theory and method the Communist communication system as a social institution was born of Hegelian-Marxist doctrine. It was shaped and interpreted by the Russian revolutionaries whose rigid, extremist, 2-valued orientation philosophy left a strong imprint. It borrowed from the experience of both the private and government-owned press under tsarist absolutism. It learned secrecy and intolerance of opposition from its own successes and failures in its struggle against the imperial government and likewise from the government's effort to control and contain nonconformist, revolutionary thought. It was tested and refined as a political institution and party weapon in the experience of the revolutionary press both at home and in exile. It developed to a considerable extent by trial and error in the early years of the new Soviet state.

Though nourished in Russia, Communist ideology was a foreign transplant in Russia as well as in China. Contrary to Marx's formula, it took roots in traditional-agrarian rather than advanced-industrial societies, among a large class of illiterate peasants. But both countries had long-established authoritarian traditions, the Russian perhaps in some ways being more absolutist than the Chinese. Both oriental despotisms experienced revolutionary upheavals brought on by the communication of Western ideas. The course of events in China differed from that in Russia, however, for in China the influence of John Stuart Mill for a time triumphed over that of Marx. But just as the ideology was a transplant, so was the concept of a newspaper or journal as a public information medium strictly a Western import. Western press systems, when introduced into Russia and China, were used first by religious institutions as organs to propagate the faith, then by business interests in the marketplace. The press thrived wherever trade and commerce flourished. Western experience has shown that modern mass communication systems attain their highest degree of influence and prestige as economically independent institutions in libertarian capitalist societies; that they attain their highest degree of structural development, capability, and mass penetration in modern, industrial, tech-

▶ From: *Voices of the Red Giants: Communications in Russia and China,* by James W. Markham. Copyright © 1967 by Iowa State University Press, Ames. Reprinted by permission of the publisher and the author.

nologically advanced societies. The evidence of Western experience also tends to show that modern mass communication systems are also products of urban communities of people with relatively high literacy and high economic and education levels.

When a Western-type press system was introduced in both countries it clashed with an environment quite alien to that which had given it birth and nourishment. Both Russian and Chinese societies were largely traditional agrarian-based societies made up of self-sufficient families and villages as the basic political units of the larger territorial subdivisions. At the base of both societies were the millions of illiterate, poverty-ridden peasants and at the top a comparatively small ruling oligarchy and bureaucracy; in between was a relatively small middle class. The masses in both countries had never heard of the Magna Charta, the rights of man, government by the consent of the governed, or a government of laws and not of men. The liberating influences of the Renaissance, the Reformation, the Industrial Revolution and the rise of the common man—forces that resulted in the concepts of individual and political liberty—were among the factors of modernization that profoundly changed Europe and America; but aside from a thin layer of wealthy intelligentsia, all these ideas never existed as far as the bulk of Russian and Chinese people were concerned. These groups of intelligentsia in both countries sought to bring about changes in their societies conducive to modernization after the Western model, first by peaceful reform, then later by revolution. Both used the press as a major instrument to promote reform and revolution —revolution that eventually toppled centuries-old dynasties. But the libertarian concept of the press's role as both mediator between the government and the governed and as a critic of government separate from and independent of both society and government hardly had a chance to take root.

But there were reasons for hope that the libertarian tradition might gain strength. In Russia centuries of Christianity under the State church had left its mark on the culture. In China the humane concepts of Confucian philosophy, imbedded deeply in Chinese tradition and civilization, offered a promising environment in which these Western ideals might grow. China differed from Russia in that she experienced for almost 100 years a period of foreign occupation in the form of territorial trade concessions to the Western powers. The Chinese could see a libertarian capitalist press operating in their own front yard. China, also unlike Russia, experienced a brief period of Republican rule in which a native Western-type press system flourished—a system in which almost all of the attributes of a libertarian press were apparent. The advent of the Communist regime abruptly halted this development and today the Communist communication system is a major link in a chain of communication and persuasion that has been successful at least in bringing to the Chinese people a rebirth of nationalism and pride in achievement. In Russia the long history of censorship and suppression was the primary heritage. It was not until the last half of the nineteenth century that the Russian press began to perceive its role as one of mass information. Since the privately owned press shared with the government-owned press responsibility for publishing, conditions did not foster the development of independent responsibility. As a consequence the Western sense of responsibility and independence of government control for mass communications was seldom envisaged and hardly ever put into practice. When the Bolsheviks came to power they were greatly impressed with the success of their propaganda methods and fully versed in the devious ways of control by the authoritarian state over mass communication and over the minds of men. They used this knowledge to consolidate political power, and to forge a stable regime based on force and fear.

Although there are important differences, the Russian and the Chinese mass communication systems today are cut from the same cloth. Both appear to represent different stages of development relating generally to each country's stage of social and economic development. The Soviet Communist media system mirrors the maturity and success the country has achieved as a first-rate world power. Still the ideal state has not been built, nor has the ephemeral socialist superman emerged. So the work of socialism must go on. On the other hand, Chinese communications reflect the tensions of a nation driving its people relentlessly in the struggle to catch up—a proud nation of extravagant ambitions and flaming nationalism, but a nation still behind in the modernizing process, still in a stage of painful transition. The Chinese system has profited from the Soviet experience and, like the Russian brand of communism, has proved to be enormously adaptive. Yet it still has much farther to go before it catches up with the other Communist giant. Moreover, it faces different and greater odds in the form of traditional values, geography, and demography. The situation has forced the Chinese regime to take extreme measures such as mass organized thought control at a time when the Soviet Union is relaxing its use of force.

Because the philosophy calls for using the media system alongside the political system to effect changes in the character of the people, both Russian and Chinese Communists have stressed the agitation function as a device for crystallizing propaganda into action. They also stress the media as focal points for party organizational work. Therefore the importance of communication systems to Communist regimes lies quite as much in the social as in the mass communications function of the media institutions. The mass media institutions, for example, provide a hierarchical base from which political organizations are built and manipulated—a system of control through which all aspects of the entire society are systematically governed from a central location. The Communists have learned that the ability to use and control information to shape and change attitudes not alone by messages in the mass media but also by face-to-face contact is fundamental to political power. Hence the Communists judge total formal and informal media performance by the extent of their combined contribution to organized action by social groups in the approved direction. From this standpoint they are concerned that the messages conform to the line quite as much because of their probable influence on the communicator of the message as because of any probable influence on the audience. Audiences, however, are playing a greater role than before in the mass communication process.

Judged by Communist standards, the mass media appear to be accomplishing their task and fulfilling their purpose, though perhaps not to the fullest extent the regimes desire. If expansion of the mass communication system is to be taken as an indication of the regime's satisfaction with it, then the Soviet regime is apparently well satisfied. Although the Soviet media have been developed rapidly, full penetration at all social levels has not been achieved. Still, the press is available on a fairly uniform basis. In China the print media have not expanded as rapidly as they are needed. In both countries the electronic media have expanded rapidly, yet because of linguistic and other barriers they still do not—in Pulitzer's phrase— "speak to a whole nation rather than a select group." The media systems are technically adequate, however, for transmitting the regime's messages to the people. Communist communication systems have demonstrated a high capability to change people and society. They do this by using mass communication to create a strong feeling of "nation-ness" and loyalty to the country, by helping prepare people to participate and to play their new roles in the new society, by promulgating and popularizing national plans and goals, by helping develop the necessary skills, and eventually by preparing the people for their country's role as a member of the family of nations—in short, to modify society and human behavior.

However rigid the dogma, Communist mass communication systems —as the Soviet system since Stalin has demonstrated—are amazingly flexible and adaptable to change. Any means, according to the ideology, is justified by the ends to be achieved. While the ends today remain the same the means have become more versatile and less rigidly bound, to meet what are rationally perceived as changing conditions. Whether the regime was in full command all the time and deliberately led, or whether it was forced by pressures to innovate, the changes of the past decade are impressive. Today's Soviet society and its mass communication system are more open, more inquiring, less motivated by terror, than they were under Stalin. The Socialist parties of Western Europe have abandoned the Marxist conception of the class struggle, and there is reason to believe that in the Soviet Union Marxism-Leninism is giving way to the modern idea of the affluent welfare state. Yet the Soviet Union remains a tightly controlled totalitarian dictatorship with its ideological and organizational foundations intact. The single party is more powerful than ever. The doctrine is revitalized and made more relevant to the needs of the times. In China the changes have not been so profound, although the Chinese at first showed ingenuity in adapting Russian methods to Chinese society. In both countries change has been reflected in the mass media, but media behavior has shown little basic change.

Since persuasion is replacing coercion and terror as a manipulative instrument in the Soviet Union, it seems that public opinion in the future will play a larger role in the communications process than it has in the past. Indeed, the very fact that persuasion is receiving greater emphasis is in itself tacit recognition that public opinion is a factor in the decisions made by the top leadership. Traditionally in Communist countries public opinion has not been considered the sovereign power. It was assumed that public opinion was completely unanimous on all important issues and revealed itself through the party and its leaders. Therefore the communications system hitherto has not been expected to reflect or necessarily to provide a basis for the development of opinion among the general public. The prevailing "public" opinion—the kind that finds expression—is either the opinion of the leaders or those opinions of others which are approved by the leaders. The channels of information are almost exclusively used by the leaders, and the information crystallized by the party provides the basis for the formulation of national policy, just as it provides the basis for the bias of the official communication line. Thus is distilled the collective wisdom of the leaders, who until the State withers away, must paternalistically see after the people's needs. The formal communication system then has the responsibility of "selling" the regime's ideas—of molding and unifying public opinion in the direction the regime wants it to go, so that in the end the regime's opinion and that of the public will be one and the same.

To maintain uniformity, Communist regimes tolerate neither oppositional media nor oppositional thought. The corollary of this situation is that mass communication serves the regimes and not necessarily the people. The function of the media becomes one that primarily concerns the processes of persuasion through monopolistic manipulation by the authorities. Under libertarian capitalistic systems, many channels and many voices competing for attention sometimes tend to drown each other out unless synchonized. In the Soviet Union and Communist China there is only one voice speaking through many channels. The messages conveyed are unwavering, positive, clear, and almost uniformly the same. These mediated messages are supplemented skillfully and reinforced by face-to-face communication and agitation leading to action. With such apparently favorable conditions for effective communication and persuasion, the potential power of Communist communications to condition, change, or

contain public opinion seems to be greater than in less regimented societies. The evidence tends to show that the systems have been successful
in changing attitudes.

Still, despite the traditional attitude toward the function of public
opinion, there is mounting evidence to indicate that what the Soviet citizen thinks—the direction of public opinion as a thing apart from the
official viewpoint—is of considerable concern to the regime. The regime
is paying more attention to public opinion mainly because it wishes to
maintain control of the society and to continue to guide the course of
popular thought. Another reason is that the regime is beginning to suspect
that the public may have a real contribution to make. Behavior that indicates sincere deference to public opinion or reaction was seen in the handling of news of the Soviet resumption of nuclear tests. The news was
broken to the Soviet public slowly and gradually. The full story of the
tests' extent was not reported at all to the people. In the Berlin situation
the Kremlin has been careful to avoid the impression among Soviet citizens that the door has been finally closed on negotiations with the United
States. In matters of civil defense the regime, quite wary of frightening
the Soviet public, has limited public display of defense measures against
the possibility of nuclear war. This does not mean, of course, that under
present conditions the expression of a genuine public opinion contrary to
the regime's will be permitted in the media. Nor does it mean that public
opinion will make itself felt directly in political action. But it does mean
that public opinion will work indirectly as a force influencing the regime's
policies and programs, both in Russia, and perhaps to a lesser extent in
China, and in this way it will make itself felt indirectly in the decision
and policy making processes. This development, if it is one, is a helpful
improvement, but it does not substitute adequately for the failure of the
mass media to serve as vehicles for the expression of individual opinion
and a broad cross-section of different shades of opinion. The chief means
of developing and crystallizing intelligent public opinion—that of free and
open discussion on all important questions—so prevalent in the Western
democracies is denied the Soviet and Chinese people. One of the most
serious limitations of Communist communication systems, then, is the
absence of the clash of opinions, an open marketplace for ideas—the
citizen's exposure to a wide range of ferment and thought on a variety
of subjects.

In fairness, exceptions to the limitation stated in the preceding paragraph must be stressed. There may exist quite a wide range of discernible
views among the Soviet people which do not run counter to established
orthodoxy on certain social and economic questions (rarely on political
questions) about which the regime has no particular position or simply
does not care either way. There also may arise some controversial matters
about which the regime, for policy reasons, hesitates to take a stand and
make its wishes known until it can whip up at least a semblance of public

support for its view; after which it is in a position to take action and make
it appear that such action was the *result* of public demand. The leaders
may have more confidence in the views of the masses than before. In any
event, admittedly the press and the other mass media can enjoy relatively
wide lattitude of public discussion and debate through letters, editorials,
and signed articles. As we have seen, such discussions may at times get
out of control. Thus, if one has in mind these areas where the regime
sees fit to permit the expression of public opinion—whether genuine or
"planted" by the party—one could argue as did Mikhail Igitkhanyan, researcher in the Institute of philosophy, in the July, 1965, issue of *Soviet
Life*, that "A highly important function of the [Soviet] press . . . [is] to
reflect all the essential shades of public opinion, to reach the truth on vital
problems through discussion." One could further state with conviction, as
Igitkhanyan did, that Soviet ". . . newspapers shape Soviet public opinion,
not by imposing a certain viewpoint on the population, but by freely presenting different viewpoints for argument." Such interpretations are valid
only when applied to those areas of public opinion the regime chooses to
leave to the mass communications media and to the people.

The introduction of public-opinion polling in recent years is a significant indication of a departure from the old assumption that official policy
and public attitudes were completely congruent—an assumption that made
it superfluous to sample public opinion on certain questions. More important, it may represent a real desire of the leadership to develop more scientific methods of assessing and understanding the society it governs. The
more captive a people are, the less likely they are to speak their minds
even when invited to do so. Hence it becomes correspondingly more difficult to know what they are thinking. For a totalitarian regime then, the
nagging problem of "engineering consent" can be somewhat eased by the
regular sampling of public opinion even on a limited scale. The information received may be useful as an index of public thought, and the people
are impressed that their opinions are considered important enough to be
sought. Still, as Paul Hollander concludes (in "The Dilemma of Soviet
Sociology," *Problems of Communism*, Vol. XIV, No. 6, Nov.-Dec., 1965,
pp. 43-44), this new concern with public opinion has "a paradoxical
quality" in that assertions of unanimity persist while at the same time
public opinion is not seen as "an autonomous force relatively independent
of the institutions of society, but rather as an integral part of them, as a
resource to be manipulated even while it is being gauged and assessed."
However, official sanction of public opinion polling on approved non-
deviant or innocuous topics together with other developments in public
discussion indicate a degree of tolerance of conflicting opinion and a growing belief on the part of the leadership that differences of opinion in areas
outside strict ideological lines may be beneficial to the public and useful
to the regime.

In theory the Communist communication system was intended to function primarily as a channel or a transmission belt to carry the message from party and government leaders down to the masses of the people. But communication was not expected to flow only in one direction. Theory envisioned a two-way flow in which the structure would provide the means by which communication could flow just as well from the bottom to the top of the hierarchy through the channels of self-criticism—both party interpersonal and media related. Experience, however, in both Russia and China indicates that the downward flow of communication literally over-whelms the feedback. Communication from the top downward has a number of advantages over communication from below. It lacks dissonance in that it speaks with one voice—consistently, systematically, and with deliberate planned purpose; the downward flow far exceeds the upward in volume and intensity; and finally, the voices from the top speak with far greater authority and credibility than the disorganized, dissonant voices from below. Thus in practice, the communication system operates for all intents and purposes as a unidirectional channel. More stress on public-opinion polling in the Soviet Union, therefore, may serve to provide more feedback and may eventually help make communication work reciprocally. China appears to be as far from instituting openly this kind of feedback channel as the Soviet Union was forty years ago.

Turning to the information function it is germane then to ask how well do the mass media, with the aid of informal communications, serve to build an informed public to provide the basis for a viable public opinion. In other words, how adequately do mass communications provide a realistic surveillance of the environment? How well do they convey reality? It seems fair to put Communist mass communications to this kind of test and to judge their performance on this kind of standard, because the average Soviet and Chinese citizen expects his media to present him with a reasonably accurate picture of his immediate environment and of the outside world. Yet, arguments of Soviet journalists to the contrary, this function is not a recognized or practiced principle of Communist systems. It seems clear that the media do reflect fairly faithfully the Soviet and Chinese governments' Promethean ambitions, plans, and goals—the struggle to reshape all facets of life in the Communist state. They reflect many of the problems encountered, and the difficulties involved. Faults are aired with the aim of providing corrections, so that the communication stream is full of the sting of unidimensional criticism. Referring to the Soviet media, Gruliow concluded they exist for one purpose, to serve the State as an instrument for containing public thought on a mass scale. If they "chance to serve the reader, that is purely coincidental," he wrote. Schramm, also speaking of the Soviet media, said they are intended to be "efficient pipelines, efficient instruments of the controlling hierarchy. And," he added, "they are held to this assignment by a strictly enforced responsibility." Obviously the adequacy of one's stock of information is essential to a realistic appraisal of and adjustment to one's environment. Just as obviously, it seems, the Communist leaders would want the people to adjust to real-life conditions. If these assumptions are correct, the communication systems should be expected to present within limited bounds a certain amount of accurate, unbiased information. Yet they are not neutral reporters of fact, except insofar as the fact may have social relevance. The extraordinary degree of reliance by the society on unofficial information sources testifies to the existence of a real need for a kind of information not being supplied. Lack of confidence in the official media is partly indicative of attitude toward the regimes and partly the result of unsatisfactory experience with the media. But if he relied solely on the official media, the average citizen would get a picture of many aspects of the environment that differs sharply from reality. Although he seldom is aware of this unless he has the opportunity to check what the media say against his own observations, he can read between the lines. He can deduce much from what the media do not say. He finds that communications picture not so much the society as it is but more as its planners want it to become.

In essence the picture the reader gets of the world, both domestic and foreign, is often one that Western readers would scarcely recognize. There is much that is not reported. Values are pictured as either right or wrong, good or bad—a world of dichotomy and of extremes. The Communist order and its goals are associated with the good, the true, and the beautiful. Enemies of the Communist state are associated with the sordid, the evil, the corrupt, the dangerous, the deceitful, and the reprehensible. Such dissident elements either at home or abroad are demonstrated to be the sole obstructionists, the only barriers to the achievement of true socialist unity and harmony. Contrary to the teachings of human experience elsewhere, Soviet and Chinese decisions as to what is right or wrong are seldom a difficult matter to determine. The slant, the position, or the Line is never depicted as uncertain, foggy, or wavering. Though perplexity may occasionally befuddle the minds of the all-powerful leaders in Moscow and Peking, the admission of such bourgeois capitalistic weaknesses almost never creeps into the stream of official communications. The general atmosphere is one of optimism; the future of socialism is bright. The communist world is getting better and more powerful every day. If it isn't, then it is the fault of capitalist warmongers, the enemies of socialism, and never the responsibility of the planners. The picture the average citizen gets from his media is one that must frequently conflict with his sense of perspective. It must be supplemented with information from other sources, if he is to have a balanced and not fragmentary view. Moreover, he cannot even expect his media to present a consistent picture over time. Emphasis may shift, frowns of displeasure may change to smiles of blandishment, from one day to the next or from one month to the next. Men,

institutions, parties, and nations may be reindexed from a favored category
to an unfavored or neutral one, or vice versa. This is the kind of confused,
fragmentary, disconnected, biased, and distorted mirror of the outside
world that is Communist communications. A second limitation of Communist communication systems, therefore, is the inadequacy of the surveillance function—the failure of mass communications to convey reality.
However, this is not to imply that the world picture the Western reader
gets from his media is perfect by any means.

Furthermore the negative effects of heavy propaganda contribute also
to the state of ignorance on the part of the Communist citizen. Most
well-educated citizens grow immune to government propaganda and agitation somewhat in the manner of an American listening to detergent advertising: he simply doesn't hear it; he may scoff at the slogans or joke at the
exaggerations, but listlessly or subconsciously he buys the advertised brand.
Often the Soviet or Chinese intellectual appears outwardly to accept the
official view, not because he is convinced, but because it has become so
much a part of his ingrained system of values, because it is useful to him
if he wishes to do well and get ahead in the society, because group pressures are exerted, or because he is afraid for other reasons to behave
differently.

The growing resistance to and immunity against propaganda is one
of the built-in limitations of Communist communication systems. Among
the others are apathy and indifference on the part of communications
personnel and other intellectuals. The problem is essentially one of stimulating and maintaining high levels of initiative and creativity in a controlled, stifling atmosphere. Another is the chronic dullness and tediousness
of media content which from time to time reaches the point of repelling
readers, thus defeating its own purpose.

Though somewhat tempered by the effect of unofficial communication channels, the mass communication system suffering from such limitations can hardly be expected to produce an enlightened public. Rather,
the media audience is more likely to be one that is filled with ignorance
and misconception, and lacking a context of meaning that creates understanding. In a democracy where public opinion provides the basis for
policy, such misrepresentations, half-truths, gaps, and distortions in the
public information stream, we believe, unless challenged and corrected,
would dangerously impair the opinion processes and functions. In Communist countries the effect may not prove disastrous, but it would seem
that over time such myopia and naïvete as mass communication messages
foster among the people cannot help but work self-defeating handicaps,
preventing the achievement of the very goals the Communists themselves
have set. Traditional fear and suspicion of the mass public by both Soviet
and Chinese regimes explains in part why they must control what the
public is told and why they are not particularly interested in broadening

the latitude of public information and knowledge. The Soviet experience seems to indicate that as a Communist regime finds itself in a position of greater strength and stability it will have less need to control the content of communications, to promulgate falsehoods, and distort reality. As stability increases a regime will have less need to use force and coercion and will turn more to persuasion to accomplish what coercion has accomplished before. Whether it also widens the spectrum of permissible expression depends upon the extent to which it believes such a widening will increase the effects of persuasion, and thus enable the media to perform their tasks more efficiently.

The crux of the problem lies in the approach which reflects the fundamental notion of the role of communications in modern society. The dilemma for Communist regimes will not be resolved—and the resulting faults in the communication system corrected—until more attention is given to the uses of mass communication for people instead of the uses of people for mass communication. The traditional atttiude can be expressed in the question, "What does mass communication do *to* people?" The question represents only part of the multidimensional role of communication in society. More stress needs to be placed on another dimension: "What do people do *with* mass communication?"

2

THE FLOW OF WORLD NEWS

UNESCO
WORLD TRENDS OF NEWS AGENCIES

Rhoda Metraux
INTERNATIONAL COMMUNICATION
   OF SCIENCE INFORMATION

Karl Erik Rosengren
INTERNATIONAL NEWS: TIME AND TYPE OF REPORT

2

THE FLOW OF WORLD NEWS

NEWS appears to be flowing well among nations today. There are some parts of the world, of course, where this cannot be said, but generally the *flow* of information across borders must be considered extremely good. Many students of international communication have shifted their concern from the *flow* (a quantitative consideration) to the *type and content* (qualitative consideration) of the information. Most scholars, however, are forced to consider the two aspects—the flow and content—together, and generally this is the treatment given the two aspects in this chapter.

It does not take great insights to recognize that flow and content are rather closely related. When, for example, news flows poorly and spasmodically from Nation A, it may reasonably be assumed that the *quality* (and most likely even press freedom) of the communications media of that nation is not very good. Numerous studies have shown that in countries where the quality of the journalism and the degree of media development are high, there is little difficulty—technologically speaking—in getting information from other nations and sending information to other nations. In some instances, however, a rather highly developed national press system will have news *flow* problems stemming from political—not technical—restrictions.

News agencies have probably been the main instruments or channels through which international news has been disseminated. Besides the five great international news agencies—the United Press International, the Associated Press, Reuters, Agence France Presse and TASS—an ever-growing number of national news agencies are filtering world information into the grassroots communities of the world.

The first article of this chapter, by UNESCO, deals with the growth and accomplishments of the news agencies and related technological advances in transmission facilities. In the second article, Rhoda Metraux, world-renowned for her outstanding work in anthropology and communication among cultures, offers hope that we may find more effective ways to use modern methods of communication to bring about a meaningful dialogue among peoples of all cultures.

In the final article of the chapter, Dr. Karl Erik Rosengren, a sociologist at Sweden's University of Lund, places the whole subject of the flow of the news in a theoretical framework, surveys much of the pertinent research on the subject and points up important directions for future research.

*   *   *   *

RELATED READING

Baechlin, Peter, and Maurice Mueller-Strauss. *Newsreels Across the World.* Paris: UNESCO, 1952.

Hohenberg, John. *Foreign Correspondence: The Great Reporters and Their Times.* New York: Columbia University Press, 1964.

IPI. *The Flow of the News.* Zurich: International Press Institute, 1953.

IPI. *Government Pressures on the Press.* Zurich: International Press Institute, 1955.

Kayser, Jacques. *Mort d'une liberté: Techniques et politique de l'information.* Paris: Plon, 1955.

Kayser, Jacques. *One Week's News: Comparative Study of 17 Major Dailies for a Seven-Day Period.* Paris: UNESCO, 1953.

Schramm, Wilbur. *One Day in the World's Press.* Stanford, Calif.: Stanford University Press, 1959.

Swindler, William F. *Phases of International Law Affecting the Flow of International News Communications.* Unpublished Ph.D. dissertation, University of Missouri (Columbia), 1940.

UNESCO. *News Agencies: Their Structure and Operation.* Paris: UNESCO, 1953.

Williams, Francis. *Transmitting World News: A Study of Telecommunications and the Press.* Paris: UNESCO, 1953.

UNESCO:

World Trends of News Agencies

SINCE THE Second World War, news agencies have come into being in large numbers, and in a great many countries. The world total of news agencies continues to grow.

The first broad wave of agency establishment or reorganization came with the post-war creation of new governments in various European countries. In all, 24 agencies began operating between 1945 and 1949. At the same time, agencies were opened or reorganized in a number of countries in Asia, North and South America and Oceania.

The expansion of news agencies was spread out rather evenly during the 1950s. New agencies came into being in Asia, North and South America, Europe and for the first time, in North and Tropical Africa.

The second broad wave of agency expansion came in 1960-62, when a total of 23 agencies were founded in the new African States as well as in Asia, North America, Oceania and the U.S.S.R.

As many as 155 news agencies are now maintained in 80 countries, compared to 96 agencies in 54 countries a decade ago. On the other hand, some 30 independent States in the developing regions still lack these basic services.

Except in Latin America, most national agencies distribute the international services of one or more of the world agencies to which they frequently supply domestic news. Although the exchange of news between countries within regions and between regions remains to a very large extent in the hands of the world agencies, bilateral agreements with neighbouring and distant countries are now common, and new ones are being drawn up each year. Certain European agencies and a few Asian agencies maintain a broad network of such agreements and have bureaux and correspondents in all continents.

In Europe, the major agencies of 16 countries co-operate through the European Alliance of News Agencies to further their common interests and promote the flow of news within the region. Asian agencies are similarly served by the Organization of Asian News Agencies, and African services by the Union of African News Agencies.

▶ From: *World Communications: Press—Radio—Television—Film,* by UNESCO. Copyright © 1964 by UNESCO and the UNESCO Publications Center, New York and Paris. Reprinted by permission of the publisher.

As the need for more regional news than is provided by the world services made itself felt, the movement towards regional solutions has gained in strength. Such agreements are also a means of strengthening the economic position of agencies which cannot afford a large network of foreign correspondents.

Technological advances in news transmission have vastly stimulated the expansion of existing news agencies since 1950 and the foundation of new ones. The period has witnessed the gradual replacement of the traditional telegraph service by the telephone and by the newer services such as telex, leased radio circuits and radio-communication to several destinations (multiple address). Radio-communication has won particular favour in the developing countries in view of its efficacy for distributing news at low cost over wide areas where telecommunication is not greatly developed.

Meanwhile, advances in the use of coaxial cables and in microwave transmission are revolutionizing the old telecommunication pattern by greatly increasing the number of channels available for press and other traffic. This development, taken in conjunction with the use of improved repeaters or "boosters" which greatly extend the range of ocean telephone cables, has already resulted in a broad expansion of world telecommunication facilities. It thus appears that, just as the early telegraph lines survived the coming of terrestrial radio, the modern telephone will become integrated with satellite radio in the world communication network of the future.

The news agencies themselves, through research and through their daily operations, have contributed greatly in post-war years to the improvement and expansion of facsimile transmission and teleprinter and telephoto services. These and other advances in telecommunication culminated on 19 July 1962 in one of the most dramatic events in news agency history. On that day the world news agencies entered the space age by using the first communication satellite to relay dispatches by telephone and teleprinter between continents. London and New York newspapers also exchanged dispatches through the satellite.

It was foreseen that three "stationary" satellites, each orbiting over the Equator at a speed synchronized with the rotation of the earth, could provide any type of telecommunication service over the whole globe. Professional organizations of the press, such as the International Federation of Newspaper Publishers and the Commonwealth Press Union, prepared for further developments in the expectation that facilities of this kind would be available to press and other users within five years.

Ironically, the conditions of modern life have at times forced a return to "new-old" techniques of communication. A somewhat fanciful example is reported by Reuters, which transmitted news dispatches by carrier pigeon in 1850 and by communication satellite in the historic experiment of 1962. The agency states that pigeons have come back as carriers of newsfilm items across metropolitan areas. Pigeons are not worried, as dispatch riders can be, by traffic jams.

Until the mid-fifties the only national agency in Africa was the South African Press Association, which began to supply domestic and foreign news to the press of South Africa, the Rhodesias and some newspapers in Portuguese East Africa in 1938. The Portuguese agencies, Lusitania and Agencia de Noticias e de Informaçoes (both founded in the mid-forties), send news to and receive news daily from Portuguese territories in Africa. The Arab News Agency, founded with headquarters in London in 1941, was set up in Cairo with the double task of collecting Middle Eastern news and supplying a varied file to Arabic-speaking countries.

Between 1955 and 1960, agencies were created in Somalia, the United Arab Republic (Egypt), Kenya, Ghana, Morocco, Senegal and Burundi.

The Middle East News, with headquarters in Cairo, now supplies national news daily in Arabic and English and foreign news in Arabic, and exchanges news with 10 non-African agencies. Morocco's Maghreb Arab Press transmits national news daily in Arabic and English, as well as foreign news received from its bureaux and correspondents abroad and from other African and non-African agencies.

News agencies were founded between 1960 and 1962 in 13 African States: Algeria, Cameroon, the Central African Republic, Congo (Brazzaville), Congo (Léopoldville), Dahomey, Ethiopia, Gabon, Guinea, Ivory Coast, Mali, Madagascar and Tunisia. Togo and Nigeria are preparing to establish agencies.

All these agencies, as well as government information services and press subscribers in countries where national agencies do not largely control news distribution, rely for world news upon European, United States or Soviet news agencies which also report African news to the rest of the world. The exchange of news between African countries is still largely carried out by AFP and Reuters and, to a lesser extent, by DPA, UPI, Tass and AP in that order. However, the Ghana News Agency transmits news in English and French daily to its London office, from where it is beamed back to West Africa and received over an area stretching from Dakar to Lagos. The Agence Ivoirenne de Presse is meanwhile spearheading plans for an exchange network among the 19 countries of the Monrovia group, to which it now sends a weekly bulletin.

The Maghreb Arab Press has proposed the creation of an African press pool in Morocco for the exchange of news among African news agencies and its distribution to the rest of the world. It has offered to put its telecommunication links with Asia, Europe and Latin and North America at the disposal of the other African agencies for the retransmission of news.

The greatest obstacle to developing adequate news agency services in Africa is poverty in telecommunications facilities. In the absence of direct links between countries, messages being sent between two points in Tropical Africa must often be routed through Paris or London. Even within countries, land-line and radio circuits are generally insufficient. The flow of news is also seriously hindered by high and often discrepant telecommunications costs, limited and expensive air mail services and by the rates charged for services from Europe and the United States. Furthermore, many African agencies are still not able to assure adequate coverage of domestic news by their own correspondents or by the staffs of subscribing newspapers.

In most African countries, the government participates in news agency operation. This varies from outright control to government assistance to a commercially operated agency.

Apart from the news agencies of Mexico, Cuba, Canada and the United States of America, there are only two news agencies in this region —the Caribbean Press Association (CPA) in the Windward Islands, and the Caribbean and Latin American News Service (CALANS) in Puerto Rico. The CPA supplements Canadian, United Kingdom and United States services to the English-speaking countries of the West Indies, while CALANS supplements services from UPI, AP and Reuters to Puerto Rico. Mexico's Informex, established in 1960, is a private agency which distributes news from correspondents in the United States, Canada, Argentina, Brazil, Chile and Spain, as well as a local service, to domestic subscribers. The Mexican press, however, obtains almost all its world news from AFP, AP and UPI. The Cuban agency, Prensa Latina, distributes news in other countries and has exchange agreements with agencies in other regions.

Canada supports two large general news agencies, Canadian Press (CP) and British United Press (BUP), a subsidiary of UPI. CP has exchange agreements with AP and Reuters, while BUP receives world-wide coverage from UPI in New York. CP maintains its own correspondents in the United States, at the United Nations and in the United Kingdom, India, New Zealand and South Africa. It also supplies news to the West Indies. BUP provides Canadian news to the United States, the Caribbean, South America, Europe and Australia.

Two of the world's largest news services are located in the United States. Associated Press, the oldest existing news agency, delivers a daily world news report to member and subscribing newspapers and radio and television stations and to news agencies. Exchange agreements with Reuters, Tass and AFP enable it to supplement its own reporting in their areas. AP maintains 110 bureaux in the United States and 57 abroad and some 2,500 permanent and thousands of part-time correspondents abroad. Altogether, AP serves 7,582 subscribers in more than 80 countries on an around-the-clock basis. It maintains an electronics laboratory which has been responsible for many innovations and improvements in news agency operations.

United Press International, which was formed when UP and INS merged in 1958, maintains 151 bureaux at home and 110 abroad, and has 10,000 full- or part-time employees. News dispatches appear in 48 languages in 111 States and territories and are received by 6,546 subscribers.

Notable technical developments in the United States include the form in which news is delivered to the press by AP. It is now sent either in justified lines in both capital and lower case letters, or in the form of paper tape for automatic typesetting. The agency operates more than 6,000 teleprinters of both types in AP bureaux and in member and subscriber offices around the world. Another important development was inaugurated by UPI in 1962. This was a computerized system for instant electronic reporting of stock market tables for newspapers. The computers furnish up-to-the-minute tables in the form of teletypesetter tape.

The greatest increase in the number of subscribers to both AP and UPI since the late fifties has occurred in the developing countries.

Although ahead of Africa and Asia in daily newspaper circulation, South America lags behind both regions in news agency development. Newspapers themselves have provided little impetus for news agency expansion, since unlike most newspapers in Africa and Asia, they receive the world news services already translated into Spanish or Portuguese. Of the 14 South American countries, seven have no general news agencies at all. Among these is Peru, which publishes 58 daily newspapers with a combined circulation of 750,000.

All agencies in Colombia and Venezuela and most of those in Chile, Argentina and Brazil, collect and distribute news only within their national borders. A special case is Surinam, where the Dutch news agency ANP supplies the press with daily news coverage in Dutch, English, Spanish and local languages. Three agencies in Argentina, Brazil and Chile have exchange agreements. Uruguay's Agencia Nacional de Informaciones (ANI) also receives the Telpress service from Buenos Aires and a service from the Chilean agency, Orbe Latino-americana, which maintains representatives in 12 Latin American capitals and distributes regional news to 22 subscribers. The Brazilian agency, Transpress, has an exchange agreement with DPA, and distributes foreign news daily. DPA (of West Germany) also exchanges with ANI (Uruguay).

But this is the total extent of regional or international news agency collaboration in South America. Throughout the region, the press and radio and television stations rely directly upon the services of AP, UPI, AFP and Reuters.

Almost all South American news agencies are privately owned, although one Brazilian agency is government controlled. There are no cooperatives.

As in the other developing regions, the inadequacy and the high cost of telecommunications facilities are the greatest obstacles to the foundation of viable news agencies. Latin American governments, at meetings sponsored by the Organization of American States, and the International Telecommunication Union, have planned the establishment of an Inter-American Telecommunication Network (RIT), which would link all countries in the Americas in a jointly-operated system. The RIT would permit the exchange of news within the Americas at costs comparable to those in Europe, and would also channel news inexpensively between South America and other regions.

News agencies now exist in 20 Asian countries, several of them maintaining more than one general news agency and one or more specialized agencies. Among these latter countries are China (Taiwan), India, Indonesia, Israel, Japan, Korea, Pakistan and the Philippines. In the Federation of Malaya, the press and the Government Department of Information are planning to establish a national agency.

Most of the 23 countries lacking an agency are small and have a low rate of literacy, Lebanon being a notable exception. Thailand has no agency, but the government news service provides the press with a summary of the Reuters file at low cost and distributes a daily domestic news bulletin free of charge. Although Hong Kong also has no local agency, it is the regional headquarters of the Pan-Asia Newspaper Alliance. Singapore, as a major centre for collection and dissemination of South-East Asian news, is able to draw on the news resources of many agencies.

The pattern of control varies from country to country. In 11 countries, agencies have an official or semi-official status, while in Ceylon, India, Israel, Japan and the Philippines they are operated as co-operatives or as joint stock companies. Indonesia, South Korea, Pakistan and China (Taiwan) maintain both official or semi-official and privately-owned news agencies.

Most of the agencies are limited in scope, their main activity being the collection and distribution of news within their own countries. However, many of them distribute international and regional news obtained principally from Reuters, AFP, UPI, AP, Tass and Kyodo. A few countries receive the NCNA (mainland China), DPA or MEN services.

Only Antara and PIA in Indonesia, ITIM in Israel, Kyodo and, to a less extent, Jiji in Japan and Viet-Nam Presse in the Republic of Viet-Nam maintain an extensive network of exchange agreements with other agencies in the region or elsewhere. Furthermore, only a few Asian agencies can afford to maintain bureaux or permanent correspondents in non-Asian centres.

In countries without a news agency, the press obtains foreign news either by subscription to world and national services of other countries, by monitored radio or from news bulletins issued by government information departments.

Among obstacles to news agency development are the poverty and small size of most newspapers in the Middle East and South-East Asia. Few of them can afford to pay agency subscriptions for wider news coverage. But, as in Africa, the great difficulty arises from the inadequacy of telecommunication facilities and disparities in communication charges. These deficiencies work to the particular disadvantage of the local agencies, since the world agencies can utilize telecommunication services from outside Asia. Such obstacles may in time be overcome through the development of telecommunication networks, now being promoted by the United Nations Economic Commission for Asia and the Far East, in co-operation with the International Telecommunication Union.

In many of the non-Arabic-speaking countries, multilingualism also raises a problem. One Indian news agency now supplies a service in eight languages but, in general, newspapers must do their own translating. French and English are widely used by agencies. In Pakistan, for example, APP distributes 50,000 words daily—all in English—to 41 newspapers, only 10 of them being English-language newspapers.

On the whole, the development of fruitful regional news exchange agreements has been slow. An agency which concentrates on regional news is Pan-Asia (Hong Kong), which maintains bureaux or correspondents in a number of Asia capitals and distributes South-East Asian news daily in English and Chinese. Plans for regional co-operation among agencies are being developed by the Organization of Asian News Agencies.

More than in any other region, news agency development in Asia is handicapped by the scripts used by the press. In the Arabic-language countries, where a simplified typewriter appeared in 1962, there is as yet no automatic teletype transmission and printing system for Arabic characters. Of the other Asian countries which employ non-ideographic or ideographic scripts, only Japan has been able to afford a tape-type facsimile system. Based upon a Chinese prototype, an ideograph teletype system was inaugurated by Kyodo in 1960, and within two years, 45 of the largest provincial dailies had installed automatic Monotype machines to receive the service. Kyodo has also begun to speed up service still further by using a telefax system to transmit whole pages. The same agency transmits news by short wave to its branches and to newspaper and radio subscribers. These are intercepted and reproduced by news agencies and newspapers in Okinawa, China (Taiwan and mainland), North Korea and the Republic of Korea.

Europe is served by a denser, more intricate system of news exchanges than any other region. Most countries subscribe, either through news agencies or through individual newspapers and radio and television stations, to the services of AP, UPI or Tass. In addition, Europe is itself the home of two world news agencies, Agence France-Presse (AFP) and Reuters.

AFP maintains 82 bureaux in cities abroad as well as 79 foreign correspondents in other cities. It exchanges national news with Reuters, AP, Tass, NCNA and DPA. Thirty-nine agencies abroad take its world service and it subscribes to the national services of 20 agencies. AFP distributes news daily to 104 countries. Although the French Government is its most important client, AFP is an autonomous organization, eight of whose directorial seats are held by French newspapers.

Reuters is a non-profit organization co-operatively owned by the newspapers of the United Kingdom, Australia and New Zealand. Reuters does not supply domestic news to British subscribers. However, it distributes overseas the news of the Press Association, Britain's leading domestic news agency. In South-East Asia and Oceania, Australian Associated Press, another Reuters partner, shares the news collection and distribution burden with Reuters.

Reuters maintains bureaux in some 60 capitals abroad and distributes news to some 110 countries. Comtelburo, its subsidiary, transmits economic news directly to over 80 countries. Apart from its agreements with other world agencies for the exchange of domestic news and its exchange arrangements with British Commonwealth agencies, Reuters has agreements with 22 agencies in Europe, 14 in Asia, five in Africa and two in North America.

Both France and the United Kingdom have co-operative agencies which collect domestic news and distribute it to provincial newspapers.

Agencies in some of the other European countries disseminate a considerable daily wordage abroad. Outstanding is DPA, which supplies a daily foreign service and has exchange agreements with 52 news agencies around the world. ADN, in Eastern Germany, has exchange agreements with all the world agencies and with 25 other agencies. The major Italian agency, ANSA, with 17 bureaux abroad, has exchange agreements with AFP, Reuters, UPI and 21 other agencies and distributes news to 150 newspapers abroad. CTK (Czechoslovakia), which has agreements with 35 agencies, including AFP, AP, Reuters and DPA, transmits news abroad daily and also issues a daily air mail bulletin. PAP (Poland) maintains 22 foreign bureaux.

In certain European countries, national news agencies are the sole source of domestic and foreign news. Among countries where national agencies have a monopoly or quasi-monopoly of news distribution are Albania, Belgium, Bulgaria, Hungary, Poland, Czechoslovakia, Eastern Germany, Rumania and Yugoslavia. But even in countries where the mass media can and do freely subscribe to foreign services, they also subscribe to the complete services of their national agencies. In addition to the five countries which publish no daily newspapers, only Ireland, Luxembourg, Cyprus, Gibraltar, Malta and Iceland have no national news agency.

Even in Europe, disparate telecommunication rates and inadequate services create problems for news agencies. In an effort to overcome these obstacles, the European Alliance of News Agencies is studying the possibility of establishing a press telecommunication network to be operated collectively by its 16 member agencies.

"Down under," fully-fledged news agencies are maintained only in Australia and New Zealand. A co-operative owned by all but one of the metropolitan dailies, the Australian Associated Press (AAP) is one of the co-proprietors of Reuters, with headquarters in Melbourne. In addition to providing a daily national and world service to member and subscribing newspapers, AAP transmits to radio and television stations and the New Zealand Press Association (NZPA). It maintains correspondents in London and New York and, jointly with Reuters, in the South-East Asian and Pacific areas. Australian United Press, which receives UPI's world service, concentrates on the collection of domestic news.

The NZPA, the major New Zealand agency, is also a Reuters co-owner. A co-operative, it distributes national and world news to forty-two dailies.

In the Pacific island groups, the small number of daily and non-daily newspapers largely rely upon the AAP, NZPA, AFP, AP, UPI and Reuters news services which are received by radio or radio-teleprinter, either by subscription or in summaries provided by local government authorities.

An exception is Tonga, where the government-owned Broadcasting Commission publishes a national news bulletin and also prepares air-mailed news for distribution abroad.

Tass, one of the world news agencies, has its head office in Moscow. As the official agency of the U.S.S.R., Tass is responsible for the distribution of world news to the 15 Union Republics and for transmission of news between Republics. It has 3,650 newspaper and magazine and nearly 40 radio and television subscribers within the Soviet Union, where it has recently speeded up news transmission by introducing newly-developed teleprinters with Cyrillic characters.

Abroad, Tass has agreements with some 30 agencies, including AFP, AP, Reuters, UPI, DPA, Kyodo, Antara, MEN and the agencies of all the popular democracies. Mass circulation newspapers in countries where national agencies do not completely control news distribution also subscribe to its service. The agency maintains communications between its four principal foreign bureaux and Moscow and with the agencies of mainland China, Czechoslovakia, Bulgaria, Rumania, Eastern Germany, Poland and Hungary.

Ten bureaux are maintained in European countries, one in Africa (where correspondents are maintained in 13 other countries), seven in Asia (plus permanent correspondents in 12 other countries), three in North American and one in Oceania. Correspondents are maintained in Canada and Mexico and in eight South American countries.

Novosti, a recently established news agency with no official governmental affiliations, supplies background information and daily "spot" news to the press in the U.S.S.R. and abroad.

Rhoda Metraux:

International Communication of Science Information

———

Given a world frame of reference, instead of a parochial point of view, it is possible that we might find new ways of formulating and presenting knowledge, and of using the modern system of communication effectively among peoples of all cultures.

THE problem of communicating scientific information, especially from the point of view of international communication, is but one facet of the larger problem of applying our knowledge of human behavior in the context of actual contemporary living, and I propose in this paper to discuss some of the general as well as some of the particular issues involved.

For some 50 years it has been apparent that we are living in a world system of communication and that a world community is in the process of emerging. Fifty years ago, there were still large areas of the world where it was possible to live without reference to anything outside the narrow boundaries of a local community; today there are almost no such pockets of isolation. Modern technology, modern political thought, contemporary ways of dressing and eating, organizing time, buying and selling, working and resting, going to school, caring for the sick, valuing the living, waging war, learning about events—all these things, in closely related versions, have a world-wide distribution.

And today we have consolidated the technical means of communicating with one another about all these things—and almost anything else we choose—irrespective of natural barriers like mountains and oceans or man-made barriers like national boundaries and even, to a certain extent, language. Twenty-five years ago, with radio, the people of an isolated Rocky Mountain mining town had access to events taking place round the world, and their judgment of these events (in contrast to their views about local events) was knowledgeable and sophisticated. At present, with television, people living in a small Indian community in Mexico can, even though they may be illiterate and may not speak Spanish, see with their own eyes events taking place in parts of the world they may never travel to or learn about through local sources of information.

▶ From: *Journalism Quarterly* (Iowa City, Iowa), Vol. 40/No. 3 (Summer 1963), pp. 332-338. Reprinted by permission of the publisher and of the author.

The real barriers have broken down, but two things, above all, hamper us in our ability to think imaginatively and constructively about the emerging world community and our best use of the technical means of communication.

The first of these is that we, in our generation, live in the widest community only in part of our lives, and it is still an almost individual matter in what part of our lives we are aware of this widest world. The man who is a banker has a different area of awareness from the farmer thinking about crops. The manufacturer of automobiles or television sets or machine tools has a different sense of what is involved from the school teacher struggling with an elementary social studies program. The biologist has a different set of world connections from the physicist. The trade union representative thinking about labor conditions has a different conception of what is important from the church mission director. The epidemiologist looks at world maps from a different point of view from that of the shipping expert. This sense of, at best, only partly shared knowledge and experience makes it exceedingly difficult to develop—or to be aware that we are developing—a style of global thinking and response which cuts across areas of special interest.

The second thing that hampers us—it would seem paradoxically—is our increasing knowledge about and sensitivity to other cultures. It was to be expected that, with increasing exposure to other cultures, the sensitivity to difference would increase and, in sophisticated societies, that an interest in systematic studies of cultural difference would become more widespread. But there is also a tendency to believe that sensitivity and sophistication in this matter are closely linked, because this has been our experience. Yet it is not necessarily the case.

Ten years ago, while I was working on a small West Indian island, a group of village boys came one afternoon to tell me about the wonderful new job they had got as porters for a team who were working on the site of a missile tracking post on one of the island's mountains. Full of enthusiasm, they described how the American in charge had sat down with them on the mountain side, while he explained what a missile was (using a stick to draw pictures on the ground) and what his plan of work was. This set off a succession of mimed scenes as different boys sketched out the behavior of various Europeans they had encountered—Frenchmen, Dutchmen, Englishmen—toward their work crews. Most of what they had to say was communicated by mimed gestures, but these were a subtle expression of their grasp of different styles of hierarchical relations.

At the time I was impressed by the slight and fragmentary quality of this people's relationship to the modern world beyond their island, by the accidental aspect of what came their way. Today I am more impressed by our lack of concern than by their lack of knowledge, and by the fragmented way in which most people—not just those living at the fringes— are taking part in the changes that are reshaping the world.

Emergence of a World Culture

For people everywhere are experiencing a revolutionary alteration of the spatial framework of their thoughts and actions, whatever they may make of the experience. Daily we are offered for our attention events that are world-wide in their coverage and reports of events that suggest their world-wide relevance, and our own activities reverberate to events taking place half a world away. An astronaut or a cosmonaut circling the globe —his flight through space observed by tracking stations linked around the globe and monitored by hundreds of millions of men and women who, through radio and television, have temporarily become parts of one vast network of communication—is only one spectacular, highly focused example of a great multitude of events. A health officer walking down the aisle of a jet plane ready to disembark its passengers at Orly or Idlewild, an academic lunch table discussion of a much disputed academic statement about race, a clumsily organized bunch of young mothers demonstrating against nuclear testing, a news broadcast about the meeting (or non-meeting) of Soviet and mainland Chinese politicians, a report of a new contraceptive device—all such events and responses to events today take place within a world-wide frame of reference.

Yet it is perfectly possible to look at many of these events from a parochial point of view. We can ask how many *Americans* knew something about space satellites before the first actual launching. We can ask how many *Americans* have what kind of understanding of terms like "race" or "species." We can ask how many *Americans*—or farmers or urban dwellers or high school graduates or women or readers of quality journals or lawyers or engineers—have what kinds of views about pesticides or have given thought to the exploration of outer or inner space. We can concentrate on the local, regional or national *American* responses to events taking place in Little Rock and Birmingham, to the moon race, to the reported effects of detergents on our water supply. Looking at what we find out, we can deplore American ignorance; we can insist that Americans must be better informed, must take a greater interest, must assume more responsibility for decisions.

But in narrowing our focus in this way we are somehow managing to dodge the central issue with all its implications, that is, the emergence of a world culture, which has been made possible by science and the application of scientific knowledge and which depends for its development on a world-wide raising of the level of knowledge, especially scientific knowledge. By insisting on the limited, parochial frame of reference, we overlook the immediate effects of intercommunication—as it already exists—even on our own lives and destinies.

The common knowledge—or ignorance—about man as a species and the use made of this knowledge—or ignorance—anywhere affect not only the social arrangements of some particular region or country but of many parts of the world today. What happens in an American city affects the decisions arrived at in an international gathering of African politicians, and their activities in turn are reflected in other activities in Europe and Asia and the Americas. We *and* all the peoples of the world need access to our best knowledge about man, as man; we *and* all the peoples of the world need to know the areas about which little or nothing is known— as yet. So, also, knowledge about the population explosion needs to be built into the thinking of all the peoples of the world; the problem cannot be dealt with piecemeal. So, too, the protection of the world's resources is dependent on a world-wide dissemination of knowledge and acceptance of good practices in relation to soil and water and minerals, plant life and living creatures.

At times it would appear that we make use of what we know about world-wide intercommunication simply to negate its possibilities by stressing the rapid spread of fad and fashion by means of the mass media, the creation of "images" shaped by half-truths, the destruction of tradition. A good world, in our imagination, is still a world with many isolating communication boundaries. We do not think of the continual establishment of new links. Indians living in the Bolivian Gran Chaco buy sun glasses and patent medicines from "Syrian" peddlers and receive as presents picture calendars made for this special purpose by a Swiss pharmaceutical house. They cannot use the calendars, for they cannot read; but nevertheless they pick up something from a wider world in which white-coated men (pictured on the calendars) make the drugs that alleviate, if they do not cure, their ailments. Fragment that it is, it is something to build on. And peoples who, just a few years ago, were even more isolated than these Chaco Indians, today are being precipitated into the modern world of plane travel, electronic equipment, schools, technical training and world politics—in the far north, for example, and in New Guinea.

Part of our handicap in using our thinking about primitive cultures arises, I think, from our acceptance of judgments made at an earlier stage of change. It took us some 400 years of contact with cultures having historically different traditions from our own to come to a full recognition of the integrity of a culture and to realize the need for moving slowly and cautiously in introducing change where the aim was to protect that integrity. We came, finally, to think of cultures as self-bounded by internal regularities of belief and behavior and shared experience. But today we need to re-examine all cultures as actually or potentially open systems; we need to re-examine what we know about diffusion and the mechanisms of using shared knowledge and practice as a medium of cross-cultural communications.

In the past, differences in the *scale* of sharing have been used to create and reinforce boundaries—between classes and special groups within cultures, and also between cultures. Today, these discrepancies in the scale of sharing constitute in themselves one of the chief barriers to the acquisition of new knowledge and patterns of behavior among those groups who for hundreds (sometimes thousands) of years have been "kept in their place" by recognized ignorance. For it should be recognized that while very limited access to knowledge (however defined) might be tragic for the unusual individual, the common bonds of ignorance among a group could constitute a kind of protection. So, in dealing with a very old peasant population, for example, we have a very different set of problems from those we must solve in dealing with a primitive or recently primitive people with access to their whole culture.

With a people who still do have access to a whole culture, the central problem is one of presenting new knowledge in such ways that they can change specifically without losing a sense of wholeness. But for a people for whom a deeply engrained reluctance to learn inclusively is linked to security, it is this learned reluctance and this acceptance of partial non-sharing which must be overcome. It is possible to see how, in the breakdown of the 19th century colonial world, this has operated in the case of those who, within their own culture, found themselves in the non-sharing position as unprivileged people in their own society. In many cases it was precisely these peculiarly placed groups who were the active rebels against the colonial system—especially as the scale of their sharing in Western culture increased. But we still have a great deal to learn about the different kinds of diffusion and rescaling of participation if knowledge is to be more widely and evenly shared.

Presenting of New Knowledge

So, also, we are somewhat handicapped by our present recognition that there are no simple, universal ways of presenting new knowledge to peoples living under different cultural systems. Given a long tradition of cross-communication and a recent great expansion of the means of communication, members of Euro-American cultures have nevertheless found it extremely difficult at times actually to communicate with one another. But this recognition is handicapping, as we also know from experience, only to the extent that we are unwilling to raise the level of analysis, on the one hand, and to attend to the finer details of the communication process, on the other. What is necessary, in fact, is greater awareness, including self-awareness, and articulateness about those aspects of a culture, including our own, which are generally carried without consciousness of them.

There is also the difficulty that we do not take full account of two of our basic premises about scientific and technical knowledge. One premise is that such knowledge is cumulative and irreversible. The other is that a body of knowledge—like a technology or a language—is formally separable from the particular culture in which, at any time, it may be imbedded. The fact that systematic knowledge, including systematic ways of transmitting and increasing the store of knowledge, is shaped by the culture in which it occurs need not prevent us from considering—with full awareness perhaps for the first time—what is intrinsic and what is extrinsic to the system. This task is perhaps a realizable one only now that, for the first time, we have the possibility of building new (and old) systems of knowledge into those aspects of human culture which are, as a world culture, coming to be shared by men of many different cultures.

Historically we may look at the immense amount of time it required to build up any one of the major branches of modern knowledge, and this encourages doubts that what is known can be learned by the members of a whole society in a short time. Furthermore, individually, having grown up in cultures in which specialization of knowledge has characterized very high levels of learning and realizing the difficulties of overcoming individual, personal limitations in such a system, we naturally are doubtful of transmitting some understanding of all the specialties to the already adult members of another culture who have not had any—let alone a long—preparation.

Yet on an experimental basis at least, it has proved feasible to instruct children in systems of knowledge with considerable success which up to now have been the prerogatives of the trained adult scholar. What has made this possible is that first class minds have set themselves the task of analyzing out basic principles (protecting the system from major distortion) and have been willing to experiment with teaching young children as well. Shall we say out of hand, then, that adults in our society —given the opportunity and adequate means—would be unable to learn what children in the sixth or third or first grade can grasp? Shall we say that it is not feasible to make such knowledge available to members of other cultures than our own?

Actually, there would be one very great advantage in ceasing to think parochially about the whole problem of the public understanding of science and technology and of the event structure of the modern world. We would be obliged to manage better than we do, at present, the problem of discovering alternative routes to knowledge and ways of combining these for world-wide dissemination. We would have to include in our thinking cultures of very different levels of sophistication about "knowledge"; we would have to include the sensory modes of communication in different ways and much more fully. We would have to face up to the problem of keeping a sense of wholeness, on the one hand, and also of overcoming the complex resistances of those who have learned how not to learn too much for their own good.

In fact, given a *world* frame of reference, it is possible that we might engage the imagination of scientists and draw on scientific talents not now involved in thinking about new ways of formulating and presenting knowledge. As long as we remain parochially limited to the problems of teaching and learning *within* a culture, it is possible to define what is being done as some kind of "improvement" of what already exists; as we know, this problem is one that engages the interest of relatively few people who are not educators by profession. But a change in the frame of reference provides a different kind of challenge.

For this reason, I have not discussed here the particular problems of, let us say, making use of international means of teaching—improving the knowledge of—populations living in cultures very closely related to our own. As long as we think mainly in terms of the United States, the United Kingdom, France, Italy, Brazil, Australia, and so on, we are beset with the problems of quite special, small-scale differences to which we, nationally and internationally, have been sensitized by long and close contact and which play some part in the maintenance of a feeling of national identity. If we shift the scale of inquiry and of performance to a much more inclusive one, we are freer to think in more inclusive terms and, therefore, in terms of genuinely new modes of presentation.

Early in World War II, when it became necessary to prepare Americans for new kinds of restrictions, such as rationing, and for rapid acceptance of various unfamiliar programs, it immediately became apparent that planning had to be based on the common features of the *national* culture (as worked out by fine-grain studies), not the particular, differentiating features of regional or local or minority group or class versions of the national culture. And it was found possible, where a plan was firmly based in the national culture, then, in the local situation, to take into account local peculiarities. Work of this kind can provide us with one model for large scale international educational programming, whether for large regions of the world or for world-wide distribution.

International Communication Program

The problem of international communication of knowledge, like the problem of cross-national communication in its most general aspects, involves serious consideration of such things as a world second language and world use of the most modern techniques of recording and retrieving information. Also involved is the planning for the technological development of less industrialized countries (such as was discussed internationally in Geneva in February 1963) in such ways as to avoid building obsolescence into new systems. It has been the considered opinion of those who have worked, on a small scale, on the problems of introducing literacy (often in connection with introducing a new, world language, such as English or French) and new knowledge, that all these things should be part of one across-the-board program. What we need to do now, of course, is to translate findings like these and the results of small, local programs —which must serve as living experiments, the only ones we have to draw on—into plans at another level of complication. If we are to embark on any such program, the first step is a definition of the set of things *most needed simultaneously* to provide a core program for the enlargement of communication. That is, essentially, the question of raising the level of knowledge of science must be bound into our most specific thinking and programming for the development of a world community.

Perhaps one of the most valuable by-products of this kind of thinking on a world scale would be that we would thereby have a fresh approach to our own parochial difficulties. The question of how to include those who have been traditionally excluded from a set of practices and those who have come to be excluded by changes in which they have not been involved is an exceedingly difficult one to answer within the framework of the existing culture. And here we must, for many purposes, think in Euro-American terms. For while there may be great differences among Euro-American cultures in the images of what specific groups within them (the old, children, women, intellectuals, manual laborers, etc.) can and should learn, the types of division made are, by and large, common within the culture area. But by thinking comparatively and on a much wider basis, we are forced to cross-cut familiar social and cultural divisions, and the results of our thinking may well have the beneficial effect of providing us with new models for thinking about local, internal problems.

Most important, the necessity of breaking traditional boundaries in order to increase the scale of our communication will carry with it the necessity of refining the scale of observation and analysis—for these two things go together. This will mean, then, that the results will be more readily applicable at whatever scale we choose—in reporting world events to a world-wide audience, or in teaching a particular group of specialists whose members happen to be residents of 20 different countries, or in devising ways for changing the image of science or scientists among school girls in Western countries, or in introducing literacy among the obstinately illiterate (that is, those for whom illiteracy has become a protective devise) wherever they may be.

Without thinking of this kind, we may, in another 50 years, have settled for a view of the world in which fragmentation is deeply engrained and in which piecemeal knowledge is part of a total system. Alternatively, we can build the foundation for shared perception and knowledge on a world-wide scale if we are willing, now, to take advantage of the newness of the means of communication we have at our command as a means of capturing the imagination of all those who need to learn—the planners and programmers, the teachers and a new world student body.

Karl Erik Rosengren:

International News: Time and Type of Report

For several reasons, the international flow of news is an important field of research. Much work has gone into the field: some hundred papers and a couple of books. Excellent investigations concerning various aspects of the subject are Adams,[1] Cutlip,[2] Galtung & Holmboe Ruge,[3] Hart,[4] Markham,[5] Schramm,[6] to mention just a few among the papers.

Yet, there is no doubt that much remains to be done. For instance, the sampling problem must be given more attention, so that the results obtained may be generalized to a well defined universe. The units of measurement must be systematically investigated, in order to obtain reliability, validity and comparability. The interest should be focused towards the theoretical aspects of the problem to a higher degree than has been the case up to now. And the time perspective must not be neglected—as only too often it is in sociological research.

In this paper a theoretical suggestion by Himmelstrand[7] concerning the time perspective will be combined with a methodological approach used by Szalai (several types of units of measurement applied on the same material).[8]

[1] J. B. Adams, "A Qualitative Analysis of Domestic and Foreign News on the AP TA Wire," *Gazette*, Vol. 10/1964, p. 285.
[2] S. M. Cutlip, "Content and Flow of AP News—From Trunk to TTS to Reader," *Journalism Quarterly*, Vol. 31/1954, p. 434.
[3] J. Galtung & M. Holmboe Ruge, "The Structure of Foreign News," *Journal of Peace Research*, Vol. 2/1965, p. 64.
[4] J. A. Hart, "Foreign News in U.S. and English Daily Newspapers: A Comparison," *Journalism Quarterly*, Vol. 43/1966, p. 444.
[5] J. W. Markham, "Foreign News in the United States and South American Press," *The Public Opinion Quarterly*, Vol. 25/1961, p. 249.
[6] W. Schramm, "Newspapers of a State As a News Network," *Journalism Quarterly*, Vol. 35/1958, p. 177.
[7] U. Himmelstrand, "Nyheter och nyheter," *Ord och bild*, Vol. 76/1967, p. 383; U. Himmelstrand, "Världen, Nigeria och Biafra. Sanningen som kom bort," *Aldus*, Stockholm 1969. (In Swedish; English edition in preparation.)
[8] Unitar Panel on Communication and Information, June 12-14, 1969: Public Information on the United Nations, *United Nations Institute for Training and Research*, New York 1969 (mimeo).

► This is an original article done for this book by Karl Erik Rosengren, Department of Sociology, University of Lund, Sweden, 1969.

"Time perspective" in this connection may mean at least three different things.

1. Most investigations on the international flow of news are cross-sectional: how many per cent of the news hole in a paper or a collection of papers are dedicated to foreign news, to news from a given country, to foreign news belonging to a certain content category (social, political, economical news etc)? But sometimes a time perspective is introduced by combining several cross-sectional investigations, as it were, one after the other. An example of this is Mott's investigation of "Trends in Newspaper Content," showing that the foreign material in the American press was growing during the first half of the 20th century; [9] another is Schwarzlose's investigation into "Trends in U.S. Newspapers' Wire Service Resources, 1934-66," showing a decline in the papers' use of more than one major press association during the period of observation.[10] The application of a time perspective in this sense is very important and somewhat neglected; it could easily be undertaken in various ways in a country like for instance Sweden, with its very long series of official statistics, and with its State libraries containing in principle everything printed in the country since a couple of hundred years. However, it will not interest us in this paper.

2. Another use of the time perspective is met with in investigations like Cutlip's, concerning the flow of the news from trunk wire over TTS into the paper.[11] That is, the investigator asks, what happens to the news as it passes through the news machinery? An interesting—but neglected—question in this connection is the following one: what are the determining factors of the varying amount of time between event and report? Cutlip had some predecessors—White's famous gatekeeper study, for instance [12]—and more followers. His is an interesting use of the time perspective. However, it will not concern us any further in this paper.

3. The third use of a time perspective is not even as common as the other two, rare as these may be. In fact, as far as I know, only Ulf Himmelstrand has treated it at some length, and even his treatment is hardly more than an outline of an argument. However, it seems to be a rather interesting outline. In principle, it consists in asking what happens to the international flow of news about a given

[9] F. L. Mott, "Trends in Newspaper Content," in W. Schramm (ed.), *Mass Communications*, 2nd ed. (Urbana: University of Illinois Press 1960).
[10] R. A. Schwarzlose, "Trends in U.S. Newspapers' Wire Service Resources, 1934-66," *Journalism Quarterly*, Vol. 43/1966, p. 627.
[11] S. M. Cutlip, *loc. cit.*
[12] D. M. White, "The 'Gatekeeper': A Case Study in the Selection of News," *Journalism Quarterly*, Vol. 27/1950, p. 383.

event or, rather, a given sequence of events (e.g., a crisis of some sort), as time passes by and new events are added to the "first" one.

In essence, Himmelstrand's approach is that of the ideal type. As something important happens and continues to happen, he says, the international communication of news about the set of events may be seen as developing in three or four phases.[13]

In the first phase, what happens is reported: hard and hot news. The details are few, however, and the basis for commentary and interpretation brittle. Therefore, what interpretation there is, is rather sketchy and loaded with clichés and prejudice. (Sometimes, there is quite a lot of this type of comment.)

In the second phase, as the pattern of events is developing, the material grows richer, the basis for interpretation firmer. There is a possibility of correcting whatever inadequacies and inadvertencies were produced during the first phase, a possibility, however, that is not always made use of.

Instead, *the third phase* may be entered, that of reduced news value of the set of events, leading to oblivion or latency. In a possible *fourth phase*, for some reasons the news value may be rising again, and this time, with the help of their archives, the mass media may produce a better picture right from the beginning. (This possibility, of course, is not always taken care of. Instead, the media may return, as it were, to phase I again.) The phases may be of varying length for different sets of events and different media.

Himmelstrand underlines that his phases are applicable mainly to really "new" news, things happening unexpectedly and/or in remote places of the world, difficult to reach for geographical or other reasons.

Himmelstrand further suggests that news and interpretation may interact in a *circulus vitiosus* to bias the total reporting of the event by a given newspaper or group of newspapers. What interpretation is made in the first phase, is rather like a projective test of the prejudices of the commentator. In the second phase these biased interpretations direct the choice among and the play up of the various news items available by then. The biased news, in return, helps create new biased interpretations, and so on, till the third phase, that of oblivion or latency, is entered. Thus, very often the second phase is characterized not so much by "better," i.e., more unbiased interpretation, as by just more interpretation than during the first phase.

Himmelstrand illustrates his argument with data gathered from the Swedish press concerning the Nigerian civil strife in 1966, and with a comparison between the reporting of the same events by the Swedish radio and BBC.

The literature concerning the international flow of news is mostly

[13] U. Himmelstrand, *loc. cit.*

ad hoc, rather poor of theoretical arguments.[14] Therefore, and because they concern a time perspective otherwise all but completely neglected, Himmelstrand's suggestions should be further looked into. Ideal type arguments as a rule are difficult to falsify. But often they may prove of great heuristic value. And in this case it so happens that data collected for quite other purposes may be marshalled in support of the argument.

In 1968, under the auspices of the United Nations, a world-wide investigation concerning news about the United Nations was carried through under the direction of Alexander Szalai. Two preliminary reports have already been issued, and a definitive report is said to follow in the near future.[15] The investigation is a really full-scale one. A great deal of material has been collected and many interesting questions have been raised. In this paper, however, only two things will be touched upon: the unit of measurement, and the time perspective in the third sense mentioned above.

In several investigations of the international flow of news, different units of measurement have been used in the same investigation.[16] Common units are column inch, number of words, number of paragraphs, number of news items. When more than one type of unit have been used, as a rule one type has been preferred, the other being used mainly as a means of validating the measurement.

In the UN investigation, too, more than one type of unit of measurement were used: number of news items and number of characters (expressed as STP—standard typewritten pages of 2,000 characters). There is nothing very new about that. But then an innovation was introduced: the different units of measurement were not seen as measuring the same concept, as in most other investigations of this kind. Instead, the two subconcepts of *amount* and *volume* of news output were introduced, amount being operationally defined as number of news items, volume as number of STP.

When amount and volume of news output were measured and plotted over time, an interesting observation was made: "Characteristic of the broken-line volume-of-output curve is that its peaks and plateaus often lag in time behind the peaks and plateaus of the amount-of-output curve. This lag seems to be due to the fact that "flashes," "spot news" and "first reports" about critical events are in general relatively brief, but if interest in the matter persists, the newsmedia on subsequent days give relatively voluminous "follow-up" and "background" stories. Thus, the time lag of the volume-of-information output behind the amount-of-

[14] For brilliant exceptions, see e.g., Galtung & Ruge, *loc. cit.*, and *Schramm, loc. cit.*
[15] Unitar Research Paper No. 1: Public Information on the United Nations, *United Nations Institute for Training and Research*, New York 1968 (mimeo); Unitar Panel; *op. cit.*
[16] Cf. G. A. Van Horn, "Analysis of AP News on Trunk and Wisconsin State Wires," *Journalism Quarterly*, Vol. 29/1952, p. 426; W. Schramm, *op. cit.*; R. W. Budd, "U.S. News in the Press Down Under," *The Public Opinion Quarterly*, Vol. 28/1964, p. 39.

information output gives a certain measure of the commentative and interpretative effort of the mass media." [17]

The quotation, of course, sounds rather like a reformulation of Himmelstrand's phase model, and *vice versa*. But Himmelstrand presented his argument in Swedish, before the mimeographed report of Szalai's. The fact that similar results have been reached independently by two qualified researchers in the field makes them worth following up. One way of doing this is by trying to combine them in a set of testable propositions forming the outline of a verbal theory of certain aspects of the flow of news. The rest of the paper will be dedicated to an effort in this direction.

Events reported in the mass media form *news*. Events may vary as to degree of *importance* and degree of *predictability*. Consequences of unpredictable events are less unpredictable than the original event. News may be *factual* and/or *interpretative* to a varying degree.

The operationalization of these basic concepts of predictability, importance, factual and interpretative news should not be too difficult. For the latter two concepts, an operationalization in the form of a code sheet for news items is already in existence.[18] For the first two, simple trichotomized ratings should be sufficient for a beginning. As the terms are understood here, it is a predictable event that a president is elected in the United States on a given day. It is an unpredictable event if, later on, he is murdered. Both are important events. A less important event is when Sweden changes her minister of agriculture. (For further refinement of the concept of importance, McNelly's operationalized concept of "meaning intensity" might be of some use. McNelly touches upon the time aspect, too.) [19]

Accepting these four basic concepts, it may be hypothesized that the more unpredictable the event, the more factual and the less interpretative its report. And the more important the event, the greater the need for interpretation. From this follows:

1. Important and predictable events will be reported at once factually and interpretatively.

2. Events that are important and unpredictable tend to be reported at first predominantly factually, then more and more interpretatively.

3. Less important events will be reported mainly factually, regardless of whether they are predictable or not.

[17] Unitar Panel, p. 25.
[18] B. H. Westley & M. S. MacLean, *Obform Coding Instructions*, University of Wisconsin, no date, (mimeo), quoted in: J. T. McNelly, "Coverage of the 1956 American Presidential Campaign in Britain's National Newspapers," *Gazette*, Vol. 4/1958, p. 33, note 11.
[19] J. T. McNelly, "Meaning Intensity and Interest in Foreign News Topics," *Journalism Quarterly*, Vol. 39/1962, p. 161.

Himmelstrand's argument may now be expressed in the terms suggested. His phase model concerns mainly events described in proposition 2, to some extent also events described in proposition 2 and followed by events described in proposition 1. Representing the two types of reporting by two curves varying over time, Himmelstrand's phase 1 may be said to last until the curve representing factual reporting has started to decline and/or the curve representing interpretative reporting has reached a given value. Phase 2 may be said to last until the curve representing interpretative reporting has started to decline. In phase 3 both curves are low, and phase 4 is marked by the sudden rise of both of them. (It may be added, that, if measured, the *quality* of both factual and interpretative reporting should rise with time).

Szalai's argument, too, may be expressed in the simple terms suggested. His observation probably represents a mix of events described in proposition 1 and 2. In terms of the relations of the two curves his argument says: the peaks and troughs of the curve representing interpretative reporting should tend to lag after the peaks and troughs of the curve representing factual reporting. The amount of lag should co-vary (negatively) with the degree of predictability.

The whole argument, of course, presupposes that the news media report available news immediately. This is not always so. In some socialist countries, for instance, at least part of the news is not published until an authoritative interpretation is available.[20] The extent of this practice is an empirical question. In some cases, it might be more rewarding to study the lag between event and report rather than that between report and comment.

So far, little has been said about the duration and composition of the event reported as news. As far as the argument in this paper concerns, it should not matter whether *event* means one single event, clearly delimited in time and space, e.g., a murder or a nomination, or whether it means a sequential set of related sub-events like a revolution.

The theory outlined, of course, may be refined by introducing additional concepts. One that is often suggested in arguments concerning the international flow of news is *distance*, physical or psychological. (Physical distance may sometimes be used as an indicator of psychological distance.) [21] *Distance*, in combination with the concepts already introduced, could be used for instance in the following proposition: The more distant the event, the more unpredictable and the less important it seems. In

[20] I am indebted to Ole Jess Olsen, Institute for Peace and Conflict Research, Copenhagen, for reminding me of this fact.
[21] Cf. R. E. Carter & W. J. Mitofsky, "Actual and Perceived Distance in the News," *Journalism Quarterly*, Vol. 38/1961, p. 223; D. R. Bowers, "A Report on Activity by Publishers in Directing Newsrooms Decisions," *Journalism Quarterly*, Vol. 44/1967, p. 43; G. Stanley, "Emotional Involvement and Geographical Distance," *The Journal of Social Psychology*, Vol. 75/1968, p. 165.

combination with hypotheses suggested above, this gives us: the more distant the event, the more factual the reporting—a hypothesis that receives some support from data gathered by Adams.[22]

The fact of this support lends further credibility to the outline of a theory of one aspect of the international flow of news presented in this paper. It motivates further research along the lines suggested by the theory. One hypothesis to be tested (along with the ones already suggested) might be the following one: The greater the distance of an event, the greater the lag between its factual and interpretative reporting, degree of importance and predictability kept constant. This proposition is somewhat more complicated than those suggested earlier in this paper, but in the present writer's opinion, it should be possible to test it.

[22] J. B. Adams, op. cit., table 3; cf. E. Östgaard, "Factors Influencing the Flow of News," Journal of Peace Research, Vol. 2/1965, p. 39, note 15. Östgaard has suggested in personal communication that the relationship between distance and degree of factual reporting may be curvilinear.

3

FREEDOM AND RESTRICTION OF COMMUNICATION

3

FREEDOM AND RESTRICTION

OF COMMUNICATION

THE whole subject of freedom and restriction of communication has become one of the main preoccupations of writers, teachers and politicians throughout the world. Although it is difficult to generalize about global trends, there are numerous indications that restrictions on the press are increasing with each passing year.

One of the main problems, of course, in any consideration of freedom of information is the problem of differing national concepts. Freedom of the press in Russia, for instance, certainly means something quite different from what it means in the United States. And, even between such countries as Sweden and the United States there are differing concepts. Therefore, it is very difficult to study such a thing as "press freedom" without falling into the trap of using one's own country as the point of departure —or as the standard for evaluating press freedom in other countries.

That freedom of information is a world problem, filled with many practical and semantic complexities, is clearly shown in the first article in this chapter. Dr. Michael Ta Kung Wei, of New Asia College's journalism department (Hong Kong), traces the international concern with freedom of information and gives special attention to the efforts of the United Nations in this area.

Governments use a wide assortment of ways to restrict or control the press; in the second article, Dr. Carter Bryan, of the University of Maryland's journalism department, discusses one of the most effective ways —economic intervention. He not only deals with economic pressures in libertarian press systems but also describes similar techniques in authoritarian and communist countries.

Dr. Joe Vogel, former professor and now with the United States Information Service in Turkey, presents in the third article a survey of the attempts by libertarian press countries to control their journalistic ethics. He discusses publishers' groups of various kinds as well as several varieties of press councils found throughout the world. This discussion brings into focus one of the most important, and controversial, questions associated with this whole area of interest: Just how much regulation and control of the press—even in the name of responsible and ethical journalism—can be permitted before a threat to press freedom occurs?

In the fourth article of this chapter, Dr. Raymond Nixon, of the School of Journalism at the University of Minnesota, provides what was probably the first systematic study of cultural and socio-economic factors in a nation and how they are related to press freedom. And, in the final article, by Dr. Ralph Lowenstein of the University of Missouri School of Journalism, the thesis is advanced that the degree of press freedom a country has is a very good indicator of that nation's general political freedom. And, in the course of his discussion, Dr. Lowenstein gives twenty-three factors used in his PICA Index to measure a country's press freedom. He believes press freedom can be measured rather accurately and presents what is probably the first systematic device for carrying out this complex task.

*   *   *   *

RELATED READING

Brucker, Herbert. *Freedom of Information*. New York: Macmillan, 1969.

Bruns, Viktor and Kurt Häntzschel. *Die Pressgesetze des Erdballs*. (10 vols). Berlin: Stilke, 1928-1931.

Chafee, Zechariah, Jr. *Government and Mass Communications*. (2 vols). Chicago: University of Chicago Press, 1947.

Eek, Hinding. *Freedom of Information as a Project of International Legislation: A Study of International Law in the Making*. Uppsala: Lundequistska Bokhandeln, 1953.

Hocking, William E. *Freedom of the Press: A Framework of Principle*. Chicago: University of Chicago Press, 1947.

Knight, Robert P. *The Concept of Freedom of the Press in the Americas*. Unpublished Ph.D. dissertation, University of Missouri, 1968.

Lowenstein, Ralph L. *Measuring World Press Freedom as a Political Indicator*. Unpublished Ph.D. dissertation, University of Missouri, 1967.

Löffler, Martin and Jean Louis Hébarre. *Form and Function of Internal Control of the Press*. Munich: C. H. Beck'sche Verlagsbuchhandlung, 1968.

Siebert, Fred, Theodore Peterson and Wilbur Schramm, *Four Theories of the Press*. Urbana: University of Illinois Press, 1956.

Terrou, Fernand and Lucien Solal. *Legislation for Press, Film, and Radio*. Paris: UNESCO, 1951.

Wiggins, James Russell. *Freedom or Secrecy*. New York: Oxford, 1964.

Michael Ta Kung Wei:

Freedom of Information as an International Problem

————

Early Attempts by Professional Organizations

THE TASK of promoting freedom of information on the international level has been partially accomplished since 1893 by international conferences of journalists. Unfortunately these meetings did nothing more than pass resolutions or pledge themselves to promote freedom of information. Little concrete action resulted, and what was accomplished was wiped out by propaganda and censorship during the two World Wars.[1]

In May, 1893, a press congress attended by journalists from all over the world was held in Chicago. Although no positive conclusion was reached, topics such as the international role of the press, the press as a defender of human rights, and the press and public morals were discussed.[2]

The Institution de l'Union Internationale Associations de Presse (International Union of Press Associations) was established in July, 1893, as the result of an international meeting of journalists in Antwerp, Belgium. Its aim was to "organize common action between associations of journalists and newspaper associations of all countries in respects of professional matters of common interest," and to "bring about international conventions and agreements concerning journalism and literary rights and property." [3]

For the next forty years, this Union held a series of congresses to discuss questions such as false news and the right of reply as a remedy for false news. It became inactive after 1935.

What is said to be the first international organization of working newspaper men, the Federation Internationale des Journalistes, was founded in 1921 in Paris. Although this Federation was primarily concerned with working conditions for journalists, it also took various steps

———

[1] William Reed, "50 Years of Resolutions Form State for UN Talks," *Editor & Publisher*, Vol. 80, No. 16, April 12, 1947, p. 17.
[2] *Ibid.*, p. 18.
[3] *United Nations Document*, E/Conf. 6/14, *The Freedom of the Press, Some Historical Notes*, Prepared by the Secretariat, February 11, 1948, p. 19.

———

► From: *Freedom of Information as an International Problem*, by Michael Ta Kung Wei. Unpublished Ph.D. dissertation, University of Missouri, Columbia/Missouri, June, 1964. Reprinted by permission of the author.

toward self-discipline within the profession, including the setting up of an International Court of Honour at the Hague in 1931.[4]

League of Nations' Freedom of Information Work

The League of Nations initiated a series of conferences beginning in 1927 with a conference of Press Experts at Geneva. This was followed by two conferences of Governmental Press Bureaux and Representatives of the Press in Copenhagen in 1932 and at Madrid in 1933.

Sponsored by the Council of the League, the Conference of Press Experts was attended by sixty-three representatives of telegraphic agencies, newspapers, international organizations of journalists and official press bureaus from thirty countries. Purposes of the conference were:

> 1. To inquire into means of ensuring more rapid and less costly transmission of press news, with a view to reducing the risks of international misunderstanding.
> 2. To discuss all technical problems, the solution of which, in the opinion of experts, would be conducive to the tranquilization of public opinion in various countries.[5]

The conference considered facilities for journalists, peacetime censorship, press rates, coding of press messages, technical press and communications improvements. Resolutions were passed on all these subjects, and legislation concerning the protection of press information was formulated. Most of these resolutions were later referred to the League Committee on Communications and Transit, and other resolutions, such as those concerning censorship in peacetime and the protection of news sources, were referred to the various governments.

The desire of the League to combat the spread of false information was expressed at the 1932 Conference of Governmental Press Bureaux and Representatives of the Press.[6] The delegates from thirty-two countries agreed that the rapid spread of accurate and abundant news was the best remedy. They insisted that measures taken to counteract inaccurate information must never be allowed to prejudice the basic freedom of the press, a freedom which, however, implied responsibility on the part of the journalist. The delegates also urged enactment of the resolution on peacetime censorship adopted by the 1927 conference, which indicated that very little had been done to carry out the resolution up to that time.

At the second conference of Governmental Press Bureaux and Representatives of the Press, the problems of false news and ways of combatting its spread were again discussed. The resolutions adopted emphasized

---

[4] Marcel Stijns, "International Cooperation of Journalists," *International Federation Journalists Information*, Vol. XI, No. 3, June-October, 1962, p. 3.
[5] League of Nations, *Conference of Press Experts*, Geneva, August 24, 1927, p. 7.
[6] *United Nations Official Records*, Economic and Social Council, Sixteenth Session, Supplement No. 12, (E/2426, May 6, 1953), p. 6.

two main themes—freedom of the press and the need for the prompt circulation of adequate and accurate information. Other resolutions recommended the creation of a committee of experts to consider technical and financial methods for combatting the spread of false news, the feasibility of bilateral and multilateral agreements regarding the prevention of false news, and the influence of newspaper reports on previous international crises.[7] Yet nothing concrete resulted from these resolutions.

The value of films and the importance of radio broadcasting were topics recognized by the League of Nations. In 1933, it sponsored the Convention to Facilitate the International Circulation of Films of an Educational Character. And in 1936 at Geneva, the League sponsored an International Convention concerning the Use of Broadcasting in the Cause of Peace. The latter convention began operations on April 3, 1938, and has been signed and ratified by twenty-two nations.[8] This appears to mark the limits of the League's efforts to promote any freedom of information on the international level.

How the UN seeks Freedom of Information

It is essential to illustrate specifically what units are responsible for this ponderousness of freedom of information. The organization and operation of the United Nations is described in its charter, signed at San Francisco on June 26, 1945, by the representatives of fifty nations. The freedom of information question has been discussed in the General Assembly and the Economic and Social Council.

When the victorious nations of World War II met at San Francisco in 1945, they had already made a decision to create a world organization that would include any potential hostile camps. It was hoped by these nations that despite the fact that the world consists of countries with heterogeneous institutions and customs based on different concepts of society and law, the United Nations would at least provide a place where contending parties could argue in the presence of others more interested in peace than in victory for either side. Most countries felt that such an organized arguing place was the best hope for preventing another world war.[9]

Although organized for peace, the United Nations has become a campaign center for truth. It believes that truth alone will make men free of the scourge of ignorance, superstition, hate and war. So states the Constitution of United Nations Economic, Social and Cultural Organization: "Since wars begin in the minds of men, it is in the minds of men that the defenses of peace must be constructed." [10]

[7] *Ibid.*, p. 7.
[8] *Ibid.*, p. 8.
[9] David Cushman Coyle, *The United Nations, And How It Works*, (New York: New American Library, 1960), p. 163.
[10] Cheever and Haviland, *op. cit.*, p. 660.

When the world delegates met in 1945 to set up a better "League of Nations," the matter of including freedom of information as a human right received more concern and support. During the drafting of the United Nations Charter, some delegates suggested that it include an elaborate declaration on human rights. However, it was finally decided that the Charter include a general obligation for member states "to take joint and separate action in co-operation with the Organization" to promote "universal respect for, and observance of, human rights and fundamental freedoms for all without distinction as to race, sex, language, or religion." [11] The fact that human rights was mentioned seven times in the Charter prompted the United Nations action in this field.

Since the United Nations is composed of official representatives from individual governments, and governments play an important role in modern mass communications, this logically leads to a practical reason for the United Nations to take up the problem of freedom of information.

The United Nations work in the field of freedom of information has fallen into two main categories: Members try to lay down a common universal standard with respect to social and legal institutions, commonly referred to as the legal approach to the concept of freedom of information; and the United Nations selects specific problems for international action to be carried out by specialized agencies—the pragmatic approach.

The pragmatic approach has led the United Nations, along with special agencies such as United Nations Economic, Social and Cultural Organization, International Telecommunications Union, and Universal Postal Union, to make numerous studies and reports regarding the production and distribution of newsprint, postal and transport service, telecommunications press rates and facilities, radio broadcasting tariff and trade practices, copyright, access to news sources, status of foreign correspondents, censorship on outgoing news dispatches, professional training and standards, independence of news personnel and similar problems.

In March, 1948, representatives from 54 governments gathered at the United Nations Conference on Freedom of Information in Geneva. Although the political post-war climate was chilly, the delegates fervently hoped to find ways and means of safeguarding and promoting world wide freedom of information. The delegates' aim was to promote peace and progress by laying down a policy for the United Nations in the field of information. The Conference in its Final Act presented a series of resolutions recommending constructive action and three draft conventions for further consideration by the United Nations.

In the meantime, the importance of an unhampered flow of information and opinion both within and between countries had been stressed again and again during World War II and during the period of prepara-

---

[11] Kent Cooper, *Barriers Down*, (New York: Farrar & Rinehart, Inc., 1942), pp. 89-91.

tion for the new world organization. Moreover, the General Assembly at its first session had declared freedom of information "a fundamental human right, the touchstone of all the freedoms to which the United Nations is consecrated," and "an essential factor in any serious effort to promote the peace and progress of the world."

In the past 20 years, one of the major works of the United Nations in the field of freedom of information has been to define the concept of freedom of information and to secure, by elaborating and adopting conventions, the observance of legal obligations emanating from the concept. To achieve this aim, four types of instruments were used, and these can be summarized as follows:

1. The Universal Declaration of Human Rights: Although it dictates only moral principles, this declaration was proclaimed on December 10, 1948 by the General Assembly as "a common standard of achievement for all peoples and all nations." Article 19 of the declaration deals with freedom of information. Derived from Article 19 was an elaboration on moral principles known as the Declaration of Freedom of Information, proposed and adopted by the Economic and Social Council of the United Nations in 1960.

2. The Draft Covenant on Human Rights: This Covenant is an international "Bill of Rights" dealing with all human rights including the rights of freedom of information. The definition of this right in the draft Covenant is broad enough to allow varying interpretations and its law must be interpreted by practice and judicial decisions. In early 1964, this Covenant on Human Rights was still in the drafting stage.

3. The Draft Convention on Freedom of Information: This Convention is designed to achieve a common standard of national law in the field of freedom of information. It allows contracting states to assume certain obligations with respect to their domestic legislation and be entitled to take action against alleged violations of the convention. It defines the scope of limitations of freedom of information. It draws the line between rights and duties, freedom of responsibility, and if adopted would become the basic law on the subject. The drafting of this convention has met great difficulty and confusion, and at the present, only four articles of the convention have been adopted by the Third Committee of the General Assembly.

4. The Convention on the International Transmission of News and the Convention on the International Right of Correction: These conventions aim at putting forth a common standard for solving practical problems in the field of freedom of information. Almost all countries have an immediate interest in facilitating the transmission of news across their frontiers, and seek to have available a remedy

in cases where, in their opinions, a misrepresentation of facts has occurred which should be corrected. The scope of these conventions is limited, but when brought into operation they might become quite useful. The Convention on International Transmission of News has been adopted by the General Assembly but has not yet been opened for signature; the Convention on International Right of Correction was ratified by the necessary six nations and entered into force as a treaty in 1962.

The enthusiasm shown at the United Nations Conference on Freedom of Information in 1948 has changed into indifference on the part of many governments. As a consequence, the achievements of the United Nations in recent years in the field of freedom of information seem insignificant. Its efforts to define and guarantee freedom of information in a document acceptable to the majority of the nations have met very little success.

Undoubtedly one of the principal causes of the failure has been the sharpening and expanding cold war. The high hopes generated during World War II by successful collaboration against a common enemy have declined, and areas of agreement diminished.

Although the cold war has most violently manifested itself in the consideration of political and security problems, no aspect of the United Nations activity has in fact been spared from its paralyzing influence. Thus, the conflict has been waged not only in the Security Council and the "political" committees of the General Assembly, but in the Third Committee and in other organs dealing with social matters. Moreover, it is understandable that no aspect of this work is more sensitive to the cold war than freedom of information. While the spoken and the printed word is the basic tool of information, it is also one of the most effective weapons of the cold war.

Directly related to the cold war have been the longstanding conflicting ideologies of different nations. Because of the conflict, the effort of the United Nations to define the concept of freedom of information has not been achieved. This is described by Professor Hilding Eek: "In the language of the United Nations, 'freedom of information' means nothing definite, constant and uncontroversial. It means only an item on the agendas of various organs of the United Nations." [12]

As reflected in the long debates in the United Nations, this ideological conflict constitutes the main obstacle which keeps the international powers from reaching a definition of a concept of freedom of information. For example, no common ground has ever been reached on the question of whether or not the information media have a primary responsibility to work positively for the cause of peace and to combat propaganda for

[12] *United Nations Official Records,* Economic and Social Council, Thirty First Session, 1961, Agenda Item 10, p. 151 (E/3443, February 2, 1961).

war, false and distorted reports. This is an issue which has come up time and again during the debates of the United Nations. While the Soviet Union opposed the Draft Convention on Freedom of Information because it did not positively set forth such obligations, the United States and other Western countries opposed the Convention because it did impose obligations and restrictions on information media.

Fundamental to most of the debates on freedom of information and a main factor in retarding progress has been the marked difference of opinion regarding the rights and freedoms versus the duties and responsibilities involved in the freedom of information concept.

The campaign for inserting "duties and responsibilities" clause in the draft conventions was strongly supported by the under-developed countries and the "new" states, freshly emerged from colonial status. They have a vivid sense of the meaning of exploitation and oppression, and they grasp at every opportunity to consolidate their hard-won gains. The resulting political alignment of the "new" and under-developed countries has in many instances cut directly across the interests of the more developed countries. This has resulted, for example, in their opposition to the Convention on International Transmission of News which would give additional facilities and opportunities to correspondents of countries with highly developed information media, without a corresponding emphasis on specific obligations and responsibilities to protect themselves. They consider the activities of such correspondents frequently harmful to the prestige and dignity of their country.

Conversely, the more developed countries such as the United States and the United Kingdom have shown an attitude reflecting their concern for both the preservation of their hard-won liberties and the possibility of abuse of the concept of responsibility. These countries see no useful purpose in ratifying international conventions on freedom of information laying down standards which they consider, in many instances, to be below levels they themselves have already attained. Some of them go so far as to express the fear that the levels they have reached would in fact be endangered by such ratification.

Although the efforts of the United Nations to promote freedom of information do not seem satisfactory to many, and despite the fact that the long debates among nations seem hopelessly deadlocked in each session, it appears to this writer that the work undertaken with respect to freedom of information is important and significant, and will contribute to the continuing work of promoting freedom of information in the future. To justify this statement, it is necessary to point out the following facts which are vital to any further development of freedom of information:

1. In the classic or historic sense, the traditional term "freedom of press" means freedom from government control. The struggle for this very freedom is as long as the history of the press itself. Not

before the end of the nineteenth century the principles of press freedom had been accepted nearly all over the world. It may be said that with a few exceptions, there now exists a common legal standard with regard to the freedom of the press which includes the following principles:

(1) The prohibition of government interference with the press in the form of censorship and similar previous restraints.

(2) The principle that any restrictions on press freedom must be applied or subject to review by the courts, and that courts alone have the right of imposing penalties.[13]

It seems clear, although the process is slow, the press has scored a major victory on the national level in the past four hundred years. It is important to point out that the United Nations has only considered this problem for less than 20 years. Furthermore, the question of freedom of information with which the United Nations must deal is far more complicated than the traditional sense of "freedom of the press," because it seeks an agreement on the international level. As the result of modern technology, the United Nations must also face the new communications techniques such as wire service, radio and television. So long as the members of the United Nations agree that freedom of information is a fundamental human right, and as long as there exists a common legal standard, freedom of information, in most nations, (stated above) the reaching of the freedom of information goal within the United Nations is only a matter of time.

2. Although delegates disagreed on how to draft conventions on freedom of information, they did agree that there is an urgent need to consider the problem.

They knew from the past experience of World War II that Nazism and Fascism had been able to mislead and dominate millions of people as much by the power of the word as by the power of the sword. They observed that wherever the dictators seized authority in any country, they proceeded to control the information media. The delegates were also aware that in the modern world, total isolation is impossible. Each country must to some extent cooperate with other countries for such things as tariffs, visas, and exchanges of currency. Since governments must deal with the problems and since the United Nations is composed of most of these governments, there is no better place than the United Nations for them to reach both short-term and long-term agreements on these matters. The same holds true with regard to freedom of information.

3. While accepting the reality of the obstacles of cold war and

[13] Hilding Eek, *Freedom of Information: As a Project of International Legislation,* (Uppsala, Sweden: Uppsala Universitet, 1953), p. 33.

conflicting ideologies, one should not, nevertheless, accept the notion that the United Nations should suspend its efforts to promote freedom of information. It must be remembered that this is the first time in history that international powers have ever had an opportunity to express their views with regard to this problem. In view of the fact that the cold war might run its course, and therefore, ideologies would be more companionable, continued study of this problem is necessary. The possibility exists that freedom of information could some day be dealt with in a climate more conducive to international understanding and cooperation. Such an opportunity, however remote its possibility, merits continued efforts.

Some other Approaches

In tracing the work on freedom of information since 1893, it is significant to point out that, with the exception of the League of Nations, the work has been primarily carried out by professional journalists, and little action has been taken by the governments. Since governments today play such an important role in communications (to be discussed in later chapters), it is encouraging, to say the least, to see that the United Nations has taken positive steps to promote freedom of information through governmental cooperation, despite the fact that the present United Nations work on the subject is far from satisfactory.

It is also important to point out that while the United Nations is working on international agreements with regard to freedom of information as a human right, the professional people are also continually striving for advancement of this freedom. For example, under the initiative of the American Society of Newspaper Editors, an International Press Institute was established in June, 1951, in Paris. Also, a Freedom of Information Center was set up at the University of Missouri in Columbia, Missouri, in 1958.[14] Their common goals, fighting for the people's right, include:

(1) The right to get information;
(2) The right to print without prior restraint;
(3) The right to print without fear of reprisal not under due process;
(4) The right of access to facilities and material essential to communication; and
(5) The right to distribute information without interference by government acting under law or by citizens in defiance of the law.[15]

---

[14] Cf. Hugh Boyd, *FOI Center Idea, 1952-58*, Freedom of Information Center Publication No. oo, Columbia/Missouri: School of Journalism, 1958.
[15] James Russell Wiggins, *Freedom or Secrecy*, (New York: Oxford University Press, 1956), p. 3.

Carter R. Bryan:

Economic Intervention: Prelude to Press Control

THROUGHOUT much of the world the rights to publish and to read the truth are either denied or under constant attack. Limitations imposed on such rights are often undisguised, but they can also be quite subtle. One of the less apparent means of abridging the freedom of the press is through economic limitations, both private and governmental.

In countries enjoying freedom of information the evolution of the press frequently has been accompanied by growth of economic conditions that tend to limit such freedom. As a consequence, governments often have felt it necessary to consider or to announce regulations applicable to the material resources and other economic factors of news publishing.

Economic developments that have evoked such regulatory actions include the industrialization of news publishing, the concentration of newspaper ownership, the growth of monopolies in auxiliary sectors of the economy, the increasing world-wide demand for newsprint, and the rising costs of news gathering and of the material requirements for publishing.

Regulation of the enterprise [1] and the material resources usually presents either of two aspects. One, it may tend toward or result in giving full force to the concept of free information—by giving free play to the economic system which is considered necessary, by helping to remove the obstacles to free information which that system might create, or by founding or assisting the special organizations needed for the proper exploitation of material resources. Or, two, such regulation may be motivated by the wish of the political authorities to restrict the right of expression and to make the press a channel of control by political leaders.

In either case the regulation of the enterprise and the material resources necessary for the publication and dissemination of information profoundly affects the freedom of such enterprises in the conduct of their activities.

---

[1] The enterprise is the economic unit incorporating the material resources used by one individual or group of individuals for the purpose of carrying out a particular social function. A press enterprise may be an individual or a collective one. It may be the property of one or more individuals, or of a group formed into a legal entity distinct from that of the individuals composing it.

► From: *Journalism Quarterly* (Iowa City, Iowa), Vol. 38/No. 1 (Winter 1961), pp. 67-75. Reprinted by permission of the publisher and the author.

Owing to the size of the economic resources required in the production and distribution of newspapers these operations are increasingly centered in large scale economic units or enterprises. This has resulted in the frequent charge that the economically weak have no voice in the news press. Is it true, as Lenin alleged,[2] that in liberal economic (capitalist) systems "freedom of the press is merely the liberty of the wealthy to buy the press . . ."? To answer this question one must consider the variety of ownership and the means of financing available to diverse opinion in such liberal economic systems.

Private Enterprise

In states where the system of private enterprise[3] prevails, the forms of ownership entities and the methods of financing news enterprises available to private persons, trade unions, political parties, co-operatives, religious societies, etc., generally depend upon the degree of economic development, the laws governing private enterprise, and the forms of economic entities that generally prevail in the individual countries. The general character of the press enterprise is determined chiefly by features peculiar to the general economic system.

A free choice can be made between any of several types of énterprise —proprietorship, partnership, corporate entity (any of a variety including funded foundations or trusts) or co-operative society—in the following states: Austria, Australia, Belgium, Canada, Denmark, England, France, Germany (West), India, Ireland, Israel, Italy, Japan, most of the Latin American states, Lebanon, Luxembourg, the Netherlands, New Zealand, Norway, the Philippines, South Africa, Sweden, Switzerland, Turkey and the United States. While in many of these countries newspapers owned by several or all these various forms of enterprise exist and compete side-by-side for the attention of readers, certain forms of ownership are peculiarly suited to individual countries. It is from this viewpoint that they will be discussed.

Throughout Scandinavia privately owned newspapers and newspapers owned by political parties, co-operative groups and endowed foundations are in useful competition. In Denmark a large number of the newspapers are the property of small shareholders of the local population. Still others are published by individual owners (although there are no "newspaper barons") and by political parties. One newspaper, *Information*, is operated by a funded foundation.[4]

---

[2] Lenin, *Theses on Bourgeois Democracy and the Dictatorship of the Proletariat* (Moscow, March 1919).

[3] The principle, in liberal systems, is that the press is a private enterprise, or in any case an enterprise independent of the political authorities, and as such is governed by a code of ordinary law based on the freedom of constitution and the private nature of all enterprises.

[4] Svend Thorsen, "Newspapers in Denmark," *Danish Information Handbook*, 1953, pp. 66-67.

According to international standards there are no great privately owned chains in Sweden. Of the six largest newspapers (all with more than 100,000 circulation), five are owned and dominated by three men. Ownership of the sixth, *Svenska Dagbladet*, one of Sweden's most influential dailies, is vested in an endowed foundation. Determination of the newspaper's general policy rests with a self-perpetuating board of 10 to 15 persons.

Among Swedish newspapers, economic concentration has gone farthest in the Social Democratic (Socialist) press. This is to be expected since most of the other newspapers were founded as a result of individual initiative while this group was launched as an avowed political weapon.[5]

In Sweden the voice of the working people is also heard through the union press, which comprises some 40 weekly and biweekly papers with a combined circulation of 1,400,000 published by organizations affiliated with the Confederation of Swedish Trade Unions. Unions of salaried employees, which are politically independent, also publish member magazines. Sweden's consumer co-operative movement's central body, *Kooperativa Förbundet* (KF, Co-operative Union and Wholesale Society), publishes the country's largest weekly, *Vi*, whose circulation is more than 600,000. Advertising and circulation generally pay the costs of producing Sweden's newspapers.[6]

In Norway most daily papers are published by independently owned companies in which the local political organizations hold a portion of the shares. But a few papers are owned by political parties in Norway; among such are Oslo's *Arbeiderbladet*, the daily organ of the Labor Party, and the Communist Party's *Friheten*, also published in Oslo. Norway also permits the formation of an entity of the nature of a foundation. It is under such an arrangement that the Trust Council of the daily paper *Verdans Gang* operates.[7]

In Great Britain there are a great variety of legal forms available for press enterprises. These enterprises usually take the shape of private companies, or, more rarely, co-operative societies. These forms also permit an original institution: the trust. Not to be confused with the cartel, the British newspaper trust is more the nature of a foundation. In general, control is exercised by certain prominent people over the operations and the development of the enterprise for the purpose of promoting its prosperity and perhaps still more, for the non-commercial purpose of safeguarding its independence and keeping it on the lines laid down by its founders. Examples of such trusts, although differing somewhat in detail,

[5] Anders Yugve Pers, *Newspapers in Sweden* (Stockholm: Swedish Institute, 1954), pp. 28-29.
[6] *Ibid.*, p. 22.
[7] Fernand Terrou and Lucien Solal, *Legislation for Press, Film and Radio* (Paris: Unesco, 1951), pp. 82-83.

are the Times Holding Company, Ltd., the Observer Trust and the Birmingham Post and Mail, Ltd.[8]

The importance to press freedom of an environment of freedom of enterprise is perhaps best illustrated in West Germany and Austria. Only 16 years ago (May 1945), after years of strict control by the National Socialist regime, during which all media of information were instruments of the state, the press of Germany and Austria ceased to exist. Today, 11 and one-half years after the end of Allied controls (September 1949), the press of West Germany presents a picture of vigor, variety and independence. As we shall see, this is in sharp contrast to the situation in East Germany and Eastern Europe.

Of West Germany's 10 largest newspapers, nine are operated as commercial enterprises. Ownership of the *Frankfurter Allgemeine*, successor (in terms of influence and reputation) to the *Frankfurter Zeitung*, with a circulation of 200,000, rests in a non-profit foundation, the five trustees of which are prominent publicists and scholars. Together with these larger papers 508 other newspapers, with 690 main editions and 774 regional or subsidiary editions, publish 17.3 million copies in West Germany and West Berlin each day.[9] These newspapers, like those of Scandinavia, represent all shades of popular political opinion and all social and economic levels. By far the greater part of them are commercially successful, and only a few are dependent on political parties or other sources for subsidization in order to exist.

Austria has 36 daily newspapers, including seven branch editions of main newspapers. Of this total seven are owned by the Communist Party, four by the Socialist Party, one by the Federal Government and one by a press co-operative. The remainder are published by privately owned commercial enterprises. Of these latter, 11 are independent in politics, five support the Austrian Peoples Party, three the Socialist Party, one the Democratic Union, and one supports conservative policies. In addition, 108 weeklies are published by co-operatives, labor unions, ethnic minority associations, political parties and commercial enterprises. The largest single publisher of weekly newspapers is the Socialist Party.[10]

In Italy, of the 95 daily newspapers published,[11] one-third are either owned or financially underwritten by political parties, while the other two-thirds are independent. The latter are owned by industry, religious groups,

[8] *Ibid.*, pp. 83-85.
[9] *Deutschland Heute* (Bonn: Federal Press Office, 1959). For a more complete survey of the West German press by the author, see "10 Years after Licensing, W. German Press Flourishes," *Editor & Publisher*, Aug. 15, 1959, pp. 11, 56.
[10] *Handbuch Osterreichs Presse Werbung Graphik* (Vienna: Verband Osterreichischer Zeitungsherausgeber [Austrian Newspaper Publishers Assn.], 1960). Added to the 35 dailies listed is *Abendpresse*, founded in October 1960.
[11] *Annuario Parlamentare*, 1960 ed., lists 97 newspapers but if *Avanti!* of Rome and Milan and *Unità*, also of Rome and Milan, are each counted as one, the total is 95.

banks and large land-owners.[12] Circulations range from a few thousand to several hundred thousand. The economic position of most Italian newspapers, however, is exceedingly precarious. The use of advertising in small provincials, comprising the majority of Italian newspapers, is very limited, and most of them, operating at a loss, are kept alive by subsidies from known and unknown sources.[13]

Dangers Arising from Concentration of Ownership

One of the chief dangers, as seen by some, to freedom of information and of the press in a system of free enterprise arises from concentration of ownership. According to this concept, true freedom of information and of the press entails diversity of opinion and requires that the means (printing presses, wire services, etc.) of expressing such diversity must be available to every trend of opinion and point of view, even though they are not among the economically powerful. Where ownership is limited to a few with interlocking interests, the means of publication of diverse opinion is necessarily limited.

The situation in Japan, where the industrial economy including the press has long been characterized by cartelization by powerful *zaibatsu* (family groups), illustrates this point. Three national dailies—*Asahi, Mainichi* and *Yomiuri*—account for 43% of the total (25 million) circulation. When two other papers of a similar character—*Sankei* and *Nihon Keizai* —are added the proportion rises to 54%.[14]

Almost all of Japan's press is privately owned and "politically independent." The "political independence" (more precisely the refusal to take an editorial position on political issues or to be identified with political movements, and the limitation of commentary to carping) of Japan's press has been carried to such an extreme degree that it has been criticized in the Western press as having "abdicated its responsibility to espouse, attack or even examine the variety of political opinion that are the stuff of democracy. It is in the grip of impartiality gone haywire. Only two of the nation's papers—the Communist *Akahata* (cir. 30,000) and the thrice-monthly Socialist *Shakai Shimpo* (circ. 80,000)—advance any creed." [15]

The tendency to concentration of ownership can be observed in other countries, notably in the United States and the United Kingdom. In Great Britain, where combinations and chains are an outstanding feature of the press organization, governmental intervention has not been thought necessary.

In the United States, the Sherman Act of 1890 and the Clayton Act

---

[12] John C. Merrill, A *Handbook of the Foreign Press* (Baton Rouge: Louisiana State University Press, 1959), pp. 103-05.
[13] Arnaldo Cortesi, "Italian Newspapers Kept Alive by Subventions and Subsidies," *Bulletin of the American Society of Newspaper Editors*, July 1, 1957, p. 10.
[14] *The Japanese Press*, 1959 (Tokyo: Nihon Shinbun Kyokai [The Japan Newspaper Publishers and Editors Assn.], 1959), pp. 6, 9.
[15] "Impartiality Gone Haywire," *Time*, Oct. 20, 1958, p. 61.

of 1914 have been found to be applicable to trade in information by decision of the Supreme Court, and, in cases involving the Associated Press, the Kansas City *Star*, the Chattanooga *News-Free Press*, the Mansfield (Ohio) *Journal* and the Wichita *Eagle*, the law has been applied to prevent monopolistic practices in the newspaper field.[16] Similar anti-trust provisions, which in principle apply in every sector of economic activity, are found in most liberal economic systems, but in most countries there is less concentration, at least in respect of newspaper and periodical firms.[17]

But, despite these laws designed to prevent monopolistic practices, is not freedom of information endangered by the development of that liberal economic system which the ordinary laws governing private enterprise are designed to promote? Is not the danger to freedom of expression increased by the fact that in auxiliary sectors of the economy on which the press enterprise is dependent—the labor force, the distributive agencies and the producers of newsprint and other material resources—the tendency towards monopoly and intervention also appears?

Dangers from Outside Monopolies

Strikes of editorial and typographical workers that interrupt the publication of newspapers are not infrequent. In some countries labor unions in recent years have demanded a voice in the editorial policy of newspapers where their members are employed. A case in point was the demand made in May 1959 by Cuba's typographical union that it have a voice in the editorial policies of the newspapers.[18]

In Japan, ominous signs that pressure may be applied to editorial policies by groups other than the government are seen. Trade unions and other businesses are cited as the sources of such pressure. In 1959, a move was reported as under way, through the Newspaper Workers Union Federation to which most of Japan's newspaper employees belong, by outside groups to try to influence the editorial policies of the nation's newspapers.[19] In Bolivia, the state-controlled trade unions (COB) have been pitted against non-conformist newspapers, and it is often from this quarter that demands for suppressions and closures originate.[20]

---

[16] Case Files, U.S. Department of Justice, Washington, D.C., Citations: *U.S. vs. Associated Press*—52 F. Supp. 362; 326 U.S.-1; *U.S. vs. Kansas City Star Co.*—240 F. 2d.-643; *U.S. vs. Chattanooga News-Free Press Co.*—1940 C.C.H. Trade Reg. Rep., 8th ed., Vol. 3, No. 15,096; *U.S. vs. Mansfield Journal Co.*—1952, C.C.H. Trade Case No. 67,216; *U.S. vs. Wichita Eagle Co.*—1959, C.C.H. Trade Case No. 69,400.
[17] Terrou and Solal, *op. cit.*, p. 92; *Guide to Legislation on Restrictive Business Practices*, Vols. I and II, 1960; *Anti-trust Legislation of the World*, Staff Office of Fair Trade Commission of Japan, Nov. 1960. The last two named works list 40 countries with liberal economic systems that have such anti-trust laws.
[18] "Cuba Printers Ask Control Editorials," Washington *Post* (UPI), May 19, 1959.
[19] *The Japanese Press*, 1959, pp. 4-5.
[20] *The Press in Authoritarian Countries*, IPI *Survey* (Zurich: International Press Institute, 1959), p. 169.

The possible use of distributive agencies as an instrument of control is seen in Viet Nam. In December 1955, the State Secretariat of Information gave a monopoly in the distribution of all newspapers published to the War Veterans Association. At the time, this association was headed by General Nguyen Ngoc Le, chief of police and security forces. There is no evidence of interference by this organization in the distribution of newspapers although the potential danger of such a system is obvious.[21]

The devastating effect on the availability of news to the public of a strike of the news distributive agencies was seen in New York when the news vendors began a strike on December 9, 1958, that lasted for 19 days.[22] Clearly the distribution of newspapers and periodicals is a problem as important as that of a publication's paper-supply or its printing, if not more so—especially in countries where the subscription system is not widespread. The cost of such distribution is high, absorbing a considerable proportion of the sale price (40% average in France).[23]

Dangers from State Intervention

Because of the high costs of production and distribution, the governments of many countries with economies based on private enterprise make available to the press both direct and indirect subsidies. In the United States and most other countries newspapers and periodicals enjoy lower postal rates. In Italy and several other countries of Europe, journalists are granted reduced railway fares and publications occasionally receive subsidies and reductions in taxes. Grants are also made to news agencies.[24] In other countries publications often receive preferred exchange treatment, government subsidized newsprint imports, advertising subsidies, etc.

Obviously all these measures of economic assistance can be used as instruments to exert pressure on the press. The exercise of such pressures is common in many parts of the world and is especially prominent in Southeast Asia, Latin America and the Middle East.

"There are some less obvious restrictions on the freedom of information," declared the Indian delegate to the second session of the General Assembly of the United Nations. "The shortage of newsprint, for example, constitutes a grave menace to the freedom of the press." [25]

While it is true that paper is the material most essential to printing, it has been only during periods of extreme economic disruption (war and early post-war periods) that shortages of newsprint have posed serious problems for the newspaper industry. Today, according to the U.S. Department of Commerce in a letter to the writer, there is a plentiful supply

21 *Ibid.*, p. 195.
22 Washington *Post* (AP), Dec. 9, 1958.
23 Terrou and Solal, *op. cit.*, p. 115.
24 Merrill, *op. cit.*, p. 105.
25 Terrou and Solal, *op. cit.*, p. 108.

of newsprint, although the cost has risen about 200% since the outbreak of World War II. With the price of newsprint today at $145 a ton, import licensing, exchange and newsprint allocation, and other forms of governmental intervention have been found necessary in a few countries that are chronic sufferers of exchange shortages.

But there are countries with authoritarian regimes (*e.g.*, Spain, Portugal, the United Arab Republic, Cuba and Indonesia) or with authoritarian tendencies that use such economic intervention as an instrument of control. In Spain the government has used its powers of price regulation and allocation of newsprint in controlling the press. It can also regulate the circulation of papers and their number of pages. It has regularly used these methods in favoring the Falangist press, which also enjoys fiscal and postal privileges.

The Franco regime has used such pressures on several occasions for silencing non-conformist publications. In fact, it used the pretext of infringement of newsprint regulations as an excuse to close down the literary reviews *Indice* and *Insula* in 1956. These magazines had published laudatory reviews of the works of exiled Spanish writers. Again, in 1958, the newsprint quota of the Madrid newspaper *Informaciones* was cut 10% for one month, because the paper's "political nuances" offended the Government. The newsprint cut from the *Informaciones* quota was divided between *Madrid* and *ABC* whose editors had hewn more closely to the Franco line.[26]

Portugal also uses restrictive or discriminatory measures such as subsidies to government papers and the inequitable distribution of newsprint. The decree of May 14, 1936, limits the number of pages of newspapers. Yet exceptions can be granted by the authorities and these obviously tend to favor government organs, since these papers can claim a special allowance of pages for space occupied by official texts.[27]

Authoritarian regimes in Latin America also have found economic regulations useful in controlling the press. In Argentina the Peron regime used a wide range of such powers, and in Colombia the dictator, Rojas Pinilla, chose quieter and more subtle methods of muzzling the press, notably through the control of newsprint. By decree of August 23, 1955, all orders for the importation of newsprint had to have the approval of the Empresa Nacional de Publicaciones which issued licenses. If these were granted, the orders could be made at the official exchange rate of 2.50 pesos per dollar with a stamp tax of 3%. Without a license the tax automatically rose to 30% and the rate of exchange to 4 pesos to the dollar. It must be stressed that this peculiarly capricious system, like the arbitrary distribution of newsprint, was consciously designed not only to

---

[26] *IPI Survey*, 1959, pp. 146-47.
[27] Richard Scott Mowrer, "Government Press Controls Capricious and Constant," *IPI Report*, Sept. 1958, p. 4.

control opinion, but to constantly prejudice the circulation of independent newspapers in favor of the *Diario Official*.[28] It now has been abolished under the liberal regime of Lleras Camargo.

In Bolivia, the government's actual control of newspapers is chiefly exercised through its control of newsprint which is used as a sword of Damocles over the heads of editors who might be tempted to criticize the government or its officials. The government office for the control of the news is copied from the similar institution created by Peron.[29]

While the control of the press exercised by the Nationalist China regime is not so systematic or severe as that installed by the Communists, the control methods have included economic pressure on independent publications.[30]

The ultimate manifestation of such economic control measures used by authoritarian regimes include confiscation, as occurred in Cuba on February 23, 1960;[31] nationalization, as decreed on May 24, 1960, in Egypt (UAR),[32] and suppression followed by "supervision" as decreed in Indonesia on October 5, 1960.[33]

Communist Economic Controls

In almost identical words the Soviet Union, the People's Republic of China and the other Communist People's Republics of the Far East and Eastern Europe guarantee the "freedom of the press." But in most cases the constitutional guarantee or its economic adjunct limits the guarantee and the means of production (plant, equipment, paper and other materials) to the "working people." [34]

These provisions represent the legal implementation of the principles laid down by Lenin when he wrote: "True freedom (of the press) will be found only in that future system . . . in which any worker (or group of workers) will be able to possess and exercise the right, enjoyed equally by all, of using the public printing works and the public paper. . . ." [35] But in a pamphlet on the press published in 1921, the father of the Bolshevik Revolution wrote: "Freedom of the press is freedom for the political organization of the bourgeoise and their agents the Social Democrats and the Social Revolutionaries. To give these people such a weapon as freedom of the press would mean facilitating the task of the adversary, helping the enemy. We do not wish to find ourselves committing suicide,

[28] *IPI Survey*, 1959, pp. 165-66.
[29] *Ibid.*, pp. 170-71.
[30] *Ibid.*, p. 186.
[31] "Cuba's Leading Newspaper, *El Mundo*, Seized," Washington *Star* (AP), Feb. 23, 1960.
[32] "All Main Newspapers in Egypt Nationalized," Washington *Star* (AP), May 25, 1960.
[33] "Indonesian Papers to be Supervised," Washington *Star* (AP), Oct. 5, 1960.
[34] Terrou and Solal, *op. cit.*; *IPI Survey*, 1959, et al.
[35] Terrou and Solal, *op. cit.*, p. 51.

and for this reason we shall not introduce freedom of the press." [36] Since the Communist Party identifies itself with the "working people," the result has been to limit the economic means of publishing to the government or to the Party or to its auxiliaries.

A Soviet law of 1932 that interprets and implements the economic corollary of the constitutional guarantee states that printing offices of any kind, including those using duplicating machines, as well as those dealing in printing equipment, may be maintained only by government agencies, co-operatives and public organizations. Moreover, even government agencies must obtain special permits to acquire printing equipment or to use printing offices and are held strictly accountable for supplies of paper, inks, type metal, etc.[37]

The distribution of newspapers to the appropriate sections of society is also closely regulated. Only 10% of a newspaper's edition is sold in the street. The rest is distributed according to a detailed plan. Each republic and region of the country receives a fixed quota of papers appearing in Moscow. Local distribution is arranged so that Party and Komsomol officials are first to receive newspapers, and administrative and economic units are next. It is almost impossible for a private person to subscribe to one of the chief papers. A Soviet citizen cannot simply buy or subscribe to the paper of his choice; he receives the paper that is specified for him according to the plan.[38]

The Chinese Communists' policy towards privately owned newspapers has not been so straightforward or simple. In this field it has been far more subtle and complex, a consequence of the Chinese version of Communist theory of the State in the transitional period of the "people's dictatorship," according to which all elements of society with few exceptions are entitled to enjoy all political rights, including that of having their own newspapers. Consequently, it was not considered advisable or expedient to ban outright all privately owned newspapers during the first phase of the revolution.

This does not mean that the privately owned newspapers were to remain uncontrolled. Privately owned newspapers with "reactionary" tendencies were outlawed at once, and in 1951 the regime began reducing the number of privately owned newspapers and changing the nature of those that remained. Since 1953, there have been only five important privately owned newspapers left in the country. None retains its former character or independent status, and, for all practical purposes, they are an integral part of the official press apparatus and are completely dependent upon the regime for the material requirements for publication.[39]

In Rumania, economic harassment of the press, begun by the Soviet

[36] *IPI Survey*, 1959, p. 14.
[37] Vladamir Gsovski, *Soviet Civil Law*, Vol. I, pp. 65-66.
[38] *IPI Survey*, 1959, p. 28.
[39] *Ibid.*, pp. 45-61.

Armistice Commission, was continued by the communist Rumanian authorities so that within two years (1947) freedom of the press had ceased. Today, there are no privately owned or independent newspapers.[40] Similarly, in Bulgaria and Albania there are no independent newspapers, and all the economic requirements for the publication of news, in terms of both production and distribution, are firmly in the hands of the State.

In the other Communist states of Eastern Europe the governments have taken firm control of the press, and a major part of this control is exercised by economic means. In each country the regime or the Party has taken ownership of the principal and best printing plants. And even in those other nominally independent printing plants all the materials needed for printing—paper, inks, metals, etc.—are owned by the State and may be obtained only by allocation, much in the Soviet pattern. In Poland, East Germany, Czechoslovakia and Hungary the control of newspapers is neither as unimaginative nor as rigid as in the USSR. But, while there are semblances of freedom, particularly during periods of "thaw," no real deviationism (criticism of the State, the Party or their objectives) is tolerated.[41]

Moreover, even during periods of relatively less control newspapers are by no means free of economic pressures. For example, during the Hungarian revolt, in which newspapers played a significant role, only one newspaper took a rightist position. It did not manage to publish more than one issue; on the following day the typographers refused to print it.[42]

Certain principles that have characterized the economic evolution peculiar to Yugoslavia since 1948 also apply to the press. Each newspaper is operated by its employees, but it is owned by what Yugoslavs call "society." They hold that "ownership by society" is not the same as ownership by the State. The system of self-administration applied to the press by the laws of June 26, 1956 has had the effect of freeing the Yugoslav press from the financial control of the State which originally, as in every Communist society, provided the necessary funds and equipment for the press enterprises. The result has been a greater degree of independence with considerably broader possibilities of expression than in other Communist countries.[43]

Conclusion

The struggle for freedom of the press continues in the free world and in some countries where freedom has ceased to exist.[44] But in many lands freedom is losing. Throughout the Communist world (except for Yugo-

[40] *Ibid.*, pp. 63-68.
[41] *Ibid.*
[42] "A Week of Freedom of the Press in Hungary," *IPI Report*, Dec. 1956.
[43] *IPI Survey*, 1959, pp. 121-35.
[44] *Ibid.*, pp. 199-201.

slavia), and in dictatorships in Spain, Portugal, Egypt, the Far East and in several Latin American countries, control of the press appears to be gaining at present on journalistic efforts to print the news freely, although certain long-term influences eventually may have an ameliorative effect.[45]

In each instance where freedom has been lost, direct government control has either been preceded or accompanied by the more subtle intervention in the management or the utilization of the resources of the press. Often this intervention is made in its initial stages "on behalf of the press" and in the name of "freedom."

Concentration of ownership in press enterprises and monopolies in auxiliary sectors of the economy may pose direct threats to press freedom and invite governmental intervention and possibly ultimate control. No freedom of the press exists without freedom of enterprise, and the wider the representation and variety of ownership the more authentic and secure is the press' freedom.

[45] On this latter point, and also for a possible method of classifying factors in degrees of press control, see Raymond B. Nixon, "Factors Related to Freedom in National Press Systems," JOURNALISM QUARTERLY, 37:13-28 (Winter 1960)—[reprinted later in this chapter].

Joe B. Vogel:

International Search for Ethical Controls

DAILY the press mounts its headline guard over the perplexities of ethics —for congressmen and government clerks, for munitions makers and draft evaders, for bank presidents or lowly bookkeepers who suddenly become wealthy philanthropists. Equally important is the question: What has the *free* press done about defining and controlling its own ethics?

Limitation to "free-press" countries seems obvious. Where there is no freedom, the journalist hardly need concern himself about his responsibilities. Some "big-brother" will define—and control—those responsibilities.

To determine what the free press has done to define its own standards of conduct, and to see what measures have been taken to control that conduct, the author made a study of 62 "free-press" countries.[1] Here, a "free-press" country is defined as any nation not classified as Communist or authoritarian in the International Press Institute Study, "The Press in Authoritarian Countries."[2]

Obviously such a classification recognizes many degrees of freedom. And some countries classified as "free" at the time of the IPI study subsequently became outstanding examples of restricted societies. (Example: Cuba.) Equally, a few countries have instituted some form of ethical definition and control since that study. (Examples: South Korea, India.)[3] However, the timing of the study provides some historical perspective to permit observation of the effect of ethical definition and control within a country.

Of the 62 nations recognized as "free-press" countries in the IPI study, journalism organizations in 29 countries had adopted or proposed some system for ethical control. In six of these nations—Italy, Indonesia,

[1] Joe B. Vogel, "Ethical Codes and Courts of Honor in the Press of the Free World," Unpublished Ph.D. dissertation, State University of Iowa, 1961.
[2] IPI Survey, *The Press in Authoritarian Countries* (Zurich: The International Press Institute, 1959).
[3] Martin Löffler, "The Problem of Internal Control of the Press," *Form and Function of Internal Control of the Press* (Munich: C. H. Beck'sche Verlagsbuchhandlung, 1968).

► This is an original article done for this book by Joe Bill Vogel, United States Information Service, Istanbul, Turkey, 1969.

Lebanon, Turkey, India, and Pakistan—controls were incomplete or in-operative. Elimination of these countries left codes of ethics and/or courts of honor for the press in 23 nations to be considered. A simple breakdown may be achieved by dividing these nations into two groupings: those where the press had some degree of government participation in its ethical orientation, and those where the press ethics and control remained entirely free of any government connection.

Government Participation in Ethical Controls

Government participated in press ethical controls in seven nations: Argentina, Chile, Cuba, France, Greece, Mexico, and Venezuela.

In general, government participated in ethical control through its granting of legal sanctions to the journalism union or associations.

None of the reported ethical controls systems with government participation makes regular reports of hearings on cases involving ethics. Only in the systematic reporting of such cases can the public gain some idea of the development or continuing effectiveness of a code. Little evidence was found to indicate that courts of honor or other devices were operating to uphold codes of ethics.

This is not to attempt to say that somewhere government and press might not work together to provide considerable degrees of freedom and responsibility to both. But a brief look at Cuba illustrates what has happened at times in several countries which tried to combine controls under press and government.

Cuba—along with Chile and Venezuela—adopted the concept of a *colegio* (a government-sanctioned professional association) in an attempt to define and control press ethics. (Back of the idea of the *colegio*—as well as the legal *syndicate* of France and several Latin American countries —is the feeling that any voluntary association of journalists will lack sufficient power to accomplish much on its own.) [4]

Cuba was the first Latin American country to provide a *colegio* for its journalists.

Article 8 of the *Estatutos del Colegio Nacional de Periodistas de la República* provided that a journalist must be a member of the *colegio* in order to work as a journalist.[5] (This is a common provision in both *colegio* and syndicate forms.) Article 10 provided that each journalist to qualify for membership (after institution of the *colegio*) must possess a certificate of aptitude from the professional school of journalists, or a certificate from a school of equal rank and character.

Within the *colegio*, journalists were expected to maintain their own disciplinary court, share with the Minister of Education control of schools

[4] Alfonso Valdebenito, *Historia del Periodismo Chileno*, quoted in Frederick Marbut, "Chile Has Law To Enforce Code of Ethics," *Quill*, April, 1960, p. 15.
[5] Vogel, p. 249.

of journalism, and institute proceedings against violators of their ethical code—or against any actions which might damage the *colegio*.

Castro forces were quick to use the *colegio* to restrict newsmen and newspapers.[6] The Castro government saw to it that newsmen who disagreed with their policies lost their *colegio* membership. Publishers were intimidated by threats and court actions, and any story—distasteful to the new regime—was killed, or "corrected" by the government-backed organization. (Similar methods in Hitler Germany helped in the takeover of that press.)

Ethical Controls Without Government Participation

National Press Councils: Of the remaining sixteen countries, six nations have national press councils, free from any government controls, generally representing the press organizations as a whole, and empowered to make decisions for the entire press. These nations are: Great Britain, Japan, Netherlands, Norway, Sweden, and West Germany.

A brief description of the formation of the earliest of these national press councils illustrates the general pattern such ethical definition and control has followed.

Swedish newsmen in 1916 and Norwegian newsmen in 1929 organized the first two national press councils.[7] The Swedish and Norwegian press councils are similar in organization and purpose.

The Swedish press council (*Pressens Opinionsnämd* or Press Fair Practices Commission) was founded by the Swedish *Publicistklubben* "to promote professional contact and consultation between the country's newspapermen" and to accomplish the following goals:

> To handle matters which may be important in setting standards for journalistic work;
>
> To safeguard the dignity and responsibility of the profession against attack from outside and dissolution from within; and
>
> To represent the Swedish press at home and abroad in all affairs of common interest which are not handled by special business or technical organizations.[8]

The *Publicistklubben* is a professional organization which includes working journalists, freelance writers, editors, and some management personnel. Associated with the *Publicistklubben* in the Press Fair Practices Commission is the *Svenska Tidningsutgivereforbundet* (Swedish Journalist's Union).

Each of the three sponsoring organizations names one man to the

[6] Vogel, p. 254.
[7] Vogel, pp. 13-53.
[8] Anders Yngve Pers, *Newspapers in Sweden*, translated by Gunnar Beckman (Stockholm: The Swedish Newspaper Institute, 1954), p. 50.

press council for a two-year term. In addition, the three organizations pick a chairman from outside the newspaper profession. Usually this fourth member—who is automatically the chairman—is a judge of one of Sweden's higher courts.

The Norwegian Press Association (*Norsk Presseforbund*) in 1929 founded the Norwegian Press Fair Practices Commission (*Det Faglige Utvalg*) to act as an ethical control on the press. The association has approximately 1,300 members, organized in regional groups. Primarily a professional association, the *Presseforbund* also incorporates in its membership the 950 members of the *Norsk Journalistlag*, a union for working journalists. The *Presseforbund*, through membership and cooperative agreement, also represents the interests of the *Norske Avisers Landsforbund* (Norwegian Newspaper Publishers' Association) and the *Periodisk Presse* (Norwegian Editors' Association). Publishers, editors, and working journalists each pick one member to form the three-member press council. Norway does not have a lay member on its council.

Swedish and Norwegian councils do not seem to have been formed under any strong pressures from government or public.[9] However, strong sentiment for the adoption of codes of ethics existed during the 1920's. The International Rotary Club, as an example, conducted a drive in the '20's to persuade all businesses and professions to adopt codes of ethics.[10] Many businesses—and many newspapers in the United States—adopted codes of ethics during the 1920's. (The ASNE Canons of Journalism was a product of this period.) Few of the codes of ethics, however, called for any enforcement, and most of the codes of ethics of the 1920's have been forgotten.

The Swedish and Norwegian attempts to uphold ethical standards of the press differed in one vital aspect from the codes of ethics of business adopted after World War I. Whereas businesses stressed adoption of their written codes of ethics—and usually forgot about enforcement—the Swedish and Norwegian press councils operated without the guidance of a code of ethics.

The Swedish Court began its work without any set of standards by which to judge cases, but in 1923 the *Publicistklubben* adopted an organizational "Code of Honor" or "Publication Rules." This Swedish code of ethics is published in pocket size and a copy is given to every beginning member of the journalistic profession. In addition the code is posted on the bulletin boards of newspapers. The code does not act as a binding and detailed set of law for the Swedish council, yet it is used by the council as a statement of principles for guidance, particularly for the lay

[9] Letters from Swedish, Norwegian Press Associations, quoted in Vogel, 167-177.
[10] Guy Gundaker, "Campaign for the International Association of Rotary Clubs for the Writing of Codes of Standards, . . ." *Annals of the American Association of Political and Social Science*, 190 (May, 1922), pp. 228-236.

member of the board who may not be acquainted with concepts of ethical journalism.

Similarly, the Norwegian council in its early years had no guiding written code of ethics for its council members. However, in 1926 the *Norsk Presseforbund* adopted a code of ethics, the *Vaer Varsom!* (Be Careful!) The code—amended in 1956—is also presented to every journalist taking his first job.

Stress must be placed here on the fact that the national press councils in Sweden and Norway represent combined efforts of publishers, editors, and working journalists. The government does not participate in press council proceedings in any fashion, except where government or a government official may be a complainant in a case. Any citizen is free to bring a case against a newspaper or a journalist. To avoid conflict with court litigation, plaintiffs must agree not to bring a case in state courts while the same case is being considered before the press councils.

There is no indication that in well over a quarter century of operation the national press councils in Norway and Sweden have jeopardized freedom of the press. (The Swedish council did make a mistake once in censuring a paper for criticizing a clergyman. A government court later found the clergyman guilty.)

Indeed, under the friendly climate of public opinion toward freedom of the press existing in these two Scandinavian countries, government legislation toward newspapers is particularly lenient. Since 1949 a new press law in Sweden, founded on experiences of the press during World War II, "categorically forbids obligatory censorship even in wartime." [11]

The Swedish press council handles from twenty to twenty-five cases a year. The Norwegian press council handles only slightly less. In both countries regular public reports are made of the results of cases heard before the councils.

Swedish journalists feel that when the council renders a verdict of guilty, the guilty paper has the moral obligation of being the first paper to print the council's verdict.[12] In addition, decisions are published by the Swedish news agency and by most other papers in the country. Details of each case—whether decided for or against the press—are also carried in the yearbook of the journalism organizations in Sweden. Publication of verdicts in Norway is handled in a similar manner.

In both countries about half of the cases tried before the councils end in verdicts against the press. However, the councils do not hesitate to uphold rights of the press or of individual journalists.

It was not until after World War II that the Swedish and Norwegian patterns for a press council were adopted in other countries. And it is

[11] Pers, p. 7.
[12] Sven Bowman, "Sweden Has 'Court of Honour:' Voluntary System of Referring Press Disputes Has Been in Operation Since 1916," *IPI Report, January,* 1953, pp. 2-3.

significant that pressures from government and public—often threatening legal or public "vigilante" control—forced, or at least encouraged, acceptance of national press councils in Great Britain, West Germany and the Netherlands. Turkey—the sixth nation to have a national press council—represents a slightly different situation. Turkish newsmen, who suffered under severe press restrictions during the Menderes regime, adopted a press council partly in an attempt to prevent irresponsibilities which might again bring on press restrictions.

In general, the newer national press councils have adopted patterns of the Swedish and Norwegian councils. However, a study of press council constitutions indicates a tendency on the part of the newer councils to consider more than responsibilities of the press.

As an example, agitation in Great Britain and West Germany for a press council arose largely over the issue of "fairness and accuracy" in the press. Yet in each country after the combined press organizations had formed a council and stated the objectives of that council, it may be seen that the supervision of "fairness and accuracy" became only one of a number of goals for the national press council. The dominant purpose of the newer national press councils—according to stated objectives—is to guard the freedom and success of the press. The British Press Council —in its fear of possible outside influence—even includes in its constitution a clause stipulating that the British Press Council may dissolve itself at any time it appears to the members that the "voluntary nature and independence of the Council are threatened." [13]

Similarly, the Japanese press council seems to have been adopted by Japanese editors and publishers (there is no representation from working journalists) primarily to preserve the freedom of the press duing a time of great sensationalism and public outcry. However, the Japanese council seems to be active in its own way in considering and settling cases.

Association Controls: The remaining ten nations have codes of ethics and/or courts of honor adopted by a single association or union of journalists in each country. These nations are the United States, Belgium, Finland, Austria, Luxembourg, Israel, Switzerland, Australia, Union of South Africa, and Great Britain and Ireland.

(Great Britain and Ireland are listed together here because the National Union of Journalists, which has an "association" code, has members in both countries. Great Britain has already been listed under those countries with a "national" court of honor.)

a. In the United States—the only country where organizations of journalists have adopted codes of ethics without any apparent intention of enforcing those ethical standards—the success or lack of success of the codes of ethics is difficult to prove. An early attempt by the American

[13] *The Press and the People: The 5th Annual Report of the General Council of the Press* (London: General Council of the Press, 1958), p. 49.

Society of Newspaper Editors to find some way to enforce its Canon of Journalism resulted in eight years of disputes between ASNE members. Finally, wearied, the editors gave up the argument, and the Canons of Journalism remain only as guideposts to press behavior.[14] One might argue for the success of U.S. press codes as ethical guideposts, but certainly the codes are little known to the general public, cannot be used by the layman to bring a complaint against a particular newspaper, and usually surface only on anniversary occasions or in journalism textbooks.

b. In Belgium, Finland, Austria, Luxembourg, Israel, and Switzerland, professional associations of journalists have disciplinary courts to enforce ethical standards. However, only in Israel did the author find evidence that the disciplinary courts have functioned at times. (Israel has since this study evolved a national Press Council). No evidence can be found to indicate that ethical controls are operating in the other countries of this group.

c. Of the remaining nations, the two important organizations to consider are the Australian Journalists' Association and the National Union of Journalists of Great Britain and Ireland.[15]

The AJA and NUJ represent attempts at ethical control by trade unions. The AJA at the time of this study continued to make regular reports of disciplinary court activities, although these reports are intended mainly for members. The AJA disciplinary councils were active, and the AJA possessed the power to enforce its decisions on its own members. However, the power of the AJA does not extend beyond the circle of its own membership. The constitution of the AJA recognizes the limits of the Union's power when it states that working journalists shall not be responsible for stories written by reporters but changed by supervisory personnel before publication in the paper.

The NUJ appears to have much the same power—and the same limitations. Since these "working journalist" unions have no power over editors and publishers, their codes and courts may have only a small influence on the final press product.

Conclusions

From the brief summaries above, the author feels that:

1. On the basis of nations studied, government participation in ethical controls does not seem to lead to enforcement of higher ethical standards. (Naturally, this does not take into consideration enforcement of those laws—of libel, as example—which tend to make a press conform to legislated standards. But this study has confined itself to what journalists feel they "ought" to do and their attempts to see that these "oughts" have some force.)

14 Vogel, pp. 61-74.
15 *Ibid.*, 133-136.

Government participation in press ethical controls may even constitute a danger to the press, as in the takeover of the Cuban press *colegio* by the Castro government. In addition to the danger of opening a way to government control of the press, any partnership between press and government takes away a part of the newspaper's vital freedom and responsibility: the freedom to criticize government and the responsibility to act as a check for the public upon government.

2. Probably the national press council—representing all journalists—provides the type of voluntary ethical control which can best define for the press the limits of freedom and responsibility.

Since the national press councils (except in Japan, as noted earlier) represent all segments of the press, the councils have some power over publishers, editors, and working journalists. At the same time, the codes and courts have something *to give* to these three elements of the press.

For the working journalist, the codes and courts offer not only yardsticks for operation, but may also form a basis for future "professionalization" of the occupation of journalism. Many journalists, of course, have always claimed to belong to a "profession." Most scholars, however, have denied that journalism is a profession since members did not have to live up to certain stated standards. Continued operation of the codes and courts, then, may raise the status of the journalist.

Publishers, naturally, resent any implication that they must share a portion of their managerial authority. Publishers—like directors of corporations—must direct their efforts toward the financial success of their business. While this need not imply that publishers would object to higher standards of journalism, it does mean that the first duty of the publisher has become the duty to assure the economic success of the press and to keep it free. The courts of honor offer a way to do this—by holding off government and public controls, and by offering a way to avoid costly litigation in civil and criminal courts.

Editors are the foremen in today's industrial news plants. As such, they are often caught between the desires of their publisher and the complaints, biases, and the difficulties their reporters experience in filling the columns of newsprint. In addition to a boost in his own status ("professionalization" again), the codes provide the editor with guidances within which he and competing editors must try to operate. Thus the courts of honor cut down on excessive competition.

3. The association courts of honor—representing primarily one segment of the press—are the least effective of all the courts of honor. Even where the association does have a disciplinary court, the association can only take action upon its own members and can do little to affect the press as a whole. (Conceivably an association representing only publishers could have an effective court of honor for the press. But, here again, the publisher's first goal must be to keep the press free—and profitable.)

4. The arguments of proponents for individual self-regulation, such as that advocated by the American Society of Newspaper Editors, cannot be dismissed. In a country which has long been accustomed to democratic processes and to a free press, this system may serve as some encouragement to higher standards. Yet, experiences in other countries seem to indicate that if a time arises when public and government become sufficiently indignant over what is felt to be abuses of press freedom, then press opponents will demand something more than a simple statement of ethics.

Similarly, it is doubtful if this type of self-regulation can be effective in a country not accustomed to long years of free press and free speech.

5. Last, the degree of success of the newer national press councils seems to indicate that enforcement of ethical "oughts" may be more important than mere definition—through a written code of ethics—of standards of responsibility of the press. Thus, a study of the national press councils might be helpful to those persons with the United Nations who labored for so many years in vain to produce a code of ethics for newspapers over the world. Though the process would be equally long, painful, and never-ending, it might be interesting to see what an international press council might do toward trying to set standards—through case studies—which could begin to serve as an international code of ethics.

The way to the adoption of any national press council—or to any enforcement of ethical principles for the press—will not be easy.

In retrospect, the author recalls receiving letters from newsmen overseas saying, in effect, that: "The code of ethics (or the plan of enforcement) you asked about for this country simply does not exist."

Recently the author sat in on a three-day conference in Istanbul as Turkish press representatives endeavored to study what had happened to their fine attempts in the early 1960's to enforce through their court of honor the high-sounding moral statements of their code of ethics. All agreed that their code and court had not been successful. Most wanted to do something to reinstate some ethical standards and enforcement. But agreement was impossible. Finally, one leading editor summed up feelings of many of those attending by stating: "Perhaps the best we can do now is to continue talking about ethical standards. At least if we keep talking, then someday we may achieve our goals."

And this advice might be the best possible for those journalists in many countries who are still trying to define and find a way to enforce ethical standards for the press.

Raymond B. Nixon:

Factors Related to Freedom in National Press Systems

IN HIS ESSAY on "The Challenge to Communication Research," [1] Wilbur Schramm makes this observation:

> If one looks at a book like *World Communications,* or at twenty articles in the *Journalism Quarterly* on twenty countries and their press, it is perfectly apparent that the literacy of each country, the gross national product, the distribution of wealth and population, and other elements are instrumentally related in some way to the pattern by which press systems have developed. But exactly how? A cross-country study of some of these variables in relation to communication systems would be revealing.

The same thought must have occurred to many other students of comparative journalism. For it long has been apparent, as Schramm suggests, that a particular kind of press or political system can develop only to the extent that certain variables—socioeconomic, cultural and otherwise —make it possible.

Yet it also has been obvious until recently that the data were inadequate to enable any large-scale comparative studies of these variables to be made. For example, until the United Nations and Unesco publications of the '50s began to appear, comparable data were lacking for most countries on even such basic factors as literacy and per capita income; the statistics still leave much to be desired. And this is to say nothing of the kinds of survey research data that require elaborate and costly field studies by qualified scholars and interviewers within each country. The paucity of data could explain why comparative analyses of communication systems have been so few, and why theory has been so slow to develop.

Happily, both the data and the theory of comparative journalism

---

[1] In Ralph O. Nafziger and David M. White (eds.), *Introduction to Mass Communications Research* (Baton Rouge: Louisiana State University Press, 1958), p. 17.

► This article, prepared by Dr. Nixon especially for this book in 1969, is basically adapted from an article by the same title which appeared in *Journalism Quarterly,* Vol. 37, No. 1 (Winter), 1960, pp. 13-28. Reprinted here, with certain changes by the author, by permission of Dr. Nixon, School of Journalism, University of Minnesota, and of *Journalism Quarterly.*

have been greatly enriched during the last 18 months by two new books. The first of these to appear was Daniel Lerner's *The Passing of Traditional Society*. In this extraordinary work, a brilliant social scientist develops a theory that clearly shows the vital functions performed by the press and other mass media in the transition from "traditional" to "modern" ways of life. A few months later came the International Press Institute's *The Press in Authoritarian Countries*, a volume completing a series of surveys in which journalists and scholars have collaborated to appraise the kinds and degrees of press control in all major countries of the world today. This is a body of new data that assumes even greater importance in the light of Lerner's analysis.

It is when appraisals like those of the IPI are compared with the kinds of data analyzed by Lerner that we begin to glimpse a partial answer to the question of *how* and *why* one press system rather than another develops. There is nothing new, of course, in being able to say that a "free press system" like that of the United States usually is found only in countries with a high rate of literacy and per capita income. But it is new to have sufficient material for determining whether these cultural and socioeconomic factors are related to press freedom and control in a definite and systematic way.

The writer undertook the present study to test the hypothesis that such relationship does exist. Accordingly, he arrayed the most recent UN and Unesco data related to national press systems alongside the information on press freedom reported by the IPI and a kindred organization, the Inter-American Press Association. The data were cross-checked with other sources for accuracy.

The results are striking, as the accompanying chart will show. And they become even more meaningful when the relevant aspects of Lerner's theory are kept in mind.

The uniqueness of the Lerner theory for journalism lies in the dynamic role that it ascribes to the mass media in the emergence and maintenance of modern society. Earlier analyses of UN and Unesco data had shown the fundamental importance of literacy. For example, Golden had found that literacy correlated at .87 with industrialization and at .84 with per capita income.[2] But this is a static relationship, bearing only indirectly upon the press and political systems. Lerner puts these cultural and socioeconomic factors into an overall theory of modernization that also includes *media* and *political* participation.

Lerner derived his hypothesis from history. Viewing the development of Western democracies, he saw that their modernization has exhibited "certain components and sequences whose relevance is global. Everywhere,

[2] H. H. Golden, "Literacy and Social Change in Underdeveloped Countries," in *Rural Society*, 20:1-7 (1955).

for example, urbanization [to which he subsumes industrialization] has tended to increase literacy; rising literacy has tended to increase media exposure; increasing media exposure has 'gone with' wider economic participation (per capita income) and political participation (voting)." This, in the older democracies, is a "historic fact."

By cross-checking the first (1951) edition of Unesco's *World Communications* with other UN and Unesco sources, Lerner obtained comparable data on 54 countries. From these he developed indices for the first four factors in his "model of modernization":

1) *Urbanization*—the proportion of a country's inhabitants living in cities over 50,000;

2) *Literacy*—the proportion of adults (*i.e.*, persons over 15) able to read in one language;

3) *Media participation*—the proportion buying newspapers, owning radios and attending movies (all combined into one index number);

4) *Political participation*—the average proportion voting in the last four national elections.

The multiple correlation coefficients of these four variables were found to be: Urbanization, .61; literacy, .91; media participation, .84; political participation, .82. Each of these coefficients represents the degree of correlation between the variable named and the three remaining variables.[3]

But this demonstration of systematic relationships among these four variables is merely the prelude to Lerner's chief contribution: the addition of the personality variable of *empathy*. Empathy, to use his simplified definition, is "the capacity to see oneself in the other fellow's situation"; it is the skill of "imagining oneself in another's shoes." He identified the more empathic individuals among 1,357 survey interviewees in six Middle Eastern countries by using the "latent structure analysis" technique of Paul F. Lazarsfeld in analyzing their responses to nine projective questions. These included such questions as: If you were made "head of the government" (or "editor of a newspaper," or "put in charge of a radio station"), "what are some of the things you would do?"

Lerner found that the more empathic individuals have more "mobile personalities"; this enables them to express opinions on a wider range of subjects. It is by providing people with vicarious or "psychic mobility" that the mass media accelerate the development of empathy and thus perform an indispensable service:

Audiences and constituencies are composed of participant individuals. People "participate" in the public life of their country by

[3] Daniel Lerner, *The Passing of Traditional Society* (Glencoe, Ill.: The Free Press, 1958), pp. 46, 63.

having opinions about many matters which, in the isolation of traditional society, did not concern them. Participant persons have opinions on a variety of issues and situations which they may never have experienced directly—such as what the government should do about irrigation, how the Algerian revolt should be settled. . . . By having and expressing opinions on such matters a person participates in the network of public communication.

The media teach people participation of this sort by depicting for them new and strange situations and by familiarizing them with a range of opinions among which they can choose. Some people learn better than others, the variations reflecting their skill in empathy.[4]

Lerner concludes that "a communication system is both index and agent of change in a total social system. This avoids the genetic problem of causality, about which we can only speculate, in order to stress correlation hypotheses which can be tested. On this view, once the modernizing process is started, chicken and egg in fact 'cause' each other to develop."

It is worth noting, however, that media participation comes *third* in Lerner's "typology of modernization." Thus, it follows urbanism and literacy, but precedes political participation and high empathy—two qualities characteristic of those societies where political democracy and press freedom have flourished.

The basic procedure used in this study—that of arranging related data on different countries in parallel columns for comparison—was so simple that little explanation seems necessary. However, since one of these variables represents a classification of qualitative appraisals by "experts" on the press, it is necessary to explain the method of classification so that the reader may judge its validity.

The UN and Unesco publications were the starting point, as they were for Lerner. Examination of these sources to the middle of 1959 indicated that reasonably comparable data could be obtained on 85 countries and territories for three variables related to national press systems:

> *Per capita national income*—defined by the United Nations as the average income per inhabitant "accruing to factors of production supplied by normal residents of the given country before deduction of direct taxation."
> *Percentage of adults (persons 15 years and older) illiterate*— illiteracy being defined by Unesco as "inability to read and write in any language."
> *Daily newspaper circulation*—a daily being "any newspaper published more than four times a week."

[4] Lerner, *op. cit.*, p. 412.

The dates selected for each variable were the latest for which comparable statistics on the largest countries could be found.

It was decided to use daily newspaper circulation, rather than a general index of "media participation" like Lerner's, partly because circulation figures were available for a larger number of countries. But further reflection revealed a much sounder reason: Since broadcasting systems in most countries outside the Western Hemisphere are either owned by the government or operated by a government-controlled monopoly, the conditions affecting press freedom relate primarily to the printed media.

The main problem of methods arose in trying to bring together "modern, precise research procedures and the more traditional broad approaches of historical . . . and journalistic appraisal." In the first place, before setting up a continuum with *freedom* at one end and *control* at the other, it was necessary to define the two terms and the various points of classification between. Secondly, a method was required for quantifying the various degrees of freedom so that this factor could be correlated statistically with other variables.

The author began by accepting the IPI's definition of an "authoritarian regime" as one characterized by "a permanent censorship or a constant and general control of the press," either by the government or the political group in power. A "free press system," by contrast, is one marked by the *absence* of such a permanent censorship or constant and general control; it is one in which private owners and independent journalists are free to supply news and opinion to the general public under statutes of libel and decency which are applicable to everyone and not capable of arbitrary and discriminatory interpretation by the ruling power. In other words, the chief criterion is the degree of control normally exercised by any official agency which has the power to interfere with the dissemination and discussion of news.

It immediately became apparent that a classification of countries according to their constitutional guarantees or statutes regarding press freedom would be of little help in determining the actual situation. Most countries have constitutions or laws that pay lip service to the principle of freedom of expression and the press, but their practices frequently are something quite different. It therefore was decided to base the classification primarily upon the situation as reported by IPI-IAPA observers and analysts.

On the basis of the two major IPI surveys (1 and 2 in the sources listed in the chart), a five-way classification was set up:

F   Free press system; normally no major government controls.
F—   Free press, but with less stability and/or more controls than F.

I   Intermediate; some characteristics of free press, but with varying kinds and degrees of authoritarian control.

A—   Authoritarian, but with less rigid press controls than A.

A   Authoritarian press system; strong controls over all mass
media.

Since journalists in the Communist countries object strongly to having their particular type of government and party controls classified as
"authoritarian," a sixth category of "C" was created for the Communist
systems, with "C—" designating countries in which there is substantial
evidence of less rigidity in enforcement.

The writer did not wish to depend upon his own unaided judgment
in classifying qualitative data. He was aware that he might have been
influenced by impressions received over the last three years on personal
visits to some 45 of the countries and territories under study. He therefore submitted his own classification to two other judges, one in Europe
and one in the United States. Both are journalists and scholars whose
principal area of research is comparative journalism.

The two judges together raised questions about seven of the 85
classifications. In each case it was a question only of moving a particular
country from one position to an adjoining position on the scale; in no
case did either judge suggest that an "F" or "F—" country should be
classified as "A" or "A—", or the reverse. In the four cases where both
judges disagreed with the writer, the classification was changed to agree
with the majority opinion.

But to what extent had two or more judges been influenced by the
same biases? How would a person who had to rely entirely on available
documentary sources classify the same countries?

A graduate student (Kenneth A. Gompertz) was assigned to work
on this problem. For information, he searched not only the IPI and
IAPA sources but also the New York *Times* and *Editor & Publisher*. In
the period since the founding of the IPI in 1951, he found reports related to press freedom in 101 countries. When he eliminated those
countries on which information was incomplete or fragmentary, 61 countries remained.

The press controls reported in these 61 countries were classifiable into
10 different categories. Three of these eventually were dropped because
of inconsistency of pattern or infrequency of occurrence. One of the categories that had to be discarded, as might be suspected, was a classification
on the basis of legal guarantees. The seven categories that appeared to
establish a "typology" were:

1)   Control through punitive action, legal and extra-legal, other
than that covered by statutes against libel and obscenity. This in-

cludes civil and criminal action, arrests, detention, jail sentences, fines and deportation. Such action was recorded only if it discriminated against the journalist, such as through the law of *desacato* ("disrespect toward authority") found in most South American countries. Such a law typifies public security measures used to control journalists considered "dangerous to public order."

2) Control of a publication's existence or very life through such action as a) seizure of newspapers, b) restriction of newsprint and other supplies, and c) permission to publish only under favorable government disposition.

3) Control of official news through governmental attitude toward official news releases (*i.e.*, that such news must be published without change) or through limited access to governmental news.

4) Control of newspaper personnel, either by direct approval or by appointment of staffs or punishment or censure.

5) Control through official censorship, either through overt censorship organs or by police or police-like actions. The existence of an office of censorship was considered control through threat even in cases where relatively little activity was reported.

6) Control of periodical content or format, ranging all the way from complete planning and policy control to pressures exerted to restrict ideological "wandering."

7) Control of periodical distribution, either directly or indirectly.

The 61 countries were "scored" on each of these controls. The resulting rank data were subjected to a Guttman-scale type of analysis to find out whether the different kinds of restriction did, indeed, cumulate.[5] This scalogram analysis produced a "model of press control" with eight types, ranging from 0 controls to 7 (Table 1).

In the listing above, the types of control are presented in the order in which they tend to cumulate. Thus a country which has control 7 (distribution) typically will have most if not all of the other controls. Again, a country with restriction 4 (control of personnel) will tend to have the controls which appear to the right of it in Table 1, but not controls 5, 6 or 7.

When the independent ratings obtained by this method for the 61 countries were compared with the classifications of these countries by the three judges, a statistical correlation of .94 was found; the correlation with the final ratings of these countries in the chart was .96.[6]

This phase of the project accomplished three things: 1) It tended to

---

[5] For a description of the method used, see Louis H. Guttman, "The Cornell Technique for Scale and Intensity Analysis," *Educational and Psychological Measurement*, 7:248-79 (1947). The coefficient of reproducibility was .92.

[6] The coefficient is tetrachoric *r*, which provides an estimate of the product-moment correlation between the two scales.

TABLE I

MODEL OF PRESS CONTROL

Control Type	METHOD OF CONTROL						
	Distribution (7)	Content-Format (6)	Censorship (5)	Personnel (4)	Official News (3)	Seizure (2)	Criminal-Civil (1)
Type 7	x	x	x	x	x	x	x
Type 6		x	x	x	x	x	x
Type 5			x	x	x	x	x
Type 4				x	x	x	x
Type 3					x	x	x
Type 2						x	x
Type 1							x
Type 0							

An "x" indicates the presence of the control category in a governmental system.

support the ratings of the three judges; 2) it pointed to the possibility of establishing an objective method for classifying types of press control; 3) it called attention (as the judges also had done) to the desirability of further shadings and qualifications in the classification scheme finally to be adopted.

For this latter reason, the five original categories on the freedom-control continuum were expanded to eight, with a ninth category possible. Thus, "F¹" was inserted between "F" and "F—" to identify five countries where the existence of a strong "free press system" was unchallenged by the judges, but where special circumstances had led to the imposition of certain controls on an emergency basis during the period studied. The "I+" symbol was added for those "Intermediate" countries where long-term tendencies since 1951 have seemed to favor press freedom, and "I—" for those in this category where the long-term development has been less favorable. Finally, a "C¹" symbol was adopted for two European Communist countries (Albania and Rumania) that had been listed for general comparison, but which could not be included among the 85 studied simply because their controls are so thorough-going as to make adequate information impossible to obtain. An "A¹" also was provided.

The scale of the "freedom-control" continuum then was expressed quantitatively, for purposes of statistical analysis, as follows:

			C—	C C¹
F F¹	F—	I+ I I—	A—	A A¹
1	2	3	4	5

These nine categories [7] made it possible to identify qualitative differences not shown by the original classification. For purposes of correlational analysis, however, the five-point numerical scale was retained (as shown above) in order to approximate the assumption of equal intervals along the continuum. In general, it was felt that the differences in degree of control were approximately equal along the five-category scale.

Support for the decision to assign the same weight to class "C" as to class "A" systems was found in the "model of press control" shown in Table 1. When the ratings of the 61 countries forming the basis of this model were compared, both the major Communist country (the Soviet Union) and the Dominican Republic, under whose military dictatorship the press system was classified as "A," fell into Type 7. This is the scale type of category in which control of the press by governmental authority is most nearly complete.

The statistical findings of this study thus strongly support the hypothesis that there is a definite and systematic relationship between the degree of freedom in a national press system and three other variables. The correlation between press freedom and each of these variables [8] is as follows:

Per capita national income	.64
Proportion of adults literate	.51
Daily newspaper circulation per 1,000 inhabitants	.63

Each of these correlation coefficients is significant at the 1% level. In other words, there is less than one chance in one hundred that the relationship could be purely coincidental.

Thus, in the world of today, wherever per capita income is high, press freedom is likely to be found—along with its necessary concomitant, political democracy. Literacy also is related to press freedom, but not so closely as per capita income.

The statistics also support what the history of the press reveals: that high newspaper circulation and press freedom tend to go together.

Discussion

In looking for specific patterns, it was noted that every country which had an annual per capita income of $600 or more in 1952-54 had then, and has today, a strong free press system. Most of these countries also

[7] In the author's second study, made five years later, a simple nine-point numerical scale was used. See "Freedom in the World's Press: A Fresh Appraisal with New Data," *Journalism Quarterly*, 42:3-14, 118-19 (Winter 1965).
[8] Because the data for the relationships between press freedom and the three independent variables did not meet the assumption of linearity, the correlation ration (eta—coefficient of curvilinear correlation) was used instead of product-moment r.)

have an adult illiteracy rate of only 1-2%. This top group in per capita income also embraced the 15 countries highest in daily newspaper circulation per 1,000 population, except for Japan.

Only two countries in the $600 or more annual per capita income group required the "F¹" classification, indicating the occurrence of certain emergency controls during recent years in what otherwise is a strong free press system. One of these countries was France, where recurrent economic and military crises appear to account for deviations from its normal pattern of freedom. The other was Finland, where the press probably is as free as any in Europe except for a law which makes it an offense to "endanger Finland's relations with her neighbors"—*i.e.*, the Soviet Union. But both these countries repeatedly have shown their determination to maintain freedom of expression, even under adverse circumstances.

Even when all countries with an annual per capita income of $300 or more were considered, only six had classifications other than "F, F¹ or F—." These were Spain, classified as "A"; Cuba, now "C"; and the four Communist countries of Europe that are most advanced industrially: Czechoslovakia, East Germany, Poland and the U.S.S.R. To these four might be added Hungary, whose more recent per capita income figures put it ahead of Poland.

Spain, as the IPI survey points out, is the only non-Communist country in the world today with an authoritarian system based upon "a well-established doctrine on information." To understand its system of press controls one must remember that the country over which General Franco gained supreme power in 1936 was, like the Tsarist Russia which the Bolsheviks took over in 1917, an old-style monarchy with strong religious underpinnings. It had been touched scarcely at all by the liberalizing influences that had led to the development of democratic institutions in Western Europe and the United States. The main difference between what happened in Spain and what happened in Russia is that Franco led a "broad" revolution which kept essentially the same elements in power, whereas the Communists appealed to long-suppressed, "deep" revolutionary forces that completely overthrew the old ruling classes in what is now the Soviet Union.

Cuba's plight points up the general instability that has characterized even the richest of Latin American countries during most of their independent existence. Essentially it grows out of the fact that these countries, as colonies of Spain and Portugal down to the early part of the 19th century, likewise were isolated from the liberalizing influences that revolutionized politics, economics, religion and the press in England and elsewhere during the 17th, 18th and 19th centuries. Even the leaders of independence movements in most Latin American countries came from a relatively small class of European descent, and their ideas did not penetrate very far down into the Indian and mestizo masses. The strong middle-class support that leads both to a stable democratic government and to a strong free press has been generally lacking, except in three countries (Uruguay, Chile and Costa Rica) where a fairly homogeneous population has helped to produce a more equitable distribution of income, and one country (Mexico) which has made consistent progress in improving the general welfare over the last 30 years.

This brings us to the five communist countries of Europe that are highest in per capita income and literacy (Czechoslovakia, East Germany, Poland, the U.S.S.R. and Hungary). These five nations stand out as the most conspicuous deviations from the general rule of a close relationship between these two variables and the existence of press freedom as defined in the Western world.

The deviation shown by these Communist countries is not as difficult to explain, however, as it might at first appear. In the first place, it must be remembered that when the Communists came to power and installed their system of press controls, the adult illiteracy rate of the Russians by their own figures was between 60 and 70%, and the old Russian Empire was on the verge of economic collapse. Moreover, it was the long-suppressed aspirations of the Russian people for a more democratic political system, as well as for economic improvement, that hastened the rise of the Communists to power. It was the need to appeal to these deep revolutionary forces—quite similar to the forces that much earlier had led to revolutions in France and England—that led the Communists to include in their political apparatus a number of democratic forms, including "freedom of the press," which in turn are counterweighted by totalitarian controls that enable the party to use the press as one instrument for achieving its social goals. These goals include the elimination of illiteracy and the raising of living standards—the same goals which the Western world had been achieving gradually over a period of years by less authoritarian methods.

From conversations with journalists in seven Communist countries during the summer of 1959, the writer feels sure that some of these journalists are sincerely convinced that their system of controls does permit them press "freedom," although of quite a different type from freedom as the West defines it. The paradox of this situation has been explained by an American historian, who points out that "man can seem to be free in any society, no matter how authoritarian, as long as he accepts the postulates of the society." To this the Western democracies have added the important concept that "man can only be free in a society that is willing to allow its basic postulates to be questioned." [9]

[9] John B. Wolf, "Man's Struggle for Freedom Against Authority," in *Social Science and Freedom* (Minneapolis: University of Minnesota, 1955), p. 1.

So far the Communist leaders of the Soviet Union have not allowed their "basic postulates" to be questioned. But now that their country has attained a high degree of literacy and industrialization, there seems to be reason for believing that it may tend increasingly to follow the pattern shown by Lerner's historical "model of modernization," and thus to manifest more of the characteristics of a truly "participant society."

As for Czechoslovakia, East Germany, Poland and Hungary, they already had attained the conditions for press freedom, along with industrialization and literacy, before they fell under Communist control as a result of developments following World War II. There is impressive evidence that they would have essentially the same kind and degree of freedom today as that of the West, except for circumstances beyond their control. These circumstances can be explained only in terms of the rise of the Soviet Union to a position of great military strength.

Already there are signs of some relaxation in the extent to which the Soviet government controls the lives of its citizens, and this is spreading to the other Communist countries of Europe. The possible benefits of an extended period of peaceful coexistence with the Western democracies are implicit in Siebert's "theory of press freedom." After an exhaustive study of the development of press freedom in the Western world, Siebert advanced as a tentative law of history that "the area of freedom contracts and the enforcement of restraints increases as the stresses on the stability of government and of the structure of society increase." [10] Obversely, as the stresses on the stability of the government and the structure of society *decrease*, the area of freedom may be expected to expand.

One of the greatest dangers in any highly centralized political system with strong press controls is that the government and ruling party can use the mass media to create whatever tensions they may regard as necessary to justify the imposition of even more rigid controls. It is no longer unusual, however, to find Communist journalists who will admit that this is one weakness of a system which they otherwise may strongly defend. In the same breath they frequently will declare that the Soviet Union today would not tolerate another dictator like Stalin. The fact that some Communists thus recognize the dangers of absolute power is one of the most hopeful signs of all.

Certainly it is in the Communist countries that still have the farthest to go along the road to literacy and high per capita income (Bulgaria, Rumania, Albania and China) that one finds the controls over the press and other institutions to be the most severe. The difference between the stern discipline of China's "great leap forward" and the more relaxed atmosphere of present-day Russia is so great, indeed, that some observers

[10] In Introduction to Frederick S. Siebert, *Freedom of the Press in England, 1476-1776* (Urbana, Ill.: University of Illinois Press, 1952).

believe the Soviet Union some day may find itself closer in many respects to the United States and the democracies of Western Europe than to its great Asian ally.

But what of those European and Asian countries with a low per capita income—some also with high illiteracy—that nevertheless have made substantial progress up the ladder toward political democracy and press freedom? It is here that one finds the clue to other factors related to press freedom that deserve careful study.

One of these countries is Japan, the other the Republic of the Philippines. Without lessening in any sense the credit due the Japanese and Filipino people, it can be said that the policies of the United States have been a contributory factor in the development of their free systems. Both Japan, since regaining its sovereignty in 1952, and the Philippines, since becoming fully independent in 1946, have shown their determination to maintain press freedom. The Japanese press, however, appears to have the stronger foundation, because of Japan's higher literacy, high per capita income and huge newspaper circulation—the fifth largest per capita in the world. The foundation in the Philippines is potentially less stable, both because of the lower literacy rate and because newspaper ownership and circulation are so heavily concentrated in one city, Manila.

The most amazing country of all is India (F—), which has attained a fairly stable democracy and free press system despite a per capita income of less than $100 a year and an illiteracy rate of 75-80%. A long period of association with British democracy and press freedom must be given some credit here, as also in Ceylon (F—) and in the present and former British dependencies elsewhere in Asia and in Africa. But one cannot explain the phenomenon of India without considering the strong personal charisma of leaders like Gandhi and Nehru, and also the possible influence of the Hindu religion.

The other Asian country with a per capita income of less than $300 which can be definitely classified as having a free press system is tiny Lebanon (F—). Almost invariably its system is rated by those familiar with the area as "the freest press in the Middle East." This can be attributed in part to a favorable geographic situation, which has helped to give it a higher per capita income than all its neighbors except Israel. But it also is probably due to a relatively long period of development as a French protectorate, and perhaps most of all to the stabilizing influence of a truce between the Christian and Moslem populations.

It is the "I" and "A" classifications that seem to be the least satisfactory. In Africa, for example, all the countries and territories except the Union of South Africa are in one sense "authortarian," not because any totalitarian government has usurped the power, but simply because in many places there would be no communication system at all unless the government provided it. The widespread illiteracy, the multiplicity of native languages and dialects, and the lack of adequate electric power in some regions to maintain even radio communication on any widespread basis—all these tend to keep most of the newly emerging African states in a strange mixture of free and authoritarian forms. In the larger and more prosperous cities inhabited by people of European descent will be newspapers much like those of the countries from which whites have come, and enjoying much of the same freedom; for the natives, the situation may be quite different. Even the press in the Union of South Africa, where democratic institutions have been developed to the highest level, must be classified as less than free because of the pressures and suspicions created by the official policy of *Apartheid*. The best that can be said for most of the newly emerging African states is that their press is in an "intermediate" state of development; "mixed" would describe the situation better as of today.

Actually, the term "authoritarian" as used by the IPI and as adopted in this study for all except the Communist countries, covers too wide a range of non-democratic systems. It includes, at one extreme, the absolutist monarchy of Yemen, which has no daily newspapers at all and depends for mass communication mainly upon a government-owned weekly and radio station. But it also includes the more democratically inclined constitutional monarchies of Libya and Ethiopia; the military dictatorships of Spain, Latin America and other areas, varying widely in their objectives if not their methods; and the still different type of authoritarian rule represented by the more dynamic United Arab Republic.

This latter type of authoritarianism, as Lerner analyzes it, seems, like Communism, to represent "people in a hurry" to obtain more of the better things of life. The violent upheavals so frequent in the Middle East can be attributed, indeed, to the fact that the demands and expectations of the people, stimulated in part by the mass media, greatly exceed their socioeconomic and cultural capacity for achievement. But if they continue to improve their economic status and their capacity for genuine media and political participation, they too may eventually succeed in establishing the conditions that make true press freedom possible.

Ralph L. Lowenstein:

Press Freedom as a Political Indicator

JOURNALISTS in democracies are usually concerned with the degree of "press freedom" that they enjoy. They are concerned not simply because this freedom involves their ability to produce the product from which they earn their livelihood, but because they believe press freedom is inextricably bound up with political freedom.

Though sometimes overlooked by political scientists, the press plays perhaps the most important role in the modern political system. It can be an avenue for freedom, or a tool for suppression. Russell H. Fitzgibbon, who has measured democratization in the 20 republics of Latin America every five years since 1945, found a stronger relationship between "free and competitive elections" and "freedom of the press" than between "free and competitive elections" and any of the remaining 13 political, social and economic criteria in his survey.[1] Other political scientists have made similar findings, though these have largely gone unreported except in the learned journals.

Press freedom, then, is of vital importance to society and should not be the concern simply of those who have a financial stake in the press. Axel Springer, West German publisher, put it succinctly when he said:

> A society of free men comes into being on the basis of free elections, and the free expression of opinion. We recognize a tyranny not only by the fact that its subjects are denied free elections, but also by the fact that they are denied a free press.[2]

Although the press in the newly-developing nations is burdened with the additional task of mobilizing the people toward national development goals, its political role should be much the same as the press in the West.

[1] Russell H. Fitzgibbon and Kenneth F. Johnson, "Measurement of Latin American Political Change," *American Political Science Review*, 55:3 (September 1961), p. 525.
[2] Axel Springer, "Deutsche Press Zwischen Konzentration und Subvention," *Kieler Vortrage*, 48 (1967), p. 4.

▶ This is an original article done for this book by Ralph L. Lowenstein, School of Journalism, University of Missouri. Portions of this article were adapted from two monographs on world press freedom written by Dr. Lowenstein and published by the Freedom of Information Center, University of Missouri.

Lucian W. Pye has written:

> Even in the most weak and unstable country the mass media must still retain to some degree one of their most basic functions: that of serving as an inspector general to the entire political system so as to provide the necessary public criticism to ensure some degree of political integrity among the power holders.[3]

It would seem to follow, then, that an accurate rating system for press freedom, if applied to every independent nation in the world at regular intervals, would enable journalists and social scientists to:

   1) Establish the precise position of any nation at any given time on a "free-controlled" political continuum.

   2) Predict the political direction in which a nation is heading.

   3) Find needed data for correlations between press freedom and other social, economic and political phenomena.

Two major weaknesses of various rating systems used in the past are that they have not used a standard set of criteria for each country judged and they have not considered factors other than those of obvious government interference. Annual surveys of world press freedom reported by the Associated Press, International Press Institute (and a survey of the Western Hemisphere by the Inter American Press Association) do not pretend to be any more than general ratings. They are based on round-up reports, primarily of government interference that has occurred in the countries mentioned. Countries listed in several of the surveys one year are not always mentioned in the next. Many countries are never listed.

Wire service surveys have been criticized because they are concerned primarily with countries where foreign correspondents have experienced difficulties.[4] The IAPA survey, concerned only with the Americas, often condenses its report on a particular country to one sentence: "There is freedom of the press." [5]

In 1963, Arthur S. Banks and Robert B. Textor sorted 99 countries into four categories with respect to degree of press freedom.[6] But since their ratings were based only upon the AP's year-end censorship reports for 1961 and 1962 and an IPI survey published in 1959, their results are open to all the criticisms already mentioned.

Up until the middle 1960's, the most significant rating system attempted was that of Raymond B. Nixon, who published his first set of

---

[3] Lucian W. Pye, "Communication, Institution Building, and the Reach of Authority," in Daniel Lerner and Wilbur Schramm (eds.), *Communication and Change in the Developing Countries* (Honolulu: East-West Center Press, 1967), p. 37.
[4] Raymond B. Nixon, "Freedom in the World's Press: A Fresh Appraisal with New Data," *Journalism Quarterly* (Winter 1965), p. 11.
[5] "Report of Inter American Press Association Committee on Freedom of the Press, Document 5." Unpublished report, mimeographed, March 19, 1960.
[6] *A Cross-Polity Survey* (Cambridge: The M.I.T. Press, 1963), Computer Printout pars. 50-52.

results classifying 85 countries in 1960.[7] After refining his methodology and scale slightly, he made another survey during 1963-64 in which he classified 117 countries. These results were published in 1965.[8] Only three men, including Nixon, were involved in classifying the countries in the first survey. In the second survey, there were four permanent judges and a fifth judge who was a specialist in one country or a group of countries. The fifth member of the panel of judges therefore varied. This panel of judges classified each country according to each member's own evaluation of the situation in the given country. Most of the final ratings represented a complete agreement; the remainder represented a consensus.[9] Nixon's studies were limited to print media only, and whereas his system was a device for *classifying*, it was not a device for *measuring*, since there was an absence of uniform and complete criteria for determining the degree of press freedom in each country.

In 1966, the Freedom of Information Center of the School of Journalism, University of Missouri, undertook a worldwide survey of press freedom, directed by the writer. In beginning the project, the Center hoped to continue it on a regular basis in the belief that it could provide not only an index, but perhaps a predictor, of political change in the nations of the world. The Center started with this definition of a "free" and "controlled" press:

A completely free press is one in which newspapers, periodicals, news agencies, books, radio and television have absolute independence and critical ability, except for minimal libel and obscenity laws. The press has no concentrated ownership, marginal economic units or organized self-regulation.

A completely controlled press is one with no independence or critical ability. Under it, newspapers, periodicals, books, news agencies, radio and television are completely controlled directly and indirectly by government, self-regulatory bodies or concentrated ownership.

The following factors were selected for measuring press freedom on the basis of their overall inclusiveness and comparability: [10]

　　1. Legal controls on the press, not including libel and obscenity laws (but including laws involving official censorship, contempt,

[7] Raymond B. Nixon, "Factors Related to Freedom in National Press Systems," *Journalism Quarterly* (Winter 1960), pp. 13-28.
[8] Nixon, "Freedom in the World's Press . . . ," p. 6.
[9] *Ibid.*
[10] For further details about the selection of these factors and the methodology of the survey in which they were employed, see Ralph L. Lowenstein, "PICA: Measuring World Press Freedom," Freedom of Information Center Publication No. 166, University of Missouri, August 1966; and Ralph L. Lowenstein, "World Press Freedom, 1966," Freedom of Information Center Publication No. 181, University of Missouri, May 1967. Detailed tables on individual factor scores in 94 different countries can be found in Ralph L. Lowenstein, "Measuring World Press Freedom as a Political Indicator," Unpublished Ph.D. dissertation, University of Missouri, 1967.

forced corrections and retractions, suspension, privacy, security, incitement to riot, etc.).

2. Extra-legal controls (threats, violence, imprisonment, confiscation, etc.).

3. Libel laws.

4. Organized self-regulation (press councils, courts of honor).

5. News and editorial personnel (all media) subject to government licensing, certification and appointment.

6. Favoritism in release of government news.

7. Media allowed to utilize services of foreign news agencies.

8. Government control over domestic news agencies.

9. Print media subject to government licensing.

10. Government control of circulation and distribution, not including postal service.

11. Degree of press criticism of local and regional governments and officials within country.

12. Degree of press criticism of national government and national officials within country.

13. Government or "government party" ownership of media (including radio, television and domestic news agencies).

14. Publications of opposition political parties banned.

15. Broadcasting and press units owned by networks and chains (concentrated ownership).

16. Government control of newsprint.

17. Government control of foreign exchange and/or purchase of press equipment.

18. Government subsidies and/or bribes to press and newsmen.

19. Government loans to media.

20. Media dependency on government advertising.

21. Tax rate on press (either higher or lower) as compared to other businesses.

22. Pressure from labor unions (to influence editorial policy, to suspend publication).

23. Number of marginal (economically insecure) press units.

In a questionnaire sent to "judges" throughout the world, each factor was followed by a five-point verbal scale, usually ranging from "none" to "all" or from "none" to "complete." In the scoring, all 23 factors were given equal weight. There was provision for each judge to score each factor "don't know" or "not applicable."

Factors 3 and 4 and Factors 14 through 23 were eliminated for any country in which most or all of the media were state owned. These factors simply did not appear to be applicable to the press in such countries. Although the Press Independence and Critical Ability (PICA) survey conducted by the Freedom of Information Center did not utilize special factors for communist nations, there are such factors that could give a better definition between the press systems of the various communist countries. The following criteria were suggested to this writer by Prof. Georges H. Mond of the University of Paris and by Leo Gruliow, editor of *The Current Digest of Soviet Press*: 1) public access to foreign publications; 2) extent of jamming of foreign broadcasts; 3) relative rigidity of the press hierarchy (the degree to which lower-level and local media are policed by central media); 4) the weight ascribed by the authorities to readers' preferences, as demonstrated by market demand, when paper supplies are being allocated among media; 5) the right to demand retraction of unfounded press accusations or criticisms; 6) restriction of public access to files of periodicals and to books published in the past; 7) penalties for transmission of manuscripts from person to person; 8) the range of aesthetic diversity permitted in theater, fiction, journals of the arts and television; 9) publication of information which does not conform to the current policy of the party; 10) publication of commentaries criticizing governmental decisions and administrative measures.

The PICA survey also made no attempt to measure "responsibility" of the press. The word "responsibility" is so subjective as to defy definition or measurement. In fact, a press system that could score at the very top of the PICA scale would probably be a completely "irresponsible" press and would exist in a country that few individuals would care to live in. PICA was attempting to measure nations on a scale ranging from "absolute" freedom to "absolute" control, though it expected no country to reach either extreme.

In addition, PICA made no attempt to measure "stability." The stability of a country, it was felt, would become apparent as future measurements progress. The position of the United States, for example, is likely to change only a fraction between measurements. But some of the more mercurial Latin American countries could be high on the scale during one measurement and very low during the next.

Some criteria for measurement were not used in the PICA survey because they were considered less meaningful in practice, too difficult to assess or not pertinent enough to press freedom *within* a country by natives of that country. Some of these were: constitutional guarantees of press freedom, access to government records, treatment of foreign correspondents, the flow of foreign publications into a country, advertising influence as a press control and foreign ownership of press units.

Finally, there were three highly unusual and perhaps unique characteristics of the judging in the PICA survey. They were:

1. PICA attempted to use both native and non-native judges to rate a particular country. If the native judges differed from the non-

natives (mostly American foreign correspondents) by more than 6 per cent of the total points possible on the scale, the native scores were discarded and only the non-natives used.

2. PICA essentially used a different set of judges for each country. No person in the world is intimately familiar with the press systems of the more than 100 independent nations of the world; individual sets of judges were therefore necessary. For the most part, these included native newsmen in the country and foreign correspondents then living in the country. The overwhelming majority of the non-native judges was composed of Americans with news experience in the United States. It was believed that they would be judging each country by the American standard of press freedom.

3. PICA is what has been referred to as a "consensus index" rather than a poll based on a sample. The Center hoped to receive a minimum of four questionnaires (two native and two non-native) from each country. To attain this goal, the Center carefully selected its judges. They were reliable and experienced men and women, representing quality newspapers, periodicals, broadcast units, news agencies and universities throughout the world.

Exactly 1,003 questionnaires were mailed out between September, 1966, and March, 1967. Each judge was asked to score the nation on the basis of conditions in 1966 only. A total of 571 questionnaires, or 56.9 per cent, was returned. About 44 per cent of them came from native judges in 85 different countries. The remaining 56 per cent came from non-native judges.

On the basis of the questionnaires returned, the Center was able to assign a PICA score to 94 of the 115 independent nations of the world with populations of more than 1 million. The maximum score a country could receive was plus-4 and the lowest score a minus-4. Table I shows how this nine-point scale was divided into seven different classifications. It also shows the results of the PICA survey for 1966. The intermediate zone was called "transitional" because this writer hypothesized at the time of the survey that those countries falling into this zone would not be stationary, but would be in the process of moving toward more freedom or more control, and that such countries would be more likely to exhibit political change than countries falling in the other categories.

Of the 115 independent nations considered, 55 had "free" press systems. This represents some 1.5 billion people. A total of 29 countries had "controlled" press systems, representing 1.3 billion people; this was largely due to the Soviet Union's 230 million people and Communist China's 760 million people falling into this category. Ten countries, representing about 434 million people, were in the "transitional" zone.

According to the PICA survey, 45.2 per cent of earth's population was free in 1966, 39.2 per cent was not free and 13 per cent was somewhere in between, at least on the basis of their press systems. The 21 countries not ranked represented only 2.6 per cent of the world's population. Thirteen of those unrated countries were in Africa, four in the Middle East, two in Asia and two in the Western Hemisphere. All but the two in the Western Hemisphere have non-complex press systems and would have been simple to score and classify. But in many of them there are few native newsmen and no foreign correspondents.

A look at the distribution of countries, by regions, into the seven classifications (see Table II) shows the Western Hemisphere to have the highest degree of press freedom of all five regions. More than 96 per cent of the population of the Western Hemisphere lived under free press conditions in 1966.

Europe is greatly polarized, with 13 of its 25 nations falling into the top two levels and 7 in the bottom level. But because of the size of Russia, 55.3 per cent of the population of Europe lived under controlled press conditions and only 41.8 per cent was subject to a free press.[11]

In the Middle East, not one country could be ranked in the top level of press freedom, and the four unranked countries would surely have fallen into the controlled division if measured completely. This means that 72 per cent of the population is exposed to a controlled press, making the Middle East the most oppressive region of the world in regard to press freedom.

In Africa, the melancholy fact is that no country in that vast continent fell into either one of the top two levels of press freedom. Although almost half of the 28 nations in Africa (North African countries were classified with the Middle East) were unranked in the survey, they represented only 17.7 per cent of Africa's population, and there is little doubt that almost all of them would fall into the "transitional" or "controlled" areas. Only 26.5 per cent of Africa's population had a free press system, and fully 37 per cent was in the transitional area, hanging somewhere between freedom and control.

Asia had more countries in the "transitional" area than did any other section of the world, but this represented only 18.4 per cent of Asia's population. India, with a population of more than 471 million, fell into the free area, somewhat offsetting the weight of Communist China at the bottom of the scale.

Only one country outside of Asia and Africa fell into the "transitional" area—Yugoslavia.

The select 16 nations in the highest category of press freedom were all within a few percentage points of each other. The PICA scores for those nations ranged from 2.53 to 3.06, with even the highest scoring nations (Norway, Switzerland and The Netherlands) almost one full point

[11] A study of Czechoslovakia in 1968 probably would show that step-by-step liberalization of the press preceded or paralleled political liberalization up until the time of the five-nation invasion of that country in August, 1968.

TABLE I

DISTRIBUTION OF INDEPENDENT NATIONS INTO SEVEN CLASSIFICATIONS OF PRESS FREEDOM ACCORDING TO PICA SURVEY, 1966

FREE — HIGH DEGREE
(2.51 to 4.00)

* Australia	* Denmark	* The Neth-	* Philippines	* United
* Belgium	* Finland	erlands	* Sweden	States
* Canada	* Guatemala	* Norway	* Switzerland	Uruguay
Costa Rica		* Peru		* Venezuela

FREE — MODERATE CONTROLS
(1.51 to 2.50)

* Austria	Ecuador	Honduras	Jamaica	* Panama
* Bolivia	* El Salvador	* Ireland	* Japan	* Singapore
* Colombia	* France	(Erie)	* Malaysia	Turkey
* Cyprus	* West	* Israel	* New	* United
	Germany		Zealand	Kingdom

FREE — MANY CONTROLS
(0.51 to 1.50)

Argentina	* China	Kenya	Morocco	Thailand
* Brazil	(Taiwan)	Lebanon	* Rhodesia	Uganda
Ceylon	Dominican	Malawi	* South Africa	Zambia
* Chile	Rep.	* Mexico	Tanzania	
	* Greece			
	* India			

TRANSITIONAL
(-0.50 to 0.50)

* Burma	* Ghana	South	Nigeria	South
Congo	Indonesia	Korea	* Pakistan	Vietnam
(Kin.)		Laos		Yugoslavia

CONTROLLED — LOW DEGREE
(-0.51 to -1.50)

Afghanistan	Iran	Jordan	Portugal	* Tunisia
Cambodia	Iraq	* Nepal	Spain	

TABLE I (continued)

CONTROLLED — MEDIUM DEGREE
(-1.51 to -2.50)

Cameroon	Hungary	* Syria
Haiti	Senegal	U.A.R.

CONTROLLED — HIGH DEGREE
(-2.51 to -4.00)

Albania	Chad	Czecho-	North	U.S.S.R.
Algeria	China	slovakia	Korea	Upper Volta
Bulgaria	(Main-	Ethiopia	Poland	
	land)	East	Rumania	
	Cuba	Germany		

UNRANKED
(Insufficient Information)

Burundi	Ivory Coast	Mali	Rwanda	Sudan
Cent. Afr.	Liberia	Mongolia	Saudi	Togo
Rep.	Libya	Nicaragua	Arabia	North
Dahomey	Malagasy	Niger	Sierra Leone	Vietnam
Guinea	Rep.	Paraguay	Somalia	Yemen

* Represents agreement between native and non-native scores; these scores were within 6 per cent of each other and were averaged to give country this placement on scale. Countries without asterisks represent, except in very few instances, assessments of non-native judges only; this indicates that native and non-native scores differed by more than 6 per cent, or no native scores were received.

below the maximum plus-4 of "absolute freedom." Several communist countries (North Korea and Albania) were about one-half point from the other end of the continuum, indicating that a very high degree of control is more attainable than a very high degree of freedom.

There were several surprising aspects to the top category. One was that Guatemala and Venezuela were able to climb these heights. Guatemala, especially, had been on and off the Inter American Press Association's blacklist in prior years and even in 1966 had left-wing guerrillas in the hills. Even so, the score supported written reports that there had been a high degree of press freedom—for both leftists and rightists—since the inauguration of civilian President Julio Cesar Mendez Montenegro in mid-1966.

Another surprising aspect was that Japan, England and New Zealand

Table II

DISTRIBUTION OF INDEPENDENT NATIONS ON PICA SCALE
FOR EACH REGION OF THE WORLD, 1966

	West. Hem. (23) *	Europe (25)	Middle East (17)	Africa (28)	Asia (22)
FREE — High Degree	7	7			2
FREE — Moderate Controls	7	6	3		4
FREE — Many Controls	5	1	2	7	4
TRANSITIONAL		1		3	6
CONTROLLED — Low Degree		2	5		2
CONTROLLED — Medium Degree	1	1	2	2	
CONTROLLED — High Degree	1	7	1	3	2
Unranked	2		4	13	2

* Number of nations (with population more than one million) in region.

did not make the top category. Japan received a minus score only on the factor of concentrated ownership, but received consistently mediocre scores on many other factors. England received high scores on a number of factors, but negative scores on almost an equal number, notably libel laws, organized self-regulation, concentrated ownership, government control of foreign exchange and number of marginal press units. New Zealand received relatively poor scores on libel laws, local and regional criticism, and national criticism.

In general, the PICA findings agreed very closely with the results of Nixon and Banks and Textor. But like any tool of this nature, however, some of the specific findings had to be considered in the light of other conditions. India's press, for example, rates considerably higher in degree of criticism than its overall score would indicate. This would indicate that the press is overcoming a number of economic controls and disadvantages to pursue its role of vigorous criticism. On the other hand, South Africa and Rhodesia display characteristics of press freedom, while denying huge segments of the population access to the press or opportunities for democratic participation.

In addition to the specific findings regarding regions of the world and individual nations, the PICA survey indicated:

1) Press freedom can be measured and probably with a good degree of accuracy.[12]

2) The standards for judging press freedom are very similar in most countries of the world. In 77 countries, both native and non-native judges returned PICA questionnaires. In 57 per cent of those countries, the scores of the native judges were in substantial agreement with the scores of non-native judges.

3) No nation will long remain half free, either in relation to its press or in relation to its politics. Those countries in the intermediate or "transitional" zone are likely to show more press and political change than countries in other zones.

This third indication is worth looking at more closely, especially in respect to political occurrences that have taken place since the conclusion of the PICA survey. If one agrees that press freedom is closely bound up with democracy, in the Western sense, then one must pay special attention to the predictive capacity of a system for measuring press freedom. No one can look at the seven levels of the PICA survey without being struck by the fact that most of those countries lying within the top two levels and the bottom three levels are relatively stable political systems, while most of those in the third ("Free—Many Controls") and fourth ("Transitional") levels are relatively unstable.

The original hypothesis when the PICA results were published in 1967 was that those countries in the Transitional zone were likely to undergo sharp political change in the near future. But it is now apparent that the third level will bear close watching, also. Journalists interested in international communications could help political scientists by keeping a close lookout for subtle (and overt) press controls that may be instituted in nations falling within these two levels. Such controls are likely to presage political changes within the country, and the sweep of these political changes is likely to be in direct ratio to the severity of the press controls instituted.

The third level is the danger zone, the warning light of the press freedom (and democracy) scale. Many of the countries at this level are sitting on the edge of a volcano. Some of them are sitting quite solidly

---

[12] Using a slightly different methodology, PICA was updated in 1967. However, fewer countries were rated during the second survey. See "World Press Freedom, 1967," *Freedom of Information Center Publication No. 201*, University of Missouri, May 1968.

on the edge, in no immediate danger of falling into the crater, but they are still on the edge. Some might have inched slightly away from the edge and, hopefully, are moving toward greater democracy and political stability. But some are leaning the other way. Argentina and Brazil are in this category, and the slide toward political and economic chaos in those countries is supposedly being prevented only by the strong hand of the military. Other countries in this zone have maintained long-time stability by one-party governments (Taiwan, Kenya and Mexico, to mention only three), a delicate political balance (Lebanon) or outright subjugation of a majority within the political entity (South Africa and Rhodesia). Greece was rated in this third category late in 1966. In April, 1967, the military coup occurred, eliminating both press freedom (such remnant as remained) and democracy at the same time. Those countries in the third level rest uneasily.

Those in the fourth (or Transitional) zone leave no question about their instability. They are in the caldron already, more likely than not to be undergoing extreme civil strife. The swaying between press freedom and press control is a good indicator of the political chaos or uncertainty existing within most of these countries.

In 1966 the Congo (Kinshasa) was emerging, under military control, out of deep civil strife, Ghana was attempting to restore democracy after the Nkrumah years, Indonesia was only recently rid of Sukarno, South Korea was facing the increasing authoritarianism of a strongman leader, Laos was in the middle of an undeclared civil war, Nigeria was on the verge of a major tribal war, the two parts of Pakistan rumbled under Ayub Khan and South Vietnam was engaged in a civil war. Changes have occurred in many of these countries since 1966.

Yugoslavia has the type of stability that would not warrant its being in this category. It was at this level, however, because it had oddly come to rest at this half-way house between freedom and control, between the Soviet Communist system and the Western free press system. It is the exception to the hypothesis, and is unlikely to move very much in either direction in the near future.

Press freedom is an excellent political indicator. The PICA survey showed that there was a scientific way of measuring press freedom, and that it could be done with a great deal of accuracy. As it now stands, PICA is a far better indicator than predictor, because frequent measurements are necessary if one is to predict political motion and direction. The Freedom of Information Center has not yet been able to solve the financial or mechanical problems attached to this need for frequency.

The Center now plans to conduct a major press freedom study every five years. But the value of such a survey would be improved if the "predictive" element could be added by studying those countries falling within the third and fourth levels of PICA at more frequent intervals.

4

NATIONAL DEVELOPMENT AND MASS MEDIA

4

NATIONAL DEVELOPMENT

AND MASS MEDIA

STUDENTS of the mass media would be hard to find who would deny that a very close relationship exists between the socio-politico-economic development of a country and the degree to which its mass communication system has advanced. Many studies have been made in the last decade which have shown that the mass media and national development are interrelated. There does, however, remain some doubt as to *cause*; i.e., whether mass media reach a high degree of development in a generally highly developed society, or whether a progressive and rapidly expanding media system brings about general national development.

In spite of such "chicken-egg" questions, there is certainly general agreement that healthy mass media are found in well-developed societies. The degree of illiteracy of a nation undoubtedly plays an important part in determining not only the health of its mass media system but of its general progress. In the first article in this chapter, a well-known British scholar, Sir Charles Jeffries, describes the problem of illiteracy throughout the world generally. And it is interesting, in noting Wilbur Schramm's article on the distribution of the mass media throughout the world, to observe how closely mass media development is related to illiteracy.

Probably the key article in this chapter is the third one by John T. McNelly. A long-time student of mass media in the development process, especially in Latin America, McNelly presents four views of mass communication's development role. He seems to favor what he calls the *pragmatic* position, which he discusses in some detail, but the reader will note that he is very cautious in making any definite decisions as to *a single theory* of mass communication and national development.

In the last article of the chapter, Floyd Arpan presents his idea of a responsible press for new or emergent nations. He seems to favor for these developing nations a kind of press which is at the same time free and responsible, saying in fact that "intelligent planning of objectives and goals, rules of operation, codes of ethics, self-discipline, will go a long way towards winning the battle for a responsible press—unencumbered by restrictions." This is, of course, a large order for a new or emergent nation's press; it would even be for the press of a well-developed nation. But there is no reason why sights should not be set high and objectives made difficult.

Although, as was seen in the preceding chapter, there does seem to be the indication that press development (and national development) is positively correlated to the degree of freedom enjoyed by the press, there are a few notable exceptions: e.g., the Soviet Union and several of the Eastern European nations. In these nations, with a controlled press, the press is well-developed, to be sure; but it may simply be that the Capitalist view of press development is quite different from the Communist view. This would be worth investigation.

* * * *

RELATED READING

Doob, Leonard W. *Communication in Africa*. New Haven: Yale University Press, 1961.

Houn, Franklin W. *To Change a Nation*. Glencoe, Ill.: Free Press, 1961.

Lerner, Daniel. *The Passing of Traditional Society*. London: Collier-Macmillan Ltd., 1958.

Mass Media in the Developing Countries. ("Reports and Papers on Mass Communication," No. 33), Paris: UNESCO, 1961.

Prakke, H. J. *Publizist und Publikum in Africa*. Cologne: Verlag Deutscher Wirtschaftsdienst, GmbH, 1962.

Pye, Lucian W. (ed.). *Communications and Political Development*. Princeton: Princeton University Press, 1963.

Schramm, Wilbur. *Mass Media and National Development*. Stanford: Stanford University Press, 1964.

Sommerlad, E. Lloyd. *The Press in Developing Countries*. Sydney, Australia: Sydney University Press, 1966.

Sir Charles Jeffries:

The World's Map of Illiteracy

IN ANY modern, civilised society, reading and writing are taken for granted as indispensable elements in a person's equipment for living. Children are taught to read and write at the earliest possible age, for the rest of their education depends on their possession of the skill of literacy. The whole social, political and economic structure of the modern community rests on the assumption that every citizen can communicate, and be communicated with by means of the written or printed word.

Yet this is a comparatively recent development in human history; and it affects, so far, only certain limited areas of the world. Some two-fifths of the world's adult population—at least 700 million men and women—cannot, at the present time, read or write.[1] Moreover, these "illiterates" are not evenly spread about the world but are, for the most part, concentrated in particular areas and countries. A study of the statistics prepared by UNESCO shows, at one end of the scale, a well-defined group of countries (including the United States, the Soviet Union, most of the European countries, Canada, Australia, New Zealand and Japan) in which the percentage of illiteracy is insignificant; and, at the other end, a group (including most of the countries of Africa and Asia, and several of those in Latin America) in which at least half—and in many cases more than three-quarters—of the adult population are classifiable as illiterate.[2]

No country or community can claim to have a population which is permanently and completely literate. Leaving infants aside, there are always, even in the most sophisticated and highly organised societies, the odd individuals who, on account of mental deficiency or some exceptional deprivation of opportunity, have never learned or, if they have learned, have forgotten how to read and write. In "advanced" societies illiteracy, as such, does not constitute a problem and they can be left out of account

[1] "Adult" in this connection, usually means "aged fifteen or over."
[2] *World Illiteracy at Mid-Century: A Statistical Study*, Monographs on Fundamental Education No. xi, Paris: UNESCO 1957.

for the purpose of the present discussion. In the statistics of illiteracy published by UNESCO in 1965 it was decided to exclude "countries or territories in which the illiteracy rate among the population aged fifteen and over was estimated at less than 5 per cent in the last census or literacy survey. This particularly applies to most European countries, the USSR, the USA, Canada, Australia, New Zealand, Japan, Argentina and Cuba." [3]

Percentages, however, always a tricky business, are never more so than in this matter of illiteracy. They may fairly be accepted as guides at the extreme ends of the scale. If we exclude from consideration countries with less than 5 per cent of illiteracy, we may reasonably regard countries with more than, say, 50 per cent as having a problem of illiteracy on their hands; and the higher the percentage the more serious and intractable the problem is likely to be. Looked at from another point of view, we may fairly say that, irrespective of percentages, any government which has more than 5 million adult illiterates in its population has an illiteracy problem. Such governments include those of Afghanistan, Brazil, China, Egypt, Ethiopia, India, Indonesia, Iran, Korea, Nigeria, Pakistan, Tanzania, Turkey and the Republic of Vietnam.

From a statistical point of view, the selection of "countries or territories" as the units for consideration is no doubt very unsatisfactory. Countries vary greatly in size and in population. The criteria adopted by different governments for estimating the extent of illiteracy also vary widely; so does the expertness of the census-takers who have to apply the criteria. A given percentage of illiteracy as stated in the records may mean one thing in one country and something rather different in another. The larger the country concerned, the less reliable the national figure may be as indicating the presence or absence of a problem of illiteracy. As the UNESCO document already referred to points out, a national average may conceal the existence of definite social groups perhaps contained within specific areas. For example, it might be found on examination that in a particular country with an apparently low illiteracy rate, the literates were in fact mainly concentrated in one or more urban centres, while the rural populations were almost completely illiterate.

Nevertheless, from a practical point of view, the question has to be considered in terms of "countries or territories"—in other words, areas controlled by separate governments. Today most of these separate governments are internationally recognised as of sovereign status, but there remain a few which are dependent on one or other of the major powers, yet are distinct and identifiable geographical and administrative entities. Wherever a problem of illiteracy exists, it is the government responsible for that place which has to deal with it, whether on its own account or

[3] Minedlit 5: *Statistics of Illiteracy*, UNESCO memorandum for the Teheran Conference, 1965, p. 2.

with help from outside as it, and it alone, may decide. While, therefore, a breakdown of illiteracy statistics according to geographical regions, races, religions or other possible divisions, may be valuable for particular purposes, what one really needs to know is which governments have an illiteracy problem on their hands and what is being or can be done about it by that government.

The basic material for studying the distribution of illiteracy is contained in the UNESCO publication *World Illiteracy at Mid-Century*, a statistical survey published in 1957. This embodies the results of earlier official and unofficial studies and gives as complete a picture as was practicable of the situation in every country of the world round about 1950. It was supplemented in 1965 by a document, *Statistics of Illiteracy*, prepared by UNESCO for the World Congress of Ministers of Education on the Eradication of Illiteracy which was held at Teheran in September of that year. This is necessarily a less complete survey than that of 1957, but it provides information, broken down into age-groups and sexes, of the position reached in 1962 in most of the countries in which illiteracy constitutes a problem.

Taking the world as a whole, the accepted figure . . . for the number of adult illiterates existing in 1950 is about 700 million, representing between 40 and 45 per cent of the world's adult population at that time. But, "taking the large number of semi-illiterates into account, people are saving with increasing frequency (at international meetings, in scientific circles, in many books and periodicals, etc.) that our world is 'a world of a thousand million illiterates.'" [4] Comparison of the 1962 figures with those of 1950 shows that, while in the interval the *percentage* of illiterates in the world population had slightly diminished from 40-45 to 38-43, the *absolute* number of adult illiterates had actually increased with the growth of the world population. There were, in UNESCO's member states, nearly 35 million more illiterates in 1962 than in 1950, despite all the work that had been done by national and international effort to deal with the problem during those twelve years. A breakdown of the illiteracy figures by continental areas gives the following results, which are based on a large number of assumptions and cannot, therefore, be regarded as fully reliable; but they are acceptable as a rough guide. Such a table is of some value as showing where most of the major areas of illiteracy will be found, but clearly further analysis is necessary. Europe cannot, as such figures would suggest, be entirely ruled out of account as an area where there are no illiteracy problems. It is, however, fair to say that, where relatively high percentages exist—as, for example, in Portugal, Greece, Yugoslavia, Bulgaria, Rumania, Malta—they may be considered as indicating short-term rather than long-

[4] Minedlit 3: *Literacy as a Factor in Development,* UNESCO memorandum for the Teheran Confernce, 1965, p. 8.

ILLITERACY PERCENTAGES BY CONTINENTAL AREAS[5]

	1950	1962
Africa	80-85	78-84
America, North and South	20-21	18-20
Arab countries	82-87	78-82
Asia and Oceania	67-71	53-57
Europe and Soviet Union	6-10	3-7

term problems, which can and doubtless will be dealt with by expansion and improvement of existing machinery for child and adult education in the countries concerned.

The figure for the American continent, again, is an average which is brought down by the very low illiteracy rate of that half of the population which lives in the United States and Canada. In fact, some of the countries of Central and South America and the Caribbean are among those in which the most serious problems of illiteracy are present. In Asia, on the other hand, Japan and Israel are almost alone in showing anything like a low proportion of illiterates, while in Africa there is no country (leaving aside the little island of St. Helena) in which less than half the adult population were classed in 1950 as illiterate, and in most of the countries the illiteracy percentage was anything from 75 to 99. The 1962 figures did not indicate any significant change in this general picture.

Passing from percentages to numbers, the official estimate of the position in 1962 was that, in the age-group fifteen to forty-four, which covers the most active section of the population, there were 94 million illiterates in Africa, 243 million in Asia, 34 million in America, and 9 million in Europe.[6]

A map of illiteracy would, therefore, show the black spots mainly grouped in certain well-defined areas: the whole of Africa; the whole of Asia (excluding the Soviet Union), with a few exceptions in relatively small geographical areas, notably Japan; the islands of the Pacific, again with a few exceptions; Central and Southern America and the Caribbean, excepting Argentina, Uruguay, the Panama Canal Zone, and some of the islands, and with a question mark concerning some other islands and some of the smaller republics. Each of these large areas includes countries differing widely in size, constitution, natural resources and historical background. To make out a complete list here would be tedious for the reader and would merely reproduce the information available in the UNESCO documents already referred to. There may, however, be some

[5] Minedlit 5, p. 7.
[6] Minedlit 3, p. 8.

advantage in taking a brief look at each region and noting some of the salient points.

The heading "Africa" covers some fifty or more separate administrative units, ranging in size from Egypt and Nigeria, with populations of well over 20 million each and formidable illiteracy figures, to the island of St. Helena with a population of 5,000 and no adult illiteracy. North and east of the Sahara desert are the African Arab states—Morocco, Algeria, Tunisia, Libya, Sudan, Egypt—whose long history of contact with oriental and occidental cultures has yet not saved them from having very high illiteracy rates. South of the Zambesi are South Africa and Rhodesia, with their special racial problems; South-West Africa; part of Mozambique, subject to the government of Portugal; and Lesotho (Basutoland), Botswana (Bechuanaland) and Swaziland, former British territories just emerging to independence. Off the coast is the great island of Madagascar, formerly part of the French colonial empire. If this were not diversity enough, there are the countries in the great land mass stretching from the Sahara to the Zambesi. It includes the ancient empire of Ethiopia; the old-established independent state of Liberia; the newly enfranchised countries which ten years ago were ruled by Britain, France and Belgium; and Angola still ruled by Portugal. Here are some twenty governments, all of which face an enormous and baffling problem of illiteracy.

The Asian picture is no less complex. The Chinese People's Republic contains at least 600 million people. Detailed information about the régime's efforts to overcome illiteracy is scanty, but there can be no doubt that great strides have been made in recent years. The prominence given to the writings of Chairman Mao Tse-tung in the "cultural revolution" of 1966-67 presupposes that these writings can be read by a wide public. Thirty million copies are said to have been produced for circulation in this connection. Posters and wall newspapers appear in profusion in streets and factories. Kurt Mendelssohn, who visited China in September 1966, found evidence of "a new high degree of literacy." [7] While, therefore, the estimated rate of illiteracy at mid-century was 50 per cent, it may well now be considerably less. India and Pakistan contain another 500 million or more people and have serious problems of illiteracy which they are striving to tackle by national effort. Ceylon, Burma, Malaysia and Indonesia all face the problem in varying degrees. So do the Arab states, Iran, Turkey, Thailand and Korea. In all, Asia is held to be the home of three-quarters of the world's illiterates. The islands of the Pacific cannot offer anything to compare with these numbers, but they comprise some twenty separate administrative units, ranging in population from a million or so (New Guinea and the British Solomon Islands) to one or two thousand,

[7] Mendelssohn, Kurt, "China's Cultural Revolution," *The Listener*, London, December 8, 1966.

and in almost all the percentages of illiteracy is high. The kingdom of Tonga is an honourable exception.

The countries of Central and South America show sharp contrasts. To some extent these are connected with the racial composition of the populations. Where a large proportion of the people is of European or part-European descent, the rate of illiteracy tends to be lower than where the majority is of indigenous origin. Thus, in Ecuador, where the illiteracy rate for the whole country is estimated at between 40 and 50 per cent, the rate for the Indian group (nearly a third of the population) is as much as 90 per cent.[8] These countries have, however, one advantage over those of Africa and Asia in that the Spanish and Portuguese languages cover the great part of the subcontinent, though some of the Indian vernaculars are still very much alive. Of the Caribbean islands it may be said that—apart from Cuba, which is not now classed as an "area of illiteracy," and Haiti, where the illiteracy percentage is something like 90 per cent and where 85 per cent of the population speak a language not yet reduced to writing [9]—the average percentage is now round about 25 per cent, variations again being due to differences of history, racial composition and geographical situation. Generally speaking, there has been steady progress in the Caribbean area during the last half-century in reducing the rate of illiteracy by the development of educational services, more particularly for girls. In the Jamaican census of 1943, the female rate was actually lower than the male, which is an unusual situation.[10]

It is beyond question that the establishment of universal illiteracy would enormously increase the human resources available for scientific and intellectual as well as economic progress. It would greatly improve the prospect of finding solutions to the problems arising from the growth in the world population. It might even affect that growth, for the undoubted statistical connection between population increase and low standard of living may also indicate a connection with a high rate of illiteracy. At any rate, it is a fact—coincidental or not—that, leaving out of account changes in population due to migration, the rise in numbers in countries with a low illiteracy rate tends to be appreciably slower than in those with a high illiteracy rate.

[8] Annual Report of the British and Foreign Bible Society, London 1963, p. 72.
[9] *Population Profile*, Population Reference Bureau Inc., Washington, D.C., September 26, 1966, p. 3.
[10] *World Illiteracy . . .*, p. 130.

Wilbur Schramm:

World Distribution of the Mass Media

WE HAVE BEEN speaking of the transition to modern communication as though it were a certainty. And, indeed, it is a certainty, barring some unforeseen event that would reverse the direction of economic and social development. The question we are considering in these pages is not *whether* the mass media will ultimately come into wide use in the developing countries as channels of information and education, but rather whether their introduction should be *hurried* so that they can do more than they are doing at present to contribute to national development.

The mass media have a particular importance at this point in history. They are the great multipliers. Just as the machines of the Industrial Revolution are able to multiply human power with other kinds of energy, so are the communicating machines of the Communication Revolution able to multiply human messages to a degree previously unheard of.

The presence of mass media makes a significant difference in the level of information *even among people who are unable to read the printed media and do not have access to the electronic media.* The fortuitous fact about the relation of information to national development is that mass communication should be available and well developed, and its use relatively well understood, when so many new countries are trying to communicate so much so quickly to so many people.

Mass communication, throughout its entire history, has been effective in combating privilege. The significance of the development of printing in the fifteenth century was not only to swing the balance from the long centuries of spoken firsthand communication toward visual and secondhand communication on a grand scale, but, more important, to extend learning beyond a privileged handful. Almost at once, the printed media became tools of political and social change. The revolutions in Europe and North America would have been most unlikely without the printed media. The development of public schools would have been most unlikely, if not impossible, without the printed media. In the nineteenth century, new developments in mass communication reached over the heads of the specially privileged and the specially educated to offer information and

▶ From: *Mass Media and National Development*, by Wilbur Schramm. Copyright © 1964 by UNESCO, Paris. Reprinted by permission of the publisher.

education to the great masses of men. Political democracy, economic opportunity, free public education, the Industrial Revolution, and mass communication were all woven together to make a great change in human life and society on several continents. Now the new electronic developments in communication have swung the balance back toward communication in which one can see and hear the communicator. They have given the developing countries potential channels of information with which to reach fantastically large audiences, to communicate with underprivileged masses despite the literacy barrier, to teach difficult skills by "showing how" they are done, to speak almost with the effectiveness of face-to-face communication.

It may well be that mass communication (and the interpersonal communication we have learned to combine with it) are about to play a key part in the greatest social revolution of all time—the economic and social uplift of two-thirds of the world's people. We are not implying that mass communication can do it alone. Without determined national leadership, adequate population and resources, and sources of capital, the most efficient communication system in the world could not bring about economic development. But this at least we can say with confidence: if the mass media or some equally potent and rapid means of information were not available, it would be utterly impossible to think of national economic and social development in terms of the timetables that are being attached to such development today.

Let us therefore see how widely available the mass media are for such use in the developing countries. Where are the facilities adequate, and where are they in short supply, for the battle of development? What is the rate of growth of these media, and what are the conditions under which they grow or lag?

The Haves and Have-Nots

Let us not harbor any delusion that the mass media are alike in all the underdeveloped countries. Quite the contrary: there is a great and sometimes astonishing variety. The media systems are as different from each other as the countries themselves. For example, in seven African countries there is no daily press except roneotyped bulletins from a government information service, and in 15 African countries there are no daily newspapers of any kind. On the other hand, throughout Latin America the press is well developed in both large and small cities. Despite lagging national economies, a highly sophisticated daily press has emerged—one example out of many is Chile. In some underdeveloped countries—Mauritania, for example—it is necessary because of lack of printing facilities to have such periodicals as exist printed outside the country. In other underdeveloped countries, like India, the printing industry is highly developed and equipped to publish in a number of languages and a variety of technical subject matters. In some countries the whole broadcasting operation depends on an ancient transmitter held together only by loving care and constant maintenance. In some almost equally underdeveloped countries, the radio stations are shining with new equipment. The writer has been in a country where the breakdown of a single projector, and the difficulty of getting someone to repair it, eliminated for months a large part of the total capability of the country for showing educational films, and in another underdeveloped country where one educational center had been given a quarter-million dollars' worth of audiovisual equipment.

Thus there is no single pattern. But as one moves from country to country one becomes aware of a condition that is more often the rule than the exception in developing countries. This is the condition of scarcity.

We can sum up the distribution of mass communication throughout the world:

1. In every respect except film making, Latin America is somewhat further developed in communication than either Asia or Africa. This is most notably true of radio and television, but also holds in the case of newspapers: per capita circulation in South America is twice what it is in Asia, and six times as much as in Africa. The busy Asian studios outproduce those of South America, but the annual attendance per person is greater in South America than in either Asia or Africa.

2. The underdeveloped regions of the world are moving along impressively toward meeting the Unesco minima in radio. The rate of growth in radio will take both Asia and Africa over the Unesco standards within a relatively few years. South America has already passed the minimum. It seems apparent that the less-developed lands are planning to depend chiefly on radio to reach their scattered and largely illiterate populations.

3. The underdeveloped regions are lagging in newspaper development. This is probably related to the development of literacy and education; and when the growth is sufficient in those two areas, we can expect faster growth in newspaper circulation.

4. But all these differences are overshadowed by the great overall difference between the parts of the world where economic development is far along and the parts where it is not. It is the same order of difference we have noted earlier, in comparisons of life expectancy, productivity, industrialization, income, and the like, and here the discrepancies are fully as spectacular as the earlier ones. In every respect, the peoples of Africa, Asia, and Latin America are have-not people in mass communication. Latin America does very well in newspapers and radio, it is true, but is still below well-developed regions, and it lags, despite its widely used common languages, in forming news agencies. The band of scarcity is no illusion. This is what Unesco was talking about when it spoke of "a dearth

of facilities over wide regions of the globe [which] prevents hundreds of millions of people from effectively enjoying freedom of information.*

The Media in the Developing Countries

Not all the differences between mass communication in the developing and the highly developed countries are quantitative ones.

One of the first things one notices about mass communication in underdeveloped countries is how the media cluster in the cities. To some extent, of course, this is true everywhere. In highly developed as well as underdeveloped countries, the newspapers, broadcasting stations, and film theaters tend to be where the concentrations of people are. But in highly developed countries, the majority of people live in urban settings; in a typical underdeveloped country 80 per cent of the people live in rural settings. Therefore, if the media concentrate on urban centers in developing countries they are really concentrating on a *minority* of the people.

To a lesser extent, radio and films also cluster in the cities. One would expect to find the studios and transmitters in the cities, of course, but one might hope to find in the rural regions a larger proportion of the radio receivers (inasmuch as radio can cover great distances) and a larger proportion of the film attendance (inasmuch as films, like radio, can jump the literacy barrier). But actually only a little more than one in ten of India's radio receivers, to take one example, are in the villages, where the rural four-fifths of India's people live, and the bulk of cinema attendance is likewise in the cities. It is spectacular in many developing countries to see the signs of the media all but vanish at the borders of the cities. One can read the morning papers in his hotel, see the young people stroll past his window carrying transistor radios, see the advertisement for the current movie across the street; then drive out of the city to spend the day in the villages, and probably see not a single newspaper, radio receiver, or film theater all day.

Why should this be? One reason is the inordinate difficulty of circulation. The newspapers have to combat inadequate roads, washouts in the rainy season, inadequate postal services. Radio and films face a lack of electricity in the villages, and lack of technically trained personnel outside the cities to repair receivers or operate film showings. In more than one country, a well-meant plan to extend the coverage of radio has failed simply because there was no one to recharge or replace a battery in an otherwise operable receiving set.

Literacy too drops off at the edge of the cities. In the cities there are concentrations of literates, even though the overall percentage may not be very high. But a village may have no more than one or two persons able and willing to read a newspaper. Serving such minuscule audiences makes an obviously difficult circulation problem.

* UNESCO, *Mass Media in Developing Countries,* Paris: UNESCO, 1961.

Money for mass media is harder to come by in subsistence economies and in the village. A villager in Burma or Malaya will be investing a sizable part of his annual cash income if he subscribes to a magazine. By the same token, a radio is a major purchase in a village. If Unesco's long-pursued goal of a five-dollar radio could be realized, it would make a considerable difference in the circulation of radio in the rural regions of developing countries.

Still another reason for impeded circulation is the language problem. The existence of Spanish (and in Brazil, Portuguese) as lingua franca may be one of the key reasons why the press has developed faster and more fully in Latin America than in Africa or Asia. Some of the language problems facing the media in Africa and Asia are fantastic. India is the classical example: 14 states with their own languages, 72 different languages spoken by at least 100,000 persons each, a national radio system that can hardly ever broadcast nationally, national wire news services that must be translated for each of the vernacular newspapers, government agricultural and community development information that must be either decentralized or translated at each state or district level.

Low circulations make for financial difficulties. When theaters are few and admission small, a developing country finds it hard to make films. In some South Asian countries, exhibitors calculate that films must run six or seven weeks at each theater in order to make a profit. Newspapers in developing countries often face a cruel financial struggle. The Unesco conferences on development of the mass media reported that only a small percentage of the papers were in sound financial position.

Newsprint costs more outside the great cities. Because of shortages of capital and foreign exchange, the smaller papers often have trouble making long-term agreements for purchase of newsprint, and therefore may have to pay premiums on prices that are already higher than their city competition pays.

News agency costs are proportionally higher on a small daily, and, if it is a local-language daily, the cost of translation must be added to the fee for the wire service. But if there is no wire news, the paper is not doing the job it should do, and is less attractive to subscribers.

Furthermore, in some countries even the wastepaper value of a newspaper is something that purchasers or subscribers take into account. They can subtract from the price of the paper the money they receive from selling the used copy. This, too, makes life harder for the smaller paper. The less advertising it has, the fewer pages it can print, and the less it will be worth as wastepaper to the subscribers.

Suppose the paper does get its head above water. Suppose it is so successful that its circulation, after three years, rises above 10,000. This is too many papers for a flat-bed and cylinder press; another press is needed. The paper faces a staggering outlay of capital if it is to grow larger—$40,000 or so for a rotary press.

Thus, although a new paper can be started inexpensively, it finds it hard to keep going and hard to grow.

Something of a phenomenon, in view of the cost problems, is the introduction of television into so many developing countries. Television is the most costly of the media to capitalize, and it requires perhaps a wider diversity of skills than any other medium. Its receiving sets are expensive, compared with radio, and repairs are more difficult and costly. Some new nations have introduced television chiefly as an aid to their educational systems; others, apparently, because television has prestige. We do not mean to imply that the introduction of television may not be economically desirable; indeed, [in some] situations it may save money as well as contribute to the speed of development. But in many places it contrasts oddly with the communication shortages one sees on every hand: shortages in machinery and technical personnel, raw film, newsprint, trained management and editorial personnel, and research.

Yet, despite the shortages, the machinery runs. Communication flows. One reason why the system works better than might be expected is that the common and traditional channels of communication are pressed into use to extend the new media. Not every country has a communication device so spectacular as the Yoruba talking drums, and yet almost every developing country has the custom of reading the newspaper to illiterates —in the coffee houses, the village square, the schoolhouse, or any other place where people congregate. Institutions like the bazaar, where for centuries people have exchanged information, now serve to carry information first planted by the mass media. Where the mass media cannot readily reach, the puppet shows, storytellers, poets, ballad singers, and dramatic groups carry some of the same information and persuasion. Radio listening and discussion groups are formed around some of the radio receivers. Leaders of many of these countries have learned to use very large public meetings with great skill, and, indeed, the crowd at a meeting may be more numerous than the readers of the local newspaper, or the listeners to a speech on the radio. Thus we must not think of the media in a developing country as standing by themselves. They fit into the larger communication system of the country; and the drums, the bazaars, the meetings, and the ballad singers all help to carry the word.

And yet, one comes away from a developing country worrying that the media numbers are so small, the coverage is inadequate, the rural targets are not being reached, the media are not being integrated fully enough with interpersonal organizations and communications. This is true, as we have said, in some places and some media more than others. In Asia, although there is usually too little chance to see films, there is a remarkable amount of film making. In Latin America, the press is well developed, and radio coverage is more extensive than in either Asia or Africa. But there is still not enough development of the media, not enough integration with the interpersonal channels, not skillful enough or general enough use to let mass communication do the job it is capable of doing.

Summary

We can sum up very briefly. The less-developed countries have less-developed mass communication systems also, and less development in the services that support the growth of mass communication. Their systems are underfinanced and underequipped, and as a result the flow of information is much less than it could be. However, there is an encouraging rate of growth throughout the developing regions, both in the mass media and in their supporting services. The question is whether it is fast enough for countries in a hurry.

Perhaps the best way to evaluate these growth rates is to calculate how long it would take the underdeveloped countries on two of the less-developed continents to reach the Unesco minima—ten copies of daily newspapers, five radio receivers, two cinema seats for every 100 persons—at their 1950-62 average rate of growth. This we have calculated,* using 1962 figures as a baseline and taking the average annual growth rate through the period as the angle of projection. If they continue to grow at this rate, it then follows that

—To reach the standard of ten copies of daily newspapers for each 100 persons would take Africa until 2035, Asia until 1992;
—To reach the standard of five radio receivers for each 100 persons would take Africa until 1968, Asia until 1970;
—To reach the standard of two cinema seats for each 100 persons would take Africa until 2042, Asia until 1981.

Is that too long? Certainly it seems an inordinately long time for Africa and Asia, at least, to wait. Of course, in making the estimate we have assumed a steady rate of growth. This may not prove to be the case. It may well be that at a certain point in the growth of literacy and education, the circulation of newspapers will rise faster, or that, at a certain point in the progress of electrification, there will be a swifter growth of cinemas. It may also be that a decrease in the rate of population growth will occur and make the per capita figures look better. This we can hope for. But the picture points to the importance of radio in the decade ahead, and calls for increased efforts to speed the growth of the other media and their supporting services. Countries in a hurry can hardly be expected to be satisfied that—at the 1950-62 rate of development—Asia would not reach Unesco minima for daily newspaper circulation until nearly the end of the century, and Africa not for 70 years!

* This estimate has been made by using the same formula as for compound interest, $A = P(1 + r)^n$, in which A is the amount to be attained at a given future time, P is the present amount, r is the rate of growth compounded annually, and n is the number of years.

John T. McNelly:

Mass Communication in the Development Process

It is too early yet to expect any full-blown theories of role of mass communication in the development of nations. But several points of view or positions have begun to emerge in this burgeoning field, depending in large part on the professional or academic backgrounds of those who hold them.

This paper will be devoted to a discussion of four general positions which have become discernible. Special attention will be focused on the fourth position in the light of a number of studies.

The Null Position

The first view of mass communication's development role is that it is of little or no significance. This might be called the *null* position. It is implied, if not overtly expressed, in the writings and discussions of development planners as well as in the non-Communist developing countries where, as Pool has pointed out, great importance generally is attached to literacy and the education of children but little importance to mass media. There also has been a tendency among many devolopment planners to assume that the really important factors in development are economic in essence: that other factors such as education, cultural advancement, political stability, and mass communication are either irrelevant or sort of "tag along" with economic development. Officials in some developing countries even suspect that mass communication can retard national progress by distracting the citizenry's attention from constructive matters toward frivolity or disruptive political or social agitation.[1]

But the *null* position becomes difficult to defend in the face of mounting evidence of relationships between mass media development and a wide range of economic, social and political variables.[2] While such studies,

[1] Ithiel de Sola Pool, "The Mass Media and Politics in the Modernization Process," in Lucian W. Pye, ed., *Communications and Political Development* (Princeton, N.J.: Princeton University Press, 1963), pp. 234-36. Cf. Pye, "Introduction," in Pye, ed., *op. cit.*, p. 15.
[2] Many studies of such relationships, using aggregate data from large numbers of countries, have followed the lead of Daniel Lerner's "Communication Systems and Social

► From: David K. Berlo, ed., *Mass Communication and the Development of Nations*, East Lansing: International Communication Institute, Michigan State University, 1968. Reprinted by permission of the author and publisher.

based on correlations, do not necessarily establish direction of causality, the data suggest that mass communication is both a cause and an effect of the development process.

Consideration of the development role of mass communication has received increasing impetus in recent years from representatives of a number of social science disciplines. Unesco reports to the United Nations have gone so far as to recommend that governments of the underdeveloped countries consider formulating national programs for development of the media as part of their planning for economic development.

The Enthusiastic Position

From this kind of recognition of mass communication's role in the development process it is possible to move to rather strong statements of the importance of that role. Assemblages of media, government and academic people gathered under Unesco auspices in developing regions of the world have been exposed to declarations which assign to the mass media a decisive role in humanity's search for peace and progress in every sphere of activity.[3] From statements of the media's important role it is not a very long leap to rather sweeping claims that sometimes can be heard in the euphoric atmosphere of gatherings of media professionals about the potential of mass communication as a sort of magic key to the whole development process. This might be called the *enthusiastic*—or as some might prefer to call it, the *oversold*—position. It can be a tempting one for journalists, statesmen and others impressed with the potency of the printed and electronic media.[4]

The Cautious Position

But the studies already mentioned on the interrelationships between mass media growth and other aspects of the development process should caution us that on one aspect is all-important. And of course the literature of communication is full of studies which caution that mass communication is not omnipotent: that the dissemination of messages by the media does not assure attention, learning, attitude change, or action, that social and cultural factors can mediate, muffle or even nullify media messages.

The limitations of the mass media can become particularly apparent in less developed countries. Language and literacy barriers, geographical

Systems: A Statistical Exploration in History and Policy," *Behavioral Science*, Vol. 2 (Oct. 1957), pp. 266-75.

[3] Unesco, *Los Medios de Información en América Latina* (Paris: Unesco, 1961), p. 7; Unesco, *Developing Mass Media in Asia* (Paris: Unesco, 1960), p. 5.

[4] President Nasser of Egypt is quoted by Lerner as seeing vast possibilities for radio as a means of leaping the literacy barrier: "Today people in the most remote villages hear what is happening everywhere and form their opinions. . . . We live in a new world." Lerner, *op. cit.*, p. 274.

isolation, entrenched local habits and poverty are among the problems of which both communicators and researchers in those countries are painfully aware. Indeed, some have despaired of even achieving direct *mass* communication in the near future over vast reaches of Asia, Africa and Latin America. They are willing instead to settle for media contacts only with relatively small elite groups or opinion leaders, who presumably can pass the word along to the masses.

This is, of course, an application of the two-step flow hypothesis, which has found ready acceptance among social scientists working abroad. But whereas, on the basis of an election campaign in Ohio, Lazarsfeld and his colleagues originally suggested that ideas *often* seem to flow from the media to opinion leaders and from them to the general public,[5] the hypothesis has evolved into a virtual doctrine in the course of its diffusion through several generations of graduate seminars to distant frontiers of social research.

This view that the media can (or should) reach the masses only indirectly through the good offices of opinion leaders or other interpersonal mediators might be labeled the *cautious* position on the development role of mass communication. This position places a heavy responsibility indeed on the shoulders of opinion leaders, wherever they may be and however they may be identified. It attempts to predict the flow pattern of information and ideas under a staggering variety of possible conditions involving diverse types of messages, topics, audiences, and cultural environments.

The empirical base of the two-step flow hypothesis in its quasi-doctrinal form, however, is being undermined both in our own and in developing cultures. Various news diffusion studies, for example, have shown that the mass media often inform vast proportions of the public directly without inter-personal mediation.[6] There is also evidence that much face-to-face communication on given topics takes place after the persons involved have received information on topics directly from the media.[7]

With respect to the diffusion of innovations, Rogers has criticized the two-step hypothesis on the grounds that neither its originators nor most of the later students of the idea "seem to have taken into account the relative importance of the communication sources at different stages in the adoption process." He suggests that perhaps the majority of individuals utilize the mass media in their awareness stage, and that interpersonal

[5] Elihu Katz and Paul F. Lazarsfeld, *Personal Influence* (Glencoe, Ill.: Free Press, 1955), p. 32.
[6] These studies are cited in Richard W. Budd, Malcolm S. MacLean Jr. and Arthur M. Barnes, "Regularities in the Diffusion of Two Major News Events," *Journalism Quarterly*, Vol. 43, No. 2 (1966), pp. 221-230.
[7] See Verling C. Troldahl and Robert Van Dam, "Face-to-Face Communication About Major Topics in the News," *Public Opinion Quarterly*, Vol. 29, No. 4 (Winter 1965-66), pp. 626-634.

communication is important for the majority of adoptors in the evaluation stage.[8] In this and other countries—and across different types of situations and topics—the two-step flow hypothesis has appeared increasingly in recent years to be an over-simplication of a complex process.

The Pragmatic Position

There seems to be an increasing recognition that we do not have yet, nor can expect to have in the near future, any one adequate theory to predict the nature of the flow of information or influence for all kinds of messages through all kinds of media to all kinds of audiences under all kinds of conditions in all kinds of developing countries.[9] The tendency seems to be, in view of this, to adopt what might be called a *pragmatic* position on the role of mass communication in development. For communication strategists this position says in effect, with respect to new types or combinations of messages or channels, "Try it and see if it works." For researchers this position implies a disposition to seek empirical evidence in the field uninhibited by rigid assumptions; to accept evidence on the effects of mass communication in other cultures even though it may be out of harmony with seemingly well-established theoretical models.

Thus, while the two-step flow may be—and in fact often is—found to be operating in a developing society, there seems to be a trend among researchers to look further into the complexity and variety of the mass communication process. The possibility appears that in the same situation in which a two-step flow carries ideas to some individuals, a flow of more than two steps may operate for others—through various opinion leaders, or to innovators first and through them to opinion leaders; or that in some cases messages may flow in just one step directly from the media to the masses; or that some other pattern or combination of patterns may be at work. The tendency seems to be to recognize mass communication in developing societies as a multi-step, multi-directional process with possibilities of immediate or long-range, simple or subtle effects. Within this process are sought regularities and patterns which may permit generalizations and hypotheses in the absence of a complete theoretical scheme.

The pragmatic position is reflected in a variety of studies in various developing areas of the world. Only a few will be cited here. But first it may be useful to refer to an investigation done in a relatively advanced country.

In a study of farmers in Holland, Van Den Ban found communication about new agricultural methods to be considerably more complicated

[8] Everett M. Rogers, *Diffusion of Innovations* (New York: Free Press of Glencoe, 1962), p. 214.
[9] *Cf.* Lucian W. Pye, "Communication Policies in Development Programs," p. 229, and Daniel Lerner, "Toward a Communication Theory of Modernization," p. 329, in Pye, ed., *op. cit.*

than a two-step process. In the first place, three-fourths of the farmers—
not just the opinion leaders—mentioned the mass media as their most
important source of initial information about the new methods. This
pattern applied both to opinion leaders and to their followers—both "are
influenced by the mass media as well as by personal influence." [10]

Direct media effects on adoption of health practices were found in
a field experiment in Ecuador by Spector and associates.[11] In the two
rural communities which received a radio treatment, that medium was
reported by the inhabitants as the most important source of both information and influence on the health practices. Interpersonal communication with neighbors often took place *after* exposure to radio, but the
neighbors seldom were cited as the most influential source in the adoption
decision.

Even in a relatively isolated rural community in the Colombian
Andes, Deutschmann and Fals Borda found some evidence of direct mass
media impact—although most influence on farm practices came from face-
to-face contacts, with some cases of the two-step flow from the media to
innovators to followers. Direct exposure to the mass media was associated
with knowledge and adoption of farm practices and with knowledge of
political affairs.[12] In other rural communities of Columbia, Rogers found
evidence that media exposure is an intervening variable among various
antecedents such as literacy and consequents such as knowledge, empathy
and innovativeness.[13]

Not all studies of media impact have taken place in rural settings.
Evidence has been reported, for example, of media exposure relationships
with knowledge of public affairs on the part of urban heads of household,
university students, and other groups.[14]

The studies mentioned here—and a mounting number of others in
progress in various parts of the world—reflect a conception of the mass
media as instruments to reach the people directly with messages of modernization, not just as accessories in essentially oral systems of communication. This broader view of mass communication seems implicit in
Lerner's model of the progression from an oral to a media system. Lerner
pictures the mass media as "mobility multipliers" which make possible

[10] A. W. Van Den Ban, "A Revision of the Two-Step Flow of Communication Hypothesis," *Gazette* (Holland), Vol. 10 (1964), pp. 237-249.
[11] Paul Spector *et al.*, *Communication and Motivation in Community Development:
An Experiment* (Washington, D.C.: Institute for International Services, November
1963).
[12] Paul J. Deutschmann and Orlando Fals Borda, *La Comunicación de las Ideas entre
Los Campesinos Colombianos* (Bogotá: Universidad Nacional de Colombia, 1962),
p. 11; and Deutschmann, "The Mass Media in an Underdeveloped Village," *Journalism
Quarterly*, Vol. 40 (1963), pp. 27-35.
[13] Everett M. Rogers, "Mass Media Exposure and Modernization Among Colombian
Peasants," *Public Opinion Quarterly*, Vol. 29 (Winter 1965-66), pp. 614-625.
[14] John T. McNelly, "Mass Communication and the Climate for Modernization in
Latin America," *Journal of Inter-American Studies*, Vol. 8, No. 3 (1966), pp. 345-357.

dramatic increases in empathy and social participation through mediated experiences. The media do this for people by "depicting for them new and strange situations and by familiarizing them with a range of opinions among which they can choose." [15]

More recent data from the Middle East strongly confirm this conception of the role of the media. Frey found in a large sample of rural Turks positive correlations between media exposure and a substantial array of cognitive, attitudinal and behavioral variables associated with modernization. Such variables also were related with indices of geographic mobility and interpersonal communication, but interestingly these latter correlations dropped to almost zero when the variation attributable to media exposure was partialed out.[16]

Frey focused particularly on the impact of mass communication in the cognitive realm, as measured by such indices as general and political knowledge, cognitive flexibility, communal responsibility, educational and occupational aspirations, and political empathy. The effects of mass communication on such variables are not very rapid or dramatic; they do not result from a single message or campaign such as is commonly studied in traditional communication research; and they cannot necessarily be traced as the direct causes of given acts of behavior. But Frey sees the mass media as a prime instrument for social change in Turkey precisely because of such long-range effects on the "climate for development." Frey observes: "The low opinion that some writers appear to have of the media as a developmental tool has spawned in a very shallow pool of evidence, based as it is largely on studies of short-run political campaigns, a few sales or participation drives, and some small-group experiments." The long-range and indirect effects of the media have hardly been studied, he adds, although one would expect these to be the very areas in which the media would be most effective.[17]

Of great potential significance, though difficult to measure, are long-range effects of mass communication on the fundamental ways in which people think and act. Pool credits Lerner and McClelland with notable contributions in having advanced "the daring thesis that the mass media can have profound characterological effects"—referring to Lerner's concept of empathy and McClelland's of achievement motivation. Pool takes special note of the fact that this thesis does not depend on the two-step flow of communication, nor on opinion leaders or organizations paralleling the media, but rather on effects which the media have directly on people. He continues:

[15] Daniel Lerner, *The Passing of Traditional Society* (New York: Free Press of Glencoe, 1953), pp. 52, 412.
[16] Frederick W. Frey, *The Mass Media and Rural Development in Turkey*, Report No. 3, Rural Development Research Project, Center for International Studies, M.I.T., Cambridge, Mass., 1966, pp. 128-29.
[17] *Ibid.*, pp. 130, 197.

This suggests that the conclusion that the effectiveness of the media in the process of modernization depends upon their being linked to a well-developed organization of face-to-face influence is too simple. It is true for certain of the potential effects of the mass media but not for others.[18]

Characterological effects of the media would be expected to be slow, subtle, cumulative and infinitely complex—involving not only many possible stages and directions but also many messages from various media at different times. And they may occur in combination with multiple influences from the social environment of each individual. Even shorter-term effects on attitudes and behavior may involve complexities of this sort. Schramm has suggested that results in the development process may proceed less from individual messages or media than from "a succession of impacts of related messages and reinforcing channels"—both mass and interpersonal.[19]

All this seems to imply a pragmatic approach on the part of planners and practitioners of communication in development as well as for researchers. Clearly it would be optimistic in the extreme to expect the emergence in the near future of an adequate general theory to explain or predict a process so complex and ramified as mass communication in social and economic development. Nevertheless there are emerging gradually some hypotheses and generalizations from studies such as those which have been cited here. Investigators have tended to look at mass communication in terms of variables which lead to it and variables which follow from it. These variables can be arranged in this kind of model or paradigm:

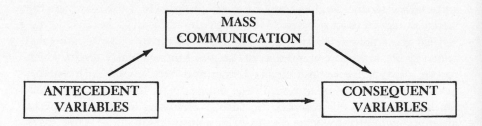

The antecedent variables tend to be factors such as education, socioeconomic status, literacy, age, and family background. The consequent variables often include knowledge, attitudes, and motivations regarding

[18] Ithiel de Sola Pool, "The Mass Media and Politics in the Modernization Process," in Pye, ed., *op. cit.*, pp. 249-53.
[19] Wilbur Schramm, *Mass Media and National Development* (Stanford, Calif.: Stanford University Press, 1964), p. 145.

modernization, empathy, opinion leadership, and innovativeness. The aspect of mass communication most commonly investigated has been exposure to the various media, but attention also has been paid to other aspects such as media availability, exposure to specific messages, and credibility of sources.

As the arrows suggest, mass communication can be studied as a dependent variable with respect to the antecedent variables, as an independent variable with respect to the consequent variables, or as an intervening variable serving as a link between the antecedent and consequent variables. And the possibility is left open in this scheme for direct effects, as the lower arrow indicates, of the antecedent variables on the consequent variables, apart from mass communication.[20] The arrows suggest predominant or probable, but not necessary, directions of causality. It is assumed that mass communication can interact with the antecedent and consequent variables in an almost infinite variety of ways to influence the development process.

Conclusion

The pragmatic position, then, differs from the null, enthusiastic and cautious positions in that it does not attempt to specify a uniform role for the mass media across all situations in all cultures. It accommodates diverse kinds of data and hypotheses. It leaves open the possibility of no media impact, a limited impact, or a heavy impact, depending upon conditions. It does not reject the possibility of direct effects on the public or indirect effects through influential persons, of immediate and measurable effects or long-range effects through almost imperceptible increments.

Mass Communication is a relatively new phenomenon which often seems difficult to handle in terms of widely-accepted theories of human behavior. Furthermore, the study of mass communication in development carries the investigator into areas of the world where even well-tested behavioral patterns may not apply. Possibilities abound for the re-examination of old theories and the building of new theories. The pragmatic position, as reflected in the studies and interpretations cited here, seems likely to describe the approach of many researchers and planners in the development field for some considerable time to come.

[20] See John T. McNelly and Paul J. Deutschmann, "Media Use and Socioeconomic Status in a Latin American Capital," *Gazette* (Holland), Vol. 9 (1963), p. 3.

Floyd G. Arpan:

What is a Responsible Press for Emergent Nations?

IN A REPORT on communications in developing nations which was published by the United Nations, the following statement appeared: *"Full, free and objective exchange of news between all people is essential to international order and understanding."* It might be assumed that in the proliferation of nations which resulted from the break-up of the old colonial empires this *"freedom of information"* philosophy would be accepted by all those who joined the United Nations. Such has not been the case, however. In many emergent countries, the cry for political freedom has not been interpreted as including necessarily the right of the individual to think, or speak, or write as he wishes.

Instead of a free press and a free flow of information, there has been a tendency to establish a controlled press, and to restrict information to that which is deemed favorable to the government in power. With the rise of the *"one-party"* governments in many of the newer nations, toleration of opposition views and criticism of government policy and officials virtually has disappeared. So, throughout the world, major struggles have developed—between those who would govern and those who demand the freedom to discuss and criticize freely. The press is aligned with the latter group. The control of the news media—newspapers, radio, television—thus has become the focal point of this struggle. The development of a free and responsible press among the newly created nations has been slowed to a "snail's pace." In 1965 it must be admitted that the objective flow of news which the United Nations deems essential to international understanding is not available from large areas of the world.

Inevitably, in my travels and work in communications in more than 50 countries, I have become involved many times in arguments over how free the press should be, the problems of ethics and responsibility, the abuses of both freedom and controls, the establishment of rules of conduct, and whether the media should govern itself voluntarily or be subject to a government-appointed body with enforceable powers. This has given me an opportunity to share views with presidents, prime ministers, cabinet ministers, members of parliament, political leaders, publishers, editors, reporters, and ordinary citizens.

▶ From: *The Journalist's World* (Brussels), Vol. II, No. 4, 1965. Reprinted by permission of author.

To many of those in government, the term *"free press"* is somehow frightening and implies that the press is entitled to pursue any policy it wishes regardless of what the national interest may be. There is a tendency on the part of government officials to equate the term *"free press"* with *"hostile press."* And, indeed, there have been occasions when opposition by the press has toppled political parties and even governments from power. In many instances, there is a mutual feeling of distrust between government and the news media.

Where the government looks askance at the term *"free press,"* so, too, do those who work in the news media have reservations concerning the term *"responsibility."* In a recent speech in Africa, Per Monsen, director of the International Press Institute in Zurich, Switzerland, analyzed the *"ominous ring"* which this term has for many newsmen. Said Mr. Monsen:

> Independent newsmen fear that, under the demand that they should be "responsible," lies the wish that they should always be in agreement with authority.
>
> They fear that, when they are urged to exercise responsibility, they are in effect being urged to support every government move uncritically.
>
> So each side, in its dealings with the other, tends to emphasize the one word—and skip over the other. Thus the journalists emphasize the word "free." Politicians and governments tend to emphasize the word "responsible"!

In large measure, whether the press is allowed to develop as a truthful news media instead of merely an instrument of propaganda depends on:

1. The stability of the government and its tolerance of, and ability to withstand, criticism.

2. The degree of self-determination permitted individual citizens, and their desire for truthful information.

3. The level of education in the country.

In general, the higher the intellectual attainment, the broader the interests of the people and the greater the need for information. (It is realized, of course, that in many of the new countries the illiteracy rate is very high. It will take a number of years of educational *"pump priming"* before a widespread ability to read and understand will eventually create a need for daily information.)

4. The financial stability attainable by the media.

Subsidized newspapers, or those paid for by governments or political parties, almost never achieve any degree of independence in their news operation. A press that is not self-supporting is usually an obligated press—obligated to do the bidding of those who pay the bills.

It should be remembered that in those countries which generally are credited with having a responsible press, the goal has not been achieved instantly nor by any magic formula. Sometimes it took a century or two to reach the desired stability, freedom, and responsibility. Often it was a difficult, painstaking, soul searching, compromising process. We should not be too impatient, therefore, if the newer countries do not achieve a high degree of press sophistication immediately. We should stand ready to help, and to provide guidance across the treacherous areas of press development.

In many countries struggling with the problems of nationhood, freedom often is mistaken for license. This leads to excesses which time and experience must temper. But the newly emergent nations do not have time on their side. They have arrived on the world scene via the "*jet age.*" Some have passed from a colonial possession to an independent nation to a participant in the United Nations—voting on world problems—all in the space of two weeks. A long, drawn-out development of their information system would be too slow for their needs. They need accurate information NOW.

It is imperative, therefore, that the new nations take giant strides toward establishing a responsible press immediately. Information, facts, truth are vitally important to their success and survival.

There is, of course, no magic formula for doing all this. Experience has shown, however, that the points which follow are vital and do provide guidelines on the road to press stability and reliability:

1. *Training of Personnel*

Many of the colonial areas had no newspapers at all. Others had newspapers owned, staffed, and operated by citizens from the colonial power. Where indigenous papers were permitted, they almost always were of extremely poor quality and edited by people who had little education or training to put out professionally oriented media. In some instances, there were persons with education and ideas who started newspapers, but except for the educated publisher there was a vacuum: those in charge of the actual production of the newspaper were ill-equipped and untrained for their jobs. Not only did they lack journalistic know-how, but they usually lacked even a general educational background, and had little sense of perspective on domestic let alone world problems. Too, with the extreme shortage of educated people in many of these newly developing areas, the government raided or conscripted almost all of the educated persons into government service. This left the news media with even fewer qualified people than they might otherwise have had.

Much attention needs to be given to this problem of training personnel for journalism. The International Press Institute (with help from one of the large foundations) is sponsoring six-month training sessions in Africa in Lagos and Nairobi, as well as staging numerous seminars for newsmen now in the profession—designed to improve and up-grade the level of performance. These seminars have been in Africa, South America, the Far East, and South East Asia. Unesco is also involved in training and seminar projects. Some of the former colonial powers have arranged to bring personnel from the newly independent areas for training in European universities. Great effort, time and money is being expended to eliminate the present shortage of trained personnel in journalism. But even with this *"crash training"* program, it probably will take years before there is an adequate supply of trained people for the communications field. Until this demand is fully met, the new nations face a difficult period of reaching their own citizens with necessary information properly reported, written and edited so that it can be understood. In a world where *"instant information"* is almost a necessity for day to day operation, the lack of trained news media personnel is a serious and dangerous problem.

2. Development of Social Consciousness

Many of the newspapers developed during the colonial period and afterward were designed to promote a point of view, defend a system, back up the government in control, serve as a medium of propaganda, help sell a policy, propagate a political point of view. Thus the press grew up as a *"power vehicle"* designed to promote causes and interests of those who paid its bills. It was concerned primarily with promoting individuals and political ideas. There was little attempt to create a real news media that was complete, fair, and truthful.

A responsible press is one which subordinates self-interest and makes the common good paramount. This is a lesson which many of those in the news media of the developing nations have not yet had time to learn. But until the news media of these countries minimize the use of the press as an instrument of personal power, not only will the press not be believed, it will not be truly effective as an instrument of information.

3. Outlining of Clear-Cut Boundaries of Independence in Operation

It is an axiom that *"the press has to prove itself."* Before it can be trusted, it must prove that it is reliable. It must have courage to fight for what it thinks is right, and not be subservient. In order to gain acceptance from the public, the newspaper has to clearly delineate the rules under which it will operate openly. It cannot say that it stands for one thing, then do another. Hypocrisy in journalism is the ultimate kiss of death. The public will not long tolerate double-dealing.

Newspapers should clearly state their policy on news, and adhere to this policy in their day-to-day handling so that readers will come to know what to expect for the money they lay down each day for a copy. Readers ordinarily tend to respect a *"balanced view"* rather than the promotion of a single viewpoint to the exclusion of all others.

The world's great newspapers became great because they earned public acceptance and respect by their everyday performance.

4. Establishment of Clear-Cut Rules of Ethical Conduct

The press in the newly developing countries must decide how far it wishes to emulate the successful news media in the older nations. Certainly the area of ethics must be faced up to. Responsibility can never be achieved without an ethical foundation. The areas of morality, fairness, truth, accuracy must be clearly spelled out, stated in such a way that both the professional journalists and the public can understand. Among some of the emergent nations, the biggest problem is to eliminate the bitterness engendered by the fight for independence, the minimizing of political emotion, the toning down of prejudice, the tempering of vindictiveness, the granting of a fair hearing to both sides of every problem. In some countries the whole concept of accuracy in news must be developed. Reporters have to be trained to a *"professional attitude"* which will drive them to check, verify, dig until they are sure, and to maintain an open and questioning mind.

5. Discipline and Controls

There is a running battle all over the world as to whether the news media should discipline themselves or whether the government should control the procedures of operation and conduct. The press usually prefers to do its own policing (but often does a bad job of it). This minimizes government control. The success of the self-disciplining idea is dependent entirely on the strength of the organization set up to do the disciplining. But discipline there must be. If the press doesn't do the job itself, the alternative is for the government to step in. It behooves the press, therefore, to take the initiative, and set up a workable self-disciplining organization.

6. Negotiation of Firm Policy on Government Limitations and Restrictions

There must be a clear-cut understanding on the part of the news media concerning the government views and policy on the press. This should not be left to chance. Agreements and understandings in advance will prevent squabbling and retribution later. Among the areas which should be clearly defined:

a) The government's policy on the control of foreign exchange for the purchase of equipment and newsprint abroad.
b) How official advertising is to be apportioned and under what terms.

c) How routine government news is to be provided; how it is to be checked.

d) Which government personnel are available as news sources, and their degree of accessibility.

e) What areas of news fall under security restrictions and who determines these restrictions.

f) Where and when censorship is to be enforced and by whom.

In the long run, the development of a responsible press by the emergent nations will depend on how well the concept of the press is understood by both the public and government. Intelligent planning of objectives and goals, rules of operation, codes of ethics, self-discipline, will go a long way towards winning the battle for a responsible press—unencumbered by restrictions.

The biggest battle being fought today is for the control of men's minds. Not only individuals, but whole nations as well, can be upset, channeled or directed to a certain course of action through the information given to, or withheld from, them. If the United Nations is ever to achieve *"international order and understanding,"* the press must do its part responsibly and well. And the newspapers in the newly emergent nations have an obligation to take their places side by side with the older established media in providing *"full, free and objective exchange of news between all peoples."* It is an obligation and a challenge which they must not sidestep.

5

PROPAGANDA AND POLITICAL COMMUNICATION

Leslie John Martin
INTERNATIONAL PROPAGANDA IN RETROSPECT
  AND PROSPECT

John C. Merrill
NATIONAL STEREOTYPES AND INTERNATIONAL
  UNDERSTANDING

Garland O. Ashley
INTERNATIONAL POWER COMMUNICATION

Ralph K. White
THE NEWS RESISTANCE TO INTERNATIONAL
  PROPAGANDA

5

PROPAGANDA AND

POLITICAL COMMUNICATION

Eᴠᴇɴ a casual observer of the media of mass communication cannot fail to notice that men's minds—nationally and internationally—are being subjected to a ceaseless and clever bombardment of messages. These messages are calculated to influence and control. Internationally, these propagandistic messages are either directed against real or potential enemies or at "neutral" message consumers who might be won over. In addition, of course, much of the international media effort is aimed at reinforcing "friendly" images held in other nations of the country engaged in the propaganda effort.

Nations use their own propaganda agencies (government-owned-and-operated) supplemented, of course, by any private or quasi-private media they have available. Many critics of the press believe that this is actually hindering world understanding and cooperation, that it is instilling suspicions and animosities among nations and thereby worsening the global psychic crisis. One of this book's editors, John Merrill, writing in *The Foreign Press* (1970), puts it this way:

> Great amounts of propaganda are in the news stream—propaganda aimed at perpetuating the psychological tug of war among nations and peoples; "exceptional" incidents which are further exaggerated by the newspapers are disseminated as important news; "eccentric" and "dangerous" people are the subject of much of the news. In short, we find that "unreal" and "alarmist" news dominates the newspaper columns. . . . Instead of being conveyors of enlightenment, the national press systems tend too often to be "press agents" for individual countries or special groups, thus doing a good job of increasing irritations and suspicions among governments and giving distorted pictures of various nations.

These are, perhaps, unnecessarily pessimistic words, but there is no doubt that "negative" information about nations takes precedence in the world's mass media over "positive" information. In the first article of this chapter, L. John Martin, a former newsman and professor and now with the USIA, places international propaganda in its historical context and presents some interesting thoughts on the future of propaganda among nations.

John Merrill, in the next article, discusses international stereotypes and their relationship to propaganda efforts, relating the whole subject to general semantics. The third article in the chapter, written by G. O. Ashley, a retired Air Force colonel and Ph.D. candidate at Missouri in 1969-70, explores the rarely discussed subject of "power communication" among nations from the perspective of international diplomacy.

In the chapter's final article, Ralph K. White gives a general critique of international propaganda, points out a growing suspicion of, and reaction to, this propaganda, and finally gives some suggestions for improving this international effort.

It is obvious to anyone with any semantic sophistication that the subject of propaganda is extremely difficult to discuss meaningfully because of its abstractness, but it may well be that the four articles in this chapter, taken together, will go a long way in defining the term in its international context and in aiding the reader in predicting new directions in this highly important area of concern.

*   *   *   *

Related Reading

Barghoorn, F. C. *The Soviet Image of the United States: A Study in Distortion.* New York: Harcourt, Brace, 1950.

Brown, J. A. C. *Techniques of Persuasion: From Propaganda to Brainwashing.* Baltimore: Penguin Books, Inc., 1963.

Domenach, Jean-Marie. *La Propagande Politique.* Paris: Presses Universitaires de France, 1962.

Doob, L. W. *Propaganda, Its Psychology and Technique.* New York: Henry Holt, 1935.

Hoffman, Arthur S. *International Communication and the New Diplomacy.* Bloomington: Indiana University Press, 1968.

Koop, Theodore F. *Weapon of Silence.* Chicago: University of Chicago Press, 1946.

Lee, John (ed.). *Diplomatic Persuaders: New Role of the Mass Media in International Relations.* New York: John Wiley and Sons, 1968.

Lippmann, Walter. *Public Opinion.* New York: Harcourt-Brace, 1922.

Lumley, F. E. *The Propaganda Menace.* New York: Century, 1933.

Martin, L. John. *International Propaganda: Its Legal and Diplomatic Control.* Minneapolis: University of Minnesota Press, 1958.

Merrill, J. C., Carter Bryan and Marvin Alisky. *The Foreign Press: A Survey of the World's Journalism.* Baton Rouge: Louisiana State University Press, 1970.

Qualter, T. H. *Propaganda and Psychological Warfare.* New York: Random House, 1962.

Smith, B. L., Harold Lasswell and Ralph Casey. *Propaganda, Communication and Public Opinion.* Princeton: Princeton University Press, 1946.

Whitaker, Urban G., Jr. *Propaganda and International Relations.* San Francisco: Howard Chandler, 1960.

White, Llewellyn and R. D. Leigh. *Peoples Speaking to Peoples.* Chicago: University of Chicago Press, 1946.

Wilson, John. *Language & The Pursuit of Truth.* Cambridge: Cambridge University Press, 1967.

Leslie John Martin:

International Propaganda in Retrospect and Prospect

PROPAGANDA is a term that has become so commonplace, hardly a day passes that it is not mentioned in the newspapers or tossed about in conversation. Its meaning ranges from "something somebody is trying to 'put across' on a person" to "a systematic attempt to influence opinion or attitude in the interest of some cause." It is in a sense closer to the latter definition that legislators tend to use the word. Yet even the legislator, as well as the social scientist, cannot avoid the connotations of the former definition. The politician has an uneasy feeling about using the word to describe the activities of his own group; he discredits the activities of his opponents by calling these activities propaganda.

Besides putting money into international propaganda, states have gone out of the way to sign treaties, especially since World War I, making important concessions to other states in exchange for a vague freedom from propaganda. Legislative bodies have drafted hundreds of statutes in an attempt to keep propaganda in check. Diplomats have cajoled, pleaded, threatened, and bargained to ward off the propaganda activities of other states. Publicists have argued vigorously on whether international propaganda, public or private, is admissible in international law.

In other words, the world is convinced today that propaganda is no mere talk. Propaganda is something that can be implanted in the minds of people, and is sufficiently potent to win battles without a fight—or to start a fight, if that is its aim. Propaganda can be dangerous for certain states at certain times, because it introduces controversy where no controversy exists, thus weakening controls. Obedience to authority is assured only where singlemindedness exists. Propaganda can cast doubts into the minds of people. It can also be used to promote international goodwill. And many international agreements have been signed, and resolutions adopted, calling upon the signatories to conduct various types of propaganda to this end.

While books and articles have been written on international propaganda and its control, few have examined the term closely enough. Fur-

▶ From: *International Propaganda: Its Legal and Diplomatic Control,* by L(eslie) John Martin. Copyright © 1958 by University of Minnesota Press, Minneapolis/Minnesota. Reprinted by permission of the publisher.

thermore, the art of international propaganda has been refined in recent years and the attitude toward it has changed, especially since World War II; so that a fresh look at the activity and its control is significant at this time.

It doesn't make much difference who first invented the term "propaganda." Suffice it to say that it has long had bad connotations. Etymologists trace the term to Pope Gregory XV. It was he who founded the *Sacre Congregatio De Propaganda Fide* in 1622 to do missionary work abroad. Already in the early nineteenth century the term had acquired its present-day derogatory connotations. W. T. Brande's *Dictionary of Science, Literature and Art,* published in 1842, says of propaganda: "Derived from this celebrated society, the name propaganda is applied in political language as a term of reproach to secret associations for the spread of opinions and principles which are viewed by most governments with horror and aversion." It should be remembered that it is some time before a lexicographer takes note of popular usage.[1]

International propaganda activities, on the other hand, are as old as history itself. One reads of the success of Joshua's propaganda in the Old Testament, and how he convinced the Gibeonites that their land had been promised to the Israelites by Jehovah. Fighting under these circumstances, the Gibeonites decided, was useless. On the other hand, Sennacherib's propaganda was unsuccessful with the Israelites, and when the intelligence officers of his ill-fated army "cried with a loud voice in the Jews' speech unto the people of Jerusalem, that were on the wall, to affright them, and to trouble them; that they might take the city," they did not meet with much success.

History provides many another example of both successful and unsuccessful propaganda. Propaganda was not recognized as a powerful force and was largely ignored, however, until about the time of the French Revolution. Among the first international incidents connected with propaganda was the one that arose out of the wartime activities of the French revolutionary soldiers. These were sent into battle armed with slogans of *Guerre aux châteaux, paix aux chaumières!* It was Robespierre's contention that France was fighting to liberate the entire universe. To assist the men in the field, the French National Assembly promised to help all nations ready to fight for their liberty, and it charged the executive power to advise French generals to assist "all citizens who have been, or shall in the future be, persecuted in the cause of freedom."[2]

---

[1] Cf. I. G. Flügel, *Vollständiges Englisch-Deutsches und Deutsch-Englisches Wörterbuch,* Vol. 1 (Leipzig, 1847), defining propaganda: ". . . originally [applied] to the spreading of religious principles, in most recent times also to the spreading of political or revolutionary principles."
[2] Decree of November 19, 1792, *Archives parlementaires de 1787 à 1860,* Vol. 53, p. 474.

The international incident was caused by Britain's reaction to this unusual activity on the part of the French. King George III spoke of the designs abroad "to destroy our happy Constitution" and "to overturn all order and all government." He told Parliament, "I cannot but view with serious disquietude the increasing indications that attempts are being made to create disorder in foreign lands with no regard for the rights of neutral states, but aiming at conquests and self-aggrandizement." [3]

The French were by no means certain that they were doing the right thing. They tried to explain away their propaganda, comparing it to Cromwell's similar activities and saying that this was only a reprisal against the illegal intervention of the allies.[4] However, they felt guilty enough to repeal the November Decree on April 13, 1793; and Britain was told that France would disavow any agent in a friendly country who sought to provoke a revolt against the established order, for this would be a violation of international law.[5] As a matter of fact, in its constitution of June 1793, France declared expressly that it had no intention of interfering with the government of any other nation.[6]

This was the beginning of world consciousness of international propaganda. Other incidents followed; but it was not until World War I that systematic propaganda was actually engaged in. It was then discovered that total war could be fought only by attacking the minds as well as the bodies of men. Without the invention and universal use of wireless communication, this would have been impossible. But by a not unusual historical coincidence, the Germans found that they were cut off from the rest of the world at the beginning of the war because the Allies controlled the cables. They were therefore forced to turn to wireless communication, and by 1915 amateurs and agents abroad were receiving daily news bulletins from Germany.

The Allies, too, saw the power of wireless communication, and they broadcast Wilson's Fourteen Points all over the world. Later the Bolsheviks used radio for revolutionary purposes. They sent revolutionary messages to all the world, and their broadcasts during the Brest-Litovsk peace negotiations were an attempt to bring pressure to bear on the German leaders. The propaganda activities of Béla Kun, the Hungarian Communist leader, after World War I worried Austria and Switzerland to such an extent that they protested vigorously. Kun was addressing his propaganda broadcasts to proletarians all over the world.

It is significant that systematic propaganda came with democracy and

[3] Albert Sorel, *L'Europe et la Révolution Française* (1889-1904), Vol. 3 (Paris, 1893), p. 227. Author's translation.
[4] Robert Redslob, *Histoire des grands principes du droit des gens* (Paris, 1923), p. 308.
[5] *Archives parlementaires de 1787 à 1860*, Vol. 58, pp. 141, 152, 133; Vol. 62, p. 3.
[6] Article 119. *Gazette Nationale ou Le Moniteur Universel*, No. 178, June 27, 1793, in *Réimpression de l'ancien Moniteur* (mai 1789-novembre 1799), Vol. 16 (Paris, 1840), p. 736.

with technical improvements in communication. It was bred in the school of revolution and came into its own about the same time as the studies of sociology, economics, and social psychology. Appealing to the common people in the days of the old diplomacy would have been considered extremely vulgar, as Harold Nicolson has put it.[7] It was the dictatorships that first organized propaganda in peacetime. Dictatorships are generally born of a revolution of the masses, who then immediately turn over the rights they have fought for to a despot. At times, the dictator, whose greed for power is seldom satisfied, attempts to spread out in search of *Lebensraum*. To do this he appeals to the masses of neighboring states, because he knows that the thought of a leader, a guardian, or a father, has strong popular appeal. Occasionally his propaganda is intended to vindicate him by explaining himself to the world.

It is not surprising, therefore, that the credit for the development of international propaganda as an instrument of foreign policy in peacetime is generally given to Lenin and Hitler. But it was Lenin and Trotsky who originated the idea of broadcasting to foreign peoples over the heads of their governments. The time was ripe for this, and they addressed themselves to a highly receptive audience. The problem of ethnic minorities had become acute following the peace treaties and the shifting of boundaries. Territorial changes were often accomplished without regard for the linguistic or national backgrounds of the population. It is not surprising, therefore, that a new feature was introduced into international radio propaganda—that of attempting to reach whole population groups by appealing to them in their own languages. To the great chagrin of the nations concerned, Soviet Russia began to broadcast in German, English, Polish, and other foreign languages from its powerful Moscow stations. Either the official protests of Finland, Estonia, Poland, Germany, Britain, the United States, and others went unheeded, or Russia merely claimed that the broadcasts were destined for the national minorities within the Soviet Union itself. At the same time Bukharin, a member of the Central Executive Committee, the Politburo, the Communist party, and the Comintern, announced in his program of 1918: "The program of the Communist Party is the program not only of liberating the proletariat of one country; it is the program of liberating the proletariat of the world, for such is the program of the 'International Revolution.' "[8]

Not that the Soviet government acknowledged its propaganda activities officially. A correspondent of an American newspaper was told that Russia was not engaged in fostering Communist propaganda abroad, and if anything of this sort was being done, the Comintern was responsible.[9]

[7] Harold Nicolson, *Diplomacy* (London, 1950), p. 168.
[8] U.S. Department of State, *Papers Relating to the Foreign Relations of the United States (1923)* (Washington, 1938), Vol. 2, p. 769.
[9] *Ibid.*, p. 766.

Later the German government used the National Socialist party as its scapegoat, and the Chinese used the Kuomintang.

It was at this time that the United States decided it could not recognize the Bolshevik government in Russia until that government had given assurances that it would concede the obligations of diplomatic intercourse to include "abstention from hostile propaganda by one country in the territory of the other." [10]

By the middle of the 1920s propaganda by most countries in most other countries had become quite commonplace. The *Völkischer Beobachter* of January 31, 1934, alleged that Poland's budget provided four million francs annually for propaganda in France. Berlin and Paris both used propaganda in the controversy over the Ruhr, and Germany and Poland used it when the Upper Silesian question arose. In 1926 Moscow and Bucharest engaged in radio warfare over Bessarabia. In Latin America radio was brought in to help in the quarrel over boundaries. Since diplomatic protests and the international conferences that attempted to regulate propaganda were ineffectual, other nations began to adopt the same tactics. Short wave was first used by the countries possessing colonies, and in this the Netherlands was the pioneer in 1927. During the French Colonial Exposition in 1931, France began to broadcast to its colonies in the French language and in the languages spoken in those territories. The BBC's Empire Service in English was inaugurated in 1932, and Germany began to broadcast to *Auslandsdeutsche* in 1933. France initiated its foreign-language programs in 1936, addressing itself in German ostensibly to the Alsatians but actually, it is thought, to the whole German people. Italy had started broadcasting in Italian to its nationals in South America as early as 1935. By 1937, however, it was broadcasting in eighteen languages. The broadcasts included programs in Arabic to the Near East. The Anglo-Italian Accord of 1938 was signed after Britain had protested to Italy about its Arabic broadcasts, and the agreement provided, among other things, that Italy would refrain from attempting to undermine the British position in this area through its propaganda. In 1938 too, Britain began broadcasting in foreign languages through the BBC, addressing the Germans and Italians directly. At the outbreak of the war in 1939, the BBC had programs in sixteen languages in its Empire, Arab, Latin American, and European services.

The United States was obviously at a disadvantage in the realm of international propaganda. Since its radio facilities were largely privately owned, it could not as a government enter into the race. The haphazard

[10] From a letter of Charles Evans Hughes to Samuel Gompers, president of the American Federation of Labor, July 19, 1923. American Foundation, Committee on Russian-American Relations, *The United States and the Soviet Union: A report on the controlling factors in the relation between the U.S. and the Soviet Union* (New York, 1933), p. 39.

and often detrimental efforts of private United States citizens to "sell" their country or, more often, their products were no match for the government-organized and subsidized propaganda of certain other states. Furthermore, the tradition of free speech and nonmeddling on the part of the government in communications activities made many suspicious when the government finally entered the race, somewhat belatedly, in 1939. Even then the United States limited its activities to the Western Hemisphere.

On the other hand, it must be remembered that the United States is in the enviable position of being practically immune to foreign radio propaganda owing to the bad reception on the North American continent of European, Asiatic, African, Australian, and even South American broadcasts. As a result, there is hardly any market for short-wave radios; and the United States, not having the regulating problems that other states have, is not so interested in the control of international propaganda as is Europe—that veritable Babel of the air. In the early days of radio this was true of other countries as well. In the 1920s, for instance, when Moscow began broadcasting in English, strong protests were voiced in the British Parliament. It was soon discovered, however, that only the most expensive British receivers were able to pick up the signals, and the broadcasts ceased to be taken seriously.

Propaganda is a term that is subject to many definitions. The definitions appear to be in agreement about one thing only: that propaganda attempts to influence the thinking of people. There is general agreement that propaganda is aimed at the minds of people, and that the attempt is to direct or strengthen their thinking along predetermined lines. While courts of law will accept the common definitions of words, they cannot pass judgment when the common definition is vague and uncertain. Occasionally, courts in the United States, for instance, have let the jury decide whether the activities of defendants were the same as those described in a law. Expert testimony is received. But in this regard both the bench and the jury cannot help but be influenced by the national sentiment of the day. This means that what is accepted as manifestly hostile propaganda in one state may be considered in quite a different light in another, or at least it may be condoned as warranted. As has been pointed out, the impact of what is said depends not so much on what is said as on the degree of friendship between the states involved.

Further complicating matters are the many treaties and resolutions that have been signed positively calling upon the signatories to engage in certain types of propaganda activities. Some of these have used the term propaganda in this connection,[11] while others have merely provided for freedom of expression in general or of a particular nature, without using the term. Thus it is not only permissible but, occasionally, desirable that

[11] Cf. Resolution 110(II) of the United Nations General Assembly.

states engage in activities designed to influence the thinking of people—their own nationals and others—about other states. The question then is whether the content of the propaganda is in agreement with the spirit of the treaty or resolution.

Much of the time it is very hard to tell what the tendency of a state's propaganda is. The content of a present-day propaganda program is far too subtle most of the time. Often it is of a nonpolitical nature, while many of the news releases and broadcasts of states contain slanted factual news and editorials on which they base their propaganda campaigns. Most, if not all of this is inspired, subsidized, and, generally, organized by the state. Of course, all communications media are potential propaganda media. Much of the propaganda contained in them is similarly too subtle to be dubbed generically as tendentious.

But let us assume a state decides that the propaganda of another state is manifestly tendentious of something undesirable. It would then, possibly, go to the numerous treaties that have been signed and look for one that bans the specific type of propaganda it feels has been perpetrated upon it. It will find that no resolution directly mentioning propaganda was ever adopted by the League of Nations. The United Nations condemns war propaganda, and propaganda likely to provoke a threat to the peace. It also recommends that measures be studied to combat false and distorted information likely to injure friendly international relations. But the United Nations does not define the two types of propaganda, and obviously each state will interpret its propaganda in the light of its own ideology.

A number of bilateral treaties were signed before World War II by certain states, especially with Russia, in which "propaganda against the other party" was banned. No such bilateral treaties have been signed since the war. But here again, propaganda against the other party will have to be defined. No state would normally admit that it is engaging in propaganda against another party. It is merely telling the truth about the other party (and itself). An international tribunal would find it difficult to adjudicate on the basis of the extant definitions. Furthermore, Russia might well plead innocent of a breach of the treaty under the *clausula rebus sic stantibus*, pointing to the fact that a cold war was being waged by the parties concerned, or that international propaganda had become so universal since the treaty was signed as to have become customary international behavior. Each contracting party might also claim violation of the treaty by the other without fear of contradiction.

Finally, the International Convention Concerning the Use of Broadcasting in the Cause of Peace could be adduced by the state. But only thirteen states have ratified it, and it has other weaknesses which have been discussed above.

The problem of hostile international propaganda has often come before the League of Nations and the United Nations, and many have argued both there and in writings that there ought to be some legislation outlawing hostile propaganda. This in itself is proof of the fact that no international law as yet exists making hostile propaganda a crime. The arguments of such protagonists of the theory as John B. Whitton and Vernon B. Van Dyke that hostile propaganda by states is a delict in international law are subject to various criticisms. Whitton advocates that warmongering propaganda on the part of states and individuals be banned.[12] On the other hand, he says that states should be allowed to conduct propaganda in support of a "licit" war; propaganda to promote aggressive wars is out, of course.[13] Elsewhere he asserts: "No state can be condemned for urging its own people to rise up and meet an unprovoked aggression. The same is true if the state is urging one foreign power to resist an unprovoked attack threatened by another foreign power." [14] The problems raised by these suggestions are obvious. Every war is licit from the point of view of the belligerent. Charles G. Fenwick has pointed out: "while jurists have been attempting to reconcile the conflict between the right of self-defense possessed by one state with the right of independence belonging to another, governments have gone ahead and done what they thought they had a right to do without finding any great difficulty in formulating a legal justification for their conduct. Thus a conflict of view has arisen not only in the field of theory, but between the jurists of one country and those of another, depending upon the foreign policies of their respective governments." [15]

Vernon B. Van Dyke adds the following footnote: "Note should be made of the fact that this statement refers to the spreading of propaganda within foreign countries. Governments are free in certain circumstances to issue and circulate within their own territory pronouncements which other governments regard as hostile to their interests (for instance, a declaration that another government is guilty of aggression), but aside from releasing the news via the radio and press, it is doubtful whether direct, official steps could legally be taken to make a foreign people cognizant of such pronouncements, unless it be done as a measure of reprisal." [16] Modern communications make this exception almost meaningless.

Whenever the problem of international propaganda has come up, its illegality in international law has been defended on two grounds: that hostile propaganda was an intervention in the affairs of another state, and that hostile international propaganda was injurious to international peace.

A number of treaties exist that do not specifically mention propa-

[12] John B. Whitton, "Propaganda and International Law," *Recueil des Cours de l'Académie de Droit International*, Vol. 72 (1948-I), p. 645.
[13] *Ibid.*, p. 609.
[14] *Ibid.*, p. 598.
[15] Charles G. Fenwick, "Intervention: Individual and Collective," *American Journal of International Law*, Vol. 39 (October 1945), p. 646.
[16] Vernon B. Van Dyke, "Responsibility of States for International Propaganda," *American Journal of International Law*, Vol. 24 (January 1940), p. 65 n.

ganda, but which forbid intervention by one state in the affairs of another. These have often been interpreted as banning hostile international propaganda. But is propaganda a form of intervention? "Intervention may or may not involve the use of force," writes Jessup.[17] But his examples of intervention without the use of force exclude propaganda, which is merely an attempt to influence people's thinking. A state may intervene in the affairs of another without the use of force, he says, "by lending open approval, as by the relaxation of an arms embargo, to a revolutionary group headed by individuals ready to accept the political or economic dominance of the intervening state. It may be accomplished by the withholding of recognition of a new government, combined with various forms of economic and financial pressure until the will of the stronger state prevails through the resignation or overthrow of the government disapproved." [18] Brierly is specific: "A mere tender of advice by one state to another about some matter within the competence of the latter to decide for itself would not be an intervention in this sense, though it might be popularly so described; the interference must take an imperative form; it must either be forcible or backed by the threat of force." [19] When it is the latter, the question is no longer one of mere propaganda. Oppenheim's definition is along the same lines, and Lauterpacht concurs: "Intervention can take place in the external as well as in the internal affairs of a State. It concerns, in the first case, the external independence, and in the second either the territorial or the personal supremacy. But it must be emphasised that intervention proper is always *dictatorial* interference, not interference pure and simple." [20]

The second argument that hostile international propaganda is injurious to international peace is one that puts the cart before the horse. Hostile international propaganda is merely an outward manifestation of an international illness. As well outlaw international misunderstandings as the fulminations that disclose them. Furthermore, the same argument that applies to the difficulty of defining propaganda in general also applies to a definition of propaganda designed to injure international harmony.

The state that considers itself injured by hostile international propaganda might then turn to international custom, as evidence of a general practice as accepted as law. Here it would find that a protest was treated according to the relative sizes of the states before World War II. That is, small states were quick to admit their guilt to large states, large states generally ignored or rejected the protests of small states, and states of

[17] Phillip C. Jessup, *A Modern Law of Nations* (New York, 1950), p. 172.
[18] *Ibid.*, pp. 172-173.
[19] J. L. Brierly, *The Law of Nations: An Introduction to the International Law of Peace*, 4th ed. (Oxford, 1949), p. 284.
[20] L. Oppenheim, *International Law*, Vol. 1, 5th ed., H. Lauterpacht, ed. (London, 1937), pp. 249-250, 250 n.

about the same size treated protests according to their current foreign policy. Since the war, however, with the world divided into two large camps, things have changed, and small states, even in the same camp, have been known to reject the protests of large states regarding their propaganda activities or those of their subjects. If states have continued to register their protests since World War II, they have apparently done so merely for the publicity or propaganda value of the protest.

Does this show a change in international custom? In the fifth edition of Oppenheim's *International Law*, Lauterpacht commented: "The series of statements and speeches made in the years 1936 and 1937 by representatives of Germany, Italy, and Russia, and containing violent attacks on the Governments and Institutions of the countries concerned, must be regarded as exceptional and as evidencing a suspension, in this matter, of the operation of an accepted rule of International Law in the relations of these States." [21] This comment is missing in the seventh edition. Perhaps it is no longer necessary, considering how widespread such propaganda has become. The argument is as false, however, as the popular interpretation of the proverb the "exception proves the rule," proves being taken to mean "establishes." The correct translation from the Latin—"the exception *tests* the rule"—is more pertinent. Here an exception rapidly developed into a custom.

An analogy may be drawn from the attitude of publicists toward propaganda in wartime. J. M. Spaight, for instance, considered it illegal to incite the civilian population in wartime in his *War Rights on Land*, a book published in 1911.[22] Thirteen years later, in the same author's *Air Power and War Rights*, he legitimizes war propaganda, because of the practice of the belligerents in World War I.[23] Lauterpacht writes: "The legitimacy, formerly controversial, of inciting enemy subjects to rise against the Government in power is now no longer disputed. During the First World War the belligerents displayed vigorous activity in that direction. Since then, the increased possibility of disseminating propaganda by aircraft and, above all, the advent of broadcasting, have revealed the wide potentialities of this weapon." [24] Hyde says much the same thing.[25] This argument should also hold true for international propaganda in peacetime.

Turning to the general principles of law recognized by civilized nations, the state that considered itself injured by hostile international propaganda would find much comfort. There is a great deal of municipal legislation on propaganda and allied subjects. But a closer examination of

21 *Ibid.*, p. 231 n.
22 James M. Spaight, *War Rights on Land* (London, 1911), pp. 146-150.
23 James M. Spaight, *Air Power and War Rights*, 3rd ed. (London, 1947), p. 333.
24 L. Oppenheim, *op. cit.*, Vol. 2, pp. 426-427.
25 Charles Cheney Hyde, *International Law: Chiefly as Interpreted and Applied by the United States*, Vol. 3, 2nd revised ed. (Boston, 1945), pp. 1838-1839.

these laws will show that they tend to protect the state on whose books they are far more frequently than they protect foreign states. In other words, it is all right most of the time if the propaganda is directed against some other state, so long as it does not harm the state which enacted the law.

When a state protects other states against hostile propaganda, it does so for one or both of two reasons. The first is the hope of reciprocity, which is the reason why immunity is granted to foreign diplomats. The second is the fear of reprisals. Large states grant no greater immunities to foreign states or their officials than they do to their own citizens and organizations. In the totalitarian countries these immunities may be great because the rights of the people are few, since the state will not stand for much independent action on the part of its citizens. In the free nations the immunities are few because the freedoms are many. Small states, fearing reprisals, grant fewer immunities to their own citizens and organizations than they do to foreign citizens and organizations.

The majority of laws that protect other states or their officials, protect them against defamation. While the propagandist may use almost any words or terms in his propaganda, not all propaganda is defamatory. In fact, propaganda has never been defined as "that which is defamatory." Libel and slander are merely incidental to propaganda, if they exist in it, and as such, they may be crimes according to the municipal law of the country in which the propagandist conducts his propaganda. But it has never been suggested that libel and slander ought to be international crimes. And even if they were delicts in international law, there is no more reason to outlaw propaganda with them than there is to outlaw the press and broadcasting because they are occasionally guilty of defamation.

This is not to say that the means do not exist to control propaganda that might cause international disunity, accelerate the advent of war, or injure the feelings of foreign states, their governments, peoples, or officials. The domestic laws of most nations—probably all nations—contain provisions for the control of propaganda, and here propaganda is interpreted in the light of the ideology of the state. States can also control propaganda activities with certain results and certain undesirable beneficiaries. Their laws provide controls over the media of communication, the content, the disseminator, and the manner of reception. The courts of many states will assume jurisdiction in cases where they consider that a crime has been committed under the laws of the state, (a) if the perpetrator is within their physical jurisdiction, (b) if he is a national of the state, and (c) even if he is an alien outside the physical jurisdiction of the state.

Aliens outside the physical jurisdiction of a state are of special interest, since they, more often than not, are the propagandists engaged in hostile international propaganda. Following a war, such aliens often fall into the hands of a state that has considered itself injured by international propaganda. What would be the fate of these aliens?

Obviously, an international crime must be one that is internationally recognized as a crime—for instance, piracy, the white slave trade, traffic in opium.[26] Propaganda, which involves controversy, cannot be included because there is generally no agreement about the criminality of its content. However, propaganda can become a crime once agreement is reached on the criminality of the content. Such agreement is possible following a war, when the defendants all belong to one side of the controversy, and the plaintiffs, who are also the judges, belong to the other side. This was the case, following World War II, in the Nuremberg trials. "We can save ourselves from . . . pitfalls if our test of what legally is crime gives recognition to those things which fundamentally outraged the conscience of the American people," Justice Robert H. Jackson stated.[27]

It should be remembered that the Nuremberg trials will serve and were intended to serve as a precedent. "I think also that through these trials we should be able to establish that a process of retribution by law awaits those who in the future similarly attack civilization," said Justice Jackson.[28] The standards laid down at Nuremberg were intended to have universal application: "We may not, in justice, apply to these defendants because they are German, standards of duty and responsibility which are not equally applicable to the officials of the Allied Powers and to those of all nations. Nor should Germans be convicted for acts or conduct which, if committed by Americans, British, French or Russians, would not subject them to legal trial and conviction." [29]

Will the law of Nuremberg apply also to propaganda? Apparently it was intended to. Not only were certain actions criminal at Nuremberg, but incitement to action was also an indictable offense. Thus Fritzsche's broadcasts were found to be noncriminal, as they were "not intended to incite the German People to commit atrocities on conquered peoples," said the court.[30] Streicher's publications, on the other hand, constituted "incitement to murder and extermination at the time when Jews in the East were being killed under the most horrible conditions." [31] And it was just as wrong for the propagandists to influence their own people as it was to influence foreign nationals.[32]

The principles of international law recognized in the charter and judgment of the Nuremberg tribunal were formulated by the International Law Commission on the direction of the United Nations General Assembly. On December 12, 1950, the principles were presented to the General

[26] Even here it is perhaps more correct to say that a universal jurisdiction, rather than an international crime, is recognized.
[27] Quoted in Telford Taylor, "Nuremberg Trials, War Crimes and International Law," *International Conciliation*, No. 450 (April 1949), p. 251.
[28] Quoted *ibid.*
[29] Quoted in Taylor, *op. cit.*, p. 353.
[30] Quoted *ibid.*, p. 271.
[31] Quoted in Taylor, *op. cit.*, p. 271.
[32] See *ibid.*, p. 333. See also Quincy Wright, "The Crime of 'War-Mongering'," *American Journal of International Law*, Vol. 42 (January 1948), p. 129.

Assembly, which invited the comments of member states.[33] Nothing further has been done about them. Nothing is likely to be done, since to accept the Nuremberg charter and judgment is as much as to say *vae victis* —woe to the vanquished!

One cannot, it has been shown, speak of the control of propaganda as such. At best the controls that exist are designed to check the act, and only secondarily the advocacy of or incitement to the act. Propaganda cannot and should not be divorced from the act it attempts to promote.

The almost universal acceptance of democracy, at least in theory, has resulted in an equally universal attempt to influence the masses in whom the power resides. As communications improved, the methods used to influence whole nations were refined. The immediate reaction of governments was to look upon this propaganda with horror. Speeches were made; recommendations to outlaw propaganda were put forward; treaties were signed. For it was apparent in those states where the people had a meaningful vote that they might be persuaded to vote not in the best interests of their own state, but for the advancement of some other state. The dictatorship, on the other hand, feared that the people might be induced to rise up and throw off their shackles.

Before long, however, it was seen that propaganda was too intangible to control internationally. Besides, its powers became universally recognized, and no state was willing to give up its right to present its point of view and make known its cause among the nations. For anything a state might say officially or through unofficial sources was dubbed propaganda, which, in fact, it was, for why should a state want to say it if not to influence others in its own interest?

The tendency since World War I has been to tighten municipal laws designed to protect a state against undesirable propaganda from without or within, while at the same time there has been a steady increase in the scientific and organized dissemination of propaganda. While this means that a state has no control over propagandists not within its physical grasp, it can, if it desires, control incoming propaganda at the receiving end through the channels and media of communication. At the same time the state is left with a freer hand in conducting its own propaganda activities. Because of changing ideologies, even within a state, the subtleties of modern propaganda, and the difficulty of definition, it is inconceivable that international law will ever control propaganda, no matter what its content, so long as the sovereignty of states is recognized. The control of propaganda will remain in the municipal laws of states and the bargaining power of diplomacy.

[33] *Yearbook of the United Nations, 1950*, p. 852.

John C. Merrill:

National Stereotypes and International Understanding

THE TEMPTATION is naturally great to launch into some type of idealistic program camouflaged as a "practical" blueprint for improving understanding among nations. Always there is the desire, almost a demand, for answers to complex problems—even when nobody really thinks that answers can be given. Such a complex problem is international understanding—or *mis*-understanding. Without a doubt many citizens of all nations have images or stereotypes of other nations which they wish, or perhaps *would* wish if they thought much about these images, to eliminate. And, certainly, these images lead to misunderstanding and even to friction among certain persons (and nations) at some times in some places under some circumstances.

Organized Programs

Misunderstanding and international friction we seem to have always had with us. It is only now, however, in an age when "small" disagreements and wars among nations can easily eliminate humanity through nuclear destruction that there is a growing desire among thoughtful persons to rid the world of international misunderstandings. Increasingly, we hear of concrete programs or proposals to eliminate harmful images of nations which are believed to cause friction and misunderstanding.

An organized and definite program as such, which would presumably eliminate stereotypes and myths thought harmful to international peace, is at most highly idealistic and perhaps even inadvisable. This does not mean, of course, that basic misunderstandings are not to be deplored. It simply means that a *program* to correct them is open to question.

The concept of a "program" itself is filled with the potentialities of the stereotype: it is suspect, it is generalized, it is a cliché which linguistically projects a well-constructed and idealized image. It is a semantic label which tends to simplify reality and cause uncritical persons to expect more than the word can deliver.

Nations, especially those segments of them which are sophisticated enough to be concerned about "images," have come to the point where they are suspicious of organized attempts to "correct" their generalized

▶ This is an original article done for this book by John C. Merrill, University of Missouri, Columbia, 1969.

ways of thinking about other countries—or about their own countries for that matter. Such attempts are considered by sensitive citizens to be false, hypocritical, and socially and politically dishonest. Unspontaneous and largely "managed" or "directed" image-making: this is the reaction of sophisticated citizens.

It is natural for Americans to have stereotypes about other nations and vice versa, however unfortunate we may feel it to be. Are we to assume that the present "stereotypes" relative to different countries are any more damaging or more erroneous than *new* stereotypes promulgated by a conscious "program" would be?

Stereotype Analysis

The whole matter might be considered from the perspective of stereotype-analysis itself. We certainly know that there is a stereotype of a stereotype, a sort of generalization about a generalization. And, we must admit that usually a stereotype is negative. Stereotypes are visualized as "bad," "unfortunate," "incomplete," "damaging to good will," "harmful," "biased," and so forth. In effect, we see stereotypes as vicious and unrealistic walls which separate peoples and keep them from getting on well together. This is basically the stereotype of the stereotype.

But an interesting question comes up at this point: What is the alternative? Is there any way to eliminate one stereotype without imposing another one over it? Is not the process of eliminating stereotypes simply the changing or modification of stereotypes? The new or revised stereotype may prove to be more effective for certain purposes than the older one, but one wonders if it will be more accurate, more *real*, or more stabilizing to society.

How can Mexicans, for instance, think of America *without* thinking in stereotypes? How can citizens of the United States think of Mexico in any other manner? Thinking itself is abstracting, selecting, focusing on certain dominant characteristics—or certain aspects of reality which fit a person's preconceived notions. Thinking, in effect, *is* stereotyping—and certainly *mass* thinking is. So we run into an imposing problem in the matter of changing *people's* stereotypes about another people: the problem inherent in the mass mind itself. Now, there are those who would immediately challenge the use of such an abstract term as "mass mind." Perhaps it should be challenged; the point is, however, that it is used quite often, and is frequently equated with "public opinion." Since these two terms, fuzzy as they may be, are actually used and in a sense take their place in social relations, they must be dealt with.

The Mass Mind and Stereotypes

To influence public opinion we must be concerned with the troublesome concept of the "mass mind." To be concerned with the "mass mind" is to be concerned with stereotypes. To be concerned with stereotypes is to be concerned with generalizations. To be concerned with generalizations is to be concerned with "images" one country might have of another.

But, again, the problem of generalization itself confronts us and re-emphasizes for us the importance of stereotypes in anything we attempt to say. *Countries,* as we know, do not have images of other countries—or of *anything* for that matter. Their *citizens* individually may have images, and it is well to remember that "citizens" is plural as is "images." If we are not careful in talking about countries, we will fall into the trap of using super-generalizations. In fact, when we speak of countries having images of other countries, we use a sort of massive stereotype. Perhaps it has grown out of the marriage of public relations to political science with the concept of "corporate image" as best man. Today many persons appear to feel that a nation (or corporation) not only can *hold* an image, but can *be* the image of some*thing* else.

It is necessary always to break such generalizations down into their parts. *Which persons* within Country A have *what kind of* stereotypes of *which segments or aspects of* Country B? When we begin thinking of national stereotypes in this fashion, we begin thinking of them as relative and individualized, and we begin wondering if they are not altogether meaningless.

But we know that they are not completely meaningless because some persons talk as if they *know* these stereotypes, as if stereotypes have meaning for them. They insist that stereotypes exist, even if only in the minds of men. So we perhaps must say that certain stereotypes of nations do in fact exist, although nobody has ever quite succeeded in getting at them even in particular individuals much less in entire nations.

Assuming the existence of national stereotypes in individual members of a society, a further question arises: Is the stereotype one has of another nation basically erroneous or basically valid? We cannot logically assume that negative or unfavorable stereotypes are *per se* more erroneous than positive or favorable ones. However, we frequently tend to make such an assumption, a fact which indicates something of our stereotype of the stereotype. Perhaps we need to realize that all is not fresh air and light in international relations or with individual nations, and that nations can have largely unfavorable characters (or images) just as specific persons can. We cannot really change the nation by manipulating its image any more than we can make a blind man read by constantly picturing him facing an open book.

Inevitable Distortion

Perhaps what we need in the area of international images or stereotypes is a *splintered or pluralistic* concept which is, indeed, indescribable. Little purpose can be seen in institutionalized destruction of national stereotypes. For the destroyer of the stereotypes places himself in the position of Truth-Holder, in the position of having the proper insights into what the stereotype *ought to be*. When he demolishes a stereotype, one would expect him to put something more valid in its place, and he himself implies he needs to do this.

We read that school children in the Soviet Union and in United States have distorted ideas of one another. This is not surprising; they undoubtedly have distorted ideas of their own classmates and their parents —or even of themselves. It might be said that everyone everywhere has distorted ideas about reality in general or about any piece of it. But what about these school children? It seems that they must change their concepts slowly through formal education and natural maturation. And, they must learn to live with the knowledge that they will always, at all times in their lives, have distorted images of one another and of other countries. This is a fact of human societies, and of the process of communication itself. Said another way: they must recognize their own human-ness and proceed on a personal basis to open their minds to ever more humanizing stereotypes. What more can they do?

It would be rather simple and greatly satisfying to suggest such panaceas as more news in the press about the respective nations, more exchange of students, more appreciative and knowledgeable tourists, better motion pictures, and books of a more "representative" type. But this is just a linguistic game played by unrealistic optimists or naïve social engineers. Such proposals are not only trite but smack too much of a trend toward stultifying consensus and a sort of universalistic morality. In fact, it relegates personal, cultural, and national differences and decisions to some negative "outcast" status.

What is rather pitiful about this national stereotype matter is that those often most concerned about it are the very ones who hold the most simplistic views. They picture whole "nations" or "the nation's children" or "the people" as having common impressions about whole groups or nations. This appears to be a rather basic form of stereotype-building in itself. It is much easier to think of "the nation" as having a stereotype of another nation than of thinking about individual persons in the nation as having differing facts, impressions, and attitudes about another nation.

Many persons will feel that this discussion completely ignores the question, that it is concerned with peripheral matters and does not squarely face the tedious job of restructuring our images of other nations. This is very far from the case. What we are saying here is that this restructuring job is a *personal* matter which each citizen of every country must undertake on his own. He must not, should not, rely on an organized campaign of restructuring. He cannot assume that at any time he has the "correct" or "right" stereotype or image of any other nation—or even of his own nation. He will have misconceptions, and they will often be based on misinformation, on biases, on ignorance, on censorship, on interest groups, and the like.

Thinking and Stereotypes

He may feel justified if he desires to blame his misconceptions on the communications media or on the "communications gap" or the "credibility gap" or whatever he desires to call it. But the fact is that he will always have this problem with him. He will always have divergent images fed to him by the media and by nature itself. He will always need to select, sift, glean, and reconstruct information for his own satisfaction and in accord with his maturity and education at that particular time. He must realize that he will always be faced with choices—in facts, opinions, experts, emphases. He must choose. And *what* he chooses determines his stereotypes, which in turn, help him make further choices.

The alternative to our rather confused system of multiple stereotypes is a closed society, an authoritarian system, in which stereotypes have been "corrected" and citizens have the same (and "right") images of other nations and of their own nation. But as long as a nation is free and open, it will be pluralistic, and as long as it is pluralistic it will have "erroneous" (or they will so appear to some persons) stereotypes. Whose stereotype is "correct" is not the question: let us assume that *all* stereotypes are wrong—"wrong" in the sense of being incomplete and non-objective. Otherwise, they would not be stereotypes.

In spite of the inadequacies of stereotypes, it is the main contention of this paper that these partial images—if we may call them that—are indispensable to public thinking, and possibly even to private thinking, about other countries. We must consider other countries in generalizations; we cannot think about the multi-faceted societies that they are or about each citizen that makes them up. We must think in broad strokes, in vivid colors, in lumps and pieces. Whether or not this is a commendable practice is not the issue; the fact remains that a human being *must* think about other nations in this way. Otherwise he cannot talk about other countries; or, at least, all he can say is, "It's too complex and differentiated for me to say anything about it."

International Implications

If we are going to talk (and think) about other nations, we must make use of stereotypes. If we want to have all favorable stereotypes, this is one thing, and we surely have the right to have them. But this does not mean that these stereotypes will be very close to the truth of the matter; in fact, a favorable stereotype may be far more misleading (and dangerous) than an unfavorable one. And, there is no evidence to lead us to believe that favorable stereotypes existing among nations lead to more "understanding" and "harmony" than do unfavorable ones.

In any discussion of relations between two nations "human values" naturally are deemed extremely important. One human value is independent determination of one's own opinions. Or, to form one's own stereotypes, if you will. This stereotype may be imperfect (it will be), but it is essential to human rights and a free society. And, to repeat, there is no reason to believe that it is *more* imperfect than it would be if it were more favorable—or in any way different from what it is.

The best way that the people of any nation can understand those of another nation is to develop, on an individual basis, a more sophisticated attitude toward the realities of language and a more patient stance toward each other. At the very root of this matter will be a changed attitude toward stereotypes—an attitude which shuns the very stereotyping of stereotypes as automatically and necessarily dangerous and vicious. The citizens of every nation must attempt constantly to think in *particulars* while realizing that the overriding tendency is for us to think in clusters, in generalizations or stereotypes.

Of course, if we take this line of thought very far we will find ourselves in the curious position of having *de*-stereotyped our thinking about one another's nations to the point that we are forced to be silent. And, perhaps *more silence* and *less communication* is really what international relations is in need of today. At least silence precipitated by a conscious determination to de-stereotype our conceptions of one another would be an intellectually healthy silence.

So, in conclusion, it might be well to emphasize several important considerations relative to national images and international understanding:

1) International understanding is so complex that it can never really be brought about by nations (or organizations therein) attempting to improve their "images" in other countries.

2) Negative stereotypes or images which citizens of countries have of other countries are not necessarily more erroneous than positive stereotypes which they may have.

3) All stereotypes or images of countries held by citizens are erroneous in the sense of being unbalanced, incomplete, and biased.

4) When we talk about stereotypes of other countries, we must talk about stereotypes held by individuals and not by nations or other collectives or entities.

5) Stereotypes are important; in fact, they are essential to thinking and communication about nations and peoples.

6) An attempt to de-stereotype our thinking about other countries is not only futile, but if taken too seriously will lead to frustration.

7) A recognition of the inadequacies of national stereotypes is useful to the student of communication, but the realistic view should be maintained that when a person eschews stereotyping, he disengages himself from reality and retreats into a world where silence and psychosis reign.

Garland O. Ashley:

International Power Communication

SOUND stock market advice also fits creatively with international power communication. In stock market lore, it is close to being axiomatic that when any good news is out, it is time to sell. Applicable to international power communication, it is evident that most of the "good news" about practiced propaganda technique is out. Much of it has been in popular print for years. So it may be a good time to disconnect from some of the "dogs," in our portfolios, of theory and practice.

"Good news," in the sense used here, means in stock market parlance that when *everyone* knows about impending profit, it is time to search elsewhere for the next profit-making adventure. In parallel, in international power communication, theory and practice of power communication were once known by only a few—hence were profitable. But as soon as "everyone knows," theory and practice are no longer profitable and become "a dog"—a bad stock. Hence, today it may be time to develop other, different, or better, forms for power communication—or recognize that any cub reporter who knows the liturgy can be as persuasive as a seasoned diplomat.

Once, the good news about international power communication was not out. It was closely guarded good news, as Machiavelli's *The Prince.* But now exposition on the techniques and commentary about its application are splurged about in so many places it becomes doubtful whether it deserves to be called good news, anymore.

Older good news about international power communication, and its propaganda technique, was once a deftly-guarded kit of tools and technique for persuasion and influence. Whatever "message sending" went on across public media was not noted and kept score on by cub reporters, as it is today. The mental kit was at a time almost solely in the hands of diplomats, certain astute military strategists, some scholarly clerics, and a core group of international economic planners.

Bulk Proliferation

The bulk of material out now is stunning, which has a pretense of connection with international power communication. The good news con-

▶ This is an original article done for this book by G. O. Ashley, University of Missouri, Columbia, 1969.

tent it may have had at a time could be said to be somewhat lost now. The actual bulk and prevalence reduces its value, for versions of it may be purchased from display racks at markets and chain stores.

It is also evident that much of the bulk has found readers. We see the slogans of it, and what used to be shibboleths of it, preened before us in print, on broadsides and banners, and across airways in broadcasting. We see it in photographs, motion pictures, and posters. It is displayed regularly on TV, where demonstrations of certain technique of it are considered "news." From many sides, youngsters not demonstrably beyond their puberty ceremonies shout and caterwaul statements they have lifted from Che Guevara's version of it. Insurgents wave copies of the so-called thought of the Chairman.

Academic writers are also contributing to the bulk. Some have what they assert is unique "theory" about international power communication, based apparently on a belief that exhortation and nagging will one day replace the power component of communication. Academic authors have even become discontented with producing critiques of each other's work. Critiques of critiques have begun to appear without the saving sign that it is a put on.

With candor, Dr. Wilbur Schramm gave us a statement of the objective of much of the proliferation now displayed. "For one thing," Schramm said, "communication research in the United States is quantitative, rather than speculative." The inapplicability of most of it to international power communication has been made manifest by many diplomats. Diplomats, over some 25 years, have tried to read and find a use for much of the outpouring. It has now been made clear there is not much. Even giving diplomats credit for being reticent about disclosing their sources, more source use of it would have been signalled, by now, if it had been useful.

It seems to stand out then that the research approach itself may preclude usefullness, for much of the bulk that fills our journals is mathematized down to a last quantum, but portends little. Over half of the disquisitions about the research beg the question of the research before they get beyond their abstract. It has become a fetish to say "more research is necessary" before the reported-on research displays it failed to achieve its ostensible purpose. While we recognize more citations have been provided, to trade off with, it is necessary to note that's about the extent of its predictability.

Meanwhile, a cacophony of international power communication shows signs of changing its form. So a diplomat who would read the bulk proliferation, to find out how he might use power communication more effectively, gets little help. Instead of obtaining useful new inductive technique, he is seemingly invited to join some type of cult. The cult apparently has as its central presumption that peace can be produced somehow from strenuous exhortation. Coercive demand seems to be the language they think is appropriate to make the lions of the world lie down straightaway with its lambs. Saying this state will produce a blessed disconnection from angry problems of international power communication neither alters the problems nor increases blessed disconnection. Hence, not much mystery goes with the evident conclusion that diplomats take little inspiration from the bulky tendentious literature on international power communication.

A Problem in Focus

A reflective look shows that the good news is out. So it becomes increasingly prospective that it may be time to sell away from reliance upon a technique that has become almost everyone's good news. As easily as we might agree to make the disconnection, however, to make it actually is another matter.

Some years back, in *The Human Use of Human Beings,* Dr. Norbert Wiener stated the international power communication problem in its three central aspects: "The commands though which we exercise our control over our environment are a kind of information we impart to it."

Our emphasis then should be on 1) commands, 2) control, and 3) imparted information.

Excluded directly by that preoccupation is almost all person-to-person communication, no matter how noteworthy it may be. The Peace Corps proponents have already demonstrated for us this takes too long, is of doubtful innoculative value during crunches, and for results achieved takes more input than the results merit.

Clearly also we need to exclude almost all crusades. The ecumenicists have made it clear there is not enough room at the top of their movement for all. All sloganeering about the "dulcet advantages" of peace should be left to them, then. When they call up or inspire a second coming, they should deserve all the credit for it. Meanwhile, power communicators should get better at their aspect of a craft of international communication.

Nor should we try to fall back on "old methods," clarified for all who will read of them by Sir Harold Nicolson. Plebes in academies get thorough grounding in those old methods. They would recognize them straightaway, even if they were brought back in a most peek-a-boo or mini-skirt façade. As Nicolson displayed, "theory" went out from the old methods on their first rude test.

To address the problem for what it is, we also have to notice diplomats have been given no new methods in modern times. There still remain as finite fundamental instruments for international power communication 1) the political art, 2) the economic inviegelment, or 3) the military threat or crunch. One would have thought, with so many selfstatedly keen minds producing such an enormity of copy on the flanks of international power communication, that something new and more substantive should have come from that great effort. Yet we note their cop out, and their ultimate recommendation during tense times that we should fall back upon techniques familiar to Talleyrand.

We see a problem then in a better focus. Serious power diplomats have a compounded problem on their hands. Publics that were once stable and that could once be addressed marginally are no longer stable. And if one tries to address them, as George F. Kennan did at Swathmore, they turn off their hearing aids, being able to anticipate the next ploy. The good news is out, then. To recognize that as Condition One of the new problem is to begin to see it correctly, for what it is.

Condition Two of the new problem involves the actual language. Traditionally, it had a form. Today, however, all the form it had that was useful is daily used in labor negotiations, teacher strikes, campus confrontations, and inter-generation coercion. A form so widely used and so inappropriately used does not have much substance left in it, for international power communication.

Condition Three is diplomatic practice. Diplomats today are compelled by a race of events, media-reported, to try to maintain old forms at the same time they want to save some of their talent to develop better ones. The Paris talks on Viet Nam are as eloquent a testimonial to this mugwumping as comes to mind.

The Shibboleth Approach

Great energy was laid on a shibboleth approach, during the Kennedy years. It worked for a period. But resort to that did not take account of modern journalism. Modern journalism has made a central pre-occupation of stripping the banner-bunting from today's shibboleth creators. A book on this hobby, *Personnel for the New Diplomacy*, didn't last past six months's exposure of its first edition. Hence its handbook role of reminding those with short memories what the word was became brief. The masthead role of the book then became a target for and casualty of modern journalism. With some help from Senator Fulbright, the jargonry recommended by that book hardly lasted in effectiveness beyond a time when the print had dried. Nor does it do to deplore this type rapid shift of events, for if the shibboleths of the book had not been unmasked at home, they would have been in a little more time by outsiders.

The steady, sustained, lastingly-secure shibboleth is no doubt something worthwhile to yearn for. As once used, to allow through those with correct credentials and to block away those without correct credentials, shibboleths were no doubt once comfortable—for fall back when one was tired. But we could usefully note the technique does not sustain international power communication, today. Those who know the correct genuflections and proper form for them might as well be practicing elocution at an academy for debutantes.

Most notably to be marked for failure, as a shibboleth *for* diplomacy from that book, was this statement. A hope was stated that diplomacy might become a "principal mechanism whereby sovereign states can communicate with one another and settle their differences short of war." Those who took that evangelistic statement to heart relinquished use of the third instrument of international power communication. It should have been made encumbent upon them to develop for the remaining two instruments far more efficacy than they have had, to date. But they were allowed to get off from that task, and retire in a happy carping about "complexity," "rates of change," "and wouldn't-it-be-nice-ifs."

Which may bring Condition Four of the new problem into a better focus, that worldwide we are believed more than we may realize. Just above, for a noble-sounding shibboleth, a group of reciters foreswore use of an ultimate instrument of diplomacy and national power. Give that all the noble attribution one may feel compelled to. But then we should note that such statements are not made in vacuums. People of predatory inclination noted those things were said. So the saying created opportunities for ill-advised predation which, upon reflection, it might have been more appropriate to dampen.

We won't try to show off any uncommon wisdom after the event noted, above. But it would appear to be foolish in an extreme to keep up that chorus, just because it was once a recommended shibboleth—designed for limited purposes. We do fault the continued chorus of it, which seems somehow in all usages to be accompanied by a holier-than-thou smirk. We are sure it is not a sustained input that helps solve a problem of international power communication. For apparently that shibboleth has fallen into such a disrepute that the only one it any longer fools is he who says it. Such as these ought to be discreet enough to count themselves out of policy circles, even when lecturing sophomores.

Condition Five needs attention next. There have been some changes which need far more thorough factor treatment, in future communication research in international power communication. Past forms of international power communication cannot be sensibly dredged up as "new breakthroughs of thought." In factoring populations, we had better begin with it given that populations are far more restive than they have ever been before, and that we shall see more of this before less of it. We ought to use as opener that the good news is out, and begin from another platform than some cumbersome arithmetical display that we have read the word. Finally, a use of non-nuclear armed forces for Mackinder-like purposes, as in Vietnam, has demonstrably come upon sorry days. To act as if it will be possible, in international power communication, to continue such adventures indefinitely is being myopic to signs of the times.

An era is in passage then. A new era will be upon us with formidable new requirements for international power communication, like as not sooner than we may become ready for. Statements such as "new needs are under intense study," as a buffonery, simply do not any longer fit.

Ambassador W. Averell Harriman prescribed in 1962 a "solution" that has come home to roost, awkwardly as chickens of thought sometimes do. He said: "The task for the United States and the West is to show that our system of freedom not only provides for human dignity but also for food, housing, education, and other fruits of the twentieth century."

We have not in the years between demonstrated that this goal can be reached in the Far East. It remains to be determined even whether we can achieve it at home, in time. Hence as an instrumental of international power communication, such epigrams ought to be bitten back from the tongue, rather than spoken. International power communication does get heard. There was no dissonance of substance connected to the Harriman "solution." It was simply proposing in "policy" what we could not deliver in fact. We had better not do much more of that.

To say diplomatic seminal understanding should have put that comment in a proper focus is correct. But it ignores a requirement to keep such ceremonial comments in diplomatic privacies. When such comments are made as "forum comments," for the media to disseminate, they become counter-productive. Condition Six of the new problem may be stated with clarity, then.

Media Coverage and Distortion

Never before in the world's history has there been such a degree and extent of diplomatic coverage, as in the media today. It should also be manifest it is not all party-line coverage. And it is international power communication in action, for advantage or increased complexity, that is having impact. The steady state of diplomatic competence one would hope for does not seem to have been abetted by that bulk of media coverage. Under such media coverage, to prevent added media distortion, communication heretofore fullsome, bland, and of multiple-entendre, would seem to need to become more bold, plausible, and blunt. If that is held to be not so, then in the climate we are in, it must follow we shall have to expect multiple *demands* from others to continue to far-outpace most concrete negotiating capability. From today's media, that is the evident proportion now.

Summed up, there is discernible a lag of thought about international power communication. The good news is out. Far too many people understand the form now and its propaganda content to keep up with "old forms." Thus it follows that unless and until forms change, increased non-communication is predictable, even while a bulk of it may increase. It takes no computational seer to discern this.

With modern journalism "interpreting" international power communication, a continued practice of its random technique shall merely add to an increasing public cacophony. It will deliver less and less actual result, all the while its volume shall increase. And much more unstructured volume of it will increase a dissonance toward it that is not in line with its objective.

We actually now see diplomats competing in the media for space and attention. The frayed art of crisis-mongering and dissimulation are much in evidence. Unstated behind it all seems to be an assumption that the public of these "performers" will stay attentive endlessly.

To the contrary, we have established enough for all to see that the publics involved are becoming increasingly restive. As if the sound and fury of it all were not enough, international power communication of late has had more and more economic overtone. But going with that overtone is the proscription that the people should stay dull and in ennui, toward the subject and its personal implications to them. It being everywhere more and more evident that the people are not going to stay dull toward international economics, then the "chorus" and "orchestration" of it we still hear becomes decidedly counter-productive. National excesses in finance are also coming back home, to be felt keenly. The media, once more, have been a latchpin for some increase in understanding of crises in international finance.

In recent journalism, exposed was the whole façade of the International Monetary Fund's adjustment proposals. Thread by thread and country by country, during 1969, the IMF's former shining reputation has begun to show many tatters. Since a journalism of frustration which began the exposé has demonstrated it can do so, with impunity, it would be uncommonly foolish to hope for a moratorium from further study of IMF's technique.

We have been on a drift, then. A discernible lag in thought about what international power communication is for seems to have overtaken us. Accordingly, on this framework, fresh thought about international power communication is indicated.

The greatest stride imaginable in it will come from those who have stamina enough to see it for what it shall have to be, rather than pretty-painting it a hue that suits them. The subject of international power communication is manifestly no longer sacred, arcane, or of great mystique. Nor shall it for much longer stay immune from trenchant analysis and critique from outsiders.

The good news is out. Minds capable of discerning a new era and its implications to diplomacy exist now. But we give the last word to Dr. Norbert Wiener: "The circuit therefore demands a certain amount of communication power in order that the message may not be swamped by its own energy."

Ralph K. White:

The New Resistance to International Propaganda

THE WORLD is more and more tired of "propaganda." This is the fundamental, all-embracing fact which every propagandist must face, and the
implications of which he must recognize, if he is even to have an entree
into the minds of those who are not already emotionally on his side.
The psychological resistances of a skeptical, propaganda-weary world must
be respected and intelligently taken into account; they cannot be simply
battered down.

American propagandists have been from the beginning more aware
of these resistances than their Communist opponents have been. Recent
evidence, however, suggests that they should be given even more weight
than they have been given in the past. There is accumulating evidence
that the special antagonism felt by neutralists toward "propaganda" coming from either side in the present East-West conflict is the greatest single
obstacle to our effectiveness, and that the greatest single factor in our being
able to beat the Communists at their own propaganda game will be our
ability to understand this neutralist skepticism and to see its practical
implications.

Recent evidence, in other words, suggests that the following propositions are, if anything, more true today than ever before:

First, our Soviet opponents have lost more than most Americans
realize by their almost continual use of the battering-ram technique. The
idea prevailing in some quarters that we lose by being less crude, less
repetitious, less "emotional" than the Russians is in the main a dangerous
misconception. Second, the chief weakness of our own propaganda is not,
as some Americans assume, that we are too gentlemanly to descend to
Soviet tactics and "fight fire with fire." It is that—at least in what we say
to the non-Communist world—we too often give the impression of being
"propagandistic." Third, the psychological resistances which the Communists fail to batter down by sheer crude repetition are equally incapable
of being circumvented by subtlety or deviousness. The way into the heart
of the skeptical neutralist lies not through artifice but through candor.

This does not mean that on the most essential points, such as the

▶ From: *Public Opinion Quarterly* (Princeton/New Jersey), Vol. 16/No. 4 (Winter
1952-53), pp. 539-551. Reprinted by permission of the publisher and the author.

danger of Soviet aggression or the necessity of collective strength to deter Soviet aggression, we need to soft-pedal our own convictions. It does not mean that we need to have any sense of guilt or apology in our role as propagandists—in the better sense of that word, involving only a large-scale effort to persuade or convince. (Probably there are few listeners to the Voice of America who do not take it for granted that it is a propaganda arm of the American Government in this non-condemnatory sense of the word propaganda. Of course we are propagandists.)

It does mean two things. First, our *actions* must be in line with our words. The propaganda of the deed is more potent than the propaganda of the word, and the propaganda of the word is effective in direct proportion to the deeds which it is able to publicize. As Secretary Acheson has put it, "what is even more important than what we say to the world is how we conduct ourselves, at home and abroad. The force of example and action is the factor which finally determines what our influence is to be."

Second, it means that our words will be most effective—at least in what we say to the non-Communist world—when the *manner* of our effort to persuade and convince is modest, reasonable, discriminating, sensitive to the kinds of skepticism existing in the minds of any particular audience, and prepared to meet that skepticism candidly and factually, as neighbor might talk to neighbor. It means that we are most effective when we depart freely, wherever the facts warrant it, from a simple black-and-white picture of the world, when we avoid all of the stock ballyhoo techniques of the radio or television advertiser as well as the manners of the table-pounding orator and the finger-wagging schoolmarm, when, instead, we cultivate the highest standards of journalism.

There is a curiously widespread assumption in the United States that the cunning Communists are past masters at the propaganda game and that we innocent democrats are rank amateurs. Actually the reverse of this assumption would be at least as easy to defend. It is true that the Communists have had successes in China, in France, in Italy; but the Communist tide seems to have been receding for some years in France, at least. Even in these countries the successes can be attributed primarily to two great assets which they have had and we have not: the existence of widespread economic distress which their class ideology is inherently well calculated to capitalize upon, and their possession of a corps of dedicated, disciplined, face-to-face agitators within each of these countries. The United States has no fifth columns within France or Italy comparable with those which Russia has in the Italian and French Communist parties. Neither of these assets, however, has any necessary direct relationship to propaganda technique as such. When it comes to evaluating Communist propaganda techniques as illustrated in the Communist press and radio, the verdict of the typical reader or listener in either eastern or western

Europe seems to be that they are boringly repetitious, obviously "propagandistic," and therefore *dull*. One Frenchman recently used a graphic gesture in describing Soviet propaganda—the gesture of an organ-grinder always grinding out the same mechanical tune.

Available figures on listenership tell the same story. For instance, in Western Germany 65 per cent of the radio listeners sampled by the Reactions Analysis Staff of HICOG said they had listened to the Voice of America, while the figure for the nearest Communist competitor of the Voice was 9 per cent. In Eastern Germany, where the Communists are in the saddle, the situation is remarkably similar; the most widely heard and respected station is not the Communist Radio Berlin but RIAS, the vigorously anti-Communist, American-directed, German-operated station in Western Berlin. Similarly, there is reason to think that the Western radios, BBC and the Voice of America, are much more listened to throughout the Satellite area than are Communist. radios in Western Europe. As for America, how many Americans even know of the existence of Moscow's programs beamed to us in English?

It is also interesting to find that the Western European verdict on Communist dullness is shared to some extent by the Communists themselves. They are beginning to realize that methodical dogmatism does not draw listeners. In the spring of 1952 there was in the Communist press of East Berlin a campaign of "criticism and self-criticism" directed chiefly against Radio Berlin, and its chief charge, realistically enough, was that this station's output was dull. Several articles called for more humor, more conversation, more "sensitivity to what is alive" (Lebensgefühl), more "creative optimism," a less schematic approach, fewer catchwords (Schlagworte), and—this from a Communist!—less of a black-and-white picture (Schwarz-Weiss-Malerei). There was also some explicit recognition that the form or technique of Western propaganda is superior: "The content (of the Communist radio programs) triumphs over the form, which is too little paid attention to, in contrast with the West, where the form usually smothers the content." The writer of this statement was perhaps intentionally vague, but he seems to be obliquely accepting a proposition which in the minds of most non-Communists in Western Europe is quite clear: the repetitiousness and the propagandistic quality of Communist propaganda make it relatively hard to listen to.

In a broader historical perspective, too, the success of the Communists' bludgeon type of propaganda is ambiguous, to say the least. Probably the most effective single piece of international communication in the twentieth century was Wilson's list of Fourteen Points, and it was not a bludgeon. The appeal lay rather in its adopting a broad statesmanlike approach, above the battle and free from vindictiveness. Hitler's propaganda bludgeon worked with the Germans, but few non-Germans were impressed, and the more winsome eloquence of Roosevelt and Churchill helped to rally a world to defeat Hitler. The Soviet bludgeon has been wielded on a large scale for thirty-five years; it has perhaps worked well with the Russians (though even this is questioned in some quarters), but world revolutionary propaganda has led to successful revolution only in the case of China. That is, it is only in China that a Communist government has attained power without the help, direct or indirect, of the Soviet Red Army, and even there the Chinese Red Army, aided by the Kremlin, had a good deal to do with it. We are free, then, to follow the present-day evidence in the direction in which it leads. We are not compelled to assume that where our methods differ from those of the Russians they are necessarily right and we are necessarily wrong.

The Real Problems of American Propaganda

The chief weakness of our own propaganda is not, as some Americans assume, that we are too gentlemanly to descend to Soviet tactics and "fight fire with fire." We use plenty of fire (of a sort quite different from that used by the Communists) in what we say to the peoples behind the Iron Curtain, and there is much reason to believe that it is effective. The great difficulty lies in what we say to the non-Communist world; the danger here is that we may appear to be too "propagandistic."

To appreciate the problem that our information program is up against, it is necessary first to distinguish very sharply between the psychological situation that confronts us on this side of the Curtain and that which confronts us on the other side. On the other side, official Communist propaganda is omnipresent, and the picture of the world that it presents is of course grossly distorted. While usually avoiding outright lying, it systematically omits any fact or idea that might modify its all-black picture of us and its all-white picture of the Kremlin. It continually and flagrantly stacks the cards. Against this flood of selected data the listener must struggle as best he can, and our information and "propaganda" are rightly designed to help him in the struggle. Necessarily, we must spend most of our time setting the record straight; and this means not only correcting the grossest lies but also taking the offensive and hitting the Kremlin hard on those vulnerable spots which the Soviet propagandist systematically covers up and glosses over. Necessarily, we must select our facts too, presenting primarily the kinds of facts that will to some extent redress the balance. We can and must "fight fire with fire" in this sense, and also in the sense that what we say must often have an emotional impact. Neither selectivity nor the occasional expression of strong emotion will impress this audience as "too prropagandistic." On the contrary, a very hard-hitting anti-Stalin political message seems to be just what most of our listeners there want. Those who are already strongly anti-Stalin (and most of those who listen apparently are anti-Stalin) usually do not seem to judge our message in terms of its judiciousness and careful discrimination. Their emotional needs are for vicarious expression of their own smouldering hatred of the Stalinist tyranny, for evidence that the strongest nation beyond the reach of Stalin's power is on their side, and for hope that, with this and other allies in the West, their day of liberation will some day come. This is what they want, and this is what they are getting. Unquestionably, too, millions listen. It would be very rash to say "millions" in Russia, but the conclusion that there are millions in East Germany and the Satellite area who listen is no longer open to serious question.

In Western Europe and other parts of the non-Communist world the psychological situation is radically different. In contrast to our listeners behind the Curtain, who are starved for straight news and for a source of hope and emotional support, our listeners throughout the free world are not starved for either news or hope. As a rule their own press and radio give them plenty of news and comment, and as a rule a good deal of it is, like what they get from America, anti-Communist. If they turn their dials to the Voice of America, they do so not as starving men but as men who have just finished a Thanksgiving dinner, and they are in a choosy mood. In addition, we cannot take it for granted that these people are favorably disposed toward America and Americans. Finally, and most important, those who incline toward neutralism are hypersensitive to what they call "propaganda" coming from *either* side. It is imperative, therefore, that we study and take into account what they mean by "propaganda."

One thing we are fairly sure of: most of those who call both us and Russians "propagandistic" do not mean that we indulge in lying as the Russians do. If this were what they meant the prospect of improvement would be dark indeed, since, platitudinous as it may sound, we are already making every effort to be scrupulously accurate on all matters of tangible fact. Occasional errors creep in, in spite of all our effort, but no major improvement is to be expected from an intensified effort to be less like the Russians in this respect.

What these critics do mean is not by any means fully clear, especially since it varies from country to country. It would seem, though, that when a Belgian or an Egyptian or an Indonesian angrily twists his radio dial in order not to hear what he calls the "propaganda" of Moscow or of the Voice of America, the chances are that in the back of his mind there is a blending of several evil images. The first is of two crudely simple black-and-white pictures of the world, each of which he believes to be a gross distortion of the complexity of reality, even when it does not contain outright lies. Then there are two giant nations struggling for world power, each looking upon the listener's own country as a pawn or tool in that struggle and each using words in a calculated effort to subject his will to its own. The last image is of the gathering storm clouds of atomic war, in which the thunder of mutual denunciation is an omen of unthinkable things to come. Calculated distortion, domination and death—these, then, are some of the connotations of "propaganda" in its present historical context. It is no wonder that "Count me out"—i.e., neutralism—is a typical reaction.

Corresponding to these three evil images, three remedies suggest themselves. Each of them is already being applied to a considerable extent, and the extent to which any one of them *should* be applied is a matter of judgment and of balancing pros and cons. It is this writer's judgment, however, that what we say to the free world would gain even more in impact if we demonstrated more candor, more respect for the listener, and a more "positive" approach.

Less Selectivity.   No one on our side questions the statement made at the beginning of this article: "The way into the heart of the skeptical neutralist lies not through artifice but through candor." No one doubts that our information program is and should be conspicuously superior to that of the Communists in candor—defining candor, provisionally, as a readiness to depart from the black-and-white picture when the available facts warrant such a departure. Yet even in the free world our task includes the countering of vicious Communist propaganda, and an awakening of those who are not aware of the nature and extent of the Soviet danger. There is a real problem, then: at what point should we draw the line between the kind of selectivity that the strengthening of the free world seems to require and the sort of non-selectivity that would demonstrate our candor and objectivity? To what extent is the selectivity which is clearly needed in our message to the Communist world also necessary or desirable in what we say to our friends and potential friends on this side of the Curtain? *How much* white or grey can we afford to admit on the "black" side of our own black-white picture, and how much black or grey on the "white" side?

The line would probably be drawn at one point by most of the professional American propagandists (e.g., desk chiefs, script-writers in the Voice of America) and at a somewhat different point by many in Congress and the general public. The professionals are likely to favor a lower degree of selectivity—that is, they are likely to put relatively more emphasis on the advantages of obvious candor and objectivity. While granting that we do not need to wash all of our dirty linen in public, they would usually feel that we should wash at least enough of it in public so that our audience could not possibly fail to notice what we are doing. Yet a fear exists—perhaps a misguided fear—that Congress and the public would see something "subversive" and insufficiently anti-Communist in the procedure if our propaganda were as candid as the professionals think it ought to be. In the interest of mutual understanding, therefore, it seems worthwhile to present in this paper the reasons why, in one person's opinion, the American information program to the non-Communist world should actually be *less* selective than it now is.

An anecdote will illustrate one of the ways in which too much selectivity could do harm. In the early days of World War II Goebbels did his best to discredit the BBC with phrases such as "the Ministry of Lies." He failed, and perhaps the most crucial single incident bringing about his failure was a news report by the BBC asserting that after a certain mission to the continent seven British planes had failed to return. The German radio had just described the same incident, stating that *five* planes had failed to return. In other words, the BBC was describing the British fortunes of battle as actually blacker than they were being described by the enemy. In this case it happens that the British were merely accurate; two planes which the Germans had seen leaving the continent were already crippled and failed to get to England when the others did. The psychological effect, however, was far greater than mere apparent accuracy would ever have achieved. It would have been worthwhile for the British to invent those two additional non-returning planes, even if they had not existed, in order to achieve a dramatic demonstration of British capacity to go beyond what was necessary in the direction of candor. Selectivity in the form of, let us say, reporting that seven British planes left the Continent (which was true, but not the whole truth) would have been a psychological mistake.

One generalization which this example illustrates is that, *where the audience has other sources of news*, comparisons are likely to be made. Applying this to our present problem, it implies that if we should soft-pedal anything that is emphasized by other news sources, Communist or non-Communist, we would not only fail to keep it from our listeners' ears but would also lose some of that credibility which is our most precious asset. This is especially true if the fact which is ignored or soft-pedaled is unfavorable to ourselves. As far as news is concerned, the soundest rule would seem to be to let *news value*—the newspaperman's conception of the inherent importance or reader-interest of an event—be almost the only criterion of what should be included or emphasized.

The experience of the British Broadcasting Corporation supports this view. The Voice of America is definitely more hard-hitting, more outspokenly anti-Communist, than the BBC, and this policy has reaped dividends in our broadcasts to Iron Curtain countries where the audiences crave hope and vicarious expression of their own hostility to the Stalinist tyranny. There the Voice of America is usually preferred just because it is in a sense more "propagandistic." On the other hand, the BBC is usually regarded as more objective than the Voice of America in the non-Communist countries where sensitivity to "propaganda" is greatest; and a major factor in its reputation is, probably, the great emphasis which it places on inclusiveness or non-selectivity in the news.

As for commentaries, selectivity has disadvantages there too. There are many topics on which an American preparing a pamphlet or a radio broadcast may hesitate to say anything at all: the Negro in America, slums in America, unemployment, corruption, our attitude toward British socialism, shifts in our policies toward Germany and Japan, MacArthur's advance to the Yalu, Franco, Chiang Kai-shek, Indochina, North Africa, the Arab refugees, our disarmament in 1945, American "imperialism" in Latin America, the perils of an arms race. On some of these topics we have a much sounder case than most of our critics realize, yet one often hesitates even to broach such a topic, knowing that any really honest treatment of it would involve certain "admissions," and knowing that every "admission" carries a certain danger.

The objection to admissions does have some factual support. There is reason to think that some listeners who are hostile enough to be looking for things to pounce on may react to an admission only by thinking "It must be true, since they admit it themselves." Because of this danger, candor is certainly not always self-evidently the best policy. But the available evidence does suggest that we should reconsider the matter; perhaps we have been too sensitive to the danger of making admissions and too insensitive to the opposite danger of losing both listeners and respect by seeming to gloss over problems which are very much present in our listeners' minds.

The evidence in favor of a need for even greater candor is impressionistic and, tentatively, experimental. The impressionistic evidence comes chiefly from the kinds of criticism of American propaganda that occur most often in the non-Communist world. With no statistics on the matter, this writer's impression is that those who criticize (and they appear to be in the minority) most often describe the Voice of America as *propagandistic* (with variants such as "table-pounding"), as *patronizing* (with variants such as "boastful," "condescending," "teaching," "didactic," and "educating"), and as simply *dull*. While there are persons who have made the very different criticism that its programs to the Free World are not "hard-hitting" enough, it is significant that this type of criticism is not frequent among our listeners in the non-Communist world. They do not often say, as some Americans do, that we are "too gentlemanly," that we should "fight fire with fire," or that we should "hit harder." What they do say, and say very often, is that we "pound the table" too hard and too much. Or they say that we are "getting to be too much like the Communists," or that the Communists are "even worse" than we are. The similarity in the pattern of adjectives is also striking. While the Communists are apparently not called "patronizing," the other two counts against us, "propagandistic" and "dull," are exactly the same as the two charges which are by all odds the most frequent in describing Communist propaganda. (Again—this is to some extent a natural reaction against the two great powers regardless of propaganda approach.)

Curiously enough, listeners do not often say in so many words that our programs are not candid enough. Yet if they were more analytical they probably would, since, in their minds, a lack of sufficient candor presumably underlies and partly accounts for each of the three defects that are most often mentioned. Greater candor would of course counteract the idea of "propaganda" in the sense of calculated distortion; similarly, more real humility (and candor about ourselves implies occasional humility) might go far toward counteracting the impression among critics that our programs are "patronizing"; and any variation from a black-white picture would be to them a welcome relief from boredom. When Anthony Eden recently spoke of the "magnificent" performance of the Red Army at Stalingrad—in a way which if anything added to the force of his later anti-Kremlin remarks—he probably accomplished three things simultaneously: he gained a little added prestige as a man who could rise above "propaganda"; he minimized any tendency of the Russians to think that he felt superior to them as Russians; and he gave a little refreshment to ears long jaded with "four legs good, two legs bad."

As far as it goes, then, the impressionistic evidence which has come to the attention of the writer supports the thesis that, in view of the changing climate of opinion in the Free World, diminished selectivity would add to the size of our audience, to our own prestige, and to the believability of everything else that we say. As for experimental evidence, preliminary results of an experiment done in Germany, with matched listening groups and controlled conditions, have turned out in favor of candor. An approach which was less selective than is now typical of the American information program appeared to be better both from the standpoint of preference for these particular programs and from the standpoint of general attitude toward the source from which these programs come.

More respect for the listener. It is hard for many Americans to appreciate the full extent of the fear of American domination that exists abroad, even among our non-Communist allies. Knowing the live-and-let-live spirit of the American people, it seems ridiculous to us that anyone should take charges of American "domination" or "imperialism" seriously. But such charges are taken seriously, and fear of our desire to use other countries as pawns in a power struggle colors much of the listening to our words. It behooves us, then, to see to it that the words themselves do not suggest any sense of superiority to the listener or any lack of understanding and appreciation of his nation and his culture. This is the least we can do to counteract the notion that we think he is, or could become, a pawn or tool.

In addition, there can be more of a person-to-person approach, with a focus on the idea of "we're all in this thing together," and without any explicit attention either to the fact that the speaker is an American or to the particular nationality of the listener. Even this, however, can be done best if the ideas and the forms of expression that are used show an intimate, easy familiarity with the listener's ways of thought.

And even this kind of thing calls for intimate *knowledge* of the listener's life and way of thought. Here we Americans are greatly handicapped by our geographical distance from our audiences. Although most of the script-writers in the Voice of America are natives of or have long lived in the country to which they are broadcasting, too often their knowledge is not up to date. Often the writer has not seen his audience for several years. An urgent need, therefore, is a greatly expanded program of rotation of personnel, to enable at least all of the creative writers of the Voice to spend two or three months refreshing their understanding of the minds, the current problems and the emotional preoccupations of the people they are talking to.

A more "positive" approach. The psychological association between denunciation of Communism and our audience's fear that we may drag them into an unnecessary war seems to be spreading in some parts of the free world. The more we denounce, the more "belligerent" they think we are, and the more they fear us. From this standpoint denunciation is the worst possible approach if we really want allies in a possible war of defense against Communist aggression. But it is not so easy to see what to do about it. If a certain people (let us say the people of India, or of Egypt) is not even really aware that the Soviet danger exists, how can we *not* talk to them about the Soviet danger? How can we justify our own policy of alliances, rearmament and fighting in Korea except against a background of Soviet aggression and the danger to all freedom which is involved if that aggression is not stopped?

The dilemma will remain regardless of all our efforts to resolve it. That is, there will necessarily be some neutralists who are so allergic to any anti-Soviet talk by us that they will always refuse to listen and always consider it further evidence of our "belligerence." But at least three things can be done to minimize the frequency of this reaction while maximizing the number of those who hear the most important elements in our anti-Soviet collective-security message:

1. To make our actions as well as our words scrupulously non-aggressive and non-provocative; to emphasize and reemphasize the official American policy of opposition to a "preventive war" or a "war of liberation," and to avoid action which would make these words sound insincere.

2. To state our accusations soberly and factually, without any of the sweeping unsupported statements which are the stock-in-trade of Soviet propaganda against us.

3. To keep down the proportion of direct and indirect denunciation of the Kremlin to that amount which is empirically found to be reasonably acceptable to a given audience, and to fill the remainder of our time with "positive" material which is not even indirectly related to the East-West conflict. Since most of our present output

to the free world is at least indirectly related to the East-West conflict (e.g., reports of the increasing defensive strength and unity of Europe) this limitation would probably cut down considerably on the present amount of direct and indirect denunciation. If we did this the chances are that we would both reassure those who now think we are "belligerent" and considerably increase the chance that they would listen to our sober and factual (but, let us hope, powerful) presentation of the essentials in the case for collective security, including the nature and dimensions of the Soviet danger.

6

SUPRANATIONAL COMMUNICATION EFFORTS

Robert P. Knight
UNESCO's INTERNATIONAL COMMUNICATION ACTIVITIES

Kurt Koszyk
THE DEVELOPMENT OF THE INTERNATIONAL PRESS
   INSTITUTE

Mary A. Gardner
THE EVOLUTION OF THE INTER AMERICAN PRESS
   ASSOCIATION

Heinz-Dietrich Fischer
EUROVISION AND INTERVISION TOWARD MONDOVISION

Nancy C. Jones
DEVELOPMENT AND FUNCTIONS OF INTELSAT

6

SUPRANATIONAL COMMUNICATION EFFORTS

A LTHOUGH some attention had been given to international cooperation in information exchange in the 1930's—and even earlier with the news agencies—it was really only after World War II that any systematic, organized efforts were made toward improving supranational communication. Naturally, as improved technology, e.g. in transportation, brought the world closer together, peoples found themselves more interested in communicating with other peoples. The organizations and technical developments which arose in the 1940's, 1950's and 1960's were inevitable results of this "one worldism" and have contributed greatly to our present concern with, and attention to, the problems of peoples in widely diverse and separated parts of the world.

One of the broadest and most important of the organizations which arose out of the ruins of World War II was the United Nations. It is with one of its divisions—UNESCO—that the first article in this chapter deals. In it, Dr. Robert Knight of the University of Missouri surveys the role of this organization in studying and improving international communication. A group, of quite a different nature, composed of internationally minded press people, began the International Press Institute in the mid-1950's, and it has played a major role in bringing together newspaper leaders from all over the world in an attempt to raise journalistic standards generally and to erase many of the narrow, nationalistic press perspectives in world journalism. In the second article, Dr. Kurt Koszyk of Dortmund, one of West Germany's leading journalism researchers, traces the evolution and achievements of the International Press Institute.

Dr. Mary Gardner of Michigan State University, a Latin American scholar, in the third article discusses an international (but not world-wide) organization—similar in many ways to the IPI but concerned with press problems of only the Western Hemisphere—the Inter American Press Association. The last two articles of this chapter are related to international activities in the field of broadcasting. Dr. Heinz-Dietrich Fischer of Cologne University first discusses the development of Eurovision and

Intervision in Europe and points the way to "Mondovision." And in the final article, Dr. Nancy Jones of the Pennsylvania State University school of journalism deals with the United Nations' efforts to improve international communication through broadcasting—especially through "Intelsat."

*   *   *   *

RELATED READING

Barber, R. B. B. *Eurovision as an Expression of International Cooperation in Western Europe*. Unpublished Ph.D. dissertation, Northwestern University, Evanston, Ill., 1963.

Codding, George A. *The International Telecommunication Union: An Experiment in International Cooperation*. Leiden, The Netherlands: Brill, 1952.

Cooper, Kent. *Barriers Down: The Story of the News Agency Epoch*. New York: Farrar and Rhinehart, 1942.

Emery, Walter B. *Five European Broadcasting Systems*. Journalism Monographs, 1. Austin, Texas: Association for Education in Journalism, 1966.

European Broadcasting Union. *Monographs* (occasional). Geneva.

Evans, F. Bowen. *Worldwide Communist Propaganda Activities*. New York: Macmillan, 1955.

Gardner, Mary A. *The Inter American Press Association: Its Fight for Freedom of the Press, 1926-1960*. Austin: Univ. of Texas Press, 1967.

IAPA. *Press of the Americas* (New York). Usually monthly; English, Spanish.

IPI. *IPI Report* (Zurich, Switzerland). Monthly; in English, German, French.

Kruglak, Theodore E. *The Two Faces of TASS*. New York: McGraw-Hill Paperbacks, 1963.

Kurta, Henryk. "The UNESCO Informational Department and the International Exchange of Information," in: *International Review of Journalism* (Warsaw, Poland), Vol. 1/No. 1 (1966), pp. 71-80.

Morris, Joe Alex. *Deadline Every Minute: The Story of the United Press*. Garden City, N.Y.: Doubleday and Co., 1957.

Nolte, Ernst. *Die faschistischen Bewegungen*. Munich: Deutscher Taschenbuch Verlag, 1966.

Storey, Graham. *Reuters Century, 1851-1951*. London: Parrish, 1951.

UNESCO. *World Communications: Press-Radio-Film-Television*. New York and Paris, 1964.

White, Llewellyn and Robert D. Leigh. *Peoples Speaking to Peoples*. Chicago: University of Chicago Press, 1946.

Robert P. Knight:

UNESCO's International Communication Activities

WHEN the United Nations General Assembly in 1962 endorsed Unesco's program for helping information media in less-developed nations, it was in a sense reconfirming the international communication role of the United Nations Educational, Scientific and Cultural Organization.

That role should not be misunderstood: It does not relate merely to developing countries. In its first years, Unesco's mass media efforts concentrated on building up media and professionalism in war-devastated nations, while breaking down barriers to the free flow of ideas; in the 1960's, the organization's communications emphasis centered on developing nations and on education; in the early 1970's Unesco's thrust apparently will be toward the use made of communications satellites, toward book production and toward getting maximum benefit from exchange of persons among nations. In other words, Unesco's international communications role has been to bridge educational, scientific and cultural gaps through the use of mass communications media.

René Maheu, Director-General since 1962, expressed this attitude in 1948 when he was a Unesco press counselor:

> . . . it is neither its [the Division of Mass Communications'] aim nor its duty to develop and extend the press, radio, and films as such. UNESCO will use these media as channels to bring education, science, and culture in the broadest sense of the words to the peoples of the world, striving to promote mutual understanding and knowledge of each other's lives.[1]

Although over the years since 1946 Unesco itself has been led by circumstances, changing world conditions and financial realities to fluctuate from an idealistic to a pragmatic position and halfway back,[2] the course

---

[1] René Maheu, "The Work of UNESCO in the Field of Mass Communications," *Journalism Quarterly*, Vol. 25, No. 2 (1948), p. 157.
[2] A clear exposition of this point is made by T. V. Sathyamurthy in "Twenty Years of UNESCO: An Interpretation," *International Organization*, Vol. 21, No. 3 (1967), pp. 614-633.

▶ This is an original article done for this book by Robert P. Knight, University of Missouri, Columbia, 1969.

of its Mass Communications Division has remained relatively steady and pragmatic. This paper will concentrate on activities of that division, charged as it is with most of the communications duties except those involving copyright and the like.

In being mainly pragmatic, Unesco generally has avoided ideological disputes. For example, it has dealt with agreements about flow of materials among countries—something concrete—rather than with the broad concept of freedom of information. (The United Nations itself has attempted to define that concept with notable lack of success as Michael Ta Kung Wei points out elsewhere in this book.)

Communications Surveys

In its first years, the late 1940's, Unesco set out to discover the technical, legislative and educational needs of the mass communications media, country by country, in what turned out to be a five-year project.[3] During those years, 29 Unesco field workers toured 126 countries and Unesco officials corresponded with persons in 31 additional nations. Questionnaires with more than 1,500 items were used to obtain press data more comprehensive than ever before available. A separate volume on television was added shortly thereafter.[4]

This massive project seemed to set the pattern for Unesco in the mass media field. It pinpointed shortages (especially of newsprint—a Unesco concern for several years); it showed the need for journalism education (a matter with which Unesco was to become more involved beginning in the mid-1950's); it recognized educational possibilities of audio and visual media; it suggested cooperative international efforts; it recommended governments recognize and help solve their own communications problems; it pointed toward the need for Unesco to aid specific countries in developing their media systems; it produced numerous studies springing from the original documentation of the surveys.

The surveys themselves continued, with new editions of *World Communications* in 1951, 1956 and 1964. Unesco mass communications data also appeared in the organization's *Basic Facts and Figures,* from 1952 until termination of the series in 1961, in the United Nations' *Statistical Yearbook* (the latest edition of which is a good source for the most current media data) and in Unesco's *Statistics of Newspapers and Other Periodicals,* 1959, and *Statistics on Radio and Television 1950-60,* published in 1963.

From 1949 to 1961 Unesco published some 20 titles in a series called

[3] Unesco, *Report of the Commission on Technical Needs in Press, Radio, Film* (Paris: Unesco, 1947, 1948, 1949); Unesco, *World Communications: Press, Radio, Film* (Paris: Unesco, 1950); Unesco, *Press, Film, Radio* (Paris: Unesco, 1952). For concise history of surveys, see pp. 13-22 in latter book.
[4] Unesco, *Television: A World Survey* (Paris: Unesco, 1953).

Press, Film and Radio in the World Today. The series apparently was motivated by what was learned in the original surveys. More than half of the titles appeared in the first three years of the series, and these focused principally on education for journalism (notably Robert Desmond's *Professional Training of Journalists*, 1949) and the role of radio and film in the educational process.

Legal and Related Aspects

Another volume in the series, *Legislation for Press, Film and Radio*, 1951, by Fernand Terrou and Lucien Solal, is one of the few books touching on a political topic which Unesco has published in its works on mass communications. Its existence has been explained as follows:

> The choice of this subject was due to two main reasons: the fact that there is a close connexion between freedom of information and that legislation, and the possibility of giving guidance to the various countries which are considering a revision of their laws in this respect.[5]

Unesco takes credit directly for two agreements intended to facilitate international circulation of educational, scientific and cultural materials (It also has had a more indirect role in other matters of this kind). Basically the Unesco agreements exempt from customs duties such items as books, newspapers, periodicals, audio-visual materials, works of art, collectors' pieces and scientific equipment. One is the Florence Agreement (proposed 1950, ratified 1952) and the other, the Beirut Agreement (proposed 1948, ratified 1954). Efforts were launched in 1967 to get Unesco member states to give a more liberal interpretation to the agreements, particularly in terms of films (which the original agreements said must be of an educational, scientific or cultural character to qualify—a condition not imposed on printed matter).[6]

To protect authors and performers—while yet maintaining a free flow of materials—Unesco sponsored the Universal Copyright Convention of 1952 (ratified 1955) and the International Convention for the Protection of Performers, Producers of Phonograms and Broadcasting Organizations (dated 1961 and ratified 1964). More recently it has considered extending copyright protection to new types of materials which have appeared on the scene.[7]

During the 1950's Unesco also published at least three books dealing with the free flow of information. Two dealt with press transmissions, *Transmitting World News*, 1953, by Francis Williams and *The Problems*

[5] Unesco, *Press, Film, Radio* (Paris: Unesco, 1952), p. 17.
[6] "Extending Application of Unesco's Two Agreements on Free Flow of Information," *Unesco Chronicle*, Vol. 15, No. 3 (March, 1969), pp. 115-116.
[7] Marie-Claude Dock, "Unesco and Copyright," *Unesco Chronicle*, Vol. 15, No. 3 (March, 1969), pp. 89-97.

of Transmitting Press Messages, 1956, produced by Unesco in cooperation with the International Telecommunication Union. The third was *Broadcasting Without Barriers*, 1959, by George A. Codding, Jr.

Reports and Papers Series

In 1952 Unesco launched a series of monographs entitled "Reports and Papers on Mass Communication." By the end of the 1960's almost 60 titles had been published, roughly half of them in each of the two decades since the series began. An analysis of subject categories may give some idea of the organization's concerns during the period:

Subject	Number of Monographs	Number Which Include This Subject As Well As a Main Subject
Films and filmstrips	16	8
Mass Media in rural and/or underdeveloped areas	14	1
Role of mass media in education	9	10
Education and research for journalism	7	2
Surveys of communications	5	7
Radio and television	4	10
Space communications	2	—
	57	95 *

A majority of the monographs tend to be practical reports outlining successful models of communications media used for a given purpose—especially education and rural development—or detailing the media needs in certain region, particularly the developing areas.

Education for Journalism

Unesco has helped establish four training centers since the mid-1950's. The first one, the International Center for Higher Education in Journalism (CIESJ), opened in 1957 at Strasbourg, a year-and-a-half after a Unesco meeting of experts endorsed a new emphasis in journalism education by the organization. A similar meeting in Ecuador in 1958 set the stage for the International Center for Higher Studies in Journalism for Latin America (CIESPAL), which opened in Quito in 1959.

The Strasbourg center concentrated on four-week refresher seminars during its first years, changing its policy in 1963 to include round-table

* Note: Some titles fit into several sub-categories.

meetings on mass communications in today's world. It also offers diplomas and degrees at the university level.[8]

In Quito, almost 500 journalism professors, journalists and other persons attended the annual two-month training course during the first 10 years of operation. At the same time, the center was leading a crusade for journalism education reform in Latin America after a CIESPAL area-wide study showed the existing curricula were not effective. In 1963 CIESPAL prepared a plan for reform and in 1965 it issued a document entitled "The Teaching of Journalism and Mass Media," based on recommendations from four regional seminars attended by 400 teachers of Journalism.[9]

In 1965 regional training institutes for Asia and Africa were founded with Unesco cooperation. The Center for Studies in Mass Communication Sciences and Techniques (CESTI) at the University of Dakar, Senegal, assists in training French-speaking African journalists through annual 10-week courses or through diploma/degree programs. Research concentrates on the elaboration of an information policy adapted to developing nations.

The Asian center is the Institute of Mass Communication at the University of the Philippines in Manila. It offers seminars and degree programs.

In addition, Unesco has assisted in the creation of other schools, some with regional and others only with national aspirations. For example, it has aided the mass communications institute (Institut d'information) at the University of Lebanon, Beirut; the School of Mass Communication at the University of Ankara, Turkey; and the Indian Institute of Mass Communication, New Delhi.

International and Regional Organizations

From its earliest days Unesco has been interested in cooperation with international and regional mass media groups. As a matter of fact, it was well on its way to establishing an independent, journalist-oriented International Institute of Press and Information in the late 1940's when that work was brought to a halt by the creation of the International Press Institute in 1951.[10]

Unesco had a direct hand in establishing the International Association for Mass Communication Research in 1957 and the International Council for Film and Television in 1959. It helped establish the Educational Film Institute for Latin America in 1956 in Mexico City and organized meetings which led to the creation of such groups as the South

[8] Hifzi Topuz, "Unesco and the Training of Journalists," *Unesco Chronicle*, Vol. 14. No. 11 (November, 1968), pp. 419-424.
[9] *Ibid.*, pp. 421-422. Also see J. Laurence Day, "How CIESPAL Seeks to Improve Latin American Journalism," *Journalism Quarterly*, Vol. 43, No. 3 (1966), pp. 525-530.
[10] *Press, Film, Radio* (1952), p. 20.

and East Asia Association of Journalism Educators in 1961 and the Union of African News Agencies in 1963. These are but a few of the regional examples which might be cited; several others deal with audio-visual media for education, book production and the like.

In 1959 Unesco published *Professional Association in the Mass Media,* with a subtitle of "handbook of press, film, radio, television organizations."

Unesco and Developing Nations

When the United Nations termed the 1960's their Development Decade, the organization was recognizing the tremendous influx of newly created nations into its fold. Freed from colonial ties, the new nations had to learn how to move forward under their own power. Unesco immediately saw a link between mass media development and economic and social development. In 1959 the Economic and Social Council already had asked Unesco to study assistance to underdeveloped countries in information media.

The study was conducted primarily through three meetings: Bangkok, January, 1960, for Asia; Santiago, Chile, February, 1961, for Latin America; and Paris, January, 1962, for Africa. Initially the results were published in monograph and document form and then were interpreted in a landmark volume by Wilbur Schramm.[11]

The reports accepted the Unesco minimum standards for mass media —in themselves a publicity achievement—of 10 copies of daily newspaper, five radio receivers, two cinema seats and two television receivers for every 100 persons in a country. Using this as a base, Schramm pointed to a "band of scarcity" circling the globe through the developing regions.

But publicizing the great lack of facilities and the time it would take to close the gaps formed only a preliminary part of a mounting Unesco campaign to improve the communications situations in the world. The other part of the campaign and the one into which Unesco thrust itself with some vigor concerned the use of the media in development, including education.

The Media and Education

Thus it was that in the mid-1960's Unesco gave increasing attention to the use of mass media for educational purposes. For example, in 1964 it launched a six-year pilot project in Senegal on the application of audio-visual materials and other media for adult education. In that same year

11 Unesco, *Developing Mass Media in Asia,* No. 30 Reports and Papers on Mass Communication (Paris: Unesco, 1960); *Mass Media in the Developing Countries: A Unesco Report to the United Nations,* No. 33 same series (Paris: Unesco, 1961) (The Spanish edition includes a report on the Santiago meeting); *Developing Information Media in Africa: Press, Radio, Film, Television,* No. 37 same series (Unesco: Paris, 1962); Wilbur Schramm, *Mass Media and National Development: The Role of Information in Developing Countries* (Stanford: Stanford University Press, 1964).

it expanded its program to stimulate book production and distribution in developing nations.[12] (Earlier Unesco had piloted teleclubs in France and Japan and had helped establish radio rural forums in India and Ghana, the latter two based on a pattern established by the Canadian government.)

In 1965 and 1966 interdisciplinary teams fanned out to 17 countries around the globe to report ways in which the electronic media and films were being used in education. Three volumes of case studies and a summary were published.[13]

Work With Individual Countries

In its second decade, Unesco began to increase its aid to individual countries, thanks to new budgetary and extra-budgetary resources provided for this purpose. Mass communications missions to individual countries took an upswing after 1955. For example, Unesco specialists advised the Costa Rican government on the establishment of a national television service; provided help to Colombian radio schools; helped develop Israeli broadcasting; helped train mass communications personnel in Mali; counseled with persons in Libya, Malaysia and Thailand about the creation of national news agencies; and helped study the reorganization of the television service in Upper Volta.

Information Services

Mass media throughout the world are entitled to use Unesco public information services. According to the Director-General's report, the press section in 1968 produced more than 700 releases; printed the monthly *Unesco Chronicle* in four languages and 400,000 copies monthly of *Unesco Courier* in 11 languages; distributed 45,000 photographs; and produced more than 500 radio programs in four languages.

Unesco and Space Communications

As a participant in space communications meetings at the international level—most of them originated by the United Nations or its agencies—Unesco during the 1960's took the position that careful steps had to be taken toward utilizing communications satellites for dissemination of educational, scientific and cultural information. In 1967 Unesco experts surveyed the possibilities of using satellites for education in India and in 1968 a smaller scale mission visited Brazil for a similar purpose. Indications were that the organization would continue to press for greater

[12] Unesco, *Report of the Director-General on the Activities of the Organization in 1964* (Paris: Unesco, 1965), p. 89. Note that the best source for Unesco information from year to year is the Director-General's annual report.
[13] Unesco-International Institute for Educational Planning, *New Educational Media in Action: Case Studies for Planners*, Vols. I, II, III, and Wilbur Schramm *et al.*, *New Media: Memo to Educational Planners* (Paris: Unesco, 1967).

involvement in determining directions in this revolutionary approach to worldwide communication.

How Unesco Operates in International Communications

A fairly consistent working pattern seems to emerge for Unesco in regard to international communication. The program for developing nations in the 1960's illustrates the pattern.

First, several years before a topic becomes a major one for Unesco, the organization begins to give the matter some consideration, perhaps with publications, perhaps with small meetings, perhaps in work in certain regions or countries. In this case, concern for developing nations can be traced to the 1940's when the technical needs surveys quickly were expanded to go beyond the developed but war devastated countries.

Next, interest is exhibited at some rather high level—the United Nations proper, Unesco itself or another agency—and some pilot projects may be launched. Then come "expert meetings," bringing together respected individuals in the field under study. The Bangkok, Santiago, and Paris meetings of 1960-1962 were of this type. The recommendations that come from such meetings usually lead to concrete action, such as the establishment of centers, organizations and the like. In this case, the United Nations' endorsement of communications aid to developed countries emerged.

Sometimes several years may elapse before a Unesco idea comes to fruition. But if the need is strong, the organization seems able to persist until some or all of its goals are achieved.

Kurt Koszyk:

The Development of the International Press Institute

It began in a small way. With the consequences of cold war politics and Korean War fighting, which had begun in June 1950, impressed in their minds, 34 newspaper editors and publishers from 15 countries met in a conference room of Columbia University, New York, in October, 1950.[1] They discussed the foundation of an International Press Institute and elected an organising committee. After being granted 35,000 dollars by the Rockefeller Foundation and the Carnegie Endowment for International Peace, the nine members of this body reunited half a year later under Lester Markel of the *New York Times* in Paris and wrote the constitution of the I.P.I.

In the preamble they set out their aims and objectives: "World peace depends upon understanding between peoples and peoples. If people are to understand one another, it is essential that they have good information. Therefore, a fundamental step toward understanding among people is to bring about understanding among the journalists of the world."

The institute declared as its main objects:

1. The furtherance and safeguarding of freedom of the press.
2. The achievement of understanding among journalists and so among peoples.
3. The promotion of the free exchange of accurate and balanced news among nations.
4. The improvement of the practices of journalism.

According to the 1952 charter only representatives of newspaper publishers and responsible members of the newspaper staffs can become members of the institute.[2] They are elected by the Executive Board of 15 members which in turn is chosen by the general assembly. Also members

[1] See: *IPI—The First Ten Years. The Story of the International Press Institute.* Zurich: IPI, 1962, pp. 12-13.
[2] *Ibid.*, pp. 18-19. Also the revised editions of the Charter of March 1955, May 1959, June 1963, June 1964, and June 1967.

▶ This is an original article done for this book by Kurt Koszyk, Director of the Institute of Newspaper Research at Dortmund and Professor of Journalism of the University of the Ruhr, Bochum/Germany.

of journalism faculties and free-lancers may become associate members of the IPI.

The First General Assembly took place in Paris in May 1952. At the same time, the first issue of the "I.P.I. Report" was published in Zurich where the Secretariat of the Institute had been located and which had sponsored national committees in 29 countries and regions.

The Institute started work with a report on "Improvement of Information," based on a questionnaire entitled "What is Needed to Improve Information on World Affairs?". Replies were received from 248 editors in 41 countries. The second survey dealt with "The News from Russia" (1952) and was the result of inquiry in 16 countries. This report had as a result the continuous negative response from all communist governments and press institutions toward all IPI activities. On Sept. 3, 1968, East Berlin *Neues Deutschland*, the central organ of the East German Socialist Unity Party (SED), printed the latest vehement attack by Prof. Dr. Franz Knipping of Leipzig concerning the "hate chorus of international reaction against the assistance of five Socialist brother countries for the sake of the CSSR," a hate chorus in which there had been the voice of "an obscure institution called IPI."[3]

Knipping accused the director of the Institute, Per Monsen, of combining his "obligatory protest with the assertion that journalists of the CSSR had gained an honorary place in the annals of international journalism." The main aim of the IPI—in the words of Prof. Knipping—was now "to undermine Socialism from within" after a period of holding back national press systems in the developing countries. Another 150,000 dollars given by the Ford Foundation in 1967 made Prof. Knipping presume that the IPI was highly integrated in the anti-socialist conspiracy of capitalism. And he found it deeply disturbing that among the members of a seminar from 21 countries in Geneva in March 1968 there had also been, for the first time, journalists from socialist countries—especially Emil Sip (Prague) who was blamed for having sent a report on the situation of the Czechoslovakian press. Knipping called the report a "Guide to organising conterrevolution by mass media."

No doubt the organisers of the Institute will be very satisfied after such attacks, since they are still greatly influenced by the ideology of the cold war period.[4] The trouble is that on one side they find it rather easy to unveil the suppression of press freedom in communist countries which are obviously understood as natural enemies of Western democracies—and on the other hand they have to judge the press systems in countries like Greece, Spain, South Africa, Brazil, Argentina, and the Philippines, which are deeply involved in the economic and military politics of the West.[5]

---

[3] *Neues Deutschland*, No. 244, Sept. 3, 1968, p. 5.
[4] See Basil Spiru, *Giftmischer*. Berlin, 1960, pp. 64-72.
[5] See Ahmed Emin Yalman (member of the Executive Board) in: *I.P.I. Rundschau*, No. 2/1954, p. 7.

Although no description of the role of the IPI should overlook these problems, it is nevertheless important to state that IPI is one of the few institutions which tries to collect material on international press relations and thus make possible a comparative examination of different national press systems. No other private or university organisation so far has had the means to do similar research with greater efficiency.

The authority of the IPI mainly derives from its close connection with the newspaper trade. In fact, among its members there are the most widely respected names in Western journalism. The attraction of the Institute is shown by the steady growth of membership: 460 in 1952, over 560 and another 104 associated members in 1955. Today the IPI has 1600 members from 60 countries. As members pay fees (40 dollars from members, 20 dollars from assoc.) and publishers give extra amounts for special projects the budget, too, has steadily enlarged from year to year. The growing importance of IPI has been acknowledged by several American foundations which support special studies, seminars, and international conferences.[6]

Although it is not easy to get a clear picture of the sources and the amounts the IPI can rely on, it is obvious that the work of the Institute would have run down some years ago, if there had not been large grants from the Ford and Rockefeller Foundations. Both foundations gave increasing amounts starting with some 30,000 dollars in 1954 and reaching about 500,000 dollars in 1965. Since 1959, this income has not been mentioned in the ordinary budget of the IPI.

The subscription income (in dollars) from members and publishers is shown below:[7]

	1959	1962	1967
Europe	33,077	39,768	46,156
North America	14,725	19,325	24,945
Asia	10,850	13,632	19,582
Oceania	2,640	3,205	4,817
Latin America and Africa	0,437	1,105	1,720
Total	61,729	77,035	97,220

The IPI's activities in Asia and in Africa are mainly based on the Ford and Rockefeller Funds.

The Asian programme started in 1965 and was based on the fact that a source of new readers had to be supplied with a new type of newspapers— a subject that had been discussed on the 1960 general assembly in Tokyo.

[6] The first Asian Conference of IPI in Tokyo 19.-23.3. 1956 was made possible by the Rockefeller Foundation.
[7] See *IPI-Rundschau* 10/11-1968, p. 22.

Newspaper circulation had jumped in most Asiatic countries,[8] and by 1966 the IPI was actively collaborating with the National Press Institutes in Korea, Japan, India, and the Philippines. Furthermore, Pakistan, Thailand, Vietnam, and Malaysia were engaged in IPI seminars. About 200,000 dollars have been spent on these activities each year.

At first just one consultant and his secretary had been sent into the offices of each of 30 newspapers. But subsequently a group of six specialists toured the area from Pusan in Korea to Kottayam in India and gave instructions about how to develop editors' facilities and management methods.[9] Many additional courses and seminars were arranged to enlarge on the programme of intensive instruction. Priority was given to the development of new designs for the ideographic press in some of the Asiatic countries and here Japanese practices helped a great deal to make ideographic newspapers more readable. The Japanese publishers association Nihon— Shinbun—Kyokai took an active part in this work. The latest development is the Chinese-Language Press Institute which opened in Hongkong on Nov. 18, 1968. It is part of the Press Foundation of Asia which tries to develop new applied forms of journalism in Asia. A plan to found a national committee in Taiwan has just been accepted after a study on press freedom there. Programmes similar to those in Asia have been undertaken in Africa under the direction of Frank Burton and Tom Hopkins. As a by-product much has been done in the respect of the emancipation of African women. In April 1966, for example, there were six female graduates of a course for journalists in Nairobi and Lagos.

The first culminating point of IPI's African work was the 1968 general assembly in Nairobi. It made obvious that the media situation in more than 50 African countries was still tremendously difficult. There are comparatively great differences between the technically and economically better developed regions and those that are less developed. IPI is prepared to collaborate with the new department of journalism at Nairobi university.

One of the deepest impressions which delegates took away from the 1968 Nairobi conference arose from the discussion on press freedom. Many of the European and American members of the IPI who had been ready to put forward very dogmatic idea of press independence had to learn that things cannot only be judged by traditional West European standards. Meetings of this kind have therefore helped to bring a more realistic attitude into the journalists' world.

In one of his many articles in the *IPI-Rundschau*, Per Monsen stated the gains and losses of press freedom.[10] IPI is not able to influence the development of press freedom in the countries without membership in

[8] See Amitabha Chowdhury (IPI director for Asia), "Asiatische Ergebnisse," *IPI-Rundschau*, 7-1966, pp. 8-12.
[9] See *IPI in Asia*. Zurich, 1966.
[10] See *IPI-Rundschau*, 4-1967, pp. 1-4.

the IPI, but the Institute's moral beliefs do influence journalists' and publishers' attitudes all over the world.

The 1967 conference in Geneva passed a resolution which defined the Institute's projects for the next five years. It said there would be further meetings of editors from different countries; a library and an information service would be built up in Zurich and press legislation would be one of the main subjects to be dealt with by the Institute. A first meeting sponsored by the Council of Europe in Salzburg in September 1968 resulted from an IPI initiative after a preliminary session of the International Jurists Commission in May 1968.

The new considerations arose from the dissatisfaction with the work IPI had done since its foundation. Again Lester Markel, the moving spirit of 1950, took the initiative. The report of his planning committee was delivered to the New Delhi general assembly in 1966 and formed the basis of the 1968 conclusions. It emphasized once more that the free flow of news between all countries remained the main problem of modern journalism. The preponderant interest of IPI in Africa and Asia as a result of the financial assistance given by American foundations was felt to be disproportionate in respect of the main task. To get a wider range of work, Markel's committee proposed:

1. research concerning the flow of news,[11] especially news exchange with the USSR.
2. seminars on the problems of news exchange.
3. a better presentation of international news.
4. studies in the origins of public opinion.
5. building up the IPI as a centre for sponsoring international news.

Although IPI work is actually co-operative and dependent on the activities of each member, the main burden is placed on the Executive Board and its president as well as on the director of the Zurich institute. The IPI Executive Board has had nine presidents so far: Lester Markel (*New York Times*), Elja Erkko (died 1965, *Helsingin Sanomat*), Oscar Pollak (died 1963, *Arbeiter-Zeitung*, Vienna), Urs Schwarz (*Neue Zürcher Zeitung*), Allan Hernelius (*Svenska Dagbladet*), Donald Tyerman (*The Economist*, London), Barry Bingham (*Courier Journal*, Louisville, U.S.A.), C.E.L. Wickremesinghe (*Dinamina*, Colombo, Ceylon), and Hans—Albert Kluthe (*Werra-Rundschau*, Eschwege, Germany).

On Oct. 18th, 1968, the Executive Board elected Ernest Meyer (Paris) as the new director of the IPI. He followed E.J.B. Rose (1952-1962), Rohan Rivett (1963), Per Monsen (1964-1968), and Anthony Brock who have shaped and realised the Institute's programmes since 1952. In his

[11] See the IPI study: *The Flow of the News*, Zurich 1953.

first report, shortly before the 1969 Ottawa general assembly, Meyer pointed out that the activities concerning press freedom were still the urgent interest of the IPI. Apart from continuous world wide studies in press freedom, single actions in favour of persecuted journalists and publishers have often been very successful. A study on journalism in the USSR was to be published by the end of 1969 and almost at the same time as a comparative study on "Slander by the Press." Earlier in 1969 Frank Burton's "African Assignment" had been delivered. *IPI Report, Les Cahiers de l'IPI,* and *IPI-Rundschau* are published monthly, Press Topics twice a month. And beneath all these activities—publications, seminars, meetings, conferences—a new financial basis has been gained recently by the World Communication Foundation which was started with the assistance of the Investors Overseas Services. IOS is ready to give 5,000 dollars each year for an IPI—Award and a basic amount of 25,000 dollars.

It is unlikely that IPI will turn to new fields. Press freedom remains a constant problem, and in the Western countries of Europe there are the questions of journalistic education and ethics as well. No doubt they will be topics of the general assemblies in Hongkong in 1970 and in Helsinki in 1971.

Mary A. Gardner:

The Evolution of the Inter American Press Association

FEW organizations have been so vilified and few have received such un-qualified praise as the Inter American Press Association.

Andrew Heiskell, chairman of the board of *Time*, once remarked that working with the IAPA had been one of his most fascinating, occasionally most irritating and, in the long run, one of the most rewarding experiences of his life.[1]

The late Demetrio Canelas, editor and publisher of *Los Tiempos*, Cochabamba, Bolivia, said simply, "I owe not only my freedom but my life to the Inter American Press Association."[2] And in 1963, Pedro Joaquin Chamorro of *La Prensa*, Managua, Nicaragua, and German Ornes of *El Caribe*, Dominican Republic, reiterated that they were among those who owed a similar debt to the association.[3]

Juan Perón and his bully-boys were more profuse in their homage. In 1951, when their efforts to take over the organization failed, they dedicated a 437-page book to denouncing the IAPA and its members. Among other things, the association was accused of defending the "imperialistic interests of Wall Street," and of "attacking national soveignty with its aggressions, its excesses, its frauds and its lies; . . ."[4] It has been notable during IAPA's existence that such accusations by dictators of the right are markedly similar to those propounded by dictators and advocates of the left.

As an organization, the Inter American Press Association is an effort by private citizens in an area most often left to government or foundation funds.[5] It has been a pioneer in the formation of an independent, profes-

[1] *XVIII Annual Meeting*, October 1962 (Mexico: Inter American Press Association, 1963), p. 75.
[2] As quoted by James G. Stahlman at the annual meeting, Nov. 1, 1955. *XI Annual Meeting*, November 1955 (Mexico: Interamerican [sic] Press Association, 1956), p. 163.
[3] *XIX Annual Meeting*, November 1963 (Mexico: Inter American Press Association, 1964), p. 43.
[4] Cincuenta y Tres Periodistas Argentinos, *Libro Azul y Blanco de la Prensa Argentina* (Buenos Aires: Organización Nacional del Periodismo Argentino, 1951), pp. 58-59.
[5] The International Press Institute has depended largely on foundation funds for its support. See *IPI Report*, August-September 1964, p. 5.

► From: *Journalism Quarterly*, Vol. 42, No. 4 (Spring 1965), pp. 547-556. Reprinted by permission of publisher and author.

sional, financially self-sufficient, inter-American pressure group. Most of its members are publications whose dues are based on circulation, although provisions exist for corporate and associate memberships. Monies from its members support the organization's operating costs.[6] By October 1965 membership was a record 750.[7]

The association traces its roots to the First Pan-American Congress of Journalists which convened in Washington, D.C., in April 1926 under auspices of the Pan American Union, and to later meetings in Mexico City (1942); Havana, Cuba (1943); Caracas, Venezuela (1945); Bogotá, Colombia (1946); Quito and Guayaquil, Ecuador (1949); and New York City (1950).[8]

IAPA's early meetings were often rowdy and disorganized affairs. Congresses were held at the convenience and the whims of governments. The expenses of delegates usually were paid by their governments. Government influence resulted in ambassadors, senators, typographers and others vaguely associated with the press being designated as delegates. Delegations sat and voted by countries, and heated arguments and nationalistic oratory occurred as delegates discussed political rather than press problems.

There were other difficulties also. Many Latin American editors and publishers were politically ambitious and saw no conflict in serving as a public official while still active in the newspaper business. They used their editorial columns to attack the opposition and to advance their own political causes. Then, once in power, "they would often go so far as to imprison editors of the opposition papers." [9]

Although the avowed purpose of the early congresses was to contribute to continental unity and to counteract pro-axis propaganda, the Communists attempted to manipulate the early meetings to their own advantage. There is considerable evidence that they wished to gain control of an international group whose membership would supply both the prestige and the organs for spreading communist propaganda. Two of the most active leaders in this movement were Carlos Rafael Rodríguez of Cuba and Genaro Carnero Checa of Peru.[10]

Rodríguez, then editor of the Cuban communist newspaper *Hoy*, has served as minister of agriculture in the Castro regime.[11] In 1960, Genaro Carnero Checa of Peru led a movement to take over the organizational

---

[6] *Charter, By-Laws and Rules*, Inter American Press Association, pp. 4-8, 17-19.
[7] Report of Robert U. Brown, executive committee chairman, to the Directors, XXI General Assembly, October 1965, English Document 1 (Mimeographed).
[8] Published volumes of the minutes of these meetings are available except for those held in Venezuela and Ecuador. The 1950 New York meeting minutes were published on newsprint by the *Trenton Times* of New Jersey.
[9] Letter from Hal Lee, executive secretary of the organizing committee, VI Inter-American Conference, March 18, 1959. (Mr. Lee died in December 1959).
[10] See the minutes of early meetings.
[11] *Hispanic American Report*, October 1964, (Vol. XVII, No. 8), p. 709.

meeting in Lima, Peru, of the Inter-American Federation of Working Newspapermen's Organization. His tactics were markedly similar to those used against the IAPA.[12]

Although it was the Mexicans who provided the impetus in 1942 for reviving the idea of inter-American press congresses, the Cubans eventually managed to have the secretariat located in their country. Leftist Cubans dominated the self-perpetuating executive committee and blocked other work by remaining in session throughout the Quito meeting of 1949. Its Treasurer, Carlos Rafael Rodríguez, never did present a report to the congresses. No dues were ever levied. The bills of the secretariat head-quarters in Havana were covered by the Cuban government.[13]

A sturdy group of newspapermen from Latin America and the United States fought to make the congresses professional meetings and to wrest control of the organization from those who wanted to use it for their own political purposes.

It was Julio Garzón, then editor of *La Prensa* (New York), who proposed at the Bogotá (1946) meeting that a standing committee on freedom of the press be formed to report annually on the state of the press in the hemisphere.[14] The work of this committee under the chairmanship of Jules Dubois of the Chicago *Tribune* later proved to be the cohesive force which held the IAPA membership together in spite of sharp personal and ideological conflicts. Its reports became the focal point and the point of controversy at most subsequent meetings.

Delegates to the Bogotá meeting generally credit its presiding officer, Dr. Alberto Lleras Camargo, former president of Colombia, with maintaining the "general constructive spirit" which prevailed and which permitted the approval of the resolution forming the freedom of the press committee.[15]

Similarly, Farris Flint of Famous Features credits Carlos Mantilla Ortega, the presiding officer of the Ecuador meeting (1949), with making possible the Flint-sponsored resolution to change the organization into one made up of individual members [16] "without reference to nationalities and completely independent of government ties, sanction, or support." [17]

Flint called Mantilla's handling of the hot and noisy sessions "masterly." [18] Mantilla wryly observed that he often had to shout and once

[12] Interview with Nicolas Pentcheff, treasurer, Inter-American Federation of Working Newspapermen's Organizations, Panama City, Aug. 12, 1962.
[13] "Background of Previous Inter-American Press Meetings," Confidential Memorandum prepared by Hal Lee, July 1, 1950.
[14] *Memoria del IV Congreso Panamericano de Prensa*, Noviembre 1946 (Bogotá: Editorial El Gráfico, 1946), p. 103.
[15] Julio Garzón, "Hemispheric Freedom Committee Appointed," *Editor & Publisher*, Dec. 14, 1946, p. 86.
[16] Interview with Farris A. Flint, Famous Features, New York, July 15, 1959.
[17] *New York Times*, July 15, 1949.
[18] Flint interview.

literally used force to maintain order. He stepped down from the chair and shook one Latin American delegate into silence.[19]

Thus the way was cleared for the tumultuous New York meeting in 1950 (an Argentine called the conference a "gangster meeting" because of the way the U.S. delegates ran it [20]) at which a small group of Latin American and U.S. members rammed through a new constitution completely revamping the association.

The New York meeting was poorly organized, a fiasco financially (a number of members quietly bailed it out), but attracted outstanding editors and publishers.[21] The association was reorganized on a professional and independent basis with each member publication having one vote and supporting the organization by paying dues based on circulation. The New York meeting marked the end of government-sponsored inter-American press congresses, and since then the IAPA has depended on the yearly dues of its members to cover expenses.

There have been numerous rowdy meetings since 1950. Peronistas tried to take over the sessions in Montevideo (1951), and in the resulting noise and confusion Tom Wallace, the IAPA president, suffered a heart attack.[22]

During the 1953 meeting, a Dominican Republic delegate swatted a Peruvian with a 300-page, one-pound freedom of the press report for calling Trujillo's regime a "stomach turning" dictatorship.[23]

In 1956, dictator Rojas Pinilla of Colombia sent emissaries to sabotage the annual meeting in Havana. Three IAPA officers and its general manager had received threats and the hotel where the meeting took place was protected by armed guards and Cuban plain-clothes men. During the sessions, Jules Dubois was challenged to a duel by one of Trujillo's stooges, and the "Rojas Colombianos screamed themselves hoarse for a day and a half, but finally were fought down by the General Assembly." [24]

Recent meetings have not been without controversy, but disagreements generally have been expressed verbally rather than physically—perhaps an indication of IAPA's growing maturity.

Exiled Cuban members took offense to an editorial appearing in the New York *Times* during the New York meeting (1961), for which they blamed Herbert Matthews. A Cuban moved that the assembly "make a pronouncement on the attitude of Mr. Matthews. . . ." [25] The incongruous

[19] Interview with Carlos Mantilla Ortega, Sub-director, *El Comercio* (Quito, Ecuador), Nov. 24, 1959.
[20] *Proceedings of the VI Inter-American Press Conference*, October 1950 (Trenton, N.J.: Trenton Times, n.d.), p. 15.
[21] Interview with Joshua B. Powers, Joshua B. Powers Inc., New York, July 14, 1959.
[22] Interview with Tom Wallace, editor emeritus, *Louisville Times*, Aug. 19, 1958.
[23] *Newsweek*, Oct. 19, 1953.
[24] Letter from James G. Stahlman, *Nashville Banner*, Oct. 22, 1958.
[25] *XVII Annual Meeting*, October 1961 (Mexico: Inter American Press Association, 1962), p. 232.

situation of an association advocating freedom of expression censuring its use was averted when cooler heads finally prevailed. The motion never came to vote.[26]

In Mexico City (1964), the IAPA Board of Directors in a joint meeting with the directors of the Inter American Educational Association discussed, among other things, the dangers of official textbooks being selected and required by the state. The two organizations adopted a resolution which said that "in a democratic society education on all levels should never be a state monopoly and that academic freedom as well as the economic independence of these institutions should always be guaranteed." [27] Citing Argentina's experience with Perón, Alberto Gainza Paz of *La Prensa* of Buenos Aires, vigorously supported the resolution.[28] This action precipitated a vitriolic editorial in the Mexican tabloid *ABC* which called Gainza Paz "the most hated man in Argentina." [29]

Indignant Argentine members voiced their objections to the editorial and called for a resolution expressing the association's "solidarity and its confidence" in Gainza Paz. A Mexican publisher dissented and violently shouted his disapproval when the presiding officer ruled him out of order. The vote of confidence passed.[30]

It could hardly be coincidental that the Mexican member who led the protest also has interests in the publication of official school texts.

These verbal barrages are rather tame when compared to the battles IAPA fought with the henchman of Rojas Pinilla, Perón, Trujillo, Somoza and Pérez Jiménez.

Today, one of IAPA's principal targets is the Castro regime although the association continues to pinpoint aggressions wherever they may occur. It recently has reported suppression of press freedom in Haiti, Paraguay, Guatemala,[31] Honduras, and the Dominican Republic.[32]

What tools of pressure did the IAPA use in its battles with Perón, Batista, Trujillo, Rojas Pinilla and other tyrants? Basically the tools of public opinion, of keeping aggressions against the press exposed to the glare of international publicity.

Foremost among these is the public arena in which the IAPA's annual freedom of the press report is documented, debated and presented. In the past, representatives of suspect nations have flocked to the assemblies, primed to attack and question the report. And member publications, non-

---

[26] *Ibid.*
[27] English Document 14 (Mimeographed), XX General Assembly, October 1964, p. 1.
[28] Personal Notes, XX General Assembly, October 1964.
[29] ABC, Oct. 21, 1964, pp. 1, 7.
[30] Personal Notes, XX General Assembly.
[31] Report of the Committee on Freedom of the Press, Board of Directors Meeting, March 1965.
[32] Report of the Committee on Freedom of the Press, XXI General Assembly, October 1965, English Document 16 (Mimeographed).

member publications and the wire services usually give the report extensive exposure throughout the hemisphere.

Firm but courteous cables generally are dispatched to the heads of states of the country in which abuses against the press have been noted. Not all replies are returned in the same vein. In 1953, when the IAPA protested the arbitrary closure of two newspapers and the imprisonment of an editor in Ecuador President Velasco Ibarra replied:

> Ignorant and insolent persons, such as yourselves, who speak without sufficient documentation, without knowledge of foregoing events, without background of facts, merit only contemptuous silence.[33]

Toward the end of his four years as constitutional president, the same Velasco Ibarra publicly praised the work of the IAPA.[34]

The association's headquarters also keeps the hemisphere informed of attacks against the press through news releases and through special bulletins on a country when the situation warrants it. Often some of the material used in the releases consists of information smuggled from the country under scrutiny.

Editorials from newspapers throughout the Americas are collected and made available to members. During the latter days of the Rojas Pinilla regime in Colombia, IAPA headquarters almost daily forwarded a packet of editorials to the dictator.[35]

The association has also sent envoys to conduct on-the-spot investigations of press conditions. Most often the envoy has been Jules Dubois, but at times Latin American IAPA members have acted as special envoys at their own expense.

IAPA presidents also have traveled at their own expense to help a fellow member. In 1954 IAPA's president, the late Miguel Lanz Duret of Mexico, jumped through a window in the Costa Rican embassy in Managua, Nicaragua, to talk with a publisher who had taken refuge there.[36]

Like Perón, Castro fiercely condemned the IAPA and yet tried to infiltrate it, especially during the early days when he was consolidating power in Cuba. Now that he is solidly entrenched and in control of all media there, he appears to give relatively scant attention to the association's activities.

It was freedom of the press which first attracted most newspapers into the association, and which served as the cohesive force to hold them together. Yet IAPA members concerned themselves with other vital services even during the association's earliest and most difficult days.

[33] *Press of the Americas*, May 1, 1953.
[34] *XII Anual* [sic] *Meeting*, October 1956 (Mexico: Interamerican [sic] Press Association, 1956), p. 95.
[35] *XI Annual Meeting*, November 1955 (Mexico: Interamerican [sic] Press Association, 1956), p. 15.
[36] *Ibid.*, pp. 200, 202.

Newsprint production, cost and availability have been discussed at almost every meeting since 1942. Newsprint supply became particularly critical for the Latin Americans after World War II and in 1951 they even proposed that U.S. publishers pledge 5% of their newsprint to Latin American members. One U.S. publisher pointedly suggested that instead of complaining, the Latin Americans do something positive about the situation.[37]

Under the leadership of Guillermo Martínez Marquez of Cuba, a permanent committee to study new sources of newsprint was appointed.[38] Sugar cane bagasse came under study as a possible raw material for newsprint, and other efforts to undertake newsprint production were studied. Although newsprint is now generally available, the report on its supply has become an annual tradition at the IAPA General Assembly.

IAPA's board of directors also decided that programs should be sponsored which would contribute to the financial stability and the professional stature of Latin American publications and perhaps make them less susceptible to political and governmental pressures.

Projects in three broad fields were considered: the education of journalists, the recognition of outstanding work by journalists, and technical aid to member publications in Latin America.

In 1952, the board of directors decided to investigate the possibilities of a scholarship program to encourage the exchange of journalists and journalism students. Under the leadership of William H. Cowles of the Spokane *Spokesman-Review* (Washington), the scholarship committee presented a comprehensive plan for such a program in 1953, and by 1955 the Scholarship Fund had been incorporated in New York State with the same board of directors as IAPA.[39]

Contributions to the fund come from both U.S. and Latin American IAPA members and donations by governments and commercial enterprises are politely rejected. By October 1965, a total of 106 scholarships for study in Latin America and the U.S. had been awarded at a cost of $244,562.87 from voluntary contributions.[40] The scholarships have been divided almost equally between North American and Latin American students.[41]

In 1952 the Mergenthaler Linotype Company offered IAPA funds to give $2,500 in prizes annually for 25 years to newspapermen of publications in the Western Hemisphere, excluding the United States.[42]

[37] Stenographic Minutes, IAPA Board of Directors' Meeting, March 1, 1951 (in IAPA files).
[38] Stenographic Minutes, IAPA Board of Directors' Meeting, Oct. 7, 1951 (in IAPA files).
[39] *Editor & Publisher*, April 2, 1955.
[40] Report of Harold A. Fitzgerald, president of the IAPA Scholarship Fund, to the Directors, XXI General Assembly, October 1965, English Document 7 (Mimeographed).
[41] *Ibid*.
[42] *VIII Annual Meeting*, October 1952 (Mexico: Inter-American [*sic*] Press Association, 1953), p. 104.

Designed as the Latin American counterpart of the Pulitzer Prizes, IAPA each year offers awards to a newspaper for outstanding service to the community, and to journalists for distinguished work in cartooning, photography, newswriting and reporting, features, columns and editorials, and for defense of press freedom.[43]

Candidates are nominated by editors or publishers. The IAPA has withheld awards when its committee felt there were no qualified nominees. The first Mergenthaler Awards were given in 1954, and, by 1965, 10 citations to publications and 49 to newsmen had been presented.[44]

At the board of directors meeting in Buenos Aires (1958), Francisco A. Rizzuto h. of *Veritas* (Argentina) proposed that two prizes for North Americans, one for a newspaper and another for a journalist, be established. The resolutions committee regretfully decided that such prizes would be too costly.

Latin American members expressed a clear desire, however, to award prizes in recognition of works furthering inter-American friendship. They quickly offered to finance them and by the time the general assembly passed the resolution, nine Latin Americans had already pledged financial support.[45] The Tom Wallace Awards, named after IAPA's first president, have been given since 1960, and perhaps the most rousing argument at the 1965 meeting involved whether an award should be withdrawn once its recipient had been designated.[46]

In 1952, IAPA members also began to look for ways to obtain more advertising for the Latin American newspapers. Carlos Mantilla of Ecuador noted in 1953 that Latin American newspapers were barely receiving one-tenth of the total publicity budget spent by the U.S. Industry in Latin America. This source of income, he maintained, was lost primarily because the Latin American newspapers and magazines failed to provide precise information concerning their circulations.[47]

The IAPA established the Office of Certified Circulation in 1954 and incorporated it under the laws of New York State in 1955. The IAPA directors felt that an enterprise which involved contractual and economic commitments should operate as an autonomous organization.[48]

International auditing firms agreed to lend their cooperation, and OCC's services were limited to IAPA members. The newspaper *El*

[43] *Memoria de la Décima Asamblea General*, Octubre 1954 (México: Sociedad Interamericana de Prensa, 1955), pp. 178-180.
[44] *Press of the Americas*, April-May 1965.
[45] *XIV Annual Meeting*, October 1958 (Mexico: Inter American Press Association, 1959), pp. 30-31.
[46] Personal Notes, XXI General Assembly, October 1965.
[47] *IX Annual Meeting, October* 1953 (Mexico: Inter-America [sic] Press Association, 1954), pp. 82-88.
[48] XI *Annual Meeting*, pp. 51-52.

Espectador and the magazine *Dominical,* both of Bogotá, Colombia, were the first to have their circulations certified.[49]

OCC, it should be noted, has never enjoyed the support from Latin American newspapers that its founders hoped it would. Many factors have mitigated against it. The Latin American publisher today is somewhat in the same position as the U.S. publisher of 40 to 80 years ago.[50] A newspaper's true circulation cannot be determined easily unless the owner desires to reveal it. Many Latin American newspaper publishers have tended to inflate their circulation figures. A true audit would be an embarrassing revelation of their deceit.

It is interesting to observe, for example, that the newspaper generally rated second in circulation in a country is more likely to subscribe to the audit service than the publication traditionally rated first. For example, *El Espectador* of Bogotá subscribed to the service before *El Tiempo* did. *La Prensa* of Lima, Peru, likewise submitted to audit while *El Comercio* did not.

Care must be taken, however, not to oversimplify the situation. There are other considerations. Deep-seated reasons exist why Latin American editors might not like to have outsiders poking into their books. Traditionally, they tend to look with suspicion upon this type of activity.

Fear that authoritarian governments might utilize legally or illegally such data to harass a publication is often quite real. Questions also might be raised concerning past income tax reports. Furthermore, an opposition newspaper might not want the government to realize how strong or weak it might be. Above all, many Latin American publishers are convinced that their national advertisers are well aware which newspaper reaches most of those who can read and who can afford to buy the advertisers' products.[51]

The cost of OCC's services also has been relatively high for Latin Americans. In 1956, John R. Reitemeyer, then chairman of the executive committee, told IAPA directors that one of the most important reasons OCC had not made rapid progress was because it was too expensive. He felt the costs of the service, which, "for a paper of 50,000 circulation might run to $1,200, are too high." [52]

After a special meeting in March 1957, OCC's board of directors revamped the organization. Voting control was transferred from publishers to a board composed of advertiser members, advertising agency members and publisher or publisher representative members. In July 1965, OCC's managing director indicated the organization had 48 members, precisely the number reported in 1961.[53]

---

[49] *Memoria de la Décima Asamblea General,* pp. 62-66.
[50] *IX Annual Meeting,* pp. 92-93.
[51] Interview with Jorge Mantilla, subdirector, *El Comercio* (Ecuador), July 16, 1959.
[52] *XII Annual Meeting,* p. 24.
[53] Letter from Charles F. Rork, OCC managing director, July 28, 1965.

It has been observed that the one burning issue which has been greatly responsible for resolving the differences of IAPA members is freedom of the press. True, the freedom of press report has often roused the greatest controversy. Yet it has served as the common cause behind which members have rallied; in the long run it has apparently surmounted the barriers of nationalism, cultural differences and personal prejudices.

Once these reprehensible but sometimes colorful aggressions no longer occur with such regularity and the excitement of battle is replaced by the monotony of war, what can substitute for this stimulus which has been the welding force of the IAPA?

John R. Herbert, Quincy *Patriot Ledger* (Massachusetts), has long felt that a "technical center" would help fill such a need.[54] When he reported as chairman of the committee on exchange of information at the assembly in Mexico in 1953, he observed that one of the major requirements in a successful battle to maintain press freedom is strong newspapers—newspapers of technical excellence and efficient management. "You can never win the fight for press freedom," he said, "with newspapers financially unsound and weak in matters of policy." [55]

In January 1954, the Research and Information Center was established as a permanent agency of the IAPA to supply technical information to members upon request. The center's members and advisers came principally from IAPA's associate members, specialists in such areas as printing, advertising and other technical aspects of journalism. Herbert was appointed president.[56]

From the beginning, however, the center's activities were fraught with problems. Attendance at its technical sessions during IAPA meetings was small and it was also beset with financial difficulties.

The center furnished services to IAPA members without charge and without a budget. IAPA policy did not permit it to accept contributions from outside sources, and the center existed through the good will and cooperation of its members and the help of Cranston Williams of the American Newspaper Publishers Association.[57]

In April 1957, the center was incorporated under the laws of New York State as an educational non-profit organization for the dissemination of technical information to IAPA members.[58] Incorporation, it was anticipated, would permit it to accept foundation funds to finance various projects. In line with IAPA policy, however, funds from governments and their agencies would not be accepted.[59]

[54] Letter from John R. Herbert, Feb. 20, 1959.
[55] *IX Annual Meeting*, p. 157.
[56] *Press of the Americas*, Feb. 1, 1954.
[57] *XI Annual Meeting*, p. 49.
[58] *Editor & Publisher*, Oct. 26, 1957.
[59] Records, IAPA Executive Committee Meetings, 1957 (in IAPA files).

Although the center arranged for the publication of the first English-Spanish dictionary of newspaper terms, convinced the American Press Institute to undertake another Latin American seminar, and continued with technical sessions at IAPA annual meetings, it was still without funds. In March 1958, its gross assets were $3.00. Very little money was available for a center which "could very well become the most important activity of the IAPA as it runs out of dictators." [60]

Largely through the persistent efforts of John R. Herbert, the Technical Center, Inc. received a $15,000 Ford Foundation grant in March 1960 to conduct a three-month survey of the technical needs of Latin American newspapers.[61] The study resulted in a $400,000 Ford grant in 1962 for five years of operation.[62]

Since that date, 10 seminars and conferences (eight in Latin America) have been held concerning such subjects as management, advertising and circulation. Harold Fitzgerald of the Pontiac *Press* (Michigan) also bolstered the center's budget by giving it eleven units of rotary press, five of which were sold to a Latin American newspaper and six to an Ohio newspaper for a total price of $97,000. Fitzgerald even helped further the center's profit by having his organization assume the cost of packing and shipping to the port of embarkation.[63]

Fitzgerald's donation precipitated additional offers of presses from the Allentown *Call & Chronicle* (Pennsylvania), the San Juan *Star* (Puerto Rico), Jack Howard of Scripps-Howard Newspapers and Andrew Heiskell of Time Inc.[64]

The center also supplies technical bulletins and the services of a technical consultant on contract. A book in Spanish on typographical problems and layout written especially for Latin America by Prof. Edmund C. Arnold of Syracuse University was distributed at the XXI General Assembly, October 1965. Plans also call for establishing a Graphic Arts Center and a Press Institute for Latin America.[65]

Herbert noted at the 1964 IAPA meeting that improvement in the news content of newspapers also has been stressed at all IAPA seminars no matter what their official topic. "This," he said, "becomes our opening prayer whether the meeting is devoted to circulation or advertising or any other subject." [66]

[60] Stenographic Minutes, IAPA Board of Directors Meeting, March 1958 (in IAPA files).
[61] *Editor & Publisher*, March 26, 1960.
[62] Edición Especial de Centro Técnico de SIP, Ciudad de México, Octubre 1964, p. 3.
[63] Report of Guillermo Gutierrez V-M, general manager, IAPA Technical Center, XX General Assembly, October 1964, English Document 5 (Mimeographed).
[64] Report by Guillermo Cespedes R., general manager, IAPA Technical Center, XXI General Assembly, October 1965, English Document 14 (Mimeographed).
[65] *Ibid.*
[66] Report by John R. Herbert to the Board of Directors of the IAPA Technical Center, XX General Assembly, October 1964, English Document 13 (Mimeographed).

It is notable that Latin American members have begun to share the costs of organizing technical seminars in their countries under the center's auspices and of paying the transportation, living expenses and token registration fees of their own representatives.[67] In addition, provincial newspapers are finally being encouraged to participate.

In 1960, this writer observed that the association tended to attract the larger and wealthier Latin American publications—newspapers whose prestige and financial stability helped make IAPA possible but which, relatively speaking, least needed IAPA's aid. Small provincial newspapers generally did not have access to IAPA's benefits because of the cost of membership and the expenses involved in attending annual meetings.[68] Furthermore, as a Latin American journalist once commented, when a small newspaper publisher is thrown in with the "dignified" owners he "feels like a humble priest in a cathedral." [69]

IAPA has since decreased dues for publications with less than 5,000 circulation and set up a promotion committee to help recruit new members. A short formal ceremony has been instituted during annual meetings to welcome new members and to provide them with special identification.[70]

The promotion committee also has produced and distributed literature about IAPA and Joshua B. Powers of Joshua B. Powers, Inc. reported in 1961 that the committee had compiled a list of prospective members. About 900 eligible newspapers located in the United States and about 70 in South and Central America did not belong to the IAPA. The latter figure, as Powers noted, is surprisingly small.[71] This is particularly true if one accepts the figures submitted in 1960-1962 to UNESCO: Argentina listed 233 daily newspapers, Brazil 291, and Mexico 189.[72]

Nevertheless, IAPA's membership has increased steadily. Some members are dropped each year because of resignations, closings, retirements, deaths or delinquent dues. Almost twice as many Latin American publications become remiss in payment of dues as U.S. publications. Even so, the total number of delinquents annually is seldom more than 30.[73]

IAPA membership increased from 597 in 1960 to 647 in 1964, and its annual operating costs rose from about $60,000 to $70,000 during the same

[67] Report of Guillermo Gutiérrez V-M.
[68] Gardner, Mary A. "The Inter American Press Association and Its Fight for Freedom of the Press." Unpublished Ph.D. dissertation, University of Minnesota, 1960. A book based on this dissertation is scheduled for publication by the Institute of Latin American Studies, University of Texas, in 1966.
[69] Interview with José María Navasal, coordinating secretary, El Mercurio (Chile), Dec. 14, 1959.
[70] XVII Annual Meeting, pp. 83-85.
[71] Ibid., p. 255.
[72] UNESCO. World Communications (Amsterdam: Drukkerij Holland N.V., 1964), pp. 177, 180, 155.
[73] See the yearly reports of the treasurer to the IAPA.

period. In October 1964 the association comprised 337 U.S. members, 284 Latin American members, 18 Canadian members and 8 from the West Indies area.[74] By the end of the 1964-65 fiscal year, membership had risen to 727 and operating costs to $76,126.36.[75] No small feat for an organization which in 1951 had to extract $7,000 in pledges from U.S. and Latin American members to defray expenses.[76]

Since its reorganization in 1950, the IAPA not only has snatched newsmen from jails, given scholarships and technical aid but also has influenced the formation and structure of other inter-American organizations.

There is evidence that the Inter-American Federation of Working Newspapermen's Organizations, although a union, benefited from IAPA's experiences, especially those concerning dissident Latin American elements. At its organizational meeting in Lima (1960), IAFWNO leaders astutely and democratically repelled a Communist attempt to take over their organization.[77]

The Inter American Education Association, established in 1962 by privately supported schools and associations, has received the direct help of IAPA members and has scheduled its annual meetings to coincide with the IAPA's.

The IAPA and the Inter-American Association of Broadcasters also have long cooperated in the defense of their members. The Panama Doctrine, adopted by the organizations in 1952, provides that any aggression against either radio or the press will be considered an attack against both and will be resisted by all means possible. The two organizations have invoked the doctrine numerous times with varying degrees of success.

IAPA probably has been responsible indirectly for more extensive news coverage of Latin America in U.S. newspapers, especially during non-crisis periods. U.S. members become interested in the problems of their colleagues and tend to publish more news about their problems.

North Americans point out that hemispheric solidarity and self-protection are among the most pressing reasons they become members. One U.S. editor perhaps expressed the feeling of many of his countrymen when he observed that if his Latin American colleagues were willing to go to jail for freedom of the press, the least he could do was to give them his moral and financial support through the Inter American Press Association.

[74] Report of John A. Brogan Jr., treasurer, to Directors, XX General Assembly, October 1964, English Document 11 (Mimeographed).
[75] Report of John A. Brogan Jr., treasurer, XXI General Assembly, October 1965, English Document 5 (Mimeographed).
[76] Stenographic Minutes, IAPA Directors Meeting, March 1, 1951 (in IAPA files).
[77] Nicolas Pentcheff interview. Also see IAFWNO's publications of the period.

Heinz-Dietrich Fischer:

Eurovision and Intervision Toward Mondovision

It was as early as 1948 that the director of Radio Lausanne (Switzerland), Marcel Bezençon, got the basic idea to establish a so-called "Program Exchange" for all members of UIR (Union Internationale de Radio-diffusion) to prove the possibilities of transmitting TV programs from one country to others. But at this time there was almost no television on the European continent, and most of his colleagues did not feel an urgent need for such an institution.

When the successor of UIR was founded February 12, 1950, under the name UER (Union Européenne de Radiodiffusion) in Geneva (Switzerland) with a technical headquarters in Brussels (Belgium), the idea of international cooperation in the field of television came up again. In the meantime Marcel Bezençon had become head of the total radio networks of Switzerland, and so he had the chance to discuss his plan of 1948 once again in the gremiums of UER. On October 5, 1950, Bezençon sent his complete concept to the main office of UER, explaining the necessity of arranging TV program exchanges *before* the establishment of the television networks in the various European countries.

Bezençon's plan contained four main suggestions: (a) exchanges of films of different kinds, (b) live transmissions of main public events in the different countries, (c) exchanges of actual news, and (d) clearing of the copyrights for all over the world. The administrative headquarters of UER asked all the 21 member countries at that time to give reactions as soon as possible, but fewer than 10 answers arrived by mid-January, 1951.[1] But in the meantime there had already been a first step of TV program exchange between two countries *without* any activity of UER: On the 27th of August, 1950, the two most developed European TV countries, France and Great Britain, had a telecast across the sea from Calais

[1] Marcel Bezençon, "Eurovision—the Pattern of the Future," in: *EBU Bulletin* (Geneva), September/October 1954, p. 567, cf. also: Paul Bellac, "Die Vorgeschichte der Eurovision. Zum zehnjährigen Bestehen der Eurovision," *Rundfunk und Fernsehen* (Hamburg), Vol. 12/No. 1 (1964), pp. 26 ff.

► This is an original article done for this book by Heinz-Dietrich Fischer, Universities of Bochum and Cologne (Germany). Parts of the article are based on lectures of the author at the School of Journalism, University of Missouri, Columbia, Mo. during the academic year 1968/69.

to Dover, and they also worked together in research on technical problems of TV transmitting in different line systems. Between the 8th and 14th of July, 1952, they also arranged a real bilateral British-French so-called "Week of TV Telecasts" between Paris and London. These first steps encouraged the UER to evaluate the idea of international program exchange not only by Radio but also by Television Broadcast.[2]

A special "Study Group," with members of the different UER countries, discussed many problems in this field during 1952 and 1953. At this time television had its early beginnings also in West Germany, Denmark, and in the Netherlands, and some of these countries tried to arrange an international TV transmission of the coronation of Queen Elizabeth II. When the coronation in London took place June 2, 1953, this event was transmitted not only by BBC in Great Britain, but also by a total of 12 TV Stations of France, the Netherlands, and the Federal Republic of Germany. During the coronation the combined radio and television programs were to last over six and one-half hours and ultimately to be translated into 41 languages besides English.[3] The result of this successful transmission encouraged many TV companies all over in West Europe to develop their technical equipment, especially their relay chains, enabling them to receive TV programs from other countries.

The most discussed problem at this time was how to transmit large parts of the World's Football (Soccer) Championship from Switzerland in the early summer of 1954. When this important sports event took place, there were already around four million TV sets with 60 to 65 million people in eight European countries receiving 31 hours of transmission. At the same time the British journalist George Campey came up with the term *Eurovision* that was used from then on for all kinds of international telecasts in Western Europe.[4]

Eurovision officially became effective on June 6, 1954, at first having a temporary network linking the TV networks of Belgium, Denmark, France, West Germany, Italy, the Netherlands, Switzerland, and the United Kingdom. For a short time the technical center was in Lille (France), but at the end of 1955 it moved to Brussels (Belgium), where it has been since that time.

Eurovision was established by linking together a number of domestic TV services, rather than constructing a new and completely integrated network; it did not produce a separate program, but only coordinated it.

[2] Cf. Donald K. Pollock and David Lyndon Woods, "A Study in International Communication: Eurovision," *Journal of Broadcasting* (Los Angeles), Vol. III/No. 2 (Spring 1959), pp. 101 ff.
[3] Russell Brooks Butler Barber, *Eurovision as an Expression of International Cooperation in Western Europe*, Unpublished Ph.D. dissertation, Northwestern University, Evanston/Ill. 1963, p. 50.
[4] Paul Bellac, "Die Vorgeschichte der Eurovision," *Publizistik* (Bremen), Vol. 9/No. 1 (January-March 1964), p. 55.

By that time three distinct TV networks existed in Western Europe: (a) the BBC network using the 405 line system; (b) a chain of West German, Danish, Swiss and Italian stations using the 625 line system; and (c) a mixed-chain of French-Belgian stations using the 819 line system and Dutch-Belgian stations using 625 lines. There were some technical difficulties because of the different line systems, but the overall picture quality was pretty good. A partial solution to the problem of languages was achieved by sending commentators to the point of organization. The commentary mixed with the sound of the events was relayed over separate circuits to the receiving countries. Synthesized commentary was also employed: In this instance an announcer in the receiving country made his commentary while observing the picture on a monitor screen.

So the programs attempted to demonstrate how television services interpret local events, and thereby promote international understanding. Besides the World Football (Soccer) Championships in Switzerland, the programs in the early phase of *Eurovision* included: a Visit to the Vatican, Queen Elizabeth II receiving units of the Royal Navy, a promenade along the Rhine River, St. Johannes' night at Tivoli Gardens in Copenhagen, the creation of a TV ballet in Brussels, and the illumination of Versailles Castle. A special series of programs was telecast during Christmas week, from December 23, 1954, to January 1, 1955. These programs included: Christmas carols from Kings College at Cambridge, Midnight Mass from Notre Dame at Paris, a "Rhythm on Ice" show from Switzerland, and a visit to Erasmus House in Brussels.[5]

Between the official start of *Eurovision* on June 6, 1954, until the end of that year, 55 different programs were relayed, covering 73 hours of transmissions.[6] By the end of 1955 most of Europe was able to participate in program exchanges without disrupting national domestic programs. Austria and some other countries inaugurated new television services and also joined the continental network. Highlights of programs broadcast during 1955 included the opening of the Four Power Conference and the Conference on the Peaceful Uses of Atomic Energy. The *Eurovision* telecasts of the 1956 Winter Olympic Games, held at Cortina d'Ampezzo in Italy, represented the most extensive operation undertaken thus far. Some fifty-four telecasts were made during the thirteen days of the games. Radiotelevisione Italiana (RAI) was the host organization, and extensive arrangements were made. It is interesting to note that two communist countries—East Germany and Czechoslovakia—were linked for the first time with the *Eurovision* network. Another event of interest televised during 1956 was the wedding of Prince Rainier III to Grace Kelly, transmitted by Radio Monte Carlo. The "Tour de France," perhaps the most famous of all cycle races, was also telecast to Western Europe in 1956

[5] Donald K. Pollock and David Lyndon Woods, *op. cit.*, pp. 104 ff.
[6] "Eurovision," *Internationales Handbuch für Rundfunk und Fernsehen* 1967/68, Hamburg: Verlag Hans-Bredow-Institut, 1967, p. E 46.

by Radiodiffusion Télévision Française. Another event was a Grand Prix d'Eurovision Competition. This represented the first program arising out of *Eurovision* itself: each nation entered a song in the contest.[7]

Luxembourg and Monaco became members of *Eurovision* in 1956, the Independent Television Authority (ITV) from Great Britain in 1957, Sweden in 1958, Norway in 1959, Finland and Yugoslavia in 1960, and in 1963 the newly founded Second German TV network ZDF (Zweites Deutsches Fernsehen) got its membership. Early in 1964 *Eurovision* had 29 active members from 26 different countries and 28 associated members from all over the world; among them were the American television companies ABC (American Broadcasting Company), CBS (Columbia Broadcasting System, Inc.), NBC (National Broadcasting Company, Inc.), the Canadian CBC (Canadian Broadcasting Corporation), the Japanese NHK (Nippon Hoso Kyokai) and the SIA (Serviços de Imprensa, Rádio e Televisão Associados) from Brazil.[8]

The number of program exchanges among member countries of *Eurovision* climbed from year to year: [9]

Year	Total number of programs transmitted	hours transmitted
1954	55	73
1955	91	115
1956 *	250	273
1957	207	259
1958	203	261
1959	292	339
1960 *	500	440
1961	679	606
1962	1427	586
1963	3110	3610
1964 *	3717	4497
1965	3115	4053
1966	3790	5212
1967	3387	4092
1968 *	6240	8250
	27063	32666

* = years of Olympic Games

[7] Donald K. Pollock and David Lyndon Woods, *op. cit.*, p. 106 ff.
[8] *Internationales Handbuch für Rundfunk und Fernsehen* 1967/68, *op. cit.*, p. E 45 ff.
[9] Compiled from: *Internationales Handbuch für Rundfunk und Fernsehen* 1967/68, *op. cit.*, p. E 46, and: *EBU Review* (Geneva), No. 98 B (July 1966), p. 26; No. 104 B (July 1967), p. 32; No. 109 B (May 1968), p. 30; No. 115 B (May 1969), p. 27.

When *Eurovision* started in 1954, in the eight member countries of that time there existed around 3,238 million TV viewers, but in 1961 this number had reached more than 28 million. In all those years the main problem for transmissions were the *different* European languages. So the main product of *Eurovision* was an international sports telecast. Between 1954 and 1961 nearly 55% of the total program contained sports of some kind.[10] But since the early 1960's, the percentage of non-sport-contents of the program grew regularly. At the end of May, 1961, a modest start was made with the relaying of news in pictures by means of the *Eurovision* network. This way of relaying news has rapidly developed into a comprehensive daily operation, involving nearly all the European members of the EBU. Other organizations outside Europe participate in the system, because they can pick up the images from the *Eurovision* network at a favorable point in Europe and relay them to their own country by airfreight or even by satellite.[11]

Since that time news and actuality programs together made up nearly 60% of all *Eurovision* activity. The value of this kind of operation was underlined by nearly all the member countries. Emphasizing that the *Eurovision* news transmissions had become "an essential source of news material," a special Study Group recommended that they should have priority over all other transmissions except live multilateral programs and that they should be scheduled every day of the year including Sundays and public holidays.[12]

In addition to *Eurovision* some of the Scandinavian countries tried to develop since October, 1959, the *Nordvision* [13] which did not progress too well. But the success of *Eurovision* in regional transmissions led the Communist-ruled countries of Eastern Europe to attempt a similar venture within their own borders. Early in 1956 some stations in East Germany and Czechoslovakia broadcast part of the *Eurovision* coverage of the Olympic hockey matches relayed from Italy, and in 1957 interconnections also were extended to Poland. The idea of an international television service of the East European countries was born in sessions of COMECON (the East European equivalent of the Common market). Since May, 1958, television experts from East Germany, Czechoslovakia, Hungary, and Poland discussed the different problems. The most developed TV system outside of East Germany was that of Czechoslovakia, and

[10] Hans Brack, "Die Union Européenne de Radiodiffusion," *Rundfunk und Fernsehen* (Hamburg), Vol. 10/1962, p. 233.
[11] J. W. Rengelink, "Eurovision news—a first step to worldwide news," *EBU-Review* (Geneva), No. 90 B (April 1965), p. 10.
[12] N.C., "News overhauls sport in the Eurovision exchanges," *EBU Review* (Geneva), No. 90 B (April 1965), p. 12.
[13] W. Bauer-Heyd, " 'Nordvision' noch in Kinderschuhen. Die Entwicklung des Fernsehens in Skandinavien," *Kölnische Rundschau* (Cologne), Vol. 14/No. 241 (October 17, 1959).

there was already a test transmission to Hungary on August 31, 1957.[14] In January, 1960, the Administration Council of OIRT (International Radio and Television Organization, usually referred by the initials of its French name, the Organisation Internationale de Radio et Télévision) decided to create the so-called *Intervision*. The foundation of this institution took place on January 31, 1960, in Budapest, and the first four members were the national TV networks of East Germany, Czechoslovakia, Hungary, and Poland.[15] On February 6, 1960, in Geneva a contract was signed which dealt with a program exchange between *Eurovision* and *Intervision*.[16]

The formal inauguration of *Intervision* came on September 5, 1960, and the program aims of the organization were declared as follows: (a) actual information, live transmissions, (b) programs dealing with the economic, social, political and cultural life of the member countries, (c) artistic programs of classical and modern authors of the member countries, (d) programs for children and youth, (e) entertainment programs, (f) transmission of main national and international sport events.[17] Membership is open to "any television organization—not only O.I.R.T. members—which accepts the *Intervision* Statutes." [18] When links became available, the Soviet Union joined in 1961, and in 1963 Bulgaria and Romania became members of *Intervision*. The coordination center was established under the supervision of OIRT in its headquarter at Prague (Czechoslovakia). It is interesting to note that Finland, which already belonged to *Eurovision*, in 1965 became a member of *Intervision*, too. Very similar to this is the situation of the television organization from Yugoslavia which is a regular member of *Eurovision*, but also an associated one to the East European network system.[19]

Intervision in the later 1960's had together 14 active member organizations.[20] *Intervision* does not, however, service as many individual stations or as large an audience as its Western European counterpart. "The most important distinction between Intervision and Eurovision is, of course, their purposes," writes a researcher, and he continues: "Intervision is intended primarily to be a transmission belt for the propaganda of the Soviet Union and its European allies. It is international television

---

[14] Hermann Deml, "Osteuropäisches Fernsehen," *Publizistik* (Bremen), Vol. 4/No. 3 (May-June 1959), p. 168 ff.
[15] Cf. "Die Entwicklung der Intervision," *Hörfunk und Fernsehen* (Munich), Vol. 16/ No. 2 (April 1965), pp. 13 ff.
[16] Hans Brack, "Die Union Européenne de Radiodiffusion," *op. cit.*, p. 233.
[17] OIRT, *Reglement der Intervision*. Prague: Organization Internationale de Radio et Télévision, 1964, p. 14.
[18] OIRT, *International Radio and Television Organization. General Information.* Prague: OIRT, undated, p. 3.
[19] Burton Paulu, *Radio and Television Broadcasting on the European Continent*. Minneapolis/Minnesota: University of Minnesota Press, 1967, p. 41.
[20] OIRT, International Radio and Television Organization. General Information, *op. cit.*, p. 3.

in the service of Marxism-Leninism." [21] Between January, 1960, and January, 1965, more than 3700 programs were transmitted by the *Intervision* network. A Russian television executive classified the programs as follows: sports, 43.5%; topical, 30.5%; cultural, 9.8%; children's, 9.4%; and entertainment 6.7%.[22] These figures show that sports has nearly the same average percentage of the program of *Intervision* than it has on *Eurovision*.

After five years of *Intervision*, Aleš Suchý, Head of the Program Coordination Center at Prague, made this statement: "I think that it can be said in general that the five-year existence of Intervention has fully proved the necessity of establishment of this international organization which is, as testified by the daily life, needed by national television organizations; using it as their effective assistant in the mutual program exchange." [23] During the first five and one-half years of existence the *Intervision* center at Prague coordinated 4,941 programs, which makes 5,413 hours of transmissions.[24] A big event like a May Day parade in Moscow gets televised all over the bloc, and in certain cases these programs are transmitted to television stations outside of the *Intervision* networks.[25]

It was already mentioned that the first step of cooperation between TV networks of both members of *Eurovision* as well as of *Intervision* took place in 1956, when East Germany and Czechoslovakia broadcast some sports events from the Olympic Winter Games in Italy, transmitted by the *Eurovision* member RAI. Since 1960, when *Intervision* was founded, there has been certain annual program exchange: In 1960 *Eurovision* transmitted to *Intervision* 74 telecasts (= 126 hours), in 1961 only 54 (= 57 hours), in 1962 not more than 38 (= 65 hours), in 1963 87 (= 128 hours), in 1964 already 240 (= 247 hours), in 1965 (January-September) 124 telecasts (= 36 hours), in 1966 199 (= 310 hours), and in 1967 174 (= 274 hours). The figures for 1960 and for 1964 indicate the big interest in sports telecasts from the Olympic Summer Games in Rome (1960) and the Olympic Winter Games in Innsbruck/Austria (1964): Among the 74 program exchanges in 1960 there were 53 of sports events, and in 1964 there were 164 sports telecasts among the total of 246 transmissions from *Eurovision* to *Intervision*.

On the other hand, there have been regular program exchanges from *Intervision* to *Eurovision*, too: In 1960 *Intervision* transmitted 33 telecasts

[21] Wilson P. Dizard, *Television—A World View*. Syracuse/New York: Syracuse University Press, 1966, p. 93.
[22] Cf. Burton Paulu, *Radio and Television Broadcasting on the European Continent*, p. 141 ff.
[23] Aleš Suchý, Intervision in 1965, in: *World Radio TV Handbook: Radio-Television 1966*, 20th ed., Hellerup/Denmark: World Radio-Television Handbook Co., 1965, p. 39.
[24] N. A. Skatschko, "Jahre der Entwicklung," *Rundfunk und Fernsehen—OIRT* (Prague), Vol. 1966/No. 2, p. 3.
[25] Cf. "Television in Eastern Europe," *Television Quarterly* (New York/N.Y.), Vol. 6/No. 3 (1967), p. 35.

(= 47 hours) to *Eurovision*, in 1961 only 17 (= 30 hours), in 1962 56 (= 104 hours), in 1963 49 (= 88 hours), in 1964 95 (= 83 hours), in 1965 (January-September) 128 (= 61 hours), in 1966 107 (= 150 hours), and in 1967 only 76 telecasts (= 131 hours). Between 1960 and 1967 *Eurovision* transmitted to *Intervision* 990 programs (= 1243 hours), and in the same period the sum of *Intervision* transmissions to *Eurovision* made 561 programs (= 694 hours). Most of these imports and exports have been cultural programs or sports events.[26]

A good example for the cooperation is the year 1964, when a couple of very important events took place which were transmitted to both parts of Europe and to other countries. The following graph [27] gives an excellent overview:

NEWS TRANSMISSIONS
TOTAL ITEMS ORIGINATED AND RECEIVED
1/1/1964 — 12/31/1964

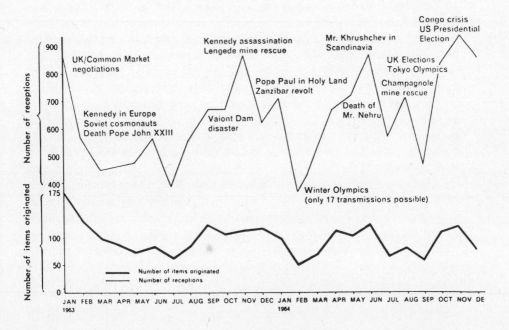

26 All figures are compiled by the author from: *Statistik des Programmaustausches zwischen Intervision und Eurovision*, unpublished material from the OIRT Center, Prague, undated (mimeographed).
27 From: *EBU Review* (Geneva), No. 90 B (April 1965), p. 13.

No country in Europe or anywhere in the world can expect to be self-sufficient in the TV field. An exciting new era began on July 23, 1962, when Europe and North America were linked by live television for the first time, through the Telstar-1 experimental communication satellite orbiting high over the Atlantic. An estimated 100 million Europeans witnessed 22 minutes of live pickups of everyday life in a dozen North American cities from Quebec to the Mexican border, during this memorable initial program. Later the same day, a North American audience of almost similar size became armchair tourists for 19 absorbing minutes as Eurovision cameras scanned from the Arctic Circle to the Mediterranean, and from the Danube to the Atlantic.[28] As a consequence of the Early Bird Satellite in 1965, the day-long transmission of live television across the Atlantic became technically possible at the very time there was increasing demand for news exchange. The new technical instruments made it possible that the number of 72 transmissions by satellites in 1964 [29] climbed to 186 in 1965.[30] The first transmission via Early Bird took place on May 2, 1965, when a two-way multiple-origin program was transmitted to mark the introduction of this new telecommunication facility. This program was rather similar in conception to the very first trans-Atlantic television program with which the satellite Telstar was inaugurated in 1962.[31]

The various developments of international television made it necessary, that Marcel Bezençon, the "father of Eurovision," in 1966 came up with the question, how the future of *Eurovision* could look like: "Will Eurovision merge into Mondovision? Probably to the extent that Mondovision is no more than a network for direct relay gradually encircling the globe and enabling any television organization to give its viewers a show picked out from some other point in the world. At first sight, and ideally speaking, there does not seem to be any insuperable barrier to this fabulous expansion." [32]

One year after these remarks *Eurovision* made another step towards Mondovision. Television services from five continents worked together for a world-wide live program under the title "Our World" on Sunday, 25th of June, 1967. This telecast was the result of two years of intensive preparation, and it was the very first step to reach a global audience for two

[28] George Jacobs, "Global report on Television," *Television Age* (New York), Vol. XV/ No. 24 (July 1, 1968), p. 22.

[29] "Eurovision program statistics," *EBU Review* (Geneva), No. 91 B (May 1965), p. 51.

[30] "Eurovision program statistics," *EBU Review* (Geneva) No. 98 B (July 1966), p. 26.

[31] J. Treeby Dickinson, "Eurovision in 1965," *World Radio TV Handbook. Radio Television 1966.* Hellerup/Denmark: World Radio-Television Handbook Co., 1966, p. 30.

[32] Marcel Bezençon, "The destiny of Eurovision—Olympus above the clouds?" *EBU Review* (Geneva), No. 98 B (July 1966), p. 13.

hours. Broadcast was between 8 and 10 p.m. Central European time, and its contents was comprised contributions of television stations in Africa, Australia, Canada, Europe, Japan, Mexico, and the United States. Because of the time zoning, viewers in the eastern United States watched it on Sunday afternoon, while in Australia and Japan it appeared on television screens early on Monday morning. This project was first put forward by the British Broadcasting Corporation in 1965 and since then developed by the EBU Television Program Committee with the assistance of the permanent staff in Geneva and Brussels.

The structure of the program was composed at a number of international conferences and technical planning commissions of 17 different broadcasting organizations. Nearly 10,000 broadcasting staff members all around the world were mobilized, and the equipment included more than a million miles of telephone line and 100,000 miles of micro-wave links. For the long-distance vision links there were four satellites over the Atlantic and Pacific, and sound circuits were also routed via the satellites; the transatlantic telephone cables provided a reserve path. The master control room and main switching center of the whole operation was located at the BBC Television Center's Studio in London. But there were set up also two regional zones for this telecast: The West Zone, with New York as sub-switching point, handled the items from Canada, the United States, Mexico, Australia and Japan, and the eastern zone, covered by the European Broadcasting Union with Brussels as switching-point, handled the sequences from Austria, Belgium, France, West Germany, Italy, Spain, Sweden und Tunisia. A system of simultaneous translation into English, French and German was set up in London, and a number of national commentators translated into their own languages where it was necessary. It was estimated that around 350 million viewers were watching this world-wide two hour program. Arrangements had also been made for a number of countries in Eastern Europe to take part in the program, but these were cancelled shortly before the start of the transmission.

The program started with a visit by television cameras to babies newly born in Japan, Canada, Denmark and Mexico. And when the transmission came to its end after two hours these babies were shown again how they looked after living for two hours in "Our World." The viewers were also shown for example scientists at work in different parts of the world in research to increase food supply, and housing development in Scotland, Canada and New York. The cameras of "Our World" were also able to show the global audience the Victorian mansion at Glassboro in the United States where at that same moment President Johnson and the Soviet Prime Minister Kosygin, were discussing the world situation. So it was really a historical day on this 25th of June, 1967, when an audience from great parts of the world was able to participate in events which happened at the same time in the various continents of "Our World." [33]

A few days after this successful event, Marcel Bezençon meditated on the future perspectives of international television: "Eurovision is no longer Eurovision. Its tight framework has been burst open by technology. Already it has Intervision as a travelling companion, and the satellites are pointing to the new paths it must follow. We are in transit between two eras . . . This process is not without its crises, its abrupt changes, fatigues, errors and thromboses. We cannot pass straight from the state of villager to that of universal man. Eurovision, Mondovision, the intensification of rapid news exchanges, and soon distribution satellites and perhaps broadcasting satellites, are going to lay bare massive and contradictory solidarities . . . One might wonder whether Eurovision in its present form will have any reason for existence in ten years' time, when broadcasting satellites will plunge their programs live into private receiving sets. . . ." [34]

As in earlier years, the program category which accounted for the longest global circuit-time in 1968 was sport. The main events were the Olympic Games: first the Winter Games at Grenoble (France) and in October, the Summer Games in Mexico. In both cases, a high proportion of the transmissions was already in color: about 56% in the case of Grenoble and about 85% in the case of Mexico City.[35] In spite of many difficulties, however, transmissions of the pictures via satellite (Intelsat III) during the Games went smoothly and reception quality was excellent. The EBU/OIRT Operations Group consisted of 160 staff members recruited from nearly all the European member organizations and in Mexico itself. The running of such a large multinational team, which had had no time to work together beforehand, was another experiment which worked satisfactorily. The European television organizations received, for selection and further distribution, 136 hours of sporting events from Mexico City.[36]

A short look to the future shows that there are several things going on since that time. Recently developed plans say that during the Olympic Summer Games 1972 in Munich a world-wide receivable program will be transmitted from 9 a.m. to 11 p.m. Central European time from all of the 32 different places of event, and that the total program will be broadcast in colour.[37] Since 1966 it has been known that Germany plans to

[33] "Our World," *Report of Activities 1967—European Broadcasting Union*. Geneva: The European Broadcasting Union, 1968, p. 3 ff.
[34] Marcel Bezençon, "Mist veils an immense horizon," *EBU Review* (Geneva), No. 104 B (July 1967), p. 10.
[35] J. Treeby Dickinson, "Eurovision in 1968," *World Radio TV Handbook. Radio Television 1969*. Hellerup/Denmark: World Radio-Television Handbook Co., 1969, p. 21.
[36] "EBU, Satellites: A Year of Transition," *Report of Activities 1968—European Broadcasting Union*. Geneva: The European Broadcasting Union, 1969, p. 7 f.
[37] Karl-Heinz Schulte, *Technische Einrichtungen für die Durchführung der Fernseh-Berichterstattung der Olympischen Spiele 1972*, Munich: Deutsches Olympia-Zentrum, May 1969.

launch a special "Olympia Satellite" toward the end of 1971 in time for the 1972 Olympic Games. Primary purpose of the satellite would be to feed Radio and Television broadcast of the Olympics to the Near East and Africa. After the Olympics, the satellite would be used for educational and informational purposes. Possible operator of these broadcasts was suggested as the *Deutsche Welle*, a station similar to the *Voice of America*. Small receiving stations might be made available to developing countries through the West German foreign aid program.[38] In all of these and similar cases Eurovision does understand its role more or less as an international coordination center for world-wide TV transmissions. In 1969 Eurovision had 29 member organizations from Europe and 56 associated institutions from all the five continents.[39] So the EBU and its subdivision Eurovision are really—according to the words of EBU's general secretary Henrik Hahr—"some kind of United Nations of Radio and Television Broadcasting." [40]

[38] Cf. Werner Büdeler, "1972 Olympic Games Prompt German Bid for TV Satellite," *Technology Week* (Washington, D.C.), Vol. 19/No. 34 (September 5, 1966), p. 19.
[39] Cf. "Eurovision," *Internationales Handbuch für Rundfunk und Fernsehen 1969/70*, Hamburg: Verlag Hans-Bredow-Institut, 1969, p. E61 ff.
[40] Horst Scharfenberg (ed.), *Studienkreis Rundfunk und Geschichte e.V.—Protokoll der Gründungsversammlung am 10. Juni 1969 in Ludwigshafen/Rhein*, Baden-Baden, 1969, p. 5.

Nancy Carol Jones:

Development and Functions of INTELSAT

WHAT has been called the "world's first operational Space Communications System" made use of one of the Earth's natural satellites, the moon. In conducting Project Diana on January 11, 1946, members of the U.S. Army Signal Corps beamed radar signals to the moon and heard an echo.[1] During the 1950's the U.S. Naval Research Laboratory continued experimentation and between 1959 and 1963 regularly relayed communications from the Washington, D.C., area to Hawaii using the moon as a reflector of radio waves. A public demonstration of this project was staged on January 28, 1960. The first official photograph transmitted via the moon came from Hawaii to the U.S. and showed men standing on the deck of the USS Hancock so as to spell out "Moon Relay."

In 1953 and 1957 the Soviet Union discussed the possibility of using large high-altitude equatorial "hanging" satellites to amplify and relay television programs to all parts of the world. Sputnik I's beep on October 4, 1957 may not have been that of a full-fledged communications satellite, but it illuminated for the world some of the potentials of outer space. At least three articles appeared in the Communist press in 1960 written by the president of the Academy of Sciences, saying Soviet scientist planned to use satellites for radio purposes. On August 6, 1961 Soviet Television viewers had their first look at a cosmonaut in flight as an astronaut orbited in Vostok II. The following year the Soviet Union accomplished a significant achievement in long-distance communication by receiving radio signals from a space rocket headed in the direction of Mars. Television pictures were sent from many of the Vostok spaceships launched during the early 1960's to Intervision, the East European network, and Eurovision, the West European counterpart.[2]

[1] National Aeronautics and Space Administration, *Satellite Communications: Six Years of Achievement, 1958 through 1964,* (Washington, D.C., March 1, 1965), p. 7.
[2] Nicolai I. Tchistiakov, "Hurdles in Space Broadcasting," *The UNESCO Courier,* November, 1966, p. 30; Jerome Morenoff, "Communications in Orbit: A Legal Analysis and Prognosis," *Communication Satellite Systems Technology,* ed. by Richard B. Marsten (New York: Academic Press, 1966), pp. 1024-25.

▶ From: *The Role of the United Nations in Communications Satellites,* by Nancy Carol Jones. Unpublished Ph.D. dissertation University of Missouri, Columbia/Missouri, August 1967. Reprinted by permission of the author.

Since the 1960's communications satellites became a national status symbol. Several nations discussed "domestic" communications satellite systems. Countries wanted to launch communications satellites for various reasons, including expansion of limited ground facilities, economic development, educational purposes and fear of unopposed propaganda from other countries. Besides the United States and the Soviet Union some other countries made valuable contributions to the development of satellites: Canada, Republic of China, France, Federal Republic of Germany, India, Japan, Thailand, United Kingdom and some others. Some of the nations also made efforts toward cooperation in the field of communications satellites. Some regional organizations of the Communist, European and Scandinavian countries were developed. In the international field the International Council of Scientific Unions, its Committee on Space Research (COSPAR) and the International Radio Union became of some importance.[3]

First half of the 1960's in the United States was occupied by organization for a commercial communications satellite system. During the summer of 1961 the Federal Communications Commission (FCC) investigated some of the problems of organizing such a system, and the FCC industrial committee reported on October 13, 1961, recommending the government set up a non-profit U.S. Satellite Corporation. On Februrary 7, 1962 the President sent the Congress a bill to establish a private corporation to operate communications satellites. Finally a compromise was made between the different plans, and on February 1, 1963, the Communications Satellite Corp. (Comsat) was established.[4] The Comsat Act specified that 50 per cent of the stock may be held by common carriers authorized by the FCC and 50 per cent may be owned by the public. Comsat has about 150,000 public shareholders and 163 communications company stockholders. Between the sale of the stock and the first annual meeting of Comsat in the fall of 1964 negotiations were conducted with foreign representatives. A set of agreements were reached July 24, 1964 and signed August 20, 1964 creating the International Telecommunications Satellite Consortium (Intelsat).

Foreign Governments or designated entities were to provide an additional $200 million as their share in creating a global communications satellite system. First satellite orbited by the international consortium was Early Bird. Soon after its launch on April 6, 1965, Early Bird perched over the Atlantic off the coast of Brazil in a synchronous orbit. An estimated 300 million persons in seventeen countries on both sides of the Atlantic watched the first public Telecast on May 2, 1965.[5]

[3] Cf. Donald Cox, *The Space Race*, Philadelphia: Chilton Books, 1962.
[4] Cf. George D. Schrader; "The Communications Satellite Corporation: A New Experiment in Government and Business," *Kentucky Law Journal*, Vol. 53, No. 4 (1965), pp. 732-42.
[5] "Electronics: The Room-Size World," *Time*, Vol. 85, No. 20 (May 14, 1965), pp. 84-85.

By December, 1965, there were forty-eight members of Intelsat: [6]

Algeria	India	Pakistan
Argentina	Indonesia	Portugal
Australia	Iraq	Saudi Arabia
Austria	Ireland	South Africa
Belgium	Israel	Spain
Brazil	Italy	Sudan
Canada	Japan	Sweden
Ceylon	Jordan	Switzerland
Chile	Kuwait	Syria
China	Lebanon	Tunisia
Colombia	Libya	United Arab Republic
Denmark	Monaco	United Kingdom
Ethiopia	Netherlands	United States
France	New Zealand	Vatican
Germany	Nigeria	Venezuela
Greece	Norway	Yemen

Membership in March, 1967, numbered fifty-six. Countries acceding during 1966 were Liechtenstein, Malaysia, Mexico, Morocco, the Philippines, Singapore and Thailand. Early in 1967 South Korea joined.[7]

Any country, organization or individual with communication facilities available may use the system by paying a standard rate, but membership in Intelsat is not required. Originally it was estimated that the global system would cost $200 million. Comsat, as manager, bills each party to the Special Agreement monthly for its share of the current obligations. Payment began in September, 1964. Each of the members was fully paid as of mid-1966. Up to that time the consortium had spent $25 million. This covered the Intelsat I phase, which was the launching of Early Bird. Launching of the synchronous Lani Bird and Canary Bird made up the Intelsat II phase. Intelsat III calls for additional launchings in 1968. For this phase of the program six new satellites each with 1,200 voice channels and total costs of $31 million are planned. Their launching would complete the basic global satellite system. The International Telecommunications Satellite Consortium also has under consideration an Intelsat IV phase, consisting of multi-purpose satellites.[8]

Members of the consortium represent more than ninety-five per cent of the expected usage of communications satellites. The United States,

[6] Charles D. LaFond, "Enthusiasm Grows for Global Comsats," *Missiles and Rockets*, January 31, 1966, p. 52.
[7] Interview with J. Raymond Marchand, March 14, 1967 at Comsat headquarters, Washington, D.C.
[8] Edwin J. Istvan, "Organization and Program of Intelsat," *Communication Satellite Systems Technology*, ed. by Richard B. Marsten, *op. cit.*, pp. 932-34.

which generates the largest telecommunications traffic, always would have a controlling voice in the consortium under the present agreement. Because Comsat was a private enterprise and some of the other countries wanted to deal on a government level, dual agreements were necessary.[9]

A Japanese law professor gave this evaluation: ". . . it is quite doubtful how much the agreement evaluates the substantive meaning of such duality and whether it has been realized or not. The reason is: The United States, at the beginning satisfied with establishing only a private Agreement among communication entities, later compromised 'formally' at the insistence of the European countries . . . The European States stood together against the United States concerning the fundamental problems, by constituting the European Conference on Satellite Communication. These states especially stressed that the communications satellite system must be a permanent world organization in its form of organization. The content of the Agreement, however, was a result of formal compromises . . . ." The same author expressed the fear that Comsat and Intelsat might be influenced through intervention and control by the U.S. government. Reference was made to UN Resolution 1962 (XVIII), providing for freedom of outer space, with this appraisal: "But in reality, freedom and equality of use of space contradict each other, and unless special aid by the United Nations or other appropriate organs is granted to the developing countries, the principle of free use of space is guaranteed only for certain highly industrialized countries at the cost and sacrifice of developing countries." [10]

Both American and foreign law professors have also studied the Comsat Act. An American scholar predicted, "In a world not sharing in a like degree the American commitment to free enterprise, its administration will present unique and absorbing problems of law and diplomacy." Another law professor from a Canadian University called the Comsat Act an "expression of a particular American ideological position" which might raise questions in international relations that probably should not be there. He continued, "Had there been a more realistic appraisal of the international significance of mechanisms of this kind, which are going to be utilized by many states, perhaps the notion of emphasizing the private corporate side might have taken a subordinate place in American thinking." [11]

[9] Asher H. Ende and Maurice Wolf, "Some Aspects of the Commercial Communications Satellite System—Impact and Problems," (Preprint 66-273 of paper presented to the AAIA Communications Satellite Systems Conference, Washington, D.C., May 2-4, 1966), p. 12.

[10] Soji Yamamoto, "Agreement Establishing Interim Agreements For a Global Commercial Communications Satellite System," *Japanese Annual of International Law*, No. 9 (1965), pp. 47-55.

[11] *Conference on the Law of Space and of Satellite Communications* (A Part of the Third National Conference on the Peaceful Uses of Space, Chicago, May, 1963, Washington, D.C.: Government Printing Office, 1964), pp. 54, 79.

An American journalist said of the Comsat Act,

> What was involved here, among other things, was the abdication
> of sovereignty, not to an international body but to private interests,
> in one of the first great national decisions of the space age. . . . The
> whole thing might have been simplified by admitting AT&T to the
> United Nations.

This article was quoted in *International Affairs,* a magazine published
in English in the Soviet Union. As might be expected, the USSR has
been the most vociferous critic of Comsat and Intelsat. On the interim
agreement, one Soviet writer said:

> The much promising declaration of U.S. statesmen on inter-
> national cooperation in space communication will remain so many
> words as long as the monopolies run the show. The first provision
> for a change for the better is to transfer the entire range of questions
> pertaining to space communication to the corresponding organiza-
> tions. There is no need to create such organizations, for they have
> existed for a long time: first and foremost the U.N. Committee on
> the Peaceful Uses of Outer Space and the International Telecom-
> munication Union.

The writer pointed out that Resolution 1962 (XVIII) at the insistence of the U.S. had sanctioned the admission of non-governmental entities to activities in outer space. He also said Resolution 1721 (XVI) that
"communication by means of satellites should be available to the nations
of the world . . . on a global and non-discriminatory basis" was being
violated.[12] Apparently the alleged discrimination was against the Communist and underdeveloped countries.

A Soviet legal publication contained this statement:

> It is not accidental that the communication system planned by
> the United States is constructed in terms of its use for telephone
> conversations alone for the purpose of a rapid repayment and receipt
> of profits. It is quite evident that a truly international system of
> global communication should be constructed for its use for purposes
> of a considerable expansion of cultural, scientific, and other asso-
> ciations.[13]

USSR representatives had been invited by the U.S. to participate in
preliminary discussions leading to the interim and special agreements, but

[12] I. Cheprov, "Global or American Space Communications System?," *International
Affairs* (Moscow), December, 1964, pp. 70, 74.
[13] G. S. Stashevsky, *Sovetskaye Gosudarstvo i Pravo* (Soviet State & Law), Moscow,
December, 1964, published in English by Clearinghouse for Federal Scientific and
Technical Information, Springfield, Va., as "Communications Satellites and Interna-
tional Law," February 18, 1965.

the invitation was ignored. Then in the late Spring, 1964, the Soviet Union requested an exploratory meeting. Soviet representatives at the meeting criticized the U.S. for commercial exploitation of space.[14] Under the quota system developed, the Soviet Union's share would be less than one-half per cent.[15]

Two British aerospace experts said although the USSR was active in communications satellite technology and had a national need for them, she could not join the international consortium under the present arrangements:

> Judging by Russian comments after the formation of Intelsat on the restrictive commercial nature of the consortium, and the conflict with the freedom of operation cited in the United Nations' resolution on the use of space, it is evident that the structure of the definitive world organisation to be determined before 1970 would have to be significantly different before Russia would become an active member.

They said there was no evidence Communist China was interested in communications satellites. But they predicted in ten or twenty years she would experience dramatic changes in requirement for a communications network. Their article continued:

> The important question is how will this organisation evolve after the interim agreements expire. . . . It seems likely that some form of international committee will still be the governing body, but that the degree of participation, ownership, and control might be significantly different. By 1970, launching vehicles other than American ones will be available, and the pattern of traffic will be substantially different from the pattern which determined the basis of the present ownership and control arrangements. It is quite likely, therefore, that the part the USA will play will be smaller and possibly not even dominating, as at present. Strongest competition can be expected from the European nations acting in harmony. By 1970 they will have gained much more experience in the field, and they will be in a stronger bargaining position including the ability to organise or join a competitive system.
>
> Secondly, will the successor to Intelsat choose to retain the Comsat Corporation as its only manager? The answer to this may well depend on what steps European and other nations take separately and collectively in planning communication satellite system research and development programmes. Comsat's position may not be in-

---

[14] Arnold W. Frutkin, *International Cooperation in Space* (Englewood Cliffs, N.J.: Prentice-Hall, 1965), pp. 161-62.
[15] G. K. C. Pardoe and L. W. Steines, "Communication Satellites—the future pattern," Part 2, *Flight International*, August 11, 1966, p. 219.

violate, and project management for post-basic phase systems may take advantage of improved European, Canadian and Japanese experiences.[16]

James McCormack, chairman and chief executive officer of Comsat, believes the corporation will be in a strong position in negotiating the definitive arrangements. He predicted:

> . . . when the Intelsat agreement comes up for renegotiation, the global system will be operating. A good many countries will have investments in earth stations designed for use with the Intelsat system.
>
> Of course, by itself this won't bring the Russians in, and it may not fully satisfy all national and regional aspirations, but it will be a going concern with a big lead over any possible rival. You should remember, too, that the bulk of Comsat's revenues comes from American customers.[17]

John Johnson, Comsat vice president in charge of international affairs, said the agreements are successful. He listed their assets:

> *First*, the concept of an international cooperative enterprise, with very widespread membership, for the purpose of sharing the exploitation of a new resource for the economic benefit of all mankind;
>
> *Second*, the effort to reduce national rivalries in a new field of economic activity by the concept of a single global system instead of competing national systems;
>
> *Third*, a form of organization which recognizes the diversity of national economic systems by permitting participation of either public or private entities on behalf of the signatory countries;
>
> *Fourth*, a form of organization which provides for a wide disparity of investment and ownership reflecting the probable extent of the use of the system by the various participants and which takes this factor into account in the decision-making process; and
>
> *Fifth*, the careful balance of political and economic factors reflected throughout the Agreements.[18]

Conclusion

One reason for establishing Intelsat was to avoid economic, technical and political problems that might result from a number of separate sys-

---

[16] G. K. C. Pardoe and L. W. Steines, *op. cit.*, pp. 219-20.

[17] "The Amazing Story of Earth Satellites: Interview with Head of Comsat," *U.S. News & World Report*, December 26, 1966, p. 62.

[18] John A. Johnson, "Satellite Communications: The Challenge and the Opportunity for International Cooperation," *Federal Communications Bar Journal*, Vol. XIX, No. 3 (1964-1965), p. 96.

tems. A single system serving all needs would still be most efficient. The Comsat-Intelsat organization has succeeded in establishing an operational system, but communications satellite technology existed and probably would have been put into operation regardless of the organizational structure chosen. Comsat-Intelsat created a complex legal tangle as well as opened the way to widespread criticism. Instead of the speed taken in launching the system, more time and effort should have been devoted to creating a comprehensive organization. Apparently technology was far ahead of man's ability to make plans for it legally, socially and politically. As a result, the victory was won by a particular American philosophy of private enterprise, without regard to other positions. Instead, the view which should have been taken was one of a broad international perspective and social benefit to mankind, rather than profit. That viewpoint will have to be considered in formulating permanent arrangements, according to the agreements.

The Soviet Union has a valid opinion in noting that communications satellites were structured around the profitable business of telephone conversations. But the asset of communications satellites seems to be in broadcasting, especially television. Cables can transmit telephone calls, although perhaps not as cheaply at the present time as communications satellites, and short wave can carry radio programs across oceans. Television, perhaps the medium with the greatest impact on international relations and underdeveloped countries, has been given a secondary position in planning.

Direct broadcasting will force this medium to the fore, if it does not become shackled by fears. By 1969 there could be demonstrations of direct broadcasting, but what effect it would have on determining the future organization is difficult to predict. Although Comsat might be able to build broadcasting satellites, the problem will be who can operate them? Solutions must be found internationally. The Comsat-Intelsat arrangement is a unique plan to cope with a fast-moving technology, although it leaves much to be desired. In the future, even greater efforts will be required to provide for such technology and make arrangements for the important implications. A dialogue would be the most effective method of bringing out the various problems, rather than meeting behind closed doors to reach a position that will set the pattern for the next generation. Some beginning has been made toward a debate and a few efforts to cope with the problems presented by the structure have been taken.

Proposal for "Univision." This area requires further study, but it seems a cultural and educational exchange of programs might promote peace. Intelsat as a specialized agency might provide a free TV channel for an experiment in "Univision." UNESCO could be instrumental in setting up a board of experts including sociologists, educators and broadcasters. A grant from the Intelsat profits might make the board possible.

This board should be a programming organization separate from the operating agency. Programs and performances from many countries as well as documentaries of the UN and member countries could be drawn upon. The objective of the board would be to select programs that promote peace and international understanding. Users of mass media tend to reinforce their existing beliefs. Experts might be able to decide on some human factors that should be reinforced. For instance, Stuart Chase's *The Proper Study of Mankind* lists thirty-three characteristics common to most societies. George P. Murdock developed a Cross-Cultural Index at Yale University. Perhaps additional sociological studies might be conducted on factors contributing to peace and means of reinforcing them by television. The board would select material to reinforce these factors.

International television seems to be the greatest asset of communications satellites. The high frequencies used for television travel only in straight lines and unlike low frequencies do not travel long distances across oceans. Even low-frequency radio at long distances is unreliable. Cables are expensive for radio and unsuited to television. Thus broadcasting, particularly television, should benefit most from communications satellites. Yet it has played a secondary role in planning. This is because television takes the equivalent of several hundred telephone calls on a satellite and does not seem worth the disruption in service. In the future, of course, with many channels, television would become more profitable. But the resources still would be limited as is the space for synchronous satellites.

Considering communications satellites may be like dancing on top of a technical volcano. Unless we are nimble enough to create patterns harnessing the great potential, much may be laid waste. Technical, economic, political, legal and social problems of communications satellites demand agility. As one educator at a communications satellite conference said, technology is neither good nor evil, but it is man's use that makes it so. One conclusion of the conference was that the technology of communications satellites was ahead of man's understanding and capacity to make use of it constructively.[19]

Present organizations should not inhibit arrangements for the future. As this survey has tried to show they can provide guideposts and waysigns. Ultimately, a structure to fit the potential and characteristics of communications satellites will have to be devised. In the future organization for communications satellites the United Nations should take its long-delayed role. This is to offer a specialized agency status to an international resource that may influence mankind as much as the alphabet, movable type and the telegraph.

[19] Charles d'Amato, Arthur Hoffman and Joseph Jones (eds.), *A Conference on Communications Satellites: Are the Users Ready?* A Report on the Proceedings. Medford/Massachusetts: Tufts University, 1966, pp. 5, 70.

THE WORLD'S PRESS

UNESCO
THE STRUCTURE OF THE WORLD'S PRESS

John C. Merrill
GLOBAL PATTERNS OF ELITE DAILY JOURNALISM

Hanno R. Hardt
THE PLIGHT OF THE DAILY PRESS IN WESTERN EUROPE

Hamid Mowlana
CROSS-NATIONAL COMPARISON OF ECONOMIC
    JOURNALISM

Heinz-Dietrich Fischer
THE INTERNATIONAL SITUATION OF MAGAZINES

THE WORLD'S PRESS

I F one hopes to keep abreast of the developments in, and growth of, the world's press, he will become extremely frustrated. The global press situation is, of course, changing very rapidly, and even organizations like UNESCO find it impossible to describe the situation while it is still fresh and valid. This unfortunate state of affairs, however, should not dissuade persons and groups from trying to provide periodically an overview of the press situation in various parts of the world.

In this chapter, several kinds of world press articles and studies are presented to indicate at least a few of the types of discussions and investigations being produced relative to the broad descriptive-analytical aspects of the world's press. It is hoped that these will also give a kind of overview of the global press and will whet the appetite of the reader for further and continuing information.

The first article, a UNESCO study admittedly somewhat dated, gives some descriptive generalizations about the world's press and provides some useful insights to growth trends in newspaper journalism in various parts of the world. In the second article, by John Merrill, the focus is narrowed to what the author calls "elite" daily newspapers; the characteristics of these "elite" are given, and representative ones (in open and closed societies) in different parts of the world are named.

Hanno Hardt, on the journalism faculty at the University of Iowa, tells of the development and current problems—and these are surprisingly serious—of the daily press of Western Europe. This analysis is especially welcome in these days where the bulk of the studies are being done in new and underdeveloped nations; continents like Europe, with highly developed press systems, are generally ignored or given brief treatment. In the next article of the chapter, Hamid Mowlana of American University in Washington, D.C., deals with the growth of journalism related to economics in seven nations of Asia. His tentative conclusion, drawn from an analysis of several rather impressive empirical studies, is that economic journalism of a nation increases as the country develops economically, and that it is only after a country becomes considerably well developed politically that economic journalism increases.

In the final article of the chapter, Heinz-Dietrich Fischer of the history faculty at the University of Cologne, discusses the magazine distribution, state of health and variety in a global context. Although many lay observers, journalists, and even some "experts" and prophets like Marshall McLuhan, are predicting pessimistic trends for the world's print media in this electronic age, the realistic student of the press cannot fail to note that generally newspapers and magazines are flourishing everywhere, except in a few isolated pockets, and the pluralism in these print media is cause for encouragement, not despair.

*   *   *   *

RELATED READING

Annuaire de la Presse française et étrangère et du monde politique: Annuaire international de la Presse. Paris: Chambre Syndicale des Editeurs d'Annuaires. (annual).

Desmond, R. W. *The Press and World Affairs.* New York: Appleton-Century-Crofts, 1937.

Dovifat, Emil (ed.), *Handbuch der Publizistik.* 3 vols. Berlin: Walter de Gruyter & Co., 1968-69.

Editor & Publisher International Year Book. New York. (annual).

Europa Year Book. London: Europa Publications Ltd. (annual).

Fischer, Heinz-Dietrich. *Die grossen Zeitungen: Porträts der Weltpresse.* Munich: Deutscher Taschenbuch Verlag, 1966.

Handbuch der Weltpresse. 2 vols. Munich-Cologne-Opladen: Westdeutscher Verlag, 1970. (Eds. H. Prakke, H.-D. Fischer & Carin Kessemeier).

IPI. *The Flow of the News.* IPI: Zurich, 1953.

Merrill, J. C. *The Elite Press: Great Newspapers of the World.* New York: Pitman Publishing Corp., 1968.

Merrill, J. C., Carter Bryan and Marvin Alisky. *The Foreign Press: A Survey of the World's Journalism.* New, enlarged edition. Baton Rouge: Louisiana State University Press, 1970.

Olson, K. E. *The History Makers: The Press in Europe from its Beginnings through 1965.* Baton Rouge: Louisiana State University Press, 1966.

Peterson, Theodore. *Magazines in the Twentieth Century.* Urbana: University of Illinois Press, 1964.

Schramm, Wilbur. *One Day in the World's Press.* Stanford: Stanford University Press, 1959.

UNESCO. *World Communications.* 4th ed. New York and Amsterdam: UNESCO: 1964.

UNESCO. *World Press.* New York: UNESCO, 1964.

UNESCO:

The Structure of the World's Press

IN MOST COUNTRIES throughout the world, the press has continued to expand during the past decade. It is significant that recent losses in certain countries of Europe and North America, where economic difficulties caused a number of newspapers to cease publication, have been offset by the establishment of new journals in the developing countries of Africa, Asia and Latin America. Meanwhile, daily newspaper circulation has increased in all regions, the present world total of 300 million copies being some 20 per cent higher than that of a decade ago.

A number of the larger individual countries scored notable advances. In the United States of America, the general-interest daily press claims a circulation of over 59 million, as against 55 million in 1954. During the same period, daily circulation has risen from 34 million to 39 million in Japan and from 30 million to 39 million in the Union of Soviet Socialist Republics.

At the same time, marked disparities persist in the pattern of press distribution. A regional breakdown shows that Europeans buy 38 per cent of the world's daily papers and North Americans 23 per cent, while Africans, Asians and South Americans, representing nearly 70 per cent of the world population, together command only 26 per cent. While the number of copies of dailies averages ten per 100 persons for the whole world— a figure suggested as a minimum of adequacy by Unesco—the level falls as low as eight copies in South America, four in Asia and just over one in Africa.

Striking technological advances in the past decade have stimulated press expansion, although in the great majority of countries, few of the new techniques have yet been applied on a broad scale. Nevertheless, it seems clear that newspaper publishing now stands on the verge of the most important technical revolution in its 400-year history.

In the field of printing itself, electronics and automation have solved many problems in production control, especially on high-speed rotary presses, as well as in actual production. This is a feat which few believed possible as little as 15 years ago.

▶ From: *World Communications: Press—Radio—Television—Film*, by UNESCO. Copyright © 1964 by UNESCO and the UNESCO Publications Center, New York and Paris. Reprinted by permission of the publisher.

There has been a vast improvement in rotary offset printing, due largely to the use of photocomposition, better inking, faster etching methods, the electronic engraving of plates and electronic control of registers. Indeed, the days of conventional printing in raised type, used since the time of Gutenberg and Caxton, appear to be numbered. Its place will probably be taken by various forms of photocomposition or filmsetting, that is, of printing plates prepared from photograph negatives, including both text and illustrations in the same process, with a great gain in speed, versatility and economy. A major result of these advances is that the need for skilled technicians will be minimized.

Within a decade or two, it seems, only the mass circulation newspapers and magazines will be printed as they are today, though they will doubtless be able to convert to the new processes eventually. The fact that, for the time being, these techniques are particularly suited to small circulation dailies, to weeklies and other periodicals is of special interest to the developing countries, as has been recently demonstrated, for example, by newspaper groups in East Africa.

Newspaper publishing has also benefited from the application of new telecommunication techniques, in association with news agency development. These advances have been made more particularly in the developed countries. In Japan, newspaper and news agency interests undertook postwar research on the facsimile transmission of ideographs, as well as on Monotype and teletypesetting, as a means of raising efficiency and conserving manpower. This culminated, in 1959, in the simultaneous publication of newspaper editions in Japanese cities hundreds of miles apart.

In 1962 a New York daily went a stage further with the simultaneous publication, by high-speed facsimile and teletypesetting, of editions in Paris and Los Angeles, the rate of transmitting material being 16 times the normal speed by cable and radio. Later in the year, the same newspaper transmitted several articles, by photo-facsimile, to its Paris edition through the first communication satellite, as well as seven pages to and from the satellite. These developments, it was foreseen, pointed the way to the simultaneous production of newspaper editions throughout whole regions and, ultimately, of "global newspapers." The subscriber would dial a telephone number and the front page of his "paper" would appear on his television screen, remaining there until he pressed a button, when it would be replaced by the second page and so on. He would, in fact, be able to view not only his local newspaper but papers in all countries in this way.

Africa has the lowest circulation level of daily newspapers among all regions of the world. There are many reasons for this, the chief among them being, perhaps, that Africa got off to a later start in press development than the other regions. Its literacy level is also the lowest of all regions. Newsprint and equipment must largely be imported. Only two

African countries, South Africa and the Federation of Rhodesia and Nyasaland, produce newsprint. Apart from a few large enterprises and a very few countries which have received bilateral or international technical assistance for the purpose, most newspapers cannot afford to maintain their own presses and consequently have their printing done under contract, usually on obsolescent machines. The lack of rapid low-cost transport is a major obstacle to distribution outside urban centres.

Circulation levels of newspapers vary greatly inside the region. In five countries, there are five to eight copies of dailies per 100 inhabitants. However, there are seven other countries which have no daily press except for roneotyped bulletins and 12 which lack dailies of any kind. Non-dailies and periodicals are generally concentrated in nine countries. Even within countries, circulation varies greatly. Publications are concentrated in urban centres, while 80 per cent of the population lives in almost inaccessible rural areas.

Nevertheless, the situation has improved in recent years. Many African governments are encouraging the development of a rural press to reinforce their literacy programmes. Ghana and Nigeria, for example, print weeklies for rural areas, most of them in vernacular languages. South Africa has many rural non-daily papers, including a number in Bantu. In Tropical Africa, many a jungle village where total illiteracy prevailed a few years ago now has access to news and information through the printed word.

A large part of the press in North Africa is nationally owned. In other parts of Africa, most of the major newspapers are European owned. However, local groups are beginning to play a role in the ownership and direction of important newspapers and magazines, especially in English-speaking countries.

In this region, the press has continued to expand both in size and scope. However, in the United States and Canada rising circulations of dailies have not kept pace with population growth. This trend has reduced the regional figure for the number of copies per 100 people from 27 to 25 since 1950.

Regional averages tend, however, to obscure the reality of progress in the less developed, predominantly Spanish-language countries. In the past decade, for example, daily newspaper circulation has more than doubled in Mexico, and has risen by 70 per cent in El Salvador, 60 per cent in the Dominican Republic and 30 per cent in Honduras. In English-speaking Jamaica, daily circulation has doubled in the same period.

Yet, real though the progress is, the results achieved to date remain painfully inadequate. Of the countries mentioned above, only Mexico has more than eight copies of dailies per 100 people, as against 42 in Bermuda, which enjoys one of the highest levels in the world.

Mexico's literacy campaign, launched some years ago, has had significant results for the press. There are now 189 dailies. All the larger towns now have their own daily and the provincial press exerts considerable influence. Its combined circulation is almost three times that of Mexico City dailies.

In the United States, which leads all countries in the total of newspapers and periodicals, an important development has been the adoption of offset printing techniques, including photocomposition, by an increasing number of small dailies as well as by weeklies. It is estimated that over 40 per cent of future purchases of press equipment in the United States will be offset. Another significant development, already mentioned, was the introduction in 1962 of long-distance facsimile composition between New York and Los Angeles and Paris, and the transmission of newspaper pages between New York and Paris by communication satellite.

Canada maintains its position as the world's largest producer and exporter of newsprint. The French-language press of Canada accounts for nearly 20 per cent of total daily circulation. Reflecting post-war immigration, there is a considerable number of newspapers and periodicals in languages other than English or French.

In the region, there has been a healthy increase in total daily newspaper circulation and in the relation between that total and the total of population in the past decade. Although only four of the 14 South American countries exceed the level of 10 copies of dailies for every 100 people, other countries are moving toward it. Circulation in Ecuador, for example, has increased by 30 per cent, in Venezuela by 60 per cent, and in Paraguay and Peru by 100 per cent.

An intensive 10-year drive to bring primary school education to everyone was launched in all the American Spanish-language countries in 1957 as a Unesco major project. This programme and the literacy campaigns accompanying it are largely responsible for the growing demand for newspapers.

Language barriers to press development in South America, which in this respect is more fortunate than the other developing regions, are almost nonexistent. But South America shares the common problems of inadequate supplies of newsprint and printing equipment. In this region, only Argentina, Brazil and Chile produce newsprint. Inadequate and costly transport is another major obstacle.

Newspaper and periodical publication is concentrated in the largest cities. Provincial centres are poorly served, and the rural press is still in its infancy. Eighty-five per cent of the region's periodicals appear in Argentina, Brazil, Colombia, Chile, Peru and Venezuela.

The daily press has also scored gains in Asia. In Pakistan, for example, circulation has increased nearly fivefold since 1955. India's daily circulation has doubled and the number of dailies has increased from 330 to 465. In Afghanistan, circulation more than tripled in the same period.

In the Middle East, Jordan has more than doubled daily circulation since 1956; Lebanon's circulation has risen by a third and Israel's by a half. Kuwait has acquired its first two dailies and Aden has increased its total of dailies from one to five.

On the Chinese mainland, where newspapers are still the major medium of communication, the press has expanded remarkably since 1955. A number of the major dailies have provincial branch offices and produce as many as five or six completely separate editions in a simplified vocabulary of about 1,000 characters. Regular daily circulation has risen by a half since 1955. Wall newspapers, however, still remain a major means of conveying information in urban and rural areas.

But though Asian circulation has risen generally, it has failed to keep pace with population growth. In the Middle East, only Israel and the Lebanon have attained satisfactory circulation levels. In the rest of Asia, only Japan, the Ryukyu Islands, Hong Kong and Singapore reach high levels.

In addition, the press in most Asian countries is concentrated in the capitals, or in a very few large cities at best. However, efforts are being made to develop a rural and semi-rural press in both national and local languages.

In many countries of the region, more dailies and non-dailies would have been established in the past decade but for the difficulty of obtaining newsprint. Acute shortages of foreign currency limit imports. Of the Asian countries which produce newsprint—India, Pakistan, Cambodia, Japan, Republic of Korea and China (Taiwan and mainland)—only Japan meets its own requirements.

There is also a widespread lack of even moderately up-to-date composing and printing machinery, which can only be obtained abroad. No country in Africa, Latin America or Asia, except Japan, manufactures such equipment.

As in the other developing regions, the press must combat low literacy levels and difficulties of distribution to large rural populations. But in Asia there is also the special problem of the Chinese ideographic script and the multiplicity of non-ideographic scripts, with a great many characters, which are widely employed in South-East Asia.

The years 1959 to 1961 saw a major technical break-through in Japanese newspaper production, in which Chinese ideographs are used. For the first time it became possible to reproduce ideographs by automatic teletypesetting, a system which is now used by some 60 per cent of all dailies owning their own printing plants. In 1959, a Tokyo daily became the world's first newspaper to use photo-facsimile and offset printing of complete newspaper pages for simultaneous printing of an identical edition in a city hundreds of miles away. The system has been extended to plants in other cities, and two other Tokyo dailies have installed systems of a similar kind for their large provincial plants.

But no automatic system to set type from perforated tape has been devised for other South-East Asian scripts or for Arabic. And in Taiwan, where the Chinese ideographic teleprinter system adapted for use in Japan was invented, no news agency or newspaper has had the funds to install it.

In most Western European countries the press has expanded rather slowly since 1955, although trends have varied considerably from country to country. In Eastern Europe, on the other hand, daily circulation has risen sharply everywhere, despite the fact that in no country except Poland has there been any significant change in the number of dailies.

The salient feature of the European press is the high circulation and general availability of daily newspapers. The United Kingdom claims more than 50 copies for every 100 persons and in Eastern Germany, Iceland, Luxembourg and Sweden the ratio is more than 40 copies. Only five European countries have less than 10 copies per 100 people. Five countries (Monaco, San Marino, Liechtenstein, Andorra and the Faeroe Islands) have no dailies. However, the first four are well supplied by neighbouring countries.

The European daily and non-daily press shows great diversity of control and editorial content. In Eastern Europe, the more important newspapers are organs of political parties and labour and youth organizations, with the national Communist party daily usually enjoying the greatest circulation.

A political press flourishes in many Western European countries, particularly in the Scandinavian countries, Belgium, Italy, Finland, Greece and the Netherlands, where almost half of all newspapers are affiliated to a political party. In several of these countries, provincial newspapers affiliated or sympathetic to a party exert considerable influence. In France and the Federal Republic of Germany, on the other hand, the thriving pre-war political press has almost ceased to exist. All large and almost all small circulation papers are politically independent.

British newspapers continue, with few exceptions, to be independent of any political party, although pronounced social and political views are often expressed. However, the trend toward concentration of daily, non-daily and periodical publications has proceeded faster and farther in the United Kingdom than in any other Western European country. Five major chains exercise wide control over the dissemination of news and opinion. One of these groups also controls newspapers in Canada, the United States, South Africa, East and West Africa and the West Indies. In addition, there are many medium-size and small London and provincial chains.

The trend toward concentration is evident in many other countries. Finland, France, the Federal Republic of Germany, the Netherlands and Norway have all lost daily newspapers, while increasing total circulation at the same time. In contrast, seven new dailies have been established in Switzerland, and 13 in Greece in the past decade.

A decline in both numbers and circulation of daily newspapers has occurred in only four European countries: the United Kingdom, Sweden,

Ireland and Spain. The United Kingdom and Sweden in fact seem to have reached saturation point, since they respectively hold first and second place among world circulation levels.

European countries include the world's second, third and fourth largest exporters of newsprint: Finland, Sweden and Norway. Austria and Eastern Germany are also large producers.

Press development in Oceania has been aided by increasing newsprint production in New Zealand, which now produces over 100,000 metric tons annually, and in Australia, which meets an increasing part of its total requirements. Post-war immigration of literate Europeans and a rising *per capita* income have also stimulated press expansion in the region.

First in size and importance is the Australian press which prints 36 copies of dailies for every 100 people and is still expanding. The post-war years have witnessed a notable development of the suburban weekly press, corresponding with the growth of population in major cities. Individual circulation figures for daily and non-daily general-interest newspapers range from 500,000 to as little as 500. Although dailies are published in all the state capitals, the most important publication centres are Sydney and Melbourne.

New Zealand is sixth in world circulation levels, with over 40 copies of daily newspapers for every 100 people. Circulation of all types of newspapers and periodicals has increased steadily since 1956.

High circulation levels in Australia and New Zealand account for the fact that Oceania holds first place for daily circulation among all regions. Only one other area in Oceania, Guam, averages more than 10 copies of dailies per 100 people.

In many of the Pacific island groups, populations are too small or too scattered to support a daily press. Thus, despite a generally high literacy rate, 11 island groups as yet have no dailies.

Small dailies have, however, lately begun publication in five island groups which previously lacked a daily press: American Samoa, Cook Islands, French Polynesia, Niue and Tonga. In the Fiji Islands, New Caledonia and Guam, the circulation of longer-established newspapers has risen rapidly. General-interest non-daily newspapers are published in many island groups and missionary, school and government periodical bulletins supply some general news.

The growth of the daily press in the Union of Soviet Socialist Republics since about 1950 far exceeds that in various other regions. Some 60 dailies have been established since 1953, and the number of copies for every 100 people has risen from 11 to just over 18. Although Russian is the common language in the U.S.S.R., each of the 15 Republics has its own official language to which its daily newspapers conform. In 1961, nearly 7,000 daily and non-daily newspapers appeared in 58 different Soviet languages.

The U.S.S.R. has 25 All-Union daily and non-daily newspapers. The world's highest circulation is claimed by a Soviet national daily with 6.3 million copies; three others range from 1.5 to 4 million copies. About 75 per cent of all dailies and weeklies are published outside Moscow, the capital.

The periodical press has also grown rapidly. The number of periodicals rose from 1,614 in 1953 to 4,121 in 1962, with total circulation between three and four times higher. Among the periodicals are 53 in foreign languages, with a total of 13,582,000 copies.

The U.S.S.R. is one of the six leading suppliers of newsprint and in 1960 exported 94,300 tons.

John C. Merrill:

Global Patterns of Elite Daily Journalism

ALTHOUGH the elite press of the world may be considered as a kind of intellectual journalistic "community," it is clearly an uneven, multi-faceted one. A seriousness of tone and purpose and a high readership among influential persons are about the only common denominators of the elite press. Its membership, because of differences in language, economic stability, degree of freedom and basic philosophy, is splintered and fragmented and suffers from too little rapport and theoretical consensus. Thus, the world's elite press is heterogeneous and pluralistic in spite of its commonalities of seriousness, general civility and influence. Struggling against great obstacles everywhere but with renewed hope and vigor, it is developing unevenly throughout the world. It falls roughly into at least three major patterns.

The first pattern is primarily *political or ideological.* Elite papers tend toward separation from government or they tend toward integration with government. While the free elite see themselves as *independent agents,* standing aloof from, and unaffected by, government, the authoritarian elite envision themselves as *partners in government,* cooperative agents of their government bent on carrying forth the socio-political system of their people.

Both groups of elite papers are dedicated to their philosophies and take their responsibilities, as they see them, quite seriously. It should be noted, however, that such a binary classification of the world's elite is too simple in reality and that all papers everywhere are free to varying degrees and restricted to varying degrees, although the character of freedom and restraint may differ significantly.

Many students of the press place considerable emphasis on "social responsibility" in determining the elite status of a newspaper. To what degree is the paper socially responsible? The answer to this question, to many, will largely determine the quality or eliteness of a newspaper. In the United States and other Western democracies, "social responsibility" is thought of generally in terms of non-authoritarianism or freedom from governmental control—coupled with some sense of "doing the right thing at the right time." In other words, "social responsibility" is the press utopia into which only libertarian-oriented newspapers may pass. This, however, seems

▶ From: *Journalism Quarterly,* Vol. 45, No. 1 (Spring 1968), pp. 99-105.

much too simple a theory and is unsatisfactory in the modern world of fragmented and pluralistic serious journalism.

It is this writer's contention that *all* conscientious and serious newspapers—regardless of what nation or political ideology they may represent—are "socially responsible." This idea was put forth in a paper in early 1965 and met with considerable objection from some quarters; however, it was also embraced by a surprisingly large number of persons who had previously failed to challenge the concept of press social responsibility being connected only to a libertarian press.[1]

Why cannot the authoritarian press or the communistic press (if there is really any difference) claim to be socially responsible also? In fact, in certain respects, a newspaper would be more "responsible" if some type of governmental supervision existed; indeed, reporters could be kept from nosing about in "critical" areas during "critical" times. And, as the Russians are quick to point out, the amount of sensational material could be controlled in the press, or eliminated altogether. Government activities could always be supported and public policy could be pushed on all occasions. The press could be more educational in the sense that more news of art exhibits, concerts, national progress and the like could be stressed. In short, the press would eliminate the "negative" and stress the "positive." Then, with one voice the press of the nation would be responsible to its society; and the definition of "responsible" would be functional—defined and carried out in the context of the existing government and social structure. This, of course, may seem unreasonable or even "treasonable" in the Western democracies, but its unreasonableness is unrealistic when projected onto the screen of international journalism.

So it would seem logical to believe that all newspapers (of any political system) which reflect the philosophy of their governmental system and try to present serious, educational reading fare are not only responsible to their society but are members of the elite press—or they are climbing into that select fraternity.

Assuming that a nation's socio-political philosophy determines its press system, and undoubtedly it does, then it follows that the nation's leading and most prestigious papers are socially responsible and form the elite. For example, the Marxist or Communist press system considers itself socially responsible, and certainly it is to its own social system. A capitalistic press, operating in a pluralistic and competitive context, would be socially *irresponsible* if suddenly transplanted into the Communist society.

The same thing might be said of the so-called "authoritarian" press system, exemplified by Spain. A critical press such as found in the United States, a press which by its pluralistic nature would tend to undermine

---

[1] John C. Merrill, "The Press and Social Responsibility," (University of Missouri: Freedom of Information Center Publication No. 001, March 1965).

national policy and disrupt national harmony, would be anathema in a nation like Spain. Spanish newspapers, the most serious like *ABC* and *Ya* of Madrid and *La Vanguardia Española* of Barcelona, are exceptionally responsible to Spanish society; and, it should be added, they supply a surprising diversity of orientations and viewpoints within the confines of the national policy.[2] In other words, the elite press of a nation, even one under considerable government control, will still prove its eliteness through its subtleties, skillful restraint and capacity to make the most of the situation in which it finds itself. In many ways, it takes more journalistic ability and acumen—as well as courage—to put out an elite newspaper in a country such as Spain than in a country like Britain or Sweden.

A second important pattern among the world's elite, and one that is even more ragged than the political one just mentioned, is that of *economic diversity*.

This pattern, of course, is related to the political context, but actually is quite different. For example, one elite paper in a libertarian nation can run into dire financial difficulties while another in the same country prospers and grows. An elite paper is not determined by how much property it owns or the profit it makes. Elite papers throughout the world exemplify a wide range of economic development and prosperity, but their overriding concern with serious news and views and their desire to influence opinion leaders manifests itself quite apart from such differences in economic health.

Naturally, there is a point below which an elite paper (or any paper) may not fall and keep up its desired level of quality. Certainly, it must have the facilities to do good printing. It must be able to pay enough to get conscientious, well-educated staff members. It must be able to receive a variety of services from news agencies, as well as to collect much national and world news with its own correspondents. It must, therefore, either have a rather sizable circulation, or it must develop a special elite readership which will offset a small circulation. Although some elite papers like *Asahi* of Japan and *Pravda* of the Soviet Union have tremendous circulations, most of the world's elite have only modest ones.[3]

The elite newspaper (especially in a libertarian nation) runs the risk of lowering its quality when it makes a bid for larger readership—at least

[2] The Monarchist *ABC* and the Catholic *Ya*, for example, often carry outspoken criticisms of municipal officials and are taken seriously in Spanish ministerial circles. *ABC*, *Ya* and *La Vanguardia* (Barcelona) have circulations of about 100,000 each, but the total daily circulation of the country is not much more than 600,000—about one copy of a paper to every 50 Spaniards.

[3] Most elite papers of the world are small—under 300,000 daily circulations. The largest are found in the USSR, Red China and Japan where *Pravda*, *People's Daily* and *Asahi* have circulations exceeding two million. A few other elite dailies, like the New York *Times* and Italy's *Corriere della Sera*, have circulations of more than 500,000.

unless it does it very slowly. For it is the popular or mass press that is after the big circulations; the elite press is after readers of discernment and influence. Unfortunately for international rationality, the public—as Leo Rosten has said—"chooses the frivolous as against the serious, the lurid as against the tragic, the trivial as against fact, the diverting as against the significant." Rosten points out that very few people in any society "have reasonably good taste or care deeply about ideas" and that even fewer appear to be "equipped—by temperament and capacity, rather than education—to handle ideas with both skill and pleasure." [4]

Most elite newspapers realize that their readership will probably be small, but they know that it is usually potent, sapient and prestigious. It should be mentioned, however, that there are some few elite papers—in nations such as Sweden where the whole public is literate and uncommonly serious—which manage to be rational and serious and at the same time furnish all types of reading material.

The third pattern of the elite press is *geographical*. And this, of course, is closely related to national development. Most of the elite are published in developed or modern countries, although there are a few that represent the developing (modernizing) or transitional nations. Europe and North America are the principal homes of the elite newspapers. This is not surprising since these two continents are the most industrialized, the most technological and most literate of all the continents. As the economic bases become stabilized, and literate and well-educated populations of other continents grow, the evenness of dispersion of the elite press throughout the world should improve significantly. Presently, however, elite newspapers are scattered about the earth in a very uneven fashion. This pattern of clusters and vast gaps greatly hinders the total impact of serious, concerned journalism in the world as a whole. It might be well to look more closely at this geographical pattern of the world's elite press.

Asia, with the exception of China, Japan and India, is virtually without an elite press. Of the three, Japan stands out for its great progress in quality journalism—and popular journalism, too, for that matter, *Asahi* is without a doubt the best quality daily in Japan and shows that an elite paper can, with editorial flexibility and sagacity, develop a large circulation within a free-market press system. *Pravda* and its counterpart in Peking, *Jen-min Jih-pao* of course, have fewer problems building circulation since Communist party members and many others find that they *need* to have these daily journals of guidance and news.

In India, the problems of the elite papers are much more acute than in either the USSR, China or Japan. There are many reasons for this, but the chief is probably the problem of too many languages. At present the major elite papers of India are published in English, understood only by the

[4] Leo Rosten, "The Intellectual and the Mass Media," *Daedalus*, Spring 1960, pp. 333-46.

educated mainly found in a few of the large cities. And, even within the English-reading public, the circulation of the English elite press is segmented since there are three very important elite dailies in the country—*The Statesman* of Calcutta, *The Hindu* of Madras and *The Times of India* of Bombay and Delhi. The vernacular languages of India, of which Hindi is the official one, have not caught on as press languages—although there are a few well-written-and-edited papers in some of them, but with little or no national or international prestige. To the language problem facing the development of the Indian elite press must be added these (generally applicable throughout Southeast Asia): low literacy rate, underdeveloped educational system, scarcity of training facilities and trained journalists, and old and inadequate printing equipment.

In Africa, outside Egypt in the extreme northeast and the Republic of South Africa in the far south, there is no significant elite press;[5] and even in these two republics considerable government sensitivity has hindered development of a truly *quality* press. Egypt, with its nationalized newspapers, would—from a Western viewpoint—have to take second place to South Africa as a nation with a pluralistic press. In South Africa, for example, in spite of government sensitivity to what it feels are press "excesses," the papers—especially those in English—show clearly that "the searchlights of inquiry and criticism are still able to shine, only slightly filtered, and to concentrate on those dark areas where a regime is most sensitive."[6] Without a doubt, South Africa has the freest newspapers on the continent, and within the English-language press are papers which are the equal in quality and tone to the elite of most nations of the world.

Johannesburg's morning *Rand Daily Mail* is a good example. It has consistently presented facts and opinion which have irritated the government, and has given its readers healthy portions of national and foreign news. Although most Afrikaans-language papers present a rather narrow pro-government picture, an important exception is *Die Burger* of Cape Town, committed generally to the policies of the Nationalist Party but often refreshingly independent and deviationist.[7] It is also interesting that in South Africa, the freest papers—generally the English-language ones— have the largest circulations. For instance, the Johannesburg *Star* (about 170,000), has a circulation of almost double the combined circulations of the city's two Afrikaans papers—the *Transvaler* and the *Vaderland*.

[5] In most parts of Africa the problems of establishing some sort of stable government while various factions are vying for political power hamper the development of any type of viable press, much less an elite press. Aside from political unrest, other problems face newspapers of the new African states: financial instability, unskilled journalists, a multiplicity of languages, high illiteracy, unsettled political direction, and a widespread absence of native national leadership.
[6] Tertius Myburgh, "The South African Press: Hope in an Unhappy Land," *Nieman Reports*, 20: 1 (March 1966), p. 6.
[7] *Ibid.*, p. 4.

The Egyptian press, although long being well-developed for the African context, has slowly but increasingly become a state-controlled press. In 1956 came the biggest blow to press freedom: President Nasser transferred the ownership of all papers to the National Union (the government party) in order to assure popular support for his regime. And in 1960 the Egyptian papers were placed in groups or units, each having an administrative council appointed by the government. Nasser claims this is not nationalization; he sees it rather as giving the ownership to "the people." In spite of this nationalization (or "people's press"), a few of the highly regarded old dailies of Cairo still provide their Arab readership with substantial amounts of serious journalism. For example, *Al Ahram* (the main mouthpiece of Nasser) gives a good (for Egypt) selection of news and features and keeps its cosmopolitan tone. Probably the most influential papers of the Arab world are still found in Egypt in spite of the fact that free, vigorous and critical Arab journalism has shifted from Cairo to Beirut, Lebanon.[8]

In the neighboring Middle East the press systems are mainly transitional—caught between the severe problems of many parts of Asia on one side and of Africa on the other. One hindrance to elite press development in this area is that these nations cannot decide whether to have their press systems (and governments) veer toward libertarianism and competition or toward authoritarianism and state planning. Governments throughout the region are generally suspicious of the press and sensitive to its criticism. The press of Israel is probably improving faster than any other in the Middle East, and has been called the most "internationally minded in the world." [9] For instance, *Maariv* of Tel Aviv with a circulation of only about 100,000, subscribes to Reuters, UPI, AP and the London *Daily Telegraph* services and has several correspondents and their families in foreign capitals.[10] And this paper, although the country's largest, is not as serious as others such as the staid *Haaretz*.

Latin America, in spite of awesome economic and literacy problems, has somehow managed to develop a rather sizable group of elite newspapers. Without a doubt, this region of the world has a far more-advanced press in all respects than is generally found in Asia and Africa. One obvious explanation for this is the fact that Spanish is the almost common language of the press of Latin America,[11] whereas in both Asia and Africa the polyglot of languages and dialects makes the development of newspapers of substantial influence and circulation extremely difficult, if not impossible.

[8] "Newspapers of the World—IX," London *Times*, March 10, 1965.
[9] "Israel's Serious Press," Service Documentaire F.I.J. (Brussels, May 1965).
[10] *Ibid.*
[11] Brazil, with its Portuguese-language press sitting like an island in a sea of Spanish, has developed an extremely vigorous and qualitative press—especially in its two largest cities, Rio and Sao Paulo. Several dailies are outstanding, with O *Estado de S. Paulo* and O *Globo* of Rio undoubtedly the best.

Many Latin American dailies meet the demands of serious readers for percipient journalism; almost every major nation south of the United States has at least one journal which is in, or aspires to, the elite press. Argentina has its *La Nación* and *La Prensa,* Chile its *Mercurio,* Peru its *Comercio,* Columbia its *Tiempo* and Mexico its outstanding trio—*Excélsior, Novedades* and *El Universal.* These and many other serious dailies of Latin America do an outstanding job of providing large proportions of scientific and humanistic news and views, with much emphasis on foreign affairs. Perhaps the Latin American serious press, like its ancestral press of Iberia, places undue stress on philosophical, theological and literary discussion; but this is simply an intellectual Latin proclivity and the elite press does well to serve it.

In Oceania, Australia alone has a press which includes newspapers of the elite type. Barriers to press growth in this sprawling island region are mainly 1) small population, 2) technological underdevelopment, 3) scarcity of trained journalists and 4) geographical isolation from the main stream of international concerns. In Australia several papers might be included among the elite and several others are aspirants. *The Age* of Melbourne is usually considered the most serious and influential. Even a paper like the same city's *Herald,* which is an afternoon journal which does not avoid appealing to all classes, furnishes some 500,000 readers a substantial diet of serious material every day. Its economic coverage and its weekly book page are especially laudable. *The Australian,* with main offices in Sydney, is developing into a truly national daily and a first-rate journal in every respect.

In North America (above the Mexican border) the elite press thrives. The *Globe and Mail* of Toronto, with a circulation of some 230,000, is Canada's only truly national daily. It is also generally considered the best of the country's dailies. Montreal's evening *La Presse,* a comprehensive afternoon daily with an exceptionally fine weekend edition, is the largest French-language daily in the Western hemisphere. In Winnipeg, Manitoba, the *Free Press* provides excellent international coverage and provides one of the most thoughtful editorial pages in North America.

Although there are elite and near-elite papers in every major section of the United States, most of them are concentrated along the East Coast and in the Middle West. In the East are such sophisticated dailies as the New York *Times,* the Washington *Post,* the *Christian Science Monitor,* the Baltimore *Sun* and the Miami *Herald.* In the Middle West a few of the leaders among the elite are the St. Louis *Post-Dispatch,* the Minneapolis *Tribune* and the Kansas City *Star.* In Kentucky, there is the Louisville *Courier-Journal;* in Georgia, the Atlanta *Constitution.* Quality papers of national and international prestige tend to fade out in the Plains and Mountain area of the West, with the Denver *Post* ruling a vast empire from its strategic position. Along the West Coast, there are the Los Angeles

Times (probably the fastest-improving U.S. daily) and the Portland *Oregonian.*

If the press of North America is well-developed and the elite papers numerous, the press of Europe (Western Europe) might be said to be *over*-developed and the elite papers *very* numerous. From Scandinavia to Spain, and from Britain to Russia, elite dailies (and weeklies) spread their serious journalism into every corner of the continent and, increasingly, into distant lands. The elite dailies of Europe are probably the most erudite and knowledgeable in the world, providing insights which Quincy Howe (former editor of *Atlas*) has said are available nowhere else.[12] European papers, says Howe, "speak with authority," and it is not only a matter "of Germans reporting on Germany, French on France and British on Britain," but also "of Germans writing about the French, the French writing about the British, and the British writing about the Germans." [13]

All types of quality papers are to be found in Europe. There are the free elite of most western Europe—led by the super-serious *Neue Zürcher Zeitung* of Switzerland, *Le Monde* of France, the *Times* and the *Guardian* of Britain and *Frankfurter Allgemeine* of West Germany. There are the authoritarian elite of Spain such as *ABC and La Vanguardia Española,* and the Communist elite such as *Pravda* and *Izvestia* of Russia and *Borba* and *Politika* of Yugoslavia. There are the dailies of Scandinavia such as Oslo's *Aftenposten,* Copenhagen's *Berlingske Tidende,* and Stockholm's *Dagens Nyheter* that combine a rather flashy typographical dress with a heavy diet of serious news and views. There are also such dailies as *Die Welt* of Hamburg and *Corriere della Sera* of Milan which are able to combine a "modern" demeanor with a solid seriousness. And, of course, there is the stolid drabness of ultra-seriousness to be found in a very special kind of prestige daily, *Osservatore Romano* of Vatican City. The European elite press offers the reader a wide selection of packaging and political orientation; there is a paper whose journalistic style and philosophy—as well as size, layout and typographical tone—appeal to any kind of serious newspaper reader.

It is interesting to note that in the areas of the world where daily journalism is most advanced and there are many elite papers, there are also the largest numbers of journalism schools and institutes, and training programs of one type or another. This concern with, or emphasis on, journalism education, of course, is coupled with a high development of education generally. In the underdeveloped nations, such as are common in Asia

---

[12] Quincy Howe, "What Americans Can Learn from the Foreign Press," Guild Memorial Lecture (Minneapolis: University of Minnesota School of Journalism, 1963).
[13] *Ibid.*

and Africa, the little emphasis on journalistic training which has been begun is still concerned chiefly with the technical aspects of journalism: typesetting, printing, newsprint acquisition and the overcoming of basic economic handicaps. On the other hand, in the more advanced nations where the elite is strongest, these elemental problems are secondary in journalism education, and concern with editorial quality, ethical standards and social responsibility comes in for more consideration.

This non-technical and non-economic emphasis or approach inevitably results in a higher quality journalism. The seriousness and size of a country's elite press undoubtedly reflects the nation's general development and cultural level, and it is reassuring to know that among the thousands of daily papers of the world, there are conscientious and intelligent journals dedicated to serious discourse and bounded together by invisible cords of pride into a fraternity of prestige and excellence.

Hanno Hardt:

The Plight of the Daily Press in Western Europe

THE PROBLEMS of deaths and mergers of daily newspapers, the powers of group ownership and their effects upon freedom of expression, are neither new nor unique to any particular country or region of the world. The development is not even very recent, although the literature of the field reflects a continuing concern about the phenomenon, as do the published reports of international organizations and legislative committees in various countries.

After World War II the press in Western Europe expanded rapidly. Free from wartime restrictions and authoritarian rules, hundreds of underground newspapers, old and new party newspapers, and thousands of individual attempts to operate newspapers contributed to an unprecedented growth of the press. The social and economic proximity of the countries of Western Europe and their integrated history after the war may provide some insights into causes and effects of the general newspaper decline and may allow some speculations as to the future of the daily press—not only in Western Europe, but in many parts of the world.

The trends of newspaper operation in several countries have been quite similar. The decrease of numbers of daily newspapers is usually accompanied by an increase in circulation of the remaining newspapers despite a variety of governmental subsidy programs to aid small- and medium-sized newspaper organizations. Following are a number of brief, country-by-country descriptions of these developments.

The Belgian press, for instance, is controlled largely by nine major publishing groups. Eleven of its 14 Flemish-language newspapers are published by four groups representing about 85% of the 1.3 million circulation. Twenty of Belgium's 26 French-language newspapers are controlled by five organizations; the largest is the Rossel-Hurbain group which acquired *La Nouvelle Gazette, La Province* and *Le Progrès* early in 1968 to increase its holdings to 35% of the 1.2 million circulation of French-language newspapers in the country. Seven daily newspapers ceased publication over the last decade; the remaining 40 newspapers are published by 18 companies. Daily newspaper circulation increases are minimal and behind increases among the weekly press, which has been able to attract a substantial number of readers (228,000 in 1968).

▶ This is an original article done for this book by the author, University of Iowa, 1969.

Denmark experienced a tremendous loss of daily newspapers from 140 in 1945 to 62 in 1967 with a total circulation of 1.8 million. Most of the newspapers simply folded; only in two cases were actual mergers reported. The *Dagbladet*, formed in 1962, is the result of a three-way merger, and the *Sjaellands Tidende* was established in 1963 by two newspapers. Most of the discontinued newspapers were small, provincial papers with circulations of only a few thousand. The Danish press is subsidized indirectly through tax advantages affecting production, sale and advertising. The Danish government also provides credit arrangements for building and improvement programs. Denmark's parliament has thus far opposed Swedish and Finnish methods of subsidizing newspapers through financial assistance to political parties.

Many of Finland's 54 daily newspapers operate at a loss; although records are not made available it is believed that of Helsinki's 10 newspapers, only five are able to meet regular operating costs. Despite official subsidies to party-affiliated newspapers the number of dailies has declined steadily from 61 with a circulation of about 1.9 million in 1957 to the present number with a circulation of about 1.6 million. The Finnish government distributed about $3.3 million in 1967 among political parties, and a large share of this money was used for the support of party newspapers. The state also subsidizes newspaper postal rates up to 72%. Circulation figures of larger newspapers in Finland show little change over time due to the increase of television and magazine advertising and a recent increase in newspaper advertising rates. Provincial newspapers, on the other hand, have reported growth rates of about 10 per cent as compared to 4 per cent among urban newspapers.

The daily newspaper press in France has undergone drastic changes since World War II. Over 100 newspapers have folded since 1946 when 203 dailies with a circulation of 15.3 million competed for readers. Today, France has 84 daily newspapers with a combined circulation of about 12 million. Hardest hit by the decline was Paris, where the number of dailies dropped from 32 to 11 and circulation from 6 to about 4 million copies, despite a population explosion which doubled the 1939 census figures. The current increase in circulation is mainly due to the expansion of the provincial press, which gained respectability and reader interest after World War II and reduced the traditional leadership role of the Parisian press from about 60% in 1939 to about 30% of the national circulation. Mergers and recognized zones of diffusion in the provinces have revolutionized the traditional structure of the provincial press. The six largest provincial groups and their circulations are *Progrès-Le Dauphiné* (1 million), *L'Quest-France* (840,000), *Dernières Nouvelles d'Alsace* and *Le Républicain* (600,000), *L'Est Républicain* (400,000), *Sud-Quest* (500,000) and *La Nouvelle République* (400,000). The Parisian press, on the other hand, has made no attempts of regrouping or restructuring, but relies on only a minimum of competition and individual ability to subsidize metropolitan dailies through extensive holdings in magazines and weekly news-papers in and around Paris. Besides tax exemptions covering aspects of production, sales and circulation, the French government also provided special postal rates for printed matter, telegrams and telephone service and underwrites 15 per cent of investments in new equipment.

In the Federal Republic of Germany, daily newspapers sharply de-clined in numbers from 225 major editions (Hauptausgaben) in 1954 and a circulation of over 16 million to 150 early in 1968, and circulation figures in excess of 20 million. About 20 larger dailies are responsible for a steady increase in circulation while small- and medium-sized news-papers made little or no progress in recent years. Over 50 percent of the total circulation is controlled by five publishing groups. They are Axel Springer (39.2), *Stuttgarter Zeitung* (3.6), *Westdeutsche Allgemeine Zei-tung* (2.5), *Süddeutscher Verlag* (2.5) and *Frankfurter Allgemeine Zeitung* (2.4). There is a notable trend towards one-newspaper towns and counties in West Germany. The government has kept the development under surveillance, but has taken no official action to curb further efforts of concentration. Federal aid in form of credits and tax relief assist small-and medium-sized newspapers. The party press, heavily subsidized in recent years by major political parties, has experienced major losses after most parties decided against further financial support.

The provincial morning newspaper in Great Britain suffered the largest loss by a trend toward fewer and larger newspapers. During the 1958-68 decade, the number of daily newspapers decreased from 121 to 114 while circulation figures dropped from 47.1 to 41.9 million. Four publishing companies control over 70% of the total circulation; they are the Daily Mirror group (26), the Daily Mail and General Trust organization (21), Beaverbrook (18) and Thomson (6). The daily newspaper industry in Great Britain is plagued by bad management, irresponsible labor unions and rising production costs, conditions shared with most of the other countries. Parliament passed the Monopolies and Mergers Bill in 1965 to control further centralization of newspaper ownership which had already resulted in 50 one-newspaper cities, and 13 cities with morning and evening papers owned by the same company, with only nine cities retaining two or more dailies. Recently, newspaper advertising suffered from the effects of a tight money market which resulted in losses of income up to 30% as compared to a similar period in 1966.

Italy's daily press has lost about 40 percent of its immediate post-World War II total of 136 newspapers, dropping to 79 in 1967 with a circulation of 5.8 million. Most of these newspapers are concentrated in the north and central sections of the country (64) with major newspaper centers in Rome (16), Milan (9) and Genoa (5). By far the largest number of newspapers (18) with almost 2.6 million circulation is con-trolled by industry and big business, including the circulation leader *Cor-*

riere della Sera(Crespi); others are *La Stampa-Stampa Sera*(FIAT), *Il Giorno*(ENI), *Il Messaggero-Secolo XIX*(Perrone), *La Nazione-Resto del Carlino*(Monti) and *La Notte*(Italcementi). The Italian government controls prices for newsprint, which is offered at lower rates to small newspapers, and provides a number of tax advantages for newspapers.

The number of daily newspapers in the Netherlands decreased from 115 in 1950 to 96 in 1967 while circulation figures during the same time increased from 2.8 to 3.7 million. Ten publishing groups control about 56 percent of the total circulation; the two largest ones, *De Telegraaf* and Nederlands Dagbladunie, decided in 1967 to cooperate closely in technical and managerial matters leaving editorial decisions unaffected by the agreement. They represent 25% or almost 1 million copies of the daily newspaper circulation. The Dutch government has adopted a number of measures to aid the press: there is no surtax on subscription, advertising and newsprint, special postal and railway express rates are available, and rebates on certain imports of newsprint are granted regularly. In addition, a compensation for losses suffered from television advertising resulted in the distribution of about $3.3 million in 1967 to dailies and weeklies which could show a noticeable loss in advertising revenue.

The number of daily newspapers in Sweden decreased from 181 in 1948 to 114 in 1967 while circulation figures increased from 2.9 to 4.2 million during the same time. The majority of the discontinued newspapers represented second newspapers in counties and towns, and resulted in a general strengthening of the one-newspaper town concept in Sweden. There were only 13 locales with more than one daily newspaper in 1968 as compared to 63 in 1948. Regardless, Swedish newspapers still sell at a ratio of about 55 copies per 100 inhabitants, which is higher than in any other European country, although Norway (47), Finland (45) and Denmark (35) also claim exceptionally high ratios. The Swedish press is supported by a state subsidy program which since 1965 distributed about $5 million to party-owned newspapers. In addition, the government allows for tax exemptions which affect production, sale and advertising costs of newspapers. The Second Press Commission in 1968 also recommended the establishment of a special loan fund and urged better coordination of distribution systems of individual newspapers.

The developments in these countries are typical for similar movements within the newspaper industry in other parts of Western Europe, with the possible exception of Greece, Portugal and Spain, where political differences affected the growth pattern of daily newspapers.

The countries represented in this discussion are examples of high, middle and low income groups in terms of *per capita* consumption expenditures after World War II; They are Belgium, Denmark, France, Great Britain, Sweden, Finland, Federal Republic of Germany and the Netherlands; and Italy, respectively. In this period Western Europe ex-

perienced an incredibly fast recovery, and economic growth led not only
to new heights of financial strength and prosperity, but also to social
changes, which may help explain the phenomenon of disappearing dailies.

The existence of an inflationary gap in most of these countries has
resulted in a steady rise of wages and cost of living, which, in turn, affected
production and replacement costs for newspaper enterprises. And while
these factors alone had some unsettling effects upon economically weaker
newspapers, there were several other developments which played a decisive
role in the decline of the number of daily newspapers. The introduction of
television, for instance, was followed by a steady increase in programming
time, especially over the last decade. In its wake came the first encounter
with commercial television and a loss of advertising revenue that was
mostly felt by newspapers and especially by those with limited circulation.
Although some efforts have been made in a number of countries to distribute television advertising profits among those newspapers most affected
by commercial television, it is obvious that these are stop-gap measures
not designed to stabilize and improve but to maintain the *status quo*. With
the advent of colored television in Western Europe, newspaper enterprises
are even more pressed for finding answers to questions of survival in a
competitive climate that makes the availability of color printing processes
not only a desirable, but a necessary condition in the fight for advertising
revenue. Governments in Western Europe again are coming to the assistance of economically weaker newspapers with credit and loan plans
designed to maintain a *status quo* of competition.

It is undoubtedly true that newspapers, which can no longer operate
without substantial losses to their owners, cannot be expected to perform
a public service without proper remuneration. However, the various government subsidy programs now in existence in Western Europe seem an
outgrowth of earlier economic policies, which supported small businesses
as a matter of principle against the rising competition of larger enterprises.
And although many of these programs may be politically expedient, they
cannot be considered long-term solutions, since they ignore the reality
of economic trends.

The dilemma of the newspaper industry in Western Europe is not
unique; the introduction of American business practices and the philosophy
of mass production have changed the character of the European business
community. The emphasis is on big business with its capability of serving
mass markets fast and efficiently, and many smaller industries have already
experienced the agonizing changes from family-operated enterprises to
larger, more efficient business establishments. Newspapers are part of an
industry whose owners and managers face similar problems. Bigness *per se*
is not bad; it seems a logical solution for publishers who realize that co-
operative planning of better production and distribution methods, for
instance, may be the fastest way to economic recovery and growth.

Underlying the fear of continuing newspaper concentrations in a few powerful organizations and the reluctance to welcome big business methods is the assumption that the safety of upholding democratic principles of a free press in a free society lies in numbers of newspapers and that diversity guarantees the operation of the system. The latest developments in Western Europe, however, have demonstrated quite clearly that the loss of a substantial number of newspapers has not affected the free flow of ideas and information. Even in countries with substantial newspaper concentrations, bigness has not interfered with the exercise of free speech and press. In addition, many of the marginal newspapers now in existence do not contribute to the welfare of the community in terms of social or political leadership, and their deaths or mergers with other newspapers will make little, if any difference in the exercise of media freedom and responsibility. Radio, television and the press on national as well as inter-European levels provide counterbalances, necessary checks and desirable diversity of ideas, while constitutional guarantees and national laws help define the parameters of press activities.

But besides economic considerations, there are social developments, which may have resulted in changes among the newspaper-reading public, thus contributing to the problem of newspaper decline.

Among the newspapers drastically affected by shrinking circulations and numbers have been the party newspapers. They flourished shortly after World War II before they decreased almost in proportion to economic recovery and rising standard of living. Unable or unwilling to detect changing interests of their readers, these newspapers remained unchanged. Without significant attempts to vary content matter and to offer additional information besides party propaganda, the party press lost readers whose political leanings were the same, but who were undergoing significant changes in their living habits.

Among the most far-reaching change has been the status of women in post-war Western Europe. Women emerge as significant factors in urban labor forces. Their emancipation resulted in new husband-wife or family relationships that affected decision-making patterns in consumer purchases and suggests that it may play a role in the selection of newspaper reading material either directly or by shifts to the women's press (e.g., women magazines) in favor of daily newspapers (e.g., the small, hometown paper, or the regional newspaper) as reflected by the large number of women's magazines in Western Europe.

Europeans now have more time; they enjoy a high standard of living and a political climate which allows them to travel without restrictions and see for themselves what life is like in Europe. Billions of them travel as tourists or television viewers and get to know their neighbors. Many others move around as laborers in seasonal or year-round jobs, adding to the flow of people and ideas across national borders. As a result, newspaper readers already disenchanted with the party press now want a product which takes into account their new interests in other people and places, but also in ideas and different viewpoints. Rome, Paris, London or Berlin are as close as the nearest television set or the person who "has been there" on his last vacation trip. Thus, larger newspapers with expert staffs and extensive coverage of the European scene in addition to their local or regional coverage are oftentimes in better positions to attract more readers and expand their circulation than small- and medium-sized newspapers, which fail to provide an equally good job.

It may well be that the failure of many daily newspapers to attract and keep readers is partly due to a lack of understanding social changes and of assessing education and educational needs (e.g., Southern Italy) of contemporary society. At the end of World War II, the European press had lost its time-honored and historically important role as a political instrument and was forced to rethink and redesign purposes and methods of daily newspaper operations. The advent of television has helped increase the pressure for newspapers to develop ideas and formulas, which match the imagination of electronic media managers and disregard previous concepts and definitions.

The diversity of ideas and viewpoints necessary for the well-being of a democratic society will be provided by a diversity of media; what has been observed in many European countries so far is the attempt to revive or keep alive 19th century ideas. They seem to die hard, and while some larger and economically stronger newspapers may see now immediate dangers, the progress of electronic media during the last two or three years may serve as an indication of the structure and impact future media may have on the newspaper industry.

BIBLIOGRAPHICAL NOTES

Among the recommended sources for the study of newspaper concentrations in Western Europe are such journals as *Journalism Quarterly, Publizistik, Gazette, Cahiers d'Etudes de Presse, presse-actualité, IPI Report, fiej-bulletin, ZV + ZV, IPI Rundschau, Il Giornalismo.*

Standard reference works and yearbooks include *Der Leitfaden* (Essen), *Willing's European Press Guide* (London), *Handbuch der Auslandspresse* (Berlin), and such national year-books as *presse française* (Paris), H. Meyn, *Massenmedien in der Bunderepublik Deutschland* (Berlin), *Willing's Guide* (London), *Handboek van de Nederlandse Pers* (Barendrecht), *Die Deutsche Tagespresse* (Bad Godesberg), and *Annuario della Stampa* (Milan).

Also useful are national reports such as *The National Newspaper Industry: A Survey* (London, 1966), *Schlussbericht von der Kommission zur Untersuchung der Gefährdung der wirtschaftlichen Existenz von Presseunternehmen und der Folgen der Konzentration für die Meinungsfreiheit in der Bundesrepublik* (Bonn, 1968), and *Report of the Royal Commission on the Press*, 1961-62 (London). A number of books deal extensively with the problem, among them are: H. Arndt, *Die Konzentration in der Presse und die Problematik des Verleger-Fernsehens* (Frankfurt, 1967), Angelo del Boca, *Giornale in Crisi* (Turin, 1968), H. Thomas, *Newspaper Crisis in Britain* (Zurich, 1967).

Hamid Mowlana:

Cross-National Comparison of Economic Journalism

NEWSPAPERS dealing with economic problems were non-existent in Korea
15 years ago, and it was not until 1959 that the first paper devoting most
of its space to economic subjects appeared in the country. Today three of
the fourteen dailies published in Seoul deal strictly with economic matters.
In India the number of specialized and business journals almost doubled
during the past decade. The 294 commerce and industry and 38 financial
papers form the largest category among specialized publications. In Thailand, where newspapers do not give much space to business and finance,
the government has been the first to publish a daily paper dealing with
economic problems.

As the developing countries move from a traditional economy toward
a modern industrial economy, we see spectacular development in their communication systems. These developments in communications, especially in
the mass media, are the results of economic, social, and political evolution
which is part of the national growth of the countries.

One such development is the growth of economic journalism which
gives birth to publications in such fields as commerce, finance, industry,
and business. Mass media spread in a direct and monotonic relationship
with a rising level of industrial capacity.[1] As economic activity spreads
throughout the country, the act of sharing and disseminating information
becomes a necessity. Changing desires of the public create new industries,
and this produces economic change. The new means of industrial production act as stimuli for altering and, indeed, remodeling the economic
system. Modernization in Pakistan's textile industry not only results in
greater coverage, but the further development of that industry spawns
the *Pakistan Textile Journal*. In a different but similar way, Bombay's
Economic Times or Bangkok's *Daily Trade News* finds readers. In short,

[1] Daniel Lerner, "Toward a Communication Theory of Modernization," in Lucian Pye,
ed., *Communication and Political Development* (Princeton: Princeton University Press,
1963), p. 336.

▶ From: "Cross-National Comparison of Economic Journalism: A Study of Mass Media
and Economic Development," by Hamid Mowlana. Published in *Gazette* (Leiden,
Netherlands), Vol. 13/No. 4 (1967). Reprinted by permission of the author and the
publisher.

as a more efficient communication system makes industrial development easier, the industrial development makes communication development easier.[2]

Let us define at the beginning precisely what we mean by economic journalism. We use the term to mean not only the process of gathering and disseminating financial news through the business press but also through the general newspaper. One purpose of this paper is to explore the interaction between economic development and the growth of economic journalism and see what correlations exist between the two. The paper does not claim to make generalizations in regard to all developing countries. Rather, the cross-national comparison is concentrated on the economic journalism of seven Asian nations—trying to establish some common factors and at the same time to analyse each country's effort to develop its economic journalism. The countries selected for this study are India, Indonesia, Korea, Pakistan, the Philippines, Thailand, and South Vietnam.

Data on the state of economic journalism in developing countries are scarce. Despite the increasingly significant role of mass media in national and economic development, little or no attention has been devoted to the study of economic journalism in the developing countries. The seven countries used for this study were selected on the basis that more data on their economic journalism were available to this author.

Economic Growth

Previous studies found a very high correlation between the measures of economic growth and the measures of communication growth. For example, Lerner found high correlations among all four of the measures—urbanization, literacy, media participation, and political participation.[3] Similarly, Greenberg found high correlation between literacy and per capita income and circulation of newspapers.[4] Doob wrote of conditions at the birth of mass communication in Africa and of the variables involved in using communication at the stage of development.[5] Farace's study of the relationship of mass media to national development indicated that "the economic-industrialization indices have high positive loadings on this factor, and appear to reflect its core."[6] He further concluded that "mass media development is interdependent with achievements in many aspects of the 'way of life' in a country."

[2] Wilbur Schramm, *Mass Media and National Development* (Stanford: Stanford University Press and Unesco, 1964), pp. 20-57.
[3] *The Passing of Traditional Society* (Glencoe: Free Press, 1958), p. 63.
[4] "Additional Data on Variables Related to Press Freedom," *Journalism Quarterly*, 38: 76-78 (Winter 1961).
[5] *Communication in Africa: A Search for Boundaries* (New Haven: Yale University Press, 1961), p. 372.
[6] "A Study of Mass Communication and National Development," *Journalism Quarterly*, 43: 305-313 (Summer 1966).

In the seven countries under study, it appears that the growth of economic journalism has run parallel to the development of the country's economy. Except in cases where a country has a long tradition of trade and political stability, such as India, the countries with relatively high per capita income and daily newspaper circulation and higher literacy have more economic papers. Further inquiry indicates that the countries with a higher rate of economic growth seem to support more economic daily and other business journals.

The state of economic journalism is closely linked with economic development. In Korea the first paper devoting most of its space to economic subjects was published only years ago.[7] Subsequent economic development, particularly during the reconstruction period following the Korean war, brought more papers in the field of economics. There are now 37 such papers in Korea, three of which are dailies.[8] The country took another step forward in the early 1960's when it attempted to develop its economy further under the Five-Year Economic Development Program.[9] In Thailand economic journalism grew simultaneously with the expansion of the Thai economy. Until recently, Thailand's provincial papers occasionally reported news of industrial and agricultural events in their areas. These reports sometimes got into the widely circulated Bangkok papers.

The steady growth of India's economy at the rate of 3.7 during 1950-60 was paralleled by an increase of economic papers. The numbers rose from 151 in 1950 to 332 in 1963.[10] Today economic papers are published in almost all important commercial and industrial centers, but the largest concentration is in such trade centers as Calcutta, Bombay, Madras, and New Delhi.

While economic news may not be as great in a country such as the Philippines which produces only primary commodities, it does exist. Economic journalism was a highly specialized subject that appealed to a few writers in the Philippines before World War II. This was due to the fact that whatever trade promotion there was before the war was intended only to intensify the trade that existed. And the Philippines, being a dependent of the United States, traded almost exclusively with the United States. As one Manila economist explained: "Why engage in export promotion when there was only one trading partner?" [11] But the Philippine economy at the end of the war was a complete wreck. Unrestrained importation of non-essential commodities inevitably followed the close of hostilities to satisfy

[7] Report of the delegation of Korea to the International Seminar on Economic Journalism, Berlin, Germany, October, 1963.
[8] *Ibid.*
[9] Chang Sun-Kap and Han Chae-Yol, "Five-Year Plan Calls for Independent Growth of Economy," *Korea Journal*, 3:3 March 1963), pp. 16-22.
[10] Report of the delegation of India to the International Seminar on Economic Journalism, Berlin, Germany, October, 1963.
[11] Interview with Agustin P. Mangila, Minister, Counselor of Office of Economic Affairs, Department of Foreign Affairs, Manila, October 19, 1963.

the thirst for consumer items to which people were accustomed before the outbreak of the war. It was soon apparent that control had to be imposed to reserve foreign exchange. It was during this period that newspapermen and newspapers in the country took interest in economics and economic journalists as such came into the picture. Although there still is not an independent economic daily in the Philippines, the daily papers, particularly in Manila, cover developments in the business world.

Against the background of economic journalism in India, the history of the business press and economic journalism in Pakistan cannot be a long one. The part of undivided India that now comprises Pakistan was relatively underdeveloped; most of the industrial, financial, and business centers were located in areas which fell to India. Accordingly the respective specialized literature was located there too. After Pakistan came into existence, a great deal of enthusiasm to move forward as fast as possible was felt in the area of reading materials as well as elsewhere. Business and financial houses published journals as far back as 1948. These journals had a hard time maintaining their existence—the economic proposition was insufficient—and many had to cease publication. Not before 1955-56 was there a change for the better. This change was due to the change in the Pakistani economic structure from purely agrarian toward a semi-industrialized state.

Today all daily newspapers in Pakistan carry at least one economic page, covering stock exchange reports, commodity prices, market surveys, and financial commentary. There is only one economic daily, the four-page *Business Post*, established in 1963.[12] There are four economic weeklies, the oldest of which is the *Economic Observer*.

There is a total of 51 economic publications in Pakistan today.

Our survey of the growth of economic journalism indicates clearly that the state of economic journalism is closely linked with economic development. The development of economic journalism in the developing countries is thus a matter of economic growth. It seems that the countries in the stage of economic "take-off" [13] or those which have completed the process exhibit remarkable growth in the field of economic journalism.

Political Implications

The press, like any other activity in an underdeveloped country, could not do more than to satisfy the curiosity of the readers. In the countries where political, social, and military problems are still high priority topics, economic news and the business press are second-rate and neglected. In-

---

[12] Reports of the delegation of Pakistan to the International Seminar on Economic Journalism, Berlin, Germany, October, 1963.
[13] See W. W. Rostow, *The Stages of Economic Growth* (Cambridge: Cambridge University Press, 1960).

donesia and South Vietnam are examples. It is only after a country achieves some political stability that economic journalism begins to increase. India and the Philippines can be cited.

A number of problems in a developing economy require special attention because they are common to most developing countries and because they affect other sectors of the political economy as well. One such problem is inflation. The very process of development tends to be inflationary. New projects have to be financed. Meanwhile the needed increase in output has to wait for projects to be finished, usually involving a time lag of several years.

Our observation shows that economic journalism is bound to grow in countries where the national development is along economic lines. As to the political implications of economic growth and the development of economic journalism, it can be argued that economic growth and the dissemination of economic news not only change economic relationships but are bound to affect political relations as well. As the industrial labor force undergoes a rapid increase and as the rural labor force finds greater employment opportunities, both are bound to press their demands more vigorously through the media.

Government Participation

Greater participation of government in the dissemination of economic news and its role as an active publisher of the business press are among the main characteristics of economic journalism in the countries under study. Although no reliable statistics are available on the number of economic journals published by government agencies in each country, a close examination shows a high degree of government participation in the diffusion of economic information.

In developing countries where 50 to 75 per cent of industry is government owned and where the government is the main economic planner, it is only logical that most of the economists will be employed by governmental agencies. In such systems government is the main entrepreneur and will not only be a leading publisher of business and economic publications but will determine their content.

Observations on the seven countries under study show that those with less political stability and a slower economic development have strict government regulations on economic news and fewer news outlets. Again South Vietnam and Indonesia are examples. The journalists interviewed expressed the lack of communications between the government and the working press on economic problems. That government has failed to acquaint the press with the new economic projects or policies can be explained by the fact that in many cases there have been no press conferences on important economic matters.

Audience and Message

The importance of economic journalism is being realized in these countries under consideration. Although this type of reporting and analysis in the daily newspaper varies in degree and intensity, it nevertheless is there. In most metropolitan newspapers of these countries it is departmentalized and published in a separate section.

Unlike the widely circulated press in advanced countries, the limited economic press of underdeveloped countries must rely on the local chamber of commerce or governmental agencies for advertising revenue.

The business press and economic journalism of developing countries face a number of problems which need attention. These include a lack of journalists trained in economics, an inadequate supply of newsprint, limited readership, and a lack of maximum freedom and facilities to collect, analyze, and disseminate news.

As to the influence of economic journalism in the countries under study, it seems that publications have played an important role in guiding the thinking of economic decision-makers and authorities on basic economic issues. Even if it cannot be measured, the influence on decision-making can be assumed to be considerable, for many suggestions of the press have been followed.

Summary

This study explores the interaction between economic development and the growth of economic journalism and seeks a basis for understanding it. The study makes a general observation on the state of economic journalism in the seven developing countries and considers the growth of economic journalism both as a possible index and agent of economic development. The initial analysis concludes that, in the countries under study, the growth of economic journalism has paralleled the nations' economic development. In countries where political, social, and military problems take top priority, economic and business news are neglected. It is only after a country achieves some political development and stability that the rate of economic journalism increases.

The study finds government is a leading publisher and disseminator of economic news and information. It concludes that the inability of many journalists to discuss economic problems and the unwillingness of economic agencies to see their problems discussed in print contribute to the failure of economic journalism in developing countries.

The survey shows, however, that economic journalism will grow in countries where economic factors dictate development. The study notes the influence of economic journalism. It hypothesizes that the accuracy, discussion, and diffusion of economic news tend to increase as the level of the economy increases. On the other hand, continuous political instability deprives the public of economic news.

Finally, the study shows that striking technological and economic advances in developing countries during 1959-65 have contributed to the development of economic journalism. The economic press has expanded both in size and scope. During this period four of seven countries have acquired financial and economic papers. None existed before.

Heinz-Dietrich Fischer:

The International Situation of Magazines

FORERUNNERS of what we call today "magazines" were annual or semi-annual publications mainly printed in Germany. As early as 1588 Michael von Aitzing published every six months the *Messrelation* containing information about the fairs of Frankfurt.[1] In 1634 Johann Philipp Abelin established in Frankfurt the famous *Theatrum Europaeum*,[2] and from 1659 on the *Diarium Europaeum* came out as a historical and political collection of European affairs.[3] Johann Rist founded in 1663 a monthly publication under the title *Monatsgespräche*, in Wedel near Hamburg.[4]

However, "France can be considered the mother of magazines"[5] because the first real magazine with varied contents was established January 5, 1665, in Paris by Denys de Sallo under the name *Journal de Sçavans*.[6] This periodical, which has appeared with short interruptions until our present times, from its very first day of publication did not use Latin, as did other publications, but the French language and was mainly oriented in philology, history, and sciences in an international scope. Soon after the foundation of this French magazine an imitation was established in England under the name *Philosophical Transactions*, edited by Henry Oldenbourg, Secretary of the Royal Society. A similar project was started in 1668 in Italy, when Francesco Nazzari founded at Rome the *Giornale de'*

[1] Cf. Felix Stieve, *Über die ältesten halbjährigen Zeitungen oder Messerelationen und insbesondere über deren Begründer Freiherrn Michael von Aitzing*, Munich: Bayer. Akademie der Wissensch., 1881.

[2] Cf. Hermann Bingel, *Das Theatrum Europaeum, ein Beitrag zur Publizistik des 17. und 18. Jahrhunderts*, Ph.D. dissertation, University of Munich 1909, Berlin: Ebering, 1909.

[3] Wilmont Haacke, *Die Zeitschrift—Schrift der Zeit*, Essen/Germany: Stamm-Verlag, 1961, p. 257.

[4] Cf. Alfred Jericke, *Johann Rists Monatsgespräche*, Ph.D. dissertation University of Leipzig, 1923, Berlin—Leipzig: de Gruyter, 1928.

[5] Roland E. Wolseley, *Understanding Magazines* (2nd ed.), Ames/Iowa: The Iowa State University Press, 1966, p. 24.

[6] Cf. Betty Trebelle Morgan, *Histoire du Journal des Sçavans. Depuis 1665 jusqu'en 1701*, Paris: La Presse Universitaires de France, 1929.

▶ This is an original article done for this book by Heinz-Dietrich Fischer, Universities of Bochum and Cologne (Germany).

Letterati which contained also book reviews on sciences and languages.[7] These and some other early periodicals had readers throughout great parts of Europe, because they were mainly oriented to well-educated people.

A big influence on the development of magazines in several European countries were the literary and moralistic periodicals from England. Daniel Defoe issued in 1704 *The Review* as the earliest example of this kind of magazine, which was "a cross between a newspaper and a magazine."[8] And especially Joseph Addison and Richard Steele's *Tatler* (founded 1709) and the famous *Spectator* (founded 1711) were the pioneers of these magazines aimed at broader audience than the mainly scientific-oriented periodicals.[9] The history of the *American Magazine* and the *General Magazine* started in 1741.[10]

During the 18th Century in most European countries magazines were —with a few exceptions—mainly made for and read by people in their own countries, although they had sometimes more liberty in expressing certain feelings than censorship and absolutism permitted to the newspapers. But in reality magazines did not have more freedom than the rest of the press, because "the Tudors in England, the Bourbons in France, the Hapsburgs in Spain—in fact practically all western Europe—utilized the basic principles of authoritarianism as the theoretical foundation for their systems in press control."[11]

Before we continue our discussion on the development of magazines in an international context we have to make clear what a magazine really is, because there is some confusion about this term: "A periodical (or magazine) possesses periodicity: it is issued at intervals more or less regular. The term appears to have been first applied, as an adjective, to the essay type of journal as distinguished from the general magazine; but by the end of the eighteenth century it was being used to designate all regularly issued publications excepting, perhaps, newspapers."[12]

In great parts of Europe the French term *journal* or its Italian equivalent *giornale* were dominating for some time, and even the English adopted the French term and Anglosized it. Nearly a century after the foundation of the *Journal de Sçavans* synonyms for the term "journal" came up in the Germanic-speaking countries. The German word *Zeitschrift*

[7] Joachim Kirchner, *Das Deutsche Zeitschriftenwesen. Seine Geschichte und seine Probleme*, Vol. 1, 2nd ed. Wiesbaden/Germany: Otto Harrassowitz, 1958, p. 16 ff.
[8] Roland E. Wolseley. *Understanding Magazines*, p. 24.
[9] Cf. Günter Graf, *Der Spectator von Addison und Steele als publizistische Erscheinung*, Unpublished Ph.D. dissertation, University of Münster/Germany, 1952.
[10] Cf. Frank Luther Mott, *A History of American Magazines*, 1741-1850, Cambridge, Massachusetts: The Belknap Press of Harvard University Press, 1957.
[11] Fred S(eaton) Siebert, "The Authoritarian Theory of the Press" in: Fred S. Siebert, Theodore Peterson, and Wilbur Schramm, *Four Theories of the Press*, Urbana, Illinois: University of Illinois Press, 1963, p. 9.
[12] Frank Luther Mott, *A History of American Magazines*, 1741-1850, p. 5 ff.

was probably first used in 1751,[13] and later on similar expressions came up in the Netherlands or in Scandinavian countries.

"The term *magazine*," says Frank Luther Mott, "has undergone some change since it was first applied to publications. The first such application seems to have been in the title of *Gentleman's Magazine*, founded in London in 1731 ... Alexander Pope ... defined magazines, in 1743, as 'upstart collections' of dullness, folly, and so on. Thus the term, as taken over from the meaning of *magazine as storehouse* ... came to be accepted as designating the whole class of *Gentleman's* imitators." [14] Finally, Frank Luther Mott makes an attempt at a definition: "While the word *magazine* is ... to be defined as a bound pamphlet issued more or less regularly and containing a variety of reading matter, it must be observed also that it has a strong connotation of entertainment." [15] There is also the term *review*, but it is much more loosely used today than it was during the 19th century. The only other more neutral-sounding term would be *periodical*, because it is "perhaps the most concise word ... , but *magazines*" is "the more popular and meaningful term" for "all types of serial publications," says Mott.[16]

So the term "magazine" from here on will be used in a very general sense, and it will be necessary to try to give a typology in a later paragraph. Especially since the early 19th century most of the old universal-oriented magazines with subscribers in several countries have died, because this century has been mainly the age of newspapers. The magazines, more and more, became mouthpieces of elite groups for the exchange of literary ideas or political opinions. But this trend toward specialization did not go so far that there were no magazines with international standards. For example, in the 19th century there were England's *Westminster Review* (founded 1824)[17] or the *Contemporary Review* (1866). Among the British historical and scientific magazines the *Economist* (1843) or the *English Historical Review* (1887) are outstanding examples. In Austria, the *Wiener Literaturzeitung*[18] (1813), and in Germany the *Hallische Jahrbücher*[19] (1838) had European readership. The revolution of 1848 was disastrous to the periodical press in Germany and very few journals survived it. Among the best-known German journals of the 19th century were

---

[13] Cf. Hansjürgen Koschwitz, "Der früheste Beleg für das Wort 'Zeitschrift,' " in: *Publizistik* (Konstanz/Germany), Vol. 13/No. 1 (January-March 1968), pp. 41 ff.
[14] Frank Luther Mott, A *History of American Magazines, 1741-1850*, p. 6 ff.
[15] *Ibid.*, p. 7.
[16] *Ibid.*, p. 9.
[17] G. L. Nesbitt, *Benthamite Reviewing. The First Twelve Years of the Westminster Review, 1824-1836*, New York: Columbia Univ. Press, 1935.
[18] Cf. Hermann Anders, *Die Wiener literarischen Zeitschriften von 1800-1815 und ihre Auseinandersetzung mit der deutschen Klassik und Romantik*, Ph.D. dissertation, University of Vienna, 1930.
[19] Cf. Else von Eck, *Die Literaturkritik in den Hallischen und Deutschen Jahrbüchern, 1838-42*, Berlin: Ebering, 1926.

the *Historische Zeitschrift* (founded 1859),[20] the *Deutsche Rundschau* (1874)[21] and the *Neue Rundschau* (1889). In the United States *The Atlantic Monthly* began its distinguished literary career in 1857. Three prominent New York weeklies were *Harper's Weekly* (1857), the *Nation* (1865) and *Outlook* (1870). By 1870 there were, for example, around 1200 periodicals in the U.S.A., close to 2400 in 1880 and nearly 3000 in 1890.[22]

The 19th century had also produced a vast flood of cheap popular magazines for light reading, like the *Penny Magazine* (1832) in England which had imitators in several countries. But these popular magazines rarely were distributed internationally. But the *English Illustrated Magazine* (1884) may perhaps be considered the parent of illustrated periodicals going to many parts of the world, where printing presses were available for the reproduction of pictures of various kinds.

Since the beginning of the 20th century a couple of new forms of magazines have arisen, a great number of them concerned with very specific problems of certain professions or sciences and not aiming at a larger audience. In pre-World-War I times in nearly all of the important countries political magazines were founded, sometimes subsidized by the governments because of their importance in foreign affairs.[23] After World War I, the world situation of magazines had changed in some respects. The Bolshevik revolution produced a great upheaval and was responsible for an enormous output of periodicals of all kinds. And also in countries outside of the Soviet Union there was increasing demand for the development of magazines which were different from those of the pre-war era.

Symptomatic of a group of mainly cultural oriented periodicals were such like the Spanish *Revista hispano-americana de Ciencias, Letras y Artes* (1921), the Swiss *Schweizerische Monatschefte* (1921), the Italian *La Cultura* (1922), the German *Deutsche Vierteljahresschrift* (1923), the French *Chronique des lettres françaises* (1923), or the Portuguese *Lusitania* (1924).[24] In Russia, the literary magazine *Novy Mir* (1925) published important works of the leading authors and made them known in other countries.[25] In February, 1922, the *Reader's Digest*[26] was founded as a

[20] Cf. Theodor Schieder (ed.), *Hundert Jahre Historische Zeitschrift, 1859-1959*, Munich: R. Oldenbourg, 1959.
[21] Cf. Wilmont Haacke, *Julius Rodenberg und die Deutsche Rundschau*, Heidelberg: Kurt Vowinckel, 1950.
[22] F(rank) L(uther) M(ot)t, "Periodicals—United States," in: *Encyclopaedia Britannica*, 15th ed., Vol. 17. Chicago—London—Toronto: Encyclopaedia Britannica, Ltd., 1956, p. 516.
[23] Cf. Wilmont Haacke, *Die politische Zeitschrift, 1665-1965*, Stuttgart/Germany: K. F. Koehler Verlag, 1968.
[24] C.T.H.W. and F.L.K., "Periodicals" in: *Encyclopaedia Britannica, op. cit.*, pp. 512 ff.
[25] James W. Markham, *Voices of the Red Giants: Communications in Russia and China*, Ames, Iowa: The Iowa State University Press, 1967, p. 229.
[26] Cf. J. Bainbridge, *Little Wonder: or the Reader's Digest and How it Grew*, New York: Reynal and Hitchcock, 1946.

magazine, which "started a new trend in size, contents, approach." And in 1923, *Time* [27] followed; it was "curt, clear, complete" [28] like no other periodical before. On the other hand, there arose a number of abstract journals, particularly in the fields of science, medicine, and technology.

The 1920's and 1930's have also been the times for the establishing of important political magazines in several countries. In Germany *Die Weltbühne,* of the later Nobel prize winner Carl von Ossietzky, had growing importance among some groups of intellectuals.[29] In England, *The New Statesman* (founded 1913), in the United States *Newsweek* (1933) and *U.S. News and World Report* (1933), were very successful. In 1936, Time, Inc. launched a weekly picture magazine under the title *Life,* which made a great success and had some imitators, chief of which was the fortnightly *Look* (1937).[30] In the Soviet Union, periodicals like the satirical *Krokodil* (1922), *Literaturnaja Gaseta* (1929) and especially the prime theoretical journal *Kommunist* (1924)[31] were "designed for both home and foreign consumption." [32] During World War II, the German minister of propaganda, Joseph Goebbels, established a weekly under the title *Das Reich* which was mainly a Nazi propaganda instrument for foreign countries.[33] After the war in many countries of the world magazines with a certain international appeal have been founded and the periodical press of the world became "extremely varied in scope, quality and general purpose. Magazines and journals range from the popular 'illustrateds' of many nations (e.g. *Stern* of Hamburg, Germany)[34] to the ultraserious journals of comment and news (e.g. *Swiss Review of World Affairs* of Zurich). There are also well-written quality 'humor' or 'satire' magazines of the *New Yorker* type such as Britain's *Punch* and Italy's *Il Borghese* and offbeat varieties such as the Soviet Union's *Krokodil.*" [35]

Without any doubt, the periodicals with a large circulation for home and domestic distribution are the news magazines of all kinds, sometimes having special international editions. Among these news magazines, the American examples of this group have the highest circulations: the leading

[27] Cf. Uwe Magnus, *Time und Newsweek: Darstellung und Analyse,* Hannover: Verlag für Literatur und Zeitgeschehen, 1967.
[28] William H(oward) Taft, *American Journalism History: An Outline,* Columbia, Mo. —Los Angeles: Lucas Brothers Publishers, 1968, p. 59.
[29] Cf. Alf Enseling, *Die Weltbühne—Organ der intellektuellen Linken,* Münster/Germany: Verlag C. J. Fahle, 1962.
[30] F(rank) L(uther) M(ot)t, "Periodicals—United States," *op. cit.,* p. 517.
[31] Foundation figures from: Karl-Marx-Universität (ed.), *Die sowjetische Presse in Dokumenten,* Leipzig: Fakultät für *Journalistik,* 1963, p. 531.
[32] James W. Markham, *Voices of the Red Giants,* p. 225.
[33] Cf. Carin Kessemeier, *Der Leitartikler Goebbels in den NS-Organen 'Der Angriff' und 'Das Reich,'* Münster/Germany: Verlag C. J. Fahle, 1967.
[34] Cf. Sherilyn C. Bennion, "Mass Magazine Phenomenon: the German 'Illustrierte,' " in: *Journalism Quarterly* (Iowa City, Iowa), Vol. 38/No. 3 (Summer 1961), pp. 360-362.
[35] John C. Merrill, Carter R. Bryan and Marvin Alisky, *The Foreign Press,* Baton Rouge, Louisiana: Louisiana State University Press, 1964, p. 7.

one is *Time* with more than 6.5 million copies, followed by *Newsweek* (2.5 million), *U.S. News and World Report* (1.63 million), *Der Spiegel* of Germany [36] (around 1.1 million), and the French *L'Express* [37] (433,000). Much smaller circulations among the news magazines have *Elseviers Weekblad* of The Netherlands (130,000); *Tiempo*, Mexico (19,000); *Shukan Asahi*, Japan (16,000); *Reporter*, Kenya (8,000); and India's *Link*, Argentina's *Veritas*, and Turkey's *Akis*.[38]

Especially *Time* magazine, with its various editions, is an excellent example of an international-oriented and global-distributed magazine, shown by the following listing from 1968: [39]

"Time" Editions	*Circulations*
United States	3,500,000
Asia	95,000
Atlantic (I)	280,000
Atlantic (II)	210,000
Australia	80,000
Brazil	18,000
British Columbia	38,000
British Islands	70,000
Canada	370,000
Canadian Students	30,000
Caribbean Sea	45,000
Common Market	66,000
Continent	145,000
East Asia	60,000
East Canada	255,000
Europe	205,000
India	25,000
India/Pakistan	35,000
Ireland	15,000
Israel	13,000
Japan	10,000
Latin America (I)	90,000
Latin America (II)	70,000
Latin America (III)	80,000
Latin America (IV)	60,000

[36] Cf. Dieter Just, *Der Spiegel: Arbeitsweise, Inhalt, Wirkung,* Hannover/Germany: Verlag für Literatur und Zeitgeschehen, 1967.
[37] Cf. Uwe Magnus, "L'Express als publizistische Opposition in der V. Republik," in: *Publizistik* (Bremen), Vol. 10/No. 4 (1965), pp. 534 ff.
[38] Circulations trom: Willy Stamm, *Leitfaden für Presse und Werbung 1969,* Essen, Germany: Stamm-Verlag, 1969.
[39] Willy Stamm, *Leitfaden für Presse und Werbung 1968,* Essen, Germany: Stamm-Verlag, 1968, p. 5/153.

"Time" Editions	*Circulations*
Latin America (V)	80,000
Mexico	10,000
Military Ed.: Asia	30,000
Military Ed.: Atlantic	10,000
Military Ed.: Overseas	40,000
Near East	18,000
Near East/Africa	70,000
New Zealand	30,000
Ontario	150,000
Philippines	13,000
Quebec	70,000
Scandinavia	20,000
South Africa	22,000
South East Asia	50,000
South Pacific	110,000
Toronto	55,000
West Canada	110,000
West Indies	22,000

More impressive than even *Time* is the situation of the U.S. magazine with the world's largest circulation, *Reader's Digest*, which is also *the* international magazine. Sixteen years after its foundation, in 1938, the magazine started a special edition for England, followed by the first foreign language edition (Spanish) for Latin America in 1940. Two years later (1942) an edition in Portuguese was founded; in 1943 followed editions in Swedish and Arabic, and after World War II French, German and a couple of other editions were started. In 1958 *Reader's Digest* was published in 13 languages in 30 different editions for distribution in over 100 countries. It was published in various English editions for the United States, Great Britain, Canada, Australia, New Zealand, and other countries of the British Commonwealth. It was also published in different French-language editions for France, Belgium, Switzerland, and Canada. The remaining editions were in Spanish, Portuguese, Swedish, Finnish, Danish, Norwegian, German, Italian, Japanese, Dutch and Arabic. Even the German edition was circulated in 58 countries, the Italian in 86, the Spanish in 71, and even the small Dutch edition in 56 lands.

The total circulation of the *Reader's Digest* international editions, including a special Overseas Military Edition, in 1958 was 8.8 million copies per month. "Each of the foreign editions has in its title the words 'selections from' or 'the best from' the *Reader's Digest* or an equivalent phrase. Every article appearing in any of these editions has first appeared in a recent or past issue of the *Digest* in the United States; but not every article published in the parent magázine is republished abroad." [40] This flexibility in contents is one of the advantages and secrets of this magazine to stay in touch with a global audience. Wood says in this respect: The foreign editors "and their staffs are citizen and residents of the country where the given edition has its chief circulation. They know national characteristics, sentiment, interests, customs, circumstances . . . Translating is done with extreme care, not only to transfer the sense and spirit of the article accurately from one language to another, but also to render the whole in the usage peculiar to the countries where the edition will be read." [41]

In 1968 the *Reader's Digest* appeared in 13 languages and 30 different basic editions and 51 regional editions with a total circulation of more than 28 million copies per month, among this around 17 million for the United States.[42] Here is an overview on the different titles of *Reader's Digest* [43]:

PUBLICATION	LANGUAGE		BASIC EDITIONS CIRC.
Reader's Digest	English	8	20,977,000
Sélection du Reader's Digest	French	4	1,405,000
Selecciones del Reader's Digest	Spanish	6	1,395,000
Seleçôes do Reader's Digest	Portuguese	1	350,000
Das Beste aus Reader's Digest	German	2	1,395,000
Het Beste uit Reader's Digest	Dutch/Flemish	2	380,000
Selezione dal Reader's Digest	Italian	1	675,000
Valitut Palat koonnut Reader's Digest	Finnish	1	165,000
Det Bedste fra Reader's Digest	Danish	1	175,000
Det Beste fra Reader's Digest	Norwegian	1	200,000
Det Bästa ur Reader's Digest	Swedish	1	355,000
リーダーズ ダイジェスト *Reader's Digest*	Japanese	1	500,000
Reader's Digest	Chinese	1	150,000
13 Publications in 13 Languages		30	28,122,000

讀者文摘

[40] James Playsted Wood, *Of Lasting Interest: The Story of The Reader's Digest*, Garden City, New York: Doubleday & Company, Inc., 1958, pp. 169 ff.
[41] *Ibid.*, p. 173 ff.
[42] Verlag Das Beste (ed.), *Die Geschichte des "Reader's Digest,"* Stuttgart/Germany: Verlag Das Beste GmbH., 1968, p. 7.
[43] Compiled from: *Reader's Digest International Editions Advertising Rates 1969* and: Verlag Das Beste (ed.), *Die Internationalen Ausgaben von Reader's Digest. Anzeigenpreisliste 1969*, Düsseldorf, Germany: Verlag Das Beste GmbH., Anzeigendirektion, 1969. Cf. also: *World-Wide Circulation of Reader's Digest (based on single issue sales),* 1968.

But the gigantic success of *Reader's Digest* has not been without any complaints, especially from Canadians: "Some publishers and members of the intelligentsia feared that the superior technical resources of American magazines and their wealth in a war-impoverished world could lead only to American cultural imperialism, and there were cries against 'Coca-Colonization' and the spread of 'a Reader's Digest culture.' Even at home there were instances of protest, as when Senator Joseph Guffey of Pennsylvania called the *Reader's Digest* a 'world cartel' and spoke of an antitrust suit, which, however, did not come about. The majority of foreign readers semed to share little of his concern, for circulations of American magazines abroad continued to rise." [44]

Besides the giants among the world's magazines in respect of their circulations there exists a small but rather influential group of elitist magazines with a certain orientation toward foreign affairs. Magazines like *Aussen-Politik* (Germany), *Chronique de Politique Etrangère* (Belgium), *Chronology of International Events* (Great Britain), *Estudos Políticos* (Spain), *International Politikk* (Norway), *Internationale Spectator* (The Netherlands), *Relazioni Internazionali* (Italy), *Foreign Affairs* (U.S.A.) or *Kommunist* (Soviet Union) and *Hung-chi* (-Red Flag) (Red China) are—more or less—theoretical discussion organs.[45] Readers of these kinds of magazines can be found in elitist groups of many countries, although the circulations of these periodicals generally are rather small. This example also demonstrates very clearly why magazines are not always necessarily mass media in the common sense because of their very limited audience group.[46]

If the German term *Weltblatt* can be defined as the "internationally distributed daily press with a permanent world-wide resonance," [47] this brings up the question if there can be found a similar expression for stressing the international reputation of magazines. It is rather difficult to do this because even weeklies are sometimes regarded as newspapers by reason of their newspaper format. In reality, the weeklies are crosses between newspapers and magazines, and there are certain reasons to group them as magazines on account of the contents. John C. Merrill has separated them from the daily press without grouping them as newspapers or as maga-

[44] Theodore Peterson, *Magazines in the Twentieth Century*, Urbana, Illinois: University of Illinois Press, 1964, p. 111.

[45] Cf. Golo Mann and Harry Pross, *Aussenpolitik*, Frankfurt/Main: Fischer Bücherei KG, 1958, p. 350. See also: James W. Markham, *Voices of the Red Giants*, pp. 225 and 397.

[46] Cf. Henk Prakke et al., *Kommunikation der Gesellschaft. Einführung in die funktionale Publizistik*, Münster, Germany: Verlag Regensberg, 1968, p. 84.

[47] Heinz-Dietrich Fischer, "Weltblatt—Weltpresse," in: Kurt Koszyk and Karl Hugo Pruys (eds.), *dtv-Wörterbuch zur Publizistik*, Munich: Deutscher Taschenbuch Verlag, 1969, p. 379.

zines: "In addition to the elite daily papers," he writes, "it should be remembered that many excellent elite weekly papers exist in a number of countries (most of them in Europe) which reinforce the international concern and reasonableness of the elite dailies. No one should minimize the extremely high-type journalism of such papers as the London *Observer* and *Sunday Times*, the *National Observer* of the United States, *Weltwoche* of Zurich, *Embros* of Athens, *Le Canard Enchâîné* of Paris, *Die Zeit* of Hamburg, *Christ und Welt* of Stuttgart, *Rheinischer Merkur* of Cologne, *Jeune Afrique* of Tunis, and *The Nation* of Rangoon." [48]

In magazines we have in the world at large a much broader spectrum of varieties than is true in newspapers which are to a certain extent much more easily groupable. Roland E. Wolseley is quite right when he says that "the breadth of the magazine field is not always realized," [49] because some directories do not contain all groups. This general uncertainty as to how to define magazines broadly makes it difficult to give a useful typology of them. Wolseley presents some magazine typologies made by other authors.[50] His own opinion is that broadly magazines today fall into two groups: (1) The consumer or general interest, and (2) the specialized, and he breaks these groups into some 13 subdivisions.[51] A large variety of groups is given by a world guide to periodicals [52] and another catalogue divides the magazines into 21 groups, most of them containing several subdivisions.[53] If one looks at these typologies critically, he discovers that there are numerous overlappings in most of them—if they are given many subgroups. Because of the mistakes made by subordination, it seems to be useful to have only a few main groups, and so Wolseley's grouping is a good example. More than a decade ago Walter Hagemann tried to describe the phenomenon of magazines by the tripartite grouping as follows: [54]

1) *Trade magazines* which are helpful for the individuals by fulfilling of their professions.
2) *Class and Group magazines* which promote the integration process of the various social groups of society.
3) *Spare time magazines* which help the readers from all of the different professions, classes and organizations to busy themselves in their leisure time.

[48] John C(alhoun) Merrill, *The Elite Press: Great Newspapers of the World*, New York—Toronto—London: Pitman Publishing Corporation, 1968, p. 53.
[49] Roland E. Wolseley, *Understanding Magazines*, p. 7.
[50] *Ibid.*, pp. 8 ff.
[51] *Ibid.*, pp. 9 ff.
[52] Cf. Karl-Otto Saur, *Internationale Bibliographie der Fachzeitschriften. World Guide to Periodicals*, 3 Vols., 5th ed. Munich: Verlag Dokumentation, 1967.
[53] Cf. Willy Stamm, *Leitfaden für Presse und Werbung 1969*, pp. 3/1 ff.
[54] Walter Hagemann, *Die Deutsche Zeitschrift der Gegenwart*, Münster, Germany: Verlag C. J. Fahle GmbH, 1957, p. 9.

Magazines from all of these three groups can be objects of international communication. Trade magazines of all kinds are often subscribed to by members of certain professions in a number of countries.
Class and group magazines are read by sympathizers abroad. And spare-
time magazines, which include as a subgroup the large number of entertainment periodicals, are also distributed across national borders.

Although there is not an exact number of the world's magazines
available, one is able to determine some points for a general orientation.
It can be estimated from UNESCO information that at least some 45,000
periodicals can be found in the world.[55] If one subtracts from this number
around 7,000 daily newspapers found by a German research team,[56] there
remains around 38,000 magazines of all kinds. It can be estimated that
the great majority of the world's magazines belong to the first and second
of Hagemann's groups, dealing with trade, class and group magazines. The
third category possibly has a smaller number by titles, but the total circulation of these magazines seems to be higher than that of the other
groups together.

Last but not least, the wide variety of magazines around the world
can be well summarized by this UNESCO description: "A periodical
other than a newspaper of general interest is a publication which appears
under the same title at regular or irregular intervals, but more than once
a year and over an indefinite period, and whose content varies widely,
ranging from information of a general nature to specialized trade, technical
and professional subjects." [57]

[55] See John C. Merrill, Carter R. Ryan and Marvin Alisky, *The Foreign Press*, p. 6.
[56] Cf. Henk Prakke, Carin Kessemeier, and Heinz-Dietrich Fischer (eds.), *Handbuch
der Weltpresse*, (2 Vols.), Cologne—Opladen: Westdeutscher Verlag (in press), 1970.
[57] UNESCO, *Statistics of Newspapers and Other Periodicals*, Paris: UNESCO, 1959,
p. 15.

BROADCASTING

UNESCO
THE WORLD'S RADIO SYSTEMS

UNESCO
TELEVISION NETWORKS AROUND THE WORLD

Wilson P. Dizard
TELEVISION'S GLOBAL NETWORKS

8

BROADCASTING

ALTHOUGH the basic technical ideas for transmitting sound mechanically were developed by Heinrich Hertz (1857-1894), it was only in the early years of the 20th century that his invention was used for practical purposes—by ships and for telegraphic transmissions. During World War I, in some cases military information was transmitted by radio, but the first real progress in radio broadcasting came after the end of the war. Early radio stations were established in Germany, Great Britain and the United States. In the late 1920's and early 1930's most countries of Europe and North America had fairly well-developed broadcasting systems.

Increasing forms of cooperation in the field of program exchange and technical aids led, in 1932, to the foundation of the International Telecommunication Union (ITU). The German radio system was the host organization of a so-called "Welt-Ringsendung" on October 27, 1935. More than 1,300 radio stations from thirty-one countries participated in an international radio broadcasting transmission under the slogan "Youth Sings Across the Borders."

On the basis of the inventions of Paul Nipkow and several other persons since 1925, the first steps in television broadcasting were taken in Germany, England and the United States. The first real test transmissions were conducted at the German Radio Exhibition in the Autumn of 1928. But it was not until April, 1934, that the first synchronized picture and sound transmissions were made. The first regular TV program began on March 22, 1935, in Berlin, and the telecasts came on three evenings a week from 8:30 to 10 p.m. When the 1936 Olympic Summer Games were held in Berlin, portions of this event were watched by a few TV viewers in the Berlin area.

Since 1941, commercial television has been authorized in the United States by the Federal Communications Commission. The first TV programs—a curiosity—in France were transmitted in 1943 by the German Occupation forces from the Eiffel Tower in Paris; they were telecast daily for five to eight hours in both German and French. After the war, television developed rapidly in many countries of the world. Since the early 1950's the European Broadcasting Union in Geneva coordinated program exchanges between different nations. This system became known as "Eurovision"; in Eastern Europe a counterpart was established as "Intervision." Many TV stations outside Europe are regular or associated members of these international networks.

It is extremely difficult to present a global overview of the radio-television situation on an international scale because these media are growing so rapidly. The main institution for research in this field so far has been UNESCO, which has published several studies. These, however, are often rather substantially out-of-date by the time they are published. The two articles in this chapter on the international situation of radio and TV broadcasting from UNESCO mainly represent the situation of the mid-1960's. However, it is believed that they will prove valuable—especially in the absence of any later systematic data. The third article of the chapter, an additional overview of the global television situation, is given by Wilson P. Dizard, a leading authority in this area.

What might well be called an "electronic communication revolution" which has come about in the 20th century is still very much in progress. Radio broadcasting especially has become more and more popular as a communication instrument in the developing countries. Cheap transistor radio receivers have made it possible for great parts of the population in Africa and Asia, for example, to be brought into a kind of "national consciousness" as they receive information and instruction previously denied them. And, in the more highly developed countries portable TV sets, efficient shortwave radio receivers and other technical improvements in broadcasting are opening new possibilities for international communication. As nations individually improve the quantity and quality of their own broadcasting systems, it appears that the emphasis in international broadcasting—at least for the next couple of decades—will be on satellite transmission and cooperative international exchange and network programming.

*   *   *   *

RELATED READING

American Broadcasting Company International, Inc. *Television in the Space Age*. Proceedings of the first Worldvision Symposium in Washington, D.C., under the auspices of ABC International, March 21, 1965.

Bellac, Paul. *Die Vorgeschichte der Eurovision*. Bern, Switzerland: Schweizerische Rundspruch-Gesellschaft, 1963.

Bogart, Leo. *The Age of Television: A Study of Viewing Habits and the Impact of Television on American Life*. New York: Frederick Ungart, 1958.

Codding, George A. *Broadcasting Without Barriers*. Paris: UNESCO, 1959.

Codding, George A. *The International Telecommunications Union: An Experiment in International Cooperation*. Leyden, The Netherlands: E. J. Brill, 1952.

Dizard, Wilson P. *Television: A World View*. Syracuse, New York: Syracuse University Press, 1966.

Haley, William J. *Broadcasting as an International Force*. Nottingham, England: Nottingham University, 1951.

Hans-Bredow-Institut (ed.). *Internationales Handbuch für Rundfunk und Fernsehen*. Hamburg: Verlag Hans-Bredow Institut für Rundfunk und Fernsehen, 1957 ff (annually).

Paulu, Burton. *Radio and Television Broadcasting on the European Continent*. Minneapolis/Minnesota: University of Minnesota Press, 1967.

Pigé, François. *La Télévision dans le Monde: Organisation Administrative et Financière*. Paris: Societé Nationale des Enterprises de Presse, 1962.

Pulling, Martin. *International Television*. London: British Broadcasting Corporation, 1963.

Schubiger, Claude. *Radio—Weltmacht ohne Grenzen*. Bern, Switzerland: Hallwag, 1942.

Summers, R. E. and H. B. *Broadcasting and the Public*. Belmont, Calif.: Wadsworth Pub. Co., Inc., 1966. See especially Ch. 2 "Systems of Broadcasting."

Tomlinson, John D. *The International Control of Radio Communications*. Ann Arbor/Michigan: Edwards Brothers, 1945.

UNESCO. *Television in the Service of International Understanding*. Paris: UNESCO, 1960.

Wagenführ, Kurt (ed.). *Jahrbuch Welt-Rundfunk*. Heidelberg—Berlin: Kurt Vowinckel, 1938.

World Radio TV Handbook. Hellerup, Denmark: World Radio-Television Handbook Co., Ltd. (annually).

UNESCO:

The World's Radio Systems

———

MANY of the problems encountered in the field of the press do not arise, or are less acute, in radio broadcasting, and the developing countries in particular are giving priority to this medium in expanding their information facilities. Since 1950, the number of radio receivers for every 100 people in all regions has increased much more rapidly than the ratio of daily newspapers. Only two regions, Africa and Asia, now average fewer than five sets per 100 people, suggested as a minimum of adequacy by Unesco. The Americas, Europe, Oceania and the U.S.S.R. exceeded this level by from 10 to 73 sets on a regional basis.

There has been a parallel increase in the number of transmitters. Numerically, the figures for North America are most outstanding. But on a percentage basis, the gains in Africa, South America, Asia, Europe and the U.S.S.R. are more significant. Africa had 140 transmitters in 1950 and 370 in 1962. The number in Europe rose during the same period from 566 to 2,700. The total more than doubled in South America, almost tripled in Asia and almost quadrupled in the U.S.S.R. It is evident that, despite the world-wide challenge of television, radio has a long and active future before it as a medium unsurpassed in speed, range and economy.

Like the press, radio in the developed regions is a well-established medium. But, again like the press, it has experienced many technical changes since 1950 and is on the threshold of new developments.

In recent years the transistor has brought 'pocket radio' within the reach of millions of people in all regions. But the transistor receiver is no longer a toy—an object of interest only because of its diminutive size. It is now a high-grade instrument capable of giving both the volume and quality of sound usually associated only with sets having four or five valves and working from power mains. The transistor receiver is smaller, lighter and needs only a small dry battery for power. It has an impressive reliability factor and very low current consumption and, hence, negligible running costs which are confined to the expense of replacing batteries.

Meanwhile, the trend towards 'miniaturization,' spurred by the revolu-

▶ From: *World Communications: Press—Radio—Television—Film*, by UNESCO. Copyright © 1964 by UNESCO and the UNESCO Publications Center, New York and Paris. Reprinted by permission of the publisher.

tion in electronics and the development of space satellites, is making for still smaller receivers and other radio equipment. Even now, the transistor is being superseded by micro-components such as the tunnel diode, which is already in mass production. Within a decade, it is expected by some technical observers, the wrist-watch radio, powered by the heat of the listener's body, will be generally available. Such developments are giving further stimulus to the mass production of low-cost receivers for use in the developing countries. These developments are moving so swiftly as to anticipate the day when there will be one receiver for every family in the world—a target which would at present require over 400 million additional sets.

Technological advances are likewise transforming the whole field of radio transmission. The past decade has witnessed the increasing adoption of frequency modulation (FM) broadcasting, which provides the listener with a high quality signal relatively free from interference and, moreover, employs hitherto unused very high frequencies in the overcrowded radio spectrum. The experience of a number of developing countries, particularly in Europe and North America, has shown that FM broadcasting for local services is capable of expansion in a way which would relieve much of the present burden in the low-, medium- and high-frequency bands and thus improve conditions for national, regional and international transmissions. The introduction of FM broadcasting is therefore of special interest to the developing countries, and particularly to tropical areas affected by solar interference.

Meanwhile, the high quality of FM transmissions has stimulated a whole industry catering to the radio-developed taste for high fidelity musical recordings. Coupled with this has been the development of stereophonic broadcasting which, by using two matched sources of sound, gives breadth, depth and movement to musical, theatrical and other programmes.

The successful operation of the first communication satellites has brought radio broadcasting, together with the press and television, into the space age. By this means, it has been demonstrated, programmes can be broadcast, free from interference, over vast areas. In addition, the satellite experiments have pointed the way to improvements in the signal to noise ratio—a vital element in broadcasting and other radio communication—and to the further development of miniature, sun-powered transmitters. All of these technical advances may be expected to enhance the effectiveness of radio broadcasting as a medium of information, education and entertainment.

Although it can now claim 2.3 receivers per 100 people, compared with only 0.7 in 1950, Africa, like Asia, still falls short of the 'Unesco minimum' of 5 sets for every 100 persons. Liberia has achieved a ratio of 7.8, the highest in Africa. Algeria, Libya, Mauritius, Morocco, Réunion, Somaliland, South Africa, Tunisia and the U.A.R. also exceed the minimum, while

Gabon and Senegal are close to it. All of the other African countries fall short of this standard.

Radio broadcasting has, however, advanced more rapidly than the press in Africa. In most countries, broadcasting services are under public control and their expansion has been actively encouraged by governments. Nevertheless a number of countries, including Basutoland and St. Helena, have no broadcasting facilities of their own. Other areas, again, rely upon programmes imported from neighbouring countries and from the United States and Europe.

There are no more than 370 transmitters for the whole continent, most of them being concentrated in a few countries. South Africa, which has 36 medium-wave and 9 short-wave transmitters, is planning to establish an FM network of 123 stations and 485 transmitters. The United Arab Republic has 26 transmitters, two of them FM; Nigeria has 27, one of them an FM transmitter; Morocco and Mozambique have 19 each and Algeria 17. Short-wave transmitters are encountered wherever there has been any significant development of broadcasting. Stations using these transmitters frequently rebroadcast overseas news, entertainment and educational programmes. Certain countries employ short-wave transmitters extensively for international broadcasting. Morocco's four short-wave transmitters, for example, are designed to cover Africa and the Middle East. The U.A.R.'s 13 short-wave transmitters beam programmes in 20 languages to the Middle East, Asia, Europe and North and South America.

Short-wave transmission has been adopted in Tropical Africa largely for reasons of economy. However, the transmissions are severely affected by solar interference from October to April, and improvement can only be made by the introduction of FM broadcasting, combined with medium-wave 'booster' services. Nigeria is one of the countries which plan to provide nation-wide medium-wave coverage within the next few years.

Poverty most seriously hinders the development of transmission services in Africa. Communal listening helps to make up for the shortage of sets, but the best long-term solution to the receiver problem may well lie in the provision of low-cost transistor sets. Programming also suffers from the lack of adequate financing and a shortage of trained staff. Furthermore, the exchange of programmes is particularly difficult in Tropical Africa due to the multiplicity of local languages and the widely differing cultural backgrounds of local audiences. English- and French-language programmes are often European-slanted and irrelevant to the interests of African listeners.

The United States is better served by radio than any other country in this region or throughout the globe. In 1962 the United States owned over one-third of the world's total of 12,500 transmitters. The American population enjoys the phenomenal ratio of 100 sets per 100 persons, with receivers in 97 per cent of all households, in 43 million motor-cars and 10 million public places.

There has been a great post-war increase in the number of transmitters and receivers despite the rapid spread of television. Since 1955, the number of FM stations has increased from 552 to 931. Of these, 187 are non-commercial, educational stations operated by colleges, universities and State or municipal authorities. Official international broadcasting is mainly conducted by the United States Information Agency through the Voice of America.

Radio also reaches 98 per cent of all Canadian households. In contrast to the United States, where all AM and most FM stations are privately owned, Canada has developed a mixed system of public and private ownership. However, in both countries, a government agency performs 'watchdog' functions over the operations and activities of broadcasters. Canada's publicly-controlled network, the Canadian Broadcasting Corporation, broadcasts educational programmes five days a week. It also broadcasts over two short-wave transmitters in 11 languages for listeners in the Americas, Africa, Europe and Oceania.

Central American republics are noteworthy for a multiplicity of small private commercial stations. Examples are the Dominican Republic with 76 AM and 9 FM transmitters for a population of approximately 3 million; El Salvador with 24 transmitters for a population of under 3 million; and Mexico with 400 transmitters (only 13 of them publicly owned) broadcasting to 3.5 million receivers. Throughout Central America, the commercial stations are required to provide free time for transmission of educational broadcasts for schools and for public interest, cultural and news programmes. In addition, most countries have at least one publicly-subsidized station which provides educational and cultural programmes.

Only five North American countries in the region fall below the level of five sets per 100 persons. As in Africa, the provision of low-cost receivers is a priority matter. The most urgent transmission problems, however, concern quality rather than quantity.

Mixed broadcasting systems operate in almost all of the South American countries, although private commercial stations out-number publicly-owned ones. While density of distribution of receivers varies widely, only Ecuador and French Guiana fall short of the level of five sets per 100 persons. Seven countries can claim over 15 sets per 100 persons, with the Falkland Islands (40 sets) and Uruguay (35 sets) heading the list.

Many stations operate on short wave for economic reasons. Of Argentina's 78 transmitters, 12 are short wave. Of Brazil's 924 transmitters, 152 are short wave and 54 are FM.

The use of radio for educational and cultural purposes has spread rapidly. Every country now uses radio as an educational aid, even if only to a limited extent. In Colombia, the Acción Cultural Popular radio schools reach 170,000 elementary school listening groups each day. Peru's Radio Nacional regularly transmits educational programmes. In addition, 14 cultural stations are operated by universities, municipalities or religious institutions. Private stations in Chile are required to broadcast the Ministry of Education's school and popular educational broadcasts, which are compulsory listening for all schools with radios. The Argentinian Ministry of Education uses the national radio system to broadcast to more than 300 schools daily. Five of Uruguay's 97 transmitters are owned by the Ministry of Public Instruction and Social Insurance which broadcasts daily courses in history, geography, science and literature for schools and the general public.

Many South American stations relay overseas or regional programmes. the majority of them provided by the BBC, Radiodiffusion-Télévision Française and United States and Argentine networks. A few countries, among them Argentina, Peru, Brazil and Ecuador, broadcast multilingual programmes to countries in the region and abroad.

In most Asian countries, broadcasting is a State monopoly and is financed through licence fees and government subsidies. Macao and the Ryukyu Islands, however, maintain private stations supported by advertising. China (Taiwan), Hong Kong, Japan, the Republic of Korea, Singapore and the Philippines maintain a mixed system.

Between 1950 and 1962, Asia's total of transmitters increased from 444 to 1,220. However, the distribution of receivers has not progressed at the same rate, the number of sets per 100 people having risen from one to two only. Only 13 countries—Aden, Bahrein, Brunei, China (Taiwan), Hong Kong, Iran, Israel, North Korea, Lebanon, Japan, Sarawak, Singapore and Syria—have five or more receivers per 100 inhabitants. On the other hand, and in contrast to Africa and South America, the press in Asia is relatively more developed than radio.

Asian broadcasting services compensate for the shortage of receivers by diffusing programmes to school and community listening centres. Heavy emphasis is laid on educational programming. Two recently-established 'radio and television universities' in mainland China have enrolled 19,000 college students. All-India Radio has established some 2,000 radio farm forums throughout the country, and more than 90,000 community listening sets are installed in villages. Special programmes are diffused to some 18,500 schools. Over 99 per cent of Japan's schools have receivers and both the State network and the private stations devote some 20 per cent of broadcasting time to educational programmes. Because of the diversity of languages, school broadcasts in Pakistan are made by regional stations rather than by Radio Pakistan's central station. However, Radio Pakistan transmits special programmes for adults in local languages from all of its stations.

Most Asian broadcasting systems must serve large populations using no generally-accepted common language. All-India Radio, which provides programmes for 432 million people, broadcasts in 51 local languages and 82 tribal dialects. Although India is an extreme example, even monolingual countries like Saudi Arabia broadcast in foreign languages because their programmes are easily received in neighbouring countries. Major languages, particularly English and French, are very commonly used.

Many Asian countries devote a large number of daily programme hours to broadcasts directed to emigrant groups in other countries, as well as to general news and cultural and background services for foreign consumption. This is particularly true of China (Taiwan and mainland), India, Israel, Indonesia, Japan, Iran, Iraq, Malaya, Pakistan and the Philippines. The BBC service in Singapore transmits in 13 languages over an area extending from Iran to Japan.

In general, most broadcasting progress has been made in transmission. Japan, for example, now has 400 transmitters, compared with 195 in 1953; Iran, 22 (5 in 1953); and the Philippines, 127 (9 in 1953). Although the distribution of sets has risen sharply in certain Asian countries, it has generally lost ground in relation to the number of transmitters. Notable exceptions are mainland China, which has 7 million receivers as against 1.5 million in 1953; Burma, 117,000 (15,000 in 1953); North Borneo, 20,000 (2,700); and Iran, 1,350,000 (174,000 in 1951).

A satisfactory level of receiver distribution could doubtless be achieved through the mass production of low-cost individual sets. An alternative would be the domestic manufacture of sets for community listening.

Europe is the sole continent where only one country (Albania) lacks adequate reception facilities. Albania has 3.7 receivers for every 100 people. Turkey, with 5.4, is just over the line. All other European countries average from 10 to 40 sets per 100 persons.

All European countries except Liechtenstein, Malta and Gozo and San Marino, have local broadcasting services. Most of the stations are publicly controlled. However, broadcasting services in Austria, the Federal Republic of Germany, Gibraltar, Iceland, Ireland, Italy, Portugal, Spain and Turkey devote some programme time to advertising. Private commercial stations in Andorra, Luxembourg and Monaco derive their entire revenue from this source.

Despite competition from other information media, broadcasting has continued to expand in Europe. Since 1952, the total of transmitters has risen from 566 to 2,700 and the average of receivers for every 100 people from 13.5 to 21. Few major changes have occurred in the principal networks, where well-established services have been operating for many years. However, FM is steadily replacing AM broadcasting because of its effectiveness in overcoming interference on the medium-wave channels generally assigned to European countries.

The movement towards FM is most pronounced in Western Europe. Belgium, which had 1 FM transmitter in 1954/55, now has 14; Norway, which had 2, has 33; Finland, which had 17, has 44; Sweden, which had 1, has 75; Switzerland, which had 2, has 61; and in the United Kingdom, the number has risen from 2 to 160. In Eastern Europe, only Eastern Germany maintains a substantial FM system. Certain countries, among them Denmark, the Federal Republic of Germany, the Netherlands, Norway and the United Kingdom, actually have fewer AM transmitters now than in 1955.

Almost without exception, European countries regularly provide programmes for schools, although the number of broadcasting hours varies widely. Educational programmes, including foreign-language courses, are also frequently broadcast to the general public. Poland's University of the Air enrolls some 200,000 student listeners. Denmark Radio conducts an 'Evening High School' and a 'Sunday University' and provides courses in seven foreign languages. The world's largest language-teaching operation is 'English by Radio,' which is beamed abroad by the BBC's London and Far Eastern stations. They transmit 150 lessons a week.

Europe's short-wave transmitters are mainly used for the foreign services operated by almost all networks. In a few countries—Iceland and Norway, for example—this service is designed for emigrant groups abroad. However, most countries broadcast in many languages to other countries in the continent and to Africa, Asia and North and South America. Broadcasts include 'spot' and background news and informational, cultural and musical programmes. Exchange systems are highly developed. The BBC sends more than 700 programmes a year to some 90 overseas broadcasting organizations. France's Radiodiffusion-Télévision Française (RTF) relayed 2,000 foreign programmes in 1960 and over 3,000 of its programmes were diffused by broadcasting services abroad. Eastern Germany exchanges programmes with broadcasting organizations in over 60 countries.

Wired relay systems are highly developed in Eastern Europe. But, with the exception of Switzerland and to a less degree the United Kingdom, Western European services broadcast almost entirely to wireless receivers.

Broadcasting services, most of them directed by governments, are more widely developed than the press in much of this region and in the island groups are the main source of news and other information. Australia averages 21.9 sets per 100 people and New Zealand 24.7. Although community sets are increasingly used in the islands, the only groups with more than five receivers per 100 persons are the Fiji Islands, French Polynesia, Nauru, New Caledonia and Norfolk Island.

Transmitters are maintained in all areas except the Cocos Islands, Nauru and Tokelau Island. New Guinea is served by the two transmitters in adjacent Papua. The Australian Broadcasting Corporation and the New Zealand Broadcasting Corporation both diffuse programmes throughout the region. Some of these are beamed direct and others are transcribed. The BBC, RTF and United States networks also supply news and educational and entertainment programmes to island areas.

In addition to the national, regional and foreign services transmitted by the Australian Broadcasting Corporation, Australia maintains 110 privately-owned stations supported by advertising. In New Zealand, where all stations are under some form of public control, there are two non-commercial networks and one which subsists on advertising. Radio Guam is commercially operated.

In comparison with other major regions, direct educational broadcasting is not highly developed in Oceania. A notable exception is Australia, which provides daily broadcasts to 94 per cent of its schools and to those in New Guinea, as well as regular programmes for adults. New Zealand offers school programmes for 3 hours a week, as well as a French-language course for adults and a programme for children under school age. The Fiji Islands service broadcasts 7 hours a week to 400 schools. The sole French Polynesian transmitter sends daily half-hour programmes to 6 schools.

Australia produces sufficient transmitters and receivers to meet its needs and also exports equipment to New Zealand and South-East Asia. Wired receivers are the salient feature of radio reception in the U.S.S.R. outnumbering wireless sets by more than two to one. The total of receivers has risen since 1950 from 13 million to 44 million, and of transmitters from 100 to 407.

The vast spaces that must be covered from the central Radio Moscow station necessitate a complex employment of long-, medium- and short-wave bands. Owing to differing zonal clock times, programmes emanating from Moscow have to be duplicated for the Urals, Siberia, Soviet Central Asia and the Soviet Far East. Supplementing the national broadcasts are programmes in local languages, which are transmitted by the various Republics, autonomous regions and territories. Listener participation in these programmes is widespread.

Programmes for listeners abroad are broadcast on short and medium waves in 40 foreign languages and eight languages spoken by Soviet citizens. The programmes are beamed to all parts of the world for about 1,000 hours a week. Broadcasts are extensively exchanged with Eastern European and Asian countries.

UNESCO:

Television Networks Around the World

AFTER only 27 years since its initial direction to a mass audience, television has established itself as a potent medium of information, education and entertainment throughout the world. It was in 1936 that the British Broadcasting Corporation inaugurated the first public telecasts. The Second World War halted television development. But, with the coming of peace, the developed countries began to turn their electronics industries to peaceful purposes, including the development of television transmitters and receivers, and at the same time established services for public viewing.

Television is now expanding with fantastic speed. In 1950, Africa, South America, Asia and Oceania had no television receivers at all and the U.S.S.R. possessed only 0.008 sets per 100 persons. Today, countries in every region maintain services, although the level of distribution of sets per 100 people ranges widely from 0.05 in Africa to 24.5 in North America. The world total of sets has risen from a mere 11 million in 1950 to 130 million in 1963. The number of transmitters has also increased spectacularly during the same period, from 130 to 2,380. Europe has registered the greatest increase of all regions—from 15 to 1,160.

International programme co-operation has become a regular feature of television development. Most exchanges so far have been made through tele-recordings. The direct transmission of programmes across frontiers has progressed rather slowly because of the need for link stations, coaxial cables and converters to permit transmissions on one line definition to be received by another system. (Broadcast definitions in use range from 405 lines with a band-width of 5 Mc/s in the United Kingdom to 819 lines and a band-width of 14 Mc/s in France, Monaco, Luxembourg, Algeria and the Belgian French-language network.)

However, 18 Western European countries now exchange programmes through Eurovision, sponsored by the European Broadcasting Union, and with the United States. Six Eastern European countries and the U.S.S.R. exchange programmes through Intervision, under the auspices of the International Radio and Television Organization, and also co-operate with

Eurovision in programme exchanges. Over a smaller area, Nordvision links the Scandinavian countries. Bilateral exchanges make available a wide range of other programmes.

Many Asian, African and South American countries are unable to meet production costs for independent programmes, or even the costs of better-quality imported programmes. As a result, their television screens often reflect the less impressive cultural standards of "popular" commercial television in the developed countries. Nevertheless, some of the developing countries are boldly imaginative in their use of television facilities for education. In Western Nigeria, for example, the Broadcasting Corporation telecasts three hours daily to all schools with receivers. These programmes are also very popular with the general public. Of Peru's five stations, the oldest, and the only non-commercial one, is owned by the Ministry of Education. Since 1960, All-India Radio has been telecasting courses on chemistry, physics, English and Hindi for secondary schools.

Some of the countries which pioneered in television are also taking advantage of the medium's great promise in the educational field. For example, the United Kingdom's publicly- and privately-owned networks transmit school programmes five days weekly during the academic year. Japan's publicly-owned educational television services now cover 42 per cent of the population.

In the United States, some 60 educational television stations operated by institutions, school systems and other groups provide a wide variety of programmes. An interesting American innovation has been the development of airborne television instruction, which has made it possible to reach schools spread over an area of 78,000 square miles (200,000 square kilometres) from a single transmitter in an aircraft flying at high altitude. This experiment indicates to some extent how communication satellites might eventually be used to accomplish a similar objective over a wider area.

Although it is the newest of the mass media, television is already experiencing the full impact of technological change. In the field of reception, both small and "full size" transistor sets, which work by battery or off the mains and can thus be used indoors or outdoors, have been developed. It is expected that, as in the case of radio, the transistor will before long be superseded by even smaller components which will make possible the production of diminutive "handbag" sets, operating in colour. Also foreseen is the manufacture of home sets with the picture tube separated from the receiver. These sets would be built into a wall for better viewing.

In the field of transmission, colour television is being actively developed in the United States, Japan, the U.S.S.R. and a number of European countries. Advances are also being made in stereophonic television. Other innovations are the use of video tape—the recording of both sound and picture on magnetic tape—rather than slowly-processed film; more "miniaturization" of cameras and, hence, more "live" coverage of news; and the development of the transistorized tape recorder, by which a picture can be seen as soon as it is recorded and thus can be edited on the spot.

Significant also is the development of closed circuit television and "pay-as-you-view" television, which better enable the viewer to see programmes of his choice. A new dimension has meanwhile been given to an old medium through "theatre-vision," described as "a marriage between the living theatre and closed-circuit television." By this means audiences in out-of-town theatres can see plays or operas transmitted hundreds of miles by telephone from a city theatre and projected on large cinema screens.

The most spectacular development in television history was the relaying, in 1962, of live programmes across the Atlantic by means of the first communication satellite. Eighteen countries in the Eurovision network participated with the United States in these exchanges, viewed by an audience of over 200 million in Europe and North America. During the first four months of the satellite's operation, 47 intercontinental transmissions were conducted, including five in colour of remarkable clarity. This inspiring co-operative effort pointed to the coming of world television, with all the diversity and enrichment it will hold for the viewer of the future.

Until 1962 the African continent remained almost untouched by television. In 1956, Morocco was the only African country with a regular service. Today, viewers in 12 countries receive telecasts; in ten of these countries—Algeria, Ivory Coast, Kenya, Morocco, Nigeria, Northern Rhodesia, Southern Rhodesia, Sierra Leone, Uganda and the U.A.R.—the services are government controlled but most of them are operated by European companies or consortiums. In Ethiopia and Libya, transmitters are operated by United States Armed Forces and programmes are directed mainly to viewers at United States air bases.

In drawing up contracts with commercial organizations, African governments have insisted on the allocation of substantial broadcasting time to educational programmes. The Nairobi station in Kenya devotes five of its 30 weekly broadcasting hours to educational programmes. In the Rhodesias, the Federal Broadcasting Corporation is required to provide school broadcasts. All three Nigerian services concentrate upon educational programming, one of them broadcasting for 3 hours a day to the 100 Western Region schools having television receivers.

Senegal, Gabon, Upper Volta, Ghana, Mauritius, Sudan and Tunisia are preparing to introduce services shortly. In the present "television" countries, current planning calls for more transmitters, the provision of communal receivers for social centres and rural communities, the encouragement of the purchase of battery-powered sets, tariff reductions on equipment and regional co-operation in programme development and standardization of line definitions.

Since 1950, the number of television receivers per 100 North Americans has risen from 5 to 24.5—by far the highest level of all regions. Oceania and Europe are distant runners-up, with averages of 7.8 and 7.2 sets respectively. With 60 million receivers, including 600,000 colour sets, the United States is better equipped with television facilities than any other country. Ninety per cent of American households had sets and viewing per home averaging more than 6 hours daily in 1962. However, for the first time in the history of television the United States has less than half the world total of sets. More than 70 per cent of programme time on the three large networks and smaller regional chains is devoted to entertainment. All revenue is derived from advertising. However, a certain amount of time is contributed gratis to public service broadcasts. Of the 60 non-commercial educational stations, 17 operate on UHF bands which cannot be received on sets in the average household. Income is derived from schools and colleges, foundations and local citizens' organizations.

Programmes are often locally produced. However, a number of regional networks are linked by live relay facilities, and the National Educational Television and Radio Centre, with which all the stations are affiliated, provides about 10 hours of films or kinescopes weekly.

Canada, which has 24 sets per 100 people, maintains a mixed system of ownership. The publicly-owned Canadian Broadcasting Corporation consists of an English and a French network. Microwave facilities link all 10 provinces for simultaneous telecasting. In addition, there are 59 private stations, most of them being affiliated to CBC networks. All Canadian stations sell advertising time. Canadian law requires that 55 per cent of all programmes be produced by Canadian companies.

Although 14 Central American and Caribbean countries maintain transmitters, they nearly all rely upon outside sources for their programmes. An exception is Cuba, where 80 per cent of all programmes are direct telecasts. Mexico also produces local programmes and tele-newsreels. But even in Mexico, with its well-developed film industry, international news material and many other programmes are imported, already dubbed, from the United States. In Bermuda, locally-produced live programmes are screened about 10 hours a week.

All stations in North America, except in the Netherlands Antilles, employ the 525-line definition used in the United States. This has facilitated the penetration of the market by American programme contractors. Furthermore, most stations are operated under contract by United States or, in some cases, United Kingdom interests. This tends to discourage the production of programmes locally or within a culturally homogeneous area linked by a telecommunication network.

Television in South America has made a strong impression in the eight countries which at present maintain services. In Chile, all stations are educational and are operated by universities. One Brazilian, one Peruvian and one Venezuelan station are government owned. Uruguay is planning to start a service under government auspices. Ecuador's sole station is operated non-commercially by a United States missionary organization. Colombia's State-owned system, which sells advertising time, reaches 45 per cent of the population through use of auxiliary stations hooked up to the main stations via the national telecommunications network. When television was inaugurated in 1954, the government imported 30,000 receivers and sold them at cost price. Venezuela's one government-owned station broadcasts educational and cultural programmes for about 6 hours a day. All other South American services are privately owned and commercially operated.

Brazil, Colombia, Venezuela and Argentina, where a considerable number of telecasts are live, all produce local tele-newsreels and other programmes. About half of Colombia's telecasts are financed and produced by the television administration. Nonetheless, South American television screens offer imported entertainment and information throughout most of the viewing hours.

Few transmitters reach rural audiences. City dwellers, on the other hand, are fairly well served by stations which operate from 5 to 15 hours a day.

The high cost of receivers, transmitting equipment and programming severely hinders television expansion in South America. The provision of battery-operated sets at low cost has been suggested as a stimulus to the medium, as has simultaneous telecasting to audiences in wide areas. The proposed Inter-American Telecommunication Network (RIT) might help to overcome obstacles to regional development by facilitating the formation of a Latin American counterpart of Eurovision. No country produces its own equipment, although Argentina now manufactures spare parts.

Although the number of transmitters in Asia has increased from one to 170 since 1950, many stations are still experimental and few can be viewed by people outside the major cities. Furthermore, 127 main stations are concentrated in Japan, which also operates 92 auxiliary and four experimental stations. With 13 million receivers, 3,000 of them colour sets, Japan is numerically led only by the United States in the number of receivers in one country, although Australia and several small European countries out-rank it in the number of sets per 100 people. The next-ranking Asian countries are Thailand, with 80,000, and Iraq with 50,000 receivers.

Except for Japan, Lebanon is the only Asian country with more than one receiver per 100 persons. However, in certain other "television" countries in Asia, audiences are larger than would be suggested by the number of receivers. Almost all the sets in mainland China are located in public meeting places and workers' clubs. When the Republic of Korea inaugurated a government-controlled station in 1961, it imported 40,000 sets from Japan and distributed them on easy credit terms, mostly for communal viewing. India's experimental station broadcasts to 150-200 people in each of 60 community centres and also transmits educational programmes to high schools in Delhi.

As yet, television exists only on an experimental basis in Cambodia, India and Kuwait. In China (mainland and Taiwan), Iran, Iraq, the Republic of Korea, Lebanon, the Philippines, the Ryukyu Islands, Saudi Arabia, Singapore, Syria and Thailand, programmes are broadcast for only a few hours a day. Programme time on Rediffusion (Hong Kong) climbs to 9 hours on Saturdays and Sundays. The introduction of television is being planned in Aden, Burma, Indonesia, Israel, Jordan, Malaya and Pakistan. Other Asian countries are not in an economic or technical position even to consider its introduction.

Except in Japan, few live programmes are produced, and throughout most of the region there is heavy reliance upon imported films and kinescopes. Owing to the rudimentary development of television in a number of countries, the medium is little used for school broadcasts in those areas.

The Asian countries producing transmitters and receivers are mainland China and Japan. Japan manufactured 3 million sets in 1960, and has now entered the fields of colour and transistorized equipment. A giant transmitter, now under construction in Tokyo, is to transmit the 1964 Olympic Games to the world through communication satellites.

Although television is extensively developed in most European countries, the density of distribution of sets and the number of hours devoted to telecasts is less than in various other developed countries, such as the United States, Canada and Australia. In the United Kingdom, for example, where more than 80 per cent of the population watch television for some 9 hours a week, the government permits the networks only 50 hours of basic programme time weekly. In France, television is on the air for only 60 hours a week.

On the other hand, the countries of Europe benefit from regional and national exchanges of a scale unparalleled elsewhere. The Western European viewer can now watch programmes which have originated in any part of Europe or the U.S.S.R. The European Broadcasting Union, through Eurovision, organizes international relays in Western Europe, and is also linked to the Intervision Eastern European network. The first live transmission from Moscow to London in 1961, an interview with the first astronaut, was relayed via the two systems. Both France and the United Kingdom now maintain terminal stations which can transmit and relay live television programmes through communication satellites.

Seven countries—Andorra, the Faeroe Islands, Greece, the Holy See, Iceland, Liechtenstein, and San Marino—have no local television systems. Some of them, however, receive broadcasts from neighbouring countries. Experimental stations have begun operating in Albania, Gibraltar and Turkey. Eleven countries—Belgium, Czechoslovakia, Denmark, France, the Federal Republic of Germany, Eastern Germany, Italy, Monaco, the Netherlands, Sweden and the United Kingdom—now claim more than five sets per 100 people.

Programme production is highly advanced in many countries, particularly in France and the United Kingdom. In 1960, Radiodiffusion-Télévision Française dispatched some 77,000 metres of television film abroad, and in 1961 the BBC contributed 116 programmes to Eurovision. Eastern Germany produces 20 film dramas a year with the co-operation of local studios.

In certain countries, including France, Italy and the United Kingdom, television for schools is being increasingly developed. In most of Europe, however, it is still in the experimental stage.

A number of countries produce receivers and transmitters for markets at home and abroad. These include Belgium, Bulgaria, Czechoslovakia, Finland, France, the Federal Republic of Germany, Eastern Germany, Hungary, Italy, the Netherlands, Poland, Spain and the United Kingdom.

In Oceania, television is well developed only in Australia, where 66 per cent of the population is within viewing range of a station. Fifty-four per cent of the live programmes on the Australian Broadcasting Commission's publicly-owned network are of domestic origin. The commercial networks devote 60 per cent of programme time to filmed material from the United States.

In New Zealand, a daily service maintained by a public body, the Broadcasting Corporation, now links the four main centres. Parliamentary debates are occasionally televised. Guam has a single station, maintained by advertising. An educational service is being established in American Samoa.

Since 1950, television has developed rapidly in the U.S.S.R. Where there were 2 transmitters, there are now 173; where there were 0.008 receivers per 100 people, there are now 3, for a total of some 7 million sets.

The U.S.S.R. was a pioneer in television. Telecasts were first made in 1931, and two stations began operating regularly in 1938. The service was resumed after the war, but to a limited audience. As late as 1954, only 700,000 sets were in use. The great period of development came later.

The Moscow Central Television Station, with two channels, is on the air for some 65 hours a week, excluding experimental colour transmissions on a third programme. Stations in other cities retransmit Moscow programmes and also produce material locally. A high percentage of viewing time is devoted to educational programmes for children and adults. They include a special programme, entitled "People's University," which offers courses in science and technology, arts and English for 2½ hours a week.

The U.S.S.R. produces transmitting equipment, as well as over 2 million receivers a year. In addition to participation in Intervision, the U.S.S.R. has exchange agreements with 22 other services throughout the world.

Wilson P. Dizard:

Television's Global Networks

AT THE BBC's new London studios there is a small room with a futuristic sign on its door. The sign reads: International Control Room. Here BBC engineers can exchange programs with over two dozen other television systems in Europe and North America. Soon, with the development of world-wide communications satellite facilities, they will be able to provide BBC viewers with programs for fifty countries. Within a decade this will extend to a hundred or more countries.

The BBC's international control room is a working symbol of the next major development in world television—the formation of regional and intercontinental networks. Such links are an old story in Europe where the pacesetting Eurovision network has been in operation for over a decade. Intervision, a Soviet-sponsored network, links eight East European countries. Fiscal, political, and geographical barriers have decreed a slower pace for similar networks in other parts of the world. Despite these difficulties, regional networks will play a key role in television's development in Latin America, the Middle East, and the Far East. In each of these areas, the first steps toward forming electronic links between national television systems have already been taken. Africa has, understandably, lagged behind in plans for regional telecasting, but even here the managers of that continent's national television systems talk confidently of TV links among themselves and with the rest of the world.

In any event, it is already clear that by the early 1970's regional and intercontinental network links will be available to a billion or more viewers in over sixty countries throughout the globe. The prospects of simultaneous sight-and-sound transmissions on such an unprecedented scale has political, economic, and cultural implications for all countries, and for American world leadership in particular. What we say about ourselves on these new links, and what is said about us by others, can seriously influence the image the world has of our national character and our international role. A closer look at the present development of these networks and their future prospects is therefore in order.

The earliest TV transmissions to cross national frontiers came from the United States. In the late 1940's, television stations in U.S. cities

▶ From: *Television: A World View*, by Wilson P. Dizard. Copyright © 1966 by Syracuse University Press, Syracuse, N.Y. Reprinted by permission of the publisher.

bordering Mexico and Canada began attracting large audiences across the border. By the early 1950's, the process became reciprocal as Canadian and Mexican television entrepreneurs began building stations with an eye on nearby U.S. audiences.

This across-the-border TV eavesdropping is now common in other parts of the world. In Europe, the largest audiences of the commercial stations in Luxembourg and Monte Carlo are nearby French, German, Belgian, and Italian viewers. Belgian and German programs have larger audiences in parts of the Netherlands than does the state-controlled Dutch station. In the Mediterranean area, the low-lying littoral provides excellent transmission conditions for long-distance telecasting. Viewers in Greece and in North Africa tuned into Italian television for years before television became a reality in their own countries. Cairo television is readily available to viewers in Lebanon, Israel, and Jordan.

In a number of cases, this factor of geographical proximity has been used to beam programs directly across borders for political purposes. The best-known example of this is in Germany where the West and East Germans conduct an elaborate, expensive form of electronic warfare aimed at attracting each other's television audiences. A similar, small example of directed Communist television programs was reported in 1963 when a Soviet station in the Arctic instituted programs in Norwegian design to attract audiences in northern Norway. A similar effort has been reported in Korea where North Korean Communist authorities have directed part of their programming efforts toward nearby South Korean viewers.

These across-the-border telecasting operations, whether random or intentional, are a small part of the new international character of television. The major emphasis is on binational, regional, and intercontinental agreements to connect television systems at all levels.

The first formal exchange of television programs on an international scale took place on August 27, 1950, between Great Britain and France. With British equipment, the inaugural program was sent from Calais to Dover. A major problem at the time was the incompatibility of British and French equipment, due largely to differences in television tube line counts. BBC and Radiodiffusion Télévision Française engineers successfully developed converter systems to a point where in July, 1952, formal bilateral exchanges of programs between the two countries were inaugurated. It is doubtful that even the most enthusiastic supporters of the exchange realized that they were taking the first practical step toward forming a link which, in little more than ten years, would reach from the Urals through Europe and across the Atlantic to California.

The initial Franco-British television exchanges were not simply an exercise in technical virtuosity or hands-across-the-Channel camaraderie. They were part of a pattern, planned several years earlier, for strengthening European cooperation in the television and radio fields. The result was the Eurovision international network whose parent organization was, and still is, the European Broadcasting Union.

Eurovision is a massive test case of the opportunities, and the limitations, involved in developing regional and intercontinental networks. It is doubtful that any area of the world will come close to European accomplishments in this field for a long time. Europe had the advantages of a relatively small geographical area, high technical competence, cultural compatibility, and, above all, a strong impulse toward regional unity at many levels. Eurovision was nurtured in the dynamics of postwar European regional cooperation, and in turn it has contributed to this movement through a unique sight-and-sound ability to dramatize it.

Eurovision's success in regional transmissions led the Communist nations to attempt a similar venture within their own borders. The result was Intervision which is—technically, at least—Eurovision's opposite number in Eastern Europe and the Soviet Union. The technical achievements of Intervision are, in fact, considerable. It is geographically the most widespread single land network, stretching from East Berlin to the Urals, with the prospect of being extended to Vladivostok on the Pacific Ocean within a few years. This latter achievement would involve a linear distance of over nine thousand miles. Intervision does not, however, service as many individual stations or as large an audience as its Western European counterpart.

There is no doubt that Europe, both East and West, has a long lead in regional network television. Geography, politics, and financial considerations are all formidable obstacles to the development of similar networks in other parts of the world. Despite these barriers, however, such regional links will become a reality on every continent within the next decade.

If current plans develop, Asia will have a regional network by 1970. This planning effort is being carried out largely under Japanese leadership. Japanese television broadcasters and equipment manufacturers are fully aware of the long-range financial benefits of their participation in television's development in the Far East. Supporting this is the Japanese government's desire to re-establish its political and economic influence in Southeast Asia—influences which are still checked by local memories of Japanese military occupation during World War II. Television offers the Japanese a uniquely effective medium for further strengthening their role as a political and economic power in the Far East.

Japanese efforts to play a leading role in Far Eastern radio and television date from the formation of the Asian Broadcasters Conference in 1957. The conference was, to a large degree, a Japanese creation. All of its early meetings, in 1957, 1958, and 1960, were held in Tokyo, where delegates were appropriately impressed by the fact that Japan has the most advanced radio and television systems in Asia. At its 1962 meeting in Kuala Lumpur, the conference voted to establish itself as the Asian Broadcasting Union. The new union came into formal being in July, 1964. It is modeled, in form and spirit, on the European Broadcasting Union. Headquartered in Tokyo, its membership includes the broadcasting systems of most major nations in the Far East, South Asia, and the Middle East.[1]

Although it is still in its formative stages, the new Asia Broadcasting Union will undoubtedly be quickly involved in a plan for regional television networks during the next few years. The initial impetus for such a plan is, of course, Japanese. In 1961, a group of Japanese equipment manufacturers and broadcasters formed a corporation known as Asiavision to explore the possibilities of directly linking the Japanese television network with other Far Eastern systems. Asiavision began as a wholly-owned subsidiary of Fuji-TV, one of the large commercial Japanese networks. Its board of directors included officials of major electronics firms. Basically it was a commercial combine, designed to explore the prospects of expanding television equipment and broadcasting sales throughout Southeast Asia.[2]

According to its original prospectus, the Asiavision link would run from Japan to Okinawa and the Philippines, crossing over to the Asian mainland via Saigon, and then on to Laos, Cambodia, Thailand, Burma, Pakistan, and India. Korean television would also be included in the network. The technical problems involved in such a link are formidable but not insoluble. Japanese engineers have plans to span the overwater segment between southern Japan and Okinawa by microwave circuits. The other overwater distances are comparable in the technical hurdles they present. More formidable, technically, is the fact that several countries, notably Cambodia, Laos, and Burma, do not have television systems. These gaps preclude any direct regional telecasting for years to come. In its early stages, Asiavision will have to restrict itself to exchanges of taped and filmed program material.

Japanese broadcasters have already had a taste of some of the political difficulties involved in their attempts to play a leading role in Asian television. Japanese offers to assist in the development of television in the Philippines have been treated warily, despite the fact that a number of stations there have been hard pressed financially in recent years. Another example of such cautiousness took place in Formosa in 1962. Fuji-TV, sponsor of Asiavision, had signed an agreement with the Chinese govern-

---

[1] Eleven such organizations are ABU charter members: Australian Broadcasting Commission, Broadcasting Corporation of China (Taiwan), All India Radio, Japan Broadcasting Corporation (NHK), Korean Broadcasting System, Radiodiffusion National Lao, Radio Malaysia, New Zealand Broadcasting Corporation, Radio Pakistan, Philippine Broadcasting Service, and the UAR Broadcasting Corporation (Cairo).

[2] It would, however, be wrong to dismiss the proposed Asiavision network simply as a Japanese commercial venture. Its organizers have an awareness of its potential political effect. One of them declared, in a 1962 Tokyo interview with the author, that Asiavision "was something like your American Peace Corps."

ment in Formosa to build a television system on commercial terms on generally regarded as favorable to both sides. Among other concessions, the Japanese planned to advertise Japanese products on Taiwan television and to provide a fixed amount of Japanese programing. In April, 1962, the Chinese parliament passed a resolution which in effect vetoed these provisions in the contract. The issue became a political one between the Japanese and Chinese foreign offices. It was settled eventually, but not without leaving a legacy of doubt about the speed with which an Asian television network might be formed.

There is no doubt that such a regional network will become a reality eventually, or that the Japanese will play a leading role in its formation. However, it is probable that the network will develop slowly, first through the exchange of filmed and taped programs, and then through limited binational microwave connections which will one day be extended to other countries in the region, probably under the auspices of the Asian Broadcasting Union.[3]

Similar political and economic difficulties have inhibited realistic planning for regional telecasting in the Middle East and Africa. The idea of a network linking Arab television systems has been discussed since television was introduced into the area in the late fifties. However, political differences within the Arab bloc have militated against any practical implementation of what would undoubtedly be an important step toward dramatizing Arab unity. The strongest force behind a regional network, if it should materialize, would be the UAR's Gamal Abdel Nasser, who has already developed Egyptian television into the best of its kind in the region. Paradoxically, the first practical move toward an Arab network has been made by an American firm, the American Broadcasting Company. In October, 1963, ABC International announced the formation of an "Arab Middle Eastern Network" consisting of TV stations in Syria, Lebanon, Kuwait, Iraq, and Jordan. The "network" is primarily a program and advertising sales arrangement, linked to ABC International's affiliations with these stations. There is, however, some significance to the fact that the network's organizing meeting in Beirut drew almost five hundred businessmen, advertisers, government officials, and station representatives.[4]

The prospects for regional television links are perhaps dimmest in Africa. It will probably be a decade before African countries move beyond bilateral program exchange arrangements to a multinational regional network.

The most practical planning in regional television outside of Europe

---

[3] Not the least of the problems facing the proposed Asian network would be the admission of the Chinese Communists into its activities. The Chinese Reds, who already have considerable television experience, are well aware of the propaganda potential of a link with other Asian television systems.

[4] *Variety*, October 2, 1963.

has taken place in Latin America. Three Central American countries are already linked directly in a small-scale version of a larger regional network that will eventually stretch from the Mexican-U.S. border south seven thousand miles to the tip of South America. The first "live" program exchanges between Latin American countries took place in 1961 when Argentinian television carried news reports of the Organization of American States conference at Punta del Este in neighboring Uruguay. A year earlier, telecommunications experts from Latin American nations, meeting in Mexico City, agreed in principle to the idea of planning a continental network.

Since that time, the international network idea has been kept alive largely by the Mexicans. It was not, however, until the Central American network began operations in 1964 that any practical moves were made to realize the plan. The network is known as CATVN—Central American Television Network. (The participants are Nicaragua, Costa Rica, Guatemala, Panama, Honduras, and El Salvador.) It was originally set up in 1960, largely under the guidance of the international division of the American Broadcasting Company of New York. As with its "Arab network" efforts in the Middle East, ABC International organized CATVN primarily as a commercial advertising and program sales organization.

It would, however, be incorrect to dismiss CATVN as a sales promotion gimmick. In fact, the nations involved have growing political and economic ties that make a television link part of a logical pattern of regional interdependence. In 1963, five of the six CATVN countries—all except Panama—formed a Central American Free Trade Area, somewhat on the model of the European Common Market. Trade barriers were eliminated on more than half the commerce between the member countries, with further reductions scheduled in 1965. A regional bank has been established as another effort to raise economic levels well above the current per capita income of 250 dollars a year. Whether it is reporting a sports event or a regional political conference, television has a role to play in the new efforts of Central American nations to strengthen each other politically and economically.

Plans are currently underway to extend "live" interconnections between CATVN's members. The success of this "subregional network" will undoubtedly have an important influence in encouraging other Latin American nations to move forward with their much-discussed plans for a network spanning the entire continent.

The next step beyond regional television networks is, of course, intercontinental television linking all areas of the world. Most speculation about world-wide television broadcasts has emphasized the role of space communications satellites (comsats). However, comsats may, in fact, play a relatively minor role in such a system. It may be more practical, financially and technically, to base the system on interlocking regional networks connected by land cable or microwave systems. TV networks in Europe, Africa, and Asia could be linked in this manner. One comsat over the Atlantic or Pacific could connect the Western Hemisphere with this Eurasian system. (The two American continents would be joined either by microwave relays or a comsat system operating on a north-south axis.) The potential role of regional networks in a global system was demonstrated at the time of President Kennedy's death. Only two communications satellites—one each over the Atlantic and Pacific—were needed in an international network that involved twenty-six countries on four continents and a viewing audience of over three hundred million persons.

There will, however, be few similar events that will enlist such worldwide interest as to justify global coverage. Most television exchanges between regional networks will involve areas with common cultural or political interests. Thus, U.S. television will probably concentrate most heavily on program exchanges with Europe and Latin America. The two regional networks in divided Europe will undoubtedly develop a more active exchange schedule.

A number of proposals for a world television network organization have been put forward in recent years. Most of these have come from American sources. In 1962, several U.S. television officials proposed that American and European broadcasters take the lead in this field. However, none of the proposals have been acted upon.[5] It will probably be several years before any active planning for world television network arrangements is begun. The chief reason, of course, is that technical achievement of such a network, through comsat and surface connections, is five to eight years in the future. In the interim, however, there will be a steady increase in the number of bilateral regional television exchanges, notably in the North Atlantic area. For the rest of the world, the question of intercontinental television may depend largely on the pace of regional network developments.

In summary, regional television networks will become a reality in all parts of the world within the next decade. The model for such arrangements will be the ten-year-old European network which has demonstrated both the opportunities and the pitfalls involved in international telecasting. A world-wide television system will be formed by the combination of communications satellites and interlocked regional networks.

The United States has, of course, an important stake in these developments. Increasingly, television is taking over Hollywood's role as the

---

[5] The proposals were made at the special European Broadcasting Union meeting held in New York shortly after the launching of the first Telstar communications satellite in 1962. There were some indications at the time that the European members of EBU resented the manner in which the Americans presented their proposals without first consulting privately with their EBU associates. See *Variety*, October 10, 1962.

chief purveyor of the American image abroad. The America that foreign viewers see on their living room screens is already a major factor in the shaping of their attitudes toward us. Equally important is the part that international television can play in defining and clarifying, as no other medium can, the realities of the rest of the world beyond their own borders. Using this gift in ways that strengthen the prospects for a democratic world order will be increasingly important for American leadership in the future.

9

ADVERTISING AND PUBLIC RELATIONS

Roland L. Kramer
INTERNATIONAL ADVERTISING MEDIA

S. Watson Dunn
THE INTERNATIONAL LANGUAGE OF ADVERTISING

Gordon E. Miracle
CLIENT'S INTERNATIONAL ADVERTISING POLICIES
    AND PROCEDURES

Bertrand R. Canfield
INTERNATIONAL PUBLIC RELATIONS

9

ADVERTISING AND PUBLIC RELATIONS

I F *advertising* of any type roughly can be defined as *commercial propaganda* for all kinds of products, business, trade and industry, and is mainly an economics-oriented function, so *public relations* may be called *idealistic propaganda* for persons, groups, institutions, etc. in behalf of their public images. In certain cases, of course, elements of advertising are merged with those of public relations, and very often public relations campaigns are nothing but a series of advertisements.

Advertising is much older than the history of newspapers or magazines; in fact, it is impossible to speculate on the origins of advertising back in the mists of pre-history. Early forms of advertising (as it is generally recognized today) were already being seen in pamphlets from the 15th and 16th centuries. Since the middle of the 17th century, newspapers have carried advertisements, and from the 19th century on, commercial announcements have been an important part of the economic base of the press.

In the world's press today we find great differences in the proportions of advertising to editorial content. Nearly no, or very few, ads can be found in the state-owned press of the Communist countries. In some Western European nations there is a proportion of about 60% editorial matter to 40% advertising, and in the United States these figures are approximately reversed.

Throughout the world there are many different concepts as to what kinds of advertisements are properly found in certain kinds of newspapers and magazines. Usually this is rather vague, and patterns of advertising use vary considerably from publication to publication and from country to country. In 1957, however, there was founded an organization of leading European dailies which proposed to cooperate and to coordinate their advertising practices—named TEAM (Top European Advertising Media). It is composed today of seventeen dailies from eleven countries, and was established largely as a cooperative institution through the initiative of the Paris daily *Le Figaro* and the Amsterdam paper *Algemeen Handelsblad*.

In late 1969 these dailies were members of this elite newspaper group: Austria: *Die Presse* (Vienna); Belgium: *Het Laatste Nieuws* (Brussels); Denmark: *Berlingske Tidende* (Copenhagen); France: *Le Figaro* (Paris), *Le Monde* (Paris); Germany: *Frankfurter Allgemeine* (Frankfurt/Main), *Süddeutsche Zeitung* (Munich), *Die Welt* (Hamburg); Great Britain: *The Daily Telegraph* (London); Italy: *Corriere della Sera* (Milan), *Il Messaggero* (Rome); The Netherlands: *Algemeen Handelsblad* (Amsterdam), *Nieuwe Rotterdamse Courant* (Rotterdam); Norway: *Aftenposten* (Oslo); Sweden: *Svenska Dagbladet* (Stockholm); Switzerland: *Neue Zürcher Zeitung* (Zurich). This is a fascinating example for international cooperation and strategy in the field of newspaper advertising.

Since the late 1920's paid messages for products of all kinds became an important factor in financing the numerous radio stations within the United States and in several other countries. And since TV was introduced in the United States, the same system was transplanted to this audio-visual medium. In most European countries, where the costs of radio and television broadcasting to some extent are paid by license fees, the daily times for commercials are limited to certain hours and are never found in other parts of the daily programs. Only Radio Luxembourg is a commercial radio station which can be received in nearly all parts of Europe, whether on medium or on short wave. And Radio Luxembourg not only has a program with commercials from many countries, it also serves in several languages its mainly entertaining program. In other parts of the world similar examples of an international radio program mainly on the basis of commercials may be found.

Although *public relations*, as a term, is one of our century, the activities of this concern have a much longer tradition. The key word in this field is the presentation of *images*—usually for institutions, countries or persons. Public relations activity tries to correct bad attitudes toward certain people or associations by changing the images people have, by using psychological aids of various kinds. Because public relations more and more has gained the connotation of a propagandistic institution, the PR departments today often prefer in their titles words like "information" or "promotion" or "news." Almost every national or international organization —such as the UN, NATO, SEATO, the Common Market and corporations, universities and the like—make use of extensive programs of public relations. Governments also have well-organized and often quite complex PR departments, under a wide variety of names, to look after their images.

In the chapter which follows, four outstanding scholars in the field of international advertising discuss various aspects of a rapidly growing emphasis. In the first article, Dr. Roland Kramer presents a survey of the situation and usefulness of international advertising media. Dr. S. Watson Dunn discusses the problems of translatability of advertisements, while Dr. Gordon E. Miracle observes the process of international advertising by special agencies. Finally, Dr. Bertrand R. Canfield gives an overview of the public relations activities in the international context.

* * * *

RELATED READING

Backman, Jules. *Advertising and Competition.* New York: New Yorker University Press, 1967.

Barton, Roger. *Advertising Agency Operations and Management.* New York: McGraw-Hill, 1955.

Barton, Roger. *Media in Advertising.* New York: McGraw-Hill, 1964.

Bernays, Edward L. *Public Relations: Principles, Cases and Problems.* Homewood/Illinois: Richard D. Irwin, 1968.

Buchli, Hanns. *6000 Jahre Werbung: Geschichte der Wirtschaftswerbung und der Propaganda.* (3 Vols.), Berlin: Walter de Gruyter, 1962ff.

Cutlip, Scott M. and Allen H. Center. *Effective Public Relations.* 3rd ed., Englewood-Cliffs/New Jersey: Prentice-Hall, Inc., 1964.

Dowd, Laurence P. *Principles of World Business.* Boston: Allyn and Bacon, Inc., 1965.

Dunn, S. Watson. *International Handbook of Advertising.* New York: McGraw-Hill, 1964.

Ellis, Nigel and Pat Bowman. *The Handbook of Public Relations.* London: Harrap, 1963.

Ettinger, Karl E. *International Handbook of Management.* New York: McGraw-Hill, 1965.

Fayerweather, John. *International Marketing.* Englewood-Cliffs/New Jersey: Prentice Hall, Inc., 1965.

Hundhausen, Carl. *Werbung um öffentliches Vertrauen: Public Relations.* Essen: Verlag Girardet, 1951.

Johnson, Malcolm M. et al. *Current Thoughts on Public Relations.* New York: M. W. Lads Publ. Co., 1968.

Oeckl, Albert. *Handbuch der Public Relations: Theorie und Praxis der Öffentlichkeitsarbeit in Deutschland und der Welt.* Munich: Süddeutscher Verlag, 1964.

Paneth, Erwin. *Die Entwicklung der Reklame vom Altertum bis zur Gegenwart: Erfolgreiche Mittel der Geschäftsreklame aus allen Zeiten und Völkern.* Munich: Verlag Oldenbourg, 1926.

Stephenson, Howard. *Handbook of Public Relations.* New York: McGraw-Hill Book Company, 1960.

Roland L. Kramer:

International Advertising Media

IN THE keen competition encountered in world markets, the American foreign trader is aided, as perhaps are the businessmen of no other nation, by the sales-producing force of advertising.

Skillfully planned and directed publicity not only at home but also abroad will overcome prejudice, combat foreign competition, establish new habits, satisfy wants, build goodwill, and thus multiply sales and lay a foundation for permanent and profitable business.

This is not to say that the businessmen of other industrial nations do not utilize advertising to good advantage. However, mass production in the United States poured such a mountain of products on the market that, in line with the purchasing power of this market, it was necessary to develop mass distribution. Thus, advertising, in all of its branches, was rapidly developed as an integral part of mass distribution.

The subject of advertising in all of its ramifications is extremely complex; and when its usefulness and application in foreign countries are considered, the most that can be attempted in chapters of this nature is to outline the highlights and sketch the principles. Details relating to the use of any one channel of advertising for any one product or service in any one country are exacting. Witness the veritable libraries of books bearing on advertising in the United States market alone.

FUNDAMENTALS OF ADVERTISING ABROAD

At the Ninth International Advertising Convention held in 1957 in New York, Arthur "Red" Motley observed the following four fundamentals of advertising abroad:

1. Create a *climate* at home on the part of top management. Try to have them think in terms of the domestic market and to take the same broad vision with regard to international operations. This is probably the most basic of all fundamentals.

2. Do not think of the overseas market as a poor market. Despite

▶ From: *International Marketing*, by Roland L. Kramer. Copyright © (second edition) 1964 by South Western Publishing Company, Burlingame, Calif.—New Rochell, N.Y. —Cincinnati, Ohio—Chicago, Ill.—Dallas, Tex. Reprinted by permission of the publisher.

the fact that a certain market may be underdeveloped, there is a market with money and it is interested in quality.

3. News is of prime importance so do not overdo prestige or age of company or establishment of a trade name or even the number of gold medals won at trade fairs since 1890 or 1870.

4. People are interested in real people, real situations, and in the use of a product. One of the great fundamentals is that people wish to believe that many other people just like themselves are doing the same thing; use the same equipment, the same product, the same service; have the same fine complexion, the same chic look; and can command the same means of traveling—by automobile.

While all channels of advertising may be used to promote a good corporate image by skillful public relations, there is basically the essential that the company, from top management down, is worthy of the image that is portrayed. This means top management backing and high ethical standards. The phrase "corporate image advertising" is commonly used. It refers to publicity of any and all sorts that will serve to give a good impression of the company that makes the products. In the view of Mr. Maynard, this is preliminary to advertising products. In general, business firms do both simultaneously; for instance, "The world-famous manufacturer of X product invites your consideration of its offerings."

International Advertising Copy

Domestic advertising copy, particularly for use in the publications field, is often found to be unsatisfactory for international advertising purposes. The form in which a story is to be told is said to depend upon the temperament and psychology of the people for whom it is intended. The "snappy" or jocular copy, which appeals to the American public, would not be satisfactory in a more conservative part of the world. Tradition, religion, and economic conditions may dictate the necessity of wording an appeal in such manner as to meet particular situations.

The Frenchman has quite definite ideas about advertising. He prefers a slogan. He will not be bothered with discursive texts (as in more disciplined countries like Germany). Loquaciousness is lost on him. He wants to be captivated and amused at the same time.

And he often gets what he wants. French advertising is original, sometimes brilliant. Despite this there is still a tendency to lose harmony between a brilliant conception and the final ad.

Another failing is the tendency, especially in women's magazines, to pack too many trade names into an ad. This brings about the pretense of its being a consumer ad when in reality it is a dealer's ad.[1]

[1] *Advertising Age*, Vol. 34, No. 21 (May 20, 1963), p. 56.

With respect to Germany, the following observation is made:

Advertising here, generally considered, is still about five years behind the U.S. The VW [Volkswagon] campaign may pave the way for more originality in the usual dead-serious German approach to advertising.[2]

Concerning Japan the comment is:

Commercials are generally couched in very polite terms and never come right out and say, "Buy Brand X Today." Such approach is offensive to delicate Japanese sensitivities. Rather the message will attempt an interesting explanation of [the] product and at the end suggest mildly that you try the product once. The most direct ads will say "XYZ Brand Please." [3]

Finally with respect to the Arab world:

Advertising to the 30,000,000 people living in seven Arab lands was almost an unknown commodity ten years ago.

But today, it's estimated that ad budgets for the seven countries are somewhere in the neighborhood of $10,000,000 annually—with most of the money going to Arab and English-language newspapers, local radio and television, cinemas and outdoor.[4]

Illustrations

The use of illustrations in international advertising calls for a knowledge of local conditions in order that they may fit required circumstances. A picture tells a story that is understood everywhere and, particularly in countries where literacy is not high, illustrations may be of greater proportionate value then copy. Color preferences are also to be found and superstitions may sometimes eliminate entirely or may strongly recommend the use of certain subjects for copy purposes. These factors are especially significant in connection with outdoor advertising, window display cards, or other illustrations that appear before the transient public, as well as packages, magazines, and catalogs.

Certain taboos are important and the successful advertiser will take note of them. A few examples will serve to illustrate this fact. Illustrations to be used for advertising in India, for example, should never show a cow—it is a sacred animal. Advertisers in Moslem countries should not forget that the purdah (a screen hiding women from the sight of men or strangers) is not extinct. An advertiser in the Sudan showed a camel in his illustration, knowing that camels are to be found there. Unfortunately he showed a Bactrian (two-humped) camel—and Sudanese camels

---

[2] *Ibid.*
[3] *Ibid.*, p. 78.
[4] *Ibid.*, p. 96.

have but one hump! Animals used to illustrate humans are not attractive or even understandable to Arabs. Allah states that a beast is a beast and a man is a man.

The symbol of three is lucky in West Africa. In the Far East white is the color of mourning among the Chinese and blue is not very lucky, but in the Far and Middle East and Africa red is a very lucky color. Color plays an important role in the lives of these people and all films should be produced in bright colors. In Greece and Cyprus, houses should be white with blue shutters, the national colors of Greece.[5]

Many a sale has been lost which may have taken years of build-up through polite correspondence—only to be thrown to the winds during a personal meeting when one of the parties violates a customs taboo.

The well-meaning American custom of patting a child on the head . . . is one example of a strong Oriental taboo where the head is held sacred. A careless flick of a cigarette into a hearth is also commonplace here in the United States but in Japan the hearth is regarded as sacred.

Our Hong Kong adviser tells that the Chinese do not, as a rule, send clocks as presents. Giving clocks as gifts is strictly taboo . . . since to the Chinese, clocks can be taken as a bad omen. An overseas advertiser should think twice before using a gift-giving angle in his clock promotions.

Perhaps because religion is a more all-pervading life force in the Orient than in the Occident, it is good business sense not to choose an advertising symbol which might offend the religious sensibilities of Eastern peoples.[6]

Translation

A common problem in copy work for international marketing is translation. If it is intended for a British public, it is important to render the copy in the King's English and to recognize differences in American and British spellings and colloquialisms. A more difficult problem is translating copy into a foreign tongue. Particularly in technical translations, as in export catalogs, there may be a complete absence of foreign synonyms for certain English words. Perhaps new words may be coined or a description may be phrased that will correctly convey the idea in the foreign language. Moreover, there is sometimes the question of a number of languages or dialects in a particular market. In India, for example, there are 14 lan-

[5] Bruno Kiwi, Director, Pearl and Dean Overseas Company, London, in *Export Trade* (January 26, 1959), p. 74.
[6] Noble de Roin, President, International Advertising Company, Denver, Colorado, in *Export Trade and Shipper* (May 12, 1958), p. 55. Mr. de Roin also quoted Elma Kelly, Managing Director, Cathay Limited, Hong Kong.

guages and any nation-wide campaign—be it visual or audio—must be planned very carefully.

FIELDS OF INTERNATIONAL ADVERTISING MEDIA

A survey of international advertising media can be only general in character, since the specific conditions that currently affect any particular method or locality are constantly changing.

International advertising media may be divided into three fields: 1. Trade or industrial; 2. Consumer; 3. Professional or ethical.

As recognized in domestic practice, *trade* or *industrial* advertising aims to reach distributors, seeking to induce them to stock the merchandise advertised, and commission sales representatives who solicit indent orders. *Consumer* advertising, on the other hand, seeks to induce consumers to purchase advertised products by name or brand from the store or outlet that serves the consumer. *Professional* or *ethical* advertising attempts to influence professional people to prescribe or to advise the use of the publicized products. Medical and dental publications come to mind in this connection. Some advertising media serve exclusively the aims of one field, but in many instances the media may be useful in more than one field.

Foreign Publications. Daily newspapers are among the most effective methods of reaching the buying public in any land. There is no civilized part of the world that does not boast of its newspaper, and the effectiveness of this medium for advertising purposes may be compared favorably with its position in the United States. Indeed, newspapers may afford a greater relative value for advertising purposes abroad than in this country. When the literacy of a people is low, the consuming population for most goods is confined largely to those highest in the economic and social scale. These are generally literate and read the dailies that are published locally. It therefore follows that an advertisement in the newspapers will reach almost the entire effective buying public.

Magazines, weekly or monthly, published abroad are also to be considered by the international advertiser. These may have a wide circulation throughout a country, and in some instances, as in the case of feminine interests, they may provide the only means of special appeal. The use of magazines is important to make United States trademarks and United States products known and to reach distributors or sales representatives who may not be covered by United States trade magazines. Generally, however, magazines in foreign countries are confined in their circulation to a certain locality where they may be of considerable, although restricted, advertising value. One or two examples will serve to illustrate these problems.

Advertising in the Benelux countries introduces problems that are not likely to be anticipated by the uninformed. According to a Belgian, Dan E. G. Rosseels, Advertising Manager of the Belgian editions of

Libelle, Goed Nieuws-Bonnes Nouvelles, and *Panorama,* a common mistake in advertising in Belgium is to consider that country as French-speaking, whereas 55 percent of the population speaks Flemish.

In the African (Rhodesia and Nyasaland) markets, the white press reaches only a small group of educated Africans.

The advertising value of foreign newspapers and magazines depends, in large measure, on the nature of the product that is advertised. From this standpoint, these advertising media must be carefully studied in order to prevent unnecessary waste of funds.

Problems in Using Foreign Publications. Several serious difficulties may confront advertisers in most foreign publications. It is generally considered that in many foreign countries advertising is behind in its development, when compared with American advertising. This not true of all publications or of all countries, but the export advertiser is likely to find a different appreciation of advertising abroad from that at home.

Some of the difficult problems that may be encountered are:

1. Difficulty of ascertaining circulation figures. There is seldom to be found abroad any complement of the ABC (Audit Bureau of Circulation) in the United States. Reliable circulation figures for all or a certain number of publications are obtained through ABC or a foreign equivalent in the United Kingdom and the Dominions (Canada, Australia, New Zealand, South Africa, India), Norway, Sweden, Denmark, Argentina, Puerto Rico, Mexico, Venezuela, and Dominican Republic. There is a slow growth abroad in appreciating the value of independent audits of circulation. Therefore, the circulation claims of foreign newspapers and magazines may or may not be accurate.

2. Ascertaining class and sex of readers.

3. Accurate analysis of the purchasing power of readers may also be difficult.

4. Political views of newspapers in foreign countries are often pronounced and the class of readers, for example, liberal, radical, progressive, and labor, may be determined from this attitude. The editorial views of some newspapers may eliminate them from consideration for advertising purposes by American exporters, particularly when these views are un-American or anti-American. In times when the national interest of the United States may not be concerned, however, anti-American editorials may not necessarily be taken seriously.

5. Ascertaining rates and space. The one-price system is an American institution and has yet to win approval throughout the world. There may be alternate haggling and bargaining in dealing with publishers abroad. Sometimes so-called "American" advertising rates are higher than for local advertisers. The higher American rate is claimed

to be due to the inclusion of an allowance for the publisher representative's commission, in addition to an advertising agency commission. The United States representatives of international publications advertising and foreign editors should be considered part of overhead.

6. Lack of uniformity of column width and page size, which results in greater production expense for the advertiser.

In addition to the national press, there are newspapers and magazines of other nationalities published in foreign countries. Some United States papers are published abroad, for example, *European Herald Tribune*. Such media may possess a wide appeal when it is considered that publications in English are read by the British, by the Americans, and by many educated local residents.

Direct-Mail Advertising

Direct-mail advertising, in its accepted sense, consists of all forms of publicity sent by an advertiser to prospective customers with the intention and hope of influencing or consummating a sale. In its most extended use by an exporting manufacturer or export house, it provides a flexible counterpart of publication advertising.

Direct-mail advertising is most effective when purchases may be made locally or where inquiries may be addressed to a local dealer or sales office. Direct-mail advertising consists principally of various forms of printed matter transmitted through the mails, for example, letters, catalogs, house organs, booklets, and a large number of miscellaneous forms such as calendars and blotters, which are so well-known in the United States.

Circularization. Circular letters, either individual or in series, are used extensively in international marketing as part of the advertising program.

Export Catalogs. Another direct-mail piece of advertising is the export catalog. An export catalog should provide the sales force necessary to sway a prospect into attention, then consideration, conviction, and finally action. It has to tell its own story and answer all manner of questions or objections that might be raised and otherwise go unchallenged. The catalog cannot argue and convince as does the salesman—it tells its story and then closes its cover.

Motion Pictures (Cinema)

International theater screen advertising is gaining increased recognition as a major, effective and growing medium.[7]

In countries too small to support quality magazines and newspapers, cinema advertising enjoys considerable success. Many theaters in small

[7] International Advertising Association, *International Advertiser,* Vol. 1. No. 1 (June, 1960), p. 10.

countries sell commercial film time. In certain areas, however, audiences have grumbled about the quality of cinema advertising, and some governments (Brazil for example) have issued decrees banning them.[8]

It is often thought that theater advertising is restricted only to the showing of "spot" commercials on the theater screen. However, in many world markets, in addition to showing spot commercials we find that they are also running soft-sell short subjects, and newsreels containing paid-for news items such as the opening of a client's store or similar promotional activity. Ever growing in importance is the use of theatres for merchandising. This includes giving out samples, distributing redeemable coupons and also lobby displays. The last three activities are generally tied in with conventional spot commercials on the screen.

Cinema advertising is world-wide. The latest estimate is that there are 140 markets in which theater advertising plays an important role. As such markets grow in importance, an organization devoted exclusively to handling cinema advertising usually is formed. These theater advertising factors are grouped together into two world-wide organizations. The oldest is the *International Screen Advertising Services* with headquarters in London, England. This organization has more than 21 large theater advertising concerns as members and through them theater commercials can be booked in more than 100 world markets.

The second world organization is the *International Screen Publicity Association*. These two organizations cooperate each year in holding the International Advertising Film Festival. Films are designed to take advantage of the large screen and generally tend toward a softer sell with emphasis on amusement values. This is out of respect to the "captive" nature of their audiences.

There are two main types of theater advertising: individual placement and package plans. Individual placement means that one orders a *specific* commercial exhibited in a specific theater for a specific time period. Package purchases involve either a number of theaters on a set circuit or the use of an entertainment vehicle such as a sportsreel, newsreel or revista short subject to encapsulate the commercial. Once spliced into such a short subject, the advertising film remains part of it during all its bookings.

Commercial Fairs and Exhibits

Commercial fairs and exhibits, held at regular intervals in many foreign cities, afford the exporter a novel method of publicity. Such events are more common and are more largely attended than are those in the United States, and in many instances they have attained a high reputation. By engaging space at a fair, distributing literature, and providing demonstrations, it may be possible to obtain good distribution connections abroad.

[8] *Advertising Age, op. cit.,* p. 93.

Among the various private and old established fairs are the Leipzig sample fairs that date from the Middle Ages. The International Sample Fair at Lyon, first held in 1419, annually attracts worldwide attention, and the same is true of the sample fair that has been held at Frankfort-on-Main since the year 1219. Of recent origin is the British Industries Fair that is held annually at London, Birmingham, and Glasgow. The Canadian National Exhibition held each year at Toronto is also wide in scope.

In recent years, as sales efforts have become more direct, American concerns have taken more interest in these events as exhibitors. Formerly they were visited almost exclusively by import buyers who found a wide display of foreign products.

Outdoor Advertising

"Outdoor advertising is one of the major advertising media throughout the world. The tremendous increase in the daily use of the automobile in many countries found corresponding increases in the importance of the outdoor medium." [9]

Outdoor advertising relates to billboards, electric or illuminated signs, and posters. As is true of every method of advertising when used abroad, it will be found that conditions vary widely throughout the world.

Aside from billboards, which are growing in number and effectiveness, located at heavily traveled points and in sporting areas, in a few countries some stores have painted advertisements which are colorful and attractive on walls, doors or metal store front closures.

A new type of display made from thousands of oversized, vari-colored sequins has made its appearance in a few countries. Usually this sign is limited to trade-marks, trade names, or simple designs. If properly located, this display has a glittering, live brilliance which attracts the eye even from a distance.

Some companies have made good use of small, permanent, all-weather enameled metal signs. Sometimes the product trademark or company name could be illustrated without the need for text matter; thus the sign was purchased in bulk for universal distribution. Frequently such signs were purchased and distributed from abroad at a considerable saving. However, companies and their foreign representatives were unanimous in their opinion that the placing of the sign must be done by the manufacturer or his own representative. . . .

The judicious distribution at sporting events of eye shades and fans with advertising messages is effective for some products, as are wall or wallet calendars. However, these are so acceptable that the advertiser must be prepared to meet a demand of astronomical proportions.

[9] International Advertising Association, *Code of Standards of Advertising Practice* (New York, 1961), p. 103.

Bus cards are good, especially for products usually bought by the bus riders. However, most buses are overcrowded; therefore interior cards are of doubtful value. The outside cards are more visible and the preferred position, those on the back of the bus.

Specific consideration should be given to permanent metal signs in areas where heat, humidity, or other severe weather conditions would make other types of outdoor signs impractical. Under the most favorable conditions, outdoor advertising is managed with the same ease and it produces the same results as in the United States. In many places, however, centralized ownership of outdoor advertising facilities is lacking, rates are not fixed, and municipal ordinances may hinder their employment. Long-range home office supervision is out of the question and branch house, dealer, or agency control over outdoor advertising of all kinds is essential.

Light standards are also equipped in some countries for carrying advertisements. It is true, however, that electric signs, including neon, are nowhere as widely to be found as in the United States; and it is generally admitted that no country has succeeded quite so well in effectively concealing landscapes behind billboards. One American company is fortunate in having a name that lends itself to ingenious Spanish advertising by means of illuminated electric signs. Admiral uses a step by step flashing message in Spanish. The first flash reveals MIRA (Spanish for look!); then follows ADMIRA (Spanish for admire!); finally, the complete name is shown ADMIRAL.

Radio

In recent years, radio advertising has attracted wide and increasing attention and American advertisers have been prompt in investigating possibilities of the radio for promoting foreign sales.

Radio advertising in international marketing is conducted almost entirely through local broadcasting stations abroad. These stations are either government owned and controlled (generally accepting no advertising) or they are independent. Many of them broadcast both long- and shortwave. Radio chains have been slow in developing in the various countries.

Radio advertising has shown vast drawing power, particularly for promoting the sale of consumer goods. This is of special value in advertising in countries with low literacy ratios, but with purchasing power for the advertised product. The number of radio listeners in an overseas area, such as Latin America, cannot be accurately determined from the estimated number of radio-receiving sets because of the installation of loud speakers at public squares, markets, cafes, drug and department stores, beaches, hotels, and amusement resorts.

Television

Television, the newcomer to the advertising media field (having been introduced in the United States as recently as 1947), is arousing the same interest abroad that it has in this country. Progress of installing television transmitting stations in foreign countries was slow due to the great expense of the equipment.

Three systems of controlling television are in effect throughout the world today:

1. The multiple enterprise system used in the United States and in Latin America.

2. The monopolistic system used, for example, in Belgium and France.

3. The combination system such as used in Italy and Great Britain.

Multiple Enterprise System. Under this system numerous broadcasting stations are permitted to operate; and they operate for commercial profit. This system is the plan used in the United States.

Monopolistic system. No commercial broadcasting is permitted under the monopolistic system. In France, for example, television is controlled by Radiodiffusion Télèvision Français (RTF). "General programs are varied in scope and content, including drama, films, newsreels, sports, panel shows, and Eurovision." The last named, Eurovision, was pioneered by RTF and BBC (British Broadcasting Company) television and consists of a network linking eight European countries—the United Kingdom, Switzerland, the Netherlands, Italy, German Federal Republic, France, Denmark, and Belgium.

Combination System. Under this system, used in Great Britain and in Italy, "prior to 1955, British TV viewers on a particular night were treated to a one and one-half hour program called, 'The Development of the Lung Fish.' Viewers were either left gasping for breath or irrevocably opposed to 'culture' in such large doses." In 1955, the Independent Television Authority (ITA) was formed and was placed under the control of the Postmaster General. All television facilities are owned, in the name of the government, by the Postmaster General who grants concessions to four private program contractors. These contractors now command 70 to 90 percent of the television audience and obtain revenue from commercials. Advertisers do not control nor sponsor programs. The commercials are sold adjacent to or within the programs.

Italy permits no live commercials; but film commercials are permitted for two and one-fourth minutes, of which only 20 seconds may be used for actual selling. The remaining one minute and fifty-five seconds must show anything considered to be quality entertainment.

S. Watson Dunn:

The International Language of Advertising

WHEN the marketing executives of Standard Oil of New Jersey tried to convince their marketing counterparts in the various Standard Oil subsidiaries, affiliates, and joint ventures in Europe that they should adopt the now famous "Tiger in your tank" campaign in each of these markets, they were told, quite emphatically I understand, that the campaign—fine as it was for the United States—just would not work in these countries. The Europeans, however, were finally persuaded to give the campaign a try, and the result is a classic success story of how to internationalize advertising. Last summer I asked the head of McCann-Erickson's Paris office why so many European businessmen had resisted the campaign, and he said many still feel you have to be a native to know how to persuade people of a given country.

Let me cite another instance before we try to decide what we mean by the "international language of advertising." Approximately a year ago Kraft Foods beamed by means of satellite a closed circuit telecast originating in New York to the company's annual international management conference in Burgenstock, Switzerland. This was part of Kraft's continuing plan, according to its present, William Beers, to find out how to use international commercial television to create an international image for the company and its products. There are, of course, a few language problems to be considered, but this is not, according to Kraft officials, as much of a problem as it might seem, because the commercials depend heavily on the visual to get their story across. Even though some of the products are regional in appeal, some, such as processed cheese, for example, are sufficiently international that they could be promoted almost anywhere in the world.

After considering these and many other examples, after supervising a series of research studies in Europe and the Middle East, and after talking at some length with many of the older and more experienced international marketers, I have come to the conclusion that we are moving quite rapidly toward an international language of advertising. It is my contention that we are building an international language of symbols,

▶ From: *Some International Challenges to Advertising*, ed. by Hugh W. Sargent. Copyright © 1967 by Department of Advertising, University of Illinois, Urbana, Illinois. Reprinted by permission of the publisher and the author.

some of which are pictorial—for example, illustrations of certain "international types" of people and logotypes like that of IBM—and some of which are word symbols understandable in any language—for example, "OK" and "marketing." It is quite possible in fact that international advertising reaches more people than any other type of message emanating from a foreign source, that Mrs. Popapopoulis in Athens or Señora Gomez in Argentina is more likely to see or hear some foreign advertising message than she is to see or hear some message from U.S. Information Agency or its counterpart in some other country. Although reliable data on international investments by advertisers are hard to come by, it is fairly clear that the top three or four U.S. advertisers spend more in foreign advertising and promotion than the U.S.I.A. has to spend on all its various operations outside the United States.

This is not to say that basic differences in cultures are lacking. In fact, I suspect that one must have a pretty good knowledge of cultural differences to be able to use international advertising effectively. Our cultural anthropologists have studied and reported on many of these differences. Edward Hall, for example, has related many of them to the problem of communication in his book, *The Silent Language*.[1] He points out that a common way for an Iranian male to communicate his manliness is to throw a temper tantrum—for example, the famous ones of Mossadegh a few years ago. Most Americans think it shows you have a low opinion of a person if you keep him waiting to see you when he has an appointment. On the other hand, many Latin Americans find it surprising that Americans should feel offended at what seems to them such a minor occurrence. Or consider how the broad humor of the Old West offends many Orientals who prefer humor in its more subtle forms.

The various *prototype* campaigns represent a recognition that there is a sort of international creative approach that works in a variety of markets. When he prepares such a campaign, the American advertiser is saying to marketing people in his foreign subsidiaries, or his licensees or distributors, that a layout or a copy theme which worked in the United States is pretty likely to work there too, provided there is a good translation of the verbal material and there is some checking to see that the ad does not violate any foreign taboos. Some companies, for example, Coca Cola and Remington Rand, appear to have had considerable success with prototype material. Some have run into resistance on the part of local marketing people, and some U.S. companies just do not bother to prepare prototype material at all.

Findings in Case and Field Studies

During these next few years many an advertiser will face the problem of determining to what extent he should internationalize his advertising.

[1] Edward T. Hall, *The Silent Language* (New York: Doubleday & Co., 1959).

In an effort to throw some light on this complicated question and to gain certain information as a guide for planning our field studies, I conducted, in 1964-1965, a series of case studies of the foreign campaigns of thirty large international advertisers.[2] Most of these were U.S. corporations and most focused on a campaign in one western European country and one underdeveloped country. We were trying to find out under what conditions sophisticated and experienced marketers were using domestic campaigns abroad. We found that one criterion was the type of product advertised. For example, six out of seven food companies we studied made only minimal effort to internationalize their promotion. It was felt by the executives concerned that food preferences and eating habits varied so much from one market to another that common appeals or ads were fruitless. On the other hand advertisers of patent medicines tended to use much the same approach in all markets—the prevention of disease or the relief of discomfort. However, in a few cases they had to change certain symbols. For example, Vicks promoted its Vaporub for the relief of cold discomfort in children in a wide variety of countries. In the Arab countries the company substituted illustrations of little boys for those of little girls since the health of a little boy is a matter of somewhat more importance there than that of a little girl. We found also that international advertising and marketing experts used certain marketing criteria to determine the transferability of campaigns: What is the competition doing? They used certain cultural criteria: Are there any real cultural or psychological barriers to acceptance of this campaign in that market? And they used media considerations: Are the media for which we designed this campaign in the U.S. available also in the new market?

We followed up these case studies with a series of field tests in France and Egypt.[3] We ended up with some very convincing evidence that the language of advertising is indeed more international than many people seem to suspect. We were trying to find out under what conditions an American advertisement would be successful in a foreign market. The five products we chose were all low-priced convenience items, and all the ads had been run in at least one American magazine. We used three variations of the illustrative material and two of the headlines and copy—all of them consistent with the original creative platform. One of the illustrations was the original as used in an American magazine, one replicated this illustration with French models and another with Egyptian models. One version of the copy and headlines consisted of an idiomatic translation into French and Arabic. The other was composed from the original by a professional copywriter of the country. The audiences consisted of a good sample of

[2] "Case Study Approach in Cross-Cultural Research," *Journal of Marketing Research* Vol. III (February 1966), pp. 13-24.
[3] See Final Report, Group Psychology Branch, Office of Naval Research, Contract Nonr 1202 (24), "Study of the Influence of Certain Cultural and Content Variables on the Effectiveness of Persuasive Communications in the International Field."

middle and upper middle class consumers in the largest city in each country and we used three measures of effectiveness for each ad. All of us who worked on the study were somewhat surprised to find how little difference there was in the effectiveness of the various versions—regardless of which measure of effectiveness you used. There was little evidence indeed to support the fact that in a case such as this you needed a local model or that you needed to attribute the message to a local—as compared with a foreign—source and only limited evidence that the message started from scratch was more effective than a good, refined translation from the U.S. original. The skill with which the material was translated was more influential in the case of France than of Egypt. I should point out, though, that the type of products chosen were ones we knew were used internationally, and the appeals featured in the ads violated no cultural or other taboos in these countries.

I should point out, too, that the audience was not a mass audience but was instead an urban, middle class one. Some people maintain that there is within each country an audience which looks for foreign symbols, foreign clothes, and foreign movies and that it prides itself on being distinct from the mass audience, so perhaps our audiences were too atypical. However, I am inclined to suspect that we have, within each country, many international audiences, one tuned to sports, another to music, another to food, and so forth. In general, the study raised as many questions as it answered. For example, why were the Egyptians more influenced by *all* versions than the French? Would the results have been different if the respondents had seen different brands of the same product instead of different products? If we had had a measure of the self-confidence or the expertise or the sophistication of these respondents would the results have been different?

Implications of Research Findings

I would like now to explore some of the implications of the developments I have been discussing—for business, for government, and for society in general.

First of all, there is the implication that some of these days you will be able to avoid the waste of starting over again when a campaign is transferred to a foreign market. And what a saving this could be! Think how scarce really good creative concepts are. And how much we need to get full use from a really good one. Think how much better it would be if we could use the original—or at least a good part of it—to communicate in another market. This implies, though, that the creative people or whoever works with them will know enough about foreign communication and culture to make needed changes but will still have the know-how and the guts to insist that foreign advertisers keep what is worth keeping.

Furthermore creative people have to be just as careful with the visual aspects of this advertising language as with the more obvious verbal pitfalls.

For example, a series of television commercials integrating white and colored persons was prepared in France for use in the United States by an American advertiser. Sometime after the commercials were in production the head of the Paris office of the American agency involved noted that one of the stars was not an American Negro, as planned, but was instead a Negro from French Africa with just enough difference in facial features to be noticeable. It was decided to recast the commercial.

I do not mean to imply that we can forget what we know and practice regarding market segmentation. Rather the developments I have been discussing mean that segmentation along national lines may become less important, that the differences between national and foreign markets will diminish, and that our markets will be segmented along more sophisticated, more meaningful demographic or perhaps even psychological lines.

This internationalization also implies that we may see a great spurt in the growth of truly international agencies and media. Although much is made these days of the fact that American agencies are establishing a multitude of offices abroad—frequently through purchase of a sizable stock interest in an ongoing agency—the fact is that a good many of these are American in name only. Many of these are native agencies with an American name and perhaps an American or two on the staff. I doubt that these need ever become truly American or even that they need have many American employees, but I think it is quite possible that their point of view might become more multinational, less parochial and nationalistic.

I would like to look also at some of the implications in fields other than advertising. For example, the field of economic growth. This is a fashionable topic these days, but most people who talk about it as applied to the underdeveloped areas worry mainly about how to increase agricultural or manufacturing output. However, I for one suspect that advertising can contribute a good deal to these economies just as it has to ours in the United States and to those of western Europe. We know that even in the days when the United States was truly one of the underdeveloped areas of the world, promotion played an important part in supporting the struggling media, in helping innovators with a real product advantage gain product acceptance, in informing consumers of product development. A lot of us have followed with interest the change in the Soviet party line since 1957 when advertising became for the first time quite respectable. Last year *Pravda* included the following:

> The more goods and products in the shops—the greater the need for advertising, for providing customers with systematic qualified information on the quality and features of one or another commodity and on where it can be bought.

The largest department store in Moscow, GUM, spends six million rubles a year ($5,400,000 at current exchange rates) on advertising and has a staff of fifty to handle print and broadcast advertising, window displays, commercials broadcast in the store, leaflets to be distributed on the counters and posters inside and outside the store. Moscow television currently carries five to ten minutes of advertising three or four times a week. We can hardly say that Russia is supporting advertising for sentimental reasons since encouraging it involved an embarrassing change in government policy. Instead we must conclude that there is substantial evidence that it contributes to that country's economic growth—even though it is a socialist economy.

Perhaps a more obvious implication of these developments lies in the field of propaganda. Arthur Meyerhoff in his *Strategy of Persuasion* insisted the United States has made a serious mistake in not "applying our sales techniques to selling ourselves and our ideas to other countries." [4] There are of course big differences between selling soap and selling our foreign policy, but there are also certain similarities. If U.S. marketers can find out how to communicate effectively with the various nations of the world, it seems highly advisable that the government use what is known to get its story across also. It is interesting to note that the new director of the U.S.I.A. is already at work exploring how advertising measurement methods can be used to test the effectiveness of some of the organization's communications program. A series of meetings devoted to this topic were held recently, and selected specialists in advertising research were invited to participate.

Most Americans are a bit wary of propaganda—even the name has a bad connotation. In addition we are inclined to be sensitive about being the big nation of the world and to worry about throwing our weight around. Consequently, the evidence is that our government's programs have been heavy on information but light on persuasion. However, if we learn how to communicate across national borders should not we share it with our government?

We should also consider the other side of the coin—the possible negative aspects of internationalizing our language. We may look back twenty years from now and wish we had not been quite so successful in our internationalizing efforts. Perhaps when we find out how to use this international language, how to apply this common denominator of persuasion, we may at the same time level some of the values and the customs that make one region so different from another. Perhaps we shall no longer be able to say about some of those charming spots in western Europe, "*Vive la différence.*" Many of them will undoubtedly retain their basic charm, but there is bound to be a certain lessening of the differences that give a country or region its basic character. If the people of Germany respond so readily to the language of the Beatles—whatever it is—and the people of Vietnam quicken to Batman, how can we avoid a certain lessening of differences in values and in customs from country to country?

[4] Arthur E. Meyerhoff, *The Strategy of Persuasion* (New York: Coward-McCann, Inc., 1965) p. 15.

Suggestions for Utilizing International Language in Advertising

Some advertisers are making out fairly well these days in using this international language of advertising. Many are not doing so well. What needs to be done?

First of all, I think we must find out a lot more about it than we know now. We must have research. Doesn't it seem strange that we have so little research evidence in the area of advertising where we are least at home and where the pitfalls are the greatest—in the international field? Most of you can probably put your hands on studies of almost any market I could name in the United States—and even if you couldn't find research evidence, you could probably make out pretty well without it. But think how different the situation is in the international field. Now I realize the problems one may run into in international research—for example, the cost, the scarcity of trained personnel, the difficulty of getting cooperation from audiences, and so on. However, these are often overestimated. At any rate they are certainly not insurmountable.

I would like to repeat a proposal I made at the Stockholm meetings of the International Advertising Association in 1963. At that time I suggested that the leading international agencies, advertisers, and media cooperate in the establishment of an international advertising research organization. More specifically I would like to suggest that we have this organization set up several international advertising experiment stations in major cities of the world—for example, New York, London, Paris, Frankfurt, and Tokyo. Campaigns from various clients and various countries would be tested simultaneously in these areas. Some evidence could be gained fairly quickly regarding the effectiveness of alternative creative or media or even overall promotional strategies. Comparisons could be made among countries and even among groups within a particular country. We have come a long way in the use of the experimental approach in advertising—note, for example, the Milwaukee Advertising Laboratory and the experimental work of Du Pont and of Ford Motor Company. My predecessor at the University of Illinois, C. H. Sandage, has for some years advocated a U.S. advertising experiment station. Why not put the same idea into effect on an international scale?

My second suggestion is that we get busy educating people for the international advertising field. There is a notion in certain firms that a person who can operate effectively in this country can do just as well in the international field. I am not at all certain this is true when I observe some of the failures in international advertising and marketing. I am proposing that we try to train people to be international communicators just as we train foreign service officers for our government and international lawyers for our big law firms. It is true that certain people have better personalities and more aptitude for the international field than others, but all can profit from the right kind of training.

What kind of education do we need to provide? I think we can benefit from the experience of the successful advertising education programs around our American universities. Emphasis would be placed on a strong liberal arts base with considerable stress on languages and social science. The international adman should know psychology, cultural anthropology, economics, and marketing. However, he should also know something of the philosophy and practice of advertising with particular emphasis on problem solving and decision making in the international field. How much more efficient it is to provide university training in these areas than to expect on-the-job training to prepare people properly.

A good deal of attention is paid these days to the problem of attracting bright, young college graduates to the business field. A lot of these students believe that the horizons in government or teaching are less confining than business and that the pay there is after all satisfactory for their needs. A program geared to international horizons just might attract students who feel that business as a whole—and particularly advertising —is a little too shallow to challenge the best that they have to offer. To work though, such a program would need a lot more support than the advertising industry has so far been willing to give to advertising education. It would need moral as well as financial support. Recently the "Adwoman of the Year," Jo Foxworth of Calkins and Holden, pointed out in a speech that "there is a particular piece of arrogance in the ad business which holds that advertising can not be learned in school . . . that it can be learned only on Madison Avenue by a process of osmosis." Miss Foxworth could not be more correct. The interesting thing is that this situation does not hold in such other creative areas as art and music or in such other business areas as accounting or business law. There it is taken for granted that a person must undergo certain training before starting his professional career.

Third, I would suggest that advertising campaigns be planned on a multinational basis. When you collect the planning facts, when you work out the media and the creative strategy, expect that it will be applied to many markets, not just to one. Assume that the segmenting is along demographic lines—age, sex, and the like—or along user lines—heavy vs. light— and that it may or may not follow national boundaries.

And, finally, I would suggest that we accept the fact that the United States is not the only country where advertising talent—creative, research or any other kind—abounds. A few years ago we could say that the *word* was in the U.S. and if you wanted to learn how to communicate through advertising you had better get your feet wet on Madison Avenue. But take a look at some of the graphics they are using in Western Europe and Japan. Or look at some of the cinema commercials from France or Italy. We can learn a lot from them—not only on how to communicate with their country, but also how to communicate in our own country.

Some of these foreign advertising examples represent the language of advertising at its creative best.

There are many more questions I might raise, but I had better not because I am not sure I can propose even tentative answers. What, for example, is the role of the verbal versus the visual in communicating in a foreign area? Is a television campaign more international than one in print? These are among the questions I would like to leave to you.

Gordon E. Miracle:

Client's International Advertising Policies and Procedures

IF advertising agencies are to grow, they must adapt themselves to the policies of their clients in such matters as the planning and preparation of promotional programs, the control of advertising budgets, the use of cooperative advertising, and the selection and use of advertising agencies.

PLANNING PROMOTIONAL PROGRAMS

A promotional program may include such activities as consumer advertising, personal selling, sales aids, and a wide range of additional promotional efforts. Planning an international promotional program involves essentially the same activities as planning domestic promotional strategy, namely: (1) setting promotional objectives; (2) deciding on the types of advertising and promotional messages; (3) selecting media; and (4) determining how much time, effort, and money to spend. Ideally, the role of the advertising agency should be essentially the same whether an international or a domestic program is being planned.

The planning of an international promotional program can be accomplished: (1) by headquarters personnel, with or without the services of a multinational agency, (2) through joint efforts of headquarters and local personnel, with the services of either a domestic agency with foreign offices, or local independent agencies; or (3) by local personnel, usually assisted by local agencies. In the case of centralized planning, the staff at headquarters may permit varying degrees of adaptation of the plan by local personnel. When planning is joint or decentralized, the company's policy may vary widely between two extremes: The company may exercise careful, centralized guidance in developing the plan, with approval of the final plan coming from headquarters; or it may allow local personnel nearly full responsibility for planning. The greater the centralized direction and control, the greater the need for closely coordinated agency service, especially by the agency's branch offices.

Among companies with subsidiaries, the trend is toward greater centralized guidance and joint planning between headquarters, subsidiaries,

▶ From: *Management of International Advertising: The Role of Advertising Agencies,* by Gordon E. Miracle. Copyright © 1966 by Bureau of Business Research, Graduate School of Business Administration, University of Michigan, Ann Arbor, Mich. Reprinted by permission of the publisher.

and their advertising agencies. But companies using licensees to manufacture abroad, or distributors to sell abroad, ordinarily depend on their
licensees or distributors to formulate the program; such manufacturers
usually confine their efforts to providing general information, guidance,
and support.

To date, most companies using licensees or distributors have not felt a
strong need for the services of an advertising agency with foreign branches
or associates. Local licensees or distributors usually work with a local
agency. However, in the future there may be increased need for centralized
services provided by an advertising agency, since the trend among companies seems to be toward greater participation by headquarters in planning the promotional programs of subsidiaries and also of licensees,
distributors, and dealers.

Joint planning of promotional programs varies from complete reliance
on mail and telephone communication to frequent travel by specialists
from the company headquarters and the advertising agency to work locally.
In some companies, the international division advertising manager (or
members of his staff) and representatives of their advertising agency participate in discussions at the planning sessions of subsidiaries. The local
advertising agency people may play a significant role at these sessions.
Under such circumstances, it is advantageous if the local agency is a
branch, or at least an associate agency, of the agency employed by corporate headquarters.

When local expertise is more important than centralized coordination
by a U.S. advertising agency, and when communication with subsidiaries
is handled primarily by mail or telephone, local associates or agency
branch offices often play a major role in planning local programs. Thus
there is relatively less need for branches; associates may be quite satisfactory.

While local advertising men abroad, including those working for
agencies, are growing increasingly capable and sophisticated, many U.S.
advertisers feel that it is desirable to implement in foreign operations the
carefully developed planning procedures and approaches employed in the
United States. Since new techniques in planning promotional programs
and solving promotional mix problems often are developed first in this
country, regular contact between U.S. and foreign personnel is desirable.
When staff members from the company and agency headquarters work
together with personnel from foreign subsidiaries and their local advertising agencies, the transfer of relevant experience from one area of the
world to another is facilitated. Under such conditions, it is likely that a
U.S. advertising agency with branches abroad can serve the client better
than a foreign agency can. Thus, an incentive exists for U.S. agencies to
expand through branch offices in which they have at least a controlling
interest.

PREPARING PROMOTIONAL PROGRAMS

An international promotional program may consist of international advertising campaigns, selling campaigns, or sales promotion campaigns, or some combination of these. Advertising campaigns, in turn, are of several types; for example, those conducted in international media, in local foreign media, or cooperative advertising with distributors. Such promotional activities as point-of-purchase displays, or press releases contributing to the reputation of the company or its products, may also be an integral part of a promotional program.

The most common media utilized are: (1) international media, such as international magazines, newspapers, and trade journals; (2) foreign newspapers, magazines, trade journals, radio and television; (3) direct mail; (4) outdoor media such as billboards and signs on moving vehicles; (5) aids for salesmen and retailers, such as brochures, point-of-purchase displays, catalogs, and manuals; and (6) miscellaneous promotional items such as calendars, blotters, and pens. It will be convenient to deal first with campaigns in international media and then proceed to a discussion of campaigns in foreign media. The discussion will emphasize those media for which advertising agency service is ordinarily utilized.

International media

Although a majority of large companies with foreign operations advertise in international magazines or trade journals, the amount they spend on these publications is relatively small compared with what they spend on foreign media; most budgets of the companies studied were between $50,000 and $350,000.

Typically, campaigns in international media are planned by the advertising manager of the international division and his staff and their advertising agency. Some advertisers and their agencies seek materials from selling locations abroad, such as suggested layouts or art work. More frequently, however, the advertising agency does the creative work without extensive guidance from abroad. Only rarely does a subsidiary or branch exercise any direct influence on preparation of advertisements for international media. Most companies utilize either a domestic or an "expert" agency to prepare and produce advertisements which are to be run in international media; thus they do not need an agency with offices abroad which can provide a full range of agency services in foreign markets.

Some companies send proofs of all "international media" advertisements to subsidiaries or distributors; some also produce engravings or plastic plates to send abroad for use either in local foreign media or foreign-based international media. Although most advertisers now perform this function themselves, some would prefer to have their advertising agency do it. If an agency is to perform this function properly on a regular basis, it must have branch offices or closely controlled associates. Of the two, advertisers tend to prefer branch offices.

Foreign media

Company policies on the preparation and placement of advertisements in foreign media range from virtually complete control by headquarters personnel to virtually complete autonomy by local personnel. To some extent the policies of companies vary according to company product lines, organization, and method of doing business abroad, but not nearly so much as might be expected. Manufacturers with similar products, selling in similar markets, often follow decidely different policies. Greater availability of competent multinational advertising agency service could result in substantial constructive improvements in the policies of many advertisers.

Centralized preparation of advertisements. Only a small proportion of companies insist that subsidiaries use centrally prepared advertisements exclusively. But those few do require comprehensive, coordinated multinational service of the type which ordinarily can be made available best by an agency with wholly owned branch offices.

As a practical matter, centralized preparation of advertisements usually requires that subsidiaries and their advertising agencies send to company headquarters their ideas and recommendations for copy themes, layout, and illustrations. Then the home office staff and its advertising agency can prepare either a prototype campaign for use or adaptation by several subsidiaries or tailor-made campaigns for individual subsidiaries. Headquarters may make all campaigns available to all subsidiaries so that the campaigns, or modified versions of them, may be requested for use wherever appropriate. Under these conditions, closet coordination, understanding, and cooperation between the advertising agency employed by headquarters and those employed by the subsidiaries is highly desirable. Moreover, from the financial standpoint, it is desirable for an agency to have foreign branch offices, or at least a close working relationship with foreign associates, so that the agency receives adequate compensation for the creative work used in those advertisements placed in foreign media by the local agencies.

Local preparation of advertisements. Companies leaving creative responsibility to subsidiaries and their local advertising agencies may provide central support, advice, and assistance, or they may simply establish broad policy guidelines. A few of the companies that provide central guidance and assistance also require that locally prepared advertisements be submitted to headquarters for approval. However, most companies do not pass final judgment on each and every creative effort produced by their subsidiaries.

Does the advantage of achieving a uniform world-wide image vary according to the characteristics of the product and market? Do companies give greater support and central guidance to those products which can be differentiated by advertising and which would gain most from a uniform well-known image? An examination of a sample of companies failed to indicate a clear pattern. For example, some producers of inexpensive consumer items, such as cosmetics, pens and pencils, and packaged goods, try to establish a uniform image and reputation, while others do not. Likewise, some manufacturers of household appliances give considerable advertising support to their local distributors, while other manufacturers give little. Although there are many reasons for the varying company policies in these areas, it seems likely that some manufacturers could use the services of a multinational advertising agency to good advantage; but often an agency with the requisite capabilities is not available. There is a need for more agencies with closely controlled branches or associates.

Central advertising assistance. The assistance which may be rendered to local personnel may range from preparing complete campaigns to giving advice only when it is solicited. The headquarters staff may prepare such aids as selling appeals, art work, photographs, sample copy or layout, complete print advertisements, complete radio commercials, and complete slide or film commercials. The materials may be intended for a variety of media, including newspapers, magazines, radio, cinema, television, direct mail, billboards; or sales promotional devices such as posters, point-of-purchase displays, catalogs, manuals, sales literature, brochures, calendars, novelties, or even dealers' signs. Although U.S. advertising agencies often prepare many of these materials for domestic use, only a few agencies are capable of preparing them for use abroad. Moreover, a domestic agency may be unenthusiastic about preparing materials which foreign agencies will use. Since advertising agencies ordinarily prefer to receive the full commission for their efforts, there is an incentive to establish branch offices abroad.

The means and frequency of providing assistance also varies. Some companies simply send out an occasional yearly corporate policy manual and corporate advertisement book containing samples of current advertisements from domestic divisions, while others regulary, transfer *all relevant materials* between *all locations*, foreign and domestic. A majority of large international advertisers have some provision for the transfer of advertising materials from headquarters to foreign subsidiaries, licensees, or distributors. But few companies provide for the transfer of materials from one foreign location to another; and it is quite rare for materials produced abroad to be transferred to, and used by, domestic divisions. The most common arrangement is for the international division to serve as a clearing house to transfer materials to foreign locations whenever the man in charge of this activity deems it appropriate. A small but growing number of companies transfer automatically to foreign locations most or all materials which are produced abroad or by the international division.

Companies transferring materials regularly prefer that an advertising agency with branches abroad handle this function. Generally, advertisers feel that there are too few agencies able or willing to do this, and even when agencies undertake this task, they often fail to handle it satisfactorily. Most agencies' clients seem to feel that there is room for considerable improvement in this aspect of agency service, although agencies with controlled branches usually handle the transferal function better than those which rely on associates.

Selection of foreign media. Selection of foreign media ordinarily is left to local personnel. The home office rarely reviews such decisions, and even then cursorily. Since media conditions differ substantially from country to country,[1] most home offices will simply establish general policy guidelines on the use of media, such as insisting on the use of measured media rather than permitting such promotional devices as cocktail parties or unauthorized premiums and novelties.

Guidelines for media policy may include a set of criteria to be used by foreign locations in evaluating media. Frequently they are about the same as the guidelines utilized by the firm in the domestic market. The criteria vary somewhat from company to company but generally include: (1) circulation and readership of print media—or set ownership, listenership, and viewership of broadcast media; (2) the character, reputation, or image of the media; (3) media rates and cost per prospect; and (4) mechanical requirements, especially as they may affect the costs of producing advertisements.

For media placement and control, advertisers often prefer an agency with branches abroad, since they may be used effectively to insure local adherence to the company's corporate media policies. Branches can be kept informed on the most sophisticated media selection techniques, which can be used when appropriate. In addition, centralized control through branches permits a company to utilize more fully what is known about its competitors' activities throughout the world, since branches can be directed to set up an effective communication system to exchange information on competitors. The use of branches also facilitates control of world-wide or regional campaigns, when and if it seems desirable to use them.

In spite of the advantages of some degree of centralized guidance, the trend is toward greater decentralization of the media selection and placement function. Nevertheless, since U.S. agencies have relatively sophisticated media selection skills, the foreign office of a multinational

[1] See for example Colin McIver, "Formulating Media Strategy for Foreign Markets," *International Handbook of Advertising*, ed. S. Watson Dunn (New York: McGraw-Hill Book Co., Inc., 1964), pp. 133-39.

agency may have an advantage over local agencies. Advertising agencies which control foreign branch offices may combine the advantages of local selection of media with those of centralized coordination, guidance, and exchange of information.

SELECTION OF ADVERTISING AGENCIES

Company policies on the selection and utilization of agencies for international advertising have a direct bearing on how agencies should organize to serve clients abroad. Since company policies on the selection of agencies for export advertising (in markets served by licensees or distributors) differ from policies on the selection of agencies for subsidiaries, it is convenient to divide the discussion along those lines.

Export advertising

Export advertising is used here to mean advertising for the purpose of promoting either a company's reputation or the sale of domestically produced products in foreign markets.

Since general criteria for selection of an export agency are about the same as for selection of a domestic agency, the company's international division or export department is likely to follow a policy similar to the company's domestic policy. In fact, frequently the agency with the domestic account has the inside track to the export account. The agency and client already have an established working relationship; the agency's personnel already are familiar with the company's products; and the experience gained in the domestic market is likely to be useful in the preparation of successful export campaigns.

In order to handle both domestic and export advertising, an agency is expected to have some experience in export advertising and to have foreign facilities to prepare and place advertisements. It is considered especially desirable for an agency to have foreign offices. However, capable foreign associate agencies often are considered acceptable—in fact, even preferred by a few.

Since not enough domestic agencies have the requisite foreign facilities, some advertisers must use a separate agency for export advertising. However, the majority of such advertisers would prefer to switch the account to the domestic agency, should it develop the capability of providing service comparable to that provided by an export agency. Opportunities exist for additional agencies to expand their international capabilities, particularly by establishing or acquiring their own branch offices.

SIGNIFICANCE FOR ADVERTISING AGENCIES

Approaches to the formulation of international promotional policies differ widely from company to company. Even among manufacturers of similar types of products, selling in similar foreign markets, there are some hard-to-explain differences in the planning process. Even more surprising, in some companies, is the marked difference in approach and procedures between the international and domestic divisions. Sometimes these differences appear justified, but in other cases a change in approach is indicated. Opportunities for advertising agencies to foster such changes are increasing. Generally, the opportunities seem to be greatest for agencies with controlled branch offices in those markets where clients require service.

The trend toward greater central participation is observable not only with regard to planning promotional programs but also in preparing, implementing, and controlling them. The major elements of international promotional programs are being coordinated and integrated to an increasing degree and, as a result, clients require cooperation and coordination among advertising agencies in several countries. Agencies with controlled branches often are better able than agencies with associates to meet the needs of their clients and to profit directly from their creative efforts, since the branches receive the full commission on local billings.

Since campaigns in international media usually are planned and controlled centrally, a domestic or "export" advertising agency often is considered satisfactory. Probably such agencies can expect to continue handling such campaigns for those clients who do not require more comprehensive international service.

However, the situation with regard to campaigns in foreign media is somewhat more complex. When an advertiser wishes to exercise some degree of central coordination or control, he typically prefers an advertising agency with a number of offices or associates abroad. The advertiser can then place the responsibility for initiating budget and campaign planning with the local subsidiary and advertising agency. They can be made responsible for establishing local advertising objectives, developing advertising strategy, selecting media, setting up media schedules, and developing a promotional budget. The local agency can maintain contact with the U.S. agency in order to ensure that all plans are in accordance with established policies and are within the framework of the total or worldwide promotional and advertising effort. Likewise, the advertiser's local subsidiary can maintain contact with the advertising staff of the corporation or international division and can coordinate with them as necessary. A majority of clients feel that if service is to be satisfactory, the local advertising agency should be a branch office of a U.S. agency.

The availability of advertising resources in the United States (especially technically competent advertising personnel), coupled with the advantages of long-term planning to determine what products to produce and sell in specified markets, makes some degree of centralized guidance and direction of advertising increasingly desirable. Probably the ideal that many companies are working to achieve combines: (1) *centralized strategic planning and policy making,* based on knowledge of corporate objectives and on information provided by the personnel of foreign subsidiaries and advertising agencies; and (2) *decentralized planning and execution of advertising and promotional campaigns,* carried out with the guidance and assistance of corporate and advertising agency personnel who can utilize experience and ideas from other countries.

Bertrand R. Canfield:

International Public Relations

A GROWING interest in public relations throughout the free world is a result of great technological, political, social, and economic changes which have given people of the emerging nations freedom of expression and recognition of the power of public opinion.

Great progress in telecommunications, making possible rapid and widespread transmission of information and ideas, has created unparalleled opportunities for people to communicate with each other and exert tremendous impact on world opinion.

The threat to the free world posed by communism and socialism is awakening the leaders of capitalistic countries to the need for exposing the fallacies of these doctrines and arousing public opinion in free nations in favor of capitalism.

United States' economic aid to foreign countries and private investments abroad make it necessary for business and government to employ public relations to protect our foreign investments and develop favorable public opinion abroad.

In undeveloped countries, expanded educational programs are making it possible for once illiterate people to read books, newspapers, and magazines and exert the power of enlightend public opinion on national and international issues.

In Europe, the Common Market of France, West Germany, Holland, Italy, Belgium, and Luxembourg has unified the European economy and created new opportunities to employ public relations to secure better understanding and good will throughout Europe. Higher living standards, rising employment, and a prosperous economy have combined to stimulate the practice of public relations.

Industrial, political, and social welfare organizations in many countries throughout the world are employing the public relations techniques, which have been originated and developed in the United States, to solve the problem of creating better understanding with employees, stockholders, neighbors, and consumers. Public relations associations have been established, and public relations departments created in government agencies, business, and social organizations in the most progressive nations.

Although the practice of public relations is making significant progress in countries throughout the world, particularly in Great Britain, Belgium, and France, public relations in the United States has attained a level of development unequaled in other countries.

Climate of Public Relations in Nations around the World

Public relations in many countries is developing in a much less favorable climate than in the United States. Established business practices and economic systems prevailing in many countries seriously handicap the development of the practice of public relations.

The traditional secrecy which surrounds the operations of many business concerns in many countries makes the management reluctant to reveal information about finances, policies, and operations. This reticence is detrimental to good public relations and restricts publicity opportunities.

European industry is monopolistic and does not recognize the desirability of cultivating the understanding and good will of the consuming public. Many large industrial enterprises are not concerned with informing and developing the good will of their employees. Industry in some countries is more interested in keeping the public in ignorance than in acquiring public understanding.

Many newspapers abroad refuse to use the name of industrial concerns in their news columns except for a consideration. News releases are only accepted from advertisers. Advertising contracts may provide that so many inches of advertising automatically entitles the advertiser to a certain number of "free news stories."

In many countries the term "public relations" has little or no meaning. It is usually used synonymously with advertising or product publicity.

In spite of these obstacles to the development of public relations, the practices of public relations in the United States are slowly being introduced abroad. The public relations associations in the principal countries, through discussions with the press and advertisers, are clarifying the meaning of public relations, adopting professional standards and codes of ethics, and securing acceptance of press publicity.

PUBLIC RELATIONS AROUND THE WORLD

In many nations of the free world, public relations is in its infancy. The term "public relations" is unknown in many languages. Modern techniques of public relations are gradually being adopted abroad as an essential function of government and business. The value of public relations is slowly being recognized through the efforts of pioneering practitioners in progressive countries who are explaining the American conception of public relations and showing how it can be used to develop public understanding by business, the professions, and government.

Much of the impetus for the development of public relations throughout the world has come from the United States. Many of the techniques which have become accepted in this country as standard practice are being adopted as public relations practices in other countries.

Public Relations in Great Britain

The substantial progress of public relations in Great Britain reflects the enterprise of the British Institute of Public Relations, the only representative organization of practitioners of public relations in the United Kingdom. Established in 1948, the Institute includes public relations officers in local and central governments, the armed forces, trade associations, industry, and counseling services.

The Institute has a 14-point development plan designed to protect and enhance the status of public relations in Great Britain and to raise the standard of practice of those engaged in public relations.

To place public relations on a par with the older professions, the Institute admits to membership only those persons who have a minimum of three years of practice, who are able to pass intermediate and final examinations of the Institute, and show evidence of professional competence. The Institute's written and oral examinations cover the principles and practice of public relations, printed material, advertising, press relations, opinion research, visual aids, and knowledge of a specialized field of public relations. The examinations are designed to evaluate a candidate's practical knowledge of the uses, techniques, and media of public relations.

To prepare candidates for admission to membership, the Institute has conducted an intermediate 60-period public relations course at the London Polytechnic consisting of lectures by practicing public relations executives supplemented with periods of field work and discussion. A final course of twelve seminars in public relations prepares for the final Institute examinations for candidates for membership. The textbook required in these courses is "A Guide to the Practice of Public Relations" published by the Institute in 1958. It was written by 24 leading practitioners who are members of the Institute and discusses the purpose and functions of public relations, the publics, consultancy, opinion research, and the media and organization for public relations in government, industry, and trade associations.

British Government Public Relations

British public relations is most highly developed in the areas of national and local government. In the central government ministries in England, the public relations officer and his staff keep the general public informed about the ministry's policies and functions. Close relations are maintained with the press through press notices, summaries, and conferences. Arrangements are made for radio and television features, photographs, news reels, and public visits. Educational campaigns and advertising are an important feature of the government public relations program.

Information service is an important function of the public relations staff in most British government ministries. Inquiry rooms are staffed to answer inquiries and provide information to the public calling in person, or by telephone, or to refer inquirers to government officials for further information. The public relations office of each ministry is also responsible for keeping the minister and officials aware of press and public opinion. Public relations offices are normally organized in three sections: press relations, publicity and inquiry, and intelligence.

In British municipal governments, the public relations officer is advised by a public relations committee and reports to the clerk of the municipal council. The public relations officer is politically impartial in his service to the corporate council and all departments of the local government. His functions include providing information and facilities to the press and other media; supervising public inquiries; arranging public meetings, lectures, and visits; producing and showing films; contacting local organizations; preparing and advising on publications; and providing the council with information on public opinion.

British Public Relations Media

The principal medium of public relations communication in Great Britain is the daily newspaper. The people of Great Britain are the greatest newspaper readers in the world, buying more than 28 million newspapers daily. Accordingly, British public relations departments usually include a press office to answer press inquiries, prepare "handouts," and arrange press conferences, entertainment, and facility visits. Press officers maintain a press information desk and reference library to answer inquiries from newspaper writers and editors. A record of all press inquiries is maintained and periodic analysis indicates trends in public interest and opinion.

Radio and television are also important media of communication with the British public which is licensed to receive programs of information, education, and entertainment broadcast by the government-owned-and-operated British Broadcasting Company. Twelve types of radio broadcasts are provided by the BBC: news, religious talks and discussions, music, drama features, documentaries, variety and light entertainment, outside programs, children's, schools, and political. Many of these programs provide public relations opportunities for noncommercial material.

The British Broadcasting Company also televises news, talks, music, drama, films, and women's, children's, and school programs. A television network supported by advertising revenue is operated by the government television authority which contracts with program companies to provide programs. Advertisers purchase time on the programs from the program companies but have no control over the content of the programs. The program companies, in addition to providing programs, pay an annual rent to the government authority for use of the broadcast facilities.

Public Relations in France

Public relations is becoming an important function in an increasing number of French commercial and industrial enterprises. French industrial public relations had its beginning in the period of economic progress following World War II, when a small group of public relations men led by Charles Louis Blondel, organized "La Maison de Verre" or "The House of Glass" which urged French managers to abandon traditional secrecy, live in "glass houses," and reveal their operations to the public. The Conseil National du Patronat Français, the leading federation of French industries, co-operated by sponsoring a program of plant visits which increased the number of plant visitors fiftyfold. Individual companies held open houses, established relations with schools, and initiated public relations programs.

In 1955, the Association Français des Relations Publiques, the French public relations association, was established to facilitate the development of public relations in France and to guide practitioners in the objectives and professional ethics of public relations. Today, 280 public relations managers and counselors are members of the Association.

The development of public relations in France has been handicapped by lack of trained, experienced practitioners; the opposition of advertising agencies and the press which looks upon public relations as "free publicity"; public prejudice against big business; the indifference of business management; and the limited public ownership of shares in corporations.

The most significant public relations programs in France are found in large industrial organizations; a few medium-sized firms confine their public relations activities to product publicity. Government agencies are also practitioners of public relations. The French Ministry of Posts and Tele-Communications, under its director of external relations, has a staff of 130 public relations field men who are responsible for community and press relations on the local level. These field men meet annually at the Ministry in Paris to hear from the Minister, Secretary General, and Director of External Relations how to improve understanding of the postal service by the public. The External Relations Department of the Ministry also produced motion pictures, a monthly publication for the general public, booklets and exhibits.

Public Relations in Italy

The organization for the advancement of public relations in Italy, Associazione Italiana per le Relazioni Pubbliche was established in Rome, in 1954, and has a membership of about 500 public relations managers and counselors. The Association has held seminars and courses for its members and staged the International Congress in Stresa in 1956 and a public relations convention in Rome in 1957. Regional public relations groups are organized in Naples and Milan.

A growing number of Italian firms are becoming interested in public relations, but there is a limited number of trained practitioners in Italy. The practice of public relations is handicapped by fundamental philosophical and psychological misconceptions concerning what public relations can and should do. Many Italian public relations departments have the conception that their major function is to prevent publication of unfavorable information about their firm's activities. Many firms which urgently need public relations are not employing public relations although they are awakening to the need for both internal and external relations. The idea that a firm can provide legitimate news is not generally recognized by either the press or industry. Italian public relations firms are actually advertising agencies. Large American and international firms operating in Italy have experienced public relations managers heading their public relations departments, but most Italian firms do not have the same concept of public relations as corporations in the United States.

Public Relations in Belgium

The Public Relations Society of Belgium, which was established in Brussels, in 1953, as the Centre Belge des Publiques Relations, has a membership of about seventy including public relations officers of industrial firms, counseling agencies, government, education, and other groups. The objective of the Society is to promote a better understanding of public relations in Belgium. The organization held its first national public relations conference in Brussels, in 1956, attended by public relations representatives of government and industry. A similar event has held in 1957. In 1958, the Society was host to the first World Congress of Public Relations, attended by 237 delegates from 23 countries, which was held in connection with the International Exhibition in Brussels. As a result of the efforts of the Society, an increasing number of Belgian private enterprises, as well as government agencies, are establishing public relations departments. The Belgian postal and broadcasting departments have instituted public relations programs. The first public relations bibliography ever published in Europe has been issued by the Society. In 1961, a Belgian Public Relations Mission was sent to the United States to study public relations in this country.

Public Relations in Denmark

A number of international corporations, as well as progressive local industrial firms, are conducting public relations programs in Denmark. Press relations is the principal activity of most Danish companies, which stage "press demonstrations" and luncheons primarily for the introduction of new products. Other public relations activities include highway safety education for children, educational materials for schools, employee education, and plant visits. Public relations is usually a function of the advertising manager in Danish industrial firms.

Public Relations in Switzerland

The Schweizerische Public Relations Gesellschaft, or the Swiss Public Relations Society, was organized in 1957 and has a membership of practitioners interested in fostering public relations in Switzerland. Much public relations work is carried on in Switzerland under different designations and in different departments, principally by advertising staffs as an auxiliary function. Some companies publish employee periodicals; consumer product manufacturers conduct plant tours; others issue publicity releases; and a few have employee suggestion systems. Since Switzerland is a country with only 5 million people and only small industrial organizations, the scope of public relations programs is limited. To communicate with the Swiss population, it is necessary to use German, French, and Italian languages. Public relations is not carried on at the management level in Swiss concerns. A completely planned public relations program is uncommon. There are few public relations counseling firms.

Public Relations in Western Germany

The Deutsche Public Relations Gesellschaft has been established in the Provence of Westphalia to further the development of public relations in West Germany.

Public Relations in Norway

The Norwegian Public Relations Society was established in Oslo, in 1949, to exchange ideas and experiences of practitioners in the field of public relations, to further the quality and ethics of the profession, and to inform the public about the public relations function. Membership in the Society is restricted to persons who are personally engaged in public relations and are responsible for the planning and execution of public relations programs. The limited membership of the Society is accounted for by the fact that few persons employed by Norwegian firms give a majority of their time to public relations work.

Business in Norway has accepted public relations to a very limited extent. Advancement of public relations is handicapped by the fact that the term, "public relations," is not found in the Norwegian language. Some of the most advanced public relations programs in Norway are those of industrial associations such as the Federation of Norwegian Industry, Norwegian Employers' Association, and Norwegian Merchant Fleet, which have public relations departments.

Public Relations in Holland

The principal organization of public relations practitioners is the Nederlands Genootschap Voor Public Relations, established in 1954. It sponsors a bimonthly public relations periodical.

Public Relations in Australia

Public relations in Australia is a growing activity with an increasing number of major industrial enterprises establishing public relations departments. The Australian Public Relations Society has two chapters: one in Sydney, New South Wales; and a second chapter in Melbourne, Victoria, with members from government, industrial, and commercial organizations.

Public Relations in South Africa

The Public Relations Society of South Africa was organized, in 1957, in Port Elizabeth, Cape of Good Hope. An educational program was established in co-operation with the University of South Africa to train practitioners in public relations.

Public Relations in the Republic of China

Public relations in the Republic of China on Taiwan (Formosa) is largely a government activity which was initiated by the Ministry of Communications, in 1952, for the purpose of increasing efficiency of workers, improving public service, developing communications, and creating public good will.

Public relations departments are now operating in the following government bureaus: postal, tele-communication, railroad, harbor, shipping, weather, civil aeronautics, highway, and diving. In addition, three government ministries have public relations staffs. Three non-government organizations, an insurance company, newspaper, and sugar corporation have public relations programs.

Several media of communication are used including radio broadcasts, motion pictures, periodicals, advertising, press publicity, and exhibits. Radio stations regularly broadcast public relations programs. Documentary films have been produced by the railway and tele-communications administrations, and government power and steamship companies. Press releases and conferences are employed by the government information bureau and other government agencies. Periodicals are published by several government bureaus. Newspaper, magazine, and outdoor advertising carry public relations messages to the public.

Opinion research is carried on by personal interviews and mail questionnaires by a leading newspaper which has polled the public on such issues as lotteries, bus transportation, and political questions. The postal and power administrations regularly survey consumers on the quality of their services.

Courses in public relations have been offered by Taiwan University, National Cheng-chi University, Taiwan Normal University, and the College of Law and Commerce. Government bureaus also train employees in public relations. The Ministry of Communication and Transportation has published a guide for employees, "Manual on Customer Relations."

Public Relations in South America

In Brazil, the Associaçio Brasileira de Relaçoes Publicas, the professional public relations association of Brazil, was established in 1956 and has three chapters in Rio de Janeiro, São Paulo, and Niterol. The first Congress of the Association was held in 1958 with an attendance of government and private industry public relations practitioners. Graduates of the public relations course of the Brazilian Public Administration School, or other courses recognized by the Association, are eligible to membership. The Association has approved a code of ethics and professional qualifications for public relations practitioners in Brazil.

The Chilean Institute of Public Relations, Santiago, Chile, was host to the Third Inter-American Public Relations Conference in Santiago, in 1962. Delegates attended from the United States, Brazil, Venezuela, Mexico, Peru, Colombia, Uruguay, and Argentina.

Public Relations in Canada

The Canadian Public Relations Society, with 478 members throughout the Dominion, includes in its membership representatives of private, government, and consulting organizations. It is adopting professional standards for qualifying practitioners of public relations following the practice of the British Institute of Public Relations in testing and certifying applicants for membership in the Society.

Public Relations in Japan

Many large industrial organizations in Japan have public relations departments which employ some of the media of communication used in public relations programs in the United States. Press conferences with important executives are arranged for editors and writers who are supplied with biographies and background material. Internal company periodicals are published by a few firms. Plant openings, open houses, and receptions are staged with guided tours, welcome by management, followed by refreshment and souvenirs. Press publicity is limited to major events such as plant openings as newspapers will not ordinarily mention a company or product in a news story. Television is rarely used for institutional messages.

Public Relations in Malaya

The Federation of Malaya Institute of Public Relations was established at Singapore, in 1962, to further the development of public relations in Malaya. The first president of the Institute is the director of Information Services, Federation of Malaya and the secretary is head of the external affairs division of the Ministry of Information and Broadcasting.

Public Relations in Other Countries

In many other countries throughout the world, public relations is on the rise with the formation of organizations to explain the functions of public relations to the business community and establish standards of qualifications and better professional training for public relations practitioners. Public relations societies have been established in the following countries: Finland, the Public Relations Society of Finland, Helsinki; Eire, the Public Relations Institute of Ireland, Dublin; India, the Public Relations Society of India, Bombay; Mexico, the Associación Mexicana de Professionales en Relaciones Públicas, Mexico City; New Zealand, the Public Relations Society of New Zealand, Auckland; Philippines, the Philippine Public Relations Society, Manila; and Sweden, Swedish Association of Public Relations, Stockholm.

INTERNATIONAL PUBLIC RELATIONS OF THE UNITED STATES

International public relations of the United States is the responsibility of the United States Information Agency, created by the President in 1953, and known abroad as the United States Information Service. The mission of the Agency is to submit evidence to the peoples of other nations that the objectives and policies of the United States are in harmony with and will advance their legitimate aspirations for freedom, progress, and peace; and to explain U.S. foreign policy, to counter hostile propaganda, and to present a balanced, accurate picture of American life and culture.

The director of the Agency reports to the President directly and through the National Security Council. He is a member of the Operations Coordinating Board which is concerned with the co-ordination of overseas programs. Foreign policy guidance is provided to the Agency by the Department of State.

The activities of the Agency are carried on by six departments: press and publications; Voice of America; television; motion-picture service; information centers including exhibits and books; and private co-operation. The public information program varies in each country depending on the literacy and educational attainment of the area. In highly literate countries, libraries and printed material of many kinds are used, but in areas where literacy is low, motion pictures, slides, exhibits, and cartoon strips are most effective.

The Voice of America is the broadcasting element of the Agency with eighteen studios located in Washington, D.C., and program centers in New York City, Munich, and Cairo to give audiences on every continent the latest news about international developments, facts about the policies of the United States, and information on our way of life. Voice of America broadcasts seven days a week, 24 hours a day, in English and 38 languages. Million-watt transmitters are located in Germany, the Philippines, Hawaii, Greece, Morocco, England, Ceylon; and, in this country, in Ohio, New Jersey, New York, and California.

The television department of the Agency prepares "live" television programing on videotape, including programs on American achievements in science, education, and culture, and portrayals of American life, which are distributed by the Agency's overseas poses in 50 countries to foreign television stations which reach an estimated audience of 160 million persons.

The motion-picture service of the Agency produces, acquires, and distributes films in 40 languages supporting U.S. foreign policy and showing American life through 210 U.S. film libraries overseas. To show films in remote areas, the Agency has 350 mobile projection units which generate their own electric power and more than 6,000 sound projectors are maintained for use by U.S. Information Service personnel and loan to foreign organizations.

The Agency maintains 161 information centers in 65 countries, each of which includes a library of American books, magazines, and newspapers to acquaint people abroad with American life and culture and promote an understanding of United States policies and objectives. In addition, centers organize classes in English, provide lecture and concert programs, arrange film showings, and sponsor exhibits and cultural events. The centers co-operate with 110 autonomous cultural centers in 31 countries which conduct similar programs. The book translation program has put into circulation some 50 million U.S. books in 50 languages. An estimated 30 million people visit the centers annually.

The Agency's Office of Private Cooperation works with private industry, associations, and individuals in bringing about a better understanding of United States' objectives overseas. Advice and assistance is given to People-to-People program committees and hundreds of projects including sports, art, music, and educational exchanges in the interest of international friendship.

Public Relations of the United Nations

The United Nations Office of Public Information, headquarters New York City, under the direction of the Undersecretary for Public Information, carries on an extensive public relations program in three areas: external relations; press, publications, and public services; and radio and visual. The objectives of the Office of Public Information are to present facts regarding problems facing the United Nations, and to create a better understanding of the long-range purposes of the United Nations.

The external program of the United Nations functions through 35 Information Centers located in the capitals of the principal member countries. The centers are responsible for working with thousands of voluntary nongovernment organizations in member countries representing art, science, social welfare, education, health, labor, and agriculture endeavors whose members are interested in promoting the aims of the United Nations. United Nations Information Centers distribute United Nations films, documentary radio programs, publications, visual materials, and press releases to create a better understanding of activities of the United Nations.

The Press, Publications, and Public Services section of the Office of Public Information is responsible for publication of the official monthly magazine, *United Nations Review*; press coverage of meetings of the General Assembly, Security Council, Economic and Social Council, and the activities of intergovernmental agencies; publication of the *Yearbook of the United Nations* and booklets about the activities of the United Nations.

Visitor services at New York headquarters include group visits, guided tours, lectures and film showings, and public inquiries and are the responsibility of the Press, Publications and Public Services section. Visual materials, including posters, charts, photographs, postcards, study kits, and flags are produced by the public inquiries unit of the Visitors' Service for sale to visitors.

The Radio and Visual section is responsible for UN radio news service consisting of news bulletins broadcast from UN headquarters in New York and Geneva, Switzerland, in 27 languages and rebroadcast by the national radio organizations of member states. Feature radio programs of 15-minute duration and 30-minute documentary programs are produced in 34 languages and broadcast over the national transmitters of 116 member and nonmember states. Recording and production facilities are provided at headquarters for delegates and news correspondents for recording reports on United Nations activities.

10

CULTURAL COMMUNICATION

Carl T. Rowan
THE CHALLENGE OF CULTURAL COMMUNICATION

UNESCO
GLOBAL OVERVIEW OF FILM SITUATION

Alphons Silbermann
MUSIC AS A COMMUNICATION FACTOR

10

CULTURAL COMMUNICATION

IN A VERY general sense *culture* has been defined by the Netherlands' sociologist P. J. Bouman as the *living style of any given society*. Although there is no generally accepted definition of *culture*, it is useful to quote one of the best-known descriptions of this phenomenon, written by the social psychologists Eugene L. and Ruth E. Hartley:

> Since "culture" is an abstraction commonly agreed to refer to the products, knowledge, traditions, skills, and beliefs that are shared by a group of people and passed on from generation to generation, its very existence is predicated on the functioning of communication.

Here the authors already touch on the interconnections between cultural elements and communication factors. One of the basic cultural products of all times and countries is the ability of expressing ideas (opinions) and feelings (attitudes) through language. And language problems up until our times have presented one of the main barriers to *intercultural communication,* which has been described by Gerhard Maletzke as "the process of the exchange of thoughts and meaning between people of differing cultures."

This exchange can occur through several kinds of interhuman contacts—by various forms of face-to-face or by intermedia communication. There are numerous kinds of possible intercultural relations, *i.e.*, interpersonal contacts by tourism, special imitations of fashions or customs, interconnections between the world's theater or music systems, gestures or general behavior patterns, etc. On the other hand, in many cases, intercultural communication is emphasized or projected by the mass media as well. Simple cross-cultural communication is already given if newspapers or magazines, books and pamphlets are made available for people in other countries, and if radio and television can be received across the national borders. Very often the language problem remains a real barrier, and so communication in many cases is only possible with an elite group who have a certain knowledge of the various languages. The best-developed form of intercultural communication by a mass medium seems to be the film in its different types: documentary film, newsreel, and especially the movies.

A German researcher, Otto Hesse-Quack, has done, for example, a pioneer study on the functional change of the contents of movies within the synchronization process from one language to another. He demonstrates the limitations, but also the various possibilities, in stressing or playing down prejudices and stereotyping between the original versions of motion pictures and their translations to other languages. Since movies belong to the world-wide distributed mass media with a great influence on the attitudes and reactions of people in many countries, this process needs further careful observation. Unfortunately, it was not possible to get a summary of Hesse-Quack's results as an article in time for inclusion in this book.

But the general *flow of culture*, nevertheless, can be demonstrated by the articles of this chapter. Carl T. Rowan discusses some basic ideas on the problem of cultural communication from the standpoint of a diplomat. An overview on the world's film situation is given by an article from UNESCO, which shows the value of this communication instrument on a global level. Dr. Alphons Silbermann, from the University of Lausanne (Switzerland) and the Sociological Institute of Cologne University, discusses in his article the communication problems of music in a general sense. In addition to this article, it would be helpful to have research on the cross-cultural communication function of *specific forms* of music, like the national anthems, folk songs, hits, and—last, but not least—jazz. Here we are already at the point between cultural and cross-national religious communication. No article was available on the international journalistic activities of the world's religions, although the editors contacted several very competent persons within this field.

However, the whole complex is described by William Stephenson, a psychologist at the University of Missouri, as the *cultural network*, in which "innumerable influences communicate to innumerable people—from many to many. Each person living in a culture is conceived of as bombarded by countless messages, the sources of which he is quite unable to recognize; what is transmitted, and what received, cannot be ascribed; and 'correction of information' is impossible. This is the network way of saying that the customary aspects of people's behavior are acquired under complex cultural conditions in which the printed word, monuments, myth, primary group, and similar conditions influence the individual without his awareness. Customary behavior is natural to him."

*   *   *   *

RELATED READING

Barnett, Homer Garner. *Innovation: The Basis of Cultural Change*. New York —Toronto—London: McGraw-Hill, 1953.
Dil, Anwar S. *The Language Factor in the Development of Emerging Nations*.

Bloomington, Indiana: Department of Education, Indiana University, 1968.

Gillin, John Lewis, and John Philip Gillin. *Cultural Sociology; A Revision of An Introduction to Sociology.* New York: Macmillan, 1948.

Hall, Stuart, and Paddy Whannel. *The Popular Arts.* New York: Pantheon Books, 1965.

Harley, John Eugene. *World-Wide Influence of the Cinema: A Study of Official Censorship and the International Cultural Aspects of Motion Pictures.* Los Angeles: University of Southern California Press, 1940.

Hesse-Quack, Otto. *Der Übertragungsprozess bei der Synchronisation von Filmen: Eine interkulturelle Untersuchung.* Munich and Basel: Ernst Reinhardt Verlag, 1969.

Hogben, Lancelot. *From Cave Painting to Comic Strip.* New York: Chanticleer Press, 1949.

Hoggart, Richard. *Uses of Literacy: Changing patterns in English Mass Culture.* Oxford—New York: Essential Books, Ltd., 1957.

Jongbloed, H. J. L. *Film production by international co-operation.* Paris: UNESCO, 1961.

Lasswell, Harold et al. *The Comparative Study of Symbols.* Stanford, Calif.: Stanford University Press, 1952.

McMurry, Ruth, and Muna Lee. *The Cultural Approach: Another Way in International Relations.* Chapel Hill: University of North Carolina Press, 1947.

Meillet, Antoine, and Marcel Cohen. *Les Langues du monde.* Paris: Centre National de la Recherche Scientifique, 1952.

Le Page, R. B. *The National Language Question. Linguistic Problems of Newly Independent States.* London—New York: Oxford University Press, 1964.

Pool, Ithiel de Sola. *Symbols of Internationalism,* Stanford, Calif.: Stanford University Press. 1952.

Rosenberg, Bernard, and David Manning White, (eds.). *Mass Culture.* New York: Free Press of Glencoe, 1964.

Rotha, Paul. *The Film till now: A Survey of World Cinema.* 3rd ed., New York: Twayne Publishers, 1963.

Smith, Alfred G. (ed.). *Communication and Culture.* New York: Holt, Rinehart and Winston, 1966.

Sorokin, Pitrim Aleksandrovich. *Sociocultural Causality, Space, Time: a Study of referential principles of Sociology and Social Science.* Durham, North Carolina: Duke University, 1943.

Stephenson, William. *The Play Theory of Communication.* Chicago: The University of Chicago Press, 1967.

Thiessen, John Caldwel. *A Survey of World Missions.* 3rd ed., Chicago: Moody Press, 1961.

Carl T. Rowan:

The Challenge of Cultural Communication

THERE IS A little something anomalous, I think, about a Communications Week banquet inviting as a speaker someone who is now charged with finding ways of not communicating with the press or with the American people. I hope the fact that you have invited me arises from your understanding something that I have recently come to understand—that there is perhaps no greater need for communication than between the people and the government of a democracy.

But I am not going to talk about the American press and the Government. I am going to talk of what communication has come to mean in the international struggle that occupies so much of the thoughts not only of the President, who spends 70 to 80 per cent of his time on it, but of other American citizens, who have come to think of this as the ever-present, everworrisome challenge to human existence.

There are some people who believe that, despite our failure to achieve a nuclear test ban, the development of these awesome weapons has virtually ruled out force as a means of solving international disputes. I say that if this is so, or if it is only partly so, then communication is a word that has become as crucial to our survival as the words "defense," "missiles" or "armaments," because communication becomes the key to the ideological struggle. It becomes the key in terms of our providing information or education in the cleanest sense of the word [not propaganda]; and it also becomes the key to psychological warfare in whatever sense you want to consider it.

Let me give you a couple of examples of communication, incidents that may seem trifling but which indicate what communication can mean. The other day I read a report from a young man in the Peace Corps in Latin America. He said he thought he had done a marvelous job of getting his Spanish in shape, but in one discussion he got his genders mixed and he said to the people living in the area, "An egg is better than a pope." Well, what he meant is an egg is better than a potato when it comes to

▶ From: *Journalism Quarterly* (Iowa City, Iowa); Special Supplement to Summer Issue, 1963: "The Challenge of Communications in Century 21," ed. by Alex Edelstein. Reprinted by permission of the publisher and of the author. This was a speech by Mr. Rowan at Communications Week, University of Washington, June 13-15, 1962.

eating the things that ought to be eaten. At another point, an old gentle-men said to him that his (the old man's) *queluca* was in very bad shape. And the young man, in a great outburst of American generosity, said, "Why, I have got two of them. One is kind of old but I would be happy to let you borrow that one." Later he discovered that this Spanish word that he thought meant "camera" actually meant "wife" in this part of Latin America.

We had an incident which was a little less trifling. Recently in a letter to the foreign minister of West Germany, Secretary Rusk used a German word which the West German official translated to mean "a breach of trust" or a "breach of confidence," when what Secretary Rusk meant was "a breach of security." This mis-translation or breakdown in communication was at the very heart of a rather interesting little flare-up between this country and West Germany.

I am going to talk tonight about cultural communication, if you will, but as I have said, essentially in world affairs. Some of you may have noted that on his return from an around-the-world trip the attorney-general spoke often and at some length about his belief that ours is perhaps the least-understood country in the world today. He made a particular plea to the Foreign Service to try to do a little better job of explaining to peoples abroad such things as our unemployment problem, the relationship of organized labor to the public and to the government, and our racial prob-lems.

The attorney-general had simply observed what a great many of us who have been so fortunate as to travel abroad have come to understand. I have detailed, for example, in *The Pitiful and the Proud* more than enough evidence that this country is woefully misunderstood. I am not going to quote from that tonight, just on the assumption that some of you may have read it, although I can tell by the royalty reports that I would not be boring too many of you with the repetition. But the attorney-general did raise what I consider to be one of the half dozen most crucial problems facing this nation today—communication across countries and across cul-tures. It may, indeed, be our most critical problem, if weapons development means there is not going to be a military solution to conflict. If we are to meet the challenge of communication, we must first ask ourselves WHY are we so woefully misunderstood.

I could cite two reasons. One is that an open society reveals many of its imperfections. It becomes fair game for the distortion, the exaggeration, and the propaganda of the Communist bloc. Secondly, and more important, we Americans have not educated *ourselves* as to where we stand on the fundamental issues over which mankind is pondering today. To put it another way, we have begun to worry about communicating with the world when we have not really solved the problem of communicating among ourselves. Under the circumstances, it should not be surprising that so many people in so many places fail to understand us.

Century 21 is, as I see it, a manifestation of the almost unbelievable change that has taken place in our world since World War II.

You move about the Fairgrounds and look at the national exhibits—those from India and Africa, as examples—and you know that these attest to gigantic political change, a political revolution since the end of World War II. A great many of us tend to think of political change primarily in terms of the new nations of Asia and Africa breaking from the metropole, from the great colonial empires. But this is only one aspect of the revolution of our time. As we move further we see evidence of a great revolution in science, a revolution that has affected travel, that since 1953, for example, has cut travel time from here to Tokyo in half. We see a great revolution in medicine that has extended the life span, wiped out diseases in many areas, and thus produced a problem of population which in itself has become a great dilemma of morals, of religion, and philosophy. We see the great revolution in weaponry to which I have referred, and of course, we see a different kind of political revolution in Russia, and China—a revolution which, some people say, is the first revolution in which one kind of tyranny was replaced by a far greater one.

Before I go into what will actually be a brief discussion of what we really want to communicate to the world—because I think this is the fundamental question we face today—that is, what is it we *wish* to communicate, let me make a statement or two about the revolution in communication, because I think that, tied in with this question of what we wish to communicate is an understanding of *how* we are going to do it. As I sit in Washington, I see that most headlines go to the summit meetings, to conferences in Geneva, to debates at the United Nations, or to other dramatic confrontations of diplomats. But as I sit there and read those cables day after day, I know that these dramatic confrontations are but the tiny visible part of that great iceberg that is known as foreign affairs. Relations between nations, and particularly maintaining peace and protecting individual liberty, has become a vastly complicated business. Most of all, it has become a business that embraces the actions and the words of all our citizens in the professions. I do not suppose it comes as any great surprise to you that those of us in the State Department are watching the debate over Medicare with just as much intentness as is the American Medical Association. We have come to understand that what our leaders say, what Congress says, and what our major organizations do about this or that piece of social legislation goes to the very heart of this important task of communicating to the world just what this country is all about.

We have come to understand that in Asia, Africa and Latin America millions of human beings do hold some rather strange notions about what we, as a nation, stand for. Each of you has read a great deal about the "ugly American"—how our tourists have created all over the world the notion that we are overwealthy, how Hollywood movies have pictured Americans as sex-crazy, as people inclined to gangsterism, and so on. But this is not the most damaging notion insofar as our foreign policy is concerned. The biggest burden, and the one most difficult to destroy, is the one that we Americans are afraid of change, either in our own country or in other parts of the world. Much of the world believes, for example, that our expressions of opposition to Communism arise solely from the fears of our "fat cats," who believe that change can only result in their having less and the great masses of the world having more.

Perhaps no other nation on earth has made a nobler effort to prove its generosity than the United States since World War II. Yet the idea persists that we are a nation of greedy people clinging stubbornly to the status quo. Why is this so, you may want to ask? What has it got to do with Medicare or with Communications Week? This idea of American greed exists in part because of this technological revolution in communication. We no longer talk about a radio network as the Voice of America. Communications facilities are such today that the man who spoke at your luncheon today, or the man who spoke in the Senate today, or maybe someone speaking at Baton Rouge, Louisiana, has become the voice of America, because they get his words in Nairobi or Lagos or New Delhi almost as quickly as they get them in Chicago today.

It is powerfully difficult for an individual in Nairobi to make a distinction between what was said yesterday by President Kennedy and what might have been said today by John Q. Smith. We are rather foolish to expect any of the peoples of Asia, of Africa or of Latin America to believe that we intend to do for them what we are unwilling to do for our own people. They do not expect us to produce great social and economic change in Latin America when every time they turn on the radio they see that some influential American is seeing Socialism and even Communism in every effort at social reform in this country, whether it is Medicare, better schooling for our youngsters, or voting rights for Negro citizens. In my opinion, our biggest burden in Latin America is the belief—and I must say it is fanned rather skillfully by pro-Communist propagandists—that when we oppose Castro and the injection of Communism in the hemisphere, what we are really opposing are the legitimate social, economic and political reforms that are being demanded by the peoples of Latin America.

I think in saying all of this I have made it clear that communication on foreign policy issues of great vitality will not, today, in Century 21, or perhaps ever again be simply a matter of nation-to-nation or government-to-government. It is going to be people-to-people. Even the most unintentional declaration is going to speed around the globe and help make that mass impression that somebody is going to label the "Image of America."

Because the average American is so deeply involved in this communication process, and because these processes are so vital to our well-being, it seems to me essential that we as a people endeavor to agree as to what it is that we want to say to the world. What *do* we wish to be the image of America? How best *can* we communicate that image to the rest of the world?

Let me discuss it in terms of what I regard as one of our great national concerns today. This concern is, of course, the preservation of our security and the maintenance of our individual freedom. If Americans see these threatened today—and I think they do—it is because they see so much of the world turmoil and upheaval that we have labelled "revolution." It is my view that there is no area in which more effective communication is required than on the attitude of the American people toward revolution.

I do not have to tell this audience that the American people today are extremely ambivalent where the question of revolution is concerned. Because of our own beginning, because of our own revolution, we feel a sort of sentimental reason to be 'for' revolution, and we find it difficult *not* to say this every now and again. But at the same time we know that there have been revolutions in Russia and in China and that these were revolutions which we regard as contrary to the human spirit. We have seen revolutions in a great many other places; in the Congo, for example, and we have said to ourselves, "Now, as a practical matter, buddy, maybe you had better stop being for revolutions." A very liberal newspaperman, Bill Shannon, said these words not too long ago. The fact is that it would be in our selfish national interest if there were no more revolutions anywhere for a good long time. There is nothing the overwhelming majority of Americans would like better than a prolonged period of stability in foreign affairs. The status quo is, from the American standpoint, a very satisfactory status quo.

We are in that sense a very status quo power. Until we have been able to assimilate and cope with some of the revolutions we have already witnessed in the Twentieth Century—such as India's rise to nationhood and its drive for industrial strength—we would prefer that there be no further distracting revolutions anywhere. No number of quotations from Thomas Jefferson or Tom Paine, reminding us how differently we felt on the matter in 1776 or in 1848 can alter the nature of our authentic emotions.

While that may be a very accurate expression of what *Americans* feel about revolutions, it is not a very accurate expression of *what is going to happen in the world*. We are not going to get that prolonged period of quietness and peace. We are not going to get any long respite in which we can sit back and enjoy the status quo. Does this mean, though, that we have to go on saying that we are for revolution, *period?* I do not think it means that at all. Everybody talking about freedom is not going there. They talk about a Chinese People's Republic and a Democratic Republic of Viet Nam. The Communists can use the words Freedom, Democracy, The People, just as freely as we can. Therefore, revolution has come to mean a great many things to a great many people. If we Americans look at this thing from the standpoint of logic, we come to the conclusion that there are *good* and there are *bad* revolutions.

Having come to that conclusion, quite naturally we decide that ours is pre-eminent among the good revolutions. Cuba would stand out as the most recent and the most bothersome example of revolution. Cuba we would regard as a shadow of larger ones in Russia and in China. However, do we want to communicate to the world a belief that ours is the *only* perfect revolution, that ours is the only national revolt truly dedicated to the rights of mankind? Do we want to communicate a suspicion that *all* the revolutions of Latin America are going to be bad ones simply because *we* do not see signs of appreciation for democracy or concern for the rights of mankind in these turbulent societies? I say that the answer is an emphatic NO; that to communicate such a belief, to communicate such fear, to communicate such suspicion would betray not only our arrogance but a lack of understanding of our own revolution and of our own development as a democracy. I say it is true that this principle of the "consent of the governed" which was the rallying cry of our own revolution is a distinctly American principle. But we should not let that blind us to a very fundamental truth, and that truth is there was a time not too long ago when Americans were unprepared, intellectually or otherwise, to accept the idea of a democracy.

I think it crucially important that we look at our own history and understand our own development. Then we become a little less smug, a little less supercilious, when we look at the developments in Africa, Latin America, or in the Far East. If we are going to communicate effectively with those caught up in the revolutions of Century 21, we shall have to stop deceiving ourselves with the contention that going back to the days of Greece's glory, democracy and a concern for the rights of the masses has always been a touchstone of Western civilization. Democracy was not exactly idolized by Plato when he said, "Democracy is a charming form of government, full of variety and disorder, and dispensing a kind of equality to equals and unequals alike." Nor was democracy idolized by the Aristotle who said, "A democracy is a government in the hands of men of low birth, no property, and vulgar employment." Then there was Clemens von Metternich, who said, "Ten million ignorances do not constitute a knowledge." And we come on down a little closer—we come, indeed, to our parent culture—and we find Benjamin Disraeli saying, "If we establish a democracy, you must in due time reap the fruits of a democracy. You will in due season have great impatience of the public burdens, combined in due season with great increase of the public expenditure. You will have wars entered into from passion and not from reason, and you will in due season submit to peace ignominiously sought and ignominiously obtained, which will diminish your authority and perhaps endanger your independence. You will in due season find your property is less valuable and your freedom less complete."

It was fairly late in our history that the voices of those who advocated democracy began to dominate the American scene. In fact, it was in 1865, on being sworn in as vice-president, that Andrew Johnson uttered these words: "Humble as I am, plebian as I may be deemed, permit me in the presence of this brilliant assemblage to enunciate the truth that courts and cabinets, the President and his advisors, derive their power and their greatness from the people." Now I hasten to point out that Johnson was drunk at the time, and indeed, there were more than a few of his contemporaries who were willing to espouse the theory that you had to be drunk to talk such nonsense. Certainly, Jefferson, Lincoln and others had espoused this principle perhaps more eloquently, and certainly with more sobriety than had Johnson, but the idea of government by the masses was for a long time to be a favorite topic of the cynical. In 1891 Oscar Wilde said, "Democracy means simply the bludgeoning 'of the people, by the people, for the people.' " And George Bernard Shaw was to say 12 years later, "Democracy substitutes election by the incompetent for appointment by the corrupt few." But—and I say in all seriousness—the lessons of our history began to seep in. Woodrow Wilson expressed his belief in democracy because it released the energies of every human being. And Silent Calvin Coolidge, in a great outburst of articulation, said in 1923, "It would be folly to argue that the people cannot make political mistakes. They can and do make grave mistakes. They know it; they pay the penalty. But compared with the mistakes which have been made by every kind of autocracy, they are unimportant." And then along came Alfred Smith in 1933 to say simply, "All the ills of Democracy can be cured by more democracy."

What these people had come to conclude is one of the things we are trying to communicate to the world today, and that is Thomas Jefferson's attitude toward mankind. You see, Woodrow Wilson said that Jefferson's immortality did not lie in any one of his achievements, but in his attitude toward mankind. And it seems clear that by the time Calvin Coolidge and Alfred Smith and Franklin Roosevelt came along, Jefferson's attitude was becoming America's attitude as the great evolutionary and elevationary force of public education became felt.

One of our great problems today is to communicate Jefferson's attitude to the peoples of many lands where democracy has faced such a hard road.

There are many Americans who still think that if there is a bad revolution in the offing, all they have to do is hold up their hand and everything is going to stay still. But that day has passed. We live in an era where the only way to deal with a potentially bad revolution is to see that a good one takes place first. And that is what we are trying to do today, to communicate this attitude of Jefferson's, in the hope that, through the Alliance for Progress, for example, we can communicate something that can be called "the right revolution."

When I talk about fomenting the right revolution, I do not mean that we go in and try to beat the Communists at the game of subversion, terror or murder in the villages of this country or that. I mean that we have to understand what it is that the peoples of the world are revolting against. The great revolutions of our time are against colonialism, political tyranny, economic, feudalism, and racial and social injustice.

There is not going to be any good revolution that does not meet the demands of the peoples to end these injustices. It will be a particular failure on our part if we fail to communicate to these great masses of the world which are rising up and crying out—in what seems to me to be a voice of unmistakable clarity—that we support their legitimate aspirations, even though we shall not be so naive as to support every act of subversion or treason to which somebody wants to attach the label of "revolution."

If you will permit me, I will summarize what I *hope* I talked about.

First, communication has become vitally important because propaganda may well have become as crucial as armaments to our survival.

Second, we have done a poor job of communicating to that restless mass that makes up most of mankind what it is that we stand for as a nation.

Third, we have not communicated a sense of national purpose because we, as a people, are too uncertain as to where we stand. We cannot communicate understanding where we have none ourselves.

Fourth, it is imperative that we, as a people, agree, because the technological revolution has made each of us a voice of America. A million conflicting voices crying out to someone else's wilderness is more than we can stand.

Fifth, perhaps the first business is for us to make up our minds where we stand with regard to the revolutions that shake three continents.

Finally, we can foment good revolutions only to the extent that our own society gives evidence of our wisdom, our humanity and our right to claim that our revolution has indeed embraced the hopes and dreams that can be shared by men everywhere.

Thank you.

UNESCO:

Global Overview of Film Situation

———

APART FROM a few countries, mainly in North America and Europe, where television has developed most extensively, the cinema has continued to expand both in terms of film production and exhibition and has retained its pre-eminent role in the world of entertainment. Since 1954, an increasing number of countries have entered into film production and, at the same time, the total number of fixed cinemas has doubled—from over 100,000 to 212,000. Their present weekly audience of 376 million equals one-eighth of the world population.

The principal gains were scored by the U.S.S.R. and the developing countries, where mobile units further expanded the cinema audience. Throughout most of Africa and Asia, however, the number of cinema seats still fell below the level of two per 100 persons, suggested as a minimum of adequacy by Unesco.

For several decades the United States, which still maintains a predominant role in world markets, was the largest producer of feature films. Since the mid-1950s, however, American output has trailed behind that of Japan, India and Hong Kong. In 1960, there were 26 countries which produced 20 or more features annually. They included 12 in Europe, 8 in Asia, 2 in North America, 2 in South America and 1 in Africa, plus the U.S.S.R.

Documentary and educational films have spread throughout the world and are being produced in increasing numbers by feature film producers, government agencies, industrial concerns, foundations and various non-profit organizations of a cultural, scientific or educational character. In many countries, the film has become an accepted part of the school curriculum, sometimes being used to enrich an already adequate course of instruction, sometimes to supplement instruction where there is a deficiency of textbooks, equipment and qualified teaching staff. With the aid of mobile units, educational and documentary films reach audiences previously uninfluenced by the cinema. Throughout Africa, Asia and Latin America, these units find their way to remote villages whose inhabitants can neither read nor write.

▶ From: *World Communications: Press—Radio—Television—Film*, by UNESCO. Copyright © 1964 by UNESCO and the UNESCO Publications Center, New York and Paris. Reprinted by permission of the publisher.

Technical progress in the film industry has continued steadily in the past decade, though perhaps without the revolutionary changes which have marked recent development of the press, radio broadcasting and television.

In the production field, there have been significant advances in camera design, with the accent on 70 mm. cameras for "wide-screen" films which put the viewer completely into the environment of the picture. Of special interest to amateurs, research workers and other specialists has been the contrasting development of 8 mm. cameras with sound. Advances have also been made in the production of colour films for screening both in cinemas and on television, as well as in stereophonic sound and optical systems which assure better images for both of the media.

There have been parallel developments in the field of exhibition. More and more cinemas throughout the world have been equipped with 70 mm. "wide-screen" projectors. The production of low-cost 8 mm. projectors has meanwhile expanded the field for amateur, research and other low-budget films. Another development, of particular interest to tropical and semi-tropical countries, is the production of projectors which use the sun as their source of light and can be employed to screen filmstrips in remote, non-electrified areas.

New types of cinemas, such as "drive-ins" for motorists and "theatro-ramas," are making a fresh appeal to potential cinemagoers and, as in the United States for example, are helping the industry to regain part of the audience lately lost to television. Some of these units, located in new suburban shopping and recreation centres with adequate car-parking space, have been more specifically classified as "drive-to" cinemas.

The development of closed-circuit television, which links groups of cinemas for the screening of special events, presages the time when the projection booth for hundreds of halls will be located in a single television station. These and other advances point the way to the gradual integration of the cinema with television.

This is, in fact, already being realized in the realm of space technology, where narrow- and wide-angle television cameras are being increasingly employed in communication, metereological, astronomical and military satellites, as well as in space exploration vehicles. The screening of film images transmitted directly to the earth from outer space may be expected to give further stimulus to what has been described as "the renaissance of the cinema." From the viewpoint both of production and viewing facilities, the development of the cinema as a mass medium is costly and no African country has as yet been able to afford the requisite double effort. The United Arab Republic is the world's fifteenth largest producer of features and a substantial producer of documentaries, but the film audience is provided with only 1.3 seats per 100 persons. Morocco and Tunisia produce an occasional feature film and, since the end of the Second World War, South Africa has produced 25 films in Afrikaans. But none of these countries averages as many as two cinema seats per 100 inhabitants.

Morocco, Tunisia and the U.A.R. have all introduced legislation designed, on the one hand, to build up their local film industries and, on the other, to attract foreign producers to their studios. Tropical Africa lacks feature production facilities of almost any kind.

In North African countries, there is growing insistence that imported films must either be dubbed or sub-titled in Arabic. The U.A.R. requires that all cinemas show an Arabic film for one week in every four.

Throughout Africa, even in the film-producing U.A.R., feature films from the United States continue to dominate cinema screens. This is as true even of French-speaking as of English-speaking countries. In recent years, the Indian film industry has established a solid foothold in Africa.

The main suppliers of newsreels are France and the United Kingdom but notwithstanding technical, economic and personnel problems, a number of African countries produce newsreel items or, periodically, complete newsreels. The periodicity varies from Dahomey's quarterly 35 mm. newsreel to the fortnightlies issued by the information services of Ghana, Senegal and Sudan. Documentary films are made in a number of countries, and both governmental and non-governmental educational films are produced from time to time in almost every African country.

Of the larger countries, only Algeria averages two cinema seats per 100 people. Three small countries—Mauritius, Melilla and St. Helena—far exceed it. However, it should be borne in mind that projection from mobile units is common throughout Africa. In Nigeria, commercial units, covering 80 towns, show to audiences of over 5,000 at each performance. These mobile vans are supplemented by units belonging to the federal and regional governments and to the British Council. The Sudan's 28 mobile units give monthly programmes in each district and the government even operates a travelling cinema on the railways for the benefit of staff at remote stations. However, millions of people living outside African administrative or commercial centres have still to see their first film.

For many years the colossus of the cinema world, the United States film industry has steadily shrunk in size and importance since the end of the Second World War. The spread of television, mounting production costs and foreign competition have all been contributing factors. By 1960, production of feature films had fallen from an average of 350 a year to a low of 211. An increasing proportion of films was being made exclusively for television networks. Meanwhile, the number of fixed cinemas within the country had fallen from 17,000 in 1952 to 12,300 in 1960, and individual annual attendance from 15 in 1952 to 12 in 1961.

Abroad, the United States film industry has also suffered. Its percentage of the world market has declined from 70 to 55 per cent since 1955. This, nevertheless, leaves it the dominant force in the film world. Up to 90 per cent of feature programmes in many countries are supplied by the United States. Non-commercial production is extensive and totalled

8,500 films in 1961. The United States also maintains some 5,000 documentary film libraries from which schools and organizations can obtain films, or where their members can view them.

Canadian cinemas have also suffered from a loss of audiences, largely due to the impact of television. Between 1957 and 1960, a total of 450 cinemas closed down and individual annual attendance dropped from 10.7 to 6.5. In other North American countries the curve of cinema attendance has been generally upwards. This is true, for example, of Mexico, which, like the United States, has experienced a drastic decline in feature production but, unlike the United States, a marked rise in attendance figures. In the whole region only the Dominican Republic, Haiti, and the Windward Islands average less than two cinema seats per 100 people.

A few other countries in the region produce films to a limited extent, chief among them being Canada and Cuba. Canada made three features in 1960. Cuba, which produced three features in 1961, now plans to make 12 a year. Canada possesses one of the world's most highly-developed educational and documentary film services. Its films, like its newsreels, are distributed in all regions. Trinidad and Tobago and Jamaica have instituted plans to encourage local production and co-productions. Occasional productions in other countries are limited to educational 16 mm. films, usually made under government auspices. Such films, together with educational films supplied gratis by foreign agencies, are sometimes projected in schools, but more often by mobile units. The region is served by 8,500 fixed cinemas which together provide 3.4 seats for every 100 people. Individual attendances average five a year.

Two countries, Argentina and Brazil, have well-established industries for the production of features, a number of which have won international awards. Both countries seek to stimulate local production by restricting the number of imported features and newsreels that can be screened in proportion to domestic films. Argentina's quota system is specifically aimed at United States films, which dominate South American screens. Two hundred United States films are allowed to be imported a year, as against an equivalent importation from all other countries combined. The screening of domestically-produced films is obligatory. Chile, Colombia, Uruguay and Venezuela produce a few features yearly.

A number of countries, among them Chile, Colombia, Peru, Uruguay, Venezuela, Argentina and Brazil, produce documentary and other short films, including newsreels or newsreel items. These are usually government sponsored, when they are not directly government produced. Government departments and private organizations maintain film libraries and projectors which are loaned to schools and organizations. Local resources are often supplemented by those of the film libraries of the British Council, the United States Information Agency, and some foreign legations. But a shortage of mobile units, coupled with poor transportation, makes it difficult to bring programmes to audiences in small villages, and the use of the cinema for educational purposes in rural areas rests in the planning stages.

More feature films are now produced in Asia than in any other region. Japan's production of 549 features in 1960 was almost half that of all the 12 major producing countries of Europe combined, and was about 2.5 times greater than United States production. India (324) and Hong Kong (273) held second and third place in the world list. Furthermore, all three countries have moved successfully into international markets, although only Japanese films have received wide acceptance in all continents. Features produced in Asia are largely designed for domestic distribution or to expatriate groups abroad.

Eight Asian countries are among the 26 nations which produced 20 or more features a year in 1960. But Ceylon, China (Taiwan), Indonesia, Israel, Lebanon, Singapore, Thailand, the Republic of Viet-Nam and Iran (which made 31 features in 1961, as compared with an annual average of 15 in the 1950s) all have a limited yearly production and release from 1 to 19 titles annually.

With regard to exhibition facilities, however, most Asian countries are poorly served. Some of the major producing countries average fewer seats per 100 persons than small countries such as Bahrain or Brunei, which rely entirely upon imported films. India has only 0.6 seats per 100 people, while Burma, which produced as many as 72 feature films in 1960, has only 1.3. In the Asian context, the number of seats is, however, sometimes deceptive. In Hong Kong, where there are only 2.6 seats per 100 people, individual annual attendance is 22.8, compared with 12 in the United States. In Lebanon, which averages 6.2 seats per 100 people, annual attendance per person is 22.5. Sarawak, with 2.6 seats per 100 persons, has an individual attendance rate of 15.7.

The great potentialities of the film for education, instruction and training in agriculture, industry and other fields are not yet widely appreciated or exploited in Asia, where the cinema is generally regarded solely as an entertainment medium. Although documentary and educational films are produced in many Asian countries, their circulation is usually limited to large cities and their environs. A few countries maintain an outstanding service. Among them is Japan, where over 1,000 educational and other documentaries were produced in 1961 and where the Ministry of Education actively encourages distribution of educational films to schools and adult audiences. In India, 957 mobile vans show weekly newsreels and about 100 documentaries a year free of charge to audiences in remote areas. All Israeli communities are within reach of either fixed or mobile cinemas which provide both entertainment and educational programmes.

Except in Japan, where individual annual attendance fell from 12.1 to 9.2 between 1957 and 1961, attendance figures have steadily risen in Asia.

Progress has been most spectacular in mainland China, where audiences have increased since 1950 from 146 million to 4 billion and the total of mobile units and ciné-clubs has risen from 7,700 to 13,800 since 1954.

Asian film production is severely handicapped by dependence on imported equipment and raw film. Only Japan is a major producer and exporter. Mainland China and India produce some equipment and India is now constructing a factory to produce raw film. Another obstacle is the existence of a distribution system which antedates local film production and favours American and European film offerings. The Indonesian Government is actively encouraging the showing of Asian films. As a result, the number of United States films distributed fell from 240 in 1957 to 130 in 1960 (out of a total of 425). In most countries, however, United States films maintain a predominant role.

European film production has expanded greatly since the end of the Second World War. But due to the greater parallel growth in Asia, Europe is no longer the largest producing region. Twelve European countries included in the world's major producers made 823 features in 1960, whereas eight Asian countries produced 1,479. Italy retains the position it has held since the early 1950s as the largest European producer, with France now running second and the United Kingdom third.

Since 1948, Europe's total of cinemas has risen by 60 per cent (in sharp contrast to North America, where the number has declined by almost one-third). However, total attendance in Europe has remained about stationary and on an annual *per capita* basis, has fallen from 11 to 9. This indicates a definite change in audience preferences, due largely to competition from television and other forms of entertainment.

In the United Kingdom, the cinema has been hardest hit by this trend. Since 1946, annual attendance per person has fallen from 33.2 (the highest in the world) to 8.7, and over 10 per cent of cinemas have closed down. The cinema has been losing ground in various other European countries. In France, for example, its audience has declined by 25 per cent since 1957. Television has been advanced as the major reason for this change in Austria, Belgium, Denmark, Finland, France, the Federal Republic of Germany, Eastern Germany, Ireland, Malta and Gozo, the Netherlands, Poland and Sweden. Yet in many other European countries with well-established television services, audiences totals have remained unchanged, as in Czechoslovakia, Norway and Portugal, or have actually increased, as in Bulgaria, Hungary, Italy, Spain, Switzerland and Yugoslavia.

Formal use of the film for education has not been fully exploited in Europe. In some countries, government services and private organizations utilize the film to a limited extent, but few countries have incorporated it as an integral part of school curricula.

Finland is one of the few countries which do so. The Netherlands, which also subsidizes the production of artistic, experimental and cultural films, produces a dozen educational films a year. The Educational Film Foundation keeps 400 projectors on revolving loan to schools. In addition, nearly 2,500 schools have their own projectors. In the Federal Republic of Germany, educational films are distributed to 33,000 academic schools, 4,000 vocational schools and to universities and technical institutes. Fourteen state and over 500 district and municipal centres also lend out educational films.

National production in most European countries is directly or indirectly subsidized. Film production is nationalized or government controlled in the Eastern European countries. In Western Europe, films are commercially produced, but their producers benefit from protective laws. In Denmark, local producers are remitted part of the box office tax. France, Italy, Portugal, Spain and the United Kingdom require exhibition of domestic films for varying periods. In France, French films must be shown for five weeks in every 13. Spain's regulations are designed to protect the fledgling industry from United States competition. The Netherlands, with almost no feature production, has an open film market, but nevertheless requires that each cinema must show non-United States films for 12 weeks in a year.

Europe is rich in film societies and clubs, as well as in film museums and archives which preserve and exhibit film classics and stimulate modern experiment. The region is also a large exporter of film equipment and raw stock. Regional collaboration is rapidly increasing. For example, 19 of Spain's films of 1961 were co-produced. In the field of newsfilm, Rumania exchanges newsreel items with 22 other countries.

In Oceania, only in Australia are feature films made, and production in that country is limited. In 1960 the sole feature produced in the Commonwealth was a foreign dramatization of an Australian novel. However, a number of Australian units make educational and documentary films. New Zealand produces a limited number of such films.

Australia is the only country in the region where television has developed extensively and, significantly, it is the only one where the cinema has lost ground in recent years. The Commonwealth's total of 35 mm. cinemas fell from 1,774 in 1956, when television began on a regular basis, to 1,579 in 1960. But throughout the region as a whole, annual attendance reaches a level of 15 per person—the second highest of all regions.

Throughout most of Oceania, exhibition facilities are adequate. Among the island groups for which figures are available, only five have fewer than two cinema seats per 100 people. Elsewhere the level is much higher.

National film boards in Australia and New Zealand promote distribution of educational and other information films. Government agencies and private institutions in the island groups maintain film libraries and arrange school programmes.

The post-war growth of the cinema audience in the U.S.S.R. has been unparalleled elsewhere. The number of fixed cinemas rose from 15,000 in 1948 to 90,500 in 1961, and 23,400 mobile units were also in use. Total attendance rose to almost 4 billion in the same period and annual individual attendances from 3 to 17.7, the highest level of any region.

In 1960, the Soviet Union was the seventh largest producer of feature films. In the same year, it also produced nearly 400 documentaries and 400 instructional films. The first stereophonic wide-screen films were made in 1955, and the first panoramic cinema in the U.S.S.R. was opened in Moscow in 1958. The rapid spread of television seems to have had no effect upon the Soviet people's interest in films.

Alphons Silbermann:

Music as a Communication Factor

THE NATURE of music has been discussed wherever and whenever music has been composed, and discussion, attempting to adapt itself to the needs of the time, swung for many centuries between the extremes of pure musical theory and philosophical and ethical reflection. Only when the invention and continuing improvement of the printing-press made it possible for enormous amounts of music to be published did it happily become necessary for scholars to preserve every composition as a precious cultural heritage.

It was at this time that the broad lines of musical evolution were laid down. It became necessary to study musicians individually, and from this necessity a vast biographical literature has arisen, as a result of which the kind of treatment once reserved for the great and in most cases dead masters is today given even the youngest composers. Thus the pendulum of musical literature has swung from pure theory through the philosophico-ethical position to the inquisitive, sensation-mongering writings, thanks to which music has almost become a literary vice. These attempts at the popularization of music—which are for the most part the result of purely commercial considerations—should not however be rejected out of hand, for they do have the effect of increasing the ordinary man's knowledge of music; a fact which should surely be welcome to all those who are in any way connected with the subject.

The fear daily grows that as a result of the continuing increase in economic production, humane values will lose their dominant place in modern society,[1] and that musicians—composers, listeners, performers and musicologists alike—will begin to lose courage and come to regard their activities as futile. Thousands of musical fortresses have been built in recent centuries, and each one contains a small amount of music which will be of interest to both the professional musician and the layman. But only when one possesses a special key can one gain access; and the forging of such a key involves such a tumult of ideas, approaches, systems and methods, that one begins to tremble at the thought of one's own ignorance.

[1] Cf. E(ric) Fromm, *The Sane Society*, London: Routledge & Kegan Paul, 1956.

▶ From: *The Sociology of Music*, by Alphons Silbermann. London: Routledge & Kegan Paul, 1963. Copyright © by the author, and reprinted by permission of the author.

Such a situation begets uncertainty, and I believe that it is in precisely this situation with regard to music that we find ourselves today. And because of our uncertainty, we restrict ourselves to guarding our cultural heritage as jealously as possible. We forbid the historian to analyse carefully the social conditions which influenced the music of the past. We forbid the psychologist to probe in any detail into the processes of artistic creation. We will not permit the educator to refine our musical responses. And only on very rare occasions do we allow the sociologist to penetrate into the musical fortress: yet it is precisely he who will be most able to illuminate the interaction between individual and individual, the individual and the group, the individual and the institution, between art and communication.

If we glance at some of the countless definitions of the word "music," we shall encounter such widely differing points of view that we may at first deem the whole subject plagued by confusion. This, however, is not the case. These different viewpoints are simply the outcome of new perceptions which result in a theory becoming more closely defined and thus limited or developed, at various intervals. Whether or not this kind of clarification, the result of contemporary ways of thinking, is satisfactory is not the present point at issue. Our summary of some of these ideas is simply meant to show how justifiably it is demanded that the question "what is music" be placed at the beginning of a work on this subject; and to show also how unwarranted it is for an author simply to select from the mass of his ideas only those which are congenial to his own method of approach. This so arbitrary, and unfortunately so frequent, practice weakens the author's thesis by supporting itself upon ideas which are a product of their time and which must therefore of necessity make way for new ones when they have outlived their usefulness.

Definitions of music will, of course, vary according to the bias of their propounders, be they theoreticians, practising musicians, philosophers, theologians, poets, doctors, psychologists, psychoanalysts or historians. Thus for Aristotle, music is a direct imitation of moral feelings, for St. Augustine the art of perfected movement. Music is the art of pleasing modulations, says Censorius; for John Cotton in the seventeenth century, it was the fitting movement of voices. The philosopher Leibniz discovers hidden arithmetical progressions in music, while the composer Rameau sees it quite simply as the science of sounds, a view confirmed in the nineteenth century by the great Combarieu, when he describes music as the art of thinking in sound. For Debussy, music is a totality of dissolved powers. While Richard Strauss sees music as a translation into sound of impressions and emotions, Stravinsky maintains that it is incapable of expressing anything at all. Moving away from the philosophers and musicians, we come to Freud, who tells us that listening to music is an undifferentiated projection of an anal significance: so that some of our most sublime experiences rest on what might be described as the basest manifestation of the human character. The depth psychologist Anton Ehrenzweig contents himself with the statement that "music has become a symbolic language of the unconscious mind whose symbolism we shall never be able to fathom." [2] The view of music as symbolism has come strongly to the fore in our day, and the following passage may be cited as being especially typical of many American thinkers: "Music is a symbolic, immediate and untranslatable presentation to our comprehension and response. Its power resides in its unique ability to dispense with portrayal, depiction and exegesis, to strike directly to the mind and the heart by symbolic articulation." [3] For Johan Huizinga the essential form of all musical activity is that of play; [4] and this belief, which is by no means held by Huizinga alone, implies recognition of the phenomenon of sociability. One author, for instance, sees in music nothing more or less than the possibility for hundreds of thousands of people to "cleanse themselves of the unclean confusions of everyday life in the real-unreal world of art," [5] while others, disliking the idea of music as a form of diversion, prefer to see it as a "gathering of souls." These rather poetic views could doubtless be attacked as being cheap and unscientific; but in our present context, they may serve as a perhaps vague, but none the less symptomatic indication of sociability.

Even the frequent invocations to the "spirit" of music—a meaningless term, whose influence should not, however, be underrated—lead us, though perhaps unintentionally, to the phenomenon of sociability. It matters little whether this "spirit" is invoked to prove that music is in a position to maintain the dignity and the freedom of man, and thus to overcome isolation, egotism, sectarianism or other regrettable manifestations; or whether one follows Confucius, who held that music, streaming forth from the human heart, is connected with the origins of human behaviour and thus has the power to contribute to the formation of societies; for again and again the power of music to condition sociability is underlined.

We may also count as forms of sociability the adventure of discovery and re-discovery of certain musical works—both of which factors are said by G. Brelet to constitute two essential coefficients of musical pleasure[6]— and also the total pleasure of understanding and enjoying a work of art. In fact the habit of hearing music is in itself a social phenomenon, if only because it establishes a form of sociability between composer and listener, composer and interpreter or between interpreter and listener, according to how one looks at it; the quantitative or dynamic strength of the sociability may for the moment be left aside. For this reason, H. H. Stuckenschmidt has rightly taken issue with those who regard modern

[2] A. Ehrenzweig, *The Psycho-Analysis of Artistic Vision and Hearing*, London: Routledge & Kegan Paul, 1953, p. 164.
[3] H. Weinstock, *Music as an Art*, New York: Harcourt Brace, 1953, p. 14.
[4] Johan Huizinga, *Homo Ludens*, Hamburg: Rowohlt, 1956, p. 157.
[5] F. Thiess. "Musik—Geheimwissenschaft oder Ereignis?," *Melos*, October, 1953, p. 284.
[6] Cf. G. Brelet, "Du plaisir musical," *Polyphonie*, Paris: Vol. 5, pp. 34 ff.

music as not being productive of a "community spirit," giving as their sole reason for this accusation the limited number of its listeners.[7] At this point it may be mentioned that it is an error to believe that in considering such social phenomena as sociability, the sociologist intends to use his findings merely in order to work out statistics or to consider certain individual public reactions.

"In what way is the musical experience socially determined?" and "In what way does the musical experience socially determine other elements?"; to the treatment of these two fundamental questions, the words of Romain Rolland are very relevant: "Art is not influenced by art alone, nor by thought alone, but by everything which surrounds us—people, things, gestures, movements, lines and light." In fact the musical experience is dependent upon so many factors that the attempt to grasp and describe them sometimes leads to despair. Yet a process of change is involved in every actual phenomenon; and to resist or even ignore this fact would lead to scant success in any scientific study. The anthropological question of whether a social fact is to be regarded as biologically predetermined or learned through cultural influence and transmitted through attitudes and examples must for the moment be left aside.

For an example we turn to racial and national character. In musical literature we find many examples of the importance of particular national characters as dependent elements. We learn, for instance, that music as an art is best practised by rather violent nations; that the staid, reserved Anglo-Saxons have never distinguished themselves in musical composition; that the Italians have never been inclined to confuse mere ingenuity with real substance; that the French are more interested in sensuous impressions than in the emotions which emanate from the sounds, etc. All these observations, which tend toward the study of differences in temperament, are subjective impressions, concerning which sociology possesses only scattered data—although the problems of race, of race in relation to mentality and culture, of racial prejudice and racial consciousness, have been exhaustively considered in sociological literature.[8]

For our purpose, it must suffice to remark that the musical experience contains a socially determinant element dependent upon race when groups having certain hereditary features in common are able to express these traits so forcibly in the musical experience that a demonstrable group differentiation comes to view. Racial phenomena and processes are biological; cultural phenomena and processes are social; and the two must therefore be considered separately in any scientific study. But in reality the biological process "race" and the social process "the musical experience"

[7] H. H. Stuckenschmidt, "Die unbedeutende Minderheit," *Melos*, May, 1952, p. 134.
[8] See H. Arendt, *Elemente und Ursprünge totaler Herrschaft*, Frankfurt: Europäische Verlagsanstalt, 1956; E. L. Hartley, *Problems in Prejudice*, New York: King's Crown Press, 1946; R. Eichenauer, *Musik und Rasse*, Munich: Lehmann, 1932; B. Bettelheim and M. Janowitz, *The Dynamics of Prejudice*, New York: Harper, 1950.

exist together, the one influencing the other in a dependent relationship: thus, as a result of this interrelationship, the musical experience becomes socially determined by the non-social factor of race. The functional-social process of taste is of particular importance at those points where the musical experience is connected with a kind of "service to the customer," as it were, established by society itself, in socio-cultural institutions such as radio organizations, in commercial undertakings like the gramophone record industry, and in such consumer groups as agents and impresarios. In such cases, music and the experience of music are, in the true sense, "measured" with the aid of statistics. And it has, from a statistical point of view, been established how far the contact of various producer and consumer groups functions quantitatively. So far as radio is concerned, I have already discussed "sense and nonsense in musical statistics" in detail elsewhere.[9]

For our present purposes, it must suffice simply to consider statistics for a moment as an example of method. When, for instance, a French researcher[10] shows that the musical world of 9999 radio listeners is made up of 500 works and 100 composers, of whom fourteen are pre-eminent in popular favour,[11] then statistics has given a certain answer. The reasons for listening, whether alone or with others, to whatever kind of music; or, to put it more fully, the motives which lead to music-making, to attending a concert, to listening to music on the radio or on records, and wholly or partly to consume the musical experience: this is a wholly different problem, which we encounter again and again in the works of philosophers and aestheticians, be it Hegel, Schelling or Schopenhauer, Hanslick, Dukas or Lalo. Summing up, we may say that physiological, emotional and mental factors constitute the total phenomenon of "hearing music," and that feeling, perception and the power to seize awarenesses are closely combined with one another in the creation of music. Nor must we forget that the effects of technological inventions and discoveries have always exerted their influence upon the most diverse motives for listening to music.

The behaviourist approach brings much new light to bear upon this problem, especially when we consider the behavioural patterns revealed in the study of "leisure" or "recreation." These are problems which, whether from a functional[12] or behaviourist[13] viewpoint, have often been the concern of sociology—especially recently, when there has been much talk of further shortening of the working day as a result of automation. What

[9] Cf. Alphons Silbermann, *La musique, la radio et l'auditeur*, Paris: P.U.F., 1954, chapter 2.
[10] A. Moles, *Théorie de l'information et perception esthétique. Etudes de Radio-télévision*, Paris: Flammarion, 1958.
[11] These composers were, in order of popularity: Mozart, Beethoven, Bach, Wagner, Brahms, Schubert, Handel, Tchaikowsky, Verdi, Haydn, Schumann, Chopin, Liszt, Mendelssohn.
[12] B. G. White, "Social Class Differences in the Use of Leisure," in: *American Journal of Sociology* (Chicago), September, 1955, pp. 145 ff.
[13] J. Vial, "Pour une sociologie des loisirs," in: *Cahiers Internationaux de Sociologie* (Paris), Vol. XIII (1952), pp. 61 ff.

we have to observe here are such leisure activities as concern the musical experience, i.e., such forms of social behaviour as are manifested by adults under the influence of other human beings or of environment, or as they originate from the need to satisfy emotional, intellectual or aesthetic desires. With younger people, and especially with children—though by no means excluding adults—we must also take into account the precedents that are set and the need for play. We observe first how leisure results in behavioural patterns which are called forth by loneliness: on the one hand idleness, lounging about, thinking, dozing and dreaming, and on the other, gadding about, wasting time, going out, taking part in excursions, sightseeing, the search for human company. Music often plays a large role, especially in the first of these two types of behaviour; as can daily be observed, especially since technology has brought the means of consuming music at the turn of a knob into the home.

Loneliness and silence are overcome—we might almost say therapeutically overcome—with the aid of music. We often hear it said: "They keep the radio on, but they don't listen to the music—all they want is noise, the louder the better." Debussy, Wagner or Monteverdi, waltzes, jazz or boogiewoogie is all the same thing to them—simply noise. The silence of loneliness must be filled in with musical background noises. This, then, is the motive for the behaviour of a large number of listeners in the consumption of the musical experience: the lonely man takes refuge in music while he does the housework, writes letters, reads novels, while he lounges about, cooks a meal, awaits a telephone call or is unable to sleep. We now come to behaviour in the consumption of the musical experience in public; and we thus approach the problem of "the masses."

It had better be said at once that a satisfactory definition of the word "mass" has not yet been found. We speak, it is true, of "mass behaviour," of the "spirit of the masses," or the "myth of the mass," of "mass hysteria," "mass reactions," "the music of the mass," etc.; but all the innumerable attempts to define the term have stumbled over the difficulty of distinguishing between "objective knowledge" and "moral value-judgments." There have, nevertheless, been fascinating accounts of the criteria of the mass, by Freud, Jung, Tarde and Le Bon among others; fascinating whether, like Le Bon,[14] they consider the "suggestibilité" of the masses, or whether, like Jung, they express an attitude of hopelessness: "It is certainly a good thing to preach reason and common sense, but what if your audience is a lunatic asylum or a crowd in a collective seizure? There is not much difference either, because the madman as well as the mob is moved by non-personal, overwhelming forces.[15] Where these writers provide us with little guidance, however, is in the question of an art-form whose means of distribution (concerts, opera, radio, etc.) enable it to be received by the masses—even

[14] Le Bon, *La psychologie des foules*, Paris: Alcan, 1895, pp. 19-20.
[15] C. G. Jung, *Psychological Reflections*, selected and edited by J. Jacobi, London: Routledge & Kegan Paul, 1955, p. 142.

though it can, as we have seen, be consumed individually by an individual, in spite of the fact that he is in close spatial connection with other people. Once again, we come upon the problem of the listener and the listeners; a problem which can easily, but unsatisfactorily, be solved by exclaiming: "There is no such thing as the individual listener. What we must consider is how listeners behave, and what they accordingly expect." [16]

Any competent sociologist would reply to this that people have not gone to such trouble to work out fine distinctions between such terms as the "active" and the "expressive" crowd, "people," "audience," "public" and "mass" so that we may now consider all of these under the collective term "mass" and completely ignore the elementary concepts of collective groupings. There can no longer be any doubt of the fact that, under certain circumstances, the "public" can become the "crowd" and that the "crowd" can become the "mass." This fact leads, in music as in other fields, to the existence of propaganda and publicity. Further, many sociologists have been able to show—without specific reference to socio-musical society—that there is less tendency for the public to become a crowd than to be swallowed up by the mass. It thus seems justifiable to consider the collective behaviour of the mass and thus to cast the net wide; for, in the sociology of music, we must consider not only the audience of three hundred people listening to chamber music in a rococo hall, but also the thirty thousand people, the mass, who wildly applaud Louis Armstrong or Frank Sinatra in a vast stadium. In many respects, the public and the mass are intermingled, a consequence of mass communication media. These media must not be overlooked in any modern study of music, and have, in fact, led to considerably increased difficulty in the observation of contemporary collective behaviour with regard to music.

These are all first and foremost considerations of quantity; but they lead none the less to the fact that the concert public can either form effective groupings or fail to do so, and that at its centre we may find sometimes the mass, sometimes the crowd. But it is by no means enough to say that when two thousand people are together in a concert hall we have to do with a public, but that three thousand constitute a mass— especially not if we have any concern for music. For, as we well know, the strife which arises from consideration of the differences between "music for the masses" and "music for a public" leads to cries of warning and fear for the life of music. But cries of warning and fear are not enough. If an illness, or even the suspicion of an illness, is to be cured, the symptoms must first be diagnosed; and in this case, the diagnosis will concern neither the quality nor the degree of the illness but the behaviour which is manifested in it.

[16] A. Grimme, "Das Ethos des Rundfunks," *Jahrbuch des Nordwestdeutschen Rundfunks*, Hamburg: 1949-50, p. 17.

When we consider the mass which consumes the musical experience, at an open air concert, a military band concert or, invisibly, from radio or television concerts, it appears to consist simply of a collection of individuals who are separate and anonymous. They are only homogeneous in so far as their mass behaviour is concerned. Since this behaviour is conditioned by no prescribed rule or expectation, it is spontaneous, innate and elementary. And since the individuals remain separate from and unknown to each other, they retain their individuality and the possibility of remaining acutely self-conscious throughout. This has the consequence that the individual, instead of reacting to the suggestions and the stimuli of those with whom he is in close intellectual or spatial connection, acts in response to the music which has demanded his attention as experience, and on the basis of impulses which the experience has awakened. It follows, then, that the behaviour of the mass in the consumption of the musical experience can be entirely conditioned by the needs of the individual and by the responses which he seeks.

It must be remarked at this point, that in sociology, music is often treated, together with the theatre, card-playing, sport, reading, cinema-going or the visiting of museums, under the heading of the "sociology of leisure," or "of recreation." Specialists in this field define leisure as free time after the carrying out of practical necessities and recreation as every activity which is carried out either in private or in groups during free time, which brings pleasure and which is not practised because of direct necessity or for deferred reward.[17] The task of this branch of sociology is chiefly to determine the typology of the different forms of leisure and recreational activity, and to consider them in relation to social class, sex, age, nationality, profession and locality. From a statistical point of view, this branch of sociology is extremely valuable: but it will concern us only when we have occasion to consider the old and painful question of whether music is a form of diversion or amusement or something quite different; a question which, as I have shown elsewhere,[18] only demands a solution by the sociologist of music when he is drawn into philosophical considerations. Even in such at first sight so different notions of the nature of music as, on the one hand, Stravinsky's view that music is a combination of tonal elements, patterns and forms, and, on the other hand, W. Pyper's view that "music is heard or performed in order to provide both musician and listener with an emotional experience," [19] there is concealed a philosophical desire to find out the truth or falsehood of Congreve's famous phrase,

[17] M. H. and E. S. Neumeyer, *Leisure and Recreation*, New York: Barnes, 1949, pp. 19 and 22; cf. also G. P. Atteberry and others in *Introduction to Social Science*, New York: Macmillan, 1947, Chap. 6; M. B. Greenbie, *The Art of Leisure*, New York: McGraw-Hill, 1935; J. Vial, "Pour une sociologie des loisirs," *op. cit.*, pp. 61 ff.
[18] A. Silbermann, *La musique, la radio et l'auditeur, op. cit.*, pp. 90 ff.
[19] W. Pyper, "Pause del silenzio," in: *Contrepoints*, Paris: Edit. de Minuit, 1946, Nr. 3, p. 5.

"Music hath charms to soothe the savage breast." Paul Hindemith has also brought up the question anew.[20] He rejects the view of the Roman philosopher Boethius, that music has the power to improve or worsen character, preferring to agree with St. Augustine, who held that music can only ennoble those who are willing to undergo the moral exertion which leads to such ennoblement. The cultivation of artistic taste is, according to Hindemith, not enough—barbarians lower music to their own level. Even from these brief examples, we see how easily the question of music as diversion or amusement can become involved with philosophy or metaphysics; and we realize the truth of Malraux' statement that "in a world of the imaginary, which only corresponded to particular wish-dreams, reason was soon obliged to call for pleasure and delight." [21]

We repeat that in sociology—with the exception of the statistics of music, which are of the greatest value in determining sociological stratification—we are faced with no such problem. For music touches the lives of human beings at a great many points. Should any man wish to embark upon a search for beauty and joy, then he will come into contact with music either creatively, interpretatively or purely receptively; and whether or not this contact contains elements of diversion or amusements is of no account.

Like the sociology of leisure and of recreation, the "sociology of the mass" is also concerned with music, in so far as it concerns the particular characteristics of the masses. The sociology of the public is also to some extent concerned with music, as is the sociological study of institutionalism: for music can be regarded as an "institutional area" which, as a result of its "most important traditional functions," is in a position "of enforcing group solidarity." [22] The study of mass communications—an important aspect of modern sociology, which considers the problem "Who says what to whom, and with what effect?"—must also necessarily consider music from the point of view of communication, distribution, propaganda and its peculiar means of expression. Herbert Spencer made mention of this last element many years ago, when he described music as a means of communicating certain ideas which could be expressed in no other way.[23]

[20] Paul Hindemith, A Composer's World, Cambridge/Massachusetts: Harvard University Press, 1952.
[21] A. Malraux, "The Imaginary Museum," in: The Voices of Silence, London: Secker & Warburg, 1954.
[22] Th. Caplow, "The Influence of Radio on Music as a Social Institution," in: Cahiers d'Etudes de Radio-Télévision (Paris), No. 3-4 (1955), pp. 278 and 286.
[23] Herbert Spencer, "On the Origin and Function of Music," in: Essays, London 1857, Vol. I. See also: W. Schramm (ed.), The Process and Effects of Mass Communication, Urbana, Illinois: University of Illinois Press, 1954; W. Hagemann, Vom Mythos der Masse, Heidelberg: Vowinckel, 1951; G. Maletzke, "Der Mensch im publizistischen Feld," in: Cahiers d'Études de Radio-Télévision (Paris), No. 3-4 (1955), pp. 292 ff; E. Barnouw, Mass Communication: Television, Radio, Film, Press, New York: Rinehart, 1956.

I I

A LOOK TO THE FUTURE

Leslie G. Moeller
THE DAILY NEWSPAPER IN TOMORROW'S SOCIETY

Lord Thomson of Fleet
NEWSPAPER STANDARDS FOR THE SEVENTIES

Hugh Cudlipp
THE ROLE OF THE PRESS IN THE LUNAR AGE

Wilson P. Dizard
FUTURE PATTERNS OF INTERNATIONAL TELEVISION

11

A LOOK TO THE FUTURE

EVERY serious student of mass communication feels he has some inkling of what the future of the mass media will bring. Theories abound and predictions pile upon predictions. While some seers of a conservative bent are talking of media virtually of the same type as we find around us today, others are conjuring up visions of elaborate push-button home systems where a person can not only select his communication immediately, flashing it before his eyes in wide vision and stereophonic sound, but will have print-out versions available at his beck and call for his files.

Many amazing technological wonders have already come about—in experimental or localized situations—and a person's wildest dreams about mass communication of the future are not beyond possibility, or even probability. George Orwell's 1984 communication systems may well seem extremely primitive to persons alive when that well-publicized year arrives. Technologically, the future seems bright. Qualitatively, as related to *content*, however, the history of mass media in recent years leads one to have some serious doubts about the communications of the next few decades.

The masses appear to be having greater and greater impact on the kinds of material furnished by the mass media. At first glance this appears quite proper, if true; for who, other than the *masses*, should decide the diet of the mass media? But, unfortunately, the tastes of the masses tend to seek rather low and, often, very anti-rational levels and are prone to drive good journalism—cultured and intelligent—into a smaller and smaller corner. As mass media become *more* mass-oriented, as undoubtedly they will, intelligent minorities will be forced increasingly to expose themselves to the output of the policy of Un-Think and of an egalitarian media concept, a situation to which they must adapt (with all the potential sickening consequences) or they must isolate themselves from the mass media altogether. In either case, this would be a tragedy. Now, the answer may be given that more universal education will bring up the desires and tastes of the masses and they will insist on having a mass media diet that will not offend the intellectual elite. This is optimism in the extreme, since the tremendous expansion of education (especially in the United

States) since World War II has hardly brought about a proportional decrease in the pap displayed in our mass media.

Certainly, any astute observer of the mass media offerings in the past decade must conclude that, if the trend is not broken, the cult of low-grade entertainment and "pseudo-event" news programming—coupled with a kind of sentimental egalitarian view of the public media of communication, will push the output of the media into lower and lower levels during the next twenty or thirty years.

Many students of the mass media are more optimistic, however, and see the situation improving. Leslie Moeller, of the University of Iowa's journalism faculty, for instance, believes that the performance of the daily newspapers in the years to come will improve. In the first article of this chapter, he presents some of his ideas about newspapers in tomorrow's society; he is writing specifically about U.S. dailies but there is no reason to believe that what he says cannot be extended to the daily press of the world.

In the second article, the world's most powerful newspaper owner— Roy Thomson (Lord Thomson of Fleet)—discusses the press of the 1970's. He sees some amazing technological—and other—changes in store for the newspaper, and he relates many of these changes to the impact of television and the tenets of Marshall McLuhan. Following the article by Lord Thomson, the outstanding British journalist and editor, Hugh Cudlipp, presents a stimulating discussion of the kind of journalism—with emphasis on content—that will be necessary for the new age, which he refers to as the "lunar age."

The final article, by Wilson P. Dizard, an outstanding scholar in the area of broadcasting, focuses on international television, with the early (and undoubtedly safe) assertion that long before 1984 television will be the most influential mass communications medium in the world. He predicts startling changes, including "a vast international communications network built around computers and space satellites." And this by 1975! He even sees, by about 1984, TV antennae raised in "the most isolated village in Africa," and the elimination of "remote places." He warns, however, that man can use television as nothing more than the "greatest entertainment circus of all time" or he can employ it as the interpreter of the world's problems. And, it is in this area of quality—or *use* of the media— that all the writers are at a loss to make any definite predictions.

*   *   *   *

RELATED READING

Because the readings related to the future of the mass media are almost altogether to be found in a large number of periodicals and scattered here and there in numerous books, the editors are not listing specific sources here. The reader may find literature related to this topic almost anywhere.

Leslie G. Moeller:

The Daily Newspaper in Tomorrow's Society

WHAT will the newspaper of tomorrow be like, as distinguished from what it is now, and from what we might wish it to be?

First of all, in such an economically tight situation, the daily newspaper can be expected to continue to be a conservative institution. It has not in the past changed methods or content quickly. There are several reasons. Much change could mean an increase in costs. Again, readers are accustomed to the paper as it is; many newspapers have had "reader difficulty" when they made sudden changes in format or content. Once a reader is lost, it is often difficult to get him back, so there is an understandable tendency to stay by the publishing recipe that has worked reasonably well, and which most other newspapers are using.

In such a circumstance, it is then probable that in the field of providing information, decision-makers will continue to give much weight, consciously or not, to their concepts of "what kind of information the public probably wants." There is no alternative; at the moment, and for at least the near future, it is imperative that the newspaper maintain the size of its audience, and so it must provide what the audience wants.

At the same time the newspaper will also provide much important and worthwhile material in which most of the audience has little or only occasional interest.

In other words, considering the nature and interests of the audience, the daily newspaper will usually continue to do much better than we have a right to expect it to do. It will not determine its content solely on the basis of the highest readership possible. It will carry much material which publishers and editors know will have low readership, but which they feel it is important to provide.

The years to come will see somewhat improved performance by daily newspapers. Many will do better in giving a broad and a deep presentation of the news, and more especially on the larger papers with bigger staffs and more sizeable news budgets.

The change may not be tremendous, and it will probably come slowly

▶ From: *The Iowa Publisher* (Iowa City/Iowa), Vol. 32/No. 10 (October, 1960), pp. 4-12. Reprinted by permission of the author.

and irregularly, but it will come. The need for the change is seen by more and more editors, it is increasingly a topic for discussion, and more and more dailies are making improvements.

Availability of personnel will be a crucial factor. Newspapers seem to be having more difficulty getting and keeping good people than was the case ten or twenty years ago. A careful examination of personnel policies is in order to make certain that newspapers of the future do have enough good quality staff people.

The presentation of news will become simpler, although progress may be slow. The habits of reporters are often hard to change; it is not enough merely to say, "Write understandably." Desk men and even executives may also be hesitant to change, or unaware of the need for change. Most newspapers do not have continuing training programs and the newspaper industry has not yet adopted the pattern of going back to school rather frequently for refresher training programs.

There are, in addition, pitfalls in simplified presentation, and many editors are conscious of them. Can we make everything simple? Is it actually possible, if we but put our minds to it, to tell everything about any topic in five hundred or a thousand words? Are we not misleading readers if we give them the impression that everything in this very complicated world can be made "easy"?

Areas of Attention to Change

The trend toward increased fairness in the news will continue. The matter of unfair news is a problem less serious than most critics imagine (except perhaps in labor news on some papers and political news on even fewer), but it still deserves attention. Editors have become quite conscious of this situation, and the situation will improve.

More attention will be given to filling important information needs of the public which are today somewhat neglected. Dr. George H. Gallup has called attention to the expressed interest of readers in getting deeper stories about health, education, religion, and finance; these fields and others, such as government and science, will be better covered. Obviously the problem on most papers will be to find writers with sufficient background to handle such assignments, and to find adequate funds (and a willingness to spend them) for this added coverage.

Whether major news will be given more of a sense of "completeness" or "roundness" is uncertain. Can we change the pattern of telling a day-to-day story in segments, in a chopped-up fashion which seldom brings the whole subject into focus? Can we get away from such background, the new entangled with the old, to the boredom of the regular reader? As it is, most newspaper demand seems to be for short stories rather than long, and there seems no great hope for increased use of summarizing stories in newspapers relying primarily on the wire services for such material.

Some progress will be made toward greater coverage of national and international news, partly because of increased awareness by editors of the need for this news, and in part because of greater reader interest. But the trend will be very mixed, and many dailies, especially the smaller, will put much emphasis on local news, usually at the expense of national and international news, because local news gives the greatest assurance of maintaining circulation. This will be especially true of the new suburban papers competing with metropolitan dailies, and the metropolitan dailies must also be "competitive," so they will tend to provide greater local coverage.

Will newspapers be less inclined to stress conflict and "trouble" in writing news and in selecting news for publication? Perhaps a little, but not much; interest in conflict is very deep, and newspapers will continue to recognize this interest. If competition among newspapers intensifies, there will be a stronger tendency to stress conflict, and even to build conflict into stories. A reduction in competition, and greater financial security for newspapers, may tend to reduce the pressure toward emphasizing conflict. In the same way, newspapers will continue to use many stories about people as people.

In the field of entertainment, daily newspapers will operate much as they have been. Comics will stay. They appeal strongly to both men and women and to young and old. (Comic books are of course not comics, but there is some similarity—and each year the United States spends more on comic books than on all texts for elementary schools and high schools.) An analysis of 40,158 items in 138 daily newspaper readership studies shows that comics had 56 per cent readership, easily topping every other type of content (the next category was war, with 34 per cent).

News management will not overlook the fact that other entertainment and service features also have high readership and high impact. They will be retained.

As for building citizen interest in public affairs, and a spirit of citizen participation in public affairs, newspapers will do more than they have been doing, but probably other changes will get more and earlier attention. It is one thing to write and print a story or an editorial; it is another thing to get it read, and it is still another and much more difficult matter to produce a spirit of action. Newspapers here must break ground with new methods and techniques.

Opinion Promotion

The newspaper will be able to do more to promote public expression of opinion through letters to the editor and in other ways. Not only is the function important, but newspaper executives are also realizing that most newspapers have for too long been engaged too much in one-way editorial-page communication. This is frustrating to many readers and also to editorial decision-makers who may not now be very clear on what readers want.

Newspapers will also be more active in advising the reader about the conduct of public affairs, primarily through the use of the editorial for purposes of persuasion. This effort will, in general, be more thoughtful, and better based in argument, since many newspapers are tending to increase editorial page staffs and are bringing more specialists to the work of the page. At the same time there are problems. Many readers do not like to feel that they are being "pushed"; they like at least the illusion of making up their own minds. Too vigorous activity by newspapers can produce a negative public reaction which will defeat the newspaper's basic purpose.

Certain problems are involved also in extending direct newspaper action in public affairs, such as in "auditing" the work of government. But such enterprises require a competent staff, and plenty of manpower. With the growth of big governmental units and the lessened contact of the individual with many of these units, the observing and auditing function of the press becomes more important. At the same time, newspapers will be wary of too extensive a "watchdog" activity; such activity makes enemies with long memories (of which newspapers already have an extensive supply), and the public strangely enough occasionally feels that "the newspapers ought to keep their hands off; they're too nosey."

These changes will probably be made somewhat slowly, and most of the changes will come first on the larger newspapers.

Need to Know the Reader

In this exciting, exacting, and difficult time, the character of the daily newspaper will in the main, as has been mentioned before, be determined by the interest of the individual citizen.

If the citizen's interests change (or if they are changed), if he wants something different in his newspaper, then it will be possible to change the newspaper. But if the newspaper is too far ahead of or too far away from his interests, the newspaper will weaken this essential contact with the reader.

First, then, comes the need to know more about what the reader of a given newspaper wants or, rather what he will tolerate as a limit of interest. Conventional readership surveys are of some help here in that they tell us something about how the reader responds to what is already being presented to him. But other approaches might give more information: an extended interview about types of news and/or interest in specific stories; or a survey in which the reader makes a forced choice among sample stories in a group; or a statement by the reader of the intensity of his interest in given stories.

Such surveys could also get information about reader interest in the types of news which the newspaper is not now presenting, information not usually gained by studying his reaction to stories which are now being printed.

And we need to know more about the man who "didn't read the paper today." We need to know *why* he didn't read the paper; only then can we do something effective to attract him, or to try to change him.

Obviously one factor with a potential for change is the nature of the newspaper itself. Merely by being published and by being available, and by being ready for some or many of the populace, it has an impact on the reader. News stories in newspapers have helped build reader interest in many fields (sports is an excellent example), almost always when a latent interest was present as a foundation.

The very nature of the newspaper, then, will in the longer run (and this could be in the order of twenty to fifty years) change the interests of many citizens, at least somewhat, *if* they are somehow exposed to the product either directly or through the influence of others who are exposed.

Some changes in citizen attitude may possibly be made through action of a more direct nature. Can we promote certain types of worthwhile content more extensively and effectively? Here again we do not know much about the appeals which are effective. Merely "calling attention" will build readership among those already predisposed toward the material, but how do we persuade readers to try *new* types of material and to develop interests in *new* fields? Until we know much more about this we must work with the tools of promotion which we now have. Here again we need the aid of all the tools of modern market research and selling; they could not be put to better use.

An important target is the opinion leader (even if he is not the specific and only target). If opinion leaders were somehow to expect greater readership from members of their groups—if, then, newspaper reading became more "the thing," a pronounced increase in such reading might result. This approach, though difficult, time-taking, and untested, would seem very much worth investigating.

Greater possibilities for changing and improving the tastes of the audience are possible through work with young people, and the probabilities of success seem greater.

If young people can be introduced early and effectively to the daily newspaper as a primary source of information and shown how it gives data for knowing the world and for making decisions about the world, and if the daily newspaper will perform effectively in providing this material, a tremendous change in American reading habits could be produced in the next ten years.

Of course, this effort succeeds only if the newspaper which the young people use as a training ground is a meaningful paper, full of substance. If it is a weak paper, or a timid paper, or a paper without much real content, exposure of young people to the newspaper may not only bring no progress; it may result in a setback in the feeling for all newspapers.

But if this effort is successful, then the reading habits of a whole generation could be changed.

Parents of course must be a basic factor in this process; they must aid through more discussion of public affairs in the home, more concern for the process of information, and more attention to encouraging the interests of their children in public life.

Reader Must Be Interested

In the effort for a fuller understanding and use of the newspaper, the citizen can be of much help. He has for too long a time taken too little real interest in the nature of newspapers. To be most effective, this interest must be continuing and thoughtful, with a due regard for the importance of the newspaper in the information process.

The citizen can aid by developing an understanding of the newspaper and its problems, and by becoming a small-scale evaluating agency for appraising the work of the newspaper. Such appraisal is welcomed now by many newspapers and it is being welcomed by more, but it is important to know also that many newspapers are still insensitive to appraisal and to criticism. This situation will change; more and more newspapers will come to appreciate public interest, and to welcome soundly made appraisal; many even now are conducting their own programs to determine public response to their newspapers.

The citizen can, of course, aid also through his own increased participation in public affairs. Such participation then makes easier the task of persuading other citizens to join in such an endeavor, which is a great problem indeed: to convince the citizen, who feels himself alone in the vast crowd, that he can be an effective agent in the society.

But the greatest gain which can be made is through the citizen's contribution to a change in pattern of mind.

As a nation, we are inclined to devote much of our non-working time to the pursuit of pleasure, and in most cases these are pleasures of physical activity or of quiescent non-thinking watching. We need then somehow to develop more public concern and regard for the active use of the mind, at once a pleasure but also an activity much in the interests of the public welfare. We do not hold the thinker in much regard, and the stereotype of the intellectual is such that he is thought of as impractical, aloof and almost not a person.

If we can change this image, if we can build a higher general regard for knowledge as knowledge, and for the practice of thought and contemplation as an endeavor for all citizens, we have then made great progress as a society. Whatever contribution the citizen can make toward developing this concept will be a very helpful contribution indeed.

Lord Thomson of Fleet:

Newspaper Standards for the Seventies

I MUST BE CAREFUL about prophecies as I may live to be proved wrong. Still, I have a right to speak because I have lived by investing in the press—by swimming with the tide of history, not against it. Obviously it is essential for a newspaper proprietor to try to assess future trends accurately if he is to make a success out of newspapers, which is what I try to do.

In estimating the trends of the seventies you have to take into account a number of factors. First there is the changing face of the consumer, the average reader whom you hope to attract. Then there are the technological developments in the production of newspapers, and their consequences. Further I think one is wise to ponder what I might call the philosophical aspects. There are a great many people, notably my fellow citizen of Toronto, Marshall McLuhan, who study the future of the mass media, who have useful things to say even if one does not agree with them all.

To take the reader first. In my lifetime the university population of the United States has grown from three million to 10 million, and in Great Britain from 20,000 to 200,000. This development is having as great an impact on the press as the introduction of universal education had in Northcliffe's day.

In his day it meant the advent of the popular press and mass circulation. In my day the spread of higher education compels us to produce more and more newspapers aimed at well-educated and sophisticated readers. The process is already well on its way in the expansion of the quality press which started in the fifties. I believe this expansion will go on and be intensified during the seventies. A symptom is the recent rapid rise in the circulation of *The Times*, traditionally the paper in Britain which above all others is aimed at minds of intellectual quality. It is selling over 400,000 copies as opposed to about 250,000 a few years ago, and its circulation is still moving upwards.

The process is aided and abetted by television, a medium which so far from militating against the written word, stimulates and arouses curiosity and a demand for deeper explanation of events.

▶ From: *The Times* (London), No. 57375, October 7, 1968, Special Supplement *The World's Press*. Reprinted by permission of *The Times*.

The production of papers for quality readers imposes new editorial techniques. It imposes the need for very rapid research which can only be done in a newspaper office by teamwork, and the recruiting and training of ever larger numbers of high class graduates as journalists to meet the requirements of more intelligent readership. It will, I believe, be very difficult for anyone in the seventies to become a journalist who has not got a good university degree—at any rate in the national press.

Population shift

Shifts of population are another factor. The establishment of new towns, satellite towns, housing and industrial estates on the fringes of existing large cities is changing the pattern of the provincial press. There is room to start local papers, with a strictly limited circulation, based on new, selfcontained units of population. I have already started two or three myself, and I believe this will be a socially healthy form of growth in the seventies, backed by new methods of production and distribution.

The present system of household delivery through retail newsagents is becoming more difficult. Alternative methods, in which newspapers undertake more of their own distribution directly, will become more common.

In Britain, although there will be an increased demand for quality papers, and opportunities for more local papers, I agree with the Economist Intelligence Unit that there will be a contraction in the total number of national newspapers during the seventies. With so many existing ones running at a loss—at least five dailies, including *The Times*, and two Sundays—this is surely bound to happen. There just is not the advertising available to maintain so many profitably, nor, I suspect, the readership demand. This situation is not peculiar to Britain.

The improvement in communications and the tendency towards larger political and economic groupings such as the Common Market will, I believe, have another effect. This is to extend the international press. We on *The Times* are already experiencing something like an upsurge in our European sales, and they are not to tourists but to residents. Papers of similar standards will in the seventies have a much wider international circulation among intelligent readers of all nations.

Even more important is the development of the press in the newly independent territories of the Afro-Asian world, where literacy is only now spreading. Here we have a press with many of the same problems which faced the British press at the beginning of the last century.

A national press cannot spring into life ready-made and similar in pattern and standards to the press of the developed countries. A national press is related to the political, educational and economic background of its country. Newspapers in developing countries have to develop with them, though it is open to us to assist where we can with capital and training, as organizations like the Commonwealth Press Union and the International Press Institute are doing. I expect the press in these countries to grow in influence and quality, but I do not expect it to achieve immediately the characteristics of the press in countries where it has had 200 years to develop.

I come now to technological development. The newspaper industry has been remarkable in the past for its lack of any radical technological innovations over a long period. Much of this has been due to the cautious attitude of management, with its vast investments in heavy conventional equipments, backed by the conservatism of the trade unions who have been suspicious of the effects of new methods on security of employment. However, technological development is upon all of us, whether we welcome it, as I do, or no. Web offset printing presses, photo-composition, computerization, satellite printing and closed-circuit television will all make their appearance in newspaper offices. Some are already there.

New methods

We do not know all the answers yet. The application of some of these new methods so far has been generally limited to smallish papers. We must find how they can be adapted to the national ones. They could lead to decentralization through simultaneous printing in many different centres, thereby bypassing the difficulties of producing national newspapers against time in one or two large centres and distributing them over long distances by road, rail and air.

Great effort will be concentrated on development of techniques for rapid high grade colour printing. This will be forced on the industry by the spread of colour television. Another possible development in the seventies could be the projection of newspapers on to television screens in the home, with selection of pages controlled by the viewer. This development is still problematic and I do not know whether by the time it can be perfected it will meet a real need.

The consequential benefits of electronic and kindred devices will be not only to produce better papers more easily, but also to reduce costs. Because newspapers will be produced in smaller buildings with fewer staff, it should be possible to redress to a great extent the imbalance between advertising and sales revenue in newspaper economy. I am not suggesting that newspapers will ever dispense with advertising as a source of revenue, but I would regard a 50-50 ratio as between advertising and sales as reasonable. I do not believe the present heavy preponderance of advertising revenue as a means of survival for some newspapers is in the long run safe or healthy for the industry.

In conclusion, I would like to make a few points about the relationship between press and television in the future, and particularly on the theories of Marshall McLuhan.

Television is, of course, in competition with newspapers in that it takes away from the volume of advertising and thereby helps to force closures. I do not believe it is in competition in the sense that Marshall McLuhan says it is.

He seems to me to be right about some things and wrong about others. He is right in saying that the modern generation are accustomed to electronic media such as television, radio and computers as a matter of course in a way which their elders were not.

I do not believe he is right in his tenet that "the medium is the message"—or, in punning terms, as he puts it, "the massage." By this I understand him to mean that a whole generation is being conditioned through electronic media, in a hypnotic sense, that they are being accustomed to think in an environment in which they develop their auditory sense, while their visual sense—the sense that relies on the printed word —becomes atrophied. I do not believe this to be true. I believe Marshall McLuhan is right in saying that the electronic media open vast new opportunities, but I do not believe the medium is the message. I believe the content remains equally important whether it is delivered through the written word or through television.

Television, like the motor car and the aeroplane in their time, is a fascinating new invention, but it is the servant, not the master, of the message it seeks to convey. There are some things it can never do as well as newspapers. Its impact is visual and instant. It cannot examine in detail and explain in the way that a newspaper can. And it is this weakness which not only allows newspapers to coexist with it, but also actively stimulates the need for quality newspapers among viewers.

For this reason I believe the press still has a great future in the seventies, provided proprietors and editors understand its real role in the age of electronics, and shape it so that it is complementary to and not just competitive with the new media.

Hugh Cudlipp:

The Role of the Press in the Lunar Age

THE YEAR 1969 will be remembered as long as the human race exists as the year when the first men were able to leave this planet, travel to and explore another, and return to tell their story—exclusively or otherwise, but certainly at great expense—on Mother Earth.

How will this capability for inter-planetary travel affect man's view of his world and of himself? The answer is—profoundly.

We knew, before Wendell Willkie told us, that this is one world. Those of us who have travelled round it by jet plane have a sense of its smallness.

The world may not yet be a global village as Marshall McLuhan has described it. But it is certainly a global city, the oceans, its lakes, the forests its gardens, the desert, its vacant lots awaiting exploitation.

We can, of course, continue to love the small suburb of that world city which we call Britain. What we can no longer do is to regard as foreign countries the suburbs over the "Kanal"—as the Germans in their wisdom call the English Channel.

Of course here in Cologne they have a slightly idiosyncrastic dialect of English. When they want to say "the winter is cold and the summer is warm" they say "Der winter ist kalt und der sommer ist warm."

Or take the French. They do not talk plainly about liberty, equality, fraternity as we do. They call it liberté, egalité, fraternité—leebertay, aygalitay, fraterneetay.

These different dialects do present some difficulties to us. And that is a pity. For not only has the effective speed of travel been multiplied by 50 in the past 150 years—other communications have actually abolished time. The transmitted message today can be received in virtually no time at all in any part of the world where they have a little electricity.

The group of suburbs we call Western Europe have stopped fighting one another, have stopped imposing tariffs on one another's products and in time they will have one town council which they will call a government.

▶ This is a slightly shortened version of a talk by the Chairman of the International Publishing Corp., Ltd., London, at the Annual Conference of the British Institute of Journalists, meeting in Cologne on September 3, 1969. Reprinted by permission of Mr. Cudlipp. The original speech was entitled "Now that Man has Set Foot on the Moon, What is the New Role of the Press on Earth?"

In the British suburb we looked on this development a bit sniffily. And when we changed our view, we had a lot of trouble from the Mayor of France, a retired General called—what was his name—Charles de Gaulle. He has given up his chain of office and we are now trying again.

And some day we shall be accepted. The Kanal, which I have crossed many times in my small boat at night, will no longer divide us spiritually or physically. We'll tunnel under it. We'll bridge over it. We are already skimming over it in Hovercrafts in a matter of hours.

We are certainly going to need a European newspaper and more than one European newspaper. The Unit of Government always requires newspapers which cover its full range.

Incidentally, the United States I believe would be healthier if the great newspapers were not simply city, or even city and state journals, but coast to coast publications. What prevents this is no longer lack of technical means: it is the dependence of U.S. newspapers on local advertising.

I am pleading for newspapers everywhere—including all those in the group over which I now preside—to be less parochial, to be interested in a wider slice of this small world, and to interest their readers in it. Not easy. Not possible to do quickly. But a goal to be aimed at over the years. We, the mass media, have to lead our readers, our viewers, our listeners.

"Nation shall speak peace unto nation"—that is the motto of the B.B.C. It is an admirable motto. I wish the B.B.C. would do more of it than they do.

*   *   *   *

Of course it may be asked—What about the newspapers in general, and what about your popular newspapers in particular? We are all to some extent vulnerable, the popular newspapers especially so.

There are two sad facts about foreign news which all newspapers have to face. The first is that readership is extremely limited. The second is that the commodity is expensive.

A newspaper which maintains a first-class foreign service will earn its reward not on this earth but only in heaven. It takes a strong editor to resist the hawk-eyed, hard-hearted accountant who, at a moment when the profits are going down, confronts him with two things: one the bill of costs, two the readership survey. Foreign news is at the top of the first; at the bottom of the second.

The answer to the accountant is this—you cannot look at costing in this piecemeal way. Some copy is naturally cheap. You can get a copious and highly printable flow from merely two or three men at Westminster. On a cost-benefit analysis the Parliamentary men might come out on top. Other copy—particularly foreign copy—may be outrageously expensive and may make only a small *quantitive* contribution to the paper.

Yet its *qualitative* value might be great. I would not wish to take a newspaper which did not have first-class men in the U.S., in Paris, in Germany, in the Far East, for example. It would be incomplete. I would like to add Moscow to the list. But it is still doubtful whether representation there is worth the high cost. Your Moscow Correspondent is not able to operate as a free journalist needs to operate. So your Soviet expert— and you must have one on any British national newspaper—may operate better, on balance, from his home base with occasional tours behind the iron curtain.

How strange it is that while Russia is itself preparing for lunar adventure, its own interior should still be kept in a mediaeval straitjacket, its people not free to travel the world, some of its best writers in prison, and one distinguished author who prefers to live abroad regarded as a foul traitor to country and creed.

*   *   *   *

British national newspapers do provide themselves with a first-class service of international news, and damn the expense. Unfortunately they are not able to make fullest use of it because of low reader interest except in times of crisis. What should we do?

Wring our hands in despair, accept the facts of life, and regard our men abroad simply as a fire brigade who will be there when the bell rings in the country they cover for a great crisis that will be of universal interest?

I do not think so.

Our foreign correspondents in this day and age are more important than most of our Ambassadors. Even the newspaper executive travelling abroad can be useful. In a major foreign country I visited a few years ago I had arranged a long and leisurely talk and exchange of views with the Prime Minister. When I mentioned to the British Ambassador that I would be seeing the Prime Minister the next day, he politely begged me to take him along with me: he had been unable to talk with the Prime Minister for the previous ten months.

Reluctantly I agreed. But the talk would have been more intimate and revealing in his absence.

In Britain *The Times, The Daily Telegraph,* and—to a lesser extent, because of expense—*The Guardian* provide a splendid foreign service. But their audience is regrettably limited. The newspapers with the vaster problem because of their vaster audience are the leading "populars," the *Daily Mirror* and the *Daily Express.*

No newspaper has splashed its money around more courageously on world-wide news coverage than the *Daily Express* over the years. All credit to it.

Its problem, like that of the *Mirror,* has always been one of presentation and interpretation. One of the more pleasurable arts of journalism to me has always been the explanation and interpretation of intricate political, economic, and foreign affairs to the wider audience. That is the essentially worthwhile reward of producing a successful popular newspaper —and in my view no popular newspaper is successful, however profitable it may be as a business, unless it succeeds in projecting to the masses a compelling and accurate picture of the material factors that govern their wellbeing and progress.

* * * *

At the *Daily Mirror* we have experimented with all kinds of techniques to interest the reader in foreign news. For some years we ran a World Spotlight page. Then we invented Mirrorscope, an endeavour to present deeper analysis and more sophisticated description by using high quality magazine techniques achieved at newspaper speed.

We have certainly interested journalists and politicians. But the ultimate test will be how many readers will find Mirrorscope compulsive reading. The result so far is greatly encouraging. Readers have to be given time to come to terms with anything new and serious you do in a newspaper. Fleet Street is littered with the corpses of brainchildren who were killed simply because nobody had the patience to let them grow and develop.

Too much change, too many brief experiments are as bad for newspapers as the opposite policy of being afraid to change anything until you are forced into desperately improvised action by a significant decline in sale.

We have experimented—and still are experimenting—in ways of interesting readers in the wider world.

We have also at I.P.C. brought over the leading journalists from France, Germany, Holland, Russia, Poland and Czechoslovakia to discuss with the Editors of the British national Press and serious periodicals the unresolved problems of Europe and the world.

* * * *

In this new lunar-nuclear world, we are faced with a paradox. We have produced the most fabulous means of communication. We can see in colour, in our own homes, the descent of the moon men into a remote ocean. We are more privileged than Cortez. We *live* on a peak in Darien.

And as the astronauts descend, the stills of the event are simultaneously bounced into our newspaper offices. To take a humbler example. In the Ulster riots, the Irish editions of the *Mirror* were able to produce the yellow flames of the burning buildings, the ominous red glow in the Belfast sky, and distribute the newspapers containing this record before the ashes were cold.

And all this is within the lifetime of newspapermen who remember when the swiftest way of sending a picture or a story between two points was often to tie a flimsy, or a spool of film, to the leg of a racing pigeon.

When I was a young reporter in Manchester I listened in awe to a member of the shooting party who years before had brought down an obstinate pigeon who endlessly circled above a newspaper office in that city on a Saturday evening—foolishly forgetting he was carrying the result of a major soccer match in London. Bang. Bang. It was edition time.

Yet there is a paradox. As the media become more and more efficient, the messages themselves are tending to become more dim. And this dimness of the message is itself a product of the processes which give us our superb communications; they are the messages of a complex, technological society.

Often today, in a newspaper office, we find ourselves coping with a cataract of messages which are either obscure because of their complexity, or meaningless because they are demagogic over-simplifications put out by politicians.

The true but obscure messages are complex simply because the problems of running an advanced industrial society are themselves complex.

*   *   *   *

How much simpler it was in the days even of our own youth when the role of government was so much smaller, when budgets were balanced —or else—and when mass unemployment was regarded as a mysterious act of God outside the province of government. In those days public finance was roughly analogous to domestic or company accounting, or at least within the realm of ordinary commonsense.

How easy it was for Chancellors such as Mr. Gladstone or Lloyd George to explain and defend their policies in clear and beautiful language made vivid and real by parables from the Bible and classical literature. Those were the days of the memorable metaphor in policies, the days of the soaring simile.

But of course, Gladstone would not understand one clause of a modern finance bill, and Lloyd George, although he was one of the earliest advocates of a Keynesian system, would be a novice in the Treasury capsule today. There is no Biblical parable to explain devaluation, re-flation, or overheating.

I suggest to you that unexciting as the prospect may be, it is no accident that grey men are propelled, or manoeuvre themselves, into the positions of power at this stage of the second half of the Twentieth Century.

The old romantics are not right for the political space age: hence the cold technicians, the committee-consensus men with guarded lips. If you doubt that we *need* them, we must admit that that's what we've got.

Whether we like it or not, we shall, I believe, get more and more men at the political controls who are the political equivalents of Aldrin, Collins and Armstrong: I hope brave, I hope self-disciplined, but naturally taciturn. Men who, justifiably or otherwise, pride themselves on being better at thinking and doing than talking and explaining.

This places new and tremendous obligations on us as professional communicators, as journalists facing the new problems on Earth in the first year man set foot on the moon.

We have to help our readers to make sense of the highly technical and complex operations of grey-men governments at home and abroad.

And, at least as far as those at home are concerned, we have to say firmly where the people and ourselves think they should take us—and stop them if they are on the wrong or undesirable course.

None of us wishes to live even in a benevolent 1984 in which good politico-technologists do good things on the people's behalf. Nobody wants a system in which the political argument is carried on in incomprehensible terms by two sets of grey men, government and opposition, while the people look inertly on and wait to have things done *for* them, and, worse, *to* them.

Somehow we as journalists have to become as good as our means of communication now are. Our basic function is to help our readers to make sense of the world, to understand how it is run, and play their part in saying how it should be run.

We must excel at the art of exposition. We must achieve what the new grey-men governments at home and abroad, either through inaptitude or ineptitude, cannot achieve for themselves.

The need, in the lunar-exploration age, is greater than ever for journalists of the highest integrity and ability who themselves understand what is going on and are capable of translating their knowledge into terms which will both interest and enlighten the ordinary man.

We are not just entertainers. But we have always to remember that if we do not interest and hold or hypnotise our readers, if we simply present them with a mass of worthy but unpalatably soggy material, we shall simply bore them and drive them away. We shall certainly fail to enlighten them.

It is wonderful to get exact knowledge about the ancient mystery of the silvery moon. It is, however, vital for men to understand what is really happening down on their habitat, Old Mother Earth. This is the mighty and exciting mission of journalism today.

Wilson P. Dizard:

Future Patterns of International Television

IN George Orwell's vision of 1984, conformity and fear are symbolized by ever-present television screens controlled by Big Brother. The vision is only partly prophetic. We probably have the wit and the will to avoid the political tyranny Orwell described. We may be less skillful in coping with the brash, ubiquitous power of television.

Long before 1984, television will be the world's most influential mass communications medium. It is already establishing its primacy in the industrialized West and in Japan; the rest of the world is catching up quickly. Television stations in over 90 countries today serve an audience of over 750 million persons. [In the] 1970's this audience will have doubled in size as national networks expand to cover all but the most isolated areas. Regional and intercontinental networks will be commonplace, making possible electronic links anywhere on earth. TV's influence will stretch from Minsk to Manila, from London to Lima, and on to the Nigerian upcountry city of Kaduna where even now bearded camel drivers and local tribesmen sit in fascinated harmony before a teahouse television set watching "Bonanza."

By 1975, television will be an integral part of a vast international communications network built around computers and space satellites. These machines will provide any kind of data instantaneously in all parts of the world to meet the needs of the new information explosion. They will carry a dialogue of experts speaking the international language of technology, and that dialogue will affect the prospects for a more stable world order. Television can be the sight-and-sound interpreter of the dialogue, making it understandable to everyone. Properly used, television can be the forum of a new age of interdependence, the only mass medium fully capable of crossing geographical, cultural, and political barriers to link men and nations in an evolving world community.

The alternative is a world struggling to meet its informational needs largely through traditional means. This is a losing race. Books and other written materials reach no more than half the earth's population. The

▶ From: *Television: A World View*, by Wilson P. Dizard. Copyright © 1966 by Syracuse University Press, Syracuse, New York. Reprinted by permission of the publisher.

other half is still functionally illiterate. Outside Europe, Japan, and the United States, newspapers are an insignificant media factor. The film medium has developed primarily as an entertainment spectacle. Only radio is still expanding at a rate which begins to match present-day mass communications needs.

Where does television fit into the pattern? At one extreme are those who conjure up Orwellian prospects of large screens feeding the mindless mass with doublespeak or, at least, Dick Van Dyke comedies. At the other extreme are the Pollyanna believers in television as an instrument for bringing people together in some sort of electronic Chautauqua. The broad confusion of intensely propounded evaluations suggests the need for consensus. For the present, we have a stunning means of reaching one another without a clear idea of what it signifies for us. The situation recalls Thoreau's doubts about building telegraph lines to Texas before one decides what to say to Texans. Television has materialized so quicky from a fast-moving technological revolution that we have not had a reflective chance to define its purpose and set its goals, here or abroad.

We can be sure only that television is here, and that there is going to be more of it very soon. Whatever its long-range implications, TV will soon be the first medium to be shared and understood by virtually everyone on earth. André Malraux once summarized the internationalization of culture by describing a film in which a Swedish actress playing a Russian heroine works for an American director to draw tears from the Chinese. But motion-picture films pale before television's unique sight-and-sound ability to bring both reality and fantasy directly to Everyman. Never was a single emotion shared by so many people as on the day in November, 1963, when three hundred million persons on four continents watched the televised funeral of a martyred American president. Television is not only a recorder of events in a revolutionary age; it is, by its persuasive immediacy, a major tool for shaping the age. Presenting with electronic impartiality not only reality but also the fantasies which cushion us from reality, it is the ultimate instrument of both confrontation and escape. Television serves this double function with a subtlety that makes it the despair of those who try to define its purposes.

Television is no longer a Western monopoly, with a Japanese extension. In a decade it has spread from a few hundred transmitters grouped largely in the North Atlantic area to over four thousand stations on five continents. It covers all of Latin America and the Middle East. In the Communist bloc, it is the most rapidly expanding mass medium, a new weapon in the regimes' propaganda arsenal. Over half of the new African nations have added television to their list of chauvinistic prestige symbols. In South Asia and the Far East, only a handful of smaller countries— Burma, Cambodia, Laos, and Ceylon—have resisted the introduction of television. For the rest of the so-called underdeveloped countries, television is perhaps the most readily available and prominently visible of the amenities of political independence and economic promise of things to come.

Equally significant is the rapid development of regional and intercontinental networks. The earliest and most successful of these has been in operation in Europe for over a decade. It is the pacesetting Eurovision network of a thousand stations in seventeen countries connected in a four thousand-mile relay. In Eastern Europe a similar Communist network, Intervision, links stations in seven countries. Geographical and political difficulties have inhibited the development of similar connections in other parts of the world. By 1975, however, such regional links will be commonplace. Five Central American nations already operate a network which will one day be part of a Latin American chain stretching from the Rio Grande to the Strait of Magellan. In the Far East, Japanese interests are promoting the idea of an "Asiavision" network linking cities from Tokyo to Karachi. Arab nationalists, led by the United Arab Republic's Gamal Abdel Nasser, see a television network as a powerful stimulus to Arab unity. Even African leaders, beset by post-independence political and economic turmoil, talk expansively of continent-wide television within the next decade.

One day within the next twenty years a TV antenna will be raised in the most isolated village in Africa. And there will no longer be any remote places. All the trivia and profundities that one man can pass on to another will be open to Everyman, staring at his living room screen.

For many this prospect conjures up images of automated Big Brother conformity. For others it augurs well for a more peaceful international order. The fact that intelligent men can draw such contradictory conclusions from the same set of facts is a rough indication of television's power and of our difficulties in understanding it. The reality of TV's global influence lies, in fact, somewhere between 1984 and Utopia.

The United States has special responsibilities in defining the potentials of world-wide use of the medium. Historically, they have set the pace of television's development both as a lightweight entertainment medium and as an instrument of informational and cultural exchange. We have a stake in the medium as a positive force serving a changing international order.

Our own national interests will be strongly influenced by our ability, through TV, to bring the sights and sounds of American life to overseas audiences. Equally important will be television's role in giving this vast audience a new image of their own societies in a fast-changing world. The flickering screen can confront them with the realities of a new world order and their relationship to it. Or it can shield them from this reality and their responsibilities by offering them a bland diet of escape programs and inane chatter.

We can affect the quality of world television to a limited but significant degree. Whatever we do will be determined largely by the activities of our own domestic television system. We cannot have one standard of conduct for television at home and another for our actions abroad. Ours is a glass-house culture, highly visible to the outside. Attempts to offer the rest of the world a sanitized version of American life at any level have always been self-defeating. The tone of our commitment to television's development as a positive international force will be set primarily by the commercial television industry and its activities here.

The question, then, is whether U.S. television is capable of representing our full national interests abroad. For the present, the answer must be a qualified no. Fault cannot be found with the technical and commercial achievements of U.S. television; American industry is the world leader in these areas. The weaknesses lie in programing limitations. We produce more television programs for export than all other nations combined; in 1966 over eighty million dollars' worth of programs were sent to over ninety countries. American programs dominate the most popular listening hours in many foreign countries because of high production quality and entertainment value.

By and large our television exports are useful, if bland, portrayals of various segments of American life. The claim that they represent a poor image of America is largely overdone. The record is better than most critics of U.S. television are willing to concede, but it still falls considerably short of a reasonable ideal. What the networks produce and sell is not always the best or the most representative either of American life of or television's potential. We need to be represented on overseas television by something more than the standard formula of cowboy serials, detective films, pratfall comedies, and an occasional news documentary. An overseas viewer would be hard put to believe, from what he sees on his screen, that contemporary America is a leader in the lively arts such as drama, architecture, painting, and sculpture, or to understand the workings of our economic system or our current struggle to build a truly democratic multiracial society. These subjects are seldom raised in the bland products that make up most of the U.S. television export package.

Censorship of allegedly "bad" television exports is no solution; it raises many more problems for a free society than it might settle. Proposals for official government subsidy to encourage a higher level of program exports, advanced in some quarters, are both politically unrealistic and otherwise unworkable. What is needed is a greater diversification of program sources within the domestic television industry. Already, signs point to such a development. The commercial networks and their affiliated stations will continue to be dominant, both politically and economically; but their dominance will be modified during the next decade by several newer forms of television operations.

Outstanding among these new forms are educational television (ETV), subscription or pay television (STV), and ultra-high-frequency channel television (UHF). Individually, none of these outlets will match the influence of the three large networks. Collectively, however, they will add a large measure of variety and competition to the American TV scene. Educational TV, already represented by more than a hundred community stations, will continue to expand and to improve in ways that will give greater dimensions to public-service television. Pay television promises to provide a high level of top-quality entertainment. Several hundred new UHF stations will complement network-controlled VHF outlets, with schedules emphasizing specialized programs for smaller audiences. Television will then be an instrument better serving both majority and minority interests.

Diversification will expand the spectrum of programs and other services available to foreign stations. The commercial networks and the Hollywood film syndicators may have a somewhat smaller share of the total export market, but the market will still be enormously profitable to them, given the steady increase in the number of overseas outlets and the popularity of American network products. The standardized light entertainment that is the networks' stock-in-trade will still get the lion's share of the overseas market. However, foreign stations also will be able to shop for programs covering other aspects of American life, produced by the operators of subscription television, educational TV, and other new elements.

But aside from these signs of developmental trends, there are a number of specific steps the United States should take to strengthen our over-all position in international television:

1. *There should be closer liaison arrangements between the industry and government to assure unified American policy, whenever practical, in international TV matters.* With the development of communications satellites and regional networks, the politics of international television are becoming increasingly complex. The U.S. networks and other elements of the TV industry find themselves often at a practical disadvantage in negotiating with state-controlled television organizations in other countries.

The United States is often inadequately represented in such negotiations simply because it does not speak with one voice as do the other countries. In the European Broadcasting Union, U.S. interests are represented by seven television organizations, only one of which (the U.S. Information Agency) represents the official government position. Although the views and the interests of all seven coincide more often than not, the members seldom speak as a united group. The result is needless downgrading of American influence in discussions of EBU policy and programing matters in which both U.S. industry and the government have an interest.

The answer to this problem lies in *ad hoc* arrangements between government and industry to assure, whenever possible, a concerted American approach. The main stumbling block to such arrangements is the industry's wariness concerning any form of official control over its overseas operations. Informal consultative machinery could be devised, however, to facilitate group decisions among the government and the major networks as well as other American TV organizations such as the National Educational Television network, commercial television film producers and syndicators, electronic equipment manufacturers, and independent television stations. Any of the participants in discussions could be free to dissociate itself from any such group decision.

2. *The United States should take the lead in forming an Inter-American Broadcasting Union.* Latin American countries have made several attempts to form a regional organization patterned on the European Broadcasting Union. They have failed mainly because they lacked a strong organizational push. The United States should vitalize this lagging effort, for its success could improve regional communications throughout the hemisphere. U.S. initiative in such a project should be worked out in ways that would quell any Latin suspicions that we might dominate the new organization. Our interests are best served by deferring to Latin sensitivities in this regard. A good working model can be found in the activities of the American Broadcasting Company (ABC) in encouraging five Central American countries to set up a regional network.

Development of a full hemisphere network could be stepped up through the use of communications satellites set up on a north-south axis. With television firmly established in most Latin American countries, such a network could greatly enhance our political and cultural relations with countries to the south and north.

3. *The American government and the television industry should establish firm policies regarding TV broadcasting by communications satellites.* This subject could be an important continuing item on the agenda of the government-industry consultative committee proposed above. Although the 1962 congressional legislation setting up the Communications Satellite Corporation specifies that the U.S.-constructed satellite system should have a clear-cut public-service function, no one has clearly defined what this function is. The corporation has put its operational emphasis on those services (telephone, teletype, etc.) which eventually promise a profitable return on the investment made by its thousands of stockholders. Television ranks relatively low on the list of profitable uses of satellite transmission time. In this instance, however, profit margins and political factors do not jibe. Because of its highly visual nature, television will be a key element in the public image of the American-built satellite system. Our national claims to responsibility in developing and operating a worldwide comsat system will depend to a large extent on television, whether it is a profitable item of business or not.

4. *American educational television should be encouraged to take a more positive role in cooperating with overseas ETV efforts, particularly in developing countries.* After a dozen years of trial-and-error experimentation, American ETV is the world leader in technical, administrative, and programing techniques for television teaching. The Japanese may make more intensive use of educational TV, but they cannot equal the American range of experience at all levels of this new and exciting teaching tool. The fruits of our experience should be made more readily available to educators and broadcasters abroad, particularly in Asia, Africa, and Latin America. By sharing our knowledge, we could strengthen educational systems in developing areas. By adapting our ETV programs for local use, we could offer to millions of students abroad a balanced, objective picture of the world around them, including the United States. In so doing, we could achieve significant political impact in correcting some of the fanciful mythologies that overseas students have about us.

The obstacle here is financing. Most U.S. educational TV systems operate on a deficit or on the thin edge of solvency. They are dependent largely on yearly appropriations from a variety of public and private sources. There are, however, precedents for making funds available to ETV groups for overseas work. A good case can also be made for involving the federal government more directly in this field. While congressmen and educators are generally reluctant to see federal funds used for direct curriculum assistance in the United States, their fears of Washington control over local education do not apply abroad. The government has already made some significant moves in this direction with its limited ETV technical-assistance projects in Nigeria and Colombia.

5. *The U.S. government should explore more intensively the direct use of television as a tool of modernization in developing countries.* Our efforts to assist television in developing countries are now concentrated on use of the medium as a classroom teaching tool. We could initiate new pilot projects to measure TV's usefulness as a conscious instrument of social change, orienting people of all ages to their individual and collective responsibilities in a rapidly changing society. The countries selected for these pilot projects would have to be chosen carefully. The danger of any intensive use of television as a social weapon is its potential as an instrument to support dictatorial regimes in the developing areas. It can be argued, for instance, that Egypt's President Nasser is employing television as a modernization tool because of its extensive schedule of popular education programs; it is also true that Egyptian television is a propaganda instrument, restricting the *political* modernization of the country.

Despite the risks, further experimentation is justified. Any powerful instrument can be dangerous, but the power of television will be needed to break the chains of ignorance and fear that impede the modernization process.

6. *The U.S. government should consider more seriously the potentialities of television as an informational and cultural tool directly supporting its political objectives.* Every American program that appears on overseas television affects, in some small degree, the international political fortunes of the United States. Overseas prejudices are confirmed, or modified, each time Danny Kaye, Lucille Ball, the Ben Cartright clan, or other such familiar faces are shown on overseas TV screens. These popular stars make television the most influential carrier of the American image to vast audiences throughout the world. Also contributing to the image is a more specialized type of program whose purpose is to support directly U.S. foreign-policy objectives. These are the programs prepared for overseas showings by the U.S. Information Agency, overseas information and cultural arm of the American government.

USIA has been in the business of overseas television since 1953 when it inaugurated a small TV operation as a subsection of the radio Voice of America. The agency's television service has expanded steadily since then; its studio facilities in Washington serve posts in over eighty countries. However, the agency TV budget is less than a fifth of the funds allotted to the Voice of America. There is a reasonable doubt whether this disparity accurately reflects the relative roles radio and television should be playing in the U.S. overseas information program.

Short-wave radio is still USIA's most important media operation directed toward Eastern Europe, the Soviet Union, Cuba, Communist China, and other areas where the agency is unable to conduct the usual information and cultural activities such as libraries and film showings. The Voice of America is also important in certain areas of Africa and Asia where, in the absence of television, radio broadcasting is the most influential mass medium. In all other parts of the world, however, the rapid expansion of TV facilities has had the uniform effect of reducing the hours of radio listening. USIA has increased the ratio of its television operations to the point where TV now accounts for about 10 percent of its annual media operations budget. The question remains whether this is an accurate reflection of television's potential for keeping overseas audiences informed on matters directly affecting U.S. foreign policy.

7. *The United States should resist attempts to restrict the free flow of news and other information over international television channels.* Censorship is a continuing threat to the full development of television as a world medium. The classic example of what can happen may be found in the history of international short-wave radio. Despite attempts during the twenties to organize this medium as a genuine instrument for the free exchange of information, radio evolved primarily as a propaganda weapon in the service of competing nationalisms. Television could fall into a similar trap. The temptation is strong in many nations to restrict participation in global television to national prestige programs. Communist and other totalitarian regimes can be relied upon to impose restrictions. Even

in many free world countries, the tradition of freedom of expression in broadcasting is more limited than it is here. Much of the free-swinging discussion that takes place on American radio and TV would be considered slanderous in other democratic countries. The United States will have to press hard to release these inhibitions against full discussion when the ground rules for international telecasting are made. Every country, including our own, will want to use international television for prestige propaganda purposes. Our concern should be to assure that the new global channels are also open to programs which offer independent viewpoints on a wide range of subjects.

Aside from reaffirming our tradition of free discussion, an "open channels" policy should prove useful in strengthening information links between the free world and Communist countries. The leadership in those countries undoubtedly will want to make use of comsat and other international TV channels to bring the story of "Socialist achievements" to free world audiences. We should encourage them to do so, provided two ground rules are observed. The first is that there should be equality in the amount and type of programs exchanged between Communist and free world nations. The second is that neither side should be allowed to impose arbitrary censorship on exchanges. Given the rapid expansion of television in Communist-dominated areas, we have everything to gain through a widened, unfettered dialogue which will reduce the psychological and informational barriers separating us from men and women in these areas.

While we are extolling the virtues of the free flow of ideas, we should make sure that we are practicing what we preach in our own TV activities overseas. We are not immune to the temptation to put our own best national foot forward and to try to slide past the less complimentary facts. It would be a mistake for us to succumb to this temptation. Our commitment to an open society would be compromised. The Italian author Cesare Pavese once wrote: "America is the gigantic theater where, with greater candor than elsewhere, is being played out the drama of us all." If we believe that our democratic pluralistic society has lessons for the rest of the world, we have no choice but to present ourselves as we are.

During the coming decades we share with the rest of mankind the need to create a more stable world order, moving beyond the present restraints of a nuclear stalemate and of social and economic disorder. This new order will be stillborn if we do not make good use of the available implements of world communications. Hundreds of millions of ordinary men and women must be made aware of the facts of a new age and of the alternatives facing us. Television will be only one of the forces in this massive effort to get the beginnings of a consensus. We can use this unique instrument as nothing more than the greatest entertainment circus of all time. Or we can employ it fully as a sight-and-sound interpreter of the problems we face, capable of reaching more people than has ever been possible with any other information medium ever invented.

12

RESEARCH IN INTERNATIONAL COMMUNICATION

Paul F. Lazarsfeld
THE PROGNOSIS FOR INTERNATIONAL COMMUNICATION
    RESEARCH

W. Phillips Davison and Alexander L. George
AN OUTLINE FOR THE STUDY OF INTERNATIONAL
    POLITICAL COMMUNICATION

Godwin C. Chu
PROBLEMS OF CROSS-CULTURAL COMMUNICATION
    RESEARCH

Gerhard Maletzke
INTERCULTURAL AND INTERNATIONAL COMMUNICATION

12

RESEARCH IN INTERNATIONAL COMMUNICATION

ALTHOUGH there had been some pioneers in the 1930's and in the early 1940's, the real boom in international or cross-national communication research started after World War II. The first intention in the United States after 1945 was "to develop an art and science of international and cross-cultural communication and opinion, in the hope of reducing international confusion and irritation" (B. L. Smith). The same author says that *international communication* should not be "restricted to campaigns of information conducted by government," because it "also includes the negotiations conducted by diplomats; the activities of international news-gathering agencies; the creation of impressions abroad by tourists and other migrants; the probably massive but generally unplanned impact of books, art works, and movies distributed in foreign countries; the international contacts of students, educators, scientists, and technical assistance experts; the negotiations and correspondence of international business interests; the activities of international missionaries and religious movements; the work of international pressure groups, such as trade unions, chambers of commerce, and political parties; international philanthropic activities. . . ."

This broad phalanx of research areas demonstrates the impossibility for the single researcher to cover all or nearly all of these fields. International communication research still is a rather young and sometimes badly arranged discipline. Because of this situation, Hamid Mowlana from the American University of Washington, D.C., on a National Conference on the Teaching of International Communication in March, 1969, made these remarks: "The increasing detachment of international communication from its parent disciplines to become a field in its own, is depriving the teacher of the use of systematic analytic framework borrowed from other fields such as anthropology, psychology, or international relations for the study and comprehension of international communication. There has not been sufficient time and experience to permit the formation of an analytic framework which can identify and define the central concepts and foundations, or precisely limit the scope of the field. Rather there exists a collec-

449

tion of diverse perspectives which try to order a vast system with nebulous boundaries. These are most difficult conditions to operate under. . . ."

But there really is no reason to be too pessimistic, because there is a steadily increasing number of research results from many countries, most of them on a graduate or general upper level. Especially for this kind of research, it is true what John C. Merrill says about *Graduate Study in Journalism and Mass Communications* (AEJ Leaflet No. 2): "The main objective of doctoral study in journalism or mass communications is to develop advanced research facility and to integrate this skill and orientation with a depth of general scholarship in mass communications. . . . The emphasis is on independent work and original research which culminates in an original dissertation or thesis." Among the various communication disciplines, especially the methods and approaches in the field of international or intercultural communication research have to be refined. James W. Markham, speaking about this research area at the Convention of the Association for Education in Journalism in Lawrence, Kansas, August, 1968, said: "I see this scholarly discipline as a vital part of a larger interdisciplinary specialized area of inquiry upon which a number of behavioral science disciplines are converging. This field has been defined as the analysis of international systems behavior."

Under these circumstances, it seems to be especially necessary to give some methodological approaches in this book, written by experts in the field of research techniques. The opening article of this final chapter is from Dr. Paul F. Lazarsfeld of New York's Columbia University who is a pioneer in this field and an outstanding scholar. The communications expert, Dr. W. Phillips Davison, and the political scientist, Dr. Alexander L. George, are authors of an interdisciplinary article. Some of the problems of cross-cultural communication are demonstrated by Dr. Godwin C. Chu from the Canadian University of Victoria. Finally, an overview about certain approaches and the distinction between international and cross-cultural communication research is given by Dr. Gerhard Maletzke who does research and teaching in West Berlin. All these authors together at least give an idea of what the difficulties are and also what the future promises for this fascinating research area.

*   *   *   *

RELATED READING

Buchanan, William, and Hadley Cantril. *How Nations see Each Other*. Urbana, Illinois: University of Illinois Press, 1953.

Farrell, R. Barry, (ed.). *Approaches to Comparative and International Politics*. Evanston, Illinois: Northwestern University Press, 1966.

Gordon, George N., Irving Falk, and William Hodapp. *The Idea Invaders*. New York: Hastings House, 1963.

Joseph, Franz M. (ed.). *As others see us: The United States through foreign eyes.* Princeton/N.J.: Princeton University Press, 1959.

Kelman, Herbert C. (ed.). *International Behavior.* New York: Holt, Rinehart and Winston, 1965.

Lerner, Daniel, and Harold D(wight) Lasswell (eds.). *The Policy Sciences.* Stanford, Calif.: Stanford University Press, 1951.

Maletzke, Gerhard. *Psychologie der Massenkommunikation. Theorie und Systematik.* Hamburg: Verlag Hans—Bredow—Institut, 1963.

Merritt, Richard L. and Stein Rokkan (eds.). *Comparing Nations. The Use of Quantitative Data in Cross-National Research.* New Haven and London: Yale University Press, 1966.

Moore, F. W. (ed.). *Readings in Cross-Cultural Methodology.* New Haven: HRAF Press, 1961.

Smith, Bruce Lannes. *International and Intercultural Communications: A Theoretical Model.* Unpublished Ph.D. dissertation The University of Chicago, Chicago, Illinois, 1957.

Sodhi, Kripal Singh, and Rudolf Bergius. *Nationale Vorurteile.* Berlin: Duncker und Humblot, 1953.

Watson, Jeanne, and Ronald Lippit. *Learning Across Cultures: A Study of Germans Visiting America.* Ann Arbor, Michigan: University of Michigan Press, 1955.

Whitaker, Urban G. *Propaganda and International Relations.* San Francisco/Calif.: Howard Chandler, 1960.

Paul F. Lazarsfeld:

The Prognosis for International Communications Research

SOMETIME during the interval between the two World Wars, communications research became a fairly well defined and well organized sub-division of social research, with a sizeable program of teaching, research and publication. At least three origins for this development can be discerned. The first was the considerable concern with the problem of propaganda that followed in the wake of the First World War. Lasswell's study of allied propaganda during the First World War[1] was a major factor in directing this concern into systematic thinking, and the Institute for Propaganda Analysis was its first institutional result. A second mainspring lay in the cultural concern with the effect of the rapidly growing mass media. The Payne Fund studies, started in the late twenties, investigated the effect of movies on children's morals, attitudes and behavior. Subsequently, the interest of the Rockefeller Foundation in the cultural effects of radio as a mass medium led to the establishment of two more permanent institutions: the Princeton Office of Radio Research and the Institute for Educational Radio at Ohio State University.

In addition to the political and cultural roots, there was a third source of stimulation, namely the commercial. As long as newspapers were the main advertising medium not much research was needed, because circulation data provided sufficient evidence of the existence and size of an audience. But the situation changed with the coming of radio. The new medium naturally led to rather fierce inter-media competition. Radio had nothing comparable to sales figures and box office receipts by which to count its audience, so it was forced to use research to find out who listened to radio programs. Research on commercial radio, in turn, led to competitive developments, especially in the magazine field; soon commercial audience research became a dominant feature of the communications research field, recruiting the aid of academicians in most of the social sciences.[2]

[1] Lasswell, Harold D., *Propaganda Technique in the World War*, New York: Alfred Knopf, 1927.
[2] It is worthwhile noting that each of the three main threads in the history of communications research is connected with one major technique: in the political sphere

---

▶ From: *Public Opinion Quarterly* (Princeton/New Jersey), Vol. 16/No. 4 (Winter 1952-53), pp. 482-490. Reprinted by permission of the publisher and of the author.

During the Second World War most government agencies made extensive use of domestic communications research. This led to a multiplication of established activities rather than to a search for new problems and new methods, a kind of freezing at the pre-war level. At the same time, international communications research made its beginning. The concern with shortwave propaganda, especially from the German side, stimulated most of the early research and writing.[3] Toward the end of the war, interest in international organization as a means of preserving peace became very strong and the possible role of communications research in the service of international cooperation was discussed. Linton published a volume on the role of the social sciences in a time of crisis,[4] including a section on the role of mass media in the building of an international authority. This article, however, was largely a re-statement of the standard Lasswell formula (Who says what to whom, and with what effect?), with examples from the international field substituted for those which had become customary in lectures and writings in the domestic field.

After World War II not much that was new happened in domestic communications research. The foundations evidently felt that they had done their part, and that from then on the new social science should be left to grow at its own pace. There were few developments in the commercial sphere because the coming of television had an upsetting effect on the financial structure of the whole communications industry, with the result that the problems of content and audiences remained minor. Furthermore, the commercial effectiveness of television was so obvious that it did not seem necessary to conduct the refined studies which were undertaken when radio was in its infancy. In short, in the domestic field the time seemed to have come for solidification and codification. The new research organizations which were established followed well-known patterns, and the textbooks were sent to press. But for a few new ideas, which will be mentioned later in this article, a period of near-stagnation might have developed. We should be grateful for the sudden upsurge of interest in international communications.

Opportunities of International Communications Research

There is no need to explain at this point where the interest comes from. It, however, seems important to clarify the special opportunities and responsibilities of international communications research as a major new development within the social sciences. These opportunities and

content analysis was prevalent; in the moral and cultural spheres most of the efforts toward effects analysis originated; the bulk of commercial research was audience analysis.
[3] See Harwood Childs and John B. Whitton. *Propaganda by Short Wave*. Princeton: Princeton University Press, 1942 and Ernst Kris and Hans Speier. *German Radio Propaganda*. New York: Oxford University Press, 1944.
[4] Linton, Ralph (ed.), *The Science of Man in the World Crisis*, New York: Columbia University Press, 1945.

responsibilities can probably best be explored within the framework of three major premises. First, it can be assumed that international communications research will have most of the talent, funds and interest which domestic communications research has commanded for the past twenty years. Consequently, since the domestic area will not have many opportunities in the years to come, the new ideas in communications research which made their appearance after the end of World War II will have to be picked up and developed in the international field if they are not to be neglected altogether. Secondly, there are certain comparative possibilities in the sphere of international communications research which will open up new and rather exciting subjects for investigation. So long as communications research struggled in one country only, to wit, in the United States, it was difficult for it to "bracket out" the pervasive features of American culture. Now, in the international field, where comparative studies between various countries will be made, these cultural variables and their role can better be discerned. Finally, there are a number of methodological problems, left relatively unsolved in the domestic field, which might be more expeditiously explored internationally.

The first premise can be somewhat reformulated along the following lines. The new groups which work in the international field are expected to redeem us from the neglects and oversights which were part of the domestic development. A few examples may serve to bring many more to the mind of the reader. Because we were partly influenced by commercial problems, there was a tendency, in domestic research, to look at audiences as a rather homogeneous mass and the emphasis, therefore, was on large-scale statistical analysis. Only in the 1940's did notable interest develop in finer differentiations. Because everyone in this country has a radio, it seems to have been assumed that except for program tastes there is not much difference between one listener and another. But listening goes on in a social context. Some people, for example, undoubtedly play the role of brokers in the field of mass media; they listen a great deal, they read a great deal and then they pass the material on to others. There are such small-scale opinion leaders in every social stratum, people who are asked by others for their advice and help. Thus, the audience to every medium is structured, with its members playing certain active or passive roles beyond the medium as it were, but also as a result of it. In the domestic field, then, it became clear that one cannot really understand the impact of mass media if one does not study how their influence is reflected and spread by the small group organizations of the whole audience—groups which may be either of a formal or informal character.

In the international field there was no such time lag in recognizing the importance of this point. In Arabic countries, for example, there are very few radios, and in entire villages there may be just one individual with a radio and only a few people who can read a newspaper. In such a situation, one cannot speak of the audience as a homogeneous group; we have to think of a kind of two-step flow in which people who get the content of the mass media directly and those who get it indirectly, through brokers of all kinds, must be distinguished. It is not enough that these different audiences and manifold processes be carefully described and studied in their implications. The problem calls for completely new statistical approaches, once we have a larger body of data. Previously, we were content to analyze the size of the total audience. Then we became interested in differences among broad social groups, noting that rich people listened to or read different things from poor people; that the old and the young, or men and women, were different in their listening, reading or viewing habits. In a third stage, the search began for psychological characteristics. Were there, for example, differences between media habits of extroverts and introverts, between isolated women and women who had many friends, etc.? International communications research requires a further step; we must now explore the sociological characteristics of the audiences. In the small towns we may ask: What is the relationship between social position and listening habits? Inversely, how does the ownership of a radio affect a man's status in the community? How should we take into account, in a country like Lebanon, the differences among the various sects which play such a role in Lebanon's political structure? What will be the relationship between the Indian caste system and the conception and reception of mass media?

The omissions of the past, incidentally, were in no way from one side only. Other disciplines committed the same sins, and it is interesting to speculate on the potentialities of international communications research for filling gaps in other social sciences as well. A striking example comes from anthropology. In the wake of the last war there developed an interest in what is called area research. The Social Science Research Council has published a monograph [5] on efforts to study certain parts of the world through a concerted effort by all branches of the social scientists. The author of this monograph, the anthropologist Julian Steward, describes in great detail how these disciplines work together to analyze the social trends of an area with special reference to problems of the United States. In the entire 200 pages of Steward's work, however, there is not a single reference to work done by communications or opinion research specialists. The terms information, public opinion, or any of the concepts with which we have become so concerned in the last twenty years are not mentioned. While he worries greatly about the relationships among the sociologist, the psychologist, and the anthropologist, he seems to be unaware that communications research exists. However, this is not a deliberate

[5] Steward, Julian H., "Area Research: Theory and Practice," *Social Science Research Council*, Bulletin No. 63, 1950.

avoidance, nor is it really as surprising as it looks at first glance. The anthropological tradition has not been primarily interested in the processes by which cultural phenomena come about. The studies which have been done on inter-cultural contact and acculturization have been mainly concerned with what one might call general morphological laws. What happens to the primitive culture, if, for example, a primitive culture and a more industrialized culture come into contact? Through what phases does it go? What changes in form does this contact bring about? The emphasis was on the changes themselves and not on the mechanisms by which they came about, while communications research, if viewed as part of the study of cultural change, would focus its attention on one of the mechanisms by which cultural changes occur. In fact, one might almost say that international communications research is a part of anthropology which has so far been neglected: the study of the processes by which the various cultures influence each other.

Comparative Research Opportunities

Now to the second point, namely that the "international" nature of the new field will probably open up a great number of new intellectual opportunities. They fall roughly into two classes: first, the possibility of studying the same social phenomena in different cultural contexts; secondly, the possibility of studying topics so unique to particular countries that they are not generally available to the social scientist.

The comparative possibilities are obvious and numerous. We take it for granted, for example, that we know what news means to people. But even in this country we have found that that is not wholly true. At the time of a newspaper strike, Bernard Berelson observed what people did when they could not get a newspaper.[6] The general expectation was that they would get their news from the radio. Actually, many people read an old newspaper. This means that they were really not concerned with the content of the day's news, but rather they wanted to engage in the nerve-soothing activity of reading small bits and pieces of stories. There can be little doubt that the meaning of news will be very different from one culture to another, and that we cannot know in advance what these variations will be. Charles Glock, in an article in this issue, elaborates on how any international information service needs to have a clearer picture of what news is, what it means to people and how it fits in with their images of themselves and others.

In addition to the possibility for cross-country comparisons, there is

[6] Berelson, Bernard, "What 'Missing the Newspaper' Means" in *Communications Research*, 1948-1949, edited by P. F. Lazarsfeld and F. N. Stanton, New York: Harper & Brothers, 1949. See also a very systematic discussion of "The Nature of News" by Wilbur Schramm in *Mass Communications*, Urbana, Ill.: University of Illinois Press, 1949.

that of selecting problems which can be studied only in certain countries and not in others. For instance, we did not learn from American research anything about the public effect of government ownership of mass media. There is no doubt that, in general, radio under government ownership in countries such as England has a greater proportion of what one might call sophisticated or educational features. But we do not know whether this is because such programs have been imposed by an enlightened elite or whether they have been, at least partly, demanded by the people. If imposed, it may well be that cultural tastes are more malleable than we think; perhaps, as a result of these more serious programs, people's tastes improve. Take, as another example, the Scandinavian countries, where there coexist two principles which we generally consider quite contradictory: stringent economic controls and complete political freedom. In America, we tend to assume that economic laissez-faire and political liberty go together. So let us study the formation of opinion and attitudes in countries where the two principles have developed independently and where economic state control has apparently not interfered with political freedom.

The use of various countries as research laboratories on specific problems bears a close relationship to some of the ideas which Harold Lasswell expresses. . . . His concept of the function of social research resembles, on a social level, the functions which, on an individual level, we have come to expect from psychoanalysis. It shows people possibilities of conduct other than the ones to which they have become accustomed. The neurotic person is unaware of other possibilities of conduct; the function of the therapist is that of bringing such other possibilities to the awareness of the individual. In the same sense, the social scientist could have a great therapeutic effect if he were to call attention to the possibilities for other solutions to social problems than the ones to which we have become accustomed. International communications research should be looked to for a large share of such contributions.

Methodological Contributions

Our third and final point combines, in a way, the two previous ones, repeating both in methodological terms. Domestic communications research has fallen short on certain technical problems. The international field permits us to experiment with methods more productively than was possible on the national scene. We usually do communications research by systematic interviewing, while the community research people rely much more on observation or participant observation. What we really need to know is the relation between the interviewing and observation techniques. What kinds of data are more easily obtained in one way, and for what kinds of information is the other technique in order? How should data collected by direct interviewing and by observation be related to each other?

It is significant that even in these early days of international communications research, such problems have already entered general discussion. At a meeting of the Viking Fund in 1951, an entire day was given to the exchange of experiences between anthropologists and what was then called "survey" people. While opinions were still fairly diffuse, and often confused, there is no doubt that international communications research will necessarily lead to some clarification. There are many problems such as the relation of information obtained from informants about other people and the information obtained directly. Sociometric methods will also enter the field, since the singling out of opinion leaders and news brokers will require methods which so far have only been used in the small group studies of the sociometrists.

One especially baffling methods problem should be mentioned here. There has been a great deal of talk in social research to the effect that, in order to do really good survey work, one needs to know the background of the community, its history, its mores, and so on. Whoever has attempted to combine this informal and general background information with formal tabulations obtained from surveys, has generally encountered serious difficulties in bringing the two together. In the international field the need for the area specialist seems especially obvious and, as this volume indicates, everyone concerned seems to stress this. However, we do not know what actually is the relation between the historical and intuitive knowledge of the area specialist who has traveled in, or lived in a community, and the precise data gathered in systematic field studies? Obviously, one of the area specialist's functions is to lead us to the right problems; in other cases he will help us to interpret our data. But this is all still quite vague. The actual potential relation between modern, precise research procedures and the more traditional, broad approaches of historical and, if you please, journalistic appraisal of a country, presents a very pressing methodological problem. Any progress on this question would have very healthy repercussions on domestic social research as well.

There is another point on which the extension of communications research to the international field should make a methodological contribution. The weakest sector of domestic communications research has always been in the field of evaluation. The effectiveness of educational programs, of efforts to promote racial understanding, and so on, has always been open to question. In a survey by Klapper [7] on our present knowledge of the effects of mass media on cultural activities, it was

---

[7] Klapper, Joseph T., *The Effects of Mass Media: A Report to the Director of the Public Library Inquiry,* New York: Bureau of Applied Social Research, October, 1950. Since the war, Carl Hovland has started a systematic series of experiments on attitude change; they might lead to a real psychological foundation of communications theory, but it is too early to appraise the Yale contribution. For an interesting programmatic statement, see Carl L. Hovland, "Changes in Attitude through Communication," *Journal of Abnormal and Social Psychology,* V. 46, July, 1951, pp. 424-437.

shown how little our literature contributes to any real knowledge, and the reasons for this deficiency were discussed. One is that so many outside stimuli impinge upon audiences that any single stimulus can have only a very small effect. There was negative feedback here; research problems were difficult, few students had the courage to engage in such work, and as a result no progress in methods was made. In the international field, we can hope that things will be different. We can expect that in a fairly stable situation such as we might find among one or two countries of the East, the Point Four program, for example, may have noticeable and rather speedy effects. After all, the introduction of a new way of plowing, or the coming of the first movie to a village, is an event of considerable importance and the research situation a fairly clear-cut one. Studies of effects under such circumstances should therefore be less discouraging, and students in the international field may be more disposed to follow them up. As the international communications research field becomes organized, one of its tasks will be to keep in close contact with all other agencies which are new to a particular country. It should not be forgotten that the Point Four activities or Mutual Security aid are also communications activities, except that in this case communication is not by exchange of symbols but by exchange of activities or objects. A combination of evaluation research methods with the activities of agencies which actually introduce new habits or new institutions into more remote countries should open up a wide area for social research experimentation. Even in the United States we know that one of the most fruitful research fields is one where a new social situation (a housing project, for example) is established. It is quite likely that the near future will bring about considerable numbers of such new situations abroad. Certainly the international communications research people should not conceive their role as involving only their traditional media. It is their task to be the evaluation officers of all contacts between the new, more industrialized countries and the older ones.

Conclusions

It is on this note that our remarks should be closed. We social scientists usually consider ourselves stepchildren on the scientific scene. We feel that we have more to contribute than we are permitted to contribute at the moment. This may or may not be the case, and the future will show what we are able to produce. Still, it should not be forgotten that the relationship between practical policy and social science should be a two-way relationship. It is not only that we should contribute to the policymaking of the United States; we should expect the policymakers also to make sure that their work contributes to the social sciences. This is imperative not merely for academic reasons but because, to a considerable extent, the national and international welfare of the country, as Lasswell points out, is tied up with the techniques of social research. The policy-makers should be joined by social scientists, not only because we can help them, but because the exclusion of the social sciences from the social events of the day impoverishes the social scientists who are themselves an important resource in a country. It is very much to be hoped that, in this sense, international communications research, because it is working in an exposed area, will contribute to the improvement of the relation between the social sciences and those groups and institutions who are the actors on the social scene.

W. Phillips Davison and Alexander L. George:

An Outline for the Study of International Political Communication

BY "INTERNATIONAL POLITICAL COMMUNICATION" we refer to the use by national states of communications to influence the politically relevant behavior of people in other national states. Thus we include the propaganda and information activities of most government agencies—especially the State and Defense Departments—and certain aspects of diplomatic communication, but we exclude the activities of the press associations and bodies which are interested principally in international education or in religious missionary activities. By "communication" we refer to the transfer of meaning, whether by written, spoken or pictorial symbols, or by various types of action. "International political communication" is thus a summary term which includes many of the activities subsumed under the terms "negotiation," "propaganda," "political warfare," and "psychological warfare."

Some Special Difficulties

Efforts to systematize the study of international political communication have, in our opinion, been unsuccessful to date. Some of the reasons why this has been the case are the following:

1. The study of international political communication cuts across the established boundaries of academic disciplines. All the social sciences, and some other disciplines, can contribute something to it; none has the complete answer. Theoretically, therefore, an expert in international political communication should have mastered all existing data bearing on human behavior.[1] No one has done this since Goethe's Faust.

2. A related reason for slow progress in this field is that the communication process is quite complex. The variables involved in communication have been summarized in the following formula:

---

[1] Cf. Marjorie Fiske and Leo Lowenthal, "Some Problems in the Administration of International Communications Research," *Public Opinion Quarterly*, Vol. 16, No. 2 (Summer 1952), p. 149. The authors report an effort to define the scope of international communications research which ended by including "practically the whole sphere of human knowledge."

▶ From: *Public Opinion Quarterly* (Princeton, New Jersey), Vol. 16/No. 4 (Winter 1952-53), pp. 501-511. Reprinted by permission of the publisher and of the authors.

Who says *what* to *whom* through what *medium* for what *purpose* under what *circumstances* and with what *effects?*

This is a convenient way of describing the chief elements of the communication process, but the variables in question are intricately related and most efforts to study and state their interrelationships have been seriously over-simplified. What we know about communication—i.e. the principles or propositions which express a relationship between two or more of these variables—is usually of only modest utility for purposes of solving a particular communication problem at a given time and place. In an operational situation we can apply our general knowledge about communication only if we supplement it with a careful "taking into account" of many of the specific components in the given situation. This means keeping many factors in the communication process in mind at once in order to get the insight we need into the concrete communication problem at hand.

The study of communication is sufficiently complicated if we confine it to the domestic scene. When we turn our attention to international political communication, where the "who" is a complicated propaganda apparatus in one culture, the "whom" is an amorphous audience in another culture, and the purposes and circumstances are bound up with all the intricacies of international relations, then it is clear that we are not yet qualified to undertake a *systematic* study of international political communication. All we can hope to do is to illuminate certain aspects of the process, and perhaps help to pave the way for more systematic study at a later date.

3. The pay-off in international communication, and in the last analysis the reason we study it, is its effect. Social scientists have had considerable success in studying audience response to certain types of domestic communication. But, as noted above, these communication situations are usually simpler than those encountered in trying to communicate for political purposes across national boundaries.

In the laboratory, for example, social psychologists are able to measuse the "learning" which takes place after selected subjects are exposed to certain carefully defined communications. And in testing the effect of certain advertising upon consumer purchases the market researcher deals with a relatively uncomplicated matter. He is able to define what he means by effectiveness—whether or not the audience likes or buys the product—and to measure the behavior which occurs as a result of his communication. The researcher's problem in studying and evaluating the effects of international communication, on the other hand, is more complicated for several reasons: (a) the researcher is faced with the fact that the communicator frequently has only a vague notion of exactly what it is that he is trying to achieve; (b) the communicator often pursues many goals with many audiences simultaneously; (c) the communication itself cannot be neatly structured in order to facilitate the researcher's job of evaluation; (d) the foreign audience is often inaccessible for direct observation and measurement; and (e) clear-cut, simple criteria of effectiveness are wanting.

As a result, while we know quite a bit about the effects of different types of domestic communications, we know only in a general way that some international communications achieve the effect that was intended, some achieve effects which were not intended, and some result in no effects at all.

4. Another difficulty is that political communication is usually—although not always—an auxiliary instrument of policy. It is used in conjunction with decisions or actions which may fall in the diplomatic, economic or military sphere. If we try to study a communication without reference to the decision or action of which it is an auxiliary, we may be in the position of examining a meaningless abstraction. Thus, study of the content of specific communications may lead us into consideration of the North Atlantic Treaty Organization, the Marshall Plan, or the tactical situation in some military theatre where surrender propaganda was successfully or unsuccessfully employed.

5. Finally, a strictly scientific approach to evaluation of international communication is often difficult to maintain because of the political and administrative conditions under which it is undertaken. International communication programs—at least in this country and in some nations abroad—do not command firm political support at home and are dependent upon the vagaries of annual budgets. As a result, agencies charged with producing international communications program are sometimes forced to combine evaluation tasks with the need for domestic public relations. In order to justify program and budget requests before those who control the purse strings, the communication agency is tempted to play up in its self-evaluation the more striking examples of its "success." This is bad from a scientific viewpoint insofar as it distorts the task, already difficult to begin with, of setting up adequate criteria of effectiveness; it may lead to the adoption of invalid, oversimplified or ambiguous criteria for this purpose. We may note that this problem is faced not only by international communications agencies but by domestic commercial agencies as well. Certainly one of the chief tasks of the student of communications is to develop methods of auditing communication programs which are both scientifically respectable and reasonably comprehensible.

Approaches to the Study of International Political Communication

In spite of the fact that systematic study of political communication is at present so difficult as to be almost impossible, international information, propaganda and psychological warfare today constitute a field of endeavor in which thousands of highly-trained individuals are employed and which promises to become more rather than less significant in the years ahead. Furthermore, international political communication has an impressive past. It played a considerable role during both world wars and—on a smaller scale—can be traced back through history to the earliest stages of international struggles for power. The subject, then, is one which the social scientist is obligated to treat if he is not to ignore a major field of human activity.

Under these circumstances, we believe that there are several directions which the study of international political communication can take. First, even if we do not know very many of the correct answers about the effects of political communication, we know some things that are *not true*. A debunking role at this stage of the game can be of considerable utility, especially if it enables the student to reject some of the nonsense about propaganda and psychological warfare which is unfortunately widespread today. One such canard, for instance, is that a nation which has an effective propaganda program can afford to cut down expenditures for its armed forces. But the more we study political communication the more we see that propaganda which is not backed up by power is unlikely to achieve its goals. Propaganda is not a substitute for armed forces; it merely complements them.

Second, we can refer to a few propositions about international communication which have been established with a fair degree of certainty. For instance, we know that an indirect approach to audiences which are in conflict with the propaganda-using nation is more likely to succeed than a direct approach. That is, one is more likely to elicit the desired type of behavior by hiding the fact that one desires it than by advertising it. Propositions such as these unfortunately do not link together to form a chain of systematic theory—they are more like isolated islands in a large sea of ignorance—but we hope that they are the beginnings of an emerging continent, and we can use them to take our bearings from time to time.

Third, one can observe that political communication campaigns in the past have been waged with a measure of success by those who have had a certain "feel" for them. These successful operators have usually been those who because of their wide experience knew what was the right thing to do, even if they did not know exactly why. Some of them have been professional propagandists and psychological warfare experts, but most have been politicians or statesmen with a rare sense of how to use the media of communication. One can group together here such strange bedfellows as Napoleon Bonaparte, Joseph Goebbels, Winston Churchill and George Creel. A study of the experience of these practitioners can contribute something toward developing a similar "feel" for the role of communication in political affairs.

Some Basic Relationships: The Role of Policy

As mentioned above, there is no standardized map that can be used in exploring the territory of international political communication—no periodic table of elements as in chemistry, or even an ongoing sequence of events as in history. Nevertheless, we must have *some* framework to hold together the relevant observations on the subject.

One of the most important of these relationships is between communication and national policy. In the absence of a clear national policy on any given issue the communicator is in the position of a swimmer treading water just to keep from going under; he is unable to strike out in any direction. Successful propaganda presupposes a clear national policy. Consequently, to understand the behavior of communicators—or propagandists—the student must be able to relate this behavior to the policy of the nation they represent.

National policy, in turn, is derived in part from the international political situation, and in part from domestic political and cultural factors. Some of these factors affect the activities of international communication specialists both directly and indirectly. Therefore, we must also consider carefully certain aspects of both the international and domestic scenes.

For instance, the distribution of power and the alignment of values in the international arena following World War II have contributed to a bi-polarization of world politics. The leaders of each of the two rival blocs are faced with two principal tasks: (1) the "internal" problem: to consolidate their own bloc of nations and peoples in order to maximize power capabilities and minimize vulnerability to outer or inner disintegrating pressures; (2) the "external" problem: to devise policies and means of dealing with the rival power bloc, e.g. developing strategies for weakening the rival power bloc, neutralizing its threat to the self, and/or for arriving at an acceptable *modus vivendi* with it.

On the domestic scene we must note that certain traditional attitudes and practices have strongly influenced the development of U.S. foreign policy, and in some cases have seriously affected our ability to form policies adequate to the exigencies of the bi-polar world. In particular, an aversion to "propaganda" and an effort to transfer the moral code of interpersonal relationships to the international plane have tended to limit the role which internationtal political communication has played in our foreign policy.

The problem of domestic constraints is, of course, not limited to the United States. The influence of domestic codes and practices on the foreign policy of some other nations is even stronger. The leaders of the Soviet Union, for instance, are bound by a self-imposed code which makes it often impossible for them to comprehend the motives for certain behavior on the part of other peoples, and it is probable that many of them sincerely believe their own propaganda to the effect that the United States is run from "Wall Street."

Communication policy—i.e. decisions as to what we want to achieve through the use of communications—is derived in part from national policy and the constraints which help shape national policy, but also from other elements in the chain represented here: audience characteristics, the conditions under which the communication is made, and the effects we want to achieve. For example, it would be unrealistic to set up as a goal for communications the achievement of behavior in our audience which we knew to be manifestly impossible. At the outset of World War II, some Allied propagandists called on the Germans to revolt and overthrow Hitler. This was poor propaganda policy, since the victorious Germans were in no mood or position to revolt, and it was soon revised.

The line in our diagram connecting "political, economic, and military policies" with "communication policy" is intended to indicate that communication is merely one tool with which we try to achieve national goals. Other tools are usually used simultaneously with it.

Communication Behavior and Action

Once communication policy is decided, specialists in the use of international communications take this policy and transform it into action: a broadcast, a leaflet, a diplomatic note, and so on. This transformation process we refer to as "communication behavior." Study of communication behavior includes consideration of the machinery by which communication policy is transformed into communication content, and also study of the personnel who operate this machinery and the techniques which they use. Thus, in concrete terms, the student of international political communication should know something about the structure, techniques and personnel of the U.S. foreign information program, the British foreign information program, the Soviet Agitprop, the diplomatic services of the major powers, and so on. Included here also are organizations designed to conduct psychological warfare in time of war.

Communication behavior results in the preparation of communication content—the part of the communication process which is visible to the audience. Also visible to the audience are various types of actions taken by the power which sponsors the communication content. These actions have certain political relevant effects on the attitudes and behavior of those who experience them or hear about them.

One of the major problems of communication policy and technique, therefore, is to find ways of controlling the interpretation which an audience will place upon events and actions. People are swayed not merely or even primarily by what is said. Even more important is what is done and what happens. Actions and events, however, can be interpreted in a variety of ways by both individual and group audiences. Communications specialists cannot be certain that events and actions will always speak for themselves in the desired manner. There are two ways of meeting this problem by means of communication: (1) The specific action or event in question can be presented by the communicator in such a way as to further the type of interpretation which is desired—that is, the propagandist "plays up" the story in a certain way, or gives it an "angle." (2) The communicator may aim at shaping the broader perspective or frame of reference of the audience in such a way that members of the audience will themselves see events and actions in the desired manner—that is, the propagandist tries to give the reader a special pair of glasses through which he is to see what takes place.

The Problem of Effect

The effectiveness of communication in influencing behavior depends in large measure on the *conditions* under which communications are sent and received. We use the term "conditions" here very broadly to include any specific characteristic of the communications act in question which falls under the parts of our formula which are underlined in the following sentence: "*Who* says *what* to *whom* in what *medium* with what *purpose* under what *circumstances* and with what *effects?*" The character imputed by an audience to the communicator—with reference, for example, to his power, prestige, reputation for credibility or sobriety, closeness to the top leadership of his own country, etc.—may affect the listeners' receptivity to what is said. Similarly, acceptance of a particular communication may be enhanced or prejudiced by the character of the medium through which it is conveyed. For example, people may be more critical of what they read in a newspaper than of what they hear over the radio or by word of mouth. The "circumstances" or setting of a given communication include such matters as its "timeliness," whether it is forced to compete with rival communications or enjoys a monopoly position, whether events support or contradict the message, whether it comes at a time of great anxiety or discontent in the audience, whether the originator of the communication seems to be winning a war or losing it, etc.

Equally important to the effectiveness of a communication are audience characteristics—the "to whom" in our communications formula. Audience characteristics vary, of course, with each audience, and it is therefore difficult to make general statements which apply to more than a few of the possible audiences which are exposed to international political communications. Nevertheless, we can call attention to various *types* of audience characteristics which are of crucial importance. We are interested here in such questions as the audience's listening, reading, or "exposure" situation, the motivations of the person who receives the communication, and the extent to which the actual listener or reader relays what he hears to others.

For our purposes, however, perhaps the most important characteristic of those who constitute the audience is their position in the political structure of the nation to which they belong. This means that an important part of our audience or "target" analysis must be to assess in detail the political structure and dynamic political processes in the country to which our communications are addressed. How is power and influence distributed? What are the contributions which different groups make to national morale and to the power potential of the state? In totalitarian societies the courses of political action open to individuals are very few; one cannot expect to influence their voting behavior, for instance, because they never have a chance to vote—or if they do it is usually a meaningless formality. Certain groups of leaders, however, may have a wider range of political choices open to them. Similarly, the way the society in question is organized, its social constraints, popular beliefs and customs, and so on, exercises an important influence on the way communicators are received and the effect they have. And finally, the members of any given group tend to react as individuals in certain patterns, and the communicator must be familiar with these patterns.

If the communications content is adequate, and geared in with other types of action, if the conditions of communication are favorable and audience characteristics are taken adequately into account, a communication may have certain effects on one or more members of the audience which receives it. But what do we mean by "effects"? They may be changes in attention or attitudes, reinforcement of existing attitudes or behavioral responses. The student is interested in all these but he is particularly concerned with actions or predispositions to actions which have political significance, since the influencing of politically-relevant behavior is the goal of international political communication.

The Complicating Role of the Past

A further caution should be given regarding the description of the communication process which has been sketched in above. It may be misleading in that it fails to indicate that each element in the process has a history. We cannot understand national policy, the conditions of communication, communication behavior, or any of the other elements unless we examine what they have been in the past as well as what they are in the present. This consideration serves as a final blow to efforts to simplify study of the subject.

This outline does not begin to cover all aspects of interest in the international communication process; it does not even provide for the inclusion of all the relevant information which is currently available. But it does, we hope, stress the relationship—even if it is a highly involved one—between national policy and the politically relevant behavioral effects of communication. With that in mind we are in a position to study and evaluate with somewhat more clearness of focus the various elements in the international political communication process.

Godwin C. Chu:

Problems of Cross-Cultural Communication Research

IN THE post-war era considerable research in mass communication has cumulated a sizable amount of empirical knowledge. Most of the experimental studies, however, were carried out against the western cultural background. We have now come face to face with the question of whether our knowledge about communication behavior can be employed with enough generality beyond the boundaries of western societies.

This question can only be answered by testing our empirical knowledge in other cultures. Findings from such cross-cultural studies will, it is hoped, provide further empirical support to our knowledge and furthermore, redefine the scope within which our current knowledge may be applied. The findings from one side will supplement the findings from the other, and at the same time generate problems to which research on the other side may provide answers. The present discussion will be limited to three technical problems: strategy of cross-cultural studies, conceptualization of research problems and methodology of cross-cultural research.

Strategy of Cross-Cultural Studies

The strategy of cross-cultural communication research is essentially one of hypothesis testing and exploratory theory building. The former provides an additional test of a previously corroborated hypothesis in a different culture. For instance, we might want to know whether the findings about one-sided versus two-sided communications (Hovland, Janis and Kelley, 1953)[1] also holds in an Oriental culture. Cross-cultural confirmation of the original hypothesis will widen the scope of its generality.

But if we fail to replicate the original findings in another culture, we would want to know what cultural factors are responsible for this failure. So, in addition to testing the original hypothesis, it will often be fruitful to explore additional propositions concerning certain important cultural variables. For instance, it may be argued that in a culture which stresses authoritarian submission, people will tend to be overly dependent and have

[1] Hovland, C. I., Janis, I. L., and Kelley, H. H. (1953), *Communication and Persuasion.* Yale University Press.

► From: *Journalism Quarterly* (Iowa City, Iowa), Vol. 41/No. 4 (Autumn 1964), pp. 557-562. Reprinted by permission of the publisher and of the author.

a high need for cognitive clarity. Therefore a persuasive communication presenting a clear-cut one-sided argument will likely be accepted, while a two-sided argument may cause confusion and doubt. It can then be hypothesized that in this type of culture, one-sided communications will be consistently more effective than two-sided communications.

In cross-cultural hypothesis testing, we sometimes adopt the straight replication approach. We would use exactly the same procedure and same materials, except for translation, and retest the hypothesis in another culture. By holding everything else constant, we can be sure within reasonable limits that whatever differences occur in the findings cannot be attributed to differences in methodology, but rather reflect cross-cultural diversities. If the replication comes up with essentially the same findings, then we will have evidence that the specific hypothesis we are testing has cross-cultural validity.

This approach, however, is likely to encounter procedural difficulties in communication research. Usually a straight replication in another culture will be feasible with psychophysical and certain other psychological experiments where culturally-based ideas, perceptions and attitudes do not constitute essential variables. For instance, it may be possible to replicate the autokinetic test (Sherif, 1937) [2] and the judgment of lines for testing group pressure (Asch, 1951)[3] in another culture without essential changes in the procedures. But if our research problem involves values, ideologies, social patterns, and experience, which may differ from culture to culture, then a straight replication is hardly feasible.

In communication research, the questionnaires and communications may not convey the same meanings when applied to a different culture. Take the fear-arousing experiments by Janis and Feshbach (1953),[4] for instance. Some of the fears employed in the communications had to do with "ugly or discolored teeth." These will become effective "fear-arousing" appeals only in the sense that the subjects are worried about having ugly or discolored teeth. In a society where people do not regard sparkling white teeth as something of a social value, having ugly or discolored teeth will not likely cause worry or fear. This is to suggest that in communication research where the original materials are phrased against one cultural background and reflect its values and beliefs, it is not at all possible to do a straight replication in another culture.

These limitations, both procedural and theoretical, make it advisable to take a different approach. Instead of replicating the same materials

[2] Sherif, M. (1937), "An Experimental Approach to the Study of Attitudes," in *Sociometry*, Vol. I, pp. 90-98.
[3] Asch, S. E. (1951), "Effects of Group Pressure Upon the Modification and Distortion of Judgments," in *Groups, Leadership and Men*, ed. by Harold Guetzkow. Pittsburgh, Carnegie Press.
[4] Janis, I. L., and Feshbach, S. (1953), "Effects of Fear-Arousing Communications," *Journal of Abnormal and Social Psychology*, Vol. 48, pp. 78-92.

and procedures, this approach calls for testing the hypothesis in another culture by use of new materials, new operational definitions, and even different procedures whenever necessary. This approach is concerned not so much with keeping the same materials and same procedures as with making the meanings of the situation and materials comparable.

This exploratory approach has one drawback. If the findings confirm the hypothesis, we shall have evidence that the generality holds not only in another culture, but also for another experiment. But if the findings fail to support the hypothesis, then we do not know whether it is because of cultural differences or because of change of procedures or measurements, which may lack reliability and validity. This is a risk the cross-cultural communication researcher will have to face. In general, the pitfalls in cross-cultural communication research are no different from those in any social studies, namely, the problems of conceptualization and measurement, in addition to the researcher's limitation of knowledge about the specific culture itself.

Conceptualization of Research Problems

We now consider the conceptualization of research problems. Let us start with a few basic assumptions about mass communication research. We wish to delimit our discussion to the investigation of the effects of communication, as reflected in changes of behavior as well as attitudes. We are interested in attitudes because they are predispositions of behavior. Also, we regard exposure to communications, the acceptance thereof, and change of one's attitudes as a type of behavior.

We assume that human behavior is goal-oriented, the goal being gratification seeking and deprivation avoidance. Acceptance of communication and change of behavior or attitudes may be due to either seeking gratification, e.g., the fulfilment of some personal needs, or avoidance of deprivation, e.g., conforming to norms to avoid sanctions.

Starting with these assumptions we can then study response to mass communications from a behavioral approach. The following analysis of communication behavior is based on the general conceptualization of Parsons (1951),[5] as well as the Lewinian concept of situational forces (Lewin, 1951).[6]

We treat response to communication as a unit of behavior, and analyze it in terms of the self, which is the audience; significant others, including the communicator; and the situation, which consists of cultural values, goals and norms—forces that may affect the reception and acceptance of the communication. This analysis suggests that in cross-cultural communication research, our choice of research topics will be guided by three broad

[5] Parson, T., Shils, E., *et al.* (1951), *Toward a General Theory of Action.* Harvard University Press.
[6] Lewin, K. (1951), *Field Theory in Social Science.* New York, Harper.

concepts: the self, the others and the situation. Miller (1961),[7] in discussing cross-cultural study of personality within the framework of interaction, uses similar concepts.

In Lewinian terms, situation is defined in terms of the forces that prompt an individual to move in various directions, resulting in tensions, goals and goal achievement. We need data on the forces, goals and barriers.

Significant others, which Parsons calls alter, include parents, siblings, spouses, associates, friends and other members of a social hierarchy. A person in this hierarchy is identified by his social roles and the specific behavior patterns required of these roles.

The self develops through interaction with others. Through interaction, a person becomes oriented to the values and norms of others and forms standards for evaluating himself. He develops stable interpersonal behavior patterns.

It is assumed that cross-cultural diversities exist with respect to these three broad concepts. Furthermore, assuming an invariant human nature, we may postulate that these cross-cultural diversities are mainly the results of differences in the situation, which also exert influence on the self and the others. All this is saying that in cross-cultural communication research, we shall keep our attention on the three broad concepts of self, others and situation, while bearing in mind that it is the situational differences underlying the three concepts that we are mainly interested in.

Take the situation first. How would the situation of receiving a communication differ from one culture to another? In terms of goals, what are the motivations for receiving a message from the mass media, for accepting the message? What forces, if any, are prompting an individual toward the mass media? What barriers exist in the culture that would tend to keep the audience away from the media and mass communication? In this category we may include such specific problems as the basic cultural values, norms and beliefs, economic activities, modes of social control, and their influences on communication effects.

About the significant others, we want to know in what social roles the communicators are perceived by the audience. How are the mass media related to the authority structure of the native culture? Are the media recognized as a potential source capable of meting out reward or inflicting punishment or both? Subsumed under this category are such familiar problems as communicator prestige, the criteria of credibility, the image of media, the roles of opinion leaders, interpersonal influence versus media influence, and social structure.

Finally we need to take a look at the self. What are the specific interpersonal response traits resultant from certain particular situational influences in that culture? How would these response traits influence the

[7] Miller, D. R. (1961), "Personality and Social Interaction," in *Studying Personality Cross-Culturally*, ed. by B. Kaplan. Evanston, Ill., Row, Peterson (pp. 271-98).

audience behavior toward persuasive communication? How would certain dimensions of self-identity that are characteristic of this culture affect people's susceptibility to communication? These are mainly problems having to do with personality and persuasibility in different cultures (Janis and Field, 1959,[8] Chu, 1964).[9]

Also, cultural differences in modal personality may necessitate reconsidering certain problems concerning the effects of communications. It may be hypothesized that in a culture where the virtue of modesty is eulogized, people will be more reserved, and attempts to change attitudes through group discussion and participation not only may be a waste of time because people are reluctant to participate, but may even boomerang because of resentment if they are forced to participate.

Methodology of Cross-Cultural Research

The methods of cross-cultural research in general have been discussed by Kluckhohn (1940),[10] Paul (1953),[11] Whiting (1954),[12] Maccoby and Maccoby (1954)[13] and Lindzey (1961).[14] Here we are mainly interested in methods of cross-cultural communication research. We may either be testing a hypothesis in one culture for comparison with data collected from another culture, or gathering data from a number of cultures to see whether empirical laws can be formulated between certain cultural variables and communication behavior. In either case we need to consider the problems of sampling and data collection.

In a cross-cultural research requiring controlled experiments, sampling will involve no more difficulty than in a western society if students are available to serve as subjects. Arrangements can usually be made with local schools.

If the research requires a survey, then sampling is likely to post a serious problem because of incomplete or out-dated census data, inaccurate maps and transportation difficulties. Take the Asian regions for instance.

[8] Janis, I. L., and Field, P. B. (1959), "A Behavioral Assessment of Persuasibility: Consistency of Individual Differences; and Sex Differences and Personality Factors Related to Persuasibility," in *Personality and Persuasibility*, ed. by C. I. Hovland and I. L. Janis. Yale University Press (pp. 29-68).

[9] Chu, G. C. (1964), "Culture, Personality and Persuasibility." Unpublished doctoral dissertation, Stanford University.

[10] Kluckhohn, Florence R. (1940), "The Participant-Observer Techniques in Small Communities," *American Journal of Sociology*, Vol. 46, pp. 331-43.

[11] Paul, B. D. (1953), "Interview Techniques and Field Relationships," *Anthropology Today*, ed. by A. L. Kroeber. University of Chicago Press (pp. 430-51).

[12] Whiting, J. W. M. (1954), "The Cross-Cultural Method," in *Handbook of Social Psychology*, ed. by G. Lindzey. Reading, Mass., Addison-Wesley (pp. 523-31).

[13] Maccoby, E. E., and Maccoby, N. (1954), "The Interview: A Tool of Social Science," in *Handbook of Social Psychology*, ed. by G. Lindzey. Reading, Mass., Addison-Wesley Publishing Co. (pp. 449-87).

[14] Lindzey, G. (1961), *Projective Techniques and Cross-Cultural Research*. New York, Appleton-Century Crofts.

With the exception of Japan and a few other areas where considerable facilities are available, surveys on a national basis would probably be extremely difficult and expensive, if not impossible. An example to follow is Deming's design of a national sample in Greece (Deming, 1950).[15] Another method worth considering is a combination of area sampling and quota sampling. This was used in a radio audience survey in Taiwan in 1960. In several cities the only data available were city maps showing the main streets. First all the blocks on the map were numbered, with no consideration to the possible differences in size. A number of blocks were then drawn at random. The interviewer was allowed to choose a designated number of respondents within a chosen block on the basis of two quota controls: sex and age. Although this was not a probability sample, and people with better education and higher economic status were likely overrepresented, yet the interviewer was unable to seek out his friends and acquaintances. Such a sample is likely to eliminate this serious source of bias mentioned by Cantril (1947).[16] Depending on the purpose of the research, we may introduce other quota controls like education, economic status in addition to sex and age.

Data collection poses another problem. In a group experiment, paper and pencil tests will ordinarily be usable although the problem of validity can be serious. Caution needs to be taken to make both the questionnaire and communications meaningful in the native culture. Materials that may violate the basic cultural mores have to be discarded.

Data collection by survey will present additional problems, mainly those of overcoming resistance and improving rapport. In most non-western societies the idea of enquiring about other's opinions is completely alien to the natives

But various attempts have been made to increase rapport in communication research in Taiwan. In a 1960 radio audience survey, it was found that tandem interviewing by a male and female interviewer met with better reception. This was possibly because the presence of a female made the interview situation less formal. However, this would mean doubling the cost of interview. In a comparative study of social effects of communications in three villages in Taiwan, it was found that courtesy calls on the farmers by the interviewer and the village elder made it easier to interview them later on.

After the interviewer has been received, there is the problem of presenting a legitimate reason for the interview. If the interviewer fails to offer a plausible explanation, then the respondent himself is likely to seek an answer of his own, which might structure his perception of the situation in such a way as to seriously impair rapport. The explanation offered should be one that is understandable to the respondent. To say that the inter-

[15] Deming, W. E. (1950), *Some Theory of Sampling*. New York, Wiley & Sons.
[16] Cantril, H. (1947), *Gauging Public Opinion*. Princeton University Press.

viewer is collecting data for research, or measuring public opinions, usually doesn't mean much to the natives. Also sociometric questions intended to reconstruct the patterns of friendship and the flow of communications in the villages failed entirely. The village people simply would not give any names. Saying things about others was regarded as gossip, and the traditional Chinese belief is: Gossip breeds trouble.

The lack of interest in things not directly concerning the natives themselves adds to the difficulties in communication research. Typically, we measure the effects of communications in terms of opinion or attitude change in a before-and-after study, where communications serve as the experimental manipulation. In a non-western society with a low literacy rate, this procedure is likely to be inapplicable because the natives usually are not aware of social issues and do not have opinions.

Generally, depending on the circumstances, the researcher may adopt either the cross-sectional or the longitudinal approach. If we can locate two communities comparable in all other respects except that one has radio, we can compare these two communities for behavioral differences and see if we can trace such differences to the use of communications. For instance, does the radio-village have a higher voting rate than the non-radio-village? If so, how is decision to vote related to having heard certain messages over the radio? This is the cross-sectional, comparative approach. The longitudinal approach is applicable where it is possible to observe a community for a lengthy period while it is being exposed to communications. For instance, what would happen when we install a television set in a secluded village? Do the villages become more conscious about personal hygiene? Do they go to the city more often? Do they adopt some of the farm methods presented on the television?

The measuring instrument in cross-cultural communication research needs reconsideration. On the one hand we need refined instruments in order to detect true differences under a false surface of indifference. This would call for the use of scales with structured response categories. On the other hand, the low literacy rate would render the Likert or Guttman type scaling technique inapplicable. Usually respondents with little education are unable to make the fine distinction between "strongly agree" and "moderately agree." A solution to this dilemma may lie in the use of judgment type scaling techniques like Thurstone's equal appearing interval scale but with fewer intervals. Instead of the usual attitude scale items to which the respondent is asked to indicate agreement or disagreement, behavioral items might be used. Even people with no education will be able to report whether they have engaged in certain kinds of behavior. For instance, instead of presenting a statement like "Religious discrimination is something bad" and then asking a Buddhist farmer to indicate his agreement or disagreement, we might ask "Do you have any friends who worship Jesus Christ?" or "Have you entertained anyone who goes to church?"

The use of behavioral items instead of the typical attitude items is suggested for several reasons. First, attitudes are abstract concepts which the natives may not be able to grasp. Even though people in an Asian village all worship their own heavenly lord, they may not be able to understand the term "religion." A term like "discrimination" is perhaps even more difficult to grasp. Secondly, the natives probably have not clearly formed their attitudes—even if they have such attitudes—and are therefore unable to verbalize them.

The use of fewer scale intervals is suggested for two reasons. First there may be the practical difficulty of sorting a number of behavioral items into say eleven scale intervals. Using five or seven scale intervals is likely to achieve higher agreement among the judges, in the relative sense of comparing the obtained spread with the possible maximum variation of a flat-topped distribution. Of course this question can be settled by empirical data. Secondly, asking eleven behavioral questions on one single topic would be tiresome to the respondent, even if eleven items of different scale scores could be constructed on the same dimension. Five or seven questions would work better.

Gerhard Maletzke:

Intercultural and International Communication

BY VERBAL definition, intercultural communication is communication between human beings of different cultures. This, of course, does beg the question a bit as to just what a "culture" is. It is not our task here to go into the deeper philosophy of the meaning of culture. Sufficient for our purposes is the general and rather simplified anthropological sense that "culture systems" are groups or populations of humans who share a variety of things in common.

" 'A culture' refers to the distinctive way of life of a group of people, their designs for living." [1]

This is a concept that can either be restricted or enlarged depending on just which perspective the observer may adopt. Observed from close up, relatively small groups of people show signs of their own "culture" which sets them apart from their neighbors; but in such instances it is really better to speak of "sub-cultures." Seen from a broader perspective, these smaller groups tend to amalgamate into a larger cultural group in the usual sense, a group which, despite many inner diversities, nonetheless reveals a substantial unity in basic beliefs and forms of experience—in customs, norms, and behavioral characteristics, and almost invariably has a common language.

Thus intercultural communication is the process of the exchange of thoughts and meaning between people of differing cultures in the sense just defined. Here the situation very soon becomes rather complicated, since we must bear in mind that the communication takes place not only between individuals as such, but also that "systems" begin to emerge here as communicating partners—even when they may, in fact, be represented by individuals. Very often these individuals are quite conscious of their "roles" as representatives of "systems" in intercultural communication.

Very often, in the American literature in particular, the phrase *international* communication is frequently used, and one can never be sure whether the authors intend to differentiate as between international and

[1] Clyde Kluckhohn, "The Study of Culture," in: Daniel Lerner and Harold D. Lasswell, eds., *The Policy Sciences*, Stanford, Calif.: Stanford University Press, 1951, p. 86.

► This is an original article done for this book by Gerhard Maletzke, Deutsches Institut für Entwicklungspolitik, Berlin.

intercultural. This may not be necessary in very general and basic approaches, indeed, not even possible. But there are other cases where the distinction is not only quite possible, but very useful, and as follows:

Whereas *intercultural* communication is an exchange of meaning between *cultures, international* communication takes place on the level of countries or nations, which is to say across frontiers. This means: *Intercultural* and *international* communication can, on occasion, be identical; but this is not always so. Very often people who belong to a common culture are separated by a state frontier, with the effect that international communication is taking place within a single culture. And, the contrary case, humans of quite differing cultures can be united in the same state, so that within this single state intercultural communication can take place. It is thus that one tends to use the word *international* when speaking of communication on the purely political level, whereas the concept of *intercultural* communication corresponds more to sociological and anthropological realities.

In conclusion, note should be made here of the fact that research in the fields of either intercultural or international communication is not to be regarded as the same thing as research in the field of comparative communication. Although there is no absolutely clear line of distinction,[2] one difference is this: at the center of all research in the intercultural communications processes stand the relation and contacts between peoples of different cultures or nations; research in the field of comparative communications studies and compares the communications system of varying cultures or countries as such, in order then to draw comparisons.

Whenever in the field of scientific research an attempt is made to study such a concrete object as intercultural communication in its full complexity, a difficulty soon arises in defining categories, arising out of the subject itself, which can be used as measuring-sticks for a scientific approach. The very complexity of the matter under study implies that it may be studied under any of several varying categories. It becomes thus the task of the researcher to adopt an analytic approach to these dimensions and categories, and then to decide which system is best, which system is fairest to the matter under study, and promises to yield the most fruitful scientific results. It is in this aspect of the matter that we must now inquire what dimensions of classification seem best for a scientific analysis of intercultural communication.

Very provisionally, and by no means pretending to be complete, there seem to be four large dimensions that can be easily distinguished and differentiated. Intercultural communication can be broken down for study purposes under:

[2] Here above all: Charles Y. Glock, "The Comparative Study of Communications and Opinion Formation," *Public Opinion Quarterly* (Princeton, New Jersey), Vol. 16/ No. 2 (Winter 1952/53), especially Note 2.

1. Scientific Disciplines,
2. Areas of Life,
3. Means and Forms,
4. Varieties of Cultures, Nations, States.

In what follows, each of these dimensions will be briefly defined—in order to locate the specific standpoint of each of the individual contributors to the Berlin Symposium on Intercultural Communication between Industrial Nations and the Developing Countries. But we should admit here that in some cases not all studies can be too neatly classified under one dimension or the other. They cannot all be pidgeon-holed.

Modern communications research, including that in the field of intercultural communication, belongs in the category of "Scientific Integration," [3] in which the approach, perspectives and methods derive from several separate disciplines—sociology, psychology, anthropology, political science, et cetera. It was precisely in this field of the comparative study of complex cultures that the old-fashioned "disciplines" proved inadequate to the task at hand, and had to make way for an "interdisciplinary" or, better still, "integrative" approach. And this is why only very few of the contributions to this symposium can be too neatly labelled as belonging to this or that specific discipline.

It becomes apparent, too, that the traditional academic disciplines are no longer enough to serve in themselves as a framework for study, or for an ordering of the material in the field of intercultural communication. The deeper reason for this is that today many of the practitioners of the traditional disciplines no longer feel satisfied with them as the ideal means to approach and integrate the new material in this field. This is the situation today which has led to the demand for interdisciplinary research and to the development of modern "Integration Sciences."

Intercultural communication takes place today in almost every sector of human activity. The most important of these would seem to be (1) Politics, (2) Science, (3) Art and Culture, (4) Economics, (5) Journalism, (6) Tourism, (7) Technics, (8) Church and Charity affairs, (9) Sport, (10) the Military Sector, (11) Institutions, Organizations etc., (12) the Personal, Private Sector.

As in every field of human endeavor, it is not always correct to try to make too absolute distinctions; indeed, because of the complexity of human life, it would be quite false to do so.

The basic psychological problem [4] in intercultural communication becomes apparent when one poses the question of understanding, non-

[3] Cf. Werner Schöllgen, "Integrierende Wissenschaften als neuer Typ von Wissenschaft," *Publizistik* (Bremen, West Germany), Vol. 5/No. 4 (July/August, 1960), pp. 195-204.
[4] Cf. Gerhard Maletzke, *Psychologie der Massenkommunikation: Theorie und Systematik*, Hamburg: Hans Bredow Institut, 1963.

understanding and mis-understanding as it takes place between cultures. In order to come to grips with this problem, we have had recourse to a concept which psychologists have been using for some time, with much success, to solve certain special problems of Psychology. It is the concept of mankind's World View or "Weltsicht."

With the mature individual, a quite specific manner and method both of apprehending and dealing with the world has already developed, which enables him to interpret and evaluate it. This relatively constant and stable World View is the product of a few inherited traits and a larger variety of living experiences in his concrete, social and cultural surroundings. The psychologists have quite a variety of concepts to deal with this situation, which may not always be quite synonymous, but in principle tend to be describing the same phenomenon, namely the fact of a definite structuring and evaluating of human experience within its environment. The various concepts for this are called either "World View" or "Cognitive Structure," "Cognitive Style" or "Private World," "Subjective Experience World," "Frame of Reference," "Subjective Value System," "Value Constellation," "Thinking Style" and other such terminology. It cannot be our task here to compare and analyse these various concepts, to find out just how they relate to one another and what shades of difference in meaning they may have, or in which psychic field they may have their special relevance.

Most social groups of humans, populations and cultures show themselves to be, or are so constituted, that they consist of people with a similar realm of experience, with the same frames-of-reference and value-systems. Moreover, these common groups or culture-specific World Views are very closely linked with the language. The common language is both an expression of the *Weltanschauung* and a determinant of it. Here we come to a series of very complicated inter-dependencies, which we can however simplify into the formula that, on the one hand, the art and manner in which one understands the world is determined to a large extent by language; but language, at the same time, is an expression of a specific group-experiencing of the world, and therefore may itself be shaped by the *Weltanschauung* as well as the wishes, expectancies and motivations of the group using it. It is from this frame of reference that we get the hypothesis that, by language-analysis, one can arrive at a direct approach to the cognitive and affective structure of the group or population which speaks this language.

From these psychological facts communications research learns the following: The extent to which individuals or groups understand one another, fail to understand, or misunderstand, is determined by the degree to which the World Views and frames of reference of the partners in communication overlap. The larger the common ground of *Weltanschauung* is, the more likely and more simple it is that there will be an adequate meeting-of-minds. The less common ground there is, the fewer frames of reference, then the more likely it is that there will be serious misunderstandings and non-comprehension. And yet, while mentioning all these things, we must also not lose sight of the fact that total understanding is never possible since, as psychoanalysis has shown, there does not exist a total and perfect self-understanding.

Since, by definition, international communication is something that takes place between people belonging to different cultures, and who in many respects live within different frames of-reference, then it follows at first that in intercultural communication there will be much narrower bounds drawn than in communications between people or groups within the same culture. Ignoring for a moment the exceptions, we can say with certainty: the extent of intercultural understanding, misunderstanding or non-understanding is determined by the extent of likenesses and differences in frames-of-reference, value systems, or World Views of the cultures involved, from their cognitive and affective distance from each other.

This concept of the psychological background of intercultural communication indicates what it really means to understand a foreign culture, and to conform to it when this is desired. It means comprehension of the foreign manner of seeing, experiencing and judging, an accommodating to the alien cognitive structure, and adopting of a foreign frame of reference. We can here only note in passing that such a process of understanding and accommodation brings with it a plethora of problems and difficulties; that, to mention only one aspect, it calls for a very high degree of empathy, and empathy is a quality that varies markedly in individuals; that there are whole cultures with greater or lesser desire and readiness to show empathy; that intercultural understanding can never be perfect in itself, and that intercultural understanding and accommodation are often a very difficult and even painful process, which can often lead to a kind of culture-shock.

It is thus that, because of the differences in frames-of-references, vertical barriers are erected between cultures, barriers which make difficult mutual comprehension or hinder it completely, and the height of which is determined by the distance between the cognitive structures of the cultures involved.

One factor that plays a role not only in international communications, but also in the development process, is the creation of conceptions or images, attitudes, prejudices and stereotypes, which develop within a given culture in reference to another.[5] These images tend to concentrate themselves on a very few marked traits, they tend to run very uniformly throughout the population, are relatively constant, and almost invariably take on a derogatory nature.[6]

[5] Cf. Herbert C. Kelman, ed., *International Behavior*, New York: Holt, Rinehart and Winston, 1965. Cf. also: William Buchanan and Hadley Cantril, *How Nations See Each Other*, Urbana: University of Illinois Press, 1953.
[6] See William A. Scott, "Psychological and social correlates of International Images," in: Herbert C. Kelman, ed., *op. cit.*, p. 72 *et seq*.

Every process of communication in the intercultural realm has to deal with these pre-dispositions. Images and attitudes play a decisive role in modifying the content and form of dialogues, they determine the process of acclimatization or comprehension, the content and form of diplomatic, journalistic or private reports on foreign countries, and many other aspects of the intercultural dialogue. It is not only among individuals, but also whole groups and even nations and populations, that one can detect two types, the xenophiles and the xenophobes, those who have an open and those who have a closed approach to foreign peoples and groups.

In the last decades there have been numerous studies in the field of social psychology concerning national images, prejudices and stereotypes, so that here we are standing on ground that has been well-researched.

International attitudes and images taken on special weight in the realm of foreign policy, which is to say in the decisions that can lead to war or peace. These decisions and their consequences are very much dependent on whether one has correctly or falsely judged the attitudes, intentions and perspectives of the other side.

If we inquire now after the functions which these images, above all in the form of stereotypes, have for people, if we ask after the drives and motives that correspond to these images, then they reveal themselves to be relievers of pressure on the ego, as means or instruments for making the world simpler, comprehensible, and without nagging questions. The differentiation and complexity of existence is subjectively eliminated, and what remain are only a few superficial, governable features. This relieving or unburdening tendency expresses itself in two psychological facts which are also most important for comprehending intercultural communication —in "self-evident truths" and in the over-estimation of one's own and the underestimation of the opponent's position.

In our previous considerations, we made the assumption that nations or cultures are separated from each other by various viewpoints and experiences, by differing frames-of-reference. We must now, however, both modify and elaborate on this model of "vertical barriers" between cultures.

International communication in general takes place not between countries *in toto*, but rather between single individuals or groups of two cultures. Thus intercultural communication does not come about haphazardly between certain people and groups, but, in by far the great majority of instances, it takes place between communications-partners who share several things in common—for example, a similar level of education, common interests, a common profession, similar motivations, et cetera. The scientist in a foreign cultural environment will invariably seek out contact with the resident scientists there, the artist with fellow-artists the athlete with other athletes; politicians, business-men, technicians, journalists, soldiers and tourists tend, when they are in foreign environments, to seek out fellow-humans with similar professions, interests, status; in short, with partners whose viewpoints and way-of-thinking will parallel theirs at least in fields of common interest. Because of this fact, there develops, right across the vertical barriers a kind of horizontal field of communication. And, without doubt, these common interests can very often be stronger and more binding than other loyalties that have been built up in various strata within the culture itself. A German scientist will very often feel more at home with a fellow-scientist from France, Nigeria, India or Venezuela than with a German farm-laborer; and technicians and businessmen from different cultures have a broader basis of understanding each other than, let us say, a Bavarian and a Holsteiner.

"Intercultures" or "Third Cultures" have thus been built up along the lines of these intercultural, horizontal, common interests. But as yet we do not have many studies about the extent, structure, or dynamics of these cultures which extend out beyond the bounds of a given culture. *Flack* in his Symposium contribution [7] does look closely at this particular problem of the type and significance of these Intercultures.

It is a wide-open question, however, how binding these Intercultures might turn out to be under serious stress—for example, during an international crisis or in time of war.

It must be reserved for subsequent research to think through the psychological and sociological aspects of intercultural communication in the special case of communication between developed and developing nations. Assuredly this can be a wide and fruitful field of research, along the following lines:

—reciprocal identification and projection;
—the roles and status relationships between developed and developing nations, which is to say the social-psychological relationships which, for example, come into play in negotiations over development aid or voting in the UNO or other international organizations;
—the question of confidence and mutual trust between the communicating partners;
—research into the psychological functions which the partners in communication may be fulfilling, as in such cases when aggressive instincts are deflected toward an external foe, or when major powers or former colonial powers are made into scapegoats in the developing nations.

"*Intercultures*" also without doubt grow up between developed and developing nations. Yet it is nonetheless quite obvious that this form of social contact takes place much more often on the level of the "élites" than in the broad masses of the people.[8] As welcome as such intercultures may be as bridges between cultures otherwise not in contact, there is a

[7] Cf. George N. Gordon, Irving Falk and William Hodapp, *The Idea of Invaders*, New York: Hastings House, 1963.
[8] Cf. Charles A. Wright, "Functional Analysis and Mass Communication," *Public Opinion Quarterly* (Princeton, N.J.), Vol. 24/No. 4 (1960), pp. 605-620.

danger that should not be overlooked, particularly in developing countries. When members of the élite in developing countries join such intercultures, then the danger exists that they are only increasing that process of alienation from their own culture which in turn only strengthens the dubious dualism already noted.

After all that has already been said, it would be superfluous to go into detail about the extraordinary practical significance that attaches to research in intercultural communication between developed and developing nations. Development aid, diplomatic negotiations, economic contacts, the exchange of students and scientists, mutual cultural and information work, will all be less testy and more successful when we know more about the situations and questions which have been raised in this study.

APPENDIX

A BIBLIOGRAPHY OF BIBLIOGRAPHIES

BIBLIOGRAPHY OF BIBLIOGRAPHIES

T HIS BOOK could only touch on a few of the principal aspects of the very broad area generally understood as "international communication." A great many fascinating subjects relative to this very broad area are missing; many of them are included in the brief "Related Readings" list at the end of each introduction for the twelve chapters of this volume.

The editors feel, however, that they should give the reader further help in ascertaining the extremely wide scope of literature in the field of international communication. This could be done by presenting an extensive bibliography here. Instead, the editors have decided to provide the reader with a "bibliography of bibliographies" in the international communication field. Some of the bibliographies which follow may not seem to have a supranational appeal if one looks only at the titles. But all bibliographies listed are concerned with international problems, also. Most bibliographic aids are in English, but several are from European countries.

In the broad field of the different communication sciences there does not as yet exist an overview of bibliographic aids—a kind of Master Bibliography of Bibliographies—and although the editors realize that all the possible titles are not listed here, they feel that the following list is at least a first step toward a full-scale bibliography of bibliographies.

Adkins, Gale R. *Books on Radio—Television—Film. A Collection of Recommendations.* Lawrence/Kansas: The University of Kansas, 1962.

Advertising Research Foundation. A *Bibliography of Theory and Research Techniques in the Field of Human Motivations.* New York: Advertising Research Foundation, 1956.

Alisky, Marvin. *Latin American Journalism Bibliography.* Mexico, D.F.: Fondo de Publicidad Interamericana, 1958.

Behn, Hans Ulrich. *Presse—Rundfunk—Fernsehen in Asien und Afrika. Eine Bibliographie in- und ausländischer Fachliteratur.* Bonn: Forschungsinstitut der Friedrich-Ebert-Stiftung, 1965.

Beuick, Marshall. *Bibliography of Public Relations.* New York: M. Beuick, 1947.

Blum, Eleanor. *Reference Books in the Mass Media. An annotated, selected Booklist Covering Book Publishing, Broadcasting, Films, Newspapers, Magazines, and Advertising.* Urbana/Illinois: University of Illinois Press, 1962.

Bömer, Karl. *Internationale Bibliographie des Zeitungswesens*. Leipzig: Otto Harrassowitz, 1932.

Bouman, Jan C. *Bibliography on Filmology—As Related to the Social Sciences*. Paris: UNESCO, 1954.

Broderick, Gertrude G. *Radio and Television Bibliography*. Washington: Government Printing Office, 1949.

Cannon, Carl L. *Journalism: A Bibliography*. New York: New York Public Library, 1924.

Cole, Barry G. and Al Paul Klose. "A Selected Bibliography on the History of Broadcasting," in: *Journal of Broadcasting*, Vol. VIII/No. 3 (Summer 1963), pp. 247-268.

Cutlip, Scott M. *A Public Relations Bibliography, and Reference and Film Guides*. Madison/Wisc.: University of Wisconsin Press, 1957.

Cutlip, Scott M. *A Public Relations Bibliography*. Madison—Milwaukee: The University of Wisconsin Press, 1965.

Draper, Benjamin. *Television—Terminology—Bibliography*. San Francisco: California Academy of Sciences, 1953.

EBU. *Selected Bibliography:* Part 1: Broadcasting in education, Part 2: Broadcasting in Society, Geneva: European Broadcasting Union, 1967ff.

Filmbuchhandlung Hans Rohr. *Filmlagerkatalog 1966/67*, Zürich: 1966, *Filmlagerkatalog 1967/68*, Zürich: 1967, *Filmlagerkatalog 1968/69*, Zürich: Verlag Hans Rohr, 1968.

Franzmeyer, Fr(itz). *Presse-Dissertationen an deutschen Hochschulen, 1885-1938*. Leipzig: Verlag des Börsenvereins der Deutschen Buchhändler, 1940, 1. Suppl. 1939 o.J. (1941).

Golter, Bob J. *Bibliography of Theses and Dissertations Relating to Audio-Visuals and Broadcasting*. Nashville/Tenn.: Methodist Publishing House, 1958.

Graham, Robert X. A *Bibliography in the History and Background of Journalism*. Pittsburgh: University of Pittsburgh, 1940.

Haacke, Wilmont. "Public-relations-Bibliographie," in: *Jahrbuch der Absatz- und Verbrauchsforschung* (Kallmünz/Germany), Vol. 3/No. 2 (1957), pp. 149-153.

Harwood, Kenneth. A *World Bibliography of Selected Periodicals on Broadcasting*, Los Angeles: University of Southern California, 1961.

Hamill, Patricia Beall. *Radio and Television—A Selected Bibliography*. Washington/D.C.: Government Printing Office, 1960.

Hansen, Donald A., and Parsons, J. Herschel. *Mass Communication, A Research Bibliography*. Santa Barbara/Calif.: The Glendessary Press, 1968.

Haverfield, Robert W. *100 Books on Advertising*. 9th ed., Columbia/Mo.: University of Missouri, School of Journalism, 1969.

Heinrich, Karl. *Film and Youth—Film und Jugend—Le film et le jeunesse. Deutsche und ausländische Bibliographie*. Frankfurt/Main: Hochschule für Internationale Pädagogische Forschung, 1959.

Herzog zu Mecklenburg, Carl Gregor. *International Jazz Bibliography—Jazz Books from 1919 to 1968*. Baden-Baden: Librairie Heitz, 1968.

Institut für Publizistik der Freien Universität Berlin. *prd—Publizistikwissen-*

schaftlicher Referate-Dienst. Köln und Opladen: Westdeutscher Verlag, 1966-1967; Munich: Verlag Dokumentation, 1968 ff. (quarterly).

Institut für Zeitungsforschung der Stadt Dortmund. "Dokumentation für Presse, Rundfunk und Film," in: *Zeitungs-Verlag und Zeitschriften-Verlag* (Bad Godesberg), Vol. 57/1960 ff. (quarterly Supplement).

Lasswell, Harold D./ Casey, Ralph D. and Smith, Bruce L. *Propaganda and Promotion Activities. An Annotated Bibliography.* Minneapolis/Minnesota: The University of Minnesota Press, 1935.

Library of Congress. *Freedom of Information. A Selective Report on Recent Writings.* Washington, D.C.: Library of Congress, 1949.

Manz, H(ans) P(eter). *Internationale Filmbibliographie 1952-1962.* Zürich: Verlag Hans Rohr, 1963. Supplement I (1963-1964), Zürich: Verlag Hans Rohr, 1964. Supplement II (1965), Zürich: Verlag Hans Rohr, 1965.

Meyersohn, Rolf. *Television Research: An Annotated Bibliography.* New York: Columbia University, Bureau of Applied Social Research, 1954.

Mitry, Jean. *Bibliographie Internationale du Cinema et de la Télévision.* 4 Vols., Paris: Institut des Hautes Etudes Cinematographiques, 1966 ff.

Mowlana, Hamid. *International Communications: A Selected Bibliography.* Knoxville/Tennessee: School of Journalism, University of Tennessee, 1967.

Nafziger, Ralph O. *Foreign News Sources and the Foreign Press. A Bibliography.* Minneapolis/Minnesota: Burgess Publishing Co., 1937.

Nafziger, Ralph O. *International News and the Press. Communications, Organization of News-Gathering, International Affairs and the Foreign Press. An Annotated Bibliography.* New York: The H. W. Wilson Company, 1940.

Nielander, William A. *A Selected and Annotated Bibliography of Public Relations.* Austin: Bureau of Business Research, University of Texas, 1956.

Peet, Hubert W. *A Bibliography of Journalism; a Guide to the books about the Press and the Pressmen.* London: Sells Ltd., 1915.

Peterson, Wilbur. *Organizations, Publications and Directories in the Mass Media of Communications.* Iowa City/Iowa: School of Journalism, The University of Iowa, 3rd. ed., 1965.

Pötter, Günter. Bibliographie zur Wissenschaft von der Publizistik, in: Wilmont Haacke; *Publizistik: Elemente und Probleme.* Essen: Stamm-Verlag, 1962, pp. 289-369.

Price, Warren C. *The Literature of Journalism. An Annotated Bibliography.* Minneapolis/Minnesota: The University of Minnesota Press, 1959.

Proehl, Friedrich-Karl. *Verzeichnis ausgewählter Hochschulschriften, 1945-1966.* Hamburg: Stiftung Wissenschaft und Presse, 1967.

Rivers, William L. *Finding Facts: A Research Manual for Journalists.* New York: Magazine Publishers Association, Inc., 1966.

Rogers, E. M. *Bibliography of Research on the Diffusion of Innovation.* East Lansing/Michigan: Michigan State University, Department of Communication, 1964.

Rose, Oscar. *Radio Broadcasting and Television: An Annotated Bibliography.* New York: H. W. Wilson Co., 1947.

Ross, Albion and Heenan, Yvonne. *English-Language Bibliography on Foreign Press and Comparative Journalism*. Milwaukee/Wisconsin: Marquette University, Center for the Study of the American Press, 1966.

Schramm, Wilbur. *The effects of Television on children and adolescents. An annotated bibliography with an introductory overview on research results*. Paris: UNESCO, 1964.

Schroeder, Theodore. *The Free Speech Bibliography*. New York—London: The H. W. Wilson Company, 1922.

Smith, Bruce Lannes, Lasswell, Harold D., and Casey, Ralph D. *Propaganda, Communication, and Public Opinion. A Comprehensive Reference Guide*. Princeton/N.J.: Princeton University Press, 1946.

Smith, Bruce Lannes, and Smith, Chitra M. *International Communication and Political Opinion. A Guide to the Literature*. Princeton/N.J.: Princeton University Press, 1956.

Sparks, Kenneth R. *A Bibliography of Doctoral Dissertations in Television and Radio*. Syracuse/New York: Newhouse Communications Center, 2. ed., 1965.

Spiess, Volker. *Bibliographie zu Rundfunk und Fernsehen*, Hamburg: Verlag Hans-Bredow-Institut, 1966

Spiess, Volker. *Verzeichnis deutschsprachiger Hochschulschriften zur Publizistik, 1885-1967*. Berlin-München: Verlag Volker Spiess and Verlag Dokumentation, 1969.

Swindler, William F. *Bibliography of Law on Journalism*. New York: Columbia University Press, 1947.

Taft, William H. *200 Books on American Journalism*. Columbia/Missouri: University of Missouri, School of Journalism, 1969.

Topuz, Hifzi. "Selected Bibliography of News Agencies," in: '*Bulletin de l'A.I.E.R.J.*' (Prague), Vol. 1966/No. 5-6, pp. 105-111.

Traub, Hans/Lavies, Hans-Wilhelm. *Das deutsche Filmschrifttum. Eine Bibliographie der Bücher und Zeitschriften über das Filmwesen*. Leipzig: Verlag Karl W. Hiersemann, 1940.

UNESCO. *Tentative International Bibliography of Works Dealing with Press Problems (1900-1952)*. Paris: UNESCO, 1954.

UNESCO. *Current Mass Communication Research—I. Register of Mass Communication Research Projects in Progress and in Plan. Bibliography of Books and Articles on Mass Communication, Published since 1 January, 1955*. Paris: UNESCO, 1957.

(Various editors). Articles on Mass Communications in U.S. and Foreign Journals. A Selected Annotated Bibliography, in: *Journalism Quarterly* (Iowa City), Vol. 7/No. 2 (1930) ff.

(Various editors). Bibliography, in: *Gazette—International Journal for Mass Communication Studies* (Leyden/The Netherlands), Vol. 1/1955 ff (quarterly).

(Various editors). Blick in die ausländische Fachpresse, in: *Publizistik* (Bremen), Vol. 2/1957 ff (annually in last edition).

Vincent, Carl. *Bibliografia generale del cinema—Bibliographie générale du cinéma—General Bibliography of Motion Pictures*. Rome: Edizioni dell' Ateneo, 1953.

Voyenne, Bernard. *Guide bibliographique de la presse.* Paris: Centre de Formation des Journalistes, 1948.

Weed, Katharine Kirtley and Bond, Richmond Pugh. *Studies of British Newspapers and Periodicals from their Beginning to 1800. A Bibliography.* Chapel Hill: The University of North Carolina Press, 1946.

Werhahn, Jürgen W., and Maiwald, Joachim W. *Bibliographie des Film- und Fernsehrechts, 1896-1962.* Baden-Baden: Verlag für angewandte Wissenschaft, 1963.

Wolseley, Roland E. *The Journalist's Bookshelf. An Annotated and Selected Bibliography of United States Journalism.* 7th ed., Philadelphia—New York: Chilton Company—Book Division, Publishers, 1961.

INDEX